By all human calculation there was no hope that the nation of Judah would be restored. But the Judeans saw themselves as a people of God rather than a geographically defined entity. They refashioned their institutions, reinterpreted their already ancient literature, lived by the Law and survived two thousand years of the most calamitous and triumphant exile in the history of man.

1948 AD

The establishment of the Republic of Israel, after the almost total extinction of European Jewry during the Nazi holocaust, marked the emergence of a new era in Jewish history, and the vindication of an indestructible faith.

This comprehensive volume examines the years between the fall of Judah and the rise of modern Israel. Solomon Grayzel, noted historian and lecturer, does not define an isolated Jewry, but illuminates the living role of the Jewish people in the social, cultural, and economic development of mankind.

Colorful as well as factual, A History of the Jews *recreates personalities, places and events as it traces the progress of a unique people through Asia, Europe and America across two thousand years.*

A
HISTORY
OF THE
JEWS

From the Babylonian Exile to the Present

5728-1968

SOLOMON GRAYZEL

A MERIDIAN BOOK

MERIDIAN
Published by the Penguin Group
Penguin Books USA Inc., 375 Hudson Street,
New York, New York 10014, U.S.A.
Penguin Books Ltd, 27 Wrights Lane, London W8 5TZ, England
Penguin Books Australia Ltd, Ringwood, Victoria, Australia
Penguin Books Canada Ltd, 10 Alcorn Avenue,
Toronto, Ontario, Canada M4V 3B2
Penguin Books (N.Z.) Ltd, 182–190 Wairau Road,
Auckland 10, New Zealand

Penguin Books Ltd, Registered Offices: Harmondsworth, Middlesex,
England

Published by Meridian, an imprint of Dutton Signet,
a division of Penguin Books USA Inc.

First Meridian Printing, January, 1984
    6   7   8   9   10   11   12   13

To

RABBI ELIAS L. SOLOMON

1878-1956

BEARER OF THE JEWISH TRADITION

PREFACE

A History of the Jews was written in a most critical period in the annals of mankind and in one of the most disastrous in the experience of the Jewish people. After similar tragic episodes in the past, such as the destruction of the Jewish state by Rome and the expulsion of the Jews from Spain, one or more contemporaries of these events undertook to summarize the history of the Jewish people and to reassure their bewildered generations about their future. So destructive have been the storms which have overwhelmed us and so stupendous are the clashing forces about us today that a modern historian, making a similar effort, would need both the narrative abilities of a Josephus and the elegiac powers of a Joseph ha-Kohen. The purpose of writing *A History of the Jews* has been much more modest. Avoiding emotionalism, it tries to tell the story as objectively as possible, giving what I believe to be a balanced picture of Jewish life and fate, in the hope of clarifying the process of Jewish development through the centuries.

In one respect, however, objectivity was impossible, and all that the reader can expect is fairness. I believe in Judaism, and I have faith in the Jewish people. One of my reasons for writing *A History of the Jews* has been my desire to fortify the spirit and strengthen the determination of my fellow Jews to persevere in the path of our ancestors, and patiently and hopefully to labor for the welfare of mankind. The struggle against injustice, oppression and tyranny, the cooperative effort to expand the human spirit and the hope of achieving a better world for all humanity have been, to my mind, the historic tasks of Jews. In such conflicts and strivings, they were bound to get hurt. But their misfortunes have been honorable wounds of the battle, to be borne with dignity. I do not consider, and have not described, the numerous tragedies of Jewish history except as gauges of the evils that had to be overcome and as tests of the vitality of the Jewish religion.

The preparation of *A History of the Jews* has in a sense been a cooperative effort. I cannot mention all those whose advice I sought; but those who have been most directly helpful deserve public acknowledgment of the thanks I owe them. First, I express my gratitude to the young men and women who during the past score of years studied in my classes at the Gratz College of Philadelphia and unwittingly helped to clarify for me the method of presenting Jewish history.

Secondly, I express my indebtedness to those friends who, at a great sacrifice of time and labor, read all or parts of *A History of the Jews* in manuscript and offered suggestions for improvement: Dr. Julius H. Greenstone, Principal-Emeritus of Gratz College; Dr. Harry M. Orlinsky of the Jewish Institute of Religion; Dr. Joshua Bloch, Chief of the Jewish Division of the New York Public Library; Professor Jacob R. Marcus of the Hebrew Union College; and Mrs. Effie Solis-Cohen. Professor Simon Greenberg, Provost of the Jewish Theological Seminary, read the sections on the Middle Ages; Professor Solomon Zeitlin of the Dropsie College read the sections dealing with the Second Commonwealth, the Talmudic Age and the Modern Period; Professior Max Arzt of the Jewish Theological Seminary read the section on the Talmudic Age; and Professor Leo L. Honor of the Dropsie College read the section on the Modern Period. In addition to all these good friends, I owe special thanks to Dr. Mortimer J. Cohen who capped many years of close friendship by putting at my disposal, not only his knowledge of facts but also his incomparable felicity of expression. I am grateful to Miss Esther Zuckerman for preparing the manuscript for the press and to her as well as to my nephew, Nathan Eig, for reading the proofs.

While I accepted many of the excellent suggestions made by these and other friends, I could not accept them all. Hence, no one is to be held responsible for any errors, of fact or of judgment, found here, except myself.

My indebtedness to Mr. William Streckfus will be obvious to anyone who examines the maps of this book. I have been aided in this respect also by the helpful criticism of Dr. Mark Wischnitzer and of my beloved teacher, Professor Alexander Marx of the Jewish Theological Seminary. Rabbi Abram Vossen Goodman gave me the benefit of his advice in connection with the map on the American colonies.

The search for illustrative material proved to be a more arduous task than I had anticipated. A number of friends assisted me in the search: Mr. M. Lutzki of the Library of the Jewish Theological Seminary; Dr. Fritz Bamberger of *Coronet*; Mr. Lee M. Friedman of Boston; my good friend, Professor Guido Kisch of the Jewish Institute of Religion; and Dr. Franz Landsberger of the Hebrew Union College. Others were liberal in lending me material and in granting me permission to copy from their books. The names of such benevolent individuals and institutions may be found in the List of Illustrations.

I should indeed be ungracious if I did not also thank The Jewish Publication Society and its President, Mr. J. Solis-Cohen, Jr., and the Publication Committee and its Chairman, Judge Louis E. Levinthal, for making the publication of this book possible. My friend and co-worker, Mr. Maurice Jacobs, Executive Vice-President of The Society, has been more than generous with his advice, encouragement and assistance.

In the course of years of teaching adolescents and adults, I have been repeatedly shocked by the prevalent ignorance of Jewish history. This ignorance has had a debilitating effect upon Jewish life. It has resulted in division rather than unity, ruinous assimilation instead of loyalty, paralyzing fear in place of courage. The thoughtless abandonment of inspiring Jewish traditions has naturally followed. I hope that *A History of the Jews* will help acquaint my fellow Jews in America and elsewhere with the sublimity of their heritage and encourage them to carry it forward into a brighter future.

SOLOMON GRAYZEL

April 21, 1947—Iyyar 1, 5707
Philadelphia, Pa.

PREFACE TO THE SECOND EDITION

Twenty years have passed since the appearance of this volume. While change is the essence of the historical process and should be taken for granted, no one could have forseen the extent of the changes that the world would undergo between 1947 and 1967. The total situation has become transformed, culturally and physically, both in Israel and in the diaspora. The slight modification made in the text of the volume in 1952-3, in order to take cognizance of the appearance of the State of Israel, no longer seemed adequate to cover the new developments; the addition of another chapter was called for in order that the full story might be told.

It is gratifying to record that the book was favorably received in the United States as well as in other countries. I am grateful to readers and reviewers who found the first edition useful and informative, and that schools and colleges have used it as a text. I can only hope that this second edition will be found equally useful.

S. G.

January 15, 1968

CONTENTS

xi

BOOK THREE

THE JEWS IN THE WEST

BOOK FOUR

RETREAT AND PROGRESS

BOOK FIVE

THE SEARCH FOR A FRIENDLY HOME

LIST OF MAPS

ALL THIS IS COME UPON US

> . . . yet have we not forgotten Thee,
> Neither have we been false to Thy
> covenant.   (Ps. 44.18)

AN INTRODUCTORY CHAPTER TO THE HISTORY OF THE JEWS

1. THE ADVENTURE OF JEWISH HISTORY

A Long Career—This book tells the story of the Jewish people, a story of continuous adventure. The Jews have lived through four thousand years. Before the dawn of the Western world the Jews were here. They began their career in Antiquity, when nations existed of whom nothing but a vague memory has survived. They lived and labored when Assyrians and Babylonians terrorized their neighbors, and Egyptian priests uttered their mysterious incantations. They are alive today, when new nations bestride the world. If the experiences of one man's life are interesting, surely the adventurous journey and miraculous life of an entire people should be even more thrilling.

The Drama of Jewish History—The history of the Jews is not the story of an isolated adventure, nor of a life lived far away from the crowded highways of civilization. On the contrary, hardly an important event happened in the history of the world but that the Jews played some part in it. Sometimes the event affected them after it happened; sometimes they themselves helped to bring the event about; but at all times they were there, anxious and eternal participants in humanity's struggle and progress. A knowledge of Jewish history, therefore, requires acquaintance with the momentous events in the history of many nations. This is why Jewish history is many times more important than one might suppose judging merely from the fact that the Jews are numerically a small

17

group. By observing the Jews, one can view the entire pageant of mankind's pilgrimage through the ages. Tragedy and almost miraculous escapes from extinction, triumphs over tremendous difficulties, great achievements in the world of culture and religion, and devotion to the welfare of humanity are characteristics of the Jewish story.

2. THE NATURE OF JEWISH HISTORY

Bigness and Greatness—Until a few years ago, before the calamity of World War II befell them, the Jews throughout the world numbered about sixteen millions. They were less than one per cent of the world's population and only about one and one half per cent of the combined populations of Europe and America. Other peoples were much bigger than the Jewish group. Moreover, the fact that they were scattered all over the world seemed to make the Jews even less important. But despite their small number and lack of concentration, their history is of tremendous significance.

Bigness has nothing to do with greatness. Someone has suggested a convincing way of demonstrating this. In the lower right-hand corner of a map of the Western world, which includes America, Europe and the western part of Asia, lies Palestine along the Mediterranean coast; Greece is a little to the northwest of it. One tiny speck on the map marks the city of Jerusalem; another marks the city of Athens. It is astonishing to realize that the culture of all the rest of the map is based on the contributions made by these two spots. Western civilization is the product of the thought and experience of these two cities. For the test of a people's greatness is not the number of its citizens, nor the size of its cities, nor the wealth of its millionaires. The real test lies in a people's effort to improve the mind, the character and the well-being of humanity, to give life new directions and to extend justice in human society. This is why the little Jewish people is of such interest and importance to the world.

The Religious Contribution—The first part of Jewish history, usually known as the history of the Hebrews, is fairly familiar. Most people have a general idea how the Hebrews originated, how they won their land and established their kingdoms. The ancient heroes of the people, the patriarchs, Joshua the conqueror, David the nation-builder, and a host of others, are well known from popular story and legend. These men influenced the world; but their influence was an indirect one. More important was the influence of the Lawgiver, the poets, writers and religious teachers of the Hebrews—the men known as the prophets. Their words have resounded through the centuries and their thoughts affect our life today. Why were the two little kingdoms, Israel and Judah, able to develop such men and such thoughts? Huge empires surrounded them; big and little nations lived on their every side. Yet, it was tiny Judah and Israel, not Babylonia or Assyria or Egypt or Philistia, that did most to enrich the spirit of mankind.

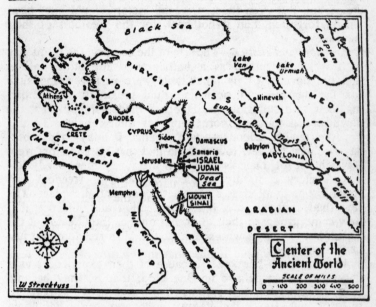

Geography and Religion—The map of the ancient world shows one reason why Judah and Israel left their impress upon humanity. To the northeast of Palestine lies the Mesopotamian valley from which sometimes Babylonia and at other times Assyria poured mighty armies into the lands of the west to satisfy their lust for booty, conquest and power. To the southwest lies Egypt, from which equally powerful armies came to join battle with those descending from the north. Between the two, on the only strip of land through which each army could move to come to grips with the other, lived the Hebrews. Though fairly fruitful, theirs was not a rich land for purposes of agriculture. Its small area was further reduced by mountains and rocky hills. The nature of their land, therefore, made it impossible for the Hebrews to become a prosperous people or to hope that as a nation they could ever rule the ancient world as upon occasions the Babylonians or the Egyptians did. Most of the Hebrews remained poor peasants, frequently oppressed. During the greater part of their history both Israel and Judah were made subject to the great empires. Time and again, they saw conquering armies march up and down their countries to victory or defeat. Whichever the direction the armies marched, or whatever the mood they felt when they returned, Israel was the victim. But even those powerful victors would have been almost forgotten, had it not been for the greatness of their victim.

Freedom and Justice—The size of the country, the frequency with which it served as a battleground for other nations and the poverty of its inhabitants were in part responsible for the development of its spiritual greatness. Remembering their own suffering, the Hebrews made sympathy for the downtrodden the very cornerstone of their religion. To this day the Jewish calendar—its Sabbaths, holidays and workdays—oblige the Jew to recall the fact that his ancestors were slaves in Egypt. David's conquests are rarely mentioned; Solomon's glory is hardly recalled; but love of freedom and equal justice to all classes of society command first place. The Jews had suffered such bitter oppression and injustice that they came to regard their God, not only as the Creator of the world, but as a God who sought to establish freedom and justice among men.

Monotheism—The Jews, because of their experiences as a nation, came to believe in One God, that is, they became monotheists. The other nations of the ancient world believed in local gods. Egypt had its own gods, and so did Babylonia and every other nation. When a nation won in battle, its leaders proclaimed that its god had conquered the god of the defeated country. The Hebrews often witnessed the defeats and victories now of one great nation and now of another. The more thoughtful among them realized that it was foolish to divide the heavens as the earth was divided, giving a nation's god rulership over a particular part of the heavens to correspond to the earth beneath it. They held it to be childish to represent God in the form of a man or an ox or a carved pole, and to pray to that image for victory against an enemy. They believed that God was the Creator of the entire world; He was Father of all humanity; His purpose was not for His people to be conquerors, but for them to set an example to mankind how "to do justice and love mercy and walk humbly with God."

Prophecy and the Bible—It took the Hebrews a long time to arrive at these great convictions. Perhaps they would never have arrived at them had not Moses risen to mold the beginnings of their history. He revived among them Abraham's ideal of monotheism; he taught them important rules of conduct. He was, however, centuries ahead of his times. Only the great men among the Hebrews, the prophets, truly understood Moses' teachings. They endeavored to make their fellow Hebrews understand them too; but, except on rare occasions, the Hebrews paid little attention to the prophets. Only after great misfortunes had overtaken them, and both Israel and Judah had been temporarily destroyed as kingdoms, did the common people accept the prophetic teachings.

These were incorporated in an extraordinary collection of books—a library in itself—that has come to be known as the Bible. The Bible has influenced the mind and happiness of the Western world more than any battle ever fought, any invention ever made or any idea ever expressed. It inspired the religion, the language, the arts, the conduct, the fears and the hopes of almost every nation on the face of the earth.

The Growing Heritage—How this happened cannot be told here. One must first understand how the thought of the prophets affected the Jews during the Babylonian Exile and after they had rebuilt their national life in Palestine. For it was not the ancient Hebrews who transmitted the Bible to the other peoples of the world, but their descendants, the Jews. The Jews were no longer satisfied merely to believe in the teachings of the prophets. They wanted to develop and apply them, and to make them part of their everyday life. They built institutions around them and defended them. When, later, their Second Commonwealth was destroyed by Rome, these institutions saved the Jewish people from utter destruction. The Jewish people, though scattered, survived. As a matter of fact, the Jews did more than survive. Just as in Palestine the Hebrews obtained a deeper understanding of truth and justice through their sufferings in cruelty and war, so their descendants in the Diaspora further developed their spirit because they experienced the evils and injustices of a later day. Through pain and suffering, through searching for means to surmount obstacles, the Jews acquired that social understanding and that human sympathy which have enabled them, individually and as a group, to make some of their richest contributions to humanity. The forces of ignorance, selfishness and brutality even today testify to this by arraying themselves against the Jewish people and making this small group the chief object of their hatred.

The Jews as the Heirs of Their Past—Explanation now of the three terms—Hebrew, Israelite and Jew—will help to avoid confusion later. These names are often used interchangeably. There is nothing wrong in this use, but it may be just as well to understand what each one means. The Hebrews were the descendants of Abraham, Isaac and Jacob; the last was also called Israel. His name was applied to the tribes who settled in Canaan and some lands near by. Later, some of the tribes became two kingdoms: Israel was the kingdom of northern Palestine; while Judah was the southern kingdom (named after one of the sons of Jacob) over which the family of David ruled. Both populations could rightly be called Hebrews, and both could be referred to as the Children of Israel. The northerners called themselves Israelites, and the southerners Judeans. Subsequently, both kingdoms were destroyed, but only the Judeans succeeded in re-establishing themselves in their old land, whereas the Israelites never restored their kingdom. Only the Judeans, therefore, played a part in later history. The word "Jew" is a modification of the word "Judean." The Jews are the last remnants of the Hebrews and the Israelites, and rightfully took over whatever hopes, tasks and glories the larger group had developed.

The Jews and their History—For several good reasons this book is limited to the history of the Jews. One reason for this is that something of the history of the Hebrews is generally, however inadequately, known. He must be a very uncultured man who does not know something about Abraham, or Joseph, or David, or Isaiah. A second reason for confining this book to the history of the Jews is that very few people know much about the history of the successors of the Hebrews. Little is to be found in modern historical writings about the Jews in connection with the Greeks, the Romans, the Middle Ages and Modern Times. Occasionally one finds a remark here or there about them. Sometimes it is a sympathetic reference to the persecutions which the Jews had to undergo. Sometimes it is an uncomplimentary opinion about their business activities or their religion. Usually the Jews are ignored as if they no longer existed. The Jews are frequently mentioned in connection with the rise of Christianity. But even here, the main interest does not lie in how the Jews lived and felt and worked, but rather in how they served as a background for the rise of Christianity, the religion adopted in the

West. Yet, the Jews themselves have a history. No one can possibly understand how the Jews survived to modern times unless he has some knowledge of the past twenty-five hundred years from the Jewish point of view. Certainly we ought to know the later period, after the rise of Christianity, much better than we do, not only because it is inherently interesting, but especially because during this period the Jews cooperated in building the world in which they lived.

The meaning of this cooperation is best described in the words of Simon Dubnow, a great Jewish historian. He said: "This latter part of Jewish history is not yet known, and many, in the thrall of prejudice, do not wish to know it. But ere long it will be known and appreciated. . . . The thousand-years' martyrdom of the Jewish people, its unbroken pilgrimage, its tragic fate, its teachers of religion, its martyrs, philosophers, champions—this whole epic will in days to come sink deep into the memory of men. . . . It will secure respect for the silvery hair of the Jewish people, a people of thinkers and sufferers. . . . It is our firm conviction that the time is approaching in which the second half of Jewish history will be to the noblest part of *thinking* humanity what its first half has long been to *believing* humanity, a source of sublime moral truth. In this sense, Jewish history in its entirety is the pledge of the spiritual union between the Jews and the rest of the nations."

3. THE CHALLENGE IN JEWISH HISTORY

The Demands of the Past—Jewish history presents a challenge to the modern Jew. The heroes of the Jewish past— thinkers, teachers and leaders—lived their lives and made their sacrifices in order that their descendants might have a fund of wisdom for inspiration and practical living. Their life and effort were wasted unless they lead to action on our part, to defend what we received from the past and, if possible, to enrich it further. In other words, Jewish history tells how generation after generation of our people grappled with problems and overcame difficulties for the sake of what they considered sacred. The story is worth telling because it may help the present generation to see its problems in better perspective and to encourage its search for helpful solutions to these problems.

The Problems of the Present—A knowledge of history does not of itself provide solutions for current problems, but it is useful in offering encouragement and suggestions. The circumstances which challenge Jewish life today are not at all the same as those which challenged it in the days of the Maccabees or when the Roman empire was at the height of its power, or upon any of the other numerous occasions when the fate of the Jews was in the balance. The problem of Jewish defense against persecution is a good illustration of how methods change in accordance with conditions. There were times when the Jews were compelled to take up the sword, and other times when they took up the pen in defense of their right to live as Jews. Sometimes a generation won its battle by proclaiming itself ready to be slaughtered; at other times it was compelled to use a plea or a bribe. Can the Jews use these methods today? To answer this question, it is necessary to study the conditions of the past struggles and compare them with present conditions. One must know the strength and weakness of the Jewish spirit then and now. Jewish history thus becomes an essential preparation for our struggle for survival. Similarly with other problems facing the Jewish group: the problem of self-regulation, that is, to what extent Jewish communal life is possible in the free environment of the United States; the problem of Jewish culture and the possibility of its further development in the Diaspora; the problems connected with modern efforts to rebuild Israel as a Jewish Homeland; and the problems connected with strengthening Jewish religious life. All of these problems are complex and interrelated. Thought, effort and sacrifice are needed for their solution; but knowledge of the past is also necessary. For none of these problems is altogether new in Jewish life; and Jewish history, which is really recorded Jewish experience, can be very helpful. The Jews are an old people and the wisdom they have acquired through their long life ought not to be neglected or wasted.

4. How Jewish History May Be Divided

Seven Ages—The history of the Jews may be divided into the following seven periods: The *Patriarchal Age,* from Abraham to the conquest of Canaan by the Israelites, tells all those beautiful and moving stories of our people's origin which have been a source of inspiration for the entire Western world. These stories, however, are only introductory to the real history of the Jewish people. This age is followed by the period of the *First Commonwealth,* from about 1200 to 586

before the Common Era. This is the age of judges, kings and
prophets, of wars, divisions and rebellions, and also of the
birth of great spiritual truths. The third period covers the history of the *Second Commonwealth*, from 586 before the
Common Era (we shall abbreviate this phrase to B.C.E. hereafter) to the year 70 in the Common Era (we shall use the
letters C.E. hereafter). This includes the story of the Babylonian Captivity, the return and the rebuilding of the Temple,
the Persian and Greek contacts with the Jews, the Hasmoneans
and the Roman control. The fourth period deals with the
Jews of the East. It relates the rise and decline of the Jews in
Babylonia and Palestine during the first thousand years of the
Common Era, the period which saw the development of the
Talmud among the Jews, and of Christianity and Mohammedanism among the Gentiles.

The fifth is that of the *Middle Ages in Europe*. It overlaps
the previous age, since the Jews of Europe trace their history
a century or two before the Common Era, while the Second
Commonwealth still existed. But the European communities
were so different in origin and development that it is impossible to discuss them along with the Jews of the East. It is the
age of Jewish settlement in various parts of Europe, Jewish
participation in the slow rise of European culture, the Crusades
and all the evils which followed them. The end of the
Renaissance (about 1520), if not the expulsion from Spain
(1492), began a new period for European Jewry. It has often
been called the Ghetto Age; but since cultural influences have
been most important in Jewish history, this period is better
named after the *Jews of Eastern Europe*, who, in their days,
developed the highest cultural activity. The seventh and last
period is the *Modern age*, dating from the time when, toward
the end of the eighteenth century, the world underwent
radical transformation after the revolutions in America and
in France.

Biblical and Post-Biblical History—The first two periods
described above are not treated in this book. The reason is
that this book seeks to present the background of present-day
Jewish life, institutions and problems. Now, the farther back
one goes, the less direct is the influence of historical events
on modern times. The Bible and its characters, of course,
have affected and still affect Jewish life. But the historical
events of biblical times have not had and do not have any
such influence. More significant and influential than the
events recorded in the Bible have been the interpretations of
these events by men who have lived during later periods.

The history of the last four periods, moreover, differs in its very nature from the history of the first three. Earlier Jewish history was the history of a people on its land and was largely concerned with politics and statesmanship. After the Second Commonwealth, and to some extent also during its existence, Jewish history has been the history of a people, physically scattered, yet working together for the development of thought, culture and religion. This is the story we try to tell, for this is what constitutes the uniqueness of the Jewish people.

BOOK ONE

THE SECOND COMMONWEALTH
586 B.C.E.—135 C.E.

**THE JEWS REBUILD THEIR NATION AND DE-
VELOP THEIR RELIGION, BUT EVENTUALLY
LOSE THE FORMER AND ENDANGER THE
LATTER**

CHAPTER I

CAN THESE BONES LIVE?

**KINGS AND SOLDIERS RUIN THE JUDEAN NATION, BUT
PROPHETS AND TEACHERS SAVE IT**

The Triumph of Hope—In the year 586 B.C.E., Judah, the
smaller of the two Hebrew kingdoms, came to its end. One
hundred and thirty-three years previously, Israel had been defeated and its upper classes, its nobles and its priests, driven
into exile never to return; now Judah, too, lost its independent existence. By all human calculations there was no hope
that the Judean nation or people would ever be restored. So
the Judeans themselves thought, both those who started out

on the long road of exile and those who remained behind in
the desolated land. But this was not the end. Due to a combination of circumstances, it was really the beginning of a more
meaningful life. Chief among these circumstances was the
fact that some Judeans regarded their people, not as a nation
whose destiny could be decided on the field of battle, but as
an instrument used by God in a great human experiment. Inspired by this idea, the leaders of the defeated nation found
means for keeping the spirit of the people alive. They refashioned their old institutions; they selected and reinterpreted
their already old literature; above all, they kept their flagging
hopes from dying. When the great opportunity came to return to their beloved homeland, the challenging moment
found the exiled Judeans ready to rebuild their national life.

1. THE CONSEQUENCES OF DEFEAT

The Destruction of Judah—For more than four hundred
years before destruction overtook it, Jerusalem had been the
capital and the pride of the Judean nation. The family of
David had ruled in it, and the descendants of Aaron had
officiated in its Temple. But kings, priests and nobles, desiring
to rule a powerful nation, yielded to the persuasion of the
Egyptians to rebel against their overlord, the king of Babylonia. In the year 597 B. C. E., Nebuchadnezzar, the mighty
king of the East, had come and forced the Judeans to surrender. He drove many of the noble families into exile in Babylonia and appointed a new king over the others. But even this
new king, Zedekiah, could not resist the promises of power
and glory which the Egyptians continued to make if Judah
would join Egypt in fighting Babylonia. Again Judah rebelled; again Egypt was driven off by the Babylonians, who
then returned, besieged Jerusalem and captured it. They
killed many people and laid the country round about in ruins,
so that the remaining peasants either fled or starved to death.
Thousands within Jerusalem were massacred. Many thousands more were taken captive by the Babylonians and driven
off to their distant land. King Nebuchadnezzar saw no need
for executing them since he felt certain that within a few
years, at most a generation, they would become lost in the
population of his vast city of Babylon and the country of
which it was the capital.

The Murder of Gedaliah—Nebuchadnezzar had not intended to destroy Judea, but merely to make it impossible for

the Judeans again to rebel. He knew that if the upper classes, or the leaders, princes and priests, were removed, the lower classes, the small merchants, the artisans, the peasants, would keep the peace. This portion of the population was therefore left undisturbed. Some sort of government was needed for Judea. Nebuchadnezzar, therefore, chose a member of a prominent Judean family, one of the nobles who had not favored the policy of alliance with Egypt, and appointed him governor. But this man, Gedaliah ben (that is, son of) Ahikam, a forthright, earnest, patriotic Judean, was murdered, soon after his appointment, by a jealous descendant of the House of David. Thereupon the men associated with Gedaliah in the government, fearing that Nebuchadnezzar would blame them for what had happened, decided to abandon completely the work of reconstruction and flee to Egypt. They compelled Jeremiah to accompany them, and it was in Egypt that the old prophet uttered his last exhortations to return to the worship of God and the observance of Mosaic traditions. To this day the Jewish calendar commemorates by a fast-day the anniversary of Gedaliah's murder, the day following Rosh ha-Shanah. For that day marked the final destruction of the first Hebrew Commonwealth. The Jews themselves completed what the Babylonians had begun.

The Fate of the Land—Nebuchadnezzar, some say, took the flight of the Judeans to Egypt as a confession of guilt. He carried another group of Judeans into Babylonian exile as a punishment for having plotted against his appointee. From every side the neighboring nations moved into Judean territory—the Ammonites from the east, the Edomites from the south, and the Samaritans from the north. They all pushed their boundaries forward into the defenseless land. Stricken, leaderless and bullied by their neighbors, the Judeans sank into national hopelessness.

The Fate of their Religion—The loss of Jeremiah was as tragic for the religion of Judea as the loss of Gedaliah was for the nation. Had he been permitted to remain, the prophet might have guided the people away from the gross superstitions of their pagan neighbors. They set up an altar on the site of the one destroyed in Jerusalem, and continued to bring sacrifices to the God of Israel. But God remained for most of them a local God, without any of that moral greatness or any of those ethical ideals which the prophets had tried to teach their ancestors. Five or six years after their great misfortune had befallen the Judean nation there was not the slightest indication that this defeated people would revive itself and become the religious teacher of mankind. That this did happen was due to what was going on among the Judeans exiled in Babylonia.

2. The Hopelessness of Exile

The Divisions among the Hebrews—While the events just described were taking place in Judea, the exiles carried off by Nebuchadnezzar were establishing themselves in Babylonia. When they arrived they found two other groups of Hebrews already there. One group consisted of their close friends and relatives. This was the group whom the Babylonians had taken into exile in the year 597 B.C.E., eleven years before the complete destruction of Jerusalem. The other group consisted of the great-grandchildren of those Israelites who had been exiled by the Assyrians one hundred and twenty-five years earlier, in 719 B.C.E., after the destruction of the Kingdom of Israel and its capital Samaria. These latter were Israelite Hebrews, not Judean Hebrews. They were descendants of the Ten Tribes, not of the Tribe of Judah.

The Babylonians were cruel conquerors. They executed the leaders of a conquered people. They sometimes kept men in prison for many long years; sometimes they sold their captives into slavery. But the Babylonians were not cruel masters. The majority of the people whom they drove into exile were permitted to live and work under certain conditions. They could not return to their own land, and they were looked down upon as a conquered people, but they were sometimes assigned land which they could till upon payment of heavy taxes. Sometimes they were permitted to settle in cities and earn their living from trade or manual labor. At first it was hard for these exiles to begin life all over again in a strange land. As time went on, however, they adjusted themselves to the new conditions. For Babylonia at this time was a prosperous country. Each Judean exile, therefore, seemed to have a personal future in Babylonia; but the Judeans as a group seemed to have no future at all.

The Lure of Babylon—Babylonia presented a contrast to Judea, and Babylon to Jerusalem. The lofty walls of Babylon, the towering domes of its temples, its hanging gardens, its massive palaces, made the Jews think of Jerusalem as small-townish. How could the Temple, even with the solemnity of its service, compare to the stateliness of the sacrificial rites of the temples of Marduk or Ishtar, chief gods of Babylon, or the simple vestments of Jerusalem's priests with the gorgeous garments of the priests of Babylon? On the streets of this conquering city, mistress of the world, men from every nation, every race and color, could be seen. In its market-stalls wares, imported from remote peoples whose very names were unpronounceable, could be admired and purchased. Its bookstalls, conducted by men known as public scribes, contained a varied banquet of wisdom and entertainment. Through this magnificent and proud city, the Judean exile walked. He was overwhelmed by it. He might hate it at first for having brought misfortune upon himself and his people. But as time went on and his personal life became easier, he was inclined to admit that there was no use struggling against anything so powerful and dazzling as Babylonian civilization. He might even be overheard admitting to his friends that, while he himself could never forget he was a Judean, it might be just as well for his children to grow up citizens of mighty Babylonia.

3. THE NEW LEADERS

The Fight against Hopelessness—The destruction of the Judean Commonwealth changed Ezekiel in Babylonia, and Jeremiah in Judah, from prophets of doom into prophets of hope. The first thing Ezekiel tried to do was to persuade the Jews that the God of Israel had not been defeated and had not abandoned them. He ridiculed the idea that Marduk was stronger than the gods of all the nations whom the Babylonians had conquered. He argued that God was the God of all the nations, and that He was using Babylonia to punish wicked peoples. The Hebrew peoples had been disloyal to Him. That was why national misfortune had come upon them. But God would certainly not continue to punish them forever (chap. 33, vv. 10–12). Nothing, he argued, was impossible for God, the Creator of the universe. The Judean nation considered itself a heap of dry bones, without life, without hope; but should God so determine, it could easily come to life again (chap. 37).

The Hebrews Must Unite—Ezekiel deplored the division among the Hebrews. These had been serious enough when the Israelites and the Judeans lived in their own countries. But for them to continue as two separate peoples when suffering a common exile was senseless. Ezekiel wanted Judeans and Israelites to look forward to being one people in one land when the time of restoration to their old country came. All the exiles faced a common present and should look forward to a common future.

Ezekiel's Assistants—This difficult task of teaching the Jews the truth about One God in the universe, keeping alive their national hopes, and uniting them into a common group, was more than one man could be expected to accomplish. Fortunately, Ezekiel was not the only one who sought these ideals. There were other prophets. We do not know their names because they left no books behind, but we do know that they existed. Moreover, another type of leader arose during this period—the scribe. The scribe was a man whose chief interest lay in the preservation of the old literature of the Hebrews. He collected the writings of famous men and the speeches of notable prophets who had spoken in Israel and Judah, and he made them available for the Babylonian exiles to read. Naturally, the scribes were not interested in gathering the writings of those prophets who had glorified the false gods, but only such writings as spoke of the God of Israel as the God of Justice and Righteousness. Since Ezekiel's ideas and the ideas of the great prophets were similar, the scribes by their literary work helped to spread the message of the Babylonian prophet and the plans he hoped to accomplish.

4. Changes in the Jewish Religion

Feasts and Fasts—The preaching of the prophets and the literature arranged and distributed by the scribes would not have been enough to keep the Jewish people alive in Babylonia. The Jews themselves, fortunately, developed their religion in such a way as to make their future more secure. They had become accustomed to rest from work on the Sabbath and on such holidays as Passover, Sukkot, and Shabu'ot. In Judea they had refrained from working on these days because their religion forbade them. In Babylonia, as we now know, many of them supposed that they no longer needed to observe their religion. Nevertheless, most of them continued to rest on such occasions. They probably argued that they were doing this in memory of the old days when their nation was free and independent. Besides the feasts and the days of rest, they also began to observe days of fasting. All of them mourned on the anniversary of the day when the wall of Jerusalem began to crumble under the attacks of the Babylonians, and on the day when the city fell. For these reasons the 10th of Tebet, the 17th of Tammuz and the 9th of Ab were observed as fast days. Such days of rejoicing and of mourning were almost enough to keep the Jews separate from the Babylonians, and to unite them in common memories.

Days of Assembly—The Jews lived in groups. It was therefore natural for those living near one another to meet on the days when they decided not to do any work in their fields or in their shops. On Sabbaths, feast days and fast days they would gather together and recall the glories of the past. They could not perform the sacrifices which the priests used to offer up on such occasions, but they could sing the songs which accompanied the sacrifices, and which the scribes had succeeded in collecting. It was most likely on such occasions that the prophets addressed the people and told them not to give up hope, and taught them how much worthier the God of Israel was than the gods whom the Babylonians worshipped. A prophet or scribe who was present read to the assembly a portion of the Torah or the written works of a prophet who had lived long before and who had urged the Judeans or the Israelites to be a godly people. These meetings thus provided the real means for the preservation of the Jews.

CHAPTER II

THE CITY SHALL BE BUILDED

THE JEWISH PEOPLE RE-ESTABLISH THEIR NATION IN THE LAND OF THEIR FATHERS

Problems of Restoration—Despite the efforts of Ezekiel and his co-workers, the future of the Babylonian Jews did not look promising. They would most likely have succumbed to the lure of their environment, had not the Babylonian empire come to a sudden and unexpected collapse. To the astonished Jews this event seemed like an act of God on their behalf, justifying all the promises of Ezekiel and the other prophets. Cyrus, conqueror of Babylonia, gave the Jews the opportunity to rebuild their nation, and many of them went back to Judea filled with joy and hope.

The returned exiles and the Judeans who had remained on their native soil were now confronted with many problems of reconstruction. Only the timely interference of prominent Babylonian Jews saved the new community and started it on the way to new greatness.

1. AN UNEXPECTED TURN OF FORTUNE

The Fall of Babylon—The change in the Jewish situation came with startling suddenness. A new and powerful kingdom had arisen to the east of Babylonia through the union of Media and Persia. In a brief war, the armies of the Babylonians were defeated and the conquerors penetrated the seemingly impregnable city. Mighty Babylon was no more; Bel and Marduk proved to be gods with feet of clay.

The Cyrus Declaration—Cyrus, king of the Medes and the Persians, had new ideas about how to govern the vast empire which he had won from Babylonia. Instead of mingling together all the conquered peoples and hoping that they would become one nation, Cyrus decided to send each nation back to its original home. He hoped that in this way each would be satisfied and grateful. In the second year of his reign (537 B.C.E.), therefore, Cyrus issued the following declaration, which may be read in the very last sentence of the Bible:

> Thus saith Cyrus, king of Persia: All the kingdoms of the earth hath the Lord, the God of heaven, given me; and He hath charged me to build Him a house in Jerusalem, which is in Judah. Whosoever there is among you of all His people— the Lord his God be with him—let him go up.

The Unknown Prophet—The Jews were overjoyed at this unexpected turn of events. Two short years before, their future seemed more or less hopeless; now they had an opportunity to revive their nation, restore their land and rebuild their Temple. We know how greatly they rejoiced from the words of a nameless prophet. Who he was really does not matter, since we have his words in the last twenty-six chapters of the Book of Isaiah. As poetry, the Great Unknown's words are among the most eloquent in the entire Bible. In one passage this prophet pictured Jerusalem mourning in her ruins, without hope of ever being rebuilt. On top of the rocky hills, a messenger suddenly appears, hastening toward the city:

> How beautiful upon the mountains
> Are the feet of the messenger of good tidings. . . .
> Hark, thy watchmen, they lift up the voice,
> Together do they sing. . . .
> Break forth into joy, sing together,
> Ye waste places of Jerusalem;
> For the Lord hath comforted His people;
> He hath redeemed Jerusalem.

2. IT IS EASIER TO DREAM THAN TO DO

Who Shall Return?—Now that the dream of a generation was about to be fulfilled, the Jews were faced with the practical labors of reconstruction. Everybody desired that Judea should be rebuilt; but the question was who should leave Babylonia and go to Judea to do the building. Not only was the journey to Judea long and hazardous, not only would life there be more rugged than in Babylonia, but many of the Babylonian Jews were already prosperous and well established in business or on farms. Moreover, the Jews in Judea were poor, and it was necessary to take money along for the rebuilding of Jerusalem. It was remarkable therefore that as many as forty-two thousand Babylonian Jews nevertheless decided to undertake the journey and the difficult task. They took with them all their worldly goods as well as the contributions of gold and silver made not only by the Jews who chose to remain in Babylonia, but also by the king out of his treasury. Most started out on foot. Some rode on camels' backs; others on donkeys. They took several months to travel the long, dusty miles of desert between Babylonia and Judea. At last they arrived. With songs and rejoicing they greeted the land of their fathers. We still have one song which commemorates this occasion in chapter 126 of the Book of Psalms:

> When the Lord brought back those that returned to Zion,
> We were like unto them that dream.
> Then was our mouth filled with laughter,
> And our tongue with singing;
> Then said they among the nations:
> "The Lord hath done great things with these."
> The Lord hath done great things with us;
> We are rejoiced.

New Troubles—Much time had to pass and many difficulties had to be overcome before the hope of restoration was realized in fact. The joy of the arrival soon passed when the newcomers looked about to see what had to be done. For something more practical than mere hope and idealism was needed for overcoming the obstacles in the way of the new community.

1. Quarrels may have broken out between the Babylonian and the Judean Jews. It is quite possible also that the Babylonian Jews laid claim to lands which had belonged to their ancestors, but which had now been cultivated for years by the Jews who had never left Judea.

2. There were also some disagreements among the returned exiles themselves. Their leaders were Zerubbabel, a descendant of the House of David, and Joshua, who was to be the high priest of the rebuilt Temple. The question now arose what to do first, to build the walls around the city, or the Temple in the city. Zerubbabel, the prince, and Joshua, the priest, were naturally on opposing sides. The prince won his desire, and the ancient walls actually began to rise.

3. The neighboring nations now interfered. They had never welcomed the idea of the Jews becoming a nation again. Ever since Gedaliah had been murdered, these neighboring peoples had been having things much their own way with the Jews. Their own populations had entered the Judean territory. They encouraged intermarriage between Judeans and members of their own peoples. If the Temple were to be rebuilt and, especially, if a wall were to surround Jerusalem, they knew that their influence would be at an end. They resorted to a despicable trick. They wrote a letter to the king of Persia charging that the Jews were plotting rebellion. The Persian king replied at once by ordering Zerubbabel to stop building the wall. Without a wall to protect his city, without an organized force to maintain order, and with quarrels and conflicts surrounding him, Zerubbabel could hardly enforce his authority.

The End of a Prince's Dream—The returned exiles were disappointed. Years passed in hard labor. The land had grown wild during their absence in exile; it would take years of back-breaking labor to restore its fruitfulness. As time went on and quarrels and hardships continued, some openly regretted that they had left their comfortable homes in Babylonia. It was one thing to dream and hope; it was quite another to toil without promise of improvement.

Eighteen years passed. Then something occurred which

aroused once more the waning hopes of the Jewish community. Revolts against the authority of King Darius broke out all over the Persian empire. It looked as though the little nations that had been mastered by Babylonia and Persia would now become completely independent. Would Zerubbabel seize this chance to gain national independence? When, however, the news from the battlefield came, it was a grave disappointment. Darius was victorious; the Persian empire stood unchanged. The enemies of Zerubbabel thereupon lost no time in informing Darius of what Zerubbabel had planned. The result was that the Jewish prince disappeared from the political scene; the Jewish dream of independence was ended; and the House of David never ruled in Judea again. Joshua, the high priest, was now in full control.

3. THE SECOND TEMPLE IS BUILT

Time to Build—Zerubbabel's failure hastened the rebuilding of the Temple. Through the years the charred ruins of the First Temple had been lying desolate on the Holy Mountain. A modest altar had been erected to replace the former beautiful one, and the priests offered the sacrifices upon it. But the scarred stones of the rest of the Temple shamed both the returned exiles and the residents of the land. Many excuses had been given for this neglect. It was necessary to build the city wall first. More money was needed than the small community possessed. The crops had not been good for several years and the people were too poor and too disheartened to engage in building.

The prophets Haggai and Zechariah, however, urged the rebuilding of the Temple immediately. Constant postponing did the people harm. They feared that the people would gradually disintegrate unless they possessed a great national symbol of which they could be proud. Zerubbabel as king might have served the purpose. When that failed, these prophets redoubled their efforts to have the Temple rebuilt. At last, in the year 517 B. C. E., the holy task was resumed.

The Samaritans: Friends or Enemies?—A new problem now arose. The Samaritans, who lived to the north of Judea, demanded the right to participate in the rebuilding of the Temple. But the Jews refused. The reason for this refusal is important. The Samaritans were almost as Hebraic as the Jews. They were, in fact, descendants of the tribes of Israel, whose kingdom had been destroyed in 719, mixed with the foreign peoples, Cuthites, settled in their territory in place of those who went into exile. Lacking spiritual guidance, these mixed Israelites permitted their religion to degenerate, even becoming halfhearted in their belief in One God. The Jews who returned from Babylonia were particularly anxious not to compromise in their conviction about One God, and they feared that the northern Israelites might have a bad influence upon the Jews. When the Samaritans found themselves barred from helping to rebuild the Temple, they were so angry that they resorted to the old trick of misinforming the Persian government that the Jews were again planning to rebel. This time, however, the Persians did not believe them. The building continued to make progress, while the leaders of the Samaritans waited for another opportunity to interfere in Jewish affairs.

Why Some Jews Wept—In the year 516 the modest Temple was completed. Exactly seventy years had passed since the First Temple had been destroyed, and about twenty-one years since the first group of exiles returned from Babylonia. The Jews, it should be noted, have continued to think of the Bablonian Exile as having lasted seventy years; for they considered the rebuilding of the destroyed Temple, not the Cyrus Declaration, as the end of the Exile.

There was great rejoicing at the dedication of the Temple. From the towns and villages the people streamed into Jerusalem and crowded on the Temple Mount to watch the priests offer up the first sacrifices and to hear the Levites sing. But joy was mingled with sorrow. Among the celebrants some very old men were present who in their youth had seen the First Temple in all its glory. The new building, hastily put up by the small and poor community, was so insignificant by contrast with the First Temple, that the old men wept in disappointment. The prophet Zechariah then prophesied and in glowing picture-words described the future of the Jewish people and the coming greatness of the House of God which, though insignificant at the moment, would in time become the dwelling-place of righteousness for all the world.

4. Ezra's Disappointment

The Second Return—Many years were to pass before that prophecy came true. Meanwhile the rebuilding of the Temple left the national situation unchanged. The Jews in Babylonia, however, did not know how bad conditions continued to be economically and religiously in Palestine. For in those days, news traveled slowly, infrequently. The Jews of Babylonia imagined that affairs in Judea were far better than they actually were. Moreover, the Jews of Babylonia, finding it hard to live as Jews, thought that it was a simple matter for the Jews of Judea to live a Jewish life.

Among the most pious of the Babylonian Jews, about a generation after the rebuilding of the Temple, was a man named Ezra. By descent he was a priest, and by profession a scribe, which means that he was a teacher of Judaism and of Jewish literature. He was loved and respected, so that when he announced that he was planning to go to Judea to live, as the pious often did, about sixteen hundred men, women and children decided to join him. With great joy and high hope the little group set out. Ezra carried letters from the Persian king ordering all his officials along the way to protect the travelers. After several months they arrived in Jerusalem.

Ezra's Grief—Ezra soon discovered how different the situation among the Jews was from what he had expected. The Temple service went on under a descendant of Joshua, but the Jews were respectful neither towards the priests nor towards the Temple. They even failed to support it properly. The neighboring peoples, chiefly the Samaritans, had as much to say about the Temple as did the Jews. Indeed, the Jews freely intermarried with the pagan peoples in the neighborhood of Judea, and the daughters of the pagans usually brought into the Jewish community their family gods, their religious notions and their own forms of sacrifice. Even the language spoken by their children was not Hebrew. Ezra believed that, unless they removed this foreign influence, the Jews could not permanently establish the belief in One God. Ezra was deeply troubled. During an entire day he would take no food. He mourned the death of his cherished dreams.

Ezra Fails—The Jews were distressed. What could they do to make Ezra feel that everything was not lost? They were willing to purify their religion, but what sacrifices would that require? At the end of three days Ezra went into conference with the leaders of the people. He told them how he felt, how hopeless the outlook for the survival of the Jews seemed to him unless they returned wholeheartedly to their pure belief in One God and the good life which that implied. They asked him whether he could lead them toward the life and beliefs he wanted them to accept. Ezra answered that he could, provided they met one very difficult condition: they must send away their foreign wives and the children born of them. He pointed out that, unless they removed the source of the evil, he could not permanently heal the evil itself.

Ezra had made a harsh request; no one realized that better than he. He was asking hundreds of men to break up their families and send those whom they loved out of their homes. At about that time the Greeks, and later the Romans, instituted similar laws against marriage with foreigners for reasons much less important than those of Ezra. He demanded this supreme sacrifice because he believed that the nation and its ideals were more important than the feelings of individual men or women. He was serving as general in a war for the preservation of the Jews, and like every general he considered his objective of greater importance than the lives of his soldiers. Under the influence of Ezra's strong personality the leaders of the Jews promised to do what he had demanded.

But the plan could not be carried through. The heartaches of the separation proved too great for the people to bear. Moreover, the pagan nations with whom the Jews had intermarried were unwilling to permit their sons, daughters and grandchildren to be sent out of the country where they had settled. These pagans threatened revenge. Ezra had no police with which to enforce his regulations upon the Jews, and no army to protect the land against outsiders. After the first expressions of willingness on the part of the Jews to obey him, Ezra saw matters settle back into what they had formerly been. Ezra was defeated.

Ezra the Teacher—Some say that Ezra was so disappointed that he returned to Babylonia and did not revisit Judea until many years later. More likely, he stayed in Judea, dwelling apart from active public life. It was well that he did so, for Ezra was not the person to deal with large masses of men. He was primarily a scribe, a man of letters, a teacher. He gathered about himself a small group of disciples and acquainted them with the great literary treasures of the Jewish people. In this way Ezra achieved more than he could possibly have accomplished by his interest in practical government. His next appearance in public life was some twenty years later, when another great figure of Jewish history arrived in Judea.

5. How Nehemiah Succeeded where Ezra Had Failed

The King's Cupbearer—News trickled through to Babylonia that the Judean community was slowly dying. Upon no

Babylonian Jew did this news have more saddening effect than upon Nehemiah, a man who stood high in the favor of the Persian king. His official title was "King's Cupbearer," probably an honorary title, having as little to do with the royal cup as, later, the official with the title "Royal Chamberlain" had to do with the royal chamber. Nehemiah was one of the king's advisers, and shared in the government of Persia. In his autobiography, which is included in the Bible as the Book of Nehemiah, Nehemiah tells how he requested a leave of absence from his duties in the government. The king, after obtaining Nehemiah's promise that he would not stay away permanently, granted him leave and appointed him military governor of Judea.

Bricks and the Sword—When Nehemiah arrived in Jerusalem, he continues, he did not at once announce publicly that he was the new governor. Instead he made the rounds of the city and the wall to see what work had to be done. Like Ezra some years before, Nehemiah came to the conclusion that the neighboring nations were deliberately obstructing the development of the Jews into a nation and of Judaism into a religion of the One God. The immediate problem was to thrust these troublemakers out of Jewish internal affairs.

A few days later Nehemiah called the leaders of the Jewish people together. Showing them the king's commission appointing him governor, he announced that he expected them to help in repairing the wall around the city. The leaders answered Nehemiah with loud objections. They pointed out that there were no men to spare for such a difficult task; they asserted that the neighboring Samaritans and Ammonites would be sure to resent the building of the wall. But Nehemiah disregarded their protests, and it soon turned out that the common people were enthusiastic about Nehemiah's plans. Without difficulty Nehemiah stirred the workmen and artisans of Jerusalem to volunteer for the building of the wall. Only the upper classes among the Jews, those who were on intimate terms with the Samaritans and Ammonites, held back. These two peoples tried their utmost to interfere with the building, and on several occasions they attacked the workmen. Nehemiah was forced to arm the people, so that each worker had a sword by his side. As soon as the outpost sounded the bugle to announce the danger of an attack, the builders would drop their trowels, seize their swords, and join the soldiers in the fighting. In an incredibly short time the wall around the city was built.

Nehemiah Orders a Reformation—The building of the

wall was but the first step towards all that Nehemiah wanted
to do. He had in the meantime established contact with Ezra,
and the two men decided what the new Jewish community
needed in order to be brought closer to the ideal which it was
to represent. Things now began to happen in quick succession. Nehemiah ordered the gates of the new wall closed at
sundown on Friday and not to be reopened till sundown on
Saturday. He did this for the sake of the Sabbath, to stop
non-Jewish merchants from making the Sabbath their market
day by bringing their wares into the city. The Jewish merchants joined the non-Jews in objecting. But Nehemiah paid
little attention to them, and, as a matter of fact, the merchants soon became used to bringing their goods to market on
another day. Nehemiah then forbade all foreign interference in internal Jewish affairs. He followed these political acts
by reform in the administration of the Temple, instituting a
regular tax for its support.

Most important of all, Nehemiah, in the spirit of the Hebrew prophets, introduced far-reaching social and economic
reforms. The prophets had always looked forward to the time
when every human being would be free and independent.
Freedom and independence among farmer-folk meant in reality the possession of land from which they drew their livelihood. To lose one's land meant poverty, then slavery. For
this reason laws existed in the Books of Moses which prevented a Jew from selling his landed property forever. If land
had to be sold, it had always to be returned to its original
owner, or to his heirs, at the expiration of a definite time, at
the end of which was the Year of Jubilee. If a man was in
debt, or had no other means of earning his livelihood, he
would ofttimes sell himself or his children into slavery. The
Jews of those days recognized slavery, much as the United
States did down to about seventy-five years ago. Judaism,
however, sought to control and make the system of slavery
more humane; and so it was forbidden for a Jew to be a
slave for more than a specified period. Before Nehemiah's arrival, the Jews had neglected to observe the laws about the
return of land to its original owners, or about the curtailment
of Jewish slavery. Poverty and suffering increased among the
population, while a few grew richer and more powerful. Such
conditions did not provide a healthy foundation for the revival of the Jewish people. Nehemiah determined to change
these evils by personal example. He announced that he would
cancel all debts due him and that he expected other wealthy

men to do the same. Whether out of fear of Nehemiah or out of shame, the others followed his example.

The First Great Assembly—As a final step in assuring the religious foundations of the Commonwealth, Nehemiah joined with Ezra in establishing the Torah as the Constitution of the new community. On the first of Tishri (Rosh Hashanah) of the year 444 B.C.E., a large number of people gathered in the court of the Temple. They watched with deep interest the priests and Levites at the service and the offering of the sacrifices. When the sacrifices had been completed, all eyes turned to the platform which had been erected in the middle of the court. Nehemiah stood there with the elders of the community and the chief priests. On it arose the dignified figure of Ezra, now an old man. In his hand was a scroll. Silence fell over the multitude as the old man raised his voice. Ezra read of God's covenant with Abraham, of the scene at Mount Sinai, of the warning given to the Hebrews that they must be a holy people, and of the religious and social laws by which that holiness was to be attained. Hours passed, and Ezra still read on. The people gave him close attention, for they were listening to their history, their destiny and their hopes. Their eyes filled with quiet tears when they thought of the great achievements expected of them. Long past midday Ezra stopped. He dismissed the people and told them to celebrate the holiday joyfully. The leaders and priests, deeply moved by the reading, stayed behind. One by one they came and made a solemn pledge to Ezra and Nehemiah to adopt the Torah from which Ezra had been reading as the fundamental law, the Constitution, of the restored state.

The Population of Jerusalem—Ezra and Nehemiah now felt that their task was almost done. Yet each of them believed that one thing more was needed to insure the permanence of their achievements. To strengthen both the national defense and their religion, Nehemiah thought it wise to bring more people into Jerusalem. Cities have always been the centers where new ideas took root, while dwellers on isolated farms or distant settlements have always been the last to give up old ideas. The reforms which Ezra and Nehemiah had introduced, though based on the teachings of the Torah and the prophets, were very different from the old ideas about religion which still prevailed among the peasants of Judea, especially those exposed to the religious influences of the neighboring pagan peoples. To bring as many Jews as possible into closer contact with the new ideas, it was necessary to bring them to Jerusalem, where these newer thoughts had greatest influence. Moreover, protection against hostile invasion could not be neglected, and Jerusalem needed human defenders in addition to the repaired wall. Nehemiah, therefore, either persuaded or compelled one in every ten of the peasant population of Judea to move into Jerusalem. The plan had the added advantage of creating an artisan class, so that Jews would not have to depend upon foreigners for skilled workmanship.

Knowledge as Strength—While Nehemiah thus strengthened the physical ramparts of the nation, Ezra performed a similar service for the people's spirit. Under his supervision, the scribes, Ezra's pupils and colleagues, undertook to spread the knowledge of the Torah and of the prophetic literature. He encouraged the reading of these books not only in Jerusalem, but in the country towns as well. Jewish tradition ascribes to Ezra the establishment of an institution which was subsequently greatly extended and became characteristic of Judaism—the reading of the Torah every Sabbath, Monday and Thursday. With this as the core, a service was eventually built up. Knowledge was to give Judaism indestructible power.

The Leaders Depart from the Scene—Despite their great accomplishments, the success of the labors of these two great leaders remained in doubt for some time. Ezra died, and Nehemiah had to return to his post in Persia. The wealthy classes among the Jews at once fell back into their old ways. Greed and pride reasserted themselves. Disregarding their vows and promises, these people revived their claims to their old debts and their former slaves. They continued their custom of marrying into families of the surrounding nations. Even the high priest permitted his son to marry the daughter of the chief Samaritan.

News of what was happening reached Nehemiah, and as soon as he could he returned to Judea. His second stay there was probably much shorter than his first, but his mere reappearance was enough to revive his earlier reforms. From that time the development of Judea went on smoothly.

The Memory of the Leaders—Twenty-four centuries have passed since Ezra and Nehemiah lived, and we can now evaluate the importance of their work. They are rightly placed among the greatest leaders that the Jewish people produced. Had it not been for them, the Jews might have become but another small pagan population like the Ammonites, or the Phoenicians, and, like them, would have been swallowed up by the Hellenistic civilization which a century later over-

whelmed the entire East. It was not national hostility that
made Ezra and Nehemiah object to the mingling of the Jews
with the pagans. The Jews were not a big nation trying to
destroy smaller ones. They were a small, weak group saving
themselves from being devoured by bigger nations. Moreover,
they were defending a way of life which at that time was new
in the world. This small people sought to be the guardian of
that way of life, or culture. Had Ezra and Nehemiah failed,
and had the Jews continued to absorb the paganism of their
neighbors, the world's loss would have been incalculably
great. The more obvious achievement of Ezra and Nehemiah
was the preservation of the independence of the Jewish nation. Hence, for centuries after, Nehemiah was acclaimed by
the Jews as the greater of the two leaders. But as time went
on, and as Judaism, the spiritual heritage of the Jewish people, became a great force in the life of the Jews and their
neighbors, Ezra's memory began to win its belated recognition and outshone that of Nehemiah. Ezra came to be called
the Restorer of the Torah, second in importance only to
Moses himself.

6. THE SILENT CENTURY

Years of Quiet Labor—After the death of Ezra and Nehemiah, it is as though a curtain fell upon Judea and hid from
sight all that went on within the tiny land. In fact, during the
century between 450 and 350 B.C.E., the entire ancient East
seems to have fallen asleep. Aside from the weak and clumsy
efforts of the Persian kings to gain control over the Greek
cities on the coast of Asia Minor, nothing new or interesting
happened within the vast empire ruled by them. The various
provinces from southern Egypt to northern India hung together loosely and lived quite peacefully. The little province
of Judea, too, was at rest in this general drowsiness. It was
one of the least important of Persia's subject states. It sent no
caravans on the highways of commerce; it launched no argo-
sies upon the sea. Consequently, no one heard of the Jews.
The Greeks, who were at that time the only people interested
in history, philosophy and geography, called the land between
the Mediterranean and the Jordan "Philistina" (Palestine), because the only people they knew in that land were the Philis-
tines who lived on the coast. Once in a while a Greek traveler
passed through the country and was impressed by the peculiar religion of its inhabitants. The Greeks, who enshrined

their many capricious gods and goddesses on Mount Olympus, were astonished to find a people who thought it a sin to make a statue of their God, who turned heavenward in prayer, and who considered their God's chief interest to be justice and righteousness. No wonder that travelers brought back stories to Greece about a strange people who lived in Palestine, a group of philosophers who worshipped the heavens.

Historical Arithmetic—What actually went on in Judea during this century can only be guessed at. Records from that period are very few, yet important changes were taking place which make that century one of the most fruitful in Jewish history. These changes were practically all intellectual and religious, therefore slow, outwardly invisible and undramatic. They did not strike the imagination sufficiently for anyone to record them. Only by subtracting the conditions of the year 450 from the changed conditions of 350, can one realize what happened during the century between the two dates. Before that subtraction is done, it is well to summarize the few facts and hints of events about which we have some information.

From the Sands of Egypt—About sixty years ago, in 1908, archaeologists in Egypt accidentally discovered letters and records which revealed the startling information that, a century and a half before Nehemiah, Jews had hired themselves out as mercenary soldiers. Around the year 600 B.C.E., the Babylonian conquerors needed soldiers to guard the southern frontier of Egypt against invasion by the Ethiopians. They hired thousands of Israelites for this purpose, gave them land in a district now called Assuan, and granted them permission to build a temple there and offer up sacrifices to their God. Later these Israelites were joined by a group of Judeans. Generation after generation the Hebrew soldier-farmers lived there side by side with native Egyptians. About the year 410, however, the Egyptians, aroused by their priests who were jealous for the Egyptian gods, destroyed the Israelite's temple. The letters recently found tell about this destruction and ask the high priest in Jerusalem and the Persian governor of Syria for aid in rebuilding the sanctuary. The Jews of Judea and of Babylonia responded to this plea and also tried to teach the Egyptian Jews to follow the rules of the Sabbath and the holidays which they had either forgotten or had never observed. The letters prove, among other things, that the movement of the Jews (Diaspora) to the West took place quite as early as their spread to the East.

Esther the Queen—The story of the Jews of Assuan is very new, while the story of Esther, Mordecai and Haman is very old and familiar. No one has as yet identified the Ahasuerus of the story of Esther. There were several kings by the name of Xerxes who might have been meant. But none of them is known to have had a wife by the name of Vashti or of Esther; none is known to have had a counselor called Haman who was replaced by another named Mordecai. Nevertheless the story does not sound impossible. The names are Persian, as is the entire atmosphere of the well-told short story. Nor is the plot difficult to believe. In a fit of drunkenness a Persian monarch removed his favorite wife, and later substituted for her another by the name of Hadassah, having also the pagan name of Esther. One of the Persian king's counselors, a vain and self-seeking person called Haman, turned out to be hostile to the Jews for no better reason than that Mordecai had hurt his vanity. Many have hated the Jews for no better cause than that, and, like Haman, have dignified their petty hates by clothing them in patriotism. In their hour of trouble Esther and Mordecai succeeded in winning the king over to the people's side by disclosing how Haman was motivated by selfish ambitions. Thus the Jews were saved and established the holiday of Purim.

High Priest in Place of King—During the First Commonwealth the Hebrews had been ruled by kings; during this, the Second Commonwealth, they were ruled by high priests. At the beginning of the Second Commonwealth, as the story of Zerubbabel proves, the Jews had been hoping for the re-establishment of the Davidic dynasty on the throne of Judah. The Persian kings would not tolerate this. They were afraid that kings among their vassal states would be tempted to plot rebellion in order to win independence. They had no such fears about high priests. Consequently high priests were entrusted with the local government of several provinces in the Persian empire, Judea among them. At this time, therefore, the Jewish government became a theocracy, which means a government headed by a priest who is supposed to be God's representative on earth. The Jews, however, never gave up the hope of some day being ruled by a descendant of David. This hope played an important part in Jewish history.

The office of high priest among the Jews was hereditary, that is, son always followed father, so that neither the Jewish people nor the Persian kings had any say about the succeeding high priest. The high priest, on his part, did not have unlimited powers in the government. He was assisted by a council from among the people, and he was responsible to an official of the Persian king. This official did not interfere much with the internal affairs of the country. He was merely concerned that the high priest should collect the taxes to be paid to the Persian government. The national council, however, did take an active part in the government. But the people did not elect this council. Its members were chosen from the important men of the country, heads of the great families among the priests and the landowners.

Scribe in Place of Prophet—As in government the high priest replaced the king, so in religious life the scribes took the place of the prophets. More prophets were not needed because the Jews now had books in which were written down the ideas of the great prophets of the past. All one had to do to know the kind of life which God wanted a man to lead was to study the sacred books. The scribes, who were the teachers, read these books before an assembled multitude and interpreted what Moses and his successors demanded of the Jewish people. Among the greatest achievements of the scribes was their final editing of the most important books of the Jewish past. What the generation of scribes down to the age of Ezra had done for the Torah and some of the prophetic books, the generations of scribes after Ezra did for other books now included in the Bible. By the end of the Persian period almost all the books of the collection now called "The Bible" were known among the people.

The New Alphabet—The influence of the scribes brought about an interesting change in the alphabet. The Israelites and Judeans, before they were exiled to Babylonia, had been using an ancient Hebrew script. While in exile, however, they learned to use a new and easier alphabet, called the Assyrian. When the scribes in Babylonia copied and recopied the ancient Hebrew literature in order to spread the knowledge of it among the exiles, they used the new script in preference to the old. Later generations of scribes continued to use it even when, like Ezra, they came to Judea and taught the Torah and the Prophets to the Jews of the Second Commonwealth. The new alphabet thus became connected with the sacred writings of the Jewish people. The ancient one continued to be used among the common people for ordinary purposes for some centuries to come. Only much later, when the Jews lost every semblance of political independence and had become a people united by its literature alone, did the alphabet of this literature come into general use, as it is among the Jews to this day.

What the Scribes Taught—Generals and statesmen decided the fate of other peoples; writers and teachers molded the destiny of the Jews. This is an oft-repeated statement and there is a good deal of truth in it. The entire transformation in the life of the Jews from this time on was the result of teaching and interpretation. The scribes encouraged knowledge; they strengthened personal character; they created literature; they formulated laws. They derived from the sacred books those ideas which were to guide their own people and, in time, inspire others.

Individual Responsibility—One of the ideas which the scribes emphasized was that true religion affects the thought and action of each individual. God wants the improvement of humanity; but this cannot be attained unless everyone improves himself. A pagan considered his duty done when he brought a gift to his Baal. A Jew, the scribes said, should indeed perform his duty in and for the Temple in Jerusalem, for the Temple was the visible reminder of God's presence among the Jewish people. But such performance was considered sheer paganism if it did not prepare a man to lead a better life.

The Jewish Sabbath—The scribes gave new meaning to the Sabbath. In ancient days only the Hebrews had any notion of a day of rest. The Babylonians, to be sure, had certain superstitions connected with every seventh day. They imagined that on that seventh day evil spirits waylaid human beings, and that therefore one should not do anything, for it was a luckless day. The ancient Hebrews had changed all that and has made the Sabbath a memorial of Creation, as is seen in the second chapter of the Book of Genesis. Ezra and Nehemiah emphasized the Sabbath as a day of rest, upon which men were to transact no business. The scribes carried Ezra's idea farther and interpreted the Sabbath as a day of holiness devoted to quiet study and religious thought.

The Second Step in the Growth of the Synagogue—The scribes used to teach their ideas to the Jewish people at the community house. In this way they advanced the development of the Synagogue as we have it today. In the days of exile in Babylonia, the Jews and Israelites had become used to meeting on Sabbaths and holidays. On such occasions portions of the Torah and the Prophets had probably been recited to give them courage and hope. It now became a firmly established part of Judaism that the people must have some portion of their sacred literature read to them. In the towns and villages of the country this may have been done in the local community house from which the government was administered and where the town council met. The details of how all this happened are not clear. This much, however, is certain, that, whereas in the days of Nehemiah the influence of the scribes was slight, a century later their ideas had become tremendously influential. They had succeeded in democratizing Jewish learning.

Missionary Judaism—On many important questions the scribes differed among themselves. Their discussions became embodied in traditional interpretations of the Bible which, under the name of Oral Law, guided the Jews of later ages. Differences of opinion must have been settled by the authority of the most respected scribe or by the experience resulting from the application of one or another view. One important question, for example, on which debate was long and heated, was that of intimate social relations between Jews and pagans. One side argued, on the basis of a view expressed in the Pentateuch, for the total exclusion of all pagans. This attitude, if adopted, would have condemned the Jews to remaining a tiny island in the midst of a sea of paganism. The opposite extreme advocated unlimited intermarriage with pagans and would have been equally disastrous for Jewish survival. A middle ground between these extremes is represented by the biblical story of Ruth the Moabite. This ancient story was offered as proof that Ruth, who was a Moabite by birth, was the mother of the most famous family of Jews, the royal family of David. It was enough, the moderate scribes asserted, that she had deliberately chosen to affiliate herself with Judaism and the Jewish people. This view made possible the growth of the people through the conversion of pagans to Judaism. Furthermore, the Book of Ruth was eventually connected with the feast of Shabu'ot, the day which commemorates the giving of the Ten Commandments. Jewish tradition thereby emphasized that Judaism may be accepted by all peoples.

Gains and Losses—How great the influence of Judaism was under the guidance of the scribes is proved by the growth of Judean territory. At the end of this century the boundaries of Judea were larger than at its beginning. Now the Jews could not possibly have conquered this new territory, since the Persian government would not have permitted local wars. The only possible explanation, therefore, is that the influence of Judaism had spread into districts which had

THE CITY SHALL BE BUILDED

indeed been portions of the first Judean Commonwealth, but which had fallen under the sway of the neighboring peoples during the intervening period. Thus the Jewish people became stronger, while the surrounding peoples were losing their identity and were soon to be swallowed up by the Greeks.

The Samaritans—One group, however, the Samaritans, was definitely lost to Jewish life. These descendants of the Israelites who lived north of Judea not only refused to join the Jews, but even became their deadly enemies after both Ezra and Nehemiah had rejected their cooperation in the national rebirth. On Mount Gerizim, near the ancient city of Shechem, they built for themselves a separate Temple. Nevertheless, despite their hostility, the Samaritans also reflected the influence of the scribes by adopting a portion of Hebrew literature. To this day their sacred writings are the Five Books of Moses and the Book of Joshua. They considered the latter book particularly significant because it described the leading part which the tribe of Ephraim played in Hebrew history, Joshua having been an Ephraimite, the tribe from which the Samaritans claimed descent.

A Century of Achievement—While all these events were taking place in little Judea, during the same century, in the Greek city of Athens, Socrates, Plato and Aristotle were speculating about the nature of man and the world. These Greeks and their successors were called philosophers, lovers of wisdom, even as the Jewish cultural leaders were called scribes, writers or lovers of literature. Both Greek philosophers and Jewish scribes were laying the foundations for a better way of life for themselves and all mankind. The philosophers hoped to attain it through the supremacy of Reason and its eternal search for truth; and the scribes through the ministry of Religion and its eternal quest for God.

CHAPTER III

THE WORLD TURNS WEST

THE GREEKS AWAKE THE EAST AND CAUSE MANY CHANGES IN THE LIFE OF THE JEWS

The New Opponent—The work of the scribes was destined before long to undergo a crucial test. Because of the scribes, Babylonian and Persian culture had not succeeded in destroying Judaism. Now a new opponent appeared—Greece, more persistent and more subtle in its efforts to lure the Jews from their way of life. This time the conflict was longer and more profound. In the course of it the whole world became changed, for out of this struggle between Greek and Jewish civilization Christianity was born, and Judaism itself was considerably modified. How the Greeks first met the Jews, and why they were sometimes friendly and at other times hostile to each other, is therefore extremely important.

1. THE COMING OF THE GREEKS

Alexander, Awakener of the East—In the year 334 B.C.E., the drowsing Persian empire was aroused by the tramp of marching armies from the West. Alexander, the young king of Macedonia, had appeared in Greece and, after uniting that divided country by force, announced that he was going to annex the entire East. A pigmy was threatening a giant! Yet it came to pass. Slow-moving, inefficient and unprogressive, Persia fell an easy prey to the youthful, ambitious, brilliant Alexander and his well-trained army. In an incredibly short time Alexander made himself ruler over all the Persian provinces, and more besides.

Alexander, unlike the Persians, did not dream of uniting all his conquests into one great empire, but wanted to merge all the conquered peoples into one great cultural unity. He admired the philosophy and the literature of Greece, but he also liked the grandeur and the wealth and the ease of life which he found in Persia. He thought it possible to combine the two and create a nation which would have the best features of both Greek and oriental civilizations. He built new cities and he enlarged old ones; and he encouraged Greeks, especially the veterans of his army, to settle in these cities and teach the native population how to live like Greeks. Within a generation the entire ancient East throbbed with new life. New ideas, new names for old gods, new methods of administration, a new language, new military tactics and, not the least, new markets for trade awakened the East from the lethargy into which it had sunk during centuries of easygoing Persian rule. The Jews, too, soon realized that they were surrounded by a new world.

Alexander and the Jews—Alexander's conquests made a tremendous impression on the Jews. He, in turn, while manifesting hostility to the Samaritans, showed special favor to the Jews and granted them self-government. He displayed respect for their religious scruples by not compelling Jewish young men to join his army, where they would have had to violate their Sabbath and other laws. Thus, the first meeting between Greeks and Jews was evidently most friendly.

2. PALESTINE AS A CAUSE FOR CONFLICT

Dividing Alexander's Conquests—No sooner had Alexander died than his generals quarreled among themselves over the control of the lands he had conquered. A long and complicated series of wars followed with Palestine at the center of the fighting. Two generals, Ptolemy and Seleucus, were especially important, since each of them established a dynasty which figures in the history of the Jews. Ptolemy gained control of Egypt, economically the most productive of all Alexander's conquests. His descendants called themselves by his name, the Ptolemies. Seleucus won for himself almost all the lands which Alexander had conquered in Asia. His descendants were called the Seleucids.

The Fate of Palestine—Both the first Ptolemy and the first Seleucus claimed Palestine as part of their kingdoms. Finally Ptolemy seized it, and Seleucus let the matter rest. His descendants, however, never gave up their claim to the land. An interesting story is told in connection with Ptolemy's capture of Jerusalem. He anticipated some difficulty in taking the city. Much to his surprise, however, the Jews did not make

the slightest effort to defend themselves. It was on Saturday.
To the Greeks, to whom the idea of Sabbath was quite unknown, it seemed ridiculous for people not to defend themselves at all times. They made sport of the Jews and called
them a foolish people. But this story shows how well the
scribes had done their work, and how deeply the reverence
for Judaism and its institutions had become ingrained in the
people during the preceding century. The scribes were destined to labor through one more century before the results of
their teaching were to be tested in the fires of a great war.

3. HELLENIZATION OUTSIDE OF PALESTINE

Emigration—For a number of centuries to come the Jews
of Palestine had more contacts with the lands to the west
than with those of Babylonia to their east. Two reasons accounted for this. In the first place, they were compelled to
look to the west because they were usually governed from
lands which lay in that direction. In the second place, trade
and commerce became active along the Mediterranean.
Therefore Jews who, in search of adventure or better opportunities to make a living, chose to leave home, as people of
every nation occasionally do, preferred to go west. Slowly
Jewish settlements grew up along the coasts of the Mediterranean, on the islands of Greece, and even along the shores of
the Black Sea. Thus began the Jewish western Diaspora, that
is, the scattering of the Jewish population. Separated from
their center of Jewish life in Judea, these emigrants had to
learn the Greek language and adopt some Greek customs and
ideas. They entered, in this way, upon the process of Hellenization (from the word *Hellas*, the Greek name for Greece).

The Jews and the Founding of Alexandria—The Jewish
community of Alexandria affords the best illustration of what
happened to the Jews under the influence of Greek, or Hellenistic, civilization. Alexandria was one of the cities planned
by Alexander and by his successor, Ptolemy, as a commercial
port. The problem of a population for the new city was
solved by bringing into it a number of people from many
conquered nations. The Greeks, of course, formed the most
important element, but from the very beginning Jews were
also in the new city. In a very short time the port of Alexandria became one of the most active commercial centers of the
world. It was no longer necessary then to force or persuade
people, including Jews, to settle there. New settlers were glad

to come, and within two generations the Jews formed an important part of the Alexandrian community.

Alexandrian Citizenship—Citizenship in a Greek city involved to some extent the matter of religion. Each city had its protecting patron god or goddess. Patriotic festivals and even games of sport, of which the Greeks were very fond, were bound up with sacrifices to the patron divinity. Consequently, when a man held a civil office, he could not avoid participating in appropriate religious ceremonies. Obviously, Jews could not take part in any such activities, and they therefore excluded themselves from full citizenship. Yet the Jews could not be called foreigners, since they had helped in founding Alexandria and had done as much as anyone to make it prosperous and important. The first Ptolemies understood all this and permitted them to organize a separate community within Alexandria. They had their own courts of law conducted in accordance with Jewish tradition and their own religious organizations. They were, to be sure, denied the honor of organizing the games, or leading in the festivals of the city, or holding public office, unless they chose to become converts to paganism. But they had the same commercial rights and the same rights to police protection as any other citizen of Alexandria. Where they resided depended upon the natural desire of people with the same background to live near one another. Like the Irish, the Italians and the modern Jews, the Jews of those days, though they had the right to live anywhere within Alexandria, preferred to concentrate in one or in several neighborhoods. Special Jewish reasons for this preference were the requirements of the Jewish religion; for example, the need of complying with the dietary laws and the desire to be near the house of study and the synagogue.

In spite of all these religious and political differences, the Jews and the other Alexandrians were friendly to one another. The city was prosperous and growing. All differences were therefore overlooked. A man by the name of Hecataeus of Abdera, one of the earliest literary men of Hellenized Egypt, spoke of the Jews in laudatory terms.

Cultural Adjustment—As the people of Alexandria prospered they became more interested in Greek culture. In fact, the time came when there was more Greek learning and philosophic thinking in this Egyptian city than in Greece itself. Jews have always been particularly hospitable to the influence of the culture about them. But, as Jews, they faced a double task. They spoke Greek; they admired Greek culture; at the same time, they insisted on remaining Jews. Therefore they had to face the problem of the Hebrew language, the language which best expressed their religious attitudes, just as modern Jews who live in the Western world have to face it at the present time. The first generation, that which came from Judea, no doubt spoke either Hebrew or Aramaic, a language resembling Hebrew, and did not understand much Greek. Perhaps the second generation understood both Hebrew and Greek. The third generation, however, understood very little, if any, Hebrew or Aramaic. Their native tongue was Greek. They read Greek books, and Greek ideas became part of their mentality. They could not read Hebrew books and, with the loss of Hebrew, they were confronted with the danger of having Judaism disappear completely from among them.

How was this danger to be met? They tried two obvious methods—the same methods used today. They encouraged their children to study the Hebrew language so that they might be able to become acquainted with Jewish ideas in their original form. They also translated the Pentateuch and, later on, other parts of Hebrew literature into Greek, so that, even though in a different language, the spirit of the Jewish people might continue to live among them.

The Legend of the Septuagint—The Jews of Egypt looked upon the translation of the Bible into Greek as such an important event that they surrounded it later with a halo of legend. They said that the act of translating the Bible was connected with a miracle. The story is told, in an apocryphal book by a certain Aristeas of Alexandria, that the second Ptolemy, surnamed Philadelphus, who reigned between 285 and 247 B. C. E., was interested in collecting a library of the finest books in the world. One day his librarian told him that he already had nine hundred and ninety-five books representing the best literature of all the nations. Nevertheless, the librarian continued, the five greatest books of all were still not to be found in his library. These books, he told the king, were those of the Jews, who called them the Five Books of Moses. Thereupon the king sent ambassadors to the high priest in Jerusalem, and asked that a copy of these books be sent to him along with men capable of rendering them into Greek. The high priest did so, sending seventy-two learned, wise and saintly scribes and a copy of the Torah. Great festivities were arranged in their honor. The king and his courtiers marveled at their wisdom and learning. Then the time came for them to get to the work of translating. Each one was placed in a separate chamber, so that without communicating with his fellows he translated the entire Torah by himself. When the task was completed, the king had the various translations compared. Behold the miracle! Not a single difference in word or letter was found among them. Because seventy learned scribes translated the Pentateuch, the Greek translation of the Bible is called the *Septuagint,* which means "the seventy." Pagans as well as Jews were so proud of the Septuagint that they declared the day of its completion an annual holiday.

4. Greeks and Jews in Palestine

The New Greek Cities—In the meantime Greek influence was spreading in Palestine too. On every side of Judea old cities that used to call themselves Ammonite, or Syrian, or Philistine, assumed new, Greek names and practiced the Greek manner of life. They adopted the Greek form of government and built Greek gymnasiums. Not only men and women, but even old gods were given Greek names. Jewish Palestine became ringed about with Greek influences.

Prosperity and Migration—The non-Jewish cities about Judea became prosperous because they took an active part in the commerce between the East and the West. Judea was also affected by the greater prosperity which resulted from the coming of the Greeks. The Jews now had a market for their products. They exported such things as grain, wine, olive oil, cheese, fruit and fish. Judea's prosperity, however, did not keep pace with that of its neighbors.

The Jewish population increased to such an extent as to make it necessary for some Jews to emigrate from Judea. Most of those who found they could not make a living in Judea settled near the borders of their own land. Jews who had sufficient money to buy a farm from its pagan owner became farmers in territory outside of Judea just as they had been in Judea. A larger number settled in the cities and became artisans or merchants. Since these places were near Judea, the Jews who moved into them could keep in touch with Jewish life much more easily than Jews who lived far away.

Hellenization in Judea—One aspect of the general situation of that day is worthy of particular attention. While almost all the ancient peoples whose names are mentioned in the Bible disappeared completely, early in the Greek period, swept away by the flood of Greek influence, the Jews remained steadfast in their own faith and their own manner of living.

They could not be attracted to the lewd, wilful and cruel gods of Olympus. In Greek games, baths and festivals, they saw occasions for self-indulgence and immorality. For the Jews of Judea did not come in touch with the highest Greek civilization, not even with as high a Greek culture as surrounded the Jews of Alexandria. Even if they had met the real Greek culture, that of the famous Greek philosophers and poets, the Jews would still have rejected it as inferior to the culture of Judaism, though they might have had some respect for it. Actually, the Judeans saw only the childishness, the brutality and the selfishness which the half-baked Greeks around them tried to present as genuine Hellenism. The scribes had done their work much too thoroughly for the Jews to be attracted by anything of this sort, let alone to adopt it in preference to Judaism. That is why more than ever before the Jews stood out as a different, unique people.

"Let Us Be Like All the Nations"—This attitude could not, however, long continue to be adhered to by all the people. There are bound to be some who feel uncomfortable unless they are with the majority, so as not to be distinguishable from everybody else. This is apt to be true especially of persons who frequently come in close contact with others, different from themselves, for example, merchants. When, moreover, being different stands in the way of greater prosperity, people have every incentive to say, "Let us stop our foolish individualism; let us be like all others." It is the eternal cry of the superficial assimilationist.

Judea was a land of peasants. It possessed only one city worthy of the name—Jerusalem. The majority of its population, the farmers, the small merchants, the artisans, were content to remain as they were. They were proud of their heritage and, judging by what they heard about the world around them, they had every right to be proud. But there were also the upper classes—the nobility, that is, the chief families among the priests who lived in Jerusalem, and the exporters and the importers, who were Judea's great merchants. These groups constantly associated with the upper classes of the surrounding peoples. Moreover, they thought in terms of economic prosperity; they wanted to make Jerusalem a great trading center, so that the caravans which traveled down to Egypt or to the coast might pass through the city. This was impossible as long as the other peoples looked upon Jerusalem as strange, foreign and barbarous. The upper-class Jews did not really want to give up Judaism. All they wanted was to make the Jews externally resemble the peoples about them.

They argued that dressing in the Greek fashion, encouraging the young people to indulge in Greek games, or reorganizing the politics of Jerusalem according to a Greek constitution, would do no harm to Judaism and might lead their neighbors to look upon the Jews as people very like themselves.

The Sons of Tobias—The principal advocates of the Hellenization of Judea were members of a family which may have traced its origin from Tobias the Ammonite with whom Nehemiah in his day had had many difficulties. For two centuries, the family, although not originally Jewish, had identified itself with the Jews and had even intermarried with the family of the high priest. They were members of the National Council which aided the high priest in the government of Judea, playing an important role in the politics of the land. About the year 230 B. C. E. one of them, Joseph ben Tobias, bought from the king of Egypt the right to collect the taxes from the entire district of Syria, consisting of Judea and all its neighbors. The system of tax-collecting in those days was for one man to pay the royal treasury a lump sum for the privilege of collecting as much as he could from the inhabitants of a district. It was a vicious system, for it enabled the collector to enrich himself at the expense of the population. Joseph took full advantage of this opportunity. He, his family and his co-workers became a great economic power in Palestine. What is more, they saw their chance to improve permanently the economic position of Jerusalem by diverting to it trade from other parts of Palestine. With increasing wealth and power their desire to rise socially also increased. More than ever they began to imitate the customs and ways of the Greeks. Thus it came about that while on the one hand they aroused the enmity of the Gentiles by their economic oppression, they tried on the other hand to imitate these same Gentiles in their manner of life.

5. LESSONS IN WISE LIVING

A Scribe's Advice—The Jews, of course, had no idea of the great life-and-death struggle which the next generation would have to wage as a result of these Greek influences. At that very time one of the scribes, Joshua ben Sirach, who may have lived in Jerusalem itself, wrote a book. He intended it as a book of instruction, a textbook in philosophy. But his philosophy differed greatly from that of the Greeks. He made no attempt to find out the laws of the physical world; he did not even attempt to describe an ideal form of government and society. He was interested in giving people practical advice on how to live. According to him the ideal life was one conducted on the lines described by Moses and the prophets. The simple peasant who worked his field, who had no ambitions for wealth and power, who served God wholeheartedly and kept peace in his family, was the man who lived wisely. Joshua ben Sirach warned against falling into the hands of wealth-seekers. A wise man will not even want to be their friend, because the rich seek to use everyone to further their own ambitions. Joshua noted the sharp division which was rising in Judea between rich and poor, but he did not realize that such distinctions had in them the elements of tragedy. Contentment with one's lot, piety and obedience to the law of God, were his recipes for the good life, and he invited all the young men to come to the school which he, like other scribes, maintained, and to listen to his instruction.

Other Books on Wisdom—Ben Sirach's book proved very popular, and yet it was not included in the anthology of the greatest Hebrew literature, the Bible. The reason was that Ben Sirach, known to have lived but recently, was not considered to have been divinely inspired. Another book, very much like that of Ben Sirach, is called the Book of Proverbs. Jewish tradition ascribes it to no less a person than King Solomon who lived about seven hundred years earlier, and that was a reason for considering it sacred. Others assert that both books were products of the same period, since both seem to reflect the influence of Greek thinking.

In contrast to these two books is a third, also probably written at this time. It is called "Koheleth" in Hebrew and "Ecclesiastes" in English, and in it one sees how deeply Greek influence penetrated the minds of many Jews. The author is a pessimist; he has a dark, unhappy view of life. He finds that everything is vain and useless. Only the last few sentences keep the book in harmony with the spirit of the rest of Jewish literature. For these last sentences argue that all earthly pleasure and power are empty, and that only piety and faith in God make for the greatest happiness. These books of wisdom present the contrast between the Hellenistic ideal of the search for individual power, with which some Jews were already infected, and the simple, pious life which the scribes held up as the greatest good.

CHAPTER IV

THE MACCABEES' FIGHT FOR SURVIVAL

THE JEWS FIGHT A WAR AGAINST TREMENDOUS ODDS AND SAVE THEMSELVES FROM PAGANISM

The Maccabean Age—The next fifty years of Jewish history (200–150 B. C. E.) were years of tremendous importance, filled with stirring events. These events transformed the Jewish people and Judaism and left their impress upon Jewish life to the present day. This age, called the Maccabean era, was as significant for the Jews as the era of the French Revolution was for Europe and America in the eighteenth and nineteenth centuries. Since almost all that happened to the Jewish people was inseparably connected with events outside of Judea, brief reference must be made to the ambitions and fortunes of the empires and kingdoms which then controlled the world and to their powerful rulers.

1. JUDEA BECOMES A SYRIAN PROVINCE

Syria's Ambition—The Seleucids nursed the ambition of reuniting all of Alexander's conquests. By the year 198 B. C. E., Antiochus III, called the "Great," took the first step in that direction when he forced Egypt to give up Palestine.

One obstacle lay in the path of the Seleucids' march to world dominion. Rome had just destroyed the power of Carthage, and was gradually acquiring supremacy over the Mediterranean lands. This event not only forced Antiochus to give up his Egyptian conquests, but to send hostages to Rome from among the royal family and to pay a huge sum of money as indemnity. Still not discouraged, Antiochus and his successor, Seleucus IV, continued to plan conquests. To further their plans and to pay the heavy indemnity to Rome, the Seleucids exacted large sums of money from the peoples subject to them. This created a great deal of dissatisfaction. The attitude of the subject peoples now revealed that neither Alexander nor the Seleucids had succeeded in making Greeks out of the masses of Asia. Uninterested in Seleucid aims, these peoples, in their anger over their additional burdens, reminded themselves of their former independence. The Seleucid empire began to crack, ultimately to fall apart, wiping out many of its superficial Greek characteristics. Such a reassertion of independence from the tyranny of the Greek Seleucids was partly responsible for the Judean rebellion under the Maccabees.

Parties among the Jews—Differences of opinion often result in political parties. When the Seleucids tried to realize their ambitions, one group of Jews favored the annexation of Judea by Syria, and another wanted Judea to remain part of the Egyptian empire. Naturally, Hyrcanus, son of Joseph ben Tobias, was on the side of Egypt, whose tax-official he was. He and his henchmen were opposed by his brothers and other wealthy men, who sided with Syria because they thought it would be victorious in the end. In all this the common people had so far taken no part. What difference could it make to them whether Hyrcanus or someone else was tax-collector, whether a Seleucid or a Ptolemy counted them among his subjects? But as soon as religious matters were involved, the common people were bound to take sides, and real political parties began to develop once more.

2. THE ATTACK ON JUDAISM

The Sanctity of the Temple—In order to gain their ends, the pro-Syrian faction curried the favor of Seleucus by revealing to him that much money belonging to his opponents was stored in the Temple. There was some truth in this. In those days, there being no banks, all temples were used for storing treasures. The sacred character of such places made it almost certain that a thief would not dare arouse the anger of a god by taking what the god protected. No doubt some of Hyrcanus' money, along with other treasures, was stored in the Temple at Jerusalem. Seleucus, ever anxious to lay his hands on more money, dispatched Heliodorus, one of his officials, to confiscate the money in the Temple. A Jewish legend tells that, when Heliodorus went into the Temple, he was confronted by a man on horseback who had him beaten to within an inch of his life. Heliodorus was scarcely able to leave the sacred place. Whatever actually happened within the Temple, the fact is that Heliodorus left without taking any of the money. Thus, the pro-Syrian group was defeated in its first attempt to gain control of Judea. They did succeed, however, in revealing to the Jewish population that the Hellenized Jews would stop at nothing in order to achieve their purpose.

The High Priest Is Removed—The pro-Syrian faction now decided to remove the high priest. That done, they could gain control of the council, and then proceed to revise the government of Jerusalem, and of all Judea, to suit their own views and interests. They felt that their plans stood a better chance of success this time because a change had taken place in the government of Syria.

Seleucus IV had died, and had been succeeded by his brother Antiochus, who had thus usurped the throne which rightfully should have gone to Seleucus' son. Now Antiochus IV, like his predecessors, also cherished the great ambition of conquering Egypt and making his empire large, strong and united. All this he hoped to achieve by means of attaching the various provinces to himself as the embodiment of Greek culture. He gave himself the surname *Epiphanes,* which means "the visible god"; in other words, he and Jupiter were to be considered identical. Worse still, he acted as though that was really the case, with the result that people began to call him *Epimanes,* "the madman."

Since Palestine, especially Judea, was the province bordering on Egypt, it was most important for Antiochus to have a loyal, Hellenized population there. Yet, that very province was the one in which Hellenization had made least progress. When, therefore, a group from among the Jews themselves came to him and proposed a way of speeding Hellenization in Judea, Antiochus was eager to fall in with their plan. The plan was a very simple one. Onias III was to be removed from office, and his Hellenized brother, Jason, was to be put in his place. In return for a sum of money Antiochus promised to grant Jerusalem a Greek constitution and the right to coin money, which would be very helpful in developing the city commercially.

The plan was carried into effect and the feelings of the common people were outraged. It was the first time since the Jews returned from the Babylonian Exile that a non-Jewish government had interfered in the succession to the high priesthood, treating the sacred office as if it were nothing more than an ordinary governorship. But worse was to come. Now that the Hellenizers had full control of Judea's government, they began to build gymnasiums within Jerusalem in which the young people were encouraged to spend a great deal of time. The young priests neglected their duties in the Temple in order to engage in sports. Greek styles in dress, Greek names, the Greek language became stylish in Jerusalem. And, worst of all, the Hellenized life brought with it looseness in religious observance, as well as the characteristically Greek looseness of morals.

Having started on the road to Hellenization, the Hellenizers themselves found that they could not stop. The more radical among them felt that progress on that road was still not fast enough. They complained to Antiochus that Jason was not sufficiently energetic. An enormous sum of money was promised the king in return for appointing a radical Hellenist to the high priesthood. Now it was Jason's turn to flee. This time the appointee, Menelaus, was not even a member of the high-priestly family. Menelaus was a man without any sympathy whatever for Jewish traditions; one whose sole ambition was to exercise power. Unfortunately for him, he found that the Temple treasury did not contain enough to pay the sum he had promised Antiochus. Consequently, Menelaus took some of the holy vessels of the Temple and sold them to raise the money he needed so badly.

The "Desolating Abomination"—To Antiochus the unwillingness of the Jews to be Hellenized was stiff-necked nonsense. If Judaism stood in his way, so much the worse for Judaism. He gave orders that Judaism must be destroyed.

A part of the Syrian army marched into Jerusalem to support Menelaus and his policy. Many of the inhabitants of the city were killed; others escaped to the hills. Only the known Hellenists remained. Orders were given prohibiting the observance of the Sabbath, the holidays and circumcision. In the Temple above the altar was placed a statue of Jupiter bearing an obvious resemblance to Antiochus. Over such a Temple Menelaus consented to remain as high priest. To that statue were brought as sacrifices the animal most detested by the Jews, the pig. An abominable act had been perpetrated on the 25th day of Kislev in the year 168 B. C. E. and, to use the descriptive expression of the Book of Maccabees, it left the Jewish people desolate.

3. THE HOPELESS OPPOSITION

The Party of Hasidim—The common people watched these events with growing horror. They ascribed them to the influence of Hellenism and to the abandonment by the upper classes of the principles of the Torah which the scribes had taught. But what could these simple, peaceful farmers and artisans do against the rich and mighty? The only way left to them was to strengthen the spirit of piety within themselves. All through the years that Hellenism gained ground among the wealthy upper classes and their imitators, Judaism had been more fervently cherished among the rest of the people and its commandments observed. The gulf between the pious, or *Hasidim*, and the impious, whom they called *Re'sha'im*, was becoming wider and more unbridgeable.

The Martyrs—With Antiochus' prohibition of the practice of Judaism, only two courses remained open to the Hasidim: to die fighting or to die as martyrs. They could not fight, since fighting required an army, which meant leadership and organization. The lower classes among the Jews had never been organized into a forceful opposition, certainly not into an army. Their leaders were the scribes. Their interests were far from political. As indicated in the early lines of the little book called *Pirke Abot* (Chapters of the Fathers), the scribes of this time were concerned about three most unwarlike things: to be very moderate in passing judgment, to raise a generation of educated men and to protect the law of the Torah. Such men could let themselves be slaughtered for their ideals, but they could not lead in fighting for them.

When, therefore, Judaism was declared illegal, and the soldiers of Antiochus spread their net over the tiny land to capture those who persisted in being Jews, the result was martyrdom for thousands. Men, women and even children gave their lives rather than violate Judaism. Undoubtedly at this time the incidents took place described in the story of Hannah, who encouraged her seven sons to die rather than abandon Judaism's religious precepts, and of Eliezer, the old man who chose death rather than mislead his younger fellow citizens by even pretending that he was not loyal to his faith. Thousands abandoned their homes at the news that a troop of Greek soldiers was coming to enforce the edict of the king. They fled to the hills where they hid till the soldiers departed. Worse even than the Greeks were those Jews who had gone over to the Hellenizers. Knowing who were the Hasidim, they did not hesitate to betray this information to the Syrians. Openly and publicly they joined the enemy.

The Sabbath in the Way—The extreme Hasidim may have been pacifists, but the ordinary Jewish peasants certainly were not. They did not permit themselves to be slaughtered without resisting. Though ill-armed and poorly led, bands of them occasionally put up a strong fight against the Syrian soldiers and their Hellenizing Jewish allies. But the latter knew how to get around their resistance; for as long as they were under the influence of the Hasidim they would not defend themselves on the Sabbath. The result was that the Syrians learned to wait till Saturdays in order to attack the Jewish bands and destroy them. The end of the Jewish people seemed to be in sight.

4. THE NEW BATTLE CRY

Mattathias and His Sons—Fortunately for the future of Judaism and humanity, the hour of greatest need brought forth the necessary leadership. Somewhat to the northwest of Jerusalem lay the little town of Modin. Peaceful farmers, its inhabitants were staunch Jews. Among the most respected were the descendants of a priestly family, called *Hashmonaim,* or Hasmoneans, perhaps because they traced their ancestry to a certain Hashmon. The head of the family during the troubled days of Antiochus was the aged Mattathias who had five sons: Simon, Eliezer, Judah, Johanan and Jonathan. Like their townsmen, Mattathias and his sons looked forward with dread to the time when the Syrians would arrive to compel obedience to the royal edict against Judaism.

The Daring Stroke—The dreaded moment soon came. In the market place of the little town, probably facing the meeting house of its citizens where the government was conducted and where religious services were held, the Syrian soldiers erected an altar. The men of Modin were assembled there. A pig was produced which the soldiers had brought with them, and Mattathias, as priest and elder, was ordered to sacrifice it to Jupiter in honor of Antiochus. Mattathias did not move. From out of the crowd a young Jew stepped forward. Judging by his dress he was a Hellenizer. Fawningly he asked permission to perform the sacrifice. There was no doubt of what would happen next: the other Jews would be asked to eat some of the sacrificial meat, and those who refused would be executed. The apostate Jew approached the animal. Erect, at attention, the soldiers stood on one side of the altar. Sullen and hopeless, the Jews of Modin stood and watched the performance. Suddenly, in the twinkling of an eye, the entire scene was transformed. The aged Mattathias, standing closest to the captain of the troops and to the apostate Jew, snatched the sword out of the captain's hand, and ran it through the body of the traitor. As the captain quickly moved forward to stop him, Mattathias stabbed him too. By common impulse, the sons of Mattathias rushed upon the soldiers before they could quite grasp what had happened. A struggle began for the weapons which the soldiers could not use at such close range. The other Jews ran to the aid of the Hasmoneans, and, in less time than it takes to tell it, the Syrian soldiers were killed and their altar completely demolished.

Beginnings of Real Opposition—"Whoever is for God, let him come unto me," is what Mattathias is said to have exclaimed when he took the first step forward. The call echoed over the entire land, across the hills of Judea and in the caves wherever Hasidim were hiding. Mattathias and the rest of the people of Modin were themselves compelled to abandon their homes in the face of larger forces of Syrians coming to avenge the death of the first group. Other peasants from the surrounding country joined the Hasmonean band. Like so many similar bands, that of Mattathias began to attack small troops of soldiers, or communities in which the Hellenist Jews were strong. There was, however, one difference between the other guerrilla bands and that of the Hasmoneans. Mattathias had decided that in order to defend all of Judaism it was necessary to give up, temporarily, one of its fundamental principles. Not for purposes of attack, but where it was a question of self-defense, the Hasmonean band took the liberty of fighting on the Sabbath. Clearly most of the Jews were ready for such a change in policy. From near and far they flocked to the banner of Mattathias and his sons, so that theirs became the most important group, the only hope for the preservation of the Jewish people.

Judah the Maccabee—The discomfort of life in the hills and the strain of campaigning were too much for old Mattathias. Before a year was up, probably in 167 B. C. E., he died. The leadership devolved upon his son Judah, who had distinguished himself above all others as head of the guerrilla band. For some reason he had acquired the surname Maccabee. Some explain this name as consisting of the first letters of each word in the Hebrew sentence of the Bible, "Who is like unto Thee among the mighty, O Lord?" This was the motto which Judah is supposed to have inscribed upon his banner. Others derive the name from *Makkebet,* the Hebrew word for hammer. Judah, according to this theory, was the hammer with which God smote the Syrians. Judah's uninterrupted successes against the Syrians and the Hellenizing Jews soon proved to his followers that the problem of military leadership was solved. Indeed, Judah may well be ranked among the great military leaders of history. Jewish history had not known so inspiring a general since David fought for the unity and independence of Israel. But credit must not be given only to the general. With recklessness born of despair, with bravery inspired by the defense of the faith they treasured, with full knowledge of the justice of their cause against tryanny and greed, the Jews were an army small in number, but mighty in power and quality. "The praise of God was in their throat, and a double-edged sword was in their hand." Thus a poet describes them whose battle-song has found a place in our Book of Psalms.

5. THE MIRACULOUS VICTORY

The First Test of Strength—In time, as the size of his forces increased, Judah felt emboldened to measure strength with larger groups of the enemy. The local Syrian commanders gathered one force after another, consisting of Syrian soldiers, Hellenizing Jews and volunteers from the neighboring peoples. Each time they thought they had the Jewish army cornered. The latter were, indeed, frightened. Characteristically, they would prepare for battle by means of fasting and prayer. Again and again able generalship and a righteous cause proved stronger than numbers and equipment. The joy of the Maccabeans, after a number of successive victories, was unbounded. Not only had they saved themselves from enslavement and death, they also gathered much needed arms and booty. What is more, they gained confidence in themselves and won more volunteers from among those Jews who had hitherto feared to acknowledge openly that their sympathies were on the Maccabean side.

The Battle of Emmaus—Antiochus realized at last that he had a full-sized rebellion on his hands in this province bordering on Egypt. It was obviously necessary for him to suppress it. Fortunately for the Jews, at that time, the Parthians in the northeast rebelled against Antiochus and sought inde-

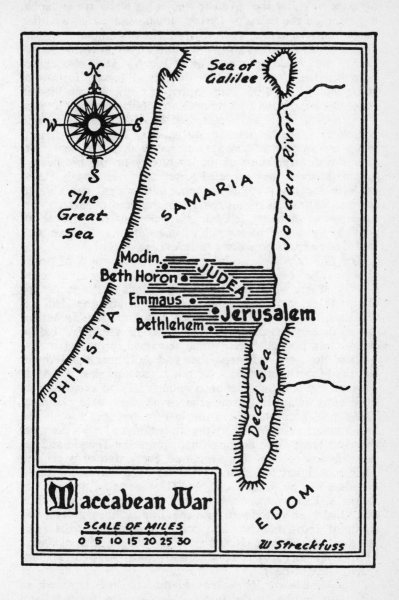

pendence from the Seleucid empire. Antiochus hurried off to fight them. He appointed as regent in his place at the capital a general by the name of Lysias. He also made him guardian of his son who was to succeed Antiochus as emperor, and he gave Lysias full power to stamp out the Judean revolt.

Like the preceding opponents of Judah, Lysias also underestimated the strength of the Maccabean forces. Instead of going himself, with his entire army, to crush the rebellion in Judea, he dispatched two subordinates, Nicanor and Gorgias. Their Syrian army was augmented by Hellenizing Jews and volunteers from the neighboring nations. These foreign peoples were so sure of the Syrian victory that they sent merchants with large sums of money to buy up the prospective prisoners whom they expected to sell as slaves. Judah, familiar with the country and its mountain passes, was able to surprise and annihilate the Syrians in the dead of night. Enormous stores of booty fell into the hands of the Maccabean soldiers. But the greatest result of this victory at Emmaus was that the road was now open to Jerusalem.

The First Hanukkah—In high spirits, with songs of praise (*Hallelu-Yah*) on their lips, the Maccabean army approached the sacred city which had been in the hands of the enemy for almost three years. The High Priest Menelaus, the Hellenizing Jews, the new pagan residents, now fled from Jerusalem just as three years previously the pious Jews had fled before them. Only a small Syrian force remained, protected by the walls of the Acra, a fortress they had built near the Temple. But the Maccabean soldiers did not advance against the Acra. Around that fort they stationed enough men to keep the garrison from interfering with other work they were planning. The simple peasants, whom the love of freedom had turned into soldiers, now dropped the sword in order to do what they had really been fighting for: cleanse the Temple and reestablish its worship. They removed every sign of paganism. They took apart the altar which had been defiled by pagan sacrifices and put aside its stones. They erected a new altar in its place. Exactly three years after the "desolating abomination" had been introduced into the Temple, they ground this statue of Zeus-Antiochus into dust, and rededicated the Temple to the worship of God. Beginning with the 25th of Kislev (165 B. C. E.), they celebrated the dedication-feast (Hanukkah) for eight days.

The Miracle of Hanukkah—Hanukkah has remained an important holiday in the Jewish calendar. The Second Book of the Maccabees, which was written considerably later, emphasizes the significance of these events by pointing out that God was concerned in the victory of Judaism. The Talmud, for its part, relates the miracle of the little cruse containing enough oil to light the Temple menorah for only one day; this oil burned on for eight days, until the priests could prepare more oil untouched by pagan hands. But the miracle of the oil, whether we think of it literally or explain it poetically, was not the only miracle of the Maccabean Revolt. It was equally miraculous that the strong were conquered by the weak, the many by the few, tyranny and greed by the cause of justice and of freedom. The story of Maccabean success, by becoming part also of the Christian tradition, has served as a means of strengthening the heart and the hands of every small group whose will it is to struggle against oppression and injustice.

6. The Peace that Was No Peace

The Hostility of the Pagans—The neighboring peoples, whenever they had the chance, had gladly helped the Syrians fight against the Jews. They not only helped them with soldiers and money, but they also started to attack the Jews in their own midst. The pagans of Jaffa, for example, drowned two hundred Jews who lived among them. Other cities committed similar atrocities. Everywhere the Jews outside of Judean territory lived in constant danger of destruction.

Foreign Expeditions—As soon as the Temple had been cleansed, Judah decided to send punitive expeditions against the Hellenized neighbors. He also wanted to prevent them from sending more assistance to the Syrians when the latter renewed the war against him, as they were sure to do. Only those cities were punished which had mistreated their Jewish inhabitants. Most of the other cities made terms with the Jews and promised to behave better. Judah certainly had no intention of annexing territory to Judea. On the contrary, wherever necessary he led the Jewish inhabitants back to their homeland. These expeditions had been hardly completed when news reached the Jews that a new army of Syrians was on the way against them.

The Siege of Jerusalem—Lysias, the viceroy himself, was leading a larger army than the Jews had ever met. Gathering his entire force, Judah went forward to meet the well-trained army which was coming to destroy him. The battle was joined not far from Jerusalem. The Maccabeans fought heroically. Eliezer, one of Judah's brothers, hacked his way through the ranks of the enemy and stabbed an elephant upon which he thought Lysias' ward, the boy King Antiochus V, was riding. In this heroic act Eliezer lost his life. Altogether it was a hopeless struggle against overwhelming odds. At the end of the day the Jews had to retire and seek the protection of the walls of Jerusalem which they had lately repaired. Lysias besieged the city. He hoped to starve the Maccabeans into submission.

Lysias' Offer of Peace—While Lysias was besieging Jerusalem, news reached him that a rival was leading a large army against Antioch, the capital of Syria. Anxious to hasten north, he made the Jews an offer of peace. In the name of Syria he promised withdrawal of all the laws against the observance of Judaism. Syria would refrain from interfering in the internal conflicts between the Hasidim and the Hellenizing Jews. Menelaus was removed from the office of high priest and executed; while Judah and his fellow leaders in the rebellion were not to be punished. On the other hand, the walls of Jerusalem were to be razed, Syria was to remain the sovereign power in Judea and to retain the right to appoint the high priest. As new high priest, Lysias offered to appoint a certain Jakim, or Eljakim, better known under his Greek name Alcimus, who had the reputation of being a mild Hellenizer. These terms, in brief, sought to restore the situation as it had existed in the days of Jason.

Why Judah Refused—Having received these terms of peace, the new council, which served as the government of Jerusalem since the Jewish victory, called a meeting. This council probably consisted of the high officers in the Maccabean army and of the respected scribes and elders who had always been identified with the hasidic cause.

The Jews had been making great sacrifices for religious freedom. Through the terms of peace offered by Lysias, that one objective had apparently been attained. They were ready, therefore, to lay down their arms and go back to their farms or workshops. Judah and a few of his followers, however, saw more clearly into the future. They did not trust Syria. They knew that no matter which side won in the Syrian civil war, that side would again interfere in the internal affairs of Judea. They also believed that the treaty of peace would restore to power that very group of aristocratic Jews who had begun the entire conflict. Had they fought and suffered for five long years in order that the large majority of Jews might again be surrendered to the greedy and the nobles who had dominated Jewish life and brought it to the brink of ruin? Judah was the leader of a mass movement from among the lower and the middle classes of Jews; he himself had been brought up among a simple farming population. He demanded that this group retain political power. Some say that Judah really wanted to have himself elected high priest. This is not likely; for Judah and the Hasidim, guided by the biblical attitude, would naturally feel that, as fighting men, the Hasmoneans had no right to the high-priestly office. Later on the Jews changed their mind. But, by that time, other factors had intervened. Yet, even if Judah hoped that he or one of his brothers could be elected, it does not disprove the good sense of his position. The fact, however, is that he lost the debate. The council, dominated by the Hasidim, decided to accept the terms of peace. Judah and a few of his followers left the city.

The Disillusioned Hasidim—It took almost no time for Alcimus, the newly-appointed high priest, to prove that Judah had been right. No sooner was he in power, the Maccabean soldiers disarmed, the walls of the city razed and Judah gone, than he showed that he had all along intended to remove the new leaders of the people and restore power to the old oligarchy. He had a number of the hasidic leaders seized and executed. No wonder that many of his former followers again sought out Judah, and the civil war in Judea was resumed in bitter earnest.

The Death of a Hero—Alcimus began to feel unsafe. He appealed to Syria, and Syria sent an army. For a while Judah did not feel strong enough to risk an open battle. But when he finally did, Judah was victorious, and the day upon which this resounding victory was gained, the 13th of Adar, was established as a half-holiday.

This, however, was Judah's last military victory. The Hellenizing Jews now saw the error of acting highhandedly, as though they, and not the Maccabeans, had been the victors. For their part, the more moderate Hasidim showed themselves ever willing to compromise in matters of political power as long as religious freedom was granted. Judah again was left with a small, poorly supported group, so that when a large Syrian force again appeared, he could hardly hope to make a stand against it. He saw himself deserted, his cause abandoned by those for whom he fought. With only eight hundred men Judah went to meet the army of Syria. Judah preferred to die in battle.

7. RESULTS OF THE STRUGGLE

A Fighting Remnant—The death of Judah ended the first phase of the Maccabean struggle. Under the leadership of Judah's surviving brothers, Simon, Jonathan and Johanan, several hundred Maccabean soldiers fled across the Jordan. From the point of view of the Syrians and the officials of Judea, they were outlaws. But to the mind of the Jews, even of those who had made their peace with the moderate Hellenizers who were now in power, these fugitives were the real patriots, the heroic remnant of that army which had fought for and won religious freedom. There was a glamour about the three brothers and their followers which attracted young men to their ranks. Jonathan, who succeeded Judah in the leadership, continued to be a constant threat to the power of the official rulers, both Jewish and Syrian.

A Memory of Victory—One permanent result of the conflict was the unfading memory of Jewish heroism. The Jews would never forget this great victory against overwhelming odds. The realization that they were excellent soldiers gave them a sense of confidence in themselves which influenced their history for centuries. But more than that, to this day the word Maccabee arouses in the Jew the memory of an heroic generation and of devoted, self-sacrificing leadership. The early Hasidim were the first martyrs in all history to the cause of religious freedom; they lead the long roll produced in later centuries under the inspiration of their example. Both types, the fighters and the martyrs, and that peerless leader, the Maccabee himself, left a number of stories which have fired the imagination of Jew and Christian down to our own day. These stories are found in the two Books of the Maccabees and in the works of Josephus.

A Feeling for Democracy—Again the fact must be emphasized that in the Maccabean conflict the masses of the Jewish people were ranged against those greedy and powerful families who had ruled the land. True, at the end of the war, after the Peace of Lysias, the old oligarchy returned to power. But the common people never forgot that they had shown themselves to be the stronger group in the nation. Thereafter, whether as the government or the opposition, they claimed a share of political power.

Religious Ideas—The war also left deep traces upon Judaism. It strengthened loyalty to the faith, and it widened the

breach between Jewish and Greek thought. It stands to reason that in the course of the next centuries, during which the
Jews continued to be surrounded by a Greek civilization, certain Greek ideas were bound to creep into the Jewish mind.
If nothing else, the larger number of Greek names, which
Jews began to give their children after this war, is an indication that Greek influences did penetrate into their life. But
consciously such penetration was not permitted. Even more
than during the age of Ezra, the Jews felt that the pagans
about them desired to destroy Judaism. Consequently, the
teachers of religion closed their minds against anything which
was obviously foreign. For this cultural antagonism Antiochus Epiphanes and the half-Greek neighbors of the Jews
must rightly be held responsible.

The events of the Maccabean period affected Judaism in
another, more direct, manner. This was the time when the
ideas of retribution and resurrection took hold of the Jewish
mind, at least of those Jews who identified themselves with
the Hasidim. The material success of the Hellenizing Jews
seemed to be a reward for their greed and their denial of
some fundamental principles of Jewish life. The Hasid, on
the other hand, the quiet, peaceful farmer, artisan or student,
who devoted himself wholeheartedly to the teachings of the
scribes, frequently found himself oppressed and downtrodden. "Where then is the justice of God?" asked the Hasidim.
In answer they turned to an aspect of Jewish thought which
had long been in process of developing, but which now
gained wide popular belief. God weighs the actions of every
human being and metes out reward and punishment after a
person's death. Moreover, there is to be a Day of Judgment,
when all human beings will be resurrected and those not
hopelessly wicked permitted to live forever. When that time
comes the nations of the world will recognize the greatness of
the Jewish people. In this way did that generation explain the
success of the wicked, the seeming failure of the righteous
and the reward obviously due to those martyrs who gave
their life for the cause of Judaism.

Contributions to Jewish Literature—Having been trained
by their scribes to be book-reading people, the Jews naturally
expressed these ideas in additions to their literature.

1) A critical period, such as that through which the Jews
passed between 200 and 150 B. C. E., always produces poetry. Poems expressing despair as well as hope, prayers for
victory, and songs to inspire confidence, were written in large

number. Many of these poems were later included in the official book of sacred poetry, the Book of Psalms.

2) This period likewise inspired the writing of several histories. Soon after the second phase of the Maccabean struggle was over, a history of the entire series of events was written by an eyewitness (about 140 B. C. E.). We call it the First Book of the Maccabees, to distinguish it from several others which deal with the same subject but were written later.

3) Still another type of literature was of a quite different kind. It was the most direct outgrowth of thinking about God's justice and about the future triumph of the Jewish people. The authors of this type of book rarely spoke of their own times directly. Usually they drew pictures of future ages when God would judge the world. When they dealt with events of their own day, they did so in terms of images and prophecies now difficult to understand. That is why these books are called apocalypses, a word which has come to mean "visions of later days." The authors, moreover, did not put their own names to the books. They preferred to ascribe them to one or another of the ancient wise men.

One such book is that found in the Bible under the name of Daniel. Daniel was the very wise man who had interpreted the vision of Belshazzar of Babylon. A book about him, or by him, may have existed for a long time. New words were put into his mouth during the Maccabean war or soon thereafter. The object of the revised book was to keep alive the courage of the Jews so that they might continue the fight for Judaism whenever called upon.

Thus the Maccabean revolt was an important event not only for the Jews of the second century before the Common Era. Because of the memories it left behind, the new ideas it created and the new literature to which it gave rise, the Maccabean struggle also influenced the Jews and all humanity to our own day.

CHAPTER V

CONFLICTS WITHIN

**THE JEWS FREE THEMSELVES FROM A FOREIGN YOKE ONLY
TO DISCOVER THAT A NATIVE YOKE CAN BE JUST AS HEAVY**

The Tragedy of Success—The heroic struggle of the Maccabees ended in only partial victory for the Jewish people and in total defeat for its heroic leaders. Judah lay dead on the battlefield; the other Hasmoneans were fugitives, their future apparently hopeless. Yet that hour of seeming defeat proved to be the hour of genuine greatness. Success, complete and overwhelming, did come soon thereafter. But the Jewish people were unable to maintain in success the idealism they had shown in the days of trouble. The later Hasmoneans, thirsting for power and glory, lost touch with Jewishness, so that their actions cast dark shadows upon the memory of their ancestors. It was an historical tragedy. The fact that all this was but natural, and that the same course of events may be traced in the history of many other nations, affords but slight comfort in view of the bitter quarrels and the acts of force and blood which the Jewish people suffered and inflicted.

1. JONATHAN AND HASMONEAN AMBITIONS

The Most Popular Man in Judea—For several years the remnants of the Maccabean army maintained themselves in the hills and wild places in the eastern part of the country and across the Jordan. With Jonathan as leader, they were the terror of Judea's Hellenizing party and its Syrian allies. Time and again the Syrians, encouraged by the Jews in power, attempted to destroy the Hasmonean band. Their efforts invariably failed. The general population of Judea looked upon Jonathan as the outstanding Jew. To all intents and purposes he became the real though unofficial head of the Jewish people.

The Great Diplomat—Jonathan did not possess the military genius of his brother Judah, but he did possess another quality more valuable in the particular state of affairs which existed between the years 150 and 140 B. C. E. Jonathan was one of the greatest diplomats the Jewish people ever produced. He saw a chance for his people to gain practical independence and greater prosperity by peaceful negotiations, and he took full advantage of the opportunity.

A few years after Jonathan's return to Judea the Syrian empire was plunged into the bloodiest civil war it had yet experienced. A pretender arose to the Syrian throne. Though he was an obvious fraud, it suited the diplomacy of Egypt and of Rome to support him against the legitimate king. Both the pretender, Alexander Balas, and the legitimate king, Demetrius II, sought help from the Syrian provinces. In attempting to win the aid of the Jews, both turned to Jonathan as the one far more able than the Hellenizing Jews to raise and lead a Jewish army. Jonathan had no interest in either side, neither in the rascally pretender nor in Demetrius who had tried several times to destroy him and had always been favorable to the Hellenizers. He waited to see who would bid highest for his aid. Each Syrian faction tried to outdo the other in heaping honors upon the Hasmonean. Before the Syrian civil war was over Jonathan was high priest, governor of Judea and member of the Syrian nobility, while Jonathan's brother, Simon, was governor of the Philistine coast.

Judea and Rome—One act of diplomacy on the part of Jonathan deserves mention, not because of the good it did the Jews at that time, but rather because of the harm it brought them almost a century later. It seemed an excellent idea for the Hasmoneans to enter into an alliance with Rome, since both they and Rome were hostile to the plans of Syria. Even Judah the Maccabee had sent an embassy to Rome, and the Senate had then declared the Jews friends and allies. In those days of slow travel, news of the Senate's action arrived only after Judah had already been defeated and killed. Jonathan sent a second embassy, to which the Senate repeated its declaration of friendship. But Rome had not the slightest-intention of sending an army to aid Jonathan. Rome was interested only in the quick breakup of the Syrian empire. The Hasmoneans knew this, but they supposed that for them to be called "Rome's friends" might make the Syrian kings think twice before attempting to destroy them. They could not foresee that in time they would have more to fear from Rome than from Syria.

Good and Bad in Jonathan's Policy—It is worth while to compare Jonathan's policy with that of Judah. Each followed a different method. Judah had striven primarily to attain religious freedom; Jonathan's first interest was the attainment of self-government for the Jewish people. Judah had fought only for the cause of the Hasidim; whereas in the case of Jonathan there is more than a suspicion that he was aiming at power and office for himself. Judah had not sought any increase in the territory of Judea; Jonathan, however, used Simon's position as governor of the coast cities practically to annex them to Jewish territory. To be sure, this was advantageous to the commercial development of the Jews, and the attainment of prosperity is the duty of every government, but prosperity had not been an essential part of the hasidic platform. All in all, it may be said that Jonathan turned the policy of the Hasmoneans from religious to secular goals. He made the Jews a factor in the politics of the time. He improved their economic position. He gained more self-government than the Hasidim had thought possible. He made himself high priest and ruler of Judea and his family the most powerful among the Jews. Judah had been an idealist and a hero; Jonathan was a diplomat and a practical statesman.

2. SIMON'S RULE

The Great Assembly—When Jonathan died, treacherously slain by a Syrian general, the Jews were faced with a critical situation. To enable them to hold on to the gains made under Jonathan, they needed a very capable leader. They naturally turned to the Hasmonean family. Of Mattathias' sons only one was still alive, Simon, a man noted for his calm wisdom, but already advanced in years.

Simon called together an extraordinary assembly. The important priests were there, the heads of the prominent families throughout the land, and possibly also the leaders of the struggle for independence. Such a gathering might have been called an Assembly of the Great; actually it was called "The Great Assembly." Such assemblies had been called on previous critical occasions; for example, to ratify the reforms of Ezra and Nehemiah, or when, around the year 198 B. C. E., allegiance had to be transferred from Egypt to Syria. But this time the personnel was somewhat different. The aristocracy which had dominated previous assemblies had in the meantime become identified with the Hellenizing Jews, so that, if they were represented at all, they were outvoted. The leaders of the hasidic party were in the majority. The Sanhedrin of a later date claimed to have developed out of this Assembly.

The Election of Simon—There was no doubt that Simon was the favorite choice for high priest and ruler. But this particular Assembly faced two difficulties. The Hasidim would have preferred a high priest from the family of Onias which they still considered the only legitimate family for the high-priestly office, and a ruler from the family of David who, to their mind, was the only one entitled to that office. The son of Onias, however, had run off to Egypt, during the Maccabean conflict, and had never joined the Maccabees in their bitter struggle for religious freedom. Thereby that family might be said to have forfeited its claims to the high priesthood. As for the Davidic family, it was impossible to say at that time who in Judea was one of their descendants, nor was it possible to send to Babylonia to find one. Simon and the Hasmoneans were still the best choice for permanent rulers. Unwilling to go contrary to God's will by choosing someone whom God had not anointed, the Great Assembly hid behind the excuse of ignorance for its final action. When they elected Simon hereditary "Ruler and High Priest," they added the saving statement "until a true prophet should arise" to indicate who was legitimately entitled to the offices.

This Great Assembly probably reorganized other departments of the Jewish government and provided for a permanent council with nation-wide representation to help the high priests.

Simon's Policy—Simon was an old man when he was elected by the Great Assembly after Jonathan's death; he was no longer capable of leading an army in battle. Beloved by the people, he faithfully and piously attended to his high-priestly and civil duties. He left the fighting to his sons. One of them was called Johanan Hyrcan or John Hyrcan. Simon's reign was indistinguishable in other respects from that of Jonathan whose policy Simon continued till his death in 135.

3. POLICY AND POLITICS

The New Generation—Simon's death (135 B. C. E.) marked the end of the heroic age of the Hasmonean struggle. The generation which for thirty-five years (170–135) had suffered and fought for its principles was dying out. The accession of John Hyrcan marked the coming into power of a new generation filled with memories of victory and proud of the nation's strength. Even the children of the aristocratic Jews were impressed by the power of the Jewish nation to win greatness and dominance by its own unaided efforts. They saw better than their parents that it was useless and unnecessary any longer to rely upon Syria to keep them in power. They felt that their future lay within the Jewish people. For a while longer the elders of this group refused to give up their policy of relying on Syria. But their influence was nearing its end. The new generation of both parties was facing a new state of affairs.

Syria's Last Victory—The Syrian king, mindful of the experiences of his predecessors, now also reconsidered his policy. It seemed wiser to come to terms with Hyrcan than to continue supporting the remnants of the Hellenizing Jews, even though at that time Syria was in a position to conquer Jerusalem. Consequently, Syria recognized Hyrcan's government on condition that Hyrcan considered himself subject to Syria and promised the Syrian king help in his military campaigns. Hyrcan had to give up all the pagan cities which his father and Jonathan had annexed, except the city of Jaffa which served as a port for Judea. All in all, the Syrian king was careful not to antagonize the Jews. He left Palestine; and the old Jewish aristocracy felt that Syria had abandoned them forever. The Hellenizing party now disappeared from the Jewish scene.

The Policy of Expansion—Judah's efforts had won religious freedom; Jonathan's gained power for the Hasmonean family and independence for Judea; Hyrcan's reign began the policy of territorial expansion. The primary objective was the attainment of greater national prosperity. Down to the time of the Maccabees, Judea had been an inland country. The pagan cities on every side held a practical monopoly of the commerce of that part of the world. They controlled the land-routes as well as the seaports. These cities, for reasons already discussed, were hostile to the Jews. Even after Judah had punished many of them, they continued their hostility and lent their aid to every Syrian effort to end Jewish resistance. Jonathan and Simon, having gained control over the Palestinian coast, used their authority to settle Jews in the port cities. Syria realized that the more prosperous the Jewish Commonwealth became the more difficult it would be to return the Jews to Syrian allegiance. That is why, as soon as the Syrian king felt able to do so, he compelled Hyrcan to give up his rule over these cities. Hyrcan, on the other hand, knew that, without control of the commercial highways, the Jewish nation would sink into weakness and insignificance. As soon as Syria was once more occupied with its internal affairs, Hyrcan recaptured the cities and resumed the policy of promoting the development of Jewish commerce.

The Conquest of Edom—When nations start on the road of conquest they do not know where to stop. Between expansion for the sake of economic welfare and expansion for the sake of power and glory is but a short step. One of the trade-routes between the northeastern lands of Asia and Egypt passed south of Judea through the territory of Idumea. Hyrcan used this as an excuse for conquering and annexing that entire country. More serious, in order to make sure of Idumea's loyalty, he actually compelled the Idumeans to adopt Judaism. Quite apart from the predicament of the Idumeans, the situation had elements of tragedy. Here was a grandson of Mattathias violating the very principle—religious freedom—which the previous generation had so nobly defended. That subsequently the Idumeans became ardent adherents of Judaism is a compliment to Judaism, but it cannot serve as justification for those who spread it by force. Other great religions, to be sure, have since then made converts at the point of the sword, and the men who did so are called heroes to this day. Judaism, too, might now have had a great many more adherents had Hyrcan's policy continued. But it is to the credit of the Jewish people that, since then, it has unanimously condemned Hyrcan's irreligious means of promoting his religion, and that even in his own day he encountered considerable opposition.

4. New Political Parties

Those in Favor—One simple way to discover who favored Hyrcan's policy is to ask who was likely to profit from it. 1) The most obvious gainers were the men of wealth, since they were ready to take advantage of the increased commercial opportunities. Their fathers and predecessors, for lesser temptations, had been ready to adjust their Judaism to the demands of Antiochus. Now the Hasmoneans themselves, and the strong Jewish nation they had brought into being, created far wider fields of enterprise than the earlier generation had even dreamed of. 2) Practically identical with the men of wealth were the aristocrats. From among such people the officials of the government were usually chosen, and they, too, generally intermarried with the wealthy families. The aristocrats, therefore, had a double interest in Hyrcan's policy. As officials they grew in power and prestige with every increase of territory; as members of wealthy families, they had the interests of their relatives and of themselves at stake. These two classes approved heartily of Hyrcan's conquests. 3) Then there were retainers, employees, and in general the men who were themselves hopeful of some day becoming rich. 4) Besides, as in every nation, there were also among the Jews men whose patriotic emotions tingled at the glory of conquest and power. 5) Finally, a group must have existed who looked upon the policy of conquest as a matter of life or death for the Jewish nation. From the history of the previous relations between their pagan neighbors and the Jews, they judged that either the Jews must destroy these neighbors or they would destroy the Jews. Palestine, as they saw it, could not remain half pagan and half Jewish.

Those Against—Just what proportion of the Jewish people the seekers after conquest made up is hard to tell. They certainly did not constitute the majority of the population. The ordinary shopkeeper, the artisan or the farmer did not see how these conquests would benefit him. There were no newspapers or magazines to explain to him just how the prosperity of the wealthy eventually seeps down to enrich the pockets of the poor. They did read the Bible, and there they found that wealth and aristocracy were not always the same as piety and wisdom. They were still under the influence of the scribes in whose teaching there was no place for wars of conquest. Above all, their sons had to do the fighting, and they themselves had to pay the taxes to defray the cost of the wars. All they saw in return was greater wealth among the aristocrats and less piety among the priests. They might applaud the conquest of the coast cities or of the Samaritans, whose Temple on Mt. Gerizim and whose claim of being Israelites had always annoyed the Jews; but they definitely opposed further conquests. Their representatives in the royal council called for peace and for concentration upon study and religious life. Thus the old conflict within the Jewish people was revived: which was more important, religious welfare or national strength?

The Pharisees—Hyrcan's reign saw the emergence of two political parties. The party of the scribes, the one opposed to expansion, became known as the Pharisee party. No one knows exactly why that name was used, or even what the word itself means. It is supposed to come from the Hebrew *pa-rosh* (פָּרֵשׁ) which means "to separate." If so, the name may imply that the king separated these men from his council, or Sanhedrin, choosing to rule only with the advice of those who favored his policy. Or it may refer to a voluntary separation of the king's opponents from the government, in protest against his policies. According to this, the name *Pharisee* would mean either "the Separated" or "the Opposition." Again, the name may have resulted from the desire of this group to have as little as possible to do with the neighboring nations. From this point of view, the word Pharisee might be an echo of that separatism which had been advocated by Ezra and Nehemiah.

The Sadducees—The opponents of the Pharisees, those who now remained in complete charge of the government, acquired the name Sadducees. It is a word even harder to explain than Pharisees. Some suppose that it had its origin in the fact that the leaders of the party were priests, descendants of the family of Zadok, the high priest under King Solomon. Of course, the adherents of the party were not only priests, but all who wanted the Jews to become, in the first place, a strong nation, gaining territory at the expense of Syria and, secondly, a prosperous nation ruled by its aristocracy, like Rome and every other nation.

Their Religious Views—Nowadays Pharisees or Sadducees are rarely spoken of as political parties, but almost always as religious parties. Such being the case, it is important to know just how the two groups differed from one another in their religious views. In general it may be said that each group drew a different conclusion from the Maccabean wars. The Pharisees, spiritual descendants of the Hasidim, argued that their religion had saved the Jewish nation. Judaism was the one factor which made them superior to the pagans about them. Therefore, everything else, the national life included, must be subordinated to religion. The Sadducees, on the other hand, argued that national power had saved the people and their religion. This did not mean that they were opposed to Judaism. On the contrary, the Sadducees applauded the forcible conversion of the Idumeans, and they were ready to pursue the same policy toward other conquered peoples. The days of open Hellenization were over, and both Pharisees and Sadducees were eager to spread Judaism among the pagans. But, while the Sadducees wanted to spread Judaism by force where they could, the Pharisees wanted to spread it by persuasion and example. And, while the Pharisees saw in the nation a means for preserving their religion, the Sadducees saw in Judaism that which Antiochus Epiphanes had seen in the

Greek religion, an instrument for uniting the State and assimilating its conquered peoples.

How Far Shall Religion Go?—Essentially, the two parties differed on how to apply Judaism to the new problems of their age, and how to interpret the Torah which was the basic authority of Jewish life. The Sadducees were in favor of a strict interpretation of the Torah; that is, they were willing to abide by every word written in the Torah, no less and no more. The Pharisees were for a liberal interpretation of the Torah, that is, they considered the Torah to be a body of principles and illustrations of these principles. They wanted to extend these principles to every possible phase of life. If they could find little support for their proposed laws in the Written Torah, they argued that there was also an Oral Torah, or teaching, a set of traditions which had been handed down to them by the scribes of former days, who in turn must have received it by tradition from their predecessors, all the way back to Moses.

A parallel to this difference of opinion on the interpretation of the Torah may be found in the history of the United States. No sooner was the Constitution adopted in 1789, than parties developed around the question of interpreting it and of applying it to new problems. There have always been Americans who wanted to interpret the Constitution broadly, and others who wanted to narrow its application. To this day American judges and lawyers argue about just what the Constitution does or does not permit the government to do. They frequently recall the arguments of the Founding Fathers and the minutes of the meetings at which various articles of the Federal Constitution were framed.

A similar situation existed among the Jews over two thousand years ago. No sooner had the Maccabees won the right for Judaism to live, than their descendants began to disagree as to just how much of their life the Torah, which has been called the Constitution of the Jewish people, should be permitted to regulate. In one sense the Pharisees made Judaism much easier by regarding biblical laws as principles. This enabled them to amend many practices to conform more closely to the changed needs of national life. But in some other respects Pharisaic Judaism was much more difficult to live by, because it insisted upon knowledge and piety in every conceivable action. Thus the Jewish people became divided on national, economic and religious policy. From divisions so profound and so bitter no good could come.

5. THE CIVIL WAR

How the Hasmoneans Came to Be Hated—As long as
John Hyrcan lived, the conflict of views did not lead to serious results. He continued to be popular with all classes. He
remembered his upbringing in the midst of the old hasidic influences, and therefore kept his private life free from
suspicion by the scribes and their adherents. His children,
however, had been reared differently. They had never known
days of poverty and defeat. They had grown up in a palace,
and they looked upon themselves as the leading aristocrats of
their nation. Moreover, the education they received was more
Greek than Jewish and more a preparation for war and conquest than for peaceful and religious leadership. They looked
upon the Pharisees with disdain and upon Pharisaic policy as
something to be eliminated. The Pharisees responded with
fear and dislike. The life and actions of the later Hasmoneans
caused the great services of the earlier ones to be almost
completely forgotten.

Aristobulus, Lover of the Greeks—The one-year reign
(104 B. C. E.) of Hyrcan's oldest son showed the Pharisees
what they were to expect from this Greek-trained Hasmonean generation. His Jewish name was Judah, but he preferred the Greek name Aristobulus. Because he was afraid
that his brothers might start a palace revolution against him,
his first act was to throw three of them into prison, where
two are supposed to have been starved to death. A few
months later another brother was treacherously murdered in
the palace. This was the sort of thing that happened regularly
in the pagan kingdoms, Egypt, Syria and others, but it
shocked and disgusted the Jews. In national policy Aristobulus continued to attack and conquer more territory from the
pagans. Boldly he assumed the title of king, though he had
sufficient regard for the sensibilities of the Pharisees, who
would have none but a member of the Davidic family as
king, not to call himself by this title (*melech*) in Hebrew.
The masses of the Jews sighed with relief when he died, after
a reign of but one year, drink, disease and the haunting fear
of rebellion having curtailed his life.

The Gathering Storm—Unfortunately, his successor was
no better. Alexander Jannai (his Hebrew name was Jonathan,
contracted into Jannai) was the only brother of Judah Aristobulus still alive in prison at Aristobulus' death. The change of

rulers brought no change of policy. For fifteen years Alexander Jannai extended his territory. The boundaries of his kingdom now included almost all the pagan cities in Palestine, so that all the commerical highways and centers of trade were practically under Jewish rule.

In the year 89 B. C. E., Alexander campaigned against the Arabs to the south. He was ambushed and lost almost his entire army. The Pharisees had been waiting for this opportunity, since until now Alexander had held them in check by means of armed might. On the following Sukkot, while Alexander was officiating as high priest in the Temple, the common people who were watching the proceedings, as if by prearranged signal, pelted him with the *etrogim* (citrons), which each one had in his hand in accordance with the ceremonial requirements of the holiday. Alexander Jannai was not the man to stand for such conduct on the part of his subjects. At his order the soldiers who were standing guard around the Temple charged into the multitude, killing hundreds of defenseless people.

Halfhearted Rebels—It was the signal for an open outbreak. Unequipped to cope with Alexander Jannai themselves, the Pharisees invited the Syrian king to help them— the successors of the Hasidim asking the Syrians to help them against a descendant of the Maccabees! The Syrians came in force, and Pharisees flocked to them in great numbers. Alexander Jannai was unable to withstand this attack and, defeated in the field, was forced to hide in the hills. Now, however, the Pharisees realized that the Syrian king would claim the fruits of the victory and resume the former Syrian authority over Judea. Thinking that Alexander and the Sadducees had been sufficiently punished, thousands of Pharisees deserted the Syrian army and went over to Alexander. With their aid Alexander Jannai was able to take the field once more and inflict a crushing defeat upon the Syrians and the remaining Pharisees.

But the patriotic rebels had failed to understand the unJewishness of their king. Restored to power, he instituted a hunt for the leaders of the rebellion against him. Many fled the country. Alexander made a horrible example of those he caught. In the garden of one of his palaces he gave a banquet to the Sadducee leaders to celebrate his victory and, in the presence of his celebrating guests, had eight hundred Pharisees crucified. This bloody deed as well as the pagan way in which it was executed, crucifixion being a method used only by the pagans to punish treason, stamped Alexander Jannai forever as one of the cruelest tyrants in Jewish history. Moreover, it made compromise between Pharisees and Sadducees utterly impossible, and was thus an important link in the chain of circumstances which led to the loss of Jewish independence.

6. GOOD QUEEN SALOMÉ

Did Alexander Repent?—A story gained currency among the Jews that on his deathbed (76 B. C. E.) Alexander Jannai advised his wife, Salomé Alexandra, whom he appointed his successor, to dismiss his own Sadducean advisers and, thereafter, to govern with the aid of the Pharisees. Perhaps the story is true. The fact is that she did change her husband's policy. She dismissed the Sadducees from their official positions and appointed Pharisees to their places in the

Sanhedrin, that is, in the Council of State which at that time was legislature and supreme court combined.

The School Law—The Pharisees now had a chance to show what they considered the proper duties of a Jewish government. They ended the policy of conquest. Instead, the Sanhedrin set about reforming the courts of law and abolishing a variety of superstitions which had begun to contaminate Jewish life. But the act which, above all others, showed what they hoped to achieve was the School Law. The Scribes had always insisted that every Jew must be acquainted with the sacred books. Ever since Ezra, scribes, like Joshua ben Sirach, had conducted schools where any man could go or send his children. These, however, had been schools of the upper grade; we should call them colleges. Elementary instruction was given at home by the father, upon whom the Bible imposed this as a duty, or by a teacher engaged for the purpose by those who could afford it. This limited the educational opportunities, since few fathers are good pedagogues, even if their knowledge suffices, and fewer still can afford the luxury of a private teacher. Gradually, to be sure, lower schools, too, had begun to come into existence. The Pharisees, however, were not satisfied with this haphazard educational system. Now that they had a chance to legislate, they, under the presidency of Simon ben Shetah, decreed that every young man was in duty bound to seek an education. Of course, farmers still did not have the opportunity to do so and eventually came to be looked down upon by the rest of the population. But at least from the larger villages, towns and cities a literate, informed Jewish people could be expected to come.

Sadducean Resentment—The Sadducees could not be satisfied with any arrangement that left them out of control of the government. The fact that the Pharisees represented the majority of the population did not matter to these aristocrats; they believed that they were the only ones fit to rule. Besides, they had some real grievances. The Pharisees had not forgotten the massacre of their leaders by Alexander Jannai at the instigation of the Sadducees. They sought revenge and got much of what they wanted, but along with it they acquired also the intensified hatred of the Sadducees. It was a cruel mistake, for, while the Pharisees were sure of the support of the majority of the population and of the justice of their cause, they should not have forgoteen that the army, the military leadership and the wealth of the land—the basis of military strength—were all on the Sadducean side.

Hyrcan and Aristobulus—One reason why Alexander Jannai preferred to have his wife rather than one of his sons follow him on the throne may have been that he had no faith in the strength of character of his older son, Hyrcan, or in the wisdom of his younger son, Aristobulus. In the situation which he left behind him, and for which he was himself largely responsible, Alexander Jannai knew that both these qualities were needed.

While Salomé was queen, Hycran acted as high priest. Lacking the gift of military leadership, he seemed to be of one mind with the Pharisees and was favored by them for the succession. Aristobulus, the younger son, possessed all the soldierly ability of the Hasmoneans, but in the peaceful policies pursued by the Pharisees he could not even look forward to military glory, let alone to the kingship which he coveted. The Saduccees were with him to a man.

The Lull before the Storm—For the nine years of her rule, from 76 to 67 B. C. E., Queen Salomé managed to maintain peace between the opposing sides. These years contrasted sharply with those that had gone before and those which were to follow. There was peace in the land, and plenty. But there was no peace in the hearts of the people, especially the Sadducees. There was lack of the sense of national welfare everywhere. Even before the queen closed her eyes, the Sadducees were on the march. She died, tired and disappointed, and left her country to face another civil war.

CHAPTER VI

ROME—IMPERIAL ROBBER

ROME, WITH CONQUEST AS ITS IDEAL, IS AIDED BY AN AMBITIOUS FAMILY IN DEPRIVING THE JEWISH PEOPLE OF ITS INDEPENDENCE

Unity that Came too Late—The Jews enjoyed independence for about eighty years and, during all that time, they could not agree among themselves how this independence should be used. Their bitter internal quarrels present a tragic spectacle. But the Jews of that age must not be condemned too hastily. Every nation throughout history has taken a long time to adjust itself to a new state of affairs, unless, as sometimes happened, external force imposed unity. France for example, after 1789, seesawed between republicanism and monarchy for more than a century; and, since 1848 at least, Germany has not been able to make up its mind about democracy or autocracy. Perhaps the United States is the best example, since the meaning of the unity attained in 1776 was not definitely agreed upon until the Civil War was fought eighty-four years afterwards.

So the Jews also had to go through a period of uncertainty and conflict until a decision could be reached concerning the men who were to rule and the ideas which were to prevail. In an important respect it speaks well for the Jews that they fought among themselves. Other nations at that time simply took it for granted that one particular class was to rule, and that a policy of force and conquest was to be followed. Not so with the Jews. There was enough intelligence and conviction and courage to question the wisdom of their leaders.

It is more than probable that in time the Jews would have arrived at some agreement among themselves. And it is also well to remember that in all likelihood the Jews would have lost their independence anyway, even if they had not weakened themselves by internal fighting. Rome, whose proud boast it became that destiny called it to rule the world by force, was casting its shadow across the East. In the face of this danger the Jewish people did unite politically. But it was too late. Then the Jews no longer had more than a slim chance to retain their independence, and even that chance was lost when a man who pretended to be one of them betrayed the Jewish people.

1. ANOTHER CIVIL WAR

The Rival Claimants—When Salomé Alexandra died, her older son, Hyrcan, who had been high priest during the queen's life, succeeded her on the throne as Hyrcan II. Already his brother, Aristobulus, was leading an army against Jerusalem. Though personal ambitions were involved, this was not merely a struggle as to who should be king. Once more Sadducees and Pharisees were arrayed against each other over the issue of what the Jewish people meant. Here, however, Hyrcan's inefficiency showed itself. He had not been able to organize an army from among the Pharisees, and he could not inspire confidence and respect in the forces still with him. He was defeated before the battle was joined for, when face to face with the army led by Aristobulus, Hyrcan's forces simply deserted him and went over to his attractive brother. Hyrcan had to make a virtue of necessity. Asserting that he had really never desired the throne, he surrendered all his honors to Aristobulus, who now became king and high priest under the name of Aristobulus II. The brothers vowed eternal peace and friendship to each other and, to strengthen the new bonds, Aristobulus' eldest son, Alexander, married Hyrcan's only daughter, Alexandra.

The Idumean Intriguer—At this time there lived in Jerusalem a man by the name of Antipater. Jewish tradition, which there is little reason to doubt, has always denied that Antipater was of Jewish birth. Both his parents are supposed to have been Idumeans, from among the nobility of that country when Hyrcan I forcibly converted its inhabitants to Judaism. Antipater was, however, a Jew by religion. A man of great ambition and shrewdness, Antipater saw in Hyrcan's situation his chance to realize a closely guarded dream of becoming a power in Judea. He easily persuaded Hyrcan that he had been unjustly deprived of his hereditary rights. Antipater had it all arranged. A word to the Nabatean Arabs to the south and east, and they would come—at a price of course—drive out the usurper and restore Hyrcan to power. Was it fear, blindness or selfishness which prompted Hyrcan to accept the plan? Aristobulus did not have enough time to prepare for so formidable a force as the Nabatean Arabs led against him. He shut himself up in Jerusalem, and both sides prepared for a long siege.

2. Rome's Faithlessness

Power and Glory—Rome was then in process of great territorial expansion. Julius Caesar was fighting his famous wars in the West, overcoming the brave resistance of the Gauls, winning new empires for Rome, and, not least important, great glory for himself. His former political ally and present rival for the favor of the Roman populace, Pompey, was in the East trying hard to equal Caesar's record. Both were plotting to gain supreme authority in Rome, and both wanted to lay the foundations for personal popularity by flattering the Roman populace with new victories won in their name. Syria had long been but a shadow of its former self; now Pompey annexed it completely and looked towards the neighboring lands to see what else he could pick off.

An Appeal for Decision—Hearing about the quarrel between the two brothers in Judea, Pompey sensed an excellent opportunity to interfere. The fact that the Nabateans had taken a hand in the dispute was not much to his liking, since their victory would make the opposition too strong. His lieutenant, Scaurus, was sent down to scare the Nabateans off. At Scaurus' command the Arabs raised the siege of Jerusalem.

Both factions now agreed to turn to Rome's powerful representative for a decision. It was like calling in a friend to arbitrate a family quarrel, for Rome had on several occasions declared itself the friend of the Jews. Moreover, each of the contending sides among the Jews feared lest Pompey aid its rival if the Roman were not flattered by being asked to arbitrate. Neither side was willing to rely altogether upon Pompey's impartiality. Aristobulus, profiting by his control of the Temple, sent Pompey a vine wrought of pure gold, one of the Temple treasures, valued at about half a million dollars. In view of his ambitions and the political situation in Rome, Pompey could hardly keep a gift of such value. He sent it on to Rome to decorate the Temple of Jupiter, where it remained for many centuries. Antipater, on behalf of Hyrcan, did not need to give anything so expensive. He understood Pompey and his politics much better than Aristobulus did. He made it perfectly clear to the Roman that a decision in favor of Hyrcan would eventually mean control of Judea, another easy conquest to boast of.

Unexpectedly, a third deputation presented itself before Pompey. It brought no gifts, it held out no promises and it came with a strange claim. While Hyrcan and Aristobulus spoke of Judea as if it were the private property of one or the other, this deputation assumed that Judea belonged to the Judeans. It was a deputation of representative Pharisees, possibly sent by the Sanhedrin. They asked Pompey to rid them of both brothers so that Judea might go back to its ancient constitution whereby the high priest ruled with the advice of a popular council.

The Iron Fist of Rome—Pompey received all three delegations and promised to study the case. In the meantime he marched his army into Judea. Somehow Aristobulus sensed that he was being led into a trap, that he was actually surrendering his power and his land without a fight. He escaped from the Roman camp and fortified himself in Jerusalem.

Pompey promptly besieged the city. Then Aristobulus, believing that he had everything to lose from a conflict with Rome, gave himself up. But his supporters, the Sadducees, refused to open the gates. Hyrcan, too, had supporters within the city. A fight between the two groups resulted in the withdrawal of the Sadducees into the Temple and the entrance of the Romans into Jerusalem. They attacked the Temple and broke through its protecting wall. The priests were performing the sacrifices. No din of war, no shouts of victory and defeat, seemed to disturb them. The Roman soldiers did not stop to distinguish between an officiating priest and a fighting Sadducee; they put both alike to the sword. But as one priest fell another would come up to continue the sacrifice where the fallen one had left off. Twelve thousand Jews are said to have perished on that day. When it was all over, Pompey entered the Temple. With characteristic Roman arrogance he penetrated into the Holy of Holies. Like all pagans of the day he must have been curious to see for himself whether it was true that the Jews did not worship images.

Pompey Decides in Favor of Rome—Jewish independence came to its end here. It was not like Rome ever to let go its prey. Called in as a friend to decide among three groups of Jews, Pompey decided in favor of Rome. The Pharisaic group was completely disregarded; the people evidently were not to be considered. It was obvious that Aristobulus would never stand for interference with his government. He was too strong a man, and was, therefore, deprived of any standing in the Judean government. On the surface, the decision in favor of Hyrcan, the older brother, seemed to accord with strict justice. But it assumes an entirely different aspect when one considers that Hyrcan was by far the weaker ruler of the two; that Antipater, now the friend of Rome—just as a little while before he had been the friend of the Nabateans—was to stand at Hyrcan's side; that Hyrcan was no longer to call himself king, but ethnarch or ruler of a people; and, finally, that Judea was incorporated into the Roman province of Syria. Moreover, all the conquests of the Hasmonean kings, all the half-Greek, pagan cities the possession of which was raising the economic standing of the Jews, were taken away from them, and placed independently under the control of the Roman governor of Syria. Pompey felt that he had done a good job, and, in order to impress the Roman Senate and populace with his great achievement, he took along Aristobulus and his two sons, Alexander and Antigonus, to march in his triumphal procession through the Roman Forum.

3. ROME AND THE IDUMEANS

The Natural Allies—Antipater and Rome, from this time on, worked together. Both were greedy for power, and both felt the hostility of the people directed against them. As a result, no matter what political mistakes the Idumeans subsequently made, Rome always forgave them. On the other hand, no matter what demands Rome made, Antipater and his sons always fulfilled them. Hyrcan II, the official ruler and high priest (63–40 B. C. E.) was nothing but a puppet in their hands. Actually Antipater ruled, and two of his sons, Phasael and Herod, were local governors, Phasael over Jerusalem and Herod over Galilee.

Rebels or Patriots—For almost a century the Jews had proudly enjoyed independence, and it stands to reason that they were not going to give it up without a fight. Pharisee and Sadducee youths were alike in their desire to drive out the national enemy. As often as Aristobulus, or either of his sons, or any of their sympathizers raised the standard of revolt, thousands flocked to it. In vain the Romans broke up the country's unity by dividing it into five administrative districts. In vain they bribed the upper classes by turning the local governments over to the Jewish aristocracy. The people still recalled the successful guerrilla warfare conducted by the Maccabean forces a century before. Any number of impetuous young men hoped to duplicate the achievements of the early Hasmoneans and their fighting bands. They, too, retired to the hills of Judea and Galilee, and emerged from their hiding-places to attack stray Roman contingents or such Jews as had made their peace with Antipater and Rome. The Jews naturally looked on these valiant, hopeful dreamers as patriots. Just as naturally, the Romans looked upon them as highwaymen and murderers. They hunted them as they would beasts of prey and slaughtered them without mercy. None of this helped to make either Rome or the Idumean family any more popular with the Jewish people.

The Humilation of the Sanhedrin—One such incident brought further proof of the stranglehold which Rome had upon Judea. Hezekiah, one of the most important of the patriot-highwaymen, was captured by Herod in Galilee. Herod had him and a number of his men summarily executed. The relatives of these men, who had the sympathy of the entire Jewish population, came to Jerusalem and lodged a strong complaint with the Sanhedrin that the least Hezekiah and his men deserved was a trial before a Jewish court of law. The Sanhedrin could not help admitting the justice of this plea. Their governing powers had been taken away by Rome, but the Jewish legal system had not been abolished, and they still considered themselves the highest judicial body. They called upon Herod to answer the charge. It was the recognized procedure for the accused to appear before the Sanhedrin dressed in black as a sign of penitence. Herod, however, impudently marched into the hall of the Sanhedrin at the head of a body of soldiers, all of them, including himself, dressed in their uniforms, swords and spears gleaming. The intention to intimidate the judges was obvious. In effect Herod was showing them that he was sure of Rome's support and so had no respect for their judicial opinions. The Sanhedrin was intimidated. A dead silence fell upon the seventy elders, a silence in which fear and humiliation were mingled. Only one of them, Shemayah, dared raise his voice. In phrases bitter with wrath and indignation he berated his associates for their cowardice. "If you will not judge this man now," he concluded, "the time will come when he will judge you and show you no mercy." This tongue-lashing awakened the Sanhedrin to its duty.

The trial was about to begin. Hyrcan, who was present in his capacity of president of the Sanhedrin, since that was a position which went with the high-priestly office, realized that Antipater's son, the favorite of the Romans, would be condemned. Hyrcan well knew that the Romans would hold him personally responsible. He quickly adjourned the meeting till the next day. Fuming at what he considered an insult to his honor, Herod was ready to order a general massacre, not only of the members of the Sanhedrin, but of everyone in Jerusalem who did not show sufficient respect for Rome. With difficulty his more cool-headed father and brother restrained him from committing an act for which the entire family might have to suffer. Still raging, Herod went off to the Roman governor of Syria and there received high honor for his signal loyalty to Rome. Again Rome and its allies showed what little regard they had for the degree of self-rule still left to Judea.

How Antipater Backed the Wrong Politician—Antipater and his sons, completely devoted to their own interests, must have been thoroughly perplexed by the civil wars which at this time broke out in Rome. A crisis was approaching between Pompey and Julius Caesar. Antipater, of course, was indebted to Pompey for all the power he had. Besides, and perhaps more important, Pompey also controlled the eastern part of the Roman empire just as Caesar controlled the West. Consequently, Antipater gave Pompey all the support he could. Even Caesar recognized that the support was valuable. In fact, in order to create trouble for Pompey, Caesar arranged to start a rebellion among the Jews. He freed Aristobulus, gave him money to raise an army in Judea and promised him his former kingdom. Warned of the plan, Antipater succeeded in having Aristobulus poisoned while he was in Greece, on the way to Judea. At the same time Antipater obtained the execution of Aristobulus' son, Alexander, on suspicion of planning to cooperate with his father.

With the defeat of Pompey, Antipater was faced with the unpleasant prospect of Caesar's revenge. He was too clever merely to wait; Hyrcan and he immediately changed sides. Caesar then confirmed Antipater and Hyrcan in their authority and granted them a certain measure of supervison over the Jews of the Diaspora. Caesar showed himself magnanimous to the Jewish people in general. He granted certain privileges to the Jews of the Diaspora and returned the port of Jaffa to Jewish rule. Thus Antipater had crawled out of a dangerous situation, and he could even claim to be a benefactor of the Jewish people.

Again the Wrong Politician—The civil war in Rome started again a few years later. Brutus and Cassius were now in control of the eastern part of the Roman empire. In great need of money, Cassius imposed a tremendous tax upon Judea. To be collected at all, the huge sum had to be collected ruthlessly. Antipater and his sons had to assist in this, thereby certainly not enhancing their popularity. Herod, in fact, distinguished himself by being first to turn in the part he was asked to collect. But Brutus and Cassius lost in the end. Would Antony and Octavius ever forgive Herod? The problem for the Idumean family was rendered the more difficult by the murder of Antipater, possibly in revenge for the murder of Aristobulus. Moreover, a deputation of Jews was going to Antony to plead with him for the removal of the Idumeans. Herod, nevertheless, decided to brazen it out, Roman fashion. He bullied the weak-kneed Hyrcan into giving him a favorable recommendation, and then went off to an interview with the new rulers of the world. What could he offer them that would counterbalance the legitimate plea of the Jewish people themselves? He could offer them his personal bravery, his daring and boldness. These were qualities the Romans could appreciate. But above all, the insistence of the popular delegations argued in favor of Herod. The Idumeans, who had always supported Roman rule, were not wanted. It was obvious that the Romans were not wanted either. Both were looked upon as foreign masters; both, therefore, had a common interest in joining forces. Antony, besides, now recalled the hospitality of Antipater and his family when he, as a dashing young captain, had seen service in Judea. Herod and Phasael came out victors again, while members of the Jewish delegation were executed on Antony's order.

4. THE LAST OF THE HASMONEANS

How the Jews Felt about Their Situation—The deputations from the people, so disdainfully and cruelly set aside, indicated how the Jews felt about the politics played with their lives and their country. The feelings of the pious Jews were expressed in a collection of poems written about this time, bearing the title, *Psalms of Solomon.* Their author was undoubtedly a Pharisee whose chief interest lay not in war and power, but in piety and right conduct. He justified the misfortunes which befell the Hasmoneans, for they had sinned and deserved punishment. Nevertheless, he could not help speaking with great bitterness of Pompey and the Romans. They had been invited as friends; the gates of the city were opened to them. But they desecrated the Temple and enslaved the people. No wonder that when the author heard of Pompey's end, he exclaimed: "Praised be the Lord who judges the whole earth with His justice." Moreover, the author feared lest the pagan neighbors in league with the Romans make life unbearable for the Jews. He prayed: "Punish us in accordance with Thy will, but deliver us not into the hands of the Gentiles." But there were also those among the Jews who were not so pious, and who, given the chance, were willing to reach for the sword. Previous rebellions had not been successful, but conditions at this time seemed to offer an excellent opportunity.

How Antigonus Made Himself King—Forced to rely upon Roman support, the Idumean brothers needed a strong Roman government. That, however, was exactly what did not exist, at least in the eastern part of the empire, for the next few years. Antony ruled over the East while Octavius took the West for himself. Now, Cleopatra, famed for her beauty and her wiles, was trying to make herself mistress of Rome by becoming the mistress of Antony. For her Antony neglected the government and let his brilliant future go to waste. Feeling no hand at the helm, the eastern Roman army became disorganized and the officials more than ever corrupt. Antigonus, Aristobulus II's youngest son, watched all this from the other side of the Euphrates, where he had found refuge with the Parthians. With their aid he invaded Judea, meeting only halfhearted Roman opposition, and arrived before the gates of Jerusalem.

Antigonus lured Hyrcan and Phasael into the Parthian camp. How bitterly he hated them! He held them responsible for years of personal suffering, for the murder of his father and brother, for the loss of Jewish independence. Phasael, knowing that he had nothing to hope for, committed suicide. As to Hyrcan, Antigonus had just enough family feeling (or it may have been fear of the reaction to such an act on the part of the Jewish people) not to have his uncle killed. He did want to disqualify him permanently for the high priesthood, and therefore did the simplest thing toward that end: he cut off the lobe of one of Hyrcan's ears, for according to Jewish law no man who was physically mutilated could serve as high priest. In addition, the Parthians took Hyrcan along with them. Antigonus entered Jerusalem and assumed the royal title and the high priesthood under the name of Mattathias (40 B. C. E.).

Antigonus as King—For about two years Antigonus had a chance to show his ability, but it cannot be said that he succeeded. To be sure, he was confronted with numerous difficulties, but the chief difficulty lay in Antigonus himself. He was not like his father, Aristobulus, nor like his grandmother Salomé; he possessed neither attractiveness nor charm, neither soldierliness nor statesmanship. Almost any other Hasmonean would have known how to use the popular dissatisfaction and Rome's temporary weakness. This last Hasmonean king was the wrong man at a time when the right one might have changed the future of the entire East.

Herod, King by Grace of Rome—Herod had refused the invitation which Phasael and Hyrcan to their sorrow had accepted. He had gathered his family, including Alexandra the daughter of Hyrcan, her daughter, Miriam or Mariamne, to whom he was betrothed, and Miriam's younger brother Aristobulus, and had fled in the direction of the Nabatean Arabs to the south. He left his family in a fortress in southern Palestine and continued on his way to Egypt where he hoped to tell his sad story to Antony. But he found that Antony had temporarily come to his senses and, having left Cleopatra, had gone off to make his peace with Octavius. Although Cleopatra tried her wiles on Herod, he paid no attention to her and went on to Rome despite the danger of crossing the Mediterranean at that season. As usual, luck was with him. He arrived safely in Rome and was greeted warmly by Antony and Octavius.

What could Herod have wanted with the rulers of the Roman empire? He certainly wanted revenge on Antigonus, and no doubt asked that Antony order the Roman armies in Syria to drive Antigonus out of Judea. With regard to the future government of the land, Herod might have been satisfied if young Aristobulus, Hyrcan's grandson and his own prospective brother-in-law, were installed in Hyrcan's place. Herod himself could then continue to be the power behind the throne and the protector of Rome's interests. Antony, however, did not see the need for such subterfuges. Why appoint a child whose future sympathies it was difficult to predict, when a man of ability and assured loyalty was at hand? The desires of the Jewish population were not considered of any importance and Herod certainly saw no objection to thus betraying Hasmonean claims. Octavius agreed. The Senate proclaimed Herod king of Judea. The ceremony of installation was followed by a banquet. The family of Antipater, whose shrewdness had dispossessed the Hasmoneans, thus attained more than they had hoped for.

The Conquest of a Kingdom—Herod, for the time being, was a king without a country. His first task was to win Judea by driving out Antigonus. In view of the bribes which the Roman generals in Syria were receiving from Antigonus, and the opposition of the Jews all over the country, Herod found this task no easy one. Letters and threats from Antony had in the end the desired effect. Jerusalem was besieged for three months, and Antigonus could hold it no longer. So great was the slaughter which the Romans instituted within the city that Herod had to take drastic measures and promise the Romans large rewards to stop it or, as he complained to the Roman officers, he might be left a king of a country without a population. Antigonus was captured and, still relying on his wits, pleaded for mercy. It was not customary for the Romans to execute a captured king, but at Herod's request to avenge his brother, it was done in this case. The Hasmonean dynasty thus came to an inglorious end along with the independence which it had so gloriously won for Judea.

CHAPTER VII

HEROD AND HIS SUCCESSORS

KING HEROD, HIS SONS AND THE ROMAN GOVERNORS WHO FOLLOW THEM MAKE THE JEWS FEEL THE FOREIGN YOKE AND PLANT THE SEEDS OF REBELLION

The Road to Misfortune—The next period of Jewish history saw the beginnings of the national calamity which overtook the Jews a century later. It is hard to refrain from wondering how different modern Jewish life would be if Herod had been a different sort of man, or if Rome and the Jews had understood each other. Until Herod's reign it was still possible to hope that the Jews and the Romans would arrive at some compromise whereby the Jews would be permitted to look upon their nation as almost independent. The Jews were a proud people. The more they felt themselves under the heel of Rome, the more they were determined to reassert their freedom. Herod was in excellent position to bring Rome and Judea to a better understanding. But he understood and sympathized with the Jews too little; he was interested in his own power too much. The result was infamy for himself and catastrophe for the people over whom he ruled.

1. HEROD'S DICTATORSHIP

The Marriage to Mariamne—Herod felt insecure upon the throne. He knew that the Jews had never liked him, and that his displacing the Hasmoneans increased their dislike. Even before the capture of Jerusalem he, therefore, married Mariamne, the granddaughter of both Hyrcan and Aristobulus. He felt that in a measure this marriage would make his claim to the throne legitimate. The marriage was not purely one of convenience; Herod and Mariamne were really in love with each other, and Herod might have been as fortunate in his family life as he was in war. But Herod never permitted personal affection to stand in the way of his ambition. Just as he had not minded hurting Mariamne and her family by accepting the throne in disregard of her brother's claims, so he did not mind hurting her again when his personal welfare was at stake. The same was true about his relationship to the Jewish people. He was very anxious for them to accept him as their king; unfortunately, he did not know how to make himself acceptable to them.

How Herod Made Himself Safe—One of Herod's first acts was the execution of forty prominent Sadducees. By committing this political murder he achieved two purposes: he rid himself of dangerous opponents and he filled his pockets. With the confiscated wealth of the executed men he was able to pay the bribes he had promised the Roman soldiers and still have enough left to pay the mercenary army with which he surrounded himself. Most of this army consisted of Jews from the Diaspora; Herod did not trust Jews from his own land. He was in constant dread lest the Jews rebel against him in favor of the Hasmoneans and he therefore rid himself of the remaining members of the family. First came the turn of young Aristobulus, Herod's own brother-in-law, who was found drowned in a pool of one of the royal palaces. Then old Hyrcan, returned from Parthia at Herod's invitation, was accused of plotting treason and executed. Herod's favorite wife, Mariamne, succumbed to the intrigues of Herod's sister and was executed despite Herod's undoubted love for her. Some years later he killed his own two sons by Mariamne on suspicion that they were plotting against him. Almost with his dying breath he ordered the execution of still another son, though this time his act was justified.

Prohibition of Politics—Herod had not the slightest intention of letting the Jews rule themselves. He deprived the Sanhedrin of every vestige of political power. Neither the Pharisees nor the Sadducees any longer exercised political influence. Only their names continued to exist for the purpose of describing two groups which differed on religious matters. Herod ruled, and through him Rome.

The Secret Opposition—It is not surprising that such a policy of suppression had the opposite effect from the one desired. Politics became an underground affair. Dissatisfaction expressed itself in secret criticism. The young people became restless and joined secret organizations for the cause of Jewish independence. These organizations, years later, united to form the dreaded revolutionary party, the Zealots. Despite the calming influence of many Pharisees, there were thousands who were ready to riot and rebel whenever an occasion presented itself. Herod was an efficient ruler and knew how to maintain peace by ruthlessness. Numberless spies ferreted out what the opponents of the king were plotting. By means of torture Herod extracted confessions from guilty and innocent alike. Naturally, the more plots were uncovered against him, the greater became Herod's sense of insecurity. That in turn resulted in greater ruthlessness and more bloodshed. Everyone was under suspicion, and everyone lived in mortal fear.

2. HEROD AND THE NON-JEWS

Fortifying His External Position—Herod, on the other hand, was clever in his relations with the pagans, and particularly shrewd in his dealings with the Romans. The death of Antony confronted Herod with a serious danger. Ever loyal to his personal friends, Herod had done all he could for Antony. He now felt that Augustus would be justified in looking upon him as an enemy. Herod, like his father under similar circumstances, hurried to meet the new ruler of the world. Removing his royal insignia, he appeared before Augustus, and, without denying his friendship for Antony and his regret at Antony's defeat, frankly offered Augustus the same friendship and loyalty which he had given the defeated Antony. This attitude appealed to Augustus. He probably saw in Herod a realist in politics, one who could be relied upon to serve Rome and Rome's master. Not only did Augustus accept Herod's offer of friendship, but, leaving him as king of Judea, Idumea, Samaria and Galilee, he even increased Herod's territory by adding to his kingdom some lands across the Jordan and some of the pagan cities along the Mediterranean coast. The friendship between Augustus and Herod remained firm for the rest of their lives.

Herod and His Pagan Subjects—The pagan cities which now fell into Herod's hands protested to Augustus. But, as they soon discovered, they need not have been afraid that Herod would discriminate against them in favor of the Jews. By sympathy and character he was more Greek than Jew and it was his dearest wish to gain the reputation of being a great Hellenistic monarch. His Gentile subjects soon understood his love of power, and he, in turn, appreciated the simplicity of their religion, the beauty of Greek art, and the charm of

Greek modes of thought. He filled his court with Greek hangers-on, mostly parasites who lived by their flattery. His most trusted adviser was an able Greek by the name of Nicolas of Damascus. Herod's ideas about government were the same as those which at that time were common throughout the Roman empire. It was government not for the sake of the people, but for, of and by men of wealth and aristocracy. The common people had only one duty—to obey their masters.

Herod Builds—According to the Greek standards of that day, a good king encouraged games and theaters and was active in building. Herod was not going to be behindhand in this respect. He reared pagan temples and amphitheaters in various Greek cities within and outside his domain. Athens, Sparta and Rhodes benefited from his liberality. He made large contributions of money to the Olympic games. He laid the foundations for and put up the central buildings of new cities. Samaria again rose from its ruins and was renamed Sebaste (Royal City) in honor of Augustus. The same was done to an old, well-situated town on the coast, which now received the name Caesarea, again in honor of the Caesar. Other cities and citadels were named in honor of Caesar's family and of Herod's, though never after a Hasmonean or a former Jewish king. So liberal did Herod show himself in all such Hellenistic activities that Augustus Caesar and his friend Agrippa could not help remarking, with the slightest touch of a sneer, that Herod's realm was far too small for his liberality. Herod's Gentile subjects did not at all mind his great anxiety to please them. To them Herod was "Herod the Great."

3. HEROD AND HIS JEWISH SUBJECTS

Hopes for Hellenization—Of course, Herod considered himself a Jew. But like so many Jews, brought up and living among non-Jews, he was overly critical of his fellow Jews and especially sorry that they insisted on being different from the other peoples of the world. Herod knew better than to force Hellenization upon his Jewish subjects; he adopted the more sensible policy of gradually introducing them to those Greek habits of life which he himself admired. As a result Jerusalem also benefited from his building activity. He erected a theater and a hippodrome within the city. Herod now imagined that a foreign visitor to his capital would feel more at home and would not look down upon him as an insignificant king of a "barbarian" people.

Efforts at Conciliation—Herod knew very well that his absorbing interest in Hellenism added to the feeling of the Jews that he was not one of them. To the best of his ability, therefore, he tried to make them change their opinion of him. Shemayah and Abtalion, the leading scholars of his day, who are mentioned in the first chapter of the "Chapters of the Fathers," were singled out by him for great honor. No doubt he performed all of the public obligations of Jewish life. From Augustus, Herod obtained the right to intervene on behalf of the Jews wherever in the Roman empire they might be annoyed. But, above all, he tried to prove that Greek temples were not his only concern by undertaking to rebuild and beautify the Temple in Jerusalem.

Herod's Temple—Almost five hundred years had elapsed since the Second Temple had been built by those who returned from the Babylonian Exile. During the intervening time the Temple had no doubt been repaired and enlarged, but it remained essentially the old building, inferior in beauty and grandeur to some of the pagan temples which dotted the land. Not only was it contrary to Herod's love of architecture to permit the Temple of his own God to remain so modest, but he thought to show his piety to the Jews by making their Temple grander than the rest. Nothing so well indicates with what suspicion the Jews regarded Herod than the fact that the leading scribes at first opposed his plan. They actually believed that once he pulled the old building down he would never replace it. To quiet their suspicions Herod had to promise that he would not touch the old building until he had built the new one around it. Under no circumstances were the services to be interrupted.

Herod engaged workmen by the thousands. Among them were many priests to build those portions not accessible to ordinary Jews. The work was started by leveling larger portions of the Temple Mount, so that the new building might be erected on a broader base. It was also made much taller, so that the white stone of which it was built from top to bottom gleamed in the bright Palestinian sun and could be seen for many miles beyond the city. On the northern and southern sides of the building were the enclosed halls or rooms where the priests prepared for the service, and where the Sanhedrin met. The large open court on the east, facing the Temple proper, was divided into several parts. Closest to the Temple was the portion set aside for the altar and the officiating priests. Next to it was the court for the Israelites who came to watch the service. By the side of that was the gallery for the women, and behind it was the court of the Gentiles. The whole area was surrounded by a wall. This is the wall, part of which remains to this day, known as "The Wailing Wall," to which Jews have gone on pilgrimage during the subsequent centuries of exile.

Herod's Flunkyism to Rome—The Temple took many years to build. Begun in the year 19 B.C.E., it was not finished till long after Herod's death, though its most essential parts were completed during Herod's lifetime. Far and wide it was said that the buildings which Herod had put up, and especially the Temple, made Jerusalem the most beautiful city of the East. The Jews themselves could not help being grateful. They thought that Herod might really be drawing closer to them. Then Herod committed a characteristic blunder. Knowing that the Jews prided themselves upon the fact that their religion tolerated no images; knowing, too, how cordially the Jews disliked being reminded of their enslavement to Rome, Herod nevertheless placed a huge Roman eagle over the most important gate of the new Temple. The feelings of the Jews were outraged. Was it not enough that Rome had robbed them of their land, must it now thrust its sharp claws also into their religion? All the good will which Herod had gained was lost by this unnecessary act of provocation. Before long a conspiracy was afoot to pull the hated eagle down. When rumors circulated that Herod was dying, a group of young men gathered before the gate on which the golden eagle was set and began to pull it down. The soldiers interfered and arrested about forty of them. Herod was so enraged at this sign of insubordination and insult to Rome, that he had the "rebels" burned alive.

Herod in History—Herod was an excellent king in certain respects. He maintained external peace in his land. He developed ports and encouraged commerce. He beautified his own and neighboring countries. He aroused the admiration not only of the pagans of the Roman empire, but also of the Jews outside Judea whose standards of value had become modified through contact with Greek civilization It is not difficult to understand why many people called Herod "the Great."

Yet the majority of Jews of his own kingdom disliked him, and Jews of later generations called him "the Wicked." The Jews of his day in Judea would probably have hated any ruler who did not lead in open opposition to Rome. Their attitude to life, moreover, their fundamental tests of good and bad were so vastly different from the Greek and Roman attitudes and values as to make the Jews a difficult people to rule. Herod, moreover, injured the interests of the Jews. In the economic struggle then raging between the Jews and the pagans of Palestine, Herod favored the pagans. Their cities prospered under his rule; the Jewish townsmen and artisans sank deeper into poverty. The Jews naturally and correctly attributed their national and economic ills to Herod's policy. They saw their difficulties as due to Herod's desire to please pagan Rome by favoring the pagan population of Judea. His personal life, his non-Jewish interests and his national and economic policies thus combined to make such an impression upon his subjects that, when Herod died, the pagans among them mourned while the Jews rejoiced.

4. HEROD'S SUCCESSORS

Augustus Decides—Herod's will had to be ratified by Rome. Three separate deputations left Jerusalem to lay their case before Augustus Caesar. Archelaus went to defend Herod's will just as it read, because by that will he was appointed king of Judea. Several of his brothers went because, as usual in Herod's family, each disliked the other, and everyone disliked Archelaus. A deputation of Jews went, too, because they wanted to present the wish of the Jewish people that none of Herod's family be permitted to succeed him. They would rather, they argued, be ruled directly from Rome than have one of the Herodians rule over them. The people's deputation obtained little consideration from Augustus. Rome was not interested in what the natives wanted; its chief interest was in holding them down. It was clear even to Augustus that Archelaus was not the man to govern Judea. He modified Herod's will slightly. Archelaus was made not king, but ethnarch (prince) of Judea, Idumea and Samaria. Antipas, another son of Herod, was made tetrarch (duke) of Galilee and part of Transjordania. A third son, Philip, was made tetrarch of another small province.

Archelaus the Fool—The story of these Herodians is soon told. Archelaus justified all the vile predictions about him. He possessed none of his father's ability. He did not even have the decency to refrain from openly violating Jewish religious sensibilities. After permitting him to rule for ten years (4 B. C. E. to 6 C. E.) Augustus removed him and sent him into exile in Gaul. His provinces were placed under the direct rule of Roman officials known as procurators.

Antipas the Crafty—Herod Antipas was the ablest of Herod's successors. He continued his father's policy of building. One of the cities he established was Tiberias, a beautiful city by the Sea of Galilee. Antipas tried not to arouse Jewish hostility against himself, but the temptation was too great, and Jewish moral requirements were too high for him. He fell in love with the wife of one of his younger brothers, and she married him, though to do so was obviously contrary to law and morals. At that time a famous and highly respected preacher, by the name of Johanan,* was traveling through Antipas' land, urging the people to lead a more godly life. He met his death because of the bold and brave manner in which he criticized Antipas for his immoral marriage. Antipas ruled over his province till the year 37 C. E., when he too was removed by Rome.

5. THE FIRST PROCURATORS

Rome and Judea—In the meantime Judea and Samaria had fallen under the direct rule of Rome, something for which the Jews had asked on several occasions. Now their request was granted, and they soon realized that, bad as the Herodians had been, they were easier to get along with than the Romans. Behind the difficulties lay the fact that the Jews completely failed to understand Rome, its aims and its policies, while the Roman officials who came to rule over the Jews failed just as completely to understand the Jews, their attitude toward life, the strictness of their moral code, and their view of religion. Clashes between the Romans and the Jews were therefore inevitable. Each clash sharpened the differences, serving to convince the Jews that Rome was cruel, greedy and wicked, and the Romans that the Jews were barbarous, stubborn and foolish. Each additional year of contact brought bloody conflict nearer.

Pontius Pilate—Six procurators followed one another in ruling over Judea and Samaria between the year 6, when Archelaus was removed, and the year 41, when another descendant of Herod was placed upon Judea's throne. Each of these procurators had his difficulties and misunderstandings with the Jews. Pontius Pilate is a good example, not only because

* See below, p. 131.

his rule was the longest (26 C. E.–36 C. E.) and his difficulties typical of the manner in which Roman and Jew failed to appreciate each other's natures, but also because, through the story of Jesus of Nazareth, his name is generally familiar.

Convinced that the Jews were barbarians who should be taught to accept the "civilization" of Rome, Pilate landed in Palestine with the intention of forcing the Jews to abandon what he considered inferior customs. He soon learned that this would not be easy to achieve. His Roman troops came into Jerusalem bearing the effigy of the emperor. Crowds of Jews went out to meet him and besought him to remove the images since, to their mind, bringing them into the sacred city was contrary to the Second Commandment. Pilate stormed and threatened. He had the unarmed crowd surrounded by soldiers with drawn swords. But the Jews would not move; they would rather die than have their city desecrated. Pilate had to give way.

Some time later the procurator decided to build an aqueduct. That was certainly a wise measure, for Jerusalem was never sufficiently supplied with water. For this purpose Pilate decided to use the money from the Temple treasury rather than money raised by taxation. To the Jews the treasury of the Temple was sacred. The money collected there could not be used for profane purposes such as civic improvements. The Jews gathered in crowds and voiced loud protests. Pilate sent soldiers disguised in civilian dress to mingle with the crowd. At a given signal they fell upon the multitude and clubbed many to death, and in the riot which ensued others were killed. Pilate won his petty triumph.

There were other such incidents both with Jews and with Samaritans. Pilate acted as master in his province. He did not tolerate the slightest disrespect for Roman orders. Life was cheap to the Romans when Roman authority was involved, and to the Jews in defense of what they considered sacred. By the time the period of rule by procurators came to a close, rebellion was secretly brewing, and sooner or later was bound to break out into the open.

CHAPTER VIII

GOVERNMENT AND WORSHIP

THE JEWS GOVERN THEMSELVES AND DEVELOP THEIR RELIGIOUS INSTITUTIONS

The Invisible Conflict—History, certainly Jewish history, is not the story of kings and wars. It is the story of the people; how they lived, and what they thought, and why they acted as they did. Even the eventual loss by the Jews of the last shred of national independence cannot be explained by the politics of the time alone. It is necessary to understand why the Jews despised the pagans as ignorant, greedy and cruel, while the pagans, at that very time, looked upon the Jews as uncivilized and superstitious. Only as we understand why each side disliked the other, can we appreciate why they eventually came to blows.

The Jews were neither a small nor an insignificant people in the days of Rome. Judea as a land was tiny, but it was the center of a religion whose adherents were widespread. Judea was a province of the Roman empire, but its institutions and traditions were already beginning to influence the world.

1. THE LAND AND ITS PEOPLE

More People and More Land—Two factors stand out as most important in the life of the Jews during the final century of the Second Commonwealth: the increase in the Jewish population, and the difference between the ideas of the Jews and non-Jews. Let us consider each factor in turn.

The small Jewish population of the days of Nehemiah, for whom Jerusalem and a few miles of surrounding territory were more than enough, grew so large several centuries later that it overflowed the boundaries of Palestine. Peace and hard labor during the Silent Century (444–333 B. C. E.) had restored to cultivation much of the Judean soil. This resulted in greater economic security which, in turn, led to a natural increase in population. Moreover, neighboring peoples threw in their lot with the Jews. By the time Alexander's successors fought over Judea, the land contained a population larger than it could support. This had definite results. One was that Jews began to migrate to other parts of the world, such as Egypt, Asia Minor and the Mediterranean islands. Another result was that the Hasmoneans, beginning with Jonathan, embarked upon a policy of expansion through conquest. To Judean territory they added the land along the coast which used to be called Philistia, the country to the north which still bears the name of Galilee, and the land to the south which belonged to the Idumeans. Many of the inhabitants of these conquered districts were compelled to embrace Judaism; most others accepted it voluntarily.*

Jewish Numbers and the Diaspora—Despite these conquests there was not enough land to accommodate the large Jewish population. It has been estimated that in the days of Rome about two and a half million Jews lived within Palestine. That is a tremendous number for so small a country, about the size of Massachusetts and Connecticut, the majority of whose inhabitants had to live by agriculture. Therefore, as time went on, ever greater numbers of Jews had to emigrate from Palestine and were dispersed over the Greek and Roman world. This scattered Jewish population has been given the name "Diaspora," which means "scattered seeds." They really were like seeds, for out of them important communities of Jews eventually grew. Strabo, a non-Jewish historian who lived during the first century, said that there was hardly a place in the world where Jews might not be found.

2. THE DIFFICULTY OF MAKING A LIVING

Jewish Farmers—The most important occupation of the Jews of Palestine was farming, but the amount of land which each peasant owned was small. Most of them just about managed to subsist on what they raised. A poor harvest or too little rain ruined them. A peasant faced with starvation was compelled to borrow from his richer neighbor. This might lead to the complete loss of his land if the next harvest was also poor. Landless, he would be forced to become a day laborer on someone else's farm or wander into the city to seek work. His richer neighbor, on the other hand, acquired large

* See the map on p. 87.

holdings of land. He could go to Jerusalem, where he lived in ease and luxury while his estate was managed by an overseer. During the Roman period the number of the poor and the landless increased and became a serious problem.

Jewish Artisans—The next occupation in order of importance was manual labor. The industrial unit was the family. Sometimes a trade would remain in a family for generations. Sometimes a locality would specialize in the manufacture of a certain product: tanning, jar-making, dyeing and many others. Some of the great teachers of this and later periods show by their names that they drew their livelihood from one or another such occupation. This proves, furthermore, that manual labor was not despised.

Manual laborers also had their difficulties. The work done by the Jews was not of the highest quality. Better articles than they made could be imported from the pagan cities of which there was a large number nearby. To make matters worse, the number of workers increased because of the immigration of the peasants into the towns.

Jewish Merchants—At the beginning of the Second Commonwealth the interest of the Jews in commerce was slight. The notion current in our day that the Jews have natural gifts for commerce finds no proof in this period, nor for a long time thereafter. The historian Josephus said of the Jews of Palestine: "We are not a commercial race." It is true, however, that during this period the Jews first began to show an interest in trade. It began with the coming of the Greeks. The half-Hellenized cities which the Greeks established in and around Palestine maintained a practical monopoly of the trade of the land. Jewish Palestine had a good many products for export: grain, wine, oil, fruit, fish from the Sea of Galilee, and tar and pitch from the Dead Sea and its neighborhood. Palestine also imported a large variety of articles. As the Jewish population increased, the Jews began to resent the fact that the profit from these exports and imports fell into the hands of those who did not consider themselves part of the Jewish people. That was an additional reason why the Hasmoneans attempted to capture and rule over the pagan cities in Palestine. During their rule Jews became actively interested in trade. They also settled in pagan cities and competed with pagan merchants. But before a Jewish merchant class became firmly established, Rome conquered Palestine. Roman policy, whether under Herod or under the procurators, was much more favorable to the pagans than to the Jews.

Work in Jerusalem—There was one city in the Jewish part

of Palestine where manual laborers and Jewish merchants
were most numerous. That city was Jerusalem. Its importance
was not due to its advantageous location, since it was not
near the sea so that it could serve as a port, nor along an
inland trade-route. It was important simply because it was the
political capital of the Jews of Palestine and the religious capital of the Jews all over the world. There the taxes and the
contributions were gathered and spent. A large number of
Jews came there as pilgrims and to perform their sacrifices in
the Temple. Since the court was there, it was the center for
all those who amounted to anything politically and socially.
That is why the permanent city population of Jerusalem
could always count upon a large amount of work and trade.
The city enjoyed a thriving business in luxuries of all kinds,
including precious stones and expensive clothes. Besides, the
Temple itself required a great deal of work. It was the greatest employer of labor, and its laborers were the best paid. It
has been estimated that at this time Jerusalem held a population approaching a million, and, during the holiday seasons,
many more than that. Naturally, therefore, whenever there
was any political or economic trouble, Jerusalem was the first
to hear of it and feel it. The masses of its population were
always ready for heroism or riot, depending upon their mood
and their leadership.

Hard Times—It is easy to see how the hard times which
overtook the Jews could be traced by them to their government. The civil wars of Rome resulted in merciless taxation
of the provinces. When peace was established Herod began
his building operations. The money which he raised from his
Jewish subjects was spent on his non-Jewish favorites and on
the building of temples and hippodromes outside of Jewish
territory. In the year 25 B. C. E. the suffering from famine
was so great that Herod went to the expense of importing
grain from Egypt. Five years later there was another economic crisis, and for that year Herod reduced the taxes by
one third. These two actions may prove either that Herod
was afraid of revolution or that occasionally he was moved to
pity. But they certainly also prove that Herod did not try to
solve the economic problem of the Jewish people, since there
is no record that he did anything to improve the condition of
the people permanently. He spent more than his country
could afford. His tax-gatherers were everywhere, and they
were merciless. It was then that a tax-collector, or "publi-
can," came to be looked upon as a tool of the oppressor, a

hopeless sinner, with whom decent people would not associate.

The cities, particularly Jerusalem, were filled with unemployed. The Temple treasury was called upon to distribute charity. But that could not go on forever. Upon Herod's death there was a loud outcry for the reduction of taxes, and especially for the abolition of the sales-tax which he had imposed. Archelaus refused to comply with this demand and thus made himself more unpopular than ever. Later the Roman procurators did reduce the taxes to some extent. But either that reduction came too late or it was insufficient.

3. POLITICS, OPEN AND SECRET

The Prohibition of Politics—Matters were made even worse by tyranny in government. Quite apart from the moral wrong of dictatorship, its political unwisdom was never so clearly proved as during the days of Herod and Rome in Palestine. The Jews were dissatisfied and wanted a change in the government. But Herod and the Romans forbade them to discuss their grievances. However such interference with individual liberty and freedom of speech worked elsewhere, it was not successful with the Jews, who had been accustomed to speak their minds freely and, for centuries, had had a council to help in the government. Moreover, they knew their Bible and considered the prophetic utterances as the words of God. They could not help applying to their own time the prophetic condemnation of a social order which permitted poverty and oppression. Herod and Rome did not understand these things. For them, the people were there to be taxed and governed, not to express their views or to assume part of the responsibility for government. Politics was outlawed.

Pharisees and Sadducees—The two parties which had existed in the Hasmonean era no longer had any part in the government of the country. The names persisted, but with a religious, not a political significance. Herod did not interfere with the debates on Oral Law, that is, the discussions and interpretations of the scribes and teachers of the Unwritten Torah, and he let the Sanhedrin judge civil and religious cases. Those among his counselors who were Jews were chosen from among those who were loyal to him personally. His authority to appoint officials enabled him to develop a small, but influential, group whose interests were tied up with himself and with Rome.

Zealots and Essenes—Political discussion, forbidden publicly, flourished in secret. The younger and more zealous advocates of Jewish independence, whether Pharisees or Sadducees in their religious views, carried on their propaganda and prepared for the day when open defiance would be possible. On the other hand, some people became so discouraged over social and economic conditions that they withdrew completely from these responsibilities and organized themselves into groups whose sole purpose was to lead a life of religious purity (Essenes*). The people were moving towards extreme views in their political life, which boded no good for the future peace of the land.

4. GOVERNMENT AND RELIGION

Local Self-Government—In the towns and villages, in internal and local matters, the Jews enjoyed the right to govern themselves. Here is where the Jewish tradition of democracy showed itself to the best advantage. Every community had its council, made up of elders and local scribes. There were also courts of law, consisting of three judges for minor cases and seven for more important ones. The Jews had no jury system, which is an Anglo-Saxon institution. In cases involving capital punishment Jewish law required the court to consist of twenty-three judges. Such large courts naturally could not exist in every community. Nor was it necessary to have so many of them. Courts, or councils, of twenty-three were to be found only in the largest cities. When the Jews enjoyed independence, these local bodies also exercised governmental duties.

The National Sanhedrin—Few institutions of the Jewish past have been surrounded with so much romance as has the Great Sanhedrin which met in Jerusalem. Jewish legend has endowed its members and its leaders with supernatural gifts, and Jewish tradition ascribed to it much of the wisdom and content of Jewish thought. When, in the beginning of the nineteenth century (in 1806), Napoleon I wanted to change the course of Jewish life in France, the method which appealed to him was to revive the Sanhedrin after it had been dead for almost two thousand years.†

It may be well at this point to recall the steps by which the

* See below, p. 130.
† See below, p. 496.

Sanhedrin came into being. The first step was taken, after the return from the Babylonian Exile, with the organization of the Council of Priests and Elders to help the high priest rule. Contemporary with this council was the Great Assembly wherein the entire nation was represented and which was called together only on very special occasions. Its last meeting was probably the one at which Simon the Hasmonean was elected hereditary ruler. Simon's successors, who started out with the best intentions of ruling democratically, continued the nationally representative body, which came to be known as the Sanhedrin, a word which in Greek means "council." To distinguish it from the local councils, the national one was called the Great Sanhedrin. Another reason for calling it "Great" was that it consisted of seventy-one members as against twenty-three in the smaller Sanhedrins.

The Great Sanhedrin differed from the modern legislature in that its members were not elected. Either the king appointed them or the members of the Sanhedrin themselves filled whatever vacancy occurred. That is why its political influence was never developed to the point of overshadowing the king. Its most important function was to serve as a court of law—a Supreme Court. Later this, too, was modified, so that, where there was the slightest suspicion of a crime being political in nature, the Herodian or Roman government took the matter into its own hands, the judicial function of the Sanhedrin being thus restricted to civil and religious matters. The decisions of the Great Sanhedrin laid the foundations for later Jewish law.

Organization of the Sanhedrin—The Great Sanhedrin was organized in an interesting way. From the earliest times of the Second Commonwealth it was customary for the reigning high priest to preside over the deliberations of the highest government body. When the Hasmonean high priests were also kings, they still considered themselves the chiefs of the Sanhedrin. Actually, however, the high priest rarely attended the sessions. His place was taken by another, called *Ab Bet-Din,* literally "Father of the Court." Including the high priest, the Sanhedrin, therefore, consisted of seventy-one members. They met in a hall set aside for them in one of the wings of the Temple, the hall known as *Lishkat ha-Gazit,* the "Hall of Hewn Stones."

It is not strange that as the members of the Sanhedrin lost in political power they gained in the affection and respect of the people. They became scholars, not politicians. And as the people inclined more and more to study and religion, they turned to the members of the Sanhedrin and their learned heads for guidance and encouragement in piety.

The High Priest—For the same political reasons the high priest lost the respect of the Jewish people. No longer the supreme ruler of the land, as he had been during the Persian and Greek periods, nor an all-powerful king, as he had been during the Hasmonean era, the high priest now was nothing more than an official appointed either by a Herodian prince or by a Roman procurator. They changed high priests at their pleasure, handing the office out to such priests as paid them most. Consider the number of changes made during a brief period before the end of the Second Commonwealth. Between the years 150 to 37 B. C. E., one hundred and thirteen years, there were only eight different high priests. But from 37 B. C. E., when Herod took charge, to 70 C. E., one hundred and seven years, twenty-eight different men occupied the high-priestly office. This was an average of something less than four years for each, although according to Jewish tradition the position was to be held for life. The Jews still looked upon the high priest with awe because he was considered the head of the Temple, their most important religious institution. But the buying and selling of the office, the corruption and ignorance of some of the priests who occupied it, and the fact that they were supporters of Rome and under the thumb of the procurators, made the Jews look elsewhere for religious inspiration.

5. THE TEMPLE AT THE HEIGHT OF ITS GLORY

The Temple and Its Beauty—To this day, when one thinks of Jerusalem as it was before the Romans destroyed it, he thinks of it as the religious capital of the Jews. The palaces of its kings and procurators, the stalls of its merchants, its political parties, its soldiers, its rabble and its visitors, all fade into insignificance before the majestic institution which crowned the city's heights and around which Jewish life revolved. It had never been as beautiful as after Herod had rebuilt it and after the Jewish people had finished embellishing it only a few years before it was destroyed. Its simple grandeur impressed every visitor, and it became known far and wide as one of the wonders of the ancient world.

Symbol of Unity—If any Jew of that age, not only in Palestine but anywhere in the world, were asked what he considered most important as an institution in Jewish life, he

would have answered that the Temple was most sacred to
him, and that for it, above all, he was ready to give his life.
No wonder that it was the ambition of every Jew, no matter
where he lived, whether in far-off Spain or deepest Asia, to
visit the Temple at least once during his lifetime, or, if he
could afford it, to spend his declining years under the shadow
of its sacred walls. Hundreds of thousands of visitors would
crowd into Jerusalem during the three major festivals of the
Jewish year: Passover, Shabu'ot, and Sukkot. There was
never enough room for them all. On such occasions the suburbs of Jerusalem would be covered with tents, as though an
army was besieging the city. The proud natives of Jerusalem
would look down upon these provincials who went gaping
through the city's streets, admiring its marvels, paying their
respects to the relics of its past, visiting its famous schools of
Torah and, above all, hurrying to the Temple whose atmosphere they wanted to breathe deeply before returning to
their distant homes.

Between the Temple and the Jews who lived outside of
Palestine the relationship was not only sentimental, but religious. Visitors streamed into Jerusalem in order to pay at the
Temple the vows they had made, or to bring there a sacrifice
in atonement for some sin committed. It seems strange,
nowadays, to think of animal sacrifices as playing so important a part in religion. As a matter of fact, the distance of a
large proportion of the Jewish people from Jerusalem made
individual sacrifices impracticable, with the result that other
religious ceremonials took the place of those in the Temple.
But as long as the Temple was in existence, the sacrificial system served as a powerful bond of union between the Jews of
Palestine and those who lived in the Diaspora.

The Service in the Temple—So dignified and awe-inspiring
was the Temple service that it left an indelible impression
upon the mind of the visitor. At the first sign of dawn on the
eastern horizon, the priest on the tower over the Temple gate
would call to the waiting priests below. The ram's horn (*shofar*) was sounded, and the heavy gate was thrown open to
admit the crowd already waiting outside. The daily service
would then begin. To the accompaniment of musical instruments the Levites chanted the psalm of the day, while the
priests brought a sacrifice for the entire Jewish people. When
that was completed, the officiating priests faced the multitude
and, with hands uplifted, pronounced the triple priestly benediction to be found in the Torah. That done, the public sacrifice for the emperor of Rome was brought. For, with the

consent of Rome, this was substituted by the Jews for the worship of the emperor which was obligatory upon all other subjects of the empire. The rest of the day was occupied with the bringing of private sacrifices: sin-offerings, thank-offerings, and offerings of other kinds, some involving the sacrifice of an animal, and others no more than a measure of flour, depending to a large extent upon the economic condition of the persons who brought them. The last sacrifice of the day was again for the entire people. Then, as night began to fall, the watching crowds were dismissed with the same priestly benediction, and the massive Temple gates were closed. Those priests who remained on duty through the night placed upon the altar all that remained of the day's sacrifices. The fire on the altar was never extinguished.

No private sacrifices were performed on the Sabbath and on holidays. On the other hand, the number of public sacrifices was increased. This addition was called the *musaf* sacrifice. The seventy additional sacrifices of bullocks brought during Sukkot were interpreted as offerings for the welfare of all humanity which was supposed to be divided into seventy nations. On the same holiday there were also extraordinary night services. While the Levites played on their instruments and sang psalms, the priests, holding torches, formed a procession around the altar and poured water at its base. The people, waving palm-branches and myrtle leaves, called out, "Lord help us, Lord prosper us *(Hosha'na)*!" The ceremony symbolically represented a prayer for rain, that water might be plentiful in a land whose chief drawback was dearth of water. The most impressive ceremony of the year was that on Yom Kippur. On that day the high priest entered the Holy of Holies, where he offered a prayer for forgiveness of the people's sins. It was a solemn day, though not a day of sorrow.

The Temple Tax—In this way, throughout the year, there went out from the Temple influences which drew the Jews together into a united religious community. No matter where the Jews lived, they knew that in the Temple at Jerusalem two daily sacrifices were offered up for them. A Jew glowed with pride when a returning pilgrim recounted the magnificence of the Temple and the impressiveness of its ritual. As a result of such feelings, no Jew neglected to send his annual contribution for the support of the Temple. There was no need to urge a Jew to pay this tax, and no collectors were sent out to gather the money. Freely and voluntarily each man paid his half-*shekel* to the local representative appointed

by each community. These sums were then dispatched to a
central treasury in each province which, in turn, sent them on
to Jerusalem. The money was put to a variety of uses. Out of
it the officiating priests were maintained, animals purchased
for the public sacrifices, and public charity disbursed in Jerusalem. There were occasions when unemployment relief consumed a large part of the funds.

Yet at the very time that the Temple was serving as a
source of pride and a bond of union among the Jews of the
world, Judaism was undergoing a transformation which was
making of the Temple a secondary institution and which was
preparing the Jewish people to survive for thousands of years
after the Temple would be no more.

6. THE SYNAGOGUE AND THE TEMPLE

The Meeting House—From the beginning of the Second
Commonwealth* the Jews had found it necessary to establish
local gathering-places where public meetings were held and
lawsuits pleaded before the local judges. There or in an ad-
joining building the scribes taught. There, too, on Sabbaths
and holidays, the people of the neighborhood gathered to
hear the Torah and the Prophets read. The center of social
life was here. From the varied activities conducted in these
houses came their name, "people's houses," or "the people's
gathering places." These names were translated into Greek by
the word "Synagogue." Now certain influences were already
at work which eventually made the Synagogue even more important than the Temple itself.

The Influence of the Pharisees—The scribes and the Pharisees followed two fundamental principles: 1) each man must
come in close and direct touch with God, and 2) knowledge
is the road to piety. Taking the last principle first, it was their
theory that a constant reading of the sacred books would encourage good actions and good thoughts. Such thoughts and
actions constantly repeated would become habits; and good
habits result in good character. Therefore, from the time of
Ezra down, the reading of portions of Torah and Prophets
became the characteristic feature of a public meeting of Jews.
Some portions were considered particularly important, for example, the declaration of God's Unity in the sentence,
Shema' Yisrael ("Hear, O Israel . . ."), and the command

* For the Babylonian roots of the Synagogue, see pp. 33, 44 above.

to love God which follows it. Hence these sentences were recited at every meeting. Other biblical portions were chosen as
appropriate for other occasions. At a later time a scholar, if
present, might be invited to explain the passage read.

The Influence of the Temple Service—The first principle
of the Pharisees, that of each man's closeness to God, also
contributed much to the development of the Synagogue service. In theory, as long as the public sacrifice was offered up
twice daily in the Temple, every Jew was represented by it.
In practice, however, those who recognized the leadership of
the scribes and Pharisees were not satisfied with such indirect
contact with God. Obviously each Jew could not perform his
own sacrifices. But he could do the next best thing—he could
recite the prayers and psalms which accompanied the performance of the sacrifice in the Temple, and he could also
read the description of the sacrifice in the Torah. Summing it
all up, therefore, there were regular services in the synagogues by the first century of the Common Era. These services consisted of: 1) a description of the public sacrifice
going on at the Temple; 2) the recital of the psalms then
being recited in the Temple; and 3) if it were a Saturday, a
holiday or a marketday (Monday and Thursday), the reading
of a portion from the Bible. There was also a growing tendency at that time to add some private prayers of the sort
which are now represented by the Silent Prayer in the Synagogue. Late in the afternoon a shorter service was instituted
to correspond to the second public sacrifice.

Where Synagogues Were to Be Found—The popularity of
the Synagogue is proved by the fact that there was no Jewish
community in Palestine or elsewhere without at least one
building dedicated to that purpose. What is even more surprising is that there were any number of synagogues in Jerusalem close by the Temple, and one within the Temple itself.
Clearly the attitude of the Pharisees had triumphed. Each
Jew sought to make his religion a personal relation between
himself and God. Though no one would have admitted it at
that time, the day was gone when Judaism depended upon
priest and sacrifice, indeed, even upon the Temple itself.

How Synagogues Were Organized—Already then the synagogues were organized somewhat elaborately. At their head
stood the most respected man of the community: *Rosh ha-
Keneset* or *Archisynagogus*. A paid official, called *Hazzan*,
was the director of the service (not the cantor, as now).
There was no official cantor in those days. Any Jew was eligible to lead the congregation in prayer. Other officials of the

community, who did their work as an act of piety, were the overseers of charity. In most instances there was no difference between the community administration and the synagogue administration. The same set of officials was responsible for both.

CHAPTER IX

EDUCATION AND THE RELIGIOUS SPIRIT

THE JEWS MAKE UP FOR THEIR PHYSICAL HARDSHIPS BY SIGNIFICANT DEVELOPMENTS OF MIND AND SPIRIT

Ideals and Their Interpreters—Rome laid its heavy hand upon the Jewish people during the very period when the Jewish religion was being further developed and purified. The ceremonies and institutions, the literature and ideas which the world calls Jewish underwent important developments during that age. Great men lived then. They were not the kings nor even the politicians, perhaps not even such as would be noticed by the mighty and the proud of Jerusalem. They were humble men. Yet they left names which have been a blessing throughout the subsequent ages, and thoughts which have influenced the world. At that time their ideas were still strange, and the world of the Greeks and the Romans did not consider them worth while. Jewish ideas, like the Jewish people, had to struggle for the right to live.

1. THE JEWS AND UNIVERSAL EDUCATON

Elementary Education—The Jews considered education as important as prayer. They traced their zeal for knowledge to the biblical command, "and thou shalt teach them to thy children." Since not all fathers can or want to teach, almost every synagogue established a school. About the year 60 C. E., the High Priest Joshua ben Gamala ordained that every community, no matter how small, must have an elementary school.

Adult Education—What must have surprised a visitor to Jewish Palestine of those days was that not only children, but that almost all adults studied. What the arena was to the Greek and Roman, the academy was to the Jew. They had a horror of ignorance, and looked down upon the unlettered man. The "proper" kind of person had his favorite teacher whose public lectures he attended and whose interpretations of the Bible he cherished and passed along.

Law and Life—Study and discussion were not altogether theoretical. One of the great principles of the scribes and their followers was the extension of religion. In the Bible there is a sentence which reads: "Ye shall be holy, for I, the Lord your God, am holy." The Pharisees undertook no less a task than to turn this ideal into a reality. They maintained that holiness could be approached, if not achieved, by a human being if he regulated his every action in accordance with biblical commands as interpreted by the scribes. Most of the regulations, to be sure, were not enforceable by the courts. The Sadducees, for example, who did not follow the principles of Pharisaic life, were no less Jews because they rejected scribal interpretations and refused to have religion invade those areas of life not definitely touched upon in the Bible. But so keen was the desire of most Jews to lead a life of holiness that they willingly accepted whatever restrictions and limitations this ideal involved.

Two Great Teachers—There were many teachers, but the most important were Shammai and Hillel, contemporaries of King Herod. Though friends, Shammai and Hillel were as different as any two human beings could possibly be in everything but their desire to make the Jews a godly people. Shammai was by nature irritable, severe and conservative. Hillel was kindly, cheerful and progressive. Tradition in numerous stories pictures Hillel as a rare human being, the ideal product of Pharisaic life. He laid the foundations of his vast learning in Babylonia, where he was born. When still a young man Hillel was attracted to the schools of Jerusalem by the fame of its great teachers. Stories tell of the suffering and hardships which, as a poor boy, alone in the large city, Hillel had to undergo in order to continue his studies. In the end his ability was recognized, and Hillel concluded his long life as the pride of Jewish scholarship, the leader of a most famous school and the honored head of the Sanhedrin.

The difference between him and his friendly rival, Shammai, is reflected in the famous story about the heathen who tried to make sport of Jewish life. Knowing that Judaism, as taught by the Pharisees, was hedged in by numerous regulations, this heathen appeared before Shammai and offered to become a Jew if the famous teacher could explain Judaism while the questioner stood on one leg without getting tired. Shammai, highly incensed, drove the scoffer out of his house. The heathen made the same offer to Hillel. Hillel smilingly replied that this request could be complied with easily. All of Judaism, Hillel said, was contained in the brief verse of the Bible (Leviticus 19.18), which reads, "Thou shalt love thy fellow as thyself," and that all the other laws and regulations of Judaism were merely extensions of this one. Deeply impressed, the heathen became serious, and, according to the story, actually became a Jew.

The points of view of both Shammai and Hillel found many adherents in that and in subsequent generations. For several centuries the followers of Shammai and the followers of Hillel engaged in earnest argument, which occasionally even led to bitterness and hostility. Finally the Hillelites prevailed. Even if his ideas had not won the minds of the Jewish people, Hillel's personality would have won their hearts. Through the long history of the Jewish people he represented the ideal Jew, combining kindliness with scholarship, simple piety with profound thought.

2. WHAT THE JEWS READ AND STUDIED

How Jewish Literature Grew—The period of the Second Commonwealth (516 B. C. E. to 70 C. E.) was an age of great literary activity. It started with the work of the scribes —Ezra, his predecessors and his successors—who sifted the literature of the preceding centuries, accepting some and rejecting others, and rewriting still others. Moreover, since a large part of the Jewish people had become interested in reading and study, an entirely new literature came into being.

Later Writings—Among the newer books some dwelt on the glories of the Jewish past and the exploits of its heroes, for example, the wisdom and loyalty of Daniel, and of Mordecai and Esther. There is a work called the *Book of Jubilees* which tells the story of the world, from Creation to the event at Mount Sinai, with a great many additional imaginative details to supplement the story in the Torah. It gives the names of Adam's children, not found in the Bible, and also the story of the Fallen Angels which, many centuries later, Milton was to retell in his *Paradise Lost*. Other books consisted of poetry, like the *Psalms of Solomon.* Still others were merely stories, like that of *Tobit,* or *Judith,* or *Susanna.* Finally, more or less authentic history was written during this age, especially the history of the Maccabean revolt.

Pseudepigrapha—In those days people took no personal pride in being authors and did not attach their names to the poems or the stories which they wrote. It may be that the men of the generation when a particular book was written still knew who its author was. His name was soon forgotten though his book remained. Sometimes, however, an author would find writings attributed to a great man of old. He would arrange them, perhaps add to them, and then call the resultant book by that man's name. For he knew that he himself was not sufficiently respected for people to pay much attention to what he wrote. He would say that he was merely republishing what had been said by a great man of an older generation: Daniel, Ezra, Enoch or even Adam. The man did not mean to tell a falsehood; all he wanted was to induce people to read his writing attentively. To such books has been given the name *pseudepigrapha,* that is, "false writings," though they should really be called "falsely ascribed writings."

Apocalypses—There was one type of book, included in the above, which at that time exerted greater influence than any other—the apocalyptic. The word *Apocalypse* means a revelation of the unknown. Part of the Book of Daniel, in the Bible, for example, is an apocalypse because it attempts to describe exactly how God, in the unknown future, would punish the sinful nations and save His pious ones. During the first century B. C. E. and the first century C. E., many apocalyptic books appeared among the Jews. The oldest and the most interesting of them is the one that bears the name of Enoch as author. This patriarch, who preceded the Flood and whom the Bible says "God took" (interpreted to mean that he never died), is here made to tell how sin and wickedness will finally disappear, and how an era of great happiness will then descend upon the earth. God will send his anointed, the Messiah, to redeem Israel from the oppressor and all of humanity from degrading sin. All this is told not in so many words, but mainly by means of arresting images. Vivid descriptions are given of God's judgment and of the Era of Peace which will follow the coming of the Messiah. In general this sort of book is weird, unreal and difficult to understand.

Why Such Books Were Popular—The Jews liked to read these books. They loved to hear about the might of their ancient heroes and about the fearful Judgment Day which God would visit upon the world. As religious people they had felt for many centuries that God could not tolerate much longer the cruelty and wickedness which they saw about them. The longer God delayed, they thought, the harsher would be the punishment which He would some day mete out to those who lived contrary to the laws of kindliness and justice.

Besides, the situation in which the Jewish people found themselves seemed contrary to God's promise. He had promised that the Jews would be the leaders and teachers of mankind, whereas actually the Egyptians, the Syrians and now the Romans had successively treated them as a conquered people. The Jews felt their moral superiority over these nations, yet these very nations were making them feel small and powerless. How was this to be explained? One explanation was that their generation was unworthy of God's promise, but that their ancestors had been worthy of it. It made them proud to think of David as the conqueror of the world, and of Solomon as the wise teacher and ruler of all the nations. But they felt even prouder when they thought of the future age when God would redeem their descendants and make the Jewish people of the future the guide and teacher of the nations. The prophets of the past had also predicted that the nations of the world would come to recognize the greatness of the God of Israel. But there was this difference between the early prophets and the visionaries who wrote apocalyptic books. The prophets had been optimistic social reformers; they saw improvement as following the natural course of life. The apocalyptists were pessimists. Before their very eyes the world was becoming worse instead of better; Israel was sinking lower instead of rising higher. There seemed to be only one way out, and that was for God Himself miraculously to intervene and to improve the world.

3. Some Jewish Beliefs

Spiritual Leadership—The Jewish teachers of the day far preferred the Torah, the Prophets and the sacred Writings to the glowing pictures of the later books. They did not, in fact, succeed at once in persuading the Jews to accept their opinion about the books to be read or the ideas to be adopted. For the sages did not establish a censorship nor did they threaten the people with punishment. They did two things: they continued to emphasize the divine nature of the books which they considered worth while; and, secondly, they selected from the other books those ideas which seemed to them to conform to what Judiasm should be and employed them in their explanations. By means of their life and their teachings the sages guided the spiritual and mental life of the people. A picture of the Judaism of that period would consist of some very old religious ideas somewhat modified, and of some new ideas which were being rapidly absorbed.

God and His Angels—The Unity of God is one of the oldest ideas of Judaism, and its very foundation. If, before the Babylonian Exile, the Jews were not altogether loyal to this idea, they prided themselves upon it during the Second Commonwealth. The more commonplace and ridiculous the pagan divinities seemed to the Jews, the more they stood in awe and respect before the God of Heaven and Earth, the Father and Creator of Mankind. They had long since stopped pronouncing God's name, since to do so indicated too much familiarity. Except when at prayer, and sometimes not even then, they spoke of God as "The Holy One, Blessed be He," or "our Father in Heaven," or simply "The Name."

As a result of Jewish contact with the Persians, the Jews had adopted the idea that God had many servants who were called His "messengers," that is, His angels. From the Persians, too, they got the idea of messengers of evil whose chief was Satan. To be sure, vague ideas on the same subject were also found in the biblical books, but there they did not assume anything like the importance which they obtained in the later literature. There was a growing danger that the Jews would look upon the angels and the devils as closer to them than God of Whom they stood in such awe. The spiritual guides of Jewish life did not desire any such development, and they stopped it. While they did not eradicate the notions about angels and devils, they made it perfectly clear that prayers were to be addressed directly to God. In the authoritative literature of the Jews angels and devils play no part. They were confined to the poetic and folk literature which expressed Jewish imagination.

Morality and Kindliness—Nothing set the Jew apart from the non-Jew of those days more than the two qualities of morality and kindliness. From the sexual immorality which characterized the life of the ancient Greeks and Romans the Jew was almost completely free. Moreover, Judaism based itself upon charity, a quality equally foreign to the rest of the ancient world. The story about Hillel and the pagan, told above, illustrates this point. But long before Hillel, a famous teacher said: "The world rests upon three things: Torah (study and observance), Worship (Temple, Synagogue), and acts of charity." These attitudes were emphasized in the later literature as well.

Resurrection—Two of the ideas which moved men most powerfully in that age were life after death and resurrection. The Jewish mind had long wrestled with the problem, and now the new literature emphasized it above everything else. The notions of a heaven and a hell gained wide belief, and connected with them was the even more agreeable idea of the dead coming to life once more, to a life that would never end. Among the Greeks and the Romans no such hope was held out. Death was the end of everything, so that life seemed hopeless and death cruel. The idea of resurrection involved also the idea of justice on earth, since only the just and the pious had hopes of eternal life. Thus, because of the belief in ultimate resurrection, Judaism made optimists of the Jews besides giving them an additional motive for living in obedience to the will of God as explained by the teachers.

The Chosen People—The Jew of that day felt that he was superior to the pagans. Their cruelty, their lewdness, their silly notions about gods, made the pagans seem lost tribes of humanity. Herein, however, the Jews saw their task: they were destined to be "the witnesses of God," the teachers of mankind. Their forefathers, the Patriarchs, had been chosen to found a new people. That new people had consecrated itself by accepting the Ten Commandments at the foot of Sinai. From this the Jews felt justified in drawing certain conclusions. One was that the Jews were a superior people, if not because of the merits of their own generation, then because of the fact that they were descendants of such illustrious ancestors. The other conclusion was that the Jewish people was not a racial group (a blood-group), but a group with a mission, that is, a group united by ideas. Anyone accepting the burden of being obedient to Torah and of exemplifying Jewish life was a good Jew even if he had been born into another people. Most Jews of that day adopted both views: they were proud of their ancestry and also willing to bear the mission which membership in the Jewish group imposed upon them.

The Messiah—One of the beliefs held by the Jews was the coming of a Messiah. This belief was soon to play an important part in the foundation of Christianity. The word *Messiah* is the Hebrew word for "an anointed one." It was applied to every king and high priest, because, before entering upon their office, these men had consecrated oil poured upon their heads. When the Second Commonwealth was established and the Persians did not permit the re-establishment of the Davidic dynasty, the Jews began to dream of the day when a descendant of David would reappear and an anointed king would once more sit upon the throne of Israel. That is why Simon the Hasmonean was elected hereditary ruler only "until a true prophet would arise" to indicate who was more entitled to the throne than he.

Then came the period of misfortune. The Hasmoneans disappointed the pious people of the land. Herod and Rome embittered the life of the nation. Poverty added to the hard lot of the people. Suffering the oppression of their conquerors, the Jews changed the old idea about a Messiah in two different ways. The majority of the Jewish people looked for the appearance of a mighty warrior who, though he was not of the Davidic family, would lead them against their enemies, destroy Rome, free the Jews and establish a reign of justice, plenty and peace. But there was another, smaller group, who thought of the Messiah as more than a human being. Unaided by ordinary weapons he would conquer the pagans, and cause the Jews and Judaism to triumph. In the Book of Enoch, written during the first century of the Common Era, the author speaks of a supernatural being, the Son of Man, who awaited a signal from God in order to go down to earth and free humanity from sin, injustice and oppression.

Torah and Wisdom—The chief belief of Judaism of that day was the belief in the Torah as the gift of God and the treasure of Israel. In the narrow sense the word Torah stands for the Five Books of Moses. But that is not what the Jews have meant by the word from that day down to our own. The word began to mean Jewish wisdom, Jewish knowledge and Jewish law. It was God's teaching, which He sent as a guide for humanity. For that reason the scribes and the teachers valued every single word of the holy books. Not the slightest of its commands could be violated. As one of them put it, it was necessary to "build a fence around the Torah." By that he meant adding rules over and above those contained in the holy books, so that a person might feel that he was a sinner long before he thought of acting contrary to biblical laws. The Pharisees of that day believed that, far from being a burden, the Torah was what distinguished the Jews from the other peoples of the world.

4. Religious Extremes

The Boethusians—It is important to remember that these ideas and beliefs were not the law of the land. A Jew of that day could believe some of them or none of them. The Boethusians, who were politically the adherents of Rome, agreed with the Sadducees in matters of religion, rejecting the belief in Resurrection, the Messiah and the reinterpretation of the Torah which was so dear to the hearts of the Pharisees.

The Essenes—At the other extreme of Jewish life was a sect bearing the name of Essenes, derived, some say, from a word which meant "self-purifiers," or "purists," while others trace their origin to the Hasidim of Maccabean times. They were a curious group of people, living in communities of their own, usually outside of cities or close to the desert. They ate together, partaking only of the simplest kinds of food, since they were vegetarians. They earned their livelihood through manual labor, and then pooled their earnings, for no one could have private possessions. They dressed in the simplest possible clothes, usually white. They washed and bathed frequently, not primarily because of a desire for cleanliness, but because outward cleanness was a symbol of inner purity. They did not disregard the Temple, but they emphasized personal piety more than public worship. They observed the Sabbath very strictly, and were very careful about private prayer.

Among the Jews generally the Essenes acquired a reputation for sanctity and mystery. This was partly due to the fact that they were credited with the possession of secret wisdom. They always lived in the open, and thus became acquainted with the medicinal power of herbs. Far and wide they were known as healers of the sick, but they did not divulge their medical knowledge to non-Essenes. The halo of mystery which surrounded them was further increased by the difficulty of getting into their society. They required a year of probation and the initiation ceremony was carried out in secret. But they did go out to preach among the people. They would appear in their strange garments and announce that the end of the world might come at any moment, for they were given to the reading of apocalyptic literature. They urged people to repent before it was too late, before the arrival of God's Great Judgment Day, when the sinners and the godless would perish.

John the Baptist—One of their most powerful preachers was a man by the name of Johanan. He went up and down the land, following the western bank of the River Jordan. Wherever he came crowds gathered to hear him. He would thrill and frighten his audiences by describing the approaching Judgment. Throughout his addresses one phrase recurred: "Repent, for the Kingdom of Heaven is at hand!" Those who were moved by his eloquence and repented, offering to lead a blameless life thereafter, Johanan invited to descend into the waters of the Jordan and bathe their bodies to indicate that they intended their spirit to be pure. Consequently, he became known as Johanan *ha-Tabol* (or *ha-Tobel*), the Baptizer, a holy man, as near to being a prophet as one could then come. His zeal for right living, as we have seen, led eventually to Johanan's death.* Indirectly, the execution of Johanan led to an even greater tragedy, that of Jesus of Nazareth.

5. JESUS OF NAZARETH

In the Footsteps of the Baptist—In Galilee, in the village of Nazareth, lived a simple and pious carpenter by the name of Joseph, and his wife, Miriam. They had several children whom they brought up in piety, and to whom they gave whatever education it was possible in their time and place to give. One of their sons, Joshua (Jesus is the Greek form of the name), distinguished himself above the other children by his greater religious devotion, love of learning and sensitiveness. As he grew older he learned his father's trade, but he never abandoned his studies, and continued to fill his mind with the words of the ancient prophets as well as of the apocalyptic writings. With many other Jews of his time he wondered when God would free His people both from the external yoke of the Romans and from the internal weight of their own sinfulness.

A critical moment occurred in Joshua's life the day Johanan the Baptizer arrived at a point on the River Jordan which was but a few hours' walk from Nazareth. The pious people of the village joined those of the towns nearby and went to hear the famous Essene preacher. Fascinated, they listened to his vivid description of the approaching Day of Judgment, and to his assurance that the Messiah would soon appear to redeem God's people and abolish all wickedness. Did they

* See above, p. 108.

want to be saved from God's wrath? Let them repent, Johanan exclaimed. The preacher made an overwhelming impression upon the sensitive spirit of Joshua.

He may even have become an Essene and remained with
this brotherhood for several years. Then, when all pious Jews
were horrified by the news that Johanan had been executed,
Joshua decided to take up the task for which the martyr had
given his life. Joshua now traveled through the land, especially Galilee. He called upon the people to repent
(teshubah), to give up their property, the possession of which
led to greed and oppression, and to observe the Divine Law
as expressed by the Torah and the prophets. His preaching,
as well as the remarkable cures he was able to effect, spread
his reputation through Galilee. Even Gentiles came to him
for cures, and though he at first refused to aid them, saying
that his business was only with the Jews, he later changed his
mind.

Disciples and Opponents—Joshua had been brought up
among the poorer class, and his wandering through the country brought him in even closer touch with the masses of the
people. He knew how hard life was for them, and he resented
the superior airs which some of the more learned assumed
towards them. It was all very well for the Jews of the cities,
who could associate with the famous learned sages, to pride
themselves upon their ability to observe all the regulations of
Pharisaic life. But what of the poor Jews of Galilee who had
neither the time nor the means to give themselves to religious
study and strict observance—should they be rejected altogether? Joshua emphasized for them those simple, straightforward principles which were the foundations of Jewish teaching.
He picked for himself several of these poor workmen, fisher-
men for the most part, and kept them as his constant compa-
nions wherever he went. He freely associated with others of
the same kind. He stayed at their homes and ate their bread,
in complete disregard of criticism by the Pharisees who were
horrified that one calling himself a teacher should act contrary
to the ceremonies which the observant Jews had taken upon
themselves. But his followers and other poor people rejoiced
in his championship of their cause. Among his disciples it was
agreed that Joshua must be the great and good deliverer
whose coming the Jews were expecting, the Messiah. The
leader of the disciples, Simon, who was also known as Peter,
was so sure of the fact that he mentioned it to Joshua and was
mildly rebuked.

The Visit to Jerusalem—Joshua and his disciples decided

to pay a visit to Jerusalem. It was close to Passover and the Holy City teemed with pilgrims from every part of the world. Like other poor pilgrims, Joshua and his friends camped in the open, on the Mount of Olives, in the suburbs of the city. Then they went to visit the Temple. A considerable number of other Galillean Jews had heard of Joshua, and, greeting him cordially, joined his group. But no sooner did the Galilean procession arrive at the Temple than trouble began. Joshua had always looked upon the Temple as God's House, the most sacred spot in the world. He was shocked, outraged, to see business going on within the Temple grounds. He did not stop to consider that foreign pilgrims had to change their ordinary money into money usable for Temple purposes, nor that people could not bring sacrificial animals with them. There were money-changers in the Temple area; there were also ugly stalls for animals close by. Joshua, the zealous preacher, the believer in Essenic purity, saw in the mixture of business and religion only godlessness and sin. He turned the tables of the money-changers over and chased the cattle-dealers away. A riot broke out in the Temple district for which Joshua and the Galileans had to bear the blame.

In the Name of Public Peace—The men responsible for public order, as well as the followers of Pharisaic teaching, saw danger in the situation. The Galileans were known to be hotheaded patriots. The Roman procurator, Pontius Pilate, was on hand with his soldiers. There was no telling what another visit by Joshua to the Temple would bring. It seemed necessary to discredit Joshua in the eyes of his followers, or to remove him from Jerusalem altogether. Some of the Pharisees felt also that Joshua was leading the Galileans away from what was considered proper Jewish custom and interpretation. In the presence of his followers, the Pharisees tried to embarrass Joshua by asking him questions about the interpretation of Jewish tradition. But he answered evasively, and the discussion was without result.

Had this peaceful method of removing the Galilean political danger been successful, the aristocratic Sadducees would not have had to put their own plan into execution. They found one of Joshua's disciples, Judas, a native of Kiriot, and paid him to point Joshua out to the high priest's police. Many explanations have been offered for Judas' action, for it seems strange that a disciple should have betrayed his master merely for money. Whatever his reasons, Judas led the police to Joshua's camping ground. It was the first night of Passover, and Joshua had been celebrating the holiday with his disciples, drinking the customary cups of wine and eating of the unleavened bread. He was arrested and led to the authorities.

Joshua and the High Priest—Since it was a holiday, no Jewish court could be called in session. Only the high priest, an appointee of Rome, and a few members of the aristocracy, who feared the common people and suspected every movement among them, were there. They wanted to find some charge against Joshua by means of which they could hold him imprisoned until after the holiday, or perhaps find out whether he really intended to cause trouble. It was at this point, according to the story, that the prisoner gave utterance to an extraordinary claim. He asserted that he was the predestined Messiah. His examiners could draw only one conclusion from such a statement, namely, that Joshua intended to start a rebellion against Rome. Whatever moved Joshua to say what he did, no one knows. Apparently, to the last moment of his life he expected the miraculous help of God. But one can guess the motives of the high priest and his friends. They wanted no messiah, for messiah meant revolution and trouble. Such occurrences had taken place before and had resulted in the death, not alone of the would-be messiah, but of those who followed him. Perhaps they should have kept Joshua in prison. Instead, they chose to deal with him harshly. Did they incidentally hope to gain praise from the procurator by proving their loyal watchfulness against the enemies of Rome? At all events, they sent their prisoner to Pontius Pilate. Joshua's declaration that he was the Messiah was a political crime, and with such crimes the Jews had no power to deal.

Joshua and Pilate—Pontius Pilate was Roman governor of Judea with a record of black cruelty. To him the Jews and their ideas had always seemed more than queer. He considered Joshua as but another claimant to messiahship, frequent among the Jews of that day. From the message sent by the high priest and from his own examination of the prisoner, Pilate judged that Joshua wanted to be king of the Jews. That obviously was treason against Rome, an offense punishable by the most gruesome of Rome's penalties, crucifixion. That very day Joshua was condemned to die on the cross.

The Tragedy of the Cross—It was Roman custom to flog the condemned before leading him forth to die. The Roman soldiers flogged Joshua in the government palace and gave him the cross upon which he was to be hung. That, too, was Roman custom; the condemned had to carry his own cross to the place of execution. Joshua and two others were marched through the streets of the city where, a few days previously, he had been received with such acclaim. He marched between Roman soldiers. From a distance several of his former friends followed him. Perhaps they also looked for a miracle to save their master. The crowds in the streets watched the sad procession. Some may have heard that this poor Galilean Jew had claimed to be the Messiah, and so they justified his fate as befitting a blasphemer. Others may have thought of him as the pilgrim who had caused a riot in the Temple. But if we understand correctly the attitude of the Jews toward Rome, the great majority must have felt heartsick to see another Jewish patriot being led to a cruel death at the hands of the Roman oppressor.

The soldiers nailed Joshua to the cross. Over his head they fastened a sign upon which they inscribed the crime for which he had been condemned to die. It read: "Jesus of Nazareth, King of the Jews." A small group of sad onlookers stood by. Were they still expecting a miracle? Was he still expecting to be saved? He could not endure the torture for long. Late in the afternoon he expired, but not before he had uttered the anguished cry: "My God, my God, why hast Thou forsaken me!" words found in the Book of Psalms.

The Hope Restored—Among the Jews it was considered a disgrace to leave a dead body exposed. Joshua's friends bribed the Romans to give his body to them. They tenderly laid it in a cave near by, covered the entrance to the cave with a huge rock, and agreed to return, in order to bring the body to proper burial. They scattered; the end of all their hopes had come. But when some of them came to keep their appointment at the cave, they found it empty. The body had mysteriously disappeared. For those who had but yesterday expected a miraculous deliverance, who had been taught that the coming of the Messiah meant the resurrection of the dead, it was not impossible to see a miracle in the emptiness of the cave. Clearly their beloved leader may have died, but he had been resurrected and taken up to heaven. Some day soon if his words were to be believed, he would return and live among them to the end of time.

The Nazarenes—This hope his followers ever refused to yield. They used to gather in the garret of the house where one of them lived. This small group of Galilean Jews used to recount the stories of Joshua's life and their experiences with him. The more they talked about him the more marvelous were the stories they found to tell. They read the holy books, and the more they read them the more references to their departed leader they thought they discovered. Someone made a collection of these references, and used them to persuade other Jews of the truth of their belief that Joshua the Nazarene was the expected Messiah. The tragedy of Joshua was now over; the glorification of Jesus had begun. But the tragedy of the Jewish people whom he had loved was continuing and was destined to be intensified in his name.

CHAPTER X

SCATTERED ISRAEL

THE JEWS BECOME SCATTERED THROUGHOUT THE THEN-KNOWN WORLD AND, WHILE MANY GENTILES LEARN TO ADMIRE THEM, SOME GENTILES HATE THEM

The Importance of the Diaspora—While Palestine struggled for liberation from the yoke of Rome, other Jewish communities were becoming increasingly important for the development of Jewish life. They tested the strength of Judaism and helped prepare it to live outside its original home.

There were then very few known lands which did not belong to the Roman empire. The boundaries of Rome were almost identical with the boundaries of civilization. Beyond were steppes, seas, deserts and savages. Within Rome's empire and its nearest civilized neighbors, the Parthians, the population was large, commerce active and mental life vigorous.

That world eventually died, and along with it the Jewish communities which had been part of it and which had contributed to its growth and grandeur. But neither the ancient civilization nor its Jewish Diaspora departed without leaving an inheritance on which our own culture has been nourished. Hence, though that world is dead, we must understand it if we are to understand ourselves. Moreover, the story of the Jews of that day is a strange and instructive one, especially instructive to us who, like them, live as a minority among a non-Jewish majority. They had problems not unlike our own at the present time; they struggled to preserve themselves, to gain the good will of their neighbors and to live in accordance with Jewish tradition as they understood it. As a result of these problems and struggles they brought about changes not only in Jewish life but also in the life of the other peoples of the world. Christianity, for example, owes to the Jews outside of Palestine almost as much as it owes to the Jews within it. Finally, the very existence of the populous and prosperous diaspora communities affected the decision of the Palestinian Jews to dare the struggle against Rome.

1. The Important Jewish Communities

The Jews of Babylonia—The only really important Jewish community not under Roman rule was the one which lived within the Parthian empire and which is familiar to us under the name of Babylonian Jewry. In the first century of the Common Era this community of Jews already had a long and distinguished past. Having come into being as a result of the Assyrian conquest of Israel in 719 B. C. E. and the Babylonian conquest of Judea in 586 B. C. E., it had redeemed these misfortunes by contributing men, money and ideas to the establishment of the Second Commonwealth. After holding the stage of Jewish life for a century and a half, this community retired to the background. Persia crumbled under Alexander's blows; the Seleucids fell heir to Greek power; they, in turn, were succeeded by the Parthians. But what these changes meant for the Jews of the land we cannot tell. For about two centuries Babylonia's Jews are all but unheard from. Probably they were of proved ability and worth, since one of the Seleucids persuaded or compelled a number of Babylonian Jews to settle farther west, in territory which this king wanted to develop. Learning had not altogether died out among them; the great Hillel was a native of Babylonia and laid there the foundations for his knowledge. Undoubtedly they had a sentimental attachment to Judea, for they were proud to entertain the exiled Hyrcan II and they used to go in large numbers to visit the Temple in Jerusalem. But now the time was approaching when their role in Jewish life would be greater than ever before.

The Jews of the Roman Empire—For the first two centuries of the Common Era, however, the Jewish communities that lived under the rule of Rome held a more central place in Jewish life than the Jewish communities of Babylonia. Jews were to be found in every corner of the empire. In Gaul and Spain, all along the northern coast of Africa, in Asia Minor, on the southern and northern coasts of the Black Sea, on the shores of the Danube, in every part of Greece and the Greek isles, and in Italy, not excepting Rome itself, there were Jewish settlements. Ultimately, of course, most of these Jews traced their origin to emigrants from Palestine. The actual, more direct focal points for settlement in the distant parts of the Roman world were three: Alexandria, Asia Minor and the city of Rome. Military force and the search for a livelihood were the two reasons which had made and which continued to make the Jews leave their homeland. In either case they did not leave because they wanted to, but rather because they could not help themselves. Once outside their own land, they chose a new home wherever chance placed them or opportunity beckoned.

The Jewish Population—It is difficult to know how many Jews lived in these scattered communities. A reasonable guess estimates that there were about eight million Jews in the world just before the conflict with Rome. Probably about one million lived in Babylonia, outside the Roman empire. About two and a half million lived in Palestine and four million in the rest of the Roman world. Jews formed two fifths of the population of Alexandria, and perhaps fifty thousand lived in Rome. Thus it has been calculated that in the first century

C. E. the Jews were ten per cent of the total population of the Roman empire. In the eastern provinces, where they lived in greatest numbers, the proportion was higher, so that they were much more conspicuous.

2. THE RESULTS OF ECONOMIC SUCCESS

Economic Opportunities—Palestine was overcrowded, and the opportunities of its Jewish inhabitants were restricted by the commercial activity of the pagans who lived in or near the land. At the same time the opportunities in the rest of the Roman empire were expanding. Out of Alexandria ships laden with grain sailed across the Mediterranean to feed the population of Rome. Jews were prominent among the exporters of this grain, both as shipowners and as sailors. Jews lived in Spain, then noted for its wine, food and mineral products. On the sea and on land the Jews were prominent merchants. Within each country, too, on a lesser scale, the Jews competed with the non-Jewish businessmen. If they were less skillful as artisans, they nevertheless helped to develop local trades. Nor must it be supposed that there were no Jewish farmers. To be sure, a newcomer into a country which had been settled for a long time could not find a farm for himself at once. Of necessity he first settled in a city and tried to be an artisan or to enter business. But every Jew looked forward to owning some land, and in time many of them realized this ambition. Below the coast of Egypt, or beyond the coasts of Spain, and in other provinces as well, Jewish farmers were frequently found.

The Jews of the Diaspora were by no means all wealthy. Most of them were poor, earning a meager livelihood from manual labor. Jewish beggars were to be seen on the streets of Rome and Alexandria. To earn a living some Jews resorted to such peculiar occupations as interpreting dreams or telling fortunes. There was a time when the Jews were famed for their fighting qualities and were hired as soldiers in various armies. This was true especially for several centuries following the Maccabean wars when everyone knew how well Jews had fought. Subsequently this occupation ceased to be common among the Jews of the Roman empire, though in Parthia Jewish mercenary soldiers continued to exist for centuries.

The Jews and Their Competitors—When the Jews arrived in any province, they were at first welcome. Their industry and ability contributed to the development of the places in which they settled. But success is always a cause for envy. In the lands of the eastern Mediterranean, pagan businessmen now saw Jews getting more and more business, some of them growing rich and influential. Naturally, they thought that if it were not for the Jews all this business would be in their own hands, and they were ready to join anyone or any movement that promised to rid them of their competitors.

3. THE RESULTS OF RELIGIOUS SUCCESS

How Judaism Spread—Such pagan businessmen soon found allies in the pagan priests and in other defenders of paganism as a religion. For not only many Jews, but Judaism had been successful. Wherever Jews settled they brought with them a contempt for paganism, its crude worship of numberless gods, its cruelty, its immorality. The Jews began to write books and pamphlets in which they tried to prove the superiority of Judaism and the truth of God's promise to prefer the Jewish people above any others. So anxious were they for the world to believe that no good could come from paganism and that everything worth while must have a Jewish origin, that they made an effort to prove that the great Greek philosophers and the wisdom of the biblical books were in perfect agreement. Some of them went even further, and asserted that Socrates, Plato and Aristotle had been influenced by the writings of Moses. The life led by individual Jews was even more helpful. Many pagans saw the greatness of the Jewish idea of God, especially that He was merciful and just. They could not help admiring the strict morality which prevailed among the Jews, and the fact that Jews felt obliged to give of their wealth to support the poor. Perhaps what attracted most attention was the refusal of the Jews to work one day in seven, devoting that day to physical rest and to prayer and study. The more intelligent pagans found this attractive, and were tempted to imitate it.

The Fearers of the Lord—Before many generations passed, wherever Jews settled, Judaism acquired converts. Outright conversion, however, was rather difficult for a Gentile, because of the numerous commandments and restrictions involved and, especially for a man, because of the demand for circumcision before one could call himself a full-fledged Jew. A peculiar situation, therefore, arose wherein a large number of pagans, particularly women, observed some Jewish rites without definitely identifying themselves with the Jewish people. There was hardly a synagogue anywhere in the Diaspora but provided space for such people, who came to be known as "fearers of the Lord." Very frequently the children of such half-Jews were brought up by their parents to be Jews in every respect. This helps to explain the large number of Jews in the Diaspora.

Pagan Opposition—Everybody fears the unfamiliar, and the vast majority of the pagans suspected Judaism as something strange and foreign. Moreover, many intellectual leaders of the time undertook to defend the beliefs and ideas in which they had been brought up. Most of them had stopped believing in the actual existence of the gods and goddesses of the Greek and Roman religion, but they continued to hold on to them as beautiful explanations of nature and natural forces. They spoke with contempt of those pagans who were interested in Judaism, which seemed to them a cold and unnatural religion. The Latin poet Horace, for example, poked fun at Romans who observed the Sabbath. Other writers found fault with the Jews, calling them "superstitious" because they believed in a God they did not see and could not describe. They branded them as haters of the divine, and proved to their own satisfaction that the Jews were also haters of humanity because they were unwilling to take part in pagan celebrations which entailed the slightest religious ceremony.

Worst of all were the libels on Judaism invented by the pagan priests. To contradict the Jewish claim that the God of Israel had led his people victoriously out of Egypt, the Egyptian priests asserted that their records told the same story differently. The ancient Hebrews, they said, were a group of slaves who had become lepers, and whom Pharaoh, upon the advice of Egypt's gods, expelled from the country. They ridiculed the Jewish idea of worshipping an Invisible God. On the contrary, they said, the Jews have, concealed in the Holy of Holies of the Temple, the image of a donkey which they worship. And, in order further to arouse feeling against the Jews, the charge was spread that every so often the Jews would capture a Greek, hide him in the Temple at Jerusalem, and eventually offer him up as a sacrifice to their God. With the spreading of stories such as these among the masses, it is no wonder that for every convert gained by the Jews, there were ten pagans who suspected the Jews for their queer ideas and feared them for their strange and mysterious customs.

4. The Results of Political Success

Religion and Politics—As though business competition and
religious differences were not enough to cause misunderstandings, a third cause developed out of the political privileges
which the Roman government granted the Jews. The source
of the trouble lay in the fact that neither Jews nor pagans
drew clear distinctions between religion and other phases of
life. Every event of public life, whether a political meeting or
a chariot race, began with a brief ceremony in honor of the
patron god or goddess of the city. To the pagans this was as
significant as standing up for the national anthem is to a
modern man under similar circumstances. But Judaism forbade its adherents to do the slightest honor to a pagan god.
Consequently the Jews could not participate in any public
function. Worse still, the Jewish population thus laid itself
open to the accusation of being unpatriotic.

God and Pagan Kings—The kings, whether Egyptian, Syrian or Parthian, were made to understand the difficult position of their Jewish subjects and they gave the Jews special
privileges, permitting them to be members of the larger political community without any of those obligations which might
be connected with pagan rites. Of course, that meant that
Jews could not be elected to local offices. On the other hand,
the early Jewish settlers did not mind this political limitation,
first because these offices were only of social consequence, but
mainly because they were happy to be free of all contacts
with paganism.

For a long time this was a generally satisfactory arrangement. Difficulties really began after the Romans conquered
Egypt and deprived it of independence. The Greek population, which had ruled Egypt for several centuries since the
time of Alexander and the first Ptolemy, resented being
merely a province of the Roman empire. Realizing this, the
Roman rulers, Julius Caesar and Augustus, tried to insure
the loyalty of at least part of the land's population. They ratified and increased the privileges of the Jews. They excused
the Jews from the worship of the goddess Roma, a worship
which was meant to indicate loyalty to the Roman empire.
Later, they were likewise excused from the worship of Caesar
and Augustus, who were considered gods. This the other
Egyptians had to do, while the Jews were expected only to
pray for the emperors. The Jews were naturally grateful for

these special favors, and the more they showed their gratitude
the more the Greeks and the native Egyptians accused them
of lacking patriotism to the land where they lived.

How the Jewish Communities Governed Themselves—
Among the privileges granted the Jews everywhere in the Diaspora, one of the most important was the privilege of organizing a separate community. The need for common worship
and the importance of the Jewish diet brought the Jews together, and also the natural social attraction of people of the
same kind for one another. They settled close together and,
before long, there were Jewish districts in most towns. In Alexandria, for example, two of the five parts into which the
city was divided were made up almost exclusively of Jews. To
be sure, many pagans lived within those neighborhoods, while
a good many of the wealthier Jews lived in other parts of the
city, but these two sections were known everywhere as Jewish. In the city of Rome there were also several districts inhabited largely by Jews.

Each of these neighborhoods had its synagogue, and every
synagogue had its necessary organization. But a synagogue
organization meant more than a society for maintaining a
house of prayer. Jewish life had rules of charity, of morals,
and laws of right and wrong which differed considerably
from the laws current among the pagans. That is why a Jewish community had a community president, and also secretaries and charity officers, called *gabbaim,* who took care of the
various activities connected with Jewish life. They also had
regular courts of law to judge cases arising between Jews. A
Jewish community had the power to punish its members for a
breach of Jewish law.

It is not certain whether the various synagogues in Rome
were united in a city-wide organization, but it is certain that
the Jews of Alexandria were so united. At their head stood a
man of their own choice whose position corresponded to that
of the ethnarchs of Judea. There was also a council of seventy members—a sort of Sanhedrin that exercised supreme
authority over the Egyptian Jews. The Jews were proud of
their communal organization, but unfortunately it caused
trouble between them and the non-Jewish residents of Alexandria. For, while the Jews had always enjoyed religious and
group autonomy, the non-Jews of Alexandria had been asking time after time for greater privileges of self-government,
which were never granted. This, the pagan Alexandrians felt,
was further proof that the Jews were a separate nation, foreigners who lived in their midst.

5. THE NEW STRUGGLE BETWEEN JUDAISM AND HELLENISM

The Accusation of Foreignness—The Jews of the Diaspora felt that the accusation of foreignness was unjustified. If to be a native meant to have helped in the founding of the new cities in the eastern part of the Roman world, then the Jews argued that many of their ancestors had also helped, especially in the case of Alexandria. If patriotism meant love of one's city and contribution to its greatness, then they were sure of their loyalty and of the fact that they had contributed and were continuing to contribute in matters of culture and material prosperity. The only difference between them and their neighbors, the Jews insisted, was a difference in religion. To be sure, they looked to Jerusalem for religious guidance, and sent their annual contribution to the Temple. These were not political, but religious ties. And so the Jews called themselves Alexandrians, or Antiochians, or Romans, and regarded themselves as good citizens as anyone else who lived in any of these cities.

The Social Pull—Of course, such arguments did not help. Pagans refused to accept Jews into high society. Jews could not obtain appointments to high political office. There were always some Jews to whom such things mattered very much, particularly if they were wealthy and not too devoted to their religion. Consequently there were always some Jews who gave up their Jewish affiliations and went over to the pagans. Among them were several who came of prominent Jewish families. One such man became procurator of Judea and subsequently led a Roman legion in the fight against Jerusalem.

The Philosophical Doubters—Of such renegades the Jewish people have had their full share in every generation. They usually contributed little more than trouble to Jewish life. More important for the Jewish people and for the world were those Jews who tried to weigh the differences and similarities between Judiasim and Greek philosophy as well as the manner of life suggested by the best minds among the pagans. Can it be possible, some Jews asked themselves, that Judaism really insists on a great many laws about food and other personal observances? They answered that question in the negative. Some poked fun at the observances prescribed in the Bible; others argued that these laws no longer applied to the Jews of their day; all agreed that what Judaism expected was no different from the teachings of the Greek philosophers, namely, that human beings live in accordance with the ideals of duty and moderation. On the other hand, there was a group of Egyptian Jews who led an ascetic life very much like that of the Essenes in Palestine.

Philo, a Jewish Preacher and Philosopher—There were many thinkers, writers and public orators among the diaspora Jews of that day, but none was more important than Philo. The works of the others were eventually lost, but Philo's writings have been preserved chiefly because of their great influence on the early Christians. His Jewish name was probably Yedidyah (Beloved of God) or David, and he belonged to one of the most highly placed Jewish families of Alexandria. He became the best interpreter of Plato's philosophy, at that time the basis of thinking in the Greek and Roman world.

Philo set for himself the task of proving to Jew and non-Jew alike that Judaism is the best possible expression of the philosophical way of life. His method was the one called allegorical. He assumed, in other words, that the Bible was not interested in telling stories about heroes such as Adam, or Abraham, or Isaac, but that it was anxious to teach a lesson in the way men should live. He did not deny, as did some of his fellow Jews, that these ancient heroes lived, or that events happened in the way the Bible narrated them. But he said that God had guided the lives of these ancient worthies so as to have them serve as illustrations of great ideals. They might represent temperance, or hospitality, or the virtue of contemplation, or any other virtue which the Greeks prized as much as did the Jews. Philo, however, was a Jew, an observant Jew; he did not agree that Jewish laws were either useless or ridiculous. Even if he could find no philosophical interpretation for a law, he would still have argued for observing it as a divine command. For Philo spoke of God as of a tremendous superhuman power. God was not like any of the Greek and Roman deities, who were merely exaggerated human beings, but a God who stood far above the world. When God desired something, that very desire created whatever God wanted. Hesitating, as all Jews did, to speak of God familiarly, Philo called God's creative will, "the *Logos*," that is, "God's Word." This term came to be important in the development of Christianity.

6. RIOTS IN ALEXANDRIA

Villainy and Prejudice—In view of what has been said about the competition between Jews and pagans and between Judaism and paganism, it need cause no surprise that in time riots started against the Jews. A few demagogues succeeded eventually in stirring up the emotions of the populace, though somewhere in the background was the greedy-eyed crowd which saw in the Jews a danger to their income. In Alexandria the chief inciter against the Jews was a foul-mouthed popular orator, called Apion, who pretended to be a philosopher, but who was generally known as "The Universal Tin Can."*

A Jewish King—Only a spark was needed to set off the inflamed passions of the Alexandrian mob. That spark was provided by a Jewish celebration in honor of a newly-appointed Jewish king. In the year 38, Gaius Caligula became emperor of Rome. He at once appointed his boon companion and fellow gambler, Agrippa, as king of Upper Galilee. Agrippa was a grandson of Herod and Mariamne, and, therefore, partly of Hasmonean blood. The appointment of a native king was generally considered as something of a restoration of Jewish independence. When Agrippa passed through Alexandria on his way to take possession of his kingdom, the Jews saw fit to celebrate in his honor. To the Alexandrian mob this was pointed out as a jibe at Egypt, which did not have a native king. On the day following the Jewish celebration the populace gathered at the amphitheater and mimicked the Jews by paying homage to the city's best known idiot whom they dressed up as a Jewish king. The fun over, the mob and its leaders became fearful of the emperor's anger, since they had mocked one of his friends. Hypocritically they resorted to patriotism. They sent a demand to the Roman governor of Egypt, Flaccus, that the Jews be made to put a statue of the Emperor Gaius in the synagogues so that they might show themselves as loyal Romans as the Egyptians who had such statues in their temples. Because of his own political fears and ambitions, Flaccus, though he knew very well that the Jews could not put statues in their synagogues and that they had an imperial privilege freeing them from any such obligation, nevertheless chose to agree with the mob. He issued the

* Literally, "The World's Cymbals."

order. When the Jews refused, he called them foreigners and publicly flogged many members of the supreme Jewish council. Thus, instead of being punished, the mob found itself encouraged to do more mischief. They waited for no second invitation, but fell upon the homes of the wealthier Jews who lived outside of the Jewish districts, and pillaged four hundred of them.

Philo's Mission—The Jews were neither weaklings nor cowards. They had clashed with the mob on previous occasions. Probably that was why the mob had not attacked the Jewish district, but confined itself to the scattered homes outside. The Jews were also unwilling to let this attack pass without retaliating. Conditions, however, were not favorable as long as the governor was their enemy and as long as the charge of lacking patriotism rested on them for refusing to put up a statue to the emperor. They decided to send a delegation to Rome to justify themselves and expose their enemies. At the head of this delegation stood Philo. The Alexandrian pagans also sent a deputation, at the head of which stood the notorious Apion. As might have been expected the mentally unbalanced Caligula was flattered by Apion's appeal to him as to a god whose statue the willful Jews refused to honor. He paid little attention to Philo, outside of asking him some foolish questions without even waiting for his answers. Having gained no satisfaction other than the recall of Flaccus, the Jewish delegation returned home, and the Jews waited for an opportunity to even the score with their enemies.

More Riots—The opportunity came when Caligula was assassinated. The Jews had been storing up arms and gathering aid from the Jews of Syria. In the ensuing riot the results were less one-sided than in the previous one. Moreover, both Jews and pagans were getting ready to resume the struggle. The new emperor, Claudius, saner than his predecessor, now took a definite stand concerning the troubles in Alexandria. He warned both sides to stop bloodshed, and, while confirming the Jews in all their previous privileges and denying new privileges to the other Alexandrians, he reprimanded the Jews for trying to win a place in the internal political life of the city.

The Problem Remains—The situation, however, remained essentially the same, since the causes for the trouble had not been removed. The Jews continued to do business, and so continued to irritate their pagan competitors. Judaism continued to assert its superiority over paganism, and the pagans refused to grant them social and political equality. The Jews could not persuade their neighbors that their connection with Jerusalem was a purely religious one, and the pagans continued to brand them as foreigners and as lacking in patriotism. Sooner or later the violence was bound to break out again.

7. CHRISTIANITY BEGINS IN THE DIASPORA

The Palestinian Nazarenes—The little group of Jesus' disciples was still in Jerusalem, waiting for his reappearance to right the evils of the world. They were poor people, mostly Galileans. At their head stood Jesus' favorite disciple, Peter (Simon), and one of Jesus' brothers by the name of James (Jacob). Since they believed that the end of the world was near, they did not work very much, but pooled their resources and led a communistic life, meeting, praying and eating together. Whenever they had a chance, they addressed crowds of simple people like themselves, or of Jews who came from the diaspora lands. With the latter, especially, they had a fair measure of success, so that in the course of a few years the Greek Jews among the believers in Jesus far outnumbered the native Palestinians. The Jews in general did not bother about the small group of their own people who added to their Judaism the belief in a messiah who had been crucified by Rome and had come to life again. The members of the new sect, for their part, did nothing to make themselves objectionable, since they observed all the regulations of Jewish life. On two occasions some of their number expressed themselves in terms insulting to the Temple, and then a group of fanatical Jews attacked them. One of these occasions caused the expulsion from Jerusalem of all the non-Palestinian believers in Jesus, since they apparently were the chief troublemakers. The others were not disturbed. Yet this brief persecution resulted in very important gains for the new sect. In the first place, those expelled had a chance to spread their ideas wherever they now went. Secondly, and even more important, a man named Saul, who came from the Greek-speaking city of Tarsus, joined the sect.

Saul of Tarsus—Saul, or Paul, to call him by his Greek name, was a very interesting man. Though his character still remains a good deal of a puzzle, his influence upon Christian life has been fundamental. In the city of Tarsus he led the life of the ordinary artisan, being a tent-maker by trade. Three things characterized him and affected his life: a body subject to some serious ailment, a gift for oratory and public disputation, and a devotion to Judaism so great as to make him impatient with its slow progress in converting the pagans. He must have spent years wondering why the ideals of Judaism, obviously so noble, failed to be accepted by the pagans and sometimes were not lived up to by the Jews. At last he made up his mind to go to Jerusalem and study Judaism at its source. Soon after his arrival he heard of the followers of Jesus, and was so incensed at the idea of Jews believing what these people believed that he joined in a riot against them. He even asked to be commissioned to go to other places, there to exterminate the new sect.

Then a strange thing happened. In a flash it came upon Paul that Judaism might be divided into laws and ideals. The Jews of Judea might observe the laws as well as the ideals, but other Jews ought to emphasize only the ideals and thereby make it easy for the Gentiles to join them. Besides, Paul saw in Jesus a great attraction to the pagan world. He decided to speak of him, not only as a messiah who had come to redeem the world, as the original followers of Jesus thought, but also as an ideal, a divine personality whose example could influence each human being, whether Jew or Gentile, and lead him to perfection. Paul became convinced and, characteristically, became terribly earnest about convincing others.

The Apostle to the Gentiles—Paul traveled through many parts of the Diaspora, especially Asia Minor and Greece. Wherever he came he went to the synagogue first. There he would preach his new doctrine. But the Jews turned angrily away from him as soon as he said something about Jesus' divinity and against Jewish observance. Even the followers of Jesus in Jerusalem strongly objected to his ideas. What Paul in his enthusiasm did not see, but the Jews of his day felt and had been taught by the Pharisees, was that ideals cannot live without observances which discipline people to realize them. Moreover, by offering a Judaism devoid of Jewish ceremonial and ritual, he was making the conversion of pagans to full Judaism quite impossible. Among the fearers of the Lord, Paul received an enthusiastic welcome. They formed the centers of the organizations (churches) which Paul founded. But as the Jews tried their utmost to prevent him from preaching his doctrine, Paul became embittered and began saying uncomplimentary things about them. He turned his attention almost exclusively to the pagans. Yet to the very end he continued to say that the Jewish people were God's chosen, and he never denied his own Jewishness. On his last appearance in Jerusalem he visited the Temple and observed all the other Jewish customs. When, however, it became known that he had violated Jewish traditions while on his travels, and when he was accused of bringing a pagan into the sacred precincts of the Temple, he was arrested. He saved himself from conviction by the Jews, but he was later condemned by the Romans and seems to have been executed in Rome.

The Results of Paul's Teachings—It is not what happened to Paul personally that is important, but rather what happened to Paul's teachings. Even while he lived, ample evidence proves that the people to whom he preached had misunderstood him. He had spoken in terms of high and noble idealism, of charity, of personal righteousness. He urged men to believe in Jesus firmly and, believing in so perfect an example of godly living, begin to lead a godly life themselves. Such righteous people could have no difficulty in meeting the awful day of God's judgment. They would surely survive it, and when the day of resurrection came, such people would surely be permitted to live again and forever. But most of the people who listened to Paul remembered only the connection between believing in Jesus and meriting God's mercy and ultimate resurrection. They skipped the middle step—the need to live godly lives. Thus, faith in Jesus came to be the only and entire basis of the religion adopted by the pagan Christians, while the Judeo-Christians, who lived in Palestine, continued to observe Jewish law.

But it was the pagan Christian attitude which won in the end. Many pagans who had admired Judaism either openly or secretly now had a chance to adopt a form of Judaism which appealed to them. It is not at all strange that Christianity spread most easily and rapidly in those cities in which Jews had lived for a long time, so that people were already acquainted with their life and religious ideas. Nevertheless, for some centuries still, it was not at all certain whether Judaism or Christianity would make the greater number of converts.

CHAPTER XI

THE WAR FOR JEWISH INDEPENDENCE

**THE JEWS OF PALESTINE FIGHT TO REGAIN THEIR INDEPEND-
ENCE, BUT ARE DEFEATED AND SEE THEIR TEMPLE GO UP
IN FLAMES**

The Irrepressible Conflict—The point has now been
reached in the story of the Jews when we must discuss the
great rebellion against Rome, the crisis which was one of the
most important turning points in Jewish history. For the Jewish state then ceased to exist and the Jewish religion had to
adjust itself to a new situation. To this day, on the 9th of Ab,
observant Jews gather in their synagogues to mourn the destruction of Jerusalem and the loss of the Temple.

Could that conflict, so tragic in its results, have been
avoided? Possibly; but it would have required more honesty
than many Roman officials were capable of, more intelligence
than most Jewish aristocrats possessed, and more patience
and submissiveness than the Jewish masses were able to practice. Under the circumstances, misunderstandings and conflicts continued, so that with each succeeding year the Jewish
people drifted nearer to rebellion against Rome.

1. THE GRIEVANCES AGAINST ROME

National Humiliation—Fundamentally the difficulty was
that the Jews felt humiliated at being treated as a conquered
province, and that the Romans were tactless in the exercise of
their power. The Romans found it fairly easy to rule over
peoples like those of Gaul or Spain, who had not yet developed a national sense like that of the Jews. Nor did Roman
rule over civilized peoples like the Egyptians or the Greeks
present as serious a problem because, after all, Rome flattered them by adopting their civilization. Jewish civilization

was not only misunderstood, but even mocked. Rome knew only force and, in the case of the Jews, force was not enough.

Religious Humiliation—Rome not only wounded the political sensibilities of the Jews but also their religious feelings. For example, for some years one of the Roman procurators kept the official robes of the high priest under lock and key. This was in the nature of a pledge that the Jews would behave themselves properly, for if they did not, the procurator might refuse to let the high priest officiate on Yom Kippur, when these garments were part of the ritual. Rome maintained soldiers within the Temple area, and these boorish men sometimes conducted themselves in an insulting manner. The most outrageous action of all was that of the half-crazy Emperor Gaius Caligula. Persuaded that he was a god, Caligula resented the refusal of the Jews to pay him divine honors. He ordered Petronius, his governor of Syria, an intelligent man, to compel the Jews to place a statue of the emperor inside the Temple. At the head of his soldiers, and carrying the statue, Petronius started for Jerusalem. In Palestine thousands of Jews blocked his road. Like the early Hasidim, they offered passive resistance. They assured Petronius that they were ready to be trodden under the hoofs of his horses rather than let him execute the emperor's order. Realizing that the people were in earnest, Petronius, at the risk of his own life, discontinued his attempt. Caligula was so enraged when he heard of Petronius' disobedience that he sent a message commanding him to commit suicide. And Petronius would have had to do it, had not news reached him of the murder of Caligula by the Romans themselves.

Corrupt Officials—Even when the Roman government was well intentioned, as no doubt it was most of the time, its representatives in Judea were often corrupt and at all times highhanded. Pontius Pilate, for example, considered the slaughter of thousands but an incident of government. Later procurators were no better. The most harmless was Tiberius Alexander, but the Jews resented his very presence because he was himself a Jew converted to paganism. His successors robbed and murdered and took bribes, so that there was neither peace nor justice in the land. The worst of all was Florus, the last procurator, who stopped at no villainy. He deliberately provoked the Jews to rebellion in order to cover up his criminal record in personal and official conduct.

2. HOSTILITY BETWEEN JEWS AND GENTILES

King Agrippa the Good—One of the most important causes for the outbreak of the rebellion was the political and economic rivalry between the Jews and the non-Jews of Palestine. Nothing revealed it more clearly than the difference in attitudes toward Herod Agrippa. Gaius Caligula had appointed Agrippa king of the northern part of Palestine. Later, Emperor Claudius enlarged Agrippa's kingdom to include Judea and Samaria, that is, all the territory which had been ruled by Herod, Agrippa's grandfather. The Jews were pleasantly surprised in this king. He had been a notorious rake, profligate, spendthrift and generally good-for-nothing. He certainly was not expected to show any Jewish sympathies. Yet no sooner had Agrippa become king, than he acquired a sense of responsibility. He became observant of Jewish tradition and law; he mingled with the common people; he even showed a desire to restore Jewish national life.

The Pagan Opposition—But the Gentiles of Palestine were not happy. They also watched Agrippa's actions and recognized that his policy was pro-Jewish. From a pro-Jewish political policy he was sure to pass into a pro-Jewish economic policy. They looked upon him as Agrippa the Bad, and went wild with joy when he suddenly died after a brief reign of barely seven years (38–44). The government in Rome, afraid that another native king of the Jews might carry through the plans which Agrippa had evidently been laying, returned Judea to the government of procurators (44–66), some of whom have just been mentioned. Agrippa's son, Agrippa II, was given a little kingdom north of Palestine. Once more the anti-Jewish policy had won.

3. JEWISH HOPES

Memories of Victory—Considering the war which the Jews undertook against the mighty power of Rome, one may well ask how it was possible for so small a people to dare fight the mistress of the world. But the Jews of that day were not insane; they felt that they had forces and expectations which would make the struggle not at all so uneven as it seemed.

Firstly, the Jews depended upon their own fighting ability. The Maccabean spirit was still alive, and the Jews were confident that what they had done to Syria two hundred years before, they could also do to Rome.

External Aid—Then, Palestine had a large population and from it a substantial army could be raised. But the Jews did not depend upon that alone; they expected to obtain aid from the numerous Jews of the Diaspora. If that population could be induced to revolt against Rome at the same time that the Jews of Palestine rebelled, Rome would have on its hands a civil war of extensive proportions. It could not then spare too many legions for the struggle in Judea.

More important still were the hopes which the Jews of Palestine placed in the Parthian empire, the rival of Rome for the possession of Syria and Asia Minor. The Jews of Palestine felt certain that their fellow Jews in Parthia would assist them, and that these Jews would easily induce Parthia to aid Judea in its fight. Every neighboring people, moreover, was persuaded that a great redeemer would arise from among the Jews who would free the world from Roman domination. If only the Jews could begin with military successes, it was fairly certain that the rest of the Roman empire in the East, with the sole exception of the Palestinian pagans, would join them in throwing off the Roman yoke.

Division in Rome—Nor was this all. The Jews were fully justified in thinking that Rome was not as strong as it seemed. There was a large faction in Rome itself which planned to rid the world of emperors and restore the republic as it had been before the days of Caesar. The murder of Emperor Gaius Caligula was one indication of such a possibility, for at that moment Rome was on the brink of civil war. Twenty years later the tyranny and the follies of Emperor Nero again drove the Roman aristocrats to another attempt at rebellion. The Jews had not forgotten that a civil war in the Syrian empire had been a powerful advantage on the side of the Hasmoneans. A similar occurrence in the Roman empire might therefore be just the time for the Jews to declare their independence.

God Is King in Zion—In all probability the ardent patriots who planned rebellion against Rome actually figured on these aids to their cause. In addition to these, however, there was one source of strength which they took absolutely for granted. This was the help of God. For the Jews had an abiding faith in the sacredness of Jerusalem and in God's preference for the Jews above the pagans. God, they thought, would never abandon His earthly habitation in Zion, or the people He had chosen to be His witnesses before a wicked world.

THE WAR FOR JEWISH INDEPENDENCE

Such were the hopes and expectations of the people. Any one of them might have justified the undertaking of the hazardous effort. Unfortunately, it so happened that none of them was fulfilled.

4. CLASS AGAINST CLASS

The Downtrodden and Oppressed—The final cause for the outbreak of the revolt against Rome was a purely internal one. There were among the Jews of that time a growing number who could look forward to nothing but a miserable existence. The Jews of Palestine continued to be predominantly agricultural. But what with the enormous taxation, the small yield of the soil, and the increase of external competition, the peasant population was being reduced to grinding poverty. Those who hopefully crowded into the cities met with disappointment. Their stomachs empty, their hearts filled with resentment, the masses of Jewish Palestine turned their minds to thoughts of destroying the injustice of the world. Whom could they blame for their plight? Obviously it was easiest to blame the foreign ruler and the non-Jewish part of the population, especially since such blame was fully deserved.

The Great and Lordly—The upper class among the Jews also came in for a great deal of condemnation. For the Jews had developed a class of rich men and aristocrats who differed in little else than religion from similar classes in Rome or Rome's provinces. Some priests and many landowners lived gaily and thoughtlessly by the side of the miserable poor. Once in a while they would bethink themselves of their suffering fellow Jews. Agrippa II, for example, spent a vast sum on paving the streets of Jerusalem chiefly in order to give employment to the poor workingmen. But such temporary measures were sure to be inadequate, especially among the Jews brought up on Torah and Jewish idealism. The masses among other peoples were not told from their childhood that all were descended from one Father, that greed is a sin and that helping one another is what is expected of a Holy People. Had the upper classes among the Jews been more intelligent, they would have done something radical to improve the situation. But they were satisfied to let nature take its course; and the course which nature took turned out to be the ruin of masses and classes alike.

The Middle Class—There was a fairly large group of people—the small merchant, the employed artisan, the comfortable peasant—who stood between the two groups mentioned above. Their sympathies might have been divided, but their impatience was exercised on both the lowly and the mighty, on the grumblers and the scolders. With whom would this middle class side in case of a crisis? On the one hand, they ardently desired peace; on the other hand, they loved their people and were proud of their faith. In this case, too, had the upper classes known how, they might have won the cooperation of the middle class against the rebels. It could have been done by taking a stronger stand against Rome, or by living a life more in conformity with what the middle class considered Jewish idealism. But the upper classes were much too anxious to please Rome, and much too critical of Jewish differences from others. And so the opportunity was lost and, when the rebellion broke out, it was directed against the wealthy and titled Jews quite as much as against Rome and her pagan allies.

5. The Steps Leading to War

Pennies for Florus—It was Florus, the procurator, who started the series of events which led to the outbreak of hostilities. Greedy beyond any of his predecessors, and completely devoid of conscience, Florus was out to gain speedy wealth at the expense of the province he governed. He sold his authority and protection, and his hirelings spread terror everywhere. Florus simply confirmed the people in their opinion of Rome. But in the year 66 he robbed the Temple itself. Then, in a crowd some Jews passed around a basket for people to throw in contributions for "poor Florus." That was an insult which the Roman could not forgive; and he loosed his soldiers upon the population. Thousands were killed that day, and the procurator threatened to do worse unless the people apologized. Persuaded by the high priest, the people agreed to offer friendly greetings to the additional soldiers whom Florus brought into the city. On Florus' orders the soldiers did not return the greeting, and when the Jews began to grumble over this added insult, they charged into the crowd trampling people under foot and murdering without mercy. In accordance with Florus' plan the soldiers made for the Temple which, once in his possession, Florus could rob at will. The Jews sensed the plot and arrived at the Temple first. Defeated in his main purpose, Florus departed from the city, leaving only a third of his soldiers behind.

The Break with Agrippa—When he heard of the events in Jerusalem, King Agrippa II hurried down from his own kingdom in order to quiet the Jewish people and prevent an open break with Rome. But instead of advising a vigorous protest to Rome, he advised submission to Florus. Thus he at once laid himself open to the accusation that he was more interested in Rome than in the honor, peace and dignity of the Jewish people. For to readmit Florus to Jerusalem meant clearing him of his previous crimes and affording him an opportunity to commit new ones. Up to that point Agrippa had the middle class, the peace-loving group, with him. Now, however, the lower class, the revolutionaries, obtained the upper hand. The king, and his sister Berenice, in danger from the fury of the mob, had to flee the city. Thereafter, throughout the entire conflict, Agrippa was on the side of Rome. He saved his delicate skin and his tiny throne at the price of his honor.

Discontinuance of the Imperial Sacrifice—Agrippa's blunder set the stage for the next step in the breach of relations with Rome. Until now the struggle had been against Florus; now a move was made against Rome itself. The son of a former high priest, Eleazar by name, held an important position in the Temple, and he persuaded his fellow priests to refuse any sacrifice on behalf of a non-Jew. Aside from being a violation of Jewish tradition which permitted the worship of the God of Israel by anyone, this order meant the ending of sacrifices for the emperor. In effect, therefore, Eleazar's act meant a refusal of allegiance to Rome. The peace party and the aristocrats strongly objected to his action. But Eleazar, with the support of the younger priests and the revolutionaries, refused to yield.

The Rising of the Masses—The aristocrats sent messengers to Florus and Agrippa asking them for aid against the revolutionaries. Florus was perfectly willing, in fact he was delighted, that the Jews should rebel, since that would clear him of all blame for his misdeeds. Agrippa dispatched a small army to Jerusalem. These joined with the Roman soldiers already in the city and captured all but the Temple. Here the most radical elements were concentrated, those who had become known as *Sicarii,* wielders of the small dagger. The fight raged within the city and especially around the Temple. The significance of this fight lay in the fact that the masses of Jerusalem fought by the side of the revolutionaries, and that, as soon as they could, they burned the archives where records of debts which people owed were kept. They also burned down the palace of Agrippa and the homes of other aristocrats who had till then ruled the city. The aristocrats who did not flee were killed.

The Murder of the Romans—The several thousand soldiers of Agrippa and Rome might have prevailed against the revolutionaries alone, but they were hopelessly outnumbered when Jerusalem's population joined them. The soldiers, besieged in one of the fortresses within the city, realized that they could fight no longer. The besiegers permitted Agrippa's soldiers to leave unharmed. Later they promised to do the same for the Romans in the fortress if they surrendered and gave up their arms. But no sooner had these soldiers come weaponless out of the fort than the rabble fell upon them and murdered them. It was a breach of faith unjustifiable even by what these soldiers had done at the command of Florus, and it gave a free hand to the enemies of the Jews within and without Palestine.

Massacres in Pagan Cities—Long before Rome decided that it had a rebellion on its hands, the pagan population of many cities took advantage of their opportunity to do away with the Jews who were their neighbors. The coastal city of Caesarea started the unhappy series of massacres. What happened in Caesarea was soon repeated in other towns with mixed populations. Bands of Jews, for their part, wandered over the land attacking pagan towns and attempting to rescue threatened Jews. Most pitiful was the case of the God-fearing pagans, who were suspected and attacked by both sides. These massacres, moreover, spread to cities outside of Palestine, the worst being a new riot in Alexandria. There the rioters, aided by troops sent by Tiberius Alexander, the renegade Jew then governor of Egypt, turned the Jewish section of the city into a heap of ruins. Clearly, the struggle was to be between the Jewish and the pagan worlds.

Defeat of a Roman Army—Cestius Gallus, the governor of Syria, moved at last against the Jewish revolutionaries. With a fair-sized army aided by auxiliary troops from among the neighboring pagan lands and cities, he made his way to Jerusalem. On the way he captured and destroyed a number of Jewish towns, including the port town of Joppa (Jaffa). He arrived before Jerusalem during the holiday of Sukkot, when the city was filled with pilgrims anxious to strike a blow for the freedom of the land. The capture of the city and, with it, the end of the revolution would have been easy had the Roman been an able general. Whether because of his incapacity or because one of his generals had been bribed by Florus not to end the war too soon, Cestius Gallus bungled the attack on the city and began a dangerous retreat through the hills surrounding Jerusalem. The Jews attacked and ambushed him at every step. Rejoicing, they returned to Jerusalem laden with booty. The unexpected had happened; a victory had been won against a Roman army. All the dreams of ultimate independence for Judea were aroused. The war against Rome began in earnest.

6. Preparations for War

The New Government—The Jews realized that Rome would not permit such a defeat to go unpunished. It was necessary to act, and act quickly, in order to prepare the country for the vengeance which Rome was bound to take. That would require money, men and thorough planning. The revolutionaries could start the trouble, but they felt themselves incapable of organizing the country to see it through. For this purpose they turned to the middle class, to those peace-lovers who had refrained from taking sides, but who, now that the die was cast, felt bound to the fate of their people. Among these was a certain Joseph son of Gorion, a former high priest by the name of Hanan, and Simon son of Gamaliel, a descendant of Hillel. These men were probably the leaders of the patriotic part of the Sanhedrin. They now constituted the government of Judea.

The Appointment of Josephus—The first step of the new government was to appoint military governors over the various districts of Palestine. Their task was to organize the defenses of the provinces, enlist men for the national army, and prepare food against the inevitable siege of various towns which the Romans would attack. Of the provinces none was more important than Galilee. For one thing, there was no doubt that the Romans would come into Palestine from the north, and thus Galilee would be the first district attacked. The longer the Romans could be held at Galilee the better chance Jerusalem would have to prepare itself for battle. A defeat of the Romans or even a hard fight against them in Galilee would hearten the rest of the country, and might result in a decision by Parthia to throw in its lot with the Jews. Besides, Galilee was one of the most fruitful districts of Palestine as well as one filled with ardent Jewish patriots. It could yield wealth and men to strengthen the Jewish cause.

The success of the Galilean campaign depended largely

upon the man sent there to organize the district. It was at this point that the new government made its most serious blunder. Suspicious of the hotheaded revolutionaries, the government chose for this important post a young man, Joseph (Josephus) son of Mattathias, a descendant of a family claiming connection with the Hasmoneans. He had received a fine Jewish education, had been to Rome, and gave the impression of being cool-headed and efficient.

Josephus' Private Motives—What the government did not know about Joseph was his character and personal ambitions. He wanted to win glory; but he also wanted to be safe. His visit to Rome had taught him to respect its might, and he became convinced that the Jews would be unable to prevail against it. Under the circumstances he was ready to do everything possible to gain power, but he was hesitant about using it against Rome. It did not take long for some of the ardent Galilean patriots to see through Joseph. His bitterest enemy in Galilee was Johanan of Gischala, who accused him of dealing very gently with the property of the Jewish aristocrats. Instead of confiscating this property of Jews who were on the side of Rome, so as to use it for fighting the battles of the Jews, Joseph simply returned the property to its owners. At last the government in Jerusalem sent men to investigate Joseph's activities and, if necessary, to remove him from office. But he was clever enough to get around all difficulties and to retain his command. Thus, instead of organizing the district for war, Joseph spent his energies in maintaining his personal authority; instead of preparing an army he prepared an alibi by which he might eventually prove to Rome that he had never really been its enemy. He built few forts; he made no attempts to inspire the wavering people with patriotic fervor; he gathered no resources for a long campaign. He left the district exposed to the enemy. His vanity and selfishness, if not outright villainy, betrayed the cause of Jewish independence at the start.

Roman Preparations—In the meantime the Romans were preparing a large and well-equipped army to quell the revolution. Emperor Nero and his advisers fully recognized the danger of letting the Jews win even a partial victory. Already after the defeat of Cestius Gallus rumors began to circulate that several other nations of the East, inspired by the example of the Jews, were making ready to join them against Rome. A strong army and a good general were needed. Nero chose Vespasian, from his youth a soldier, not a brilliant but a reliable man, who had fought successfully against the Ger-

mans and the Britons. He assigned three experienced legions
to Vespasian, in addition to several contingents of cavalry.
When Vespasian arrived at Antioch, in Syria, he called upon
and received further reinforcements from the Syrian kings
who were subordinate to Rome, including several thousand
soldiers from Agrippa. Altogether the Roman gathered an
army of over sixty thousand well-trained and excellently
equipped men. With these he began the march south into
Galilee.

7. The Reduction of the Country (67–68 C. E.)

The Conquest of Galilee—The arrival of the Romans at
once reduced the forces gathered by Joseph. Insufficiently
trained, and uninspired, many left his ranks. Moreover, now
it became apparent to what extent Joseph had failed to rally
the support of the important cities of the province. One after
another they opened their gates to Vespasian, for it was perfectly clear to them that Joseph could bring them no help.
The most serious loss of this nature was the city of Sep-
phoris, the best fortified and the most strategically placed city
in Galilee. The towns and villages which did not surrender
were utterly annihilated by the Romans. After a few feeble
efforts at fighting scattered portions of the Roman army, Joseph gave up open battles and shut himself and his army behind the walls of Jotapata.

The Fall of Jotapata—Once inside the fort, where cleverness and bravery rather than equipment and experience were
needed, the small Jewish army gave an excellent account of
itself. Time and again they beat off the enemy; repeatedly
they made sorties and inflicted heavy losses upon the Romans. Vespasian himself was slightly wounded in the course
of battle. Individual Jews distinguished themselves by acts of
great bravery. But it was all in vain against the battering
rams and the superior equipment of the Romans, who eventually made a breach in the wall and began their rush into
the city. The Jews fought them hand to hand, and poured
boiling oil upon them from above. Obviously a direct assault
even through a breach in the wall was not the way these
people could be defeated. Only through information given by
a Jewish traitor were the Romans enabled to march stealthily
into the town. And then there was no pity and no mercy for
the Jews within.

The Traitor Joseph—Long before the city fell Joseph had

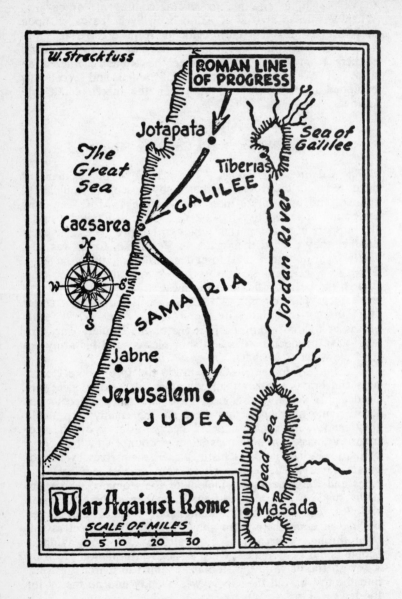

planned to escape. But this time his soft words and persuasive logic failed. His own soldiers kept watch on him to prevent his desertion. When the city fell, Joseph was not among the slain. While the Jewish soldiers were making the Romans pay dearly for their lives, their commander sought safety in a cave and a few days later surrendered to the Romans.

All this Joseph himself records in the great book he, under his Roman name, Flavius Josephus, wrote some years later in order to justify himself for his desertion of the Jewish cause, as well as to flatter the family of Vespasian and the Romans. He pretended to believe that it was all preordained by God, and that God had granted him prophetic powers so that he could foresee the results of the war. Perhaps it was his "gift of prophecy" which saved his life, but it was far more likely to have been the proof he produced of his loyalty to Rome even while he was leading the Jewish army against the Romans. A more convincing proof was his willingness to serve Rome against the Jews from then on, for he was attached to the staff of the Roman general. His special assignment was to weaken the morale of the Jewish fighters.

Galilee in Roman Hands—The capture of Joseph did not stop the fighting in Galilee. All other available Jewish forces were concentrated near Tiberias, by the shore of the Sea of Galilee. The Romans sent a strong force to that city. The Jews, fighting from rafts and boats on the sea as well as from the shore, put up a brave struggle. But they were overpowered, and the remnants of the army fled toward Judea. With that the Jewish defense of Galilee practically ended. The Romans destroyed and killed wherever there was the slightest suspicion of continued rebellion. Then Vespasian went into winter quarters to await further developments among the Jews as well as the outcome of important events in Rome.

Results of Galilee's Fall—With this fertile and populous province lost, little short of a miracle could have saved the Jewish cause. The comparative ease with which Galilee was conquered discouraged whatever other peoples might have been planning to join the Jews in their revolt. Only the royal family of Adiabene, which had become converted to Judaism a generation before, sent men and food. Certainly Parthia was unwilling to support a cause apparently bound to fail. Nor had the Jews of the Roman Diaspora shown themselves ready to lend assistance, and whatever they might have done under the inspiration of success in Galilee, the time for such action was now over. But the worst result of all was the effect of the fall of Jotapata upon the situation in Jerusalem.

Emperor Vespasian—Indirectly the fall of Galilee had another result. While Vespasian was occupied in Palestine, Nero's follies brought about a revolution and a brief civil war in Rome. Nero himself committed suicide, and several candidates appeared for his place. Three emperors followed each other inside of one year, and affairs in Rome were in complete disorder. At this point the armies of the East proclaimed Vespasian as their candidate for imperial power. Now, it is safe to say that had Vespasian not won a speedy victory over the Jews in Galilee, no one would have thought of him as a candidate for the supreme power. As it was, Vespasian went to Rome to preside over the Roman empire, leaving his son, Titus, who had been with him through the Galilean campaign, in Palestine to subdue the Jews. Here again one of the Jewish hopes was shattered, for if Vespasian's candidacy had met with any real opposition, he would have had to withdraw his legions from Palestine and the Jews might have won at least an easier peace. Everything seemed to work out to their disadvantage.

8. THE SIEGE OF JERUSALEM

The Fall of the Moderate Government—When the news first reached Jerusalem that Jotapata had fallen, there was great sorrow for the heavy blow to the national cause, and admiration for the brave defenders of the fortress. Joseph ben Mattathias was especially mourned, for the news had it that he was among the slain. But the truth soon came out that Joseph was a traitor and had gone over to the enemy. Naturally, the people who had appointed him to command in Galilee were now blamed for the great defeat. The conclusion was drawn that they, too, were traitors. Every member of the government was executed by the Zealots.

Civil War in Jerusalem—Who was to rule now? The moderate party still had the majority of the solid Jerusalem population behind it; the Zealots, however, were young and armed. In the fight which broke out in the city the moderates gained the upper hand and drove the Zealots within the Temple area. The Zealots now called in the Idumean contingent. For the Idumeans had become ardent Jewish patriots and were easily persuaded that the moderate group was ready to surrender Jerusalem to the enemy. They came in the dead of night and fell upon the moderate fighters. The streets of Jerusalem ran with Jewish blood, and the Zealots assumed command.

But that was not the end. Among the patriots themselves there were rival groups. Johanan of Gischala, he who had been Joseph's strongest opponent and had escaped to Jerusalem after Jotapata's fall, was the leader of one band. Eleazar ben Simon was the head of another, while Simon ben Giora was the head of a third. They fought with each other incessantly, apparently not caring how much of the provisions stored up by the former government was being destroyed, nor how they weakened the manpower and the defenses of the city. Vespasian and Titus patiently permitted them to wear each other out, since with every passing day Jerusalem was growing weaker.

Titus' Siege of Jerusalem—Slowly Titus and his army approached Jerusalem, reaching it early in the spring of the year 70. Only then did the fighting within the city cease, and the three rivals for power now became rivals for glory. The Romans made their camp on Mount Scopus and began their siege of the city and their work with the battering rams. Time and again the Jews would rush out of the city and attempt to destroy the military machine of the Romans. Nevertheless, within fifteen days a breach was made in the outermost wall, which Agrippa I had begun and which the moderate government had hurriedly completed. The middle wall did not last much longer. It was behind the first and oldest wall that the Jews made their longest stand. The Romans faced it with a wall of their own from the top of which they hurled stones and arrows upon the defenders. The Jews repulsed attacks, undermined the opposing wall, made sorties and routed portions of the enemy force. But their food and their forces were growing insufficient, while the entire population of the city, together with many refugees, were crowded behind the wall. From the beginning of the siege Titus would not permit the civil population to leave the city, lest that relieve the pressure of hunger within. Such people would be crucified within sight of the defenders. Nevertheless, large numbers preferred to take the chance of slipping through the Roman lines to the certainty of starvation within the city. The Jews for their part forbade flight because it showed the Romans how poorly Jerusalem was supplied, and indicated to them that the city's fall was near.

The fighters would not give up. The time had come to redeem the oath every Zealot had taken, to die fighting rather than surrender to Rome. On several occasions Titus sent Jo-

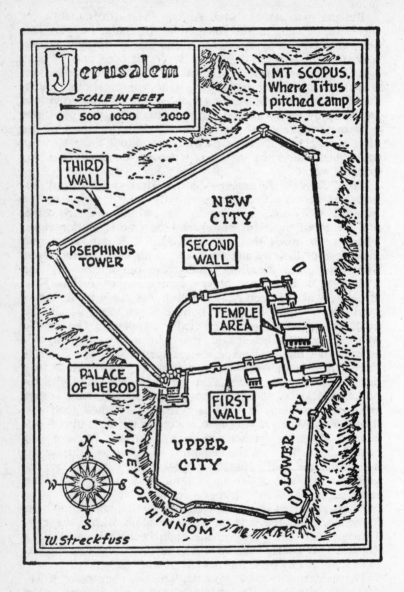

Jerusalem

SCALE IN FEET
0   500 1000   2000

MT SCOPUS,
Where Titus
pitched camp

THIRD
WALL

NEW
CITY

PSEPHINUS
TOWER

SECOND
WALL

TEMPLE
AREA

PALACE
OF HEROD

FIRST
WALL

LOWER CITY

UPPER
CITY

VALLEY OF HINNOM

W. Streckfuss

seph the traitor to address the Jews on the wall and persuade them to surrender. But the Jews greeted Joseph with insulting names and with a hail of stones.

The Fight for the Temple—Finally the fortress of Antonia fell, and all that was left for the Jews to defend was the Temple area, which was also surrounded by a fairly strong wall. This was the last stand for Jerusalem. Here the Jews felt they would be invincible, since God would not permit His Holy Place to be destroyed. Regardless of war and famine, the sacrifices in the Temple had been going on as usual, until there was nothing to sacrifice. The 17th day of Tammuz, when the sacrifices were discontinued, is still observed as a fast day by many Jews. For three more weeks the defenders held out. On the 9th of Ab, Titus ordered that the gates be set on fire, and, as soon as these were consumed, his soldiers rushed in. The slaughter which then commenced is beyond description. To the Jews life was no longer worth living, now that they were sure that God had abandoned them, that His sacred building, the Shrine of His people, was in flames.

Why Was the Temple Burned?—Was it accident or design that set the Temple afire? On the night of the 9th of Ab, Titus held a council with his generals to decide whether the Temple should be permitted to remain. Joseph, in his history, says that Titus was opposed to its destruction. But Joseph always defended Titus before the Jews, and he was not above telling a falsehood when it suited his purpose. It is hard to believe that Titus' orders would have been disobeyed in so important a matter. On the other hand, the Romans had every reason to suppose that with the destruction of the Temple they would destroy the Jewish people and the Jewish faith. The Jewish religion had been the cause of conflict with the Roman officials so often, it had been the pride of the Jews in the Diaspora to such an extent, that to destroy it might be considered an act of piety toward the gods of Olympus as well as an assurance of the ultimate achievement of greater unity within the empire. The burning of the Temple could not have been an accident.

As soon as he saw the Temple in flames Titus dashed within. Like all pagans, he was anxious to find out whether the Jews were telling the truth in saying that theirs was a religion without images. Like Pompey more than a century before, Titus went to the Holy of Holies and pulled the curtain aside. Was he impressed or disappointed to find only a small, bare room? Whatever the effect upon him, his sacrilegious act so offended the Jews that they placed him forever alongside of

Nebuchadnezzar, Haman and Antiochus, in the gallery of their enemies. The Romans may have called him "The Joy of the World"; among the Jews he has been known as "Titus the Wicked."

9. THE END OF THE WAR

Scattered Resistance—Though continued fighting was now useless, the remnants of the Zealot forces refused to surrender. One group escaped from the burning Temple into the Upper City, where they held out for several days. Smaller groups of Zealots still defended fortresses along the Jordan. In the course of the following year these were reduced. The longest and bravest fight was put up by the defenders of Masada, on the western shore of the Dead Sea, where Eleazar, a descendant of an ancient and noted family of patriots, led a band of dauntless men. Their fight was hopeless and they knew it. When the Romans finally penetrated within the fort, they were greeted by the stillness of death. The defenders had died by their own hands.

The Dead and the Captured—How many lost their lives during the course of the war? That is a difficult question, though, according to Josephus, the dead numbered many hundreds of thousands. There were also many thousands sold into slavery or condemned to work in the mines. From among the captured, Titus picked seven hundred handsome young men to march in his triumphal procession in Rome and subsequently to be enrolled among the gladiators. To their own misfortune the two leaders of the fight in Jerusalem were also captured. Johanan of Gischala, perhaps because he was sickly and would not make a good appearance in the parade, was condemned to life imprisonment. Simon ben Giora was chosen for the triumphal procession and eventual execution.

The Triumphal Procession—It was the first victory won by the new imperial family, and they were eager to make the most of it. Titus and Vespasian shared the chief glory and received the applause of Rome's population as they rode through the crowds which lined the Forum. Behind their chariot Simon ben Giora was led in chains, as well as the other unfortunate captives who were thus forced to add to the pride of the national enemy. The golden table which stood in the Temple hall, the musical instruments used by the Levites, and the seven-branched Menorahs which were part of its furnishings, were carried by Roman soldiers and later were deposited in one of the pagan temples. It was a glorious day for Rome, and to commemorate it the Romans afterwards erected an arch on the spot overlooking the Forum where the procession first came into sight. The arch still stands; it is called the Arch of Titus. On its inner panels is carved a portion of that day's parade—soldiers carrying the sacred vessels. In further commemoration of the great triumph Vespasian had the coins of that time inscribed with the words *Judaea Capta,* "Judea has been taken."

CHAPTER XII

SURVIVAL OR EXTINCTION

THE JEWS, WITH A CHOICE BETWEEN TWO METHODS OF KEEPING THE JEWISH PEOPLE ALIVE, CHOOSE THE WAY OF FORCE AND ARE AGAIN DEFEATED

End or Beginning?—Thus ended the second attempt of the Jews to maintain a state of their own. It had not been merely a fleeting effort. From the year 538 B. C. E., when the exiles received Cyrus' permission to return from Babylonia to Judea, to the year 70 C. E., when the triumphant Titus watched the Temple go up in flames, over six hundred years had gone by. During this time the Jewish nation had grown both physically and spiritually. Scribes and Hasidim, Hasmoneans and Pharisees, teachers and writers had added greatly to the luster of the Jewish name and to the thought and faith of the entire world. Was all that to end now, or was the Jewish nation to rise again after a period of Roman exile? It was natural for the Jews to hope that still another chance at state-building would be offered them. But the Roman empire was not the Babylonian; conditions were different, and the chance for which the Jews of that day waited was not destined to come till centuries turned into millennia and ancient into modern times. Yet for the Jews of that day the question was pressing; they wanted a state and they wanted it at once. The story of the Jewish desire for statehood and how that desire led to further heroic but unsuccessful conflict must be told now, before we turn to the story of that inner strength by which the Jewish people was able to live long beyond the time when the grandeur that was Rome crumbled into dust.

1. THE RESULTS OF THE JEWISH DEFEAT

Destruction and Homelessness—In the year 71 both the land and the people lay exhausted under the heel of the conqueror. The Romans had ruthlessly destroyed the fertile fields and the orchards from which the rebels might have drawn sustenance. It would take many years before the soil could be cultivated again to the same extent as before. The cultivators also were missing. Numerous cities had been destroyed, along with the peasant population which had taken refuge in them or whose homes had lain on the Roman line of march. Thousands more, especially from among the younger men and women, were now slaves in foreign lands, as far off as Gaul or Spain.

Loss of Political Rights—Even before the war, the Jews had enjoyed but little political independence. But at least they occasionally had a native king, and they always had a Sanhedrin which represented the shell of self-government. Now there could be no more Sanhedrin, because from the point of view of Rome there was no longer a Jewish nation. Palestine was to be governed by a military representative of the emperor. Whatever little towns or villages survived the destruction continued to have their own local organizations. Such local governing bodies, however, were responsible to no central Jewish authority, but to Rome and its soldiers in Palestine.

Loss of the Center of Jewish Life—Losing the war deprived the Jews of a central Jewish authority. This was felt by the diaspora Jews to an even greater extent than by the Palestinians. The Jews of the world had looked to Palestine —to its teachers, its Sanhedrin and its synagogues—for guidance in Jewish religion and customs. It used to be easy to define a Jew in the days before the war. A Jew was one who believed in the One God, in the Torah as God's way, and in the Temple as the only place where sacrifices could be brought to Him. Now all this was at an end. There was no Jerusalem and no Temple. The various sects and interpretations of God's law remained. With nothing to bind them together as the Temple had done, it was almost certain that the

Jewish people would fall apart into small groups, too weak to resist the pull of the environment, and destined eventually to merge with the pagans, or with some other group which might claim a belief in monotheism.

Loss of Jewish Prestige—Losses actually occurred. Until the war, the Jews of the world had held their heads high. They claimed the special protection of God. Their Temple with its reputation for hoary antiquity and unparalleled splendor was one of the wonders of the ancient world. Their numbers and the security of their position in the Diaspora added to the respect in which most pagans held them. People may have disliked them for this very pride, or tried to get rid of them because of the economic competition which they offered, but they did not look down upon them. This, too, was changed by the disastrous war. Pagan priests now said that the Jewish God had been vastly overrated. Others proclaimed that God had abandoned the Jews and that it was, therefore, dangerous to be on their side or to follow them.

Worst of all, the Roman government did something which made the Jews ridiculous. An outward symbol of their loyalty to the Temple had been the small annual sum which Jews the world over used to send for its support. It so happened that about the time when the Jewish Temple was burned the Romans began to rebuild the Temple of Jupiter in Rome. The Romans now ordered the Jews to send the same annual sum, not to Jerusalem, but to the Temple of Jupiter on the Capitoline Hill of Rome. This was a deliberate insult. The sum involved was petty. The real point was, that despite the pride of the Jews in the God of heaven, they had to pay tribute to the Olympian god who presumably had conquered Him and was entitled to be His heir. The pagans considered it a huge joke on the Jews. Moreover, this tribute was imposed not only upon the Jews of Palestine who had rebelled, but upon the Jews of the Diaspora, who had considered the war little concern of theirs. The shame of it was unbearable to some, so that many tried to avoid paying this *Fiscus Judaicus*. From trying to pose as pagans it was an easy step to becoming pagans.

Converts and Christians—Under the circumstances, conversions to Judaism, very frequent until then, became more rare, at least for some time to come. There was, however, one sect of Jews that could claim converts to a greater extent now than when the Temple was in existence. The Jews who were known as believers in the Messiah of Nazareth, or Christians, had never considered the Temple of as great importance as did the other Jews. Some of them had gotten into trouble because of this view as long as twenty years before the outbreak of the rebellion. During the rebellion the Christians, who had till then used Jerusalem as their center of activity, moved out of the city to a small town on the other side of the Jordan. The group was so small and insignificant that the Jews disregarded this unpatriotic action. But when the Temple lay in ruins and the Jewish nation was expected to disappear, the Christians intensified their propaganda. They told all prospective converts that the destruction of the Temple was proof that God had abandoned the Jews, that He no longer wanted a Temple, and that they, who believed in Jesus as the Messiah, were the only true Jews. In other words, the Christians were able to point to the Temple ruins and say: "We expected this, and it is as it should be." No wonder that after this period conversions to Christianity were proportionately more numerous than conversions to Judaism. Before long, the Gentiles among the Christians far outnumbered the Jews among them. But it must be remembered that everyone —Jews, Christians and Romans—still looked upon Christianity as a sect of Judaism.

2. THE DIASPORA REBELLION (115–117)

The Choice Before the People—How could the Jewish people survive the losses, the disorganization and the shame? At this very critical moment in the history of the Jewish people, there were some who did not believe that the loss of the war was necessarily fatal to Jewish life; study and Jewish action would guarantee the continuance of the people. But this was so unusual a point of view that most of the people of that day did not take it seriously. Can a people live without a political state? That generation of embittered fighters felt that it could not be done. Either the Jews must regain their national state or be prepared to disappear.

The Diaspora Discovers Its Jewishness—The Diaspora to the west of Palestine had given very little aid during the first rebellion. This was due to its loyalty to Rome and its unwillingness to be considered part of the Jewish nation. Yet, when the war was over, these Jews realized that the rest of the world refused to make any such distinction. Rome made them pay the irritating and insulting tax to Jupiter's Temple, and the pagans mocked at them as though they had also been involved in the Judean struggle. Too late they understood that the misfortune of Jerusalem was their misfortune too. Moreover, fugitives from Palestine and redeemed slaves from among the captives told of Roman cruelty and Jewish heroism, stirring their hearers to await the time when the score could be evened. A brief attempt to do so was made in Egypt a year or two after the Jewish defeat. But it was quickly put down and, in punishment, the Temple of Onias, which had functioned until then in the little town of Heliontopolis, was ordered closed.

Emperor Trajan and the East—For a generation the state of affairs remained practically unchanged. The Roman government had become somewhat more friendly, but the pagan neighbors of the Jews were more irritating than ever. Then, about the year 110, Emperor Trajan began to plan another campaign in the East. Parthia, the rival of the Roman empire in Asia, was weak at the time, and Trajan dreamed of becoming another Alexander the Great by conquering Persia and India as well. In order to conduct a successful campaign in that part of the world it was considered advisable to have the good will of the Jews, both because Judea was a border province and because so many Jews lived in the western portion of Parthia. Trajan's government seems to have given the Jews of Palestine a promise to permit the rebuilding of the Temple.

Trajan then started on his great campaign against Parthia. He quickly overran the district on the other side of the Euphrates where the Jews were thickly settled. He conquered the kingdom of Adiabene, situated in the territory that was once Assyria, whose royal family had become Jewish two generations before. He then continued eastward, following the footsteps of Alexander. But he had to turn back. In the rear of his army the provinces he had just conquered rebelled. Among the fighters for Parthia, threatening to cut off Trajan's return and thus capture and annihilate his army, were the Jews of Parthia who were anything but enthusiastic about coming under the rule of Rome, the destroyer of Jerusalem. Trajan was forced to abandon all thought of further conquest, and turned his attention to the rebellion of the Jews.

The Rebellion in Cyprus, Egypt and Cyrene—These were not the only troubles of the Roman empire in the year 115. At the very time when the Jews of Babylonia, or Parthia, were rising against the new conquerors of their country, a violent rebellion was started by the Jews in the lands of the eastern Mediterranean. One of the frequent racial riots broke out in Cyrenaica, that is, North Africa west of Egypt.

Usually in such riots the pagans could count upon the help of the Roman soldiers to stop the Jews from putting up a good defense. But at this time almost no Roman soldiers were available, all of the regular army having been sent to Trajan's aid in Parthia. Consequently the Jews were able to fight back and to carry the battle into the places where the pagans resided. What is more, the Jews of the island of Cyprus, and those of Egypt joined in the fighting.

The riot became a war. The Jews of the three districts involved organized regular armies and took a bloody revenge for all they had had to bear during the half century before. Trajan hurriedly sent Turbo, one of his generals, to restore order. Turbo's soldiers were joined by the pagan population of the affected districts. They attacked the Jews, both the fighters and the peaceful population, more mercilessly than the Jews had attacked them. In the island of Cyprus every single Jew was killed, the total running into thousands. A law was adopted never to permit a Jew to set foot on the island even if he were shipwrecked near by. In Egypt and Cyrene the Jewish population was treated with almost equal ferocity. Thereafter the once flourishing Jewish community of Alexandria was definitely on the downgrade.

3. The Second Judean Revolt (132–135)

Inaction in Palestine—For several reasons the Judean Jews did not take advantage of the rebellion in the Diaspora to the east and the west of them as everyone expected them to do. Sporadic outbreaks of fighting by the more enthusiastic Jews gave Trajan an excuse to send his most ruthless general, Tineius Rufus, who had put down the uprising of the Parthian Jews, to be the governor of Judea. With stern ruthlessness he wiped out every trace of rebelliousness in Palestine. On the whole, however, it is pretty clear that the Jews of Palestine did not want to fight this time. In part this was due to the influence for peace exercised by the great rabbis of the day. More important was the fact that the Jews still believed in the promise given them by Trajan to restore the Temple, which probably meant also to rebuild Jerusalem. There was no use fighting for that which could be had in peace.

A Broken Promise—Rome had promised, but would Rome keep its promise? Objections began to pour in upon Rome from the pagans of Palestine and also from the Samaritans. They did not want Jerusalem rebuilt and Judaism raising its head again. The matter dragged on for years. Trajan was succeeded by Hadrian, a man of greater pagan culture and therefore of deeper opposition to any but a pagan faith. Then Rome promised to redeem its pledge as soon as the emperor could visit Palestine and investigate the matter on the spot. At last, in 130, Hadrian came to Judea. He was a great builder; he hated to see once flourishing cities lie in ruins. He ordered Jerusalem rebuilt. But it was to be a pagan city, to be called Aelia Capitolina! It was to have an altar; but it was to be a pagan altar, dedicated to Jupiter whose high priest Hadrian was.

Mistake or Policy?—Hadrian may simply have failed to understand the sacredness which the Jews attributed to the place. Judaism meant nothing to him. As to the Jews, this was a terrible blow to them. For fifteen years the peace-loving intellectual leaders of the people had held them in check. They had kept the Palestinian Jews from joining the diaspora rebellion by preaching faith in the pledged word of Rome. Now Rome was doing worse than going back on its word; it was offering a deliberate insult, and adding to the joy of every enemy of the Jewish people. Moreover, soon thereafter Hadrian issued another decree, applicable to the whole Roman empire, which was interpreted as prohibiting circumcision. Consequently the Jews saw in Hadrian another Antiochus Epiphanes. And where there was an Antiochus, a Maccabee was bound to arise.

Akiba, Supporter of Rebellion—As the situation appeared to the Jews in the year 130, they were faced with the choice of perishing in cowardly fashion or of fighting to the death on the field of battle. Since there were still several millions of them in Palestine, and since the idea that the Jewish people could survive only in a political state still lived in the hearts of the majority, they saw no alternative but to fight. Provincials and city-dwellers, peasants and scholars rose as one to defend their honor and to restore their state.

The most influential among the leaders of this second revolt was the eighty-year-old scholar, Rabbi Akiba ben Joseph, who had risen from an ignorant shepherd to be the most outstanding teacher of Judaism. He had been to Rome and had believed in Rome's promises. But now that Judaism was threatened, he used his prestige and influence to stir up revolt. Having visited Babylonia and become acquainted with the Jews of the Parthian empire, he may have hoped that they would again rise to fight Rome. Whatever his reasons, he traveled through Palestine and helped organize thousands of soldiers in the fight for an independent Judea.

Simeon Bar Kochba—Who was to lead the fight? The aged Akiba certainly could not do so. It had to be someone younger and more energetic. Just such a man was found in the person of Simeon, a native of the town of Koziba. Strong, imaginative and inspiring, he gave promise of becoming a second Judah the Maccabee. Akiba was pleased with him. He called him God's anointed, in other words, messiah. For most Jews still believed in a messiah of flesh and blood who would be sent by God to redeem the Jewish people. Accepting the biblical sentence, "A star (*kochab*) has come forth from Jacob," as a reference to the Messiah, the old scholar and patriot changed Simeon's name from *Bar Koziba*, "the man of Koziba," to *Bar Kochba*, "the son of the star." The Jews who flocked to his banner from every corner of the land enthusiastically endorsed Akiba's phrase. Under Bar Kochba's leadership hundreds of thousands gathered, making up by numbers for their lack of weapons, and by burning zeal for their lack of military training. In a valley hidden among steep and rocky hills Bar Kochba had his headquarters. Every mountain swarmed with Jewish rebels. This time there were no divisions in their ranks. They were ready to teach Rome, by Rome's own method, that Jews and Judaism could not be destroyed.

Rome's Answer—It was not until the year 132, when Hadrian was already back in Rome, that the actual outbreak of the rebellion took place. When the extent of Jewish preparation became known, Hadrian realized that he would have a hard struggle. As commander he appointed Julius Severus, a man who had had a great deal of experience in fighting untrained but determined provincials. Again a Roman army, aided by the pagan neighbors of the Jews, marched into Palestine. Once more began that slaughter and destruction which had laid waste the land just sixty years before.

Jerusalem Won and Lost—Before the arrival of Julius Severus, Bar Kochba met with considerable success against the local Roman soldiers. Jerusalem was taken by the Jews; an altar was built on the Temple Mount; the building of a wall was begun. But with the coming of the regular Roman army all energies had to be directed to meeting the Romans in the field. Severus refused to meet the Jews in open battle. He was afraid of being overwhelmed by their superior numbers. He played upon Bar Kochba's lack of experience. He harassed the Jews. He waited until they divided their forces and then attacked each part separately. He laid the land waste and prevented supplies from reaching the Jewish army. He wore down their strength and dispelled their enthusiasm. Within two years he drove them out of Jerusalem. which they had failed to fortify sufficiently.

The Fall of Bettar—In the end Bar Kochba was forced to shut himself and a considerably reduced army in the fortified town of Bettar to the southwest of Jerusalem. For some weeks the Jews held out against the Roman siege, and might have held out longer had not spies shown the Romans a secret way into the town. The Jewish army was destroyed. Thousands upon thousands of them, exhausted by the siege, fell fighting in and outside of Bettar. Simeon Bar Kochba was among the dead. The Romans also suffered heavy losses, but the Second Revolt was over.

4. SHALL JUDAISM SURVIVE?

Jewish Losses—"Is this the end?" the surviving Jews must have asked themselves in the year 135. Five hundred and eighty thousand men are said to have been killed in battle alone. Tens of thousands more must have fallen before the relentless destruction carried out by the Romans. The slave markets were again glutted with Jewish captives. Judea lay desolate, and the Jewish people were in mourning.

The Prohibition of Judaism—Hadrian decided that this must be the end. It was obvious to him that as long as this strange people kept up their curious religion they would consider Rome an oppressor and would refuse to become one with the Roman population. Even before the fighting was over, Jerusalem began to be rebuilt as a pagan city. By a strange chance, the foundations of the new city were laid on the usual day of misfortune for the Jews, the 9th of Ab. Jews were prohibited from coming near the city. Thereafter, annually on that day many would come from every part of the country and bribe the Roman soldiers to let them weep over the ruins of their former glory. Hadrian prohibited the practice of Judaism. He forbade circumcision, the observance of the Sabbath, and the fixation of the calendar which was so important for the celebration of the holidays. He also forbade the meeting of the Academy and *Bet Din* (court) established by Johanan ben Zakkai at Jabne at the end of the first revolt.* In fact, he prohibited study and teaching. Anyone found studying the Torah was punished by death.

The Martyrs—These laws did not stop the Jews from observing their religion; they only forced the people to defy Rome. The Roman officials did not attempt to punish the ordinary Jews. They decided that, if the religious leaders were kept from instructing the Jewish masses, the common people would in time yield to Roman demands. It was upon the great teachers of Judaism, therefore, that Rome's hand lay heaviest. A number of them fell victim to Rome during and after the revolt. The foremost among these was Rabbi Akiba. The aged sage refused to stop studying. "Just as a fish cannot live outside of water," he would say, "so the Jewish people cannot live outside of Torah." He was condemned to be flayed alive, and with his last breath he exclaimed: "Hear, O Israel, the Lord is our God, the Lord is One."

Judaism Refuses to Die—Nevertheless, despite enemies and losses, the Jews continued to live. Even their national hopes were not completely destroyed. They still waited and hoped for the Parthian empire to grow strong and come to their deliverance, or for divine intervention to save Jerusalem from pagan hands. They certainly did not give up their laws and ceremonies, their beliefs and their study. In time the Romans came to realize the uselessness of persecuting Judaism. The academies were reopened, and though Palestine never revived from the blow struck at the Jews during the second revolt, it still remained for two generations the center of Jewish life everywhere. The first choice, the way of the sword for keeping the Jews alive as a group, had failed. The second choice, the way of the spirit, was now entered upon with enthusiasm. For a very long time to come the Jews were destined to be "a kingdom not of this earth"—a people without physical boundaries, a group who lived not by the strong arm, like Esau, but by the spiritual qualities of Jacob.

* See below, pp. 184 ff.

BOOK TWO

THE SUPREMACY OF THE EAST
(70–1000)

JUDAISM SAVES THE JEWISH PEOPLE FROM EXTINCTION

INTRODUCTION

JEWISH HISTORY BECOMES DIFFERENT FROM THE HISTORY
OF OTHER PEOPLES

Not the History of a Land—The history of a people has
almost always been the history of a nation in a land. The history of the United States has been largely the history of the
colonies and the United States on the American continent.
The history of the English people, for the most part, has been
identical with the history of England. The same is true of
France, of Germany and of other nations. Until the destruction of the Jewish Commonwealth in 70 C. E., this was also

true of the Jews; the history of the Jewish people was inseparable from that of the Jewish land. The history of the Jewish communities in the Diaspora, in lands outside of Palestine,
was connected with Palestine as the territorial center of
Judaism. From 70 C. E. the situation changed. For a while
Palestine continued to hold the central place in Jewish life.
Then it became transformed into a dream, a goal, an ideal,
while the most important events in Jewish history took place
elsewhere, now in one land and now in another.

The Miracle of Jewish Survival—Nevertheless we can
speak of the history of the Jewish people. For, although the
Jews were no longer a nation, in the usual sense of a territorial group, they still continued to feel united. That is one of
the outstanding marvels in all human history. When Assyria
was destroyed, there ceased to be any Assyrians; when Egypt
was conquered, there were no longer any Egyptians, except in
so far as the people who live in that land are still called by
that name. The Jews, however, still survive, although Judea
was conquered and the Jewish nation destroyed almost nineteen hundred years ago. The reason for this most unusual situation is that the Jewish Idea, or Judaism, was made more
important than the Jewish land and Jewish national life.

This did not happen all at once. No group of Jews came
together and said: "Our nation is no more. Come, then, let us
survive by creating a Jewish way of life!" The process of
creating such an imperishable life had started with the Pharisees, indeed even farther back, with Ezra. But during the period that we are going to discuss now, it was strengthened
and developed to work under all circumstances. If we compare the national territory to the body of a people and the
national culture to its soul, then we may say that in all other
peoples the body kept the soul alive, whereas in the case of
the Jews, the soul, for these many centuries past, has kept the
Jewish people alive.

The Wandering Spirit—There is a current belief that the
Jews are a wandering people. This is not altogether true, for
Jews rarely leave their birthplace of their own free will. The
fact is, however, that ever since the Greek and Roman periods Jews have lived in almost every known land. Naturally,
the Jews of each country have a history of their own, based,
to a large extent, upon the history of that country. But to
study all these countries at the same time would be very con-
fusing. Therefore, we shall take one segment of the Jewish
people, inhabiting one part of the world, and study it up to a
certain point in Jewish history. Later we shall return and

study what had been happening in the meantime to other Jews in other countries. In this section we shall continue with the history of the Jews of Palestine and the rest of the Eastern world, because this part of the Jewish people then played the most important role in insuring Jewish survival. Without the intellectual and religious work done by the Jews of Palestine and Babylonia during the first thousand years of the Common Era, the Jews elsewhere, who became more important during the second thousand years, would never have remained Jewish.

Culture in the East—Much of the story of Eastern Jewry is the story of books. This is natural, because books, thoughts, traditions have been the guides of Jewish life. Here, too, something so providential happened as to amount to almost a miracle. Had the Jews of Palestine moved west instead of east, they would have been completely under the influence of the Roman empire at a time when its culture was decaying, its libraries being pillaged and burned and its classical knowledge forgotten. The East was, in many respects, more civilized than the West, and the cultural influences of the more favorable surroundings helped to stimulate the Jewish mind. Thus Judaism suffered no dark ages. Later, when the light of the East began to dim, that of the West grew brighter at the very time when circumstances compelled the Jews to seek new homes in that direction.

CHAPTER I

THE NEW FOUNDATION

THE JEWS PREVENT THEIR OWN DESTRUCTION BY DEVELOPING THEIR LAWS AND CEREMONIES

The Way of the Spirit—It had been hard for the Jews to accept defeat in the year 70 as final. Time and again they tried their fortune in war with Rome, but, as often as they tried, they failed. The difficulty was, as we have seen, that most Jews did not believe it possible to survive without some form of national life. Not even the tragic results of Bar

Kochba's attempt convinced them of the futility of using the sword, and they continued to look for opportunities to fight Rome even after the year 135. But, as time went on, a growing number of them became convinced that another way existed for insuring their survival—the way of Jewish life suggested by Johanan ben Zakkai. As that second way was adopted, as that idea became rooted and developed in the minds of the Jews, the people gradually transformed itself from a nation like any other into a group united by invisible bonds, living in a land of the spirit, ruled by the laws of God. They laid down the sword of the soldier and raised high the more lasting pen of the scholar. This was the process which went on in Palestine between the years 70 and 200.

1. WHAT ROME COULD NOT DESTROY

Judaism and Jewish Customs—Rome might destroy the Jewish nation, the city of Jerusalem, the Temple and the Sanhedrin. It might kill hundreds of thousands of men and women and lay waste the land of Israel. But there were some portions of Jewish life which Rome could not touch, namely, those which did not exist in any physical form, but were nevertheless part of the people's being. The Jewish idea of God's unity and uniqueness and the Jewish concept of human brotherhood, and many other ideals and attitudes which were part of Judaism, survived the Roman victory. The customs which had grown up during the previous centuries were also not subject to death by the sword. Such were the obligation to rest on the Sabbath, the custom of observing as holy the days upon which important events had taken place, the dietary laws and any number of other traditions within and outside the Jewish home. These traditions were not connected with the Temple or with national life, but they were widespread, being observed wherever Jews lived.

Jewish Learning—Nor could Rome destroy the Torah. For centuries, ever since Ezra, the Jews had considered study an essential part of living as Jews. Such study embraced not only the books now called the Bible, but all the other legal and literary works written primarily under the guidance of the Pharisees. The common folk were satisfied with the study of the written Torah and its homiletic interpretations, but the educated concerned themselves mainly with the still largely unorganized laws and traditions which had come to be known as the Oral Law. This love of study was universal among the Jews. Rome could not destroy all the books in Jewish possession, and certainly not the desire to study them. Therefore, as long as the Jewish schools continued to teach, the Jewish people was assured of life.

The Synagogue—The Synagogue, too, remained indestructible. By the year 70, synagogues were in existence everywhere in Palestine and in the Diaspora. True, Rome might and probably did destroy the synagogue buildings in rebellious Palestine. But for synagogues, buildings were not altogether necessary. Far more important than the synagogue building were the activities within the synagogue—the prayers recited, the traditions followed, even the social gatherings. These communal activities formed a bond of union and gave encouragement for continued living as Jews.

Memories and Hopes—Above all, Rome could not destroy the memories and the hopes of the Jewish people. Every book of the Bible and every teaching of an ancient sage aroused memories of the glories of the past. This gave the Jews a sense of pride and prevented them from being absorbed by the pagans among whom they lived. These memories also fortified their trust in the glorious future promised them by prophet and by sage. Moreover, every ceremony in Jewish life was connected with an event or an ideal, and further distinguished the Jews from their neighbors in mental outlook as well as in behavior. Ceremonials and observances were often so practiced and interpreted as to keep alive the hope for freedom, for justice, for kindliness on the part of all humanity, as well as for the eventual restoration of the Jewish people. Such memories and hopes were deepened and strengthened during the dangerous period which followed the unsuccessful rebellions against Rome.

Messianic Hopes—One of the hopes, which began to come into greater prominence at this time, was that of the Messiah. In place of a human messiah, the idea of a divine deliverer, a restorer of David's kingdom, a founder of universal righteousness and international justice, in a word, a supernatural Messiah, acquired a firm hold upon the imagination of the Jewish people. The ideas of the Essenes, upon which the founders of Christianity had drawn some generations earlier, were now further developed among all the Jews and helped to make their sad lot more tolerable by hopes for a happy future.

2. A STATESMAN OF THE SPIRIT

Johanan and Vespasian—Out of this indestructible material the Jewish people was eventually rebuilt. The man who formulated the plan and showed the method was Johanan ben Zakkai, who therefore stands out as one of the greatest statesmen and leaders in the long story of the Jewish people. The beginnings of his plan go back to the days of the siege of Jerusalem by Titus. Johanan ben Zakkai, a firm believer in the views of Hillel, was at that time the most respected of the Pharisees. The Jewish people were to him not merely a nation like any other. The Jews must live by the spirit, not by the sword—so Johanan thought—and the war against Rome was therefore a mistake. When he saw the end of Jerusalem approaching, Johanan decided that the time had come for him to act.

A famous story tells what happened after this. Some of Johanan's pupils announced that their master had died and asked permission to carry his body for burial outside of Jerusalem. Theirs was a dangerous mission, doubly dangerous, since the suspicious Zealots were on one side of the walls and the cruel Romans on the other. But they managed to carry the living Johanan beyond the lines of danger, where he rose out of his coffin and made his way to Vespasian, the Roman general.

No greater contrast can be imagined than that between Johanan ben Zakkai and Vespasian when they faced each other during their interview. Rome and Jerusalem were personified in them—the Sword versus the Spirit. Vespasian knew that the man before him was a very influential man, whose good will would have restraining effect upon the moderates among the Jews in and outside of Palestine. He was ready to grant almost any request that Johanan might make. One can imagine Vespasian's astonishment when all that Johanan requested was permission to open a school in a little town by the seacoast which the Jews called Jabne and the Romans Jamnia. Vespasian, knowing how much he was willing to grant, must have thought the request ridiculous and Johanan a foolish old man. He certainly would not have believed that that school would save the Jewish people, keep it alive for many hundreds of years, and prove, more than any other single event in history, that Spirit is mightier than Sword.

The School at Jabne—Johanan went from the Roman

camp directly to Jabne, now crowded with refugees from Galilee and Judea, and settled down to await the outcome of the siege of Jerusalem. He knew what had to be done to keep Jewish courage alive after the inevitable defeat, to hold the Jews united after the Temple was destroyed, to maintain what was most valuable in the Jewish way of life after the Jews became more widely dispersed. A few scholars too old to fight, or too certain of the war's uselessness, gathered about him, meeting at stated times in the courtyard of his home to study, discuss and plan. Before many months passed by, the school at Jabne was known wherever Jews lived.

The New Sanhedrin—Johanan's plans soon matured. His object was not only to study, but to replace the destroyed institutions by new and equally respected ones. The Sanhedrin, for example, which used to meet in Jerusalem and which Jews everywhere had looked upon as the central legislative and judicial body, could meet no more. Rome had forbidden its revival as it forbade everything else that pertained to Jewish national life. Quietly Johanan ben Zakkai gathered seventy-one scholars, the number that used to sit in the Sanhedrin, organized them under similar officers, and set for them the same functions. But this was to be an unofficial body, not recognized by Rome, and, therefore, having no authority to enforce its decisions. Johanan depended upon the respect which he and his fellows commanded among the Jews, and upon the regard which Jews always had for learning. Above all, he knew that as religious questions arose, the Jews would naturally turn to this group of scholars, who were thus to constitute a religious legislature and supreme court of law.

Synagogue in Place of Temple—Even more than the Sanhedrin, the Temple had stood out as the foremost institution in Jewish life. What was to take its place? The role of the Synagogue in Judaism had been increasing at the expense of the Temple.* The sacrificial ceremonies, to be sure, were picturesque and awe-inspiring; but they bore hard on the poor, since sacrifices were expensive. Furthermore, prayer was considered much more desirable than sacrifice for the satisfaction of the innermost religious needs of the Jews. The destruction of the Temple hurt Jewish pride and unity; the discontinuance of the sacrifices was a blow to tradition. Actually, however, the Synagogue was ready to fulfill all of Judaism's spiritual needs.

* For the origin and early development of the Synagogue, see above, pp. 120 ff.

Johanan's main task was to persuade the Jews to admit into the Synagogue some of the ceremonies of the Temple other than the sacrifices. This would make the Synagogue the heir to the Temple. The ceremonies, the retention of which Johanan suggested, were among the most impressive of the Temple service: namely, the priestly benediction, the sounding of the *Shofar* on Rosh Hashanah (which he vainly urged even for the Sabbath), and the *lulab* procession during the entire holiday of Sukkot. These ceremonies, somewhat modified, form part of the synagogue ritual to this day.

The Discipline of Observance—A body of Jewish traditional observances had long been accumulating. These observances (or *mitzvot*) assumed an additional importance at this time as bonds of union among widely scattered communities. As long as the nation was in existence, uniform religious observances were not essential. Sadducees could differ from Pharisees, and Essenes could differ from both. Now, however, it became one of the tasks of Johanan ben Zakkai and his colleagues to abolish as many differences as possible. Both Sadducees and Essenes disappeared. Any man refusing to follow the decisions of the *Bet Din* as to what was or was not traditionally Jewish weakened Jewish life by loosening the ties which bound him to the group.

Who Were the Rabbis?—Johanan ben Zakkai and his colleagues made study more important than it had ever been. Jewish knowledge was to identify a Jew. The nobility of blood which had existed among the Jews before the destruction of the Jewish state was to be replaced by a spiritual nobility of the mind and spirit. This spiritual nobility, the most respected group among the Jews, especially in Palestine, came to be known as *rabbis*. The word *Rab* originally meant "great one," and *Rabbi* is "my superior," like *Monsieur* in French. Before long it came to mean "my teacher," and after a while became a title of honor granted, as we shall see, upon the attainment of a certain degree of knowledge. Members of the *Bet Din* especially had to possess this degree. The head, or *Nasi*, of the *Bet Din* was addressed by the title *Rabban*.

3. THE NASI

The House of Hillel—Rabban Johanan ben Zakkai was already an old man when he established the *Bet Din* at Jabne and started to rebuild Jewish life upon spiritual foundations. Who was to succeed him and carry on the unfinished work?

It required a man not only respected for his learning, but one whose very name would convey authority among the Jewish people everywhere. It was inadvisable to select someone from the aristocratic priestly families, for most of them had been too sympathetic to Rome and, therefore, would be unacceptable to the Jews. Nor could Johanan and the *Bet Din* pick a man who had been identified too closely with the rebellion, since that would arouse the suspicions of Rome.

There was one family which best met most of the requirements: that of the renowned Hillel. The name Hillel was remembered with awe and affection by all the Jews. So weighty had been his authority, that to be a descendant of his came to be accepted as a mark of the highest spiritual nobility. His son, or it may have been his grandson, Gamaliel the Elder, had also been the head of the Sanhedrin, and so too had the latter's son, Simon, whom it is probable that the Zealots killed, on the suspicion of being pro-Roman, during the war against Rome. A son of this Simon, also called Gamaliel, now lived in Jabne, and the *Bet Din* fixed on him to succeed Rabban Johanan ben Zakkai as its *Nasi*.

Rabban Gamaliel of Jabne—Gamaliel, in addition to the fame of his family, had one other quality very necessary for that time. He saw the need of unifying Jewish life quite as clearly as Johanan ben Zakkai had, and he possessed the stubborn energy which such a task required. He was younger and unfortunately felt less learned than many members of the *Bet Din*. Therefore, he tried to accomplish by the exercise of authority what Johanan had done by persuasion.

The Defense of Democracy—Trouble was bound to arise when Gamaliel's desire to do everything possible to fortify Jewish unity led him to enforce too strictly his own authority and the opinions of the majority. An example will serve to illustrate the attitude of the Jewish scholars towards the suppression of minority opinion. The Synagogue had modeled itself after the Temple so that there were as many services daily in the Synagogue as there had been public sacrifices in the Temple: a morning service and an afternoon service every weekday, and an additional service on Saturdays, New Moons and holidays. There had been no evening service in the Temple and, therefore, no official evening service in the Synagogue. Gamaliel took advantage of a growing religious custom to recite evening prayers, to unite Jewish life further by making evening services an obligation upon every Jew. He forced his views through the *Bet Din*. Rabbi Joshua, however, a poor man but a highly respected scholar, persisted in his own view that, legally, the recital of evening prayers was voluntary. Angered, Gamaliel administered a public rebuke to Joshua. This was too much for the other members of the *Bet Din;* they resented Gamaliel's harsh exercise of authority. In their desire to show him that he had exceeded the limitations of his office, they deposed him and elected as *Nasi* a young priestly aristocrat by the name of Eleazar ben Azariah. Soon, however, the *Bet Din* realized that it had struck a serious blow at the object dear to all of them, the unity of Jewish life. Moreover, Gamaliel had accepted his humiliation with such good grace that his colleagues repented of having removed him. Gamaliel was thereupon restored to office, though Eleazar continued to enjoy official honors. The *Nasi* had learned his lesson, and thereafter recognized that Jewish life had no room for arbitrary authority.

Rome and the Bet Din—Some years later, after the dynasty of emperors established by Vespasian had given place to another, the Roman government recognized the folly of trying to destroy Judaism. Rome would not give policital independence to Judea, but it saw no objection to a religious organization by Jews. Thus, toward the end of the first century, the *Bet Din* was recognized as an official institution and given control over internal Jewish affairs. The *Nasi,* as head of the *Bet Din,* could appoint judges and enforce their decisions. He supervised the schools and all other institutions of the Jewish community. Only matters of taxation and the like were left in the hands of the Roman administrator of the provinces. Actually, the powers of the *Bet Din* and the *Nasi* were much greater than those officially granted them, since they had not only legal authority over the Jews in Palestine but also their voluntary allegiance wherever they lived, both in the Roman empire and in Parthia. The Jews recognized their religious authority, and gladly sent contributions for their maintenance. Jewish unity was again established.

4. INTELLECTUAL LIFE IN DANGER

The Second Trial of Arms—The mass of the Jewish people did not quite realize the importance of what was going on at Jabne. We have already seen how this attitude brought about the diaspora rebellion in the years 115–117, as well as the Judean rebellion under Bar Kochba in 132, along with their disastrous consequences for all the Jews. The Bar Kochba rebellion endangered all that Johanan and Gamaliel had achieved.

Study Prohibited—The outlawing of the *Bet Din* and the prohibition of Jewish observances were accompanied by a decree forbidding the study of the Torah. This the leaders of the Jews could not permit. There must have been many who, like the famous Rabbi Akiba ben Joseph, risked capture by the Roman soldiers by continuing to study and teach. An interpreter of Judaism to the very end, he welcomed his martyrdom and the torture to which the Romans subjected him, so the story runs, because it enabled him to fulfill the biblical command: "And thou shalt love the Lord thy God with all thy heart, and all thy soul, and all thy might."

Ordination and Judah ben Baba—Another martyr for the same cause was Judah ben Baba. His "crime" was the granting of ordination (*Semichah*). When a student was considered sufficiently learned and mature to teach and to interpret the Bible, his teacher or another learned man went through a ceremony by which the pupil was given the right and authority to teach. As a sign of this authority he was henceforth called "Rabbi." This ceremony carried with it a sense of the sacred, for in the view of the people of that day it connected the one ordained with "the Chain of Tradition" which led directly back to Moses and Mount Sinai by way of the scribes, the prophets and the elders whom Moses himself had ordained.

Rome prohibited ordination after the Bar Kochba rebellion. It decreed death to the one giving and to those receiving this authority, as well as the destruction of the town in or near which the ceremony took place. The situation for Judaism was serious. So many of the young scholars had fallen during the war, that the next generation was threatened with a lack of religious leadership and all of the Jewish people with a break in the Chain of Tradition upon which they based their claim to being a "holy people." Rabbi Judah ben Baba, an old man, thereupon picked five young but highly promising students, took them to a place between two towns, so that neither town could be blamed, and hurriedly ordained them. The ceremony was hardly over when the Romans, notified by spies, were upon them. The old teacher urged his pupils to run for their lives, while he himself remained to receive the punishment of the enemy. He was killed; but the newly ordained young men remained to continue Jewish teaching.

What Must a Jew Die For?—Like Rabbi Akiba, Rabbi Judah ben Baba, and others, the Jewish population of Palestine could no longer resist the Romans, but they were ready to let themselves be martyred rather than obey Rome's law against Judaism. Such an attitude threatened the destruction of the entire Jewish population. Thereupon a number of religious leaders gathered to consult about the fundamentals of Judaism. Their discussions turned upon the following questions: 1) Is study more important than observance, or observance of the laws of Jewish living more important than study of the Torah? 2) What are those basic laws of Jewish life which a Jew ought to die for rather than violate? After lengthy and thorough consideration they finally decided: 1) Study is more important than observance, since knowledge of the Torah is bound to lead to obedience of its wise laws, whereas observance without intelligent understanding of the background offers little hope for a future. 2) There are only three fundamentals of Judaism for which a man or a woman must prefer death to transgression—the worship of idols, adultery, and the shedding of innocent blood. Any other law of Judaism may be transgressed if it is a question of life.

5. The Second Reconstruction

Judea Deserted—One permanent result of the Bar Kochba rebellion was the loss of Jewish population in Palestine, especially in the province of Judea. Those spared from the Roman sword fled from Roman oppression to other parts of the world, above all to that portion of the Parthian empire already famous in Jewish history under the name of Babylonia. Neither the Babylonian nor the Palestinian Jews realized as yet that this transfer of population was but the beginning of a transfer of religious strength and authority. That was to become apparent several generations later. In the meantime it was clear that Judea was completely destroyed.

Galilee Leads—The stubborn adherence of the Jewish people to their religious laws and customs overcame, in the course of years, Rome's efforts to destroy them. A new administration in Rome made Jewish life easier. Permission was given for the *Bet Din* to be reconstituted (about 150 C. E.), with Simon II, the son of Gamaliel of Jabne, as its *Nasi*. The schools were reopened, and among the new teachers the five men, whom Rabbi Judah ben Baba had given his life to ordain, became most prominent. One was Rabbi Meir, a brilliant mind and an extraordinary preacher. Rabbi Simon ben Yohai, who for many years had hidden from Roman power, now came out of his cave in the desert. These refugees from

Judea were indescribably poor. Some had to borrow an outer garment before they could venture into the street. Study was their sole comfort; knowledge their only wealth. Yet it was now clearer than ever (clearer even than during Johanan ben Zakkai's day), that the survival of the Jewish people as a separate group, and the survival of Judaism along with its ideals, would be assured "not by might nor by power, but by My spirit."

6. LITERATURE AND ORAL TEACHING

Biblical Books and Their Imitations—Since the intellectual and literary activity of the Jews of the second century (C. E.) has exercised an enormous influence on Jewish life down to the present day, it is necessary to see what books the Jews had been writing and reading, and which of the many books in their possession they accepted as worth while and which they rejected as valueless or harmful. The Bible, by this time, was in the form in which we now have it. None among the Jews questioned its division into the three parts—the Torah, the Prophets, and the Writings—each part somewhat less sacred than the preceding.

One thing, however, is quite certain—the Jews never stopped writing books. Any number of other books appeared during the latter part of the Second Commonwealth, as we have already seen,* and after the war against Rome. Some of them are still in existence; others have long been lost. There are two interesting facts about these books outside of the Bible. One is that they were all imitations of one or another book of the Bible: narratives, prophecies, psalms and proverbs. The second fact about these books is that the Jews forgot them.

The Rejected Literature—Why were these books forgotten? Some of them were written in Greek and therefore could not become popular among the masses of the Jews, especially in Palestine. Others were neglected and forgotten during the transfer of so large a portion of the Jewish population from Palestine to other parts of the world. Moreover, these books were, on the whole, not well written; they lacked literary excellence. Judged by the biblical book upon which each one seems to have been modeled, the superiority of the biblical book in style and interest is immediately apparent. Besides,

* See above, pp. 124–6.

many of these books advocated religious laws which differed
from the legislation favored by the Pharisees and the rabbis.

The most important reason for the rejection of a good
many of them was the inferiority of their ideas. Many imitators of the prophetic books of the Bible tried to encourage
the belief in the miraculous deliverance of the Jews and the
miraculous survival of Judaism. They also overstressed the
glories of "the Other World" (the world after death) and of
"the World to Come" (the world after the arrival of the Messiah). The leaders of Judaism feared that these ideas could
easily be emphasized too much. The rabbis wanted to save
the Jewish people by the life and labor of the Jews of each
generation. They sought to make Judaism a religion which
stressed the need of making this world a better place to live
in, rather than neglect this world for the world to come after
death and resurrection. Finally, these books were hard to distinguish from Christian works which soon appeared, written
in the same languages and propagating the same ideas. To
avoid confusion it was considered best to discourage the reading of the entire literature. A number of the rejected books
were, in fact, accepted by the early Christians and are still to
be found in the Bible of the Catholic Church. Such books are
generally known as "The Apocrypha."

The Oral Teaching—One part of the Bible was never imitated. So great was the awe in which the Torah was held that,
while men wrote more prophecy or more poetry or more history, no one dared to write any more Torah. Even the traditions and the legislation which had originated during the Second Commonwealth, some of which no doubt went back as
far as Ezra, had not been written down. It would have been
considered sacrilegious to do so, for it would have meant
writing a book to supplement the Written Torah. Judges and
teachers taught these traditions to their pupils orally. Thus,
the distinction between the "Oral Teaching" (or as some people prefer to call it, "Oral Law") and the "Written Teaching"
(or the "Written Law," the Five Books of Moses) still held
in the second century of the Common Era.

The Schools of the Rabbis—The Oral Teaching was taught
in the schools of Judea which were transferred to Galilee
after the Jewish defeat in the second war against Rome. The
school conducted by Rabbi Akiba, whose fame as a teacher
attracted a great many pupils in the days before Bar Kochba,
can serve as an example of the others. The object of his
teaching was a double one: to show how the various existing
laws and customs of Jewish life were based upon statements

and principles contained in the Torah, and, secondly, to derive out of the words of the Torah guidance for the changed conditions of Jewish life in his own day and for the future. He and his pupils and the other rabbis ingeniously derived even from the sacrificial laws, which were no longer applicable, principles and rules of conduct useful to their own times. They considered not a word, or a letter, or even a dot in the Torah as superfluous.

Books of Legal Interpretation—Most of the teaching was done by lectures, and most of the pupils had good enough memories to retain what their teachers told them. When the schools were reopened in Galilee, there was great fear that the teachings of the previous generation, that of Akiba for example, would be forgotten. As a result the important comments of these rabbis were collected and perhaps written down in the form of commentaries on the four last books of the Torah.

Ethical Instruction—Law was not the only subject of study by the Jews. Ethics and morality were considered just as essential. As a matter of fact, the most important ethical principle, that of justice, was the foundation of all the legal studies just described. That is why the Jews looked upon all their laws as religious laws, since their aim was to train the human character and discipline it in the ways of godliness. But advanced students, like the rabbis and their pupils, did not need to have the ethical foundations repeated to them at every step; consequently they were interested in the laws and their just application. The vast majority of the people, however, who were not students, had to be told again and again how beautiful and desirable it was for all human beings to live in peace and harmony, in accordance with the standards of justice.

The rabbis did not neglect this part of their duty. Many of them interpreted every statement of the Bible not only legally for the advanced students, but also ethically for the people in general. Sometimes the same man was a teacher of law as well as a preacher. The most noted example of this was Rabbi Meir, whose fame as a preacher attracted enormous audiences. Such public lectures were also based on biblical stories and statements, including those of Abraham, Isaac and Jacob, the kings and the prophets. The preacher appealed to the emotions and the imagination of the people. He tried to give hope and courage to the individual, and strengthen the self-esteem of the group. There was clearly less need for collecting such interpretations of the Bible, since every generation has its preachers, and every preacher must be left to interpret the words of the Bible as he likes, in order to make the best appeal to the people of his day. At a much later time, as we shall see, these interpretations were also collected, and to this day are still in use under the name of *Midrash*. Such interpretations were known by the name *Agada*, which means "narration."

7. JUDAH THE PRINCE AND PALESTINE'S LEADERSHIP

Threats to the Leadership of Palestine—After the defeat of Bar Kochba, Jews in the Diaspora believed that they could no longer look to the old homeland for leadership. The Palestinian Jewish community was now smaller in number than several others, especially the Babylonian. Among the emigrants from Palestine were many promising scholars, so that Palestine was threatened with a loss of intellectual leadership as well. It looked for some time as though Rome would never relax its anti-Jewish legislation. For all these reasons the long supremacy of Palestine in Jewish life seemed to be permanently ended. But when, under the rule of Emperor Antoninus Pius (138–161), Rome did relax its hostility, and the *Bet Din* was re-established and the schools reopened, the religious leaders of Palestine felt that they could resume their directing influence among the Jewish people.

The Patriarchate at Its Height—The danger of Palestine's loss of leadership seemed to be definitely over when the *Nasi* Simon died and his son Judah succeeded him. Few among the rabbis have left so deep an impression on Jewish life as Judah. Social position, wealth, learning, organizing ability, statesmanship and piety combined to make him one of the most extraordinary men of his time. The Jews stood in great awe of him, and subsequent generations have spoken of him as "Judah the Prince," or "Our Holy Teacher," or simply "Rabbi," without need for a proper name. His prestige as well as his authority were enhanced when Rome recognized him as hereditary head of the Jewish people, with the title of Patriarch.

Ordination Restricted—Judah wanted to make sure that Jewish religious leadership would forever depend upon Palestine and he therefore decided to confine ordination to the Holy Land. He did not want to restrict the spread of Jewish learning, but he made the granting of ordination depend upon the consent of the Patriarch, and then refused to ordain scholars unless he was certain that they had no intention of emigrating and thus continuing the Chain of Tradition in some other land. One of the most promising young scholars of that day was a man by the name of Abba, who, because of his size, was nicknamed *Arika* ("the Long"). Now, Abba was a Babylonian, and made no secret of his intention to go back there. Time and again Abba attempted to obtain ordination from the Patriarch Judah, but was always refused. Eventually Abba Arika returned to Babylonia without ordination.

8. THE MISHNA

Too Many Authorities—Later events proved Judah the Prince mistaken in his efforts to establish Palestine's supremacy by means of the personal authority of the Patriarch. Jewish history did not develop in the way the great Patriarch anticipated, for soon after Judah's death Palestine lost its leading place among the Jewish communities of the world. Its influence has, indeed, remained to guide the Jews; but it has been an influence founded on books rather than on persons, and especially on the contribution made by Judah himself when he compiled the code of laws known as the *Mishna*.

Judah the Prince undertook this work because such a code was necessary in order to avoid confusion. There had been many teachers, and each one of them had left his interpretation as to what the duties of a Jew were to be under any set of circumstances. Anyone wanting to know the law or tradition on some matter might have to decide among a large number of opinions and might in the end overlook the authoritative decision. Several important teachers had in fact already tried their hand at setting down the important principles of Jewish law, but their prestige had not been great enough to make their decisions acceptable without dispute by their successors. The great learning of Judah and his position as Patriarch combined to make the code arranged by him the final authority on any subject.

Contents of the Mishna—The Mishna is not a commentary on the Bible. It is arranged according to subject matter, like any code of laws. It is divided into six sections (or "Orders"), which, in turn, are subdivided into treatises. For example, in the agricultural section one treatise discusses the exact regulations for observing the biblical command that a farmer leave the border of his field unharvested so that a poor man might be free to take whatever is left there. Curiously enough the same section contains a treatise, the first in the Mishna, which discusses the laws of prayer and benedictions (*Berakot*). The reason is that in the Jewish mind the yield of the soil and the enjoyment of life in general are intimately associated with the gratitude due to God. Another example of an interesting treatise is one in the section dealing with sacrifices. It is called *Hulin* and sets forth the laws of slaughtering animals for daily use as food. It was placed there because such slaughtering (*shehita*) is a semi-sacred procedure, the slaughterer (*shohet*) being obliged to recite a benediction over each animal.

The Treatise "Abot"—One treatise belonging to the fourth section (*Nezikin*) deserves special mention for two reasons. First, it has always been extremely popular among the Jews. Secondly, it is unusual to find a treatise of this kind in a code of laws. It consists of five chapters in which are outlined the principles that should guide the private conscience of every Jew, particularly if he is a scholar. In addition, it contains many ethical statements by famous rabbis, like the one which says that the world rests upon three ideals: Truth, Justice and Peace. Rabbi Judah no doubt included it because Jewish Law and Ethics are inseparable.

Style and Language of the Mishna—Judah wrote the Mishna in Hebrew, although during his day, and long before his time, the ordinary language spoken by the Jews in Palestine was Aramaic, a Semitic language related to Hebrew. For it was Judah's hope to revive Hebrew speech among the Jews, especially among those of Palestine. He used simple Hebrew, and clear, short sentences. Next to the Bible, the Mishna has exerted most influence on the Hebrew language as spoken and written to this day.

Tannaim and Their Achievements—The scholars or rabbis of the period between Johanan ben Zakkai and Judah the Prince are generally known by the name *Tannaim*, students, from an Aramaic word, the singular of which is *Tanna*. The period during which they worked is therefore known as "The Tannaitic Age." That was the age during which the binding ties of Jewish life changed from national institutions, like a land and a government, to religious institutions, like the Synagogue and the regulations of daily life. It was then that the achievements of the religious leaders over the more than five hundred years of the Second Commonwealth were crystallized into definite rules of conduct. These rules, in turn, were summed up in logical order by Judah the Prince. The Mishna became a companion to the Bible. More than ever before the Jews now became "The People of the Book."

CHAPTER II

AN ABANDONED HOMELAND

A NUMBER OF FACTORS MAKE IT IMPOSSIBLE FOR PALESTINE TO RETAIN ITS PLACE AS THE CENTRAL COMMUNITY AMONG THE JEWS

The Expiring Motherland—No efforts by the Patriarch Judah or his successors could arrest the social and economic forces sapping the strength of the Palestine Jewish community. Like a mother, Palestine had nursed the Jewish people from its infancy. It had seen the Jews grow into a small but mature and influential nation. Even after many of its children had scattered to the four corners of the earth, Palestine continued to provide them with food for their spirit. For their part, the dispersed Jewish communities still looked upon it as the Motherland, heeded its directions and contributed to its institutions. The Palestine community itself was not aware that its day of influence and authority was drawing to a close, that twilight was falling upon the Holy Land and a long and terror-filled night. Palestine's Jews of the third and fourth centuries hopefully looked upon their political and economic misfortunes as temporary. By the time the country actually and unmistakably ceased to be their homeland, it had provided the Jewish people with enough spiritual sustenance in the form of books, traditions and ideals to maintain it until the day comes when its life is revived and its position re-established.

1. CAUSES FOR THE DECLINE OF PALESTINE

Roman Misgovernment—Given slightly better economic opportunities, after the Roman emperors relaxed their laws against Judaism, the Jews would have restored themselves and their country to prosperity. However, such opportunities did not come during the next century, or ever after. The Roman government was always in the hands of wealthy aristocrats, interested in increasing the size of their estates, in enriching themselves no matter how they impoverished the masses of the people. The governors sent to rule over Palestine were of similar character. They taxed the people mercilessly, while doing nothing to improve their conditions. One of them told the Jews of Palestine that, if he could, he would tax the air they breathed. Roman officials were utterly corrupt and made it impossible for a poor man to defend his interests.

Roman Wars—Another difficulty of that period was the constant enmity between the Roman and the Parthian, or Persian, empires, each trying to expand at the expense of the other. Palestine was near the Roman frontier, so that it was always being threatened or, at least, disturbed. Moreover, on several occasions the Jews themselves are said to have taken a hand in the conflict, seeing an opportunity to throw off the yoke of Rome. The most serious of these revolts is supposed to have taken place in 351, with the result that the largest Jewish cities in Palestine were destroyed.

Gentile Competition—Friction between the Jews and Gentiles in Palestine had long existed, and under Rome it had increased rather than diminished. There were, as we have seen,* political, economic and religious reasons for this. The Jews, defeated, impoverished, bled white, most of them small farmers, suspected the Gentile merchants of taking advantage of them. Life was harder for the Jews now, the weaker part of the population, since Rome continued to work hand in hand with the Gentiles. That too, was cause for loss of Jewish population. It was perhaps too much to expect the Gentiles to realize that the emigration of the Jews would soon reduce the entire country to economic impotence.

2. THE TRIUMPH OF CHRISTIANITY

The Parting of the Ways—The antagonism between Jew and Gentile showed its worst results after many of the pagans of Palestine had adopted the Christian religion. This change of religion happened slowly. The first followers of Jesus,

---

* See above, pp. 139–42, 153.

themselves pious Jews, were as horrified as were the Jews by
Saul's (Paul's) arguments against Jewish ceremonies. There
were, therefore, two kinds of believers in Jesus: those who
continued to look upon themselves as members of the Jewish
people, and those who would have nothing to do with the
Jews. Before long, the second kind, who preferred to call
themselves Christians, became very much more numerous
than the first kind. For the most part of Gentile origin, these
Christians took over with them into Christianity many of the
antagonisms which had characterized them as pagans. They
certainly had no interest in the continuance of the Jewish
group, whether as a nation or a religion.

Until the Bar Kochba revolt, 132–135, the difference between Judaism and Christianity was not clear even to most
Jews. The Roman government, the pagans and many Jews
looked upon Christianity as a heretical sect in Judaism. The
Jewish Christians, who like Jesus and his immediate disciples
believed in the need for following Jewish traditions, used to
attend the synagogues and participate in Jewish life. But during the revolt it became clear to the Jews that neither Jewish
Christians nor Gentile Christians wanted the Jews to win. On
the contrary, the Christians were rather anxious to have the
Jews defeated since the latter looked upon Bar Kochba as a
messiah, and his victory would destroy many Christian claims
for Jesus. Some Christians were active against the Jews. As a
result the Jews adopted regulations which successfully excluded all Christians from the synagogues and from Jewish
life in general. For example, the Jews included in their *Ami-
dah* (the Eighteen Benedictions) a prayer asking for the disappearance of sectarians. Thereafter, there was no more hope
of reconciliation. For several centuries the Jewish Christians
lingered as a separate sect in the East; then they disappeared
completely. Judaism had given birth to a new religion; and
the daughter was turning against the mother.

The Victory of the Church—Not only did the Christians
fail to help the Jews in their struggles to maintain themselves
in Palestine, they even denied the right of the Jewish people
to continue to exist. They claimed the Jewish holy books for
themselves, with the addition, of course, of the books which
described the life of Jesus and the first Christians. They asserted that the Jews did not understand their own Bible. Furthermore, the Christians said that God had abandoned the
Jews, and that they, the Christians, were the true Israel, the
people whom God had chosen.

The Jews naturally resented all such claims and tried to

keep Christianity from growing. They did not yet give up the hope that the pagans would choose Judaism instead of Christianity. But the Christians were much more active in proselytizing, and they kept on gaining adherents. The persecutions which they occasionally had to suffer from the Roman government did not stop them. In fact, the social and economic conditions prevailing in the Roman empire helped the spread of Christianity. Roman society was divided into a small number of wealthy aristocrats and a great majority of poor people who could look forward to nothing during their life on earth. A shining vision of life beyond the grave held out to them comfort, hope and satisfaction. Christianity emphasized such a life after death; it also stressed the old Jewish ideals of human brotherhood and charity and thus made the strongest possible appeal to the downtrodden and oppressed.

By the year 300 there were so many Christians in the Roman empire that Emperor Constantine found it to his advantage soon thereafter to declare Christianity the official religion. Now the Christians had the upper hand. Unfortunately the more ambitious and politically-minded among their leaders began to do everything possible to bring about the humiliation, if not the destruction, of their Jewish rivals. They knew only too well that Judaism still retained powers of attraction and they therefore persuaded the emperors to enact and enforce a number of anti-Jewish laws. Jews dared no longer carry on missionary work; they were forbidden to convert to Judaism even their pagan slaves, and they could not own a Christian slave. Churchmen discouraged social contacts between Jews and Christians and completely forbade intermarriage between members of the two religions; for they knew that in those days, more often than not, the non-Jewish party to a marriage soon became Jewish. Some churchmen called Jews and Judaism by the vilest names in order to keep Jews and non-Jews apart. Thus further obstacles were added to the continuance of Jewish life in Palestine.

3. AN UNFINISHED BOOK

The Palestinian Academies—Throughout this period, despite war and other misfortunes, the Jews of Palestine kept up their studies. The completion of the Mishna by Judah the Prince served as a further incentive for discussing and applying the laws and customs of Jewish life. More teachers arose, and more students came to their academies. Every town had its school for children. One teacher expressed the view which all the Jews entertained on the subject of education, when he said: "The world is sustained on the breath of the children who study in the elementary schools." No adult was considered worthy unless he spent some time in study. It was Judah's Mishna which now became a sort of textbook, every sentence of which gave rise to discussion.

A Saint and an Ex-Highwayman—Of the many teachers (*Amoraim*) who lived and taught in Palestine during the century and a half after the death of Judah the Prince, none was more important than Rabbi Johanan bar Nappaha, who gained a reputation for purity of life and kindliness. Johanan was the son of a blacksmith, which indicates that he started life as a very poor man. But he became a great scholar and had thousands of pupils. Among these was one who in his youth had been a gladiator and highwayman. This was Simeon the son of Lakish who, persuaded by Johanan, gave up his sinful occupation and began to study. In time Simeon became Johanan's brother-in-law and his most helpful colleague. The two are usually mentioned together because between them they kept alive the tradition of learning in the dying Jewish community of the Holy Land.

The Palestinian Talmud—By the time another generation of students grew to maturity in the academies of Palestine, it was clear that the torch of learning was not destined to burn there much longer. Neither in quality nor in quantity did the scholars of Palestine at all compare with their predecessors or with those who, at that very time, were studying and teaching in Babylonia. This was dangerous not only for the future of Palestinian learning, but even for its past. All that had been achieved by generations of great men was likely to be lost, completely forgotten. That is why the schools spent their time, during the greater part of the fourth century, in reviewing what had been discussed by the teachers who had preceded them. Each treatise of the Mishna was taken up separately, and the important statements and discussions about it noted, whether these discussions were of an ethical or a legal nature. The collection of these discussions and elaborations of the Mishna was called *Gemara*, while the Mishna and Gemara combined are called *Talmud*. To distinguish the resultant work from a similar one in Babylonia a century and a half later, this one is called the *Palestinian Talmud*, or the *Jerusalem Talmud*, though of course the city of Jerusalem was not the place where the academies worked.

An Uncompleted Task—The scholars of Palestine never

really completed the collection of the opinions and discussions which they had set out to compile. After the year 350, when the effects of all the difficulties previously described showed themselves most clearly, there was not enough intellectual energy for so important an undertaking. Consequently the Palestinian Talmud was never quite finished. It has remained difficult to understand, and never gained the popularity which has always been-enjoyed by the Talmud produced later on in Babylonia. Only the more learned among the Jews have been interested in it.

4. THE TEMPLE AND A ROMAN EMPEROR

A Glimmer of Hope—Quite unexpectedly, in the midst of all the troubles besetting the Jews of Palestine and of the Roman empire, hope of a brighter future was held out to them by an emperor of Rome himself. In 361 Julian became the sole ruler of the empire, and he at once tried to change the religious policy of his predecessors of the previous half century. He was bitterly opposed to Christianity, and among the Christians he is known to this day as Julian the Apostate, that is, "the one who abandoned the true religion." As part of his policy of restoring the religious situation that existed before the year 325, Julian wrote the Jews a friendly letter, promising to remove many of the laws passed against Judaism and, much to everyone's surprise, also to rebuild the Temple in Jerusalem.

Disappointment—No doubt the Jews looked upon all this as a stroke of good fortune and as a promise of even better days to come. According to one report, made by a Christian of the next generation, the Jews actually started to rebuild the Temple, but an explosion and fire destroyed everything before the work was much advanced. This the Christians interpreted as proof of God's opposition to both Julian and the Jews. The Jews of that time left no such story behind, so that we know nothing at all about the actual rebuilding, or even whether it was ever begun. In any event, what destroyed any prospect of a rebuilt Temple was not miraculous fire, but rather the fact that Julian lived for only about two years after becoming emperor. With his death on the field of battle vanished any chance for a revival of Jewish Palestine.

5. The Last Patriarchs

Faded Glory—Looking back at the history of the Patriarchate, one can see that its decline began after the death (219) of Judah the Prince. The *Bet Din* lost much of its influence, while the powers of the Patriarch increased. But although Judah's descendants had more political influence, they did not have his learning and ability. Unfortunately, too, they acquired all the faults of aristocrats. They looked down upon the people; they did not associate intimately with the scholars; they led the life of princes in the midst of the poverty of the Palestinian Jewish population. They did not realize that their importance rested upon their usefulness in encouraging learning and the maintenance of Jewish customs and traditions. On their part, the Jews of Palestine began to look upon the Patriarch as a tax-gatherer and merely a social ornament.

Powers of the Patriarch—Despite their criticism the Jews were happy that such an institution existed; for the Patriarch was a living sign of the continued life of the Jewish people. On the other hand, despite his interest in his social position, every Patriarch continued to perform useful tasks for the Jews. He represented their interests before the Roman government, and occasionally used his influence to make things easier for Jews outside of Palestine also. He appointed officials in the Jewish communities in Palestine, and frequently was asked to ratify elections and make appointments elsewhere in the Roman empire. He saw that the judges were competent and that markets were properly conducted. In a word, the Patriarch headed the Jewish government wherever the Romans gave the Jews a chance to conduct their own affairs. Moreover, one of his most important functions was to fix the calendar, a matter of vital interest to the Jews everywhere, but of no concern to the Romans.

The Patriarch and the Calendar—In the days of the Temple the calendar used to be announced by the Sanhedrin. Later it was announced by the Patriarch and the *Bet Din*. The people did not have access to chronometric tables by which they could calculate seasons and dates; they were guided by these official announcements which the Patriarch would transmit through emissaries dispatched to every part of the Diaspora. There were, however, a considerable number of Christians who also waited for the Patriarch's calendrical information. For a great many Christians still observed the holidays common to Judaism and Christianity, especially Passover (Easter), at the same time as the Jews, just as many of them observed the Jewish Sabbath rather than the Christian Sunday. This dependence on Judaism irked the Christian clergy, and about the middle of the fourth century they prevailed upon the Roman government to forbid the Patriarch to send emissaries with such information. To avoid having Jewish life sink into chaos, the Patriarch of that day made public the rules governing the Jewish calendar. From then on any mathematically-minded man in every diaspora community could and did arrange the years, months and holidays according to a fixed formula.

The Last Patriarch—The family of Hillel long continued as Patriarchs to rule over the Jewish people; generation after generation, the Patriarch at his death was succeeded by his son. Unfortunately, when Gamaliel VI died, in 425, he left no son to succeed him. No doubt there were relatives, one of whom should have been chosen. But which one? The choice, it seems, had to be made by the Roman government. There was delay; and in the meantime some Christian bishops prevailed upon the emperor to discontinue the Patriarchate altogether. In 429, the Roman government announced the abolition of the office.

Achievements of the Patriarchate—In this way was ended an institution which had existed for about three and a half centuries and which had done much for the survival of the Jewish people. Immediately after the defeat by Rome in the year 70, when Jewish prospects were very dim, the Patriarchate had served unofficially as a rallying point for Jewish hopes. When Jewish laws had to be codified, it was one of the Patriarchs, Judah the Prince, who produced the best code. When dark days came upon the Jews of Palestine, and its population emigrated in large numbers, the Patriarchs kept alive the dignity of the homeland and its position as the center of Jewish life. Through those long centuries when Jewish life was being organized elsewhere, the Patriarch in Palestine kept Jewish thoughts and hearts united about himself. By the time there was no longer any Patriarch, other ways had developed to maintain Jewish unity intact.

6. The Legacy of Palestine

Farewell to Canaan—Up to this point the Land of Israel and the Jews who lived in it have held the center of the stage in the drama of the Jewish people. From now on other lands and other Jewish communities are going to come to the fore. The children of Israel, after having lived in that land for over fifteen hundred years, had for the most part gone to seek other homes and friendlier neighbors. Not that there were no more Jews within the boundaries of Palestine, and not that Palestine was no longer destined to produce ideas and spiritual treasures for the Jewish people; but the Jewish community was so small, and the conditions under which it lived so bad, that it was no longer able to lead. The leadership which it relinquished was at once taken up by another, stronger, more happily situated Jewish community. Before turning to that community, it is well to sum up what Palestine had done for the Jewish people till this point in Jewish history.

Religion—First and foremost, Judaism had developed in Palestine and had been carried out of it to ennoble the life and direct the activity of Jews all over the world, and, incidentally, also of non-Jews. Its location, in the heart of the ancient world, was favorable to the development of the idea of One God, the Creator of all humanity, the One Ruler of all the world. This idea was deepened and spread by the prophets, almost all of whom had lived and preached in Palestine. It finally took hold of the mind of the people who, under the guidance of scribes and rabbis, developed a manner of life which other nations came to admire and finally imitate in a modified form.

Laws—The laws and customs of the Jews which developed during their life in Palestine are really part of Judaism, but they have been so important that it is worth while to list them as a separate legacy of Palestinian life. In the end they were all summarized in the Mishna which became the subject of study for the Jews outside of Palestine, where the laws were modified to fit diaspora life. Within Palestine the study of the Mishna resulted in the Palestinian Talmud.

Literature—During the fifteen hundred years of Jewish life in Palestine there was never a generation which did not produce important books. As a result of this great and constant literary creation, not only the Jew, but all humanity possesses the Bible, the books included in the Apocrypha, great poetry, novels, dramas and visionary writings, as well as a rich heritage of marvelous legends and tales which have served to inspire and entertain Jews and Gentiles alike.

Unity—Palestine also bequeathed to the Jews a sense of unity, of common purpose, without which the Jewish group would never have been able to survive. It had accustomed the people to think of themselves as one body devoted to the service of their way of life. Kings, Temple, and Patriarchs successively kept the hearts of the Jews bound together.

Palestine as a Memory—Palestine kept the Jews united long after it had stopped being the home of the most important community of Jews. It did this by means of the affection which the Jews forever cherished for the land of their fathers. The glories of the past, the spiritual achievements of prophets, scribes, Maccabees, rabbis, all combined to stir the imagination of the Jews in the subsequent, darker periods of Jewish history. The era of Jewish control of Palestine has since then stood out as the most spiritually creative period of the people's history.

Palestine as a Hope—No Jew has ever thought of the end of that era without a pang of regret. No wonder, therefore, that there has always been an ardent hope for the re-establishment of Palestine as the homeland of the Jewish people. How such a return was to be achieved was never quite clear. The Jews of one generation might use practical means, while those of another might simply pray for a return through the miraculous intervention of God. But the hope was always there, connected with other hopes for peace and justice, for quiet labor and spiritual achievement, not alone for the Jews but for all mankind.

CHAPTER III

THE BABYLONIAN COMMUNITY

THE ANCIENT LAND OF BABYLONIA BECOMES THE CENTER
OF JEWISH LIFE AT THE VERY TIME THAT PALESTINE IS
DECLINING

Changing Centers of Life—One of the most remarkable facts in the history of the Jews is that they have never been without a central leadership. No sooner was one important Jewish community destroyed or fallen into decay, than another came into being. Even before the one center realized that it was destined to give up the leadership of the scattered Jewish people, the next was developing the ability to resume where the former was leaving off. At the point of the story which we have now reached, such a transfer of leadership took place from Palestine to Babylonia.

By the time Rome succeeded in driving the Jewish community of Palestine into poverty, ineffectiveness and obscurity, the Jewish community in Babylonia had awakened from a slumber of centuries and was ready to carry on. Safe in this land to the east of Palestine, the Jews established schools and led an active intellectual life, continuing the traditions of Judaism begun and developed in Palestine. Jewish life in the twentieth century and its problems cannot be properly understood without knowing about the work of the Amoraim and Geonim, or the meaning of such terms as Talmud and Responsa, which are connected with the life of the Jews in Babylonia more than a thousand years ago.

1. A COMMUNITY IN RESERVE

Mental Slumber and Physical Vigor—The Jews of Babylonia had little to complain of. The various governments treated them well and rarely interfered with their religious life. But this religious life depended for its inspiration upon Palestine. Until the time of Ezra, Babylonian Jews had been more progressive than the Palestinian ones; but after Ezra's time, Palestinian intellectual and religious activity far outstripped similar activity among the Jews who remained in Babylonia. It seems as though, after making a number of steps forward in the development of Judaism, the Babylonian community became tired and sat back to let Palestine do the rest. But the Babylonian Jews were very helpful to the Jews of Palestine during times of crisis. Their dislike of Rome was as great as that of the Palestinian Jews themselves. On several occasions they looked forward with anticipation to the possibility of Parthia's victory over Rome and the eventual incorporation of Palestine into the Parthian empire. Failing that, they received with hospitality the refugees from Palestine whenever Roman persecution or general bad times drove people out of the Holy Land. The downfall of the Hasmoneans, the defeat of the year 70, the failure of Bar Kochba, were three occasions when the Babylonian Jewish population received a large influx of Palestinian refugees. But during the intervening periods, too, a steady stream of Palestinians flowed toward Babylonia, as it did toward other diaspora lands throughout the later centuries of Palestine's history.

To Palestine for an Education—The Babylonian Jews, like their coreligionists everywhere, were always interested in study and established schools. Their intellectual activity, however, was not as profound nor as intensive as in Palestine. When a man showed an unusual desire to continue his studies, he would go to Palestine, and sometimes would remain there. This is what happened to the famous Hillel, who was born in Babylonia around the year 75 B. C. E., but who went to Palestine to complete his education and stayed there to become the head of the Sanhedrin. His example was followed by any number of others, some of whom must have returned to their birthplace and eventually raised the cultural level of the Babylonian population. The most outstanding example of this latter type was Abba Arika, or, to use the name by which he is better known, Rav.

2. Some Passing Difficulties

Changing Dynasties and Pagan Priests—The peaceful life of the Jews of Babylonia was interrupted in the third century of the Common Era by two tragedies. In 226, a few years after Rav's return to his native country, a brief civil war occurred as a result of which one dynasty gave place to another. It was bad enough for the Jews that the friendly ruling house of the Parthians was displaced, but even worse was the fact that the Persian kings, who ascended the throne, were allied with the fire-worshipping priests of the Zoroastrian religion. Extremely fanatical, they began a systematic persecution of anyone who differed from them. The Jews followed a number of religious customs which the Zorastrian priests considered objectionable, for example, the lighting of candles in celebration of Sabbaths and holidays, the ritual slaughter of clean animals, the burial of the dead, and the like.

Had this persecution continued indefinitely, Jewish life in Babylonia would have been destroyed. Fortunately, the second king of the new Persian dynasty did not have to depend upon the priests to the same extent as his father, so that he curbed their activity against the non-Zoroastrian population. By about the year 260, after more than twenty-five years of hardship, Jewish life began to return to normal. There are scholars who believe that this difficult period helped Judaism, since it turned the minds of many Jews to a deeper study of their religion, and thus aided in the establishment of schools and the spread of learning.

Roman Invasion—No sooner was the religious persecution beginning to abate, than another misfortune befell the Jews living in Babylonia. The periodic warfare between Rome and the Persian empire broke out anew in 258. Just when it looked as though Rome might be defeated, it received aid from the newly-founded kingdom of Palmyra. The Persians were driven back, and the Palmyrans invaded Babylonia, which lay nearest to them. Many Jewish settlements were destroyed, particularly the city of Nehardea where the oldest and most famous Jewish academy had been located.* These wounds, too, were soon healed, although the academy at Nehardea was never restored. Instead an academy was founded in near-by Pumpeditha which was destined to become famous in Jewish history as the great rival of the equally famous academy at Sura.

3. HOW THE JEWS GOVERNED THEMSELVES

Descendants of David—One of the most interesting institu-

* For a description of the academies, see below, pp. 218–20.

tions of Jewish life in Babylonia was that which came to be known as the Exilarchate. The word *Exilarch* means "Head of the Exile," and is a translation of the Aramaic term *Resh Galuta* used by the Jews. The mere existence of a head for the Jewish people indicates that the Parthian government and its successor, the Persian, recognized the Jews as a separate group, with problems of its own and with need for a distinct organization. What makes the Exilarch even more interesting is the fact that he was a descendant of the ancient ruling dynasty of Judea, the House of David. The four closing sentences of the Second Book of Kings in the Bible speak of the last king but one of Judea who was eventually pardoned by his captor, the king of Babylonia, and given high rank in the Babylonian court. Very likely his descendants continued to hold this rank also under the subsequent rulers of the land. The Jews naturally looked up to them with respect, and some time during the period when Babylonian Jewry was hidden from sight, the Parthian government made these descendants of David official heads of the Jews. No ruling house in the world continued uninterruptedly for so long to hand authority down from father to son. Considering that the Exilarchate lasted beyond the year 1000 C. E., the House of David can be said to have exercised authority for more than two thousand years.

Powers and Duties—When we first hear of the Exilarch, about the year 200 C. E., we find him possessed of certain powers and duties. His influence derived from the fact that the Jews of Babylonia enjoyed the right to rule themselves in accordance with Jewish law, in other words, they possessed autonomy. The Exilarch appointed judges and was himself the final court of appeal. In his name punishment was inflicted upon condemned Jews who might be made to suffer imprisonment, stripes or excommunication from the Jewish community. He also collected the taxes from the Jews of the entire country, and turned over a portion of this money to the supreme authorities of the land. Since there were certain cities in the Persian empire in which the Jews formed the largest portion of the population, these cities were to all intents under the direct and complete government of the Exilarch and his officers, even to the extent of supervising their markets and guarding the walls which surrounded them. Clearly the Exilarch was an important and influential personage.

Community Life—Theoretically every official, in every Jewish community of Babylonia, was appointed by the Exilarch; practically, however, he did no more in many instances than ratify the men chosen by the community itself. Each community had its head who, with his seven advisers, formed the Community Council. They, divided into a number of committees, supervised the usual civic activities such as charity collection and distribution, the synagogue and other communal property, and the schools which every city was expected to have. They also appointed the officers of the city to maintain order and check weights and measures. Thus every Jewish community was practically an independent municipality.

Communal Property—Every Jewish community was compelled by its very nature to possess certain property. For example, there had to be a synagogue building and, in many instances, a separate administration building. There also had to be a *mikvah,* or ritual bath. Moreover, a cemetery had to be established. Finally, the larger cities, those which enjoyed the presence of a talmudical academy (*yeshiba*), must have had a *Bet Midrash* ("House of Study") in addition to the synagogue.

4. How the Babylonian Jews Earned Their Livelihood

Farming—The most important occupation of the Babylonian Jews was farming. Nowadays that part of the world (Iraq) is a considered poor agriculturally; its soil yields little. But in ancient times it was highly productive. This difference is easily explained. The ancient Babylonians took advantage of the proximity of the two rivers to crisscross their land with irrigation canals.* The dryness of the climate was in this way overcome, so that the Babylonian farmer needed rain as little as did the Egyptian, whose river Nile overflowed its banks. These canals were very carefully tended by the farmer under government supervision. Farmers from their Palestine days, the Jews naturally became farmers in Babylonia as well. A few of them had large tracts of agricultural land which they parcelled out among others who leased smaller farms or rented them, paying with an agreed share of the produce. A large number possessed small farms of their own. Still others were merely farmhands who worked for a daily wage. The Talmud, that great literary achievement of Babylonian Jewry, is full of references to the life of the farmer; it also contains

* For the Tigris and Euphrates rivers see the map on p. 208.

laws regulating the wages, leases and other matters in which
an agricultural population would be naturally interested.

Cattle-Raising and Winegrowing—The raising of cattle was
another important occupation among those Jews, though it
was not considered as respectable as farming. For some reason it was looked down upon, and shepherds were held in
low esteem. Still another occupation was the growing of
products from which wine could be made. This included not
only grapes, but also dates from which a mildly intoxicating
liquid could be pressed.

Commerce—There were always some Jews who engaged in
business, and as time went on their numbers increased. For
the most part this commerce was local. The same canals
which were used for irrigation purposes were also used to
transport goods to various parts of Babylonia, for the two
rivers were thus connected. This, in turn, developed a shipping industry as well as a group of Jewish boatmen. Wine,
fruit and grain moved up and down the rivers, and were then
taken for export to foreign lands. Despite the repeated wars
with Rome, there was a constant interchange of goods between the Roman and the Persian empires. Undoubtedly
there were Jewish merchants who dealt with the lands farther
east. Silk was imported from China, and various other articles of luxury from India. Babylonian Jewry thus in a sense
served as a bridge between Europe and the Far East.

Manual Labor—In the cities another important class of
Jews were those who hired themselves out by the day or the
week. Masons, carpenters, tailors, potters, weavers, the entire
gamut of manual workers thronged the towns. Early in the
morning those who had no shop of their own might be seen
gathered in the market place, waiting for an employer to
come and hire them. Here again, a great variety of laws in
the Talmud testify to the interest which the rabbis of that day
took in regulating the relations between employer and em-
ployee.

5. How the Babylonian Jews Lived

The Number of Jews in Babylonia—It is a great pity that
the Jews of that day, like other people, did not keep records
of their population. Only a rough guess is possible, based
upon the manner of life and the numbers mentioned here and
there in the Talmud. One may estimate that about the year
70 C. E. the Jews of Babylonia numbered around a million.
They continued to increase both naturally within Babylonia and

by immigration from Palestine, so that between the years 200 and 500 they may have reached the two million mark. Thereafter the Jewish population began to decline, for reasons which will be discussed later.

Rich and Poor—The statement that this period was a comparatively happy one for the Jews of Babylonia must not leave the impression that all the Jews at that time were rich, or even well-to-do. All it means is that they were permitted to earn their livelihood undisturbed, and that there was little destitution among them. But there were some whose income from land, from the brewing of liquors and from commerce set them apart and enabled them to live more comfortably. The city of Mahoza, for example, during the fourth and fifth centuries, became noted for the number of wealthy people who lived in what for those days were considered palatial homes.

Life at Home—But one must not get exaggerated notions; even these "palaces" were probably less comfortable than ordinary homes nowadays. They had a number of rooms for sleeping quarters; they had a reception-hall, and a porch. A small garden near the house helped the inhabitants to endure the discomfort of the warm climate. Yet all this was infinitely more comfortable than the way the vast majority of the population lived. Theirs were small houses made of soft brick. It was unusual for them to have more than two rooms, and, if there was a second story, it could be reached only by means of a ladder from the street. In the famous city of Sura, most of the streets were narrow and not especially clean. Consequently life was crowded and uncomfortable. Articles of furniture were few. As to the food, among the poorer people it consisted of bread, vegetables and fruit. It is especially interesting to find that raw meat was considered a delicacy, for they did not have meat very often. Clearly such living conditions are far below the standard of the average person in our own day, but this manner of living was quite the usual one in those days among non-Jews, too.

The Family—From the earliest times the family was considered a sacred Jewish institution. The ties between husband and wife, parent and child, were highly treasured. Few things were considered as important as peace within the home. That is one reason why the Jews practiced monogamy, in spite of the fact that the Bible permits a man to have more than one wife, and in spite of the fact that the Gentile Babylonians frequently had more than one wife. There were cases of Jews practicing polygamy; but such cases were rare. Because of the insistence upon a quiet, dignified family life, great care was exercised in the selection of a husband or a wife for one's son or daughter. For it was the parents who usually did the choosing in the first place, though among the Jews it was considered proper for the young man or woman to have the final word. One of the chief requirements in the choice of a mate for one's child was that the family standing of the proposed in-laws should not be much lower than one's own. A man who insisted upon marrying too far beneath his social standing could be publicly cut off from his family. Young people married early; the usual age for a boy was eighteen and for a girl even younger. Children were considered a blessing, and a childless marriage could be dissolved. The community held the parents responsible not only for the education of the child, but also for its preparation for life, that is, for earning a living.

Slaves—In the wealthier homes there was still another member of the family, the slave. Jewish slaves among Jews were comparatively rare, and where any such existed they had to be treated in accordance with biblical law and released after the sixth year. Moreover, Jews considered it their duty to redeem fellow Jews from slavery among Gentiles. But non-Jewish slaves among Jews were not uncommon. In such cases, however, the slave frequently became partly Jewish, that is, a certain number of Jewish laws and customs had to be observed by him. In the end, many of these were freed and were eventually absorbed by the Jewish people. But as long as they were within a family, they were treated as members of the family, so that their lot was far from hard.

6. RELIGIOUS LIFE

Prayer and Observances—Following the traditions of the Pharisees, the Jews of Babylonia adopted the principle that Judaism must influence every aspect of life. The synagogue was the tallest and handsomest building in a Jewish community. Prayers and benedictions accompanied every act. The Bible, as interpreted by the rabbis, and the Mishna were the standard works for the guidance of life. This had not always been the case. When Rav first returned from his studies in Palestine (around 220) and undertook a journey through the Jewish settlements in Babylonia, he was shocked at the ignorance of the Jews about matters of Jewish observance. He decided there and then to establish himself in the midst of this ignorant population, open a school, and instruct the people in proper Jewish living. He succeeded so well that within a generation that part of Jewish Babylonia became the model for the rest of the country.

Education—Always important in the life of the Jews, education made rapid strides forward during the three centuries after the return of Rav from Palestine. The biblical law, "Thou shalt teach them to thy children," seemed to leave elementary education in the hands of the father of the family. The result was that where the father did not know much, the child would know even less. Rav bent his energies to raising the standards of education among the adults. He brought to Babylonia the idea which had long been current in Palestine, that an ignoramus was to be despised. As soon as that idea took root, young and old became interested in acquiring knowledge, for a man's social standing became dependent not so much upon family and wealth as upon cultural achievements. Before long, there was hardly a Jewish community, no matter how small, which did not consider the education of its children a matter of the highest importance. No idea became more characteristic of Jewish life than that study is a religious duty. What is still more remarkable is that in the matter of study there were no distinctions between rich and poor; all studied the same material with the same zeal. In fact, one of the famous talmudic sayings has it "Watch over the children of the poor, for out of them will knowledge come forth." The Jewish people became a cultural democracy.

Law and Life—The ultimate aim of education was not merely to acquire information, but what was more important, to establish good habits of life. They studied the laws which regulated man's relations to God, and also those which guided man's relations to his fellow man. Philanthropy and business, wages and the rules of common politeness, morality and ethics were as much part of their religious studies as were synagogue regulations and the rules of penitence for sins committed. The attitudes towards one another were as much a subject for discussion as the observance of the Sabbath. There was no difference in their attitude towards Law, Ethics and Morals; all were part of Religion.

For this reason the literary work, the Talmud, which these Jews left behind as a great spiritual heritage for us to study, is of the greatest interest and importance.

CHAPTER IV

THE SEA OF LEARNING

THE BABYLONIAN SCHOLARS STUDY AND TEACH AND DE-
BATE, FINALLY PRODUCING AN ENCYCLOPEDIA OF JEWISH
KNOWLEDGE WHICH IS CALLED THE TALMUD

The Story of Another Book—Literature is of great importance to a social group. For good literature not only reflects
the way of life which exists, it also stimulates and helps to
create new ways of living and modes of thinking in accordance
with the group's highest ideals. To the Jews, literature has
been, in addition, a matter of life or death. Their literature,
and the strength of mind and character which it developed,
enabled the Jewish people to survive through all the difficult
days of their long history.

No book, next to the Bible, played so important a role as
that book, or series of books, known by the name of "Talmud." Consequently, no Jewish history can be complete without discussion of the manner in which this voluminous work
came into being. We have already discussed how the Palestinian Talmud grew out of study in Palestinian academies; now
we turn to the story of the more important similar work
which was produced by the scholars of Babylonia.

1. BABYLONIA, HEIR TO PALESTINE

Another Link in the Chain—When Judah the Prince refused to permit ordination (*Semichah*) outside of Palestine,
his object, as we have seen, was to keep the Chain of Tradition connected with the Holy Land. Because, from Moses
through the Tannaim until his day, Jewish learning and authority had originated in Palestine, Judah and all the Jews
thought that this should and would continue throughout the
indefinite future. To some extent this belief was justified.
Even though they did not possess regular ordination, the fact

that ultimately the learning of later teachers could be traced back to the Tannaim made the Jews look upon their teaching as possessing great authority. Now the link which connected these later teachers with the Tannaim was the man whom we have already met, Abba Arika, or Rav, who had been a pupil of Judah the Prince. The teachers of Babylonia, who came to be known as *Amoraim,** continued the traditions of Rav and in turn transmitted their learning to European scholars. In this way, modern rabbis may consider themselves links in the Chain of Tradition.

Rav and His Memories—The first and foremost Babylonian Amora was Rav. Upon his return to his native Babylonia, he brought with him the learning he had acquired in Palestine, a thorough knowledge of the Mishna, a wide acquaintance with that imaginative interpretation of the Jewish past which was called *Agada,* and a deep, sincere piety. Characteristically, he preferred to go out among the common people whom he hoped to teach and from among whom he hoped to raise a generation of Jews as informed in the traditions of Judaism as were the Jews of Palestine. He settled in Sura and there opened a modest school. Before long, young and old were attracted by his charm and his learning. He preached to them; he taught them; he inspired them. The times were rather difficult, for this was the period when the newly-established Persian dynasty, allied to the Zoroastrian priests, persecuted the Jews. Rav sustained the courage of the people. He also prepared inspiring new prayers for them, some of which are still used in synagogues to this day: the one beginning with the words *'Alenu le-shabeah* which is recited at the end of every service and in which, with beautiful simplicity, God's reign is invoked over all the world; and the prayer recited on Sabbath morning preceding the appearance of the new moon, which describes the kind of life one would like to be blessed with during the coming weeks. These prayers illustrate the spiritual impulse which Rav gave to the Jews of Babylonia.

Samuel of Nehardea—An academy already existed, in Nehardea, at the time of Rav's return from Palestine. How long it had been in existence is not known, but its most famous scholar at the time of Rav was Samuel. He was a distinguished man, justly proud of his knowledge of medicine, astronomy and law. He admired Rav, and Rav admired him.

---

* The teachers in Palestine in the post-Mishna period are also called Amoraim. See above, p. 201.

When the head of the academy of Nehardea died, Rav was offered the position, and he refused it in favor of Samuel. Thus, these two illustrious men stood at the head of two influential schools. Rav was an expert in religious law, Samuel in civil law. One rule of Jewish life was established by Samuel which turned out to be of the utmost importance to the Jews in subsequent ages when they lived scattered among many nations. Briefly stated this principle was: "The law of the land is law." This has come to mean that the civil laws of the countries where Jews live must be obeyed even though they may conflict with the laws by which they would have guided themselves if they had been independent. Of course, this principle did not refer to religious laws; it helped enormously, however, to make Jewish life more adaptable to diaspora environments.

The Academy at Pumpeditha—The war which broke out between Persia and Rome around the year 260 caused the destruction of Nehardea. The academy which had existed there never revived. Its activity was transferred to a neighboring town, Pumpeditha. Thereafter the academy of Pumpeditha supplemented the work of that at Sura. The organization of both was the same; both taught the same subject matter. Sometimes the one, sometimes the other was the head and center of Jewish life.

2. How the Academies Did Their Work

Head of the Academy—At the head of each academy stood a famous scholar, the successor respectively of Rav and Samuel. He was called *Rosh ha-Yeshiba*, which means, literally, "Head of the Academy." He was selected for this office by the more prominent scholars of the academy, but the selection had to be ratified by the Exilarch. The duties of the head were to lead the discussion and preside over the debate which followed. Many famous men held this position; some famous for their vast amount of knowledge, others for their ability to analyze a point and present an argument. It speaks well for the love of learning on the part of the Babylonian Jewish population that the students of one academy did not hesitate to move over to the other when its head was the greater scholar.

The Students—Anybody could be a student at the academy; there were no requirements for admission, no tests, no system of promotions except after one had reached the rank of a recognized scholar and possessed the necessary moral requirements. Anyone who could follow the discussion was welcome to stay, and anyone who could not follow soon became discouraged of his own accord. Now, in order to follow the discussion the student had to know the fundamental subjects, that is, the Bible, the Mishna and most important statements on Jewish law by previous teachers. In other words, no one could really profit from the work at the academy unless he had had an elementary education in one of the many schools found in every Jewish settlement of any size, and which were under the supervision of the local Jewish community. Nor was there any limit set on the age of the student at the academy. A man might be a student all his life if he could afford it.

There were no classes in the academy. All the pupils, old and young, met together in one lecture-hall and listened to the same lecture. The more prominent scholars sat closest to the dais from which the head conducted the debate, and they took the leading part in it. Some of the students may have taken notes. All the studying, however, was based on memory. It is astonishing how much these students remembered. One explanation is that even after leaving the lecture-hall, they continued the discussion, so that the subject matter stuck in their minds. All this, it must be recalled, was considered the study of the Oral Law, so that no textbooks existed, with the possible exception of the Mishna which every student was expected to know by heart.

Subject Matter—The Mishna was the beginning and the basis of every discussion, but it was not the only subject matter. The head of the academy would begin his lecture with a quotation from the Mishna, but then he would add to it the opinions of other Tannaim and Amoraim which either agreed with or differed from the mishnaic statement. This would be followed by various attempts to apply the law under discussion to any number of situations which might arise in the daily life of the Jews in Babylonia, whether in the home, the field or the workshop. As time went on, this subject matter increased in volume, since each generation added its own opinions for the next one to remember. It stands to reason that the scholars did not always agree about the interpretation of the original mishnaic statement or about the manner in which the law should be applied. It is these differences of opinion that led to the long discussions in the academies.

There was also a lighter side to the work of the academies. Every once in a while the seriousness of the discussions was interrupted by a story which someone told to illustrate a point, or by a moral maxim usually, though not necessarily, derived from the life of the Jews. Frequently interpretations of biblical verses or stories were presented which appealed to the imagination and which helped to glorify the past of the Jewish people and keep alive their hopes. These stories, parables and maxims had little to do with the study of the law, but the Jewish student was interested in such material which, at the same time, we call history and ethics.

Kallah Months—One of the most interesting phases of the work of the Babylonian academies was the popular education carried on during two months of the year. In Ellul, the month preceding Rosh Hashanah, and in Adar, the month preceding Passover, workers and farmers streamed to the academies. On one occasion they numbered as many as twelve thousand. Apparently these people, occupied throughout the rest of the year, gave up these two months to concentrated study under the direction of famous scholars. Thus they became familiar with the latest decisions in Jewish law and with the latest interpretations of Jewish life. In this way, the results of the study carried on by the Amoraim became widespread among the general population. In this way, too, the entire Jewish community of the land became united in heart, thought and observance. Such a gathering was called *Kalla.*

3. THE TALMUD BECOMES A BOOK

Gathering the Fruit—Studying of the kind just described went on without much change for a century and a half after Rav established the academy of Sura. Around the year 400, however, it was realized that a change was necessary. The difficulty was that so many discussions of importance had taken place, so many good ideas had been expressed, that confusion was bound to result unless it could be decided what was to be remembered and what forgotten. It was found undesirable to trust the memory or judgment of any one scholar. Here was a situation very much like the one which had prompted Judah the Prince to compile the Mishna so as to organize the discussions of the preceding centuries. For generations the tree of Jewish knowledge had been growing luxuriantly; the time had come for a discriminating scholar to harvest its fruit.

Rav Ashi's Great Undertaking—Such a scholar was Rav Ashi. He became the head of the academy at Sura toward the end of the fourth century, and there he began a systematic review of the work done during the century and a half before his time. One by one he examined the treatises of the Mishna and sifted the material, he and his colleagues choosing the worthwhile from the less important and surrounding each mishnaic statement with the legal discussions and thoughts which it had aroused. Again, this material was not all legal material: ethics, history, legend remained side by side with law. But when, after about fifty years of this sifting process, Rav Ashi died, any student could easily find out what he was expected to know and what he might ignore. Ashi's successors continued the work, following his method and taking up for discussion those treatises of the Mishna which he had had no time to review.

More Trouble—It was fortunate that this process was near completion by the year 470. For at about that time a new wave of persecution swept over the Persian empire and deeply affected the Jewish community of Babylonia. Mazdaism, a movement toward social and economic radicalism, temporarily gained control over the Zoroastrian religion. The radicals directed their hostility against all—Christians, conservative Persians, as well as Jews—who disagreed with them. As usual, political and economic difficulties lay behind these persecutions, for Persia was suffering from bad government, military defeats and an inadequate supply of food for the population. Like everyone else, the Jews were impoverished. But in addition they were subjected to restrictions which forced them to close the academies and discontinue their studies. Even their private religious practices were interfered with, among these the reciting of *Shema' Yisrael*, since that implied a denial of the two rival gods in which the Zoroastrians believed.

For some thirty years the Persian empire suffered terrible misfortunes and its Jewish population harsh persecutions. A number of teachers were executed and, what was worse from the Jewish point of view, the dominant sect of priests attempted to force immorality upon the entire population. As a result the Jews rebelled. The Exilarch, at that time a young man by the name of Mar Zutra, gathered a small army of Jews and succeeded in establishing himself as an independent ruler over a tiny Jewish kingdom. For seven years he maintained himself in power, but he was then defeated and publicly executed.

4. Saboraim and the End of an Era

Order Restored—About the year 500, quiet returned to the Persian empire; the Zoroastrian priests lost their influence, and the spirit of persecution abated. The Jews tried to restore their life as it had been thirty years previously; but they did not completely succeed. Communal institutions resumed their functions; the Exilarchate was restored, though not to its former official standing; the academies reopened at Sura and Pumpeditha. Intellectual activity, however, could not be restored to its old vigor. For thirty years there had been little study, so that students were few and these few were ill-equipped to carry on the work of former generations.

Thinkers—When work was resumed in the academies, it was found most fortunate that the previous century's activities had produced a definite collection of the important discussions. The new scholars, those of the sixth century, did not dare or were unable to add new material. That is why it is generally said that the Babylonian Talmud was completed by the year 500. That, too, is why the scholars of the next century are no longer called Amoraim, lecturers or expounders, but Saboraim, "men who reflect or reason." They had before them a collection of discussions briefly and concisely noted. But what had been easy enough for the former sages to understand, the new students could not grasp as readily. They had to stop and think. The best the most learned among them could do was to make these notes more understandable for themselves and their successors by setting them in better order, by expanding some parts of them, and by adding a word or phrase here and there to indicate how the discussions were to be read. No one had done this for the Palestinian Talmud, which, therefore, remained obscure. The Babylonian Talmud is also far from easy to read and study, but if not for the work of the Saboraim it would have been very much more difficult.

Characteristics of the Babylonian Talmud—Had not the persecution intervened at the end of the fifth century and thus interrupted the work of Rav Ashi's successors, the Talmud might have become an even bigger work than it is and might have included much more information than it does. As it is, it contains discussions on only about half of the treatises of the Mishna. Fortunately, Rav Ashi and the others had worked primarily over those treatises which contained material of importance to Jewish life in the Diaspora. As a result the Babylonian Talmud afforded a better basis for life in later diaspora lands where Jews and non-Jews lived side by side.

The Jews of Babylonia were more concerned with commerce than were those of Palestine. As a result, the Babylonian Talmud proved to be in this respect, too, more useful for the Jews of a later day. Such treatises as dealt with agriculture in Palestine, or with laws of ritual purity which applied only to the Holy Land, were largely left out of the record of Babylonian discussions. Not that such matters were completely omitted from the discussions, but both Amoraim and Saboraim clearly indicated that they did not consider them of importance in actual life. On the other hand, subjects like prayer, the holidays, business conduct, family life were thoroughly discussed and decided in terms which applied to conditions in the Diaspora. This was another reason why the Babylonian Talmud was much more popular among the Jews of the subsequent era than was the Palestinian.

Talmud and Bible—Next to the Bible, the Talmud is the most important product of the Jewish mind. There have, indeed, been times when the Jews paid more attention to Talmud than to Bible. This is not surprising, for the Jews have looked upon the Talmud as the Bible in action, as the principles of the Bible applied to daily life. The same insistence upon human equality and personal freedom, the same love of justice and hope for a better society which the prophets had spoken of, shine through every discussion of the Tannaim and the Amoraim. Scribes and Pharisees had long before established the principle that it is not enough to believe in ideals, but that these ideals must be given meaning through application to human activities. One may talk grandly about human equality or about love as a basis for religion. Such talk comes pretty close to hypocrisy if a man does not *act* accordingly. The rabbis therefore assumed that not mere expressions of faith but the development of personal and social habits is the best expression of the godly life. The human will must be shaped, controlled, regulated and directed so that, even if a man forgets the fundamental principles expressed by the prophets, he will live according to them because such is the law. From this point of view, the Talmud was all the more essential for the very reason that the Jews had no central government. A government is able to apply the principles set down in a constitution which speaks in general terms. But individual men or women cannot be trusted to interpret the constitution properly. The tendency of an interpereter is to give himself the benefit of every doubt. The Talmud applies the fundamental principles to as many actual situations as the Tannaim and Amoraim met in their day. Consequently, the Jews have been correct in asserting that the Talmud is a link in the Chain of Tradition which leads in a straight path back to Moses and Sinai.

The Effect of the Talmud—As new situations arose in later days, the Jews turned to the Talmud for guidance. Not finding exact duplications of the conditions which confronted them, they nevertheless found parallels. This is what led to the writing of so many commentaries to the Talmud and so many codes of law based upon it. The Spanish commentaries and codes differed from the French, and the French from the Polish. All of them, however, hark back to the original text. The Talmud thus served as a unifying element among the Jews. It prescribed the fundamentals of their life. It helped to bind them together in action and in thought. It even united them in language, for in later Jewish writing, whether in books or in private correspondence, the language and the phraseology of the Talmud were used. Its legal discussions were not the only part of the Talmud to exercise influence on the Jews. The stories, the parables and the ethical maxims scattered among the discussions played an equally extraordinary part in shaping the Jewish character. From now on we shall meet the Talmud again and again as a force in the survival of the Jewish people. We shall see how it kept alive their hopes and courage, their culture and their faith in God.

CHAPTER V

MOHAMMEDANISM—A NEW MASTER

MOHAMMED BRINGS TO THE ARABS A NEW RELIGION, TO THE CHRISTIANS A NEW RIVAL, AND TO THE JEWS A NEW POLITICAL MASTER

The Second Daughter—In another part of the Eastern world developments were taking place destined to have a far-reaching effect upon civilization and upon the Jewish people. The tribes who lived on the western fringe of the vast Arabian desert had for centuries played an insignificant role in the activities of the peoples to their north and west. They could not, however, permanently shut their minds to the ideas common among their neighbors. Gradually the teachings of Judaism, and to some extent of Christianity, began to make themselves felt among the Arabs. Once more the fundamental thoughts of Judaism triumphed and gave birth to another religion. Judaism now mixed with Arab culture to produce Mohammedanism, just as six centuries previously it had mixed with Roman-Greek culture to give birth to Christianity. The adoption of this religion by the Arabs revolutionized the entire world of that day.

1. A CORNER OF THE DIASPORA

When Did Jews Come to Arabia?—No one knows when Jews first settled in the Arabian peninsula. It may be that some chose the cities of its western coast when, during the period of the Hasmoneans, Palestine became too small to hold the growing Jewish population, and numbers of Jews went forth to seek homes in Syria and Egypt and lands still more distant. It is also possible that when the Nabatean Arabs invaded Palestine, as they did on several occasions, they took away some captives who eventually made their way farther south. The defeat of the Jews by Rome in 70, and the ill effects of the unsuccessful rebellions, no doubt increased the Jewish population in this part of the Eastern world. It is certain that by the middle of the fifth century Jews were to be found as far as the southernmost tip of the Arabian peninsula, in the kingdom of Yemen.

A Jewish Kingdom—In this fruitful and delightful part of Arabia an incident occurred a century before Mohammed which proves the presence and influence of Jews. Early in the sixth century the king of Yemen, named Dhu Nowas, and presumably also a part of his people, became converts to Judaism. He changed his name to Joseph and assumed the role of defender of the Jews. He resented the harsh treatment of the Jews by the emperors of the Eastern Roman empire and threatened to avenge them on the Christians. Directly west of Yemen, across the Red Sea, was the Christian kingdom of Abyssinia. Politics and religious zeal prompted the emperor of Byzantium, that is, of the Eastern Roman empire, to urge the king of Abyssinia to invade Yemen. King Joseph was de-

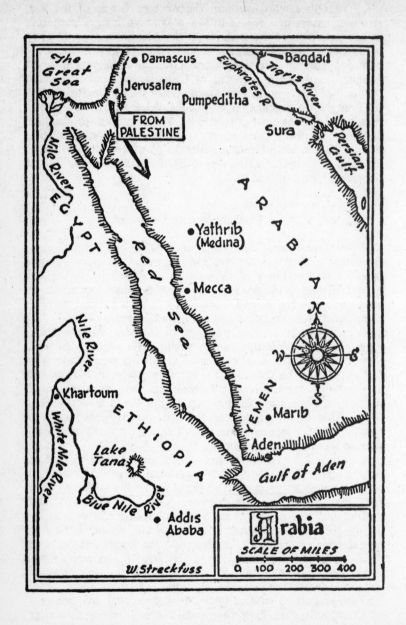

feated. Riding his horse up a tall cliff which overlooked the sea, he committed suicide by jumping into the water. A number of Jewish Yemenites must have moved northward to seek homes among other Arab peoples.

Jewish Arab Tribes—By the sixth century Jews were to be found in and near Mecca and Yathrib (Medina), the two important cities of Arabia. This part of the world was not organized politically into one unit; its population was still divided into tribes, even where the people lived close together in cities. The Jews of Arabia were also divided into about half a dozen different tribes, torn apart by jealousies and occasionally resorting to war. They differed from their pagan Arab neighbors in religion only.

Judaism in Arabia—Far from the centers of Jewish culture in Palestine and Babylonia, the Arabian Jews possessed little learning. They did know and revere the Bible. Their knowledge of the Bible was such that they, as well as the Christians, were called by the Arabs "the People of the Book." While they were inferior, in this and in other respects, to other Jews, they were superior to the pagans around them. Their belief in the unity of God, their higher personal morality, their dignified observance of Jewish feast and fast days, their rest from work on the Sabbath and their refusal to permit a fellow Jew, even of a different tribe, to remain in slavery, left a deep impression upon their neighbors. In this way their presence and example prepared the mind of the heathenish Arabs for the acceptance of a higher form of religion.

2. Mohammed and the Jews

The Education of a Prophet—Mohammed's childhood and youth were spent in the city of Mecca where he belonged to one of the most powerful Arab tribes. He was poor, and consequently received little of the education which a wealthier Arab child would have received. But he was gifted with intelligence and with a mind which absorbed information. From being a mere camel-driver he soon rose to be the leader of a caravan and the manager of his employer's business. He became what we now call an exporter, and his business trips frequently took him to Palestine. Both on his trips and at home, he came in contact with Jews and Christians. He became acquainted with their views of the world, with the stories connected with their faith, with their customs and their manner of worshipping God. As a result, he contrasted the paganism of the Arab masses with the loftier ideas of Christians and Jews. He spent much time with the Jewish inhabitants of Arabia, and the more he talked with them the more he became convinced that it was desirable and possible to change the religion of his people.

The Prophet and Islam—Before long Mohammed began to work out his plan. Clearly he was more favorably impressed with the Jewish idea of the unity of God than with the Christian idea of the Trinity. He announced himself a prophet, the chief prophet, the greatest that ever lived, greater even than Moses, and greater than Jesus upon whom he also looked as one of the prophets. Asserting that revelations, or prophecies, came to him through an angel, he had them written down as he uttered them after coming out of the trance into which he occasionally fell. These prophecies were subsequently put together into a book which Mohammed meant to rival the Bible of the Jews and the Christians. The Mohammedans still regard it (the Koran) as God's latest message. In his prophecies Mohammed forbade many of the pagan practices which prevailed among the Arabs: he prohibited sacrifices; he instituted prayer; he outlined a life of morality and ethics modeled upon that of the Jews and the Christians; and, as in these two religions, he promised the faithful the rewards of joy after death. His religion assumed the name of "Islam," a word related to the Hebrew *Shalom* (its adherents were called "Moslems"), but in Western lands it was given the name Mohammedanism, after its founder, Mohammed.

When Mohammed began to preach his new ideas, he met with a great deal of opposition. His own fellow tribesmen resented the things he said about the old religion of the Arabs. After he had been proclaiming his new faith for a few years, he had won only a small number of followers, and, in the year 622 of the Common Era, he was forced to flee from his home in Mecca. This event subsequently marked that year as the year 1 of the Mohammedan calendar, for it was Mohammed's arrival at the neighboring town of Yathrib, renamed Medina, which began the series of successes that established Islam.

Jewish Critics—Mohammed fully expected to find among the Jews greater appreciation than he did among the pagan Arabs. It seemed to him that he had taken over so many elements of Judaism that the Jews ought to hail him as their leader and recognize in him the great prophet and redeemer of mankind for whose coming they were hoping. But the Jews from among the Jewish tribes that lived in or near

Yathrib would have nothing to do with him. They saw in him a man no better than any other, for in his personal life Mohammed was not much more moral than his pagan relatives. They laughed at him for his ignorance of the Bible, for Mohammed had never really studied it thoroughly and, as a result, made some bad mistakes. They absolutely refused to have anything to do with some of the methods and ideas which Mohammed set forth, for many pagan customs remained part of the Islam he preached. They were horrified by his claim of being superior to Moses. Soon Mohammed realized that with very few exceptions the Jews would not follow him. He became angry, filled his new revelations with accusations against the Jews, and decided to destroy them.

Disunion and Death—Had the Jewish tribes joined forces to oppose Mohammed, they would surely have defeated him and saved themselves. But mutual jealousies among them kept them apart. Mohammed attacked the Jewish tribes one by one, destroying each one in turn, confiscating their property, sometimes killing the men and enslaving the women, sometimes sending the whole tribe into exile. This destruction of the Jews accomplished two things for Mohammed. He could now point out that God was on his side and always gave him victory, and he could use the Jewish booty to support his movement and lure more people to his camp. The result was that a large number of Arabs joined him. Thus, Mohammed's victory over the Jews helped him strengthen among the Arabs the very ideas which he had borrowed from the Jews. The same strategy aided Mohammed in his conquest of the non-Jewish tribes of Arabia. One by one he destroyed them as independent tribes and forced them to adopt his religion. That done, these Arabs soon realized that Mohammedanism really was superior to the paganism in which they had till then believed. Before Mohammed's death, only ten years after his flight from Mecca, all Arabia rang with the cry, "Allah is God and Mohammed is His prophet!"

3. MOHAMMEDAN CONQUESTS AND THE JEWS

Growing Power—Before another century had passed Mohammedanism ruled over Persia and Palestine, North Africa and Spain. It was a remarkable growth, and can be accounted for by the strength of the forces behind the new religion and by the weakness of the heirs to the former Roman empire. That empire had been disintegrating for some time. The invasions of the barbarian peoples had sapped its strength in the West and bad government had weakened it in the East.

Conquest of Palestine—Palestine during the fifth and sixth centuries had become depopulated, the Jews displaced by Christians, Jewish cultural opportunities considerably reduced, and the slight degree of autonomy abolished with the ending of the Patriarchate. To be sure, Jews continued to live there; synagogues and schools were maintained; but they were constantly interfered with by the emperors of the Eastern Roman empire. One emperor especially, Justinian I (527–565), tried to make their religious and social life as difficult as possible. He interfered with what went on even inside the synagogues, telling the Jews what Greek translation of the Bible they might or might not use and prohibiting the interpretation of the Bible according to the imaginative, hope-inspiring Midrash. He expected that, in this way, the Jews might be induced to abandon Judaism.

The actual effect was to make the Jews hope for the time when Christians would lose control of the country. This happened toward the beginning of the seventh century, when Emperor Heraclius was defeated by the king of Persia. The Jews helped the Persian king free the land from Roman rule. Some years later, however, the Christians reconquered Palestine, and the Jews paid dearly for having formerly sympathized with Persia.

Only a few years later, in 635, the Arabs appeared upon the scene. Romans as well as Persians were completely unprepared to meet this new adversary. Mohammed, in the Koran, had promised eternal bliss to any soldier falling on the field of battle, and Islam's soldiers fought fiercely to gain either more territory on earth or greater joy in heaven. Within little more than a year Palestine and Syria were in Mohammedan hands. A new period now began for the Jews of the Holy Land. They were not granted complete freedom; they, like the Christians, were heavily taxed. But they were permitted to settle wherever they pleased, even in Jerusalem; they could reopen their schools; they could pray in their synagogues without interference. Slowly Jewish learning revived and the Jews of Palestine were thus enabled to make further contributions to Jewish culture.

Conquest of Persia—Just one year later the Persians were driven out of Babylonia and, after a few years more, all of Persia was Mohammedan. Here, too, the Jews sighed with relief at the coming of the invaders. The reason was much the same—religious persecution. For while the Mohammedans were starting on their road to conquest, the Persian government, for some obscure reason or for no reason at all, began another persecution of its Jewish subjects.

The Exilarch at this time was a man named Bustanai. Whatever truth there may be in the stories connected with his name, it is known that, when the Mohammedans invaded Persia, Bustanai was in flight before the Persian king who had deprived him of his position and was seeking his life at the same time that he was mistreating the other Jews. It was natural, therefore, for Bustanai and the Jews to welcome the overthrow of the persecutor. One cannot tell how much help the Jews gave to the Mohammedans. It is doubtful that the Mohammedans needed help, for Persia turned out to be very weak. But the establishment of the Mohammedans as masters of Babylonia and Persia meant the restoration of Bustanai to the Exilarchate and the reopening of the academies of learning.

Conquest of Egypt—While one army of Mohammedans was conquering Asia, another invaded Egypt. At this time the Jews of Egypt were few in number. The large and important Jewish community which had existed in that land had suffered blow after blow. It never recovered from the revenge which the pagan inhabitants of Egypt had taken for the Jewish rebellion against Rome in 115–117 C. E. The reduced community suffered further from persecutions by the Christians, the most bloody one being the one organized by Bishop Cyril of Alexandria in 415. Most of the remaining Jews fled farther west in northern Africa. For the next two hundred years a tiny Jewish community led a shadowy existence in Egypt. As a matter of fact, the whole of Egypt fell far below the state of wealth and culture which had characterized it in earlier centuries. In 640 the Arab Mohammedans easily conquered the country and started it on a new career. Gradually Jews wandered back and settled there. Under the influence of the Jews of Palestine and Babylonia, Jewish life once more became active and Jewish culture revived.

4. THE CONQUEST OF NORTH AFRICA

Origin of North African Jewry—Stories, more or less credible, agree that the Jewish settlement in North Africa was of very ancient date. It may, indeed, be true that individual Israelites came there as early as the days of King Solomon, in whose time cities established by Tyrian and Sidonian colonists were active commercially. Jews are known to have lived in Cyrenaica (Tripoli) soon after the reign of Ptolemy I, in the third century B. C. E. Their numbers were augmented by fugitives from Antiochus Epiphanes of Syria before he was defeated by the Maccabean armies. One of these refugees was Jason of Cyrene, who wrote a book describing the Maccabean war. Josephus, the Jewish historian who lived two centuries later, described Cyrenaica as the center of a large Jewish population. A further increase in Jewish numbers came as a result of the defeat of the Jews by Rome in 70 C. E. So large was the Jewish population of Cyrenaica in the next generation that, in the ill-fated uprising of 115–117, the Jews almost overcame their pagan neighbors and the Roman armies.* Rome's fearful vengeance caused many to flee farther west into the territory then known as Mauretania and now as Tunisia, Algeria and Morocco. Other Jews from the former population of Cyrenaica fled completely beyond the reach of Rome into the desert to the south. Such is the explanation how the Sahara desert first acquired Jewish tribes toughened by a fighting tradition and possessed of physical characteristics which, it is said, still make them approximate very closely the original Jewish population of Palestine.

An Era of Political Opportunity—Pagan Rome established order in its world and grew tolerant. Under its rule the Jews of North Africa lived in peace for two hundred years after the diaspora rebellion. Their position changed but slightly for the worse after Christianity became the dominant religion of the empire early in the fourth century. Then the Vandals came, that Germanic tribe which wandered across Gaul and Spain and established a kingdom in North Africa (430). The Jews were growing in power and prestige at that time. Many North African pagans were choosing between Judaism and Christianity, and the Vandals were tolerant in religious matters. In the sixth century, Belisarius, Emperor Justinian's general, attempted to reconquer North Africa for the Roman empire. That, however, was only a passing storm, although it probably caused additional Jews to flee southward into the desert. Generally speaking, the fifth and sixth centuries saw the growth of Jewish cities and, perhaps, of independent Jewish kingdoms, as the following story of a Jewish queen indicates.

The Mohammedan Invasion—In the second half of the seventh century the Moslem armies moved westward from

* See above, pp. 173–4.

Egypt and carried everything before them. Diah Cahena, a member of a Jewish royal dynasty, placed herself at the head of an army composed of Berbers, Christians and Jews, and fought the advance of the Mohammedans beyond Tunisia. She defeated them, and the Christian bishops along with the pagan Berbers rejoiced in her triumph. The Jews were not so happy, partly because they saw her falling too deeply into debt to her pagan and Christian helpers, and partly because she outraged them by being more warrior than Jewess. The Christians, too, turned out to be ungrateful. When, after five years of preparation, the Mohammedans returned to do battle, the Christian bishops entered into negotiation with them. Diah Cahena, deserted alike by her Christian and her Jewish subjects, retreated, destroying everything in her way. Her army was reduced in numbers and she died in battle. Her son then turned Moslem and later took part in the Mohammedan conquest of Spain when, in the year 711, the Mohammedans crossed the narrow straits and took possession of almost the entire peninsula.

Thus, in little less than one hundred years, Mohammedanism had spread from the half-forgotten Arabian desert to include lands as far apart as the northern border of India and the Pyrenees south of France. Babylonia, Palestine and Egypt were theirs, the cradles of ancient civilization. These lands began to nourish a new culture, certain to affect the culture of their Jewish inhabitants.

5. JUDAISM AND MOHAMMEDANISM

Religious Rivalry—The Mohammedans were as anxious to convert the Jews to Mohammedanism as they were to convert the Christians. But through many years of living in the midst of a much larger number of believers in another religion, whether Christianity or Zoroastrianism, the Jews had learned to resist pressure. Equally important was the fact that the Jews were far more educated and better informed about their religion than the adherents of other religions with whom they came in contact. What had the Mohammedans to offer them which the Jews did not have? The Mohammedans admitted the sacredness of the Bible, and the Koran did not compare with the Bible for idealism and religious power. The Mohammedans admitted the greatness of the Jewish past and even claimed Abraham as their ancestor—since they traced their origin to Ishmael, brother of Isaac—and Moses and the prophets as their teachers. They adopted the Jewish idea of God's unity. They looked upon Palestine as a Holy Land. On the other hand, they did not have the great cultural tradition of the Jews; they could not lay claim to the heroism and the hopes of the Jewish people. All they could offer was physical comfort and political success. To a spiritually advanced people like the Jews that was not enough. Wherever the Mohammedans came they found Jews, and they soon discovered that, with very few exceptions, Jews adhered obstinately to their old faith despite threats or promises.

The Pact of Omar—The Mohammedans established a code of laws by which the Jews and the few Christians who remained in the lands which they conquered were forced to live. It was known as "The Pact of Omar." Its object was to make it perfectly clear that members of another religious group were inferior to Mohammedans. Non-Mohammedans were forbidden to speak disrespectfully of Mohammed and his religion. They could not prevent one of their number from joining Islam. The taxation which non-believers had to bear was always to be heavy. No new synagogues could be built, though old ones could be repaired. No synagogue (or church) could tower higher than a neighboring mosque. Members of another religion could not ride on horses, but only on mules; nor could they carry swords. In general, non-Moslems were to be so dressed as to be easily distinguishable from Moslems.

This last regulation was of unusual importance. Two centuries after Omar I, the Khalif Mutawakkil, in 850, ordered that non-Moslems be forced to wear a yellow patch on their sleeves as well as a yellow head-covering. Subsequent khalifs made changes in these symbols of non-belief, some making them more odious and others disregarding them entirely. The Christians of Europe, however, learned this system of separation from the Mohammedans and, several centuries later, imposed similar regulations upon the Jews who lived among them.

The regulations contained in the Pact of Omar were, on the whole, not as severe as they might have been. Moreover, at the beginning of Mohammedan domination even these rules were not enforced too strictly, and, before long, Jews were holding high positions of trust and honor under various khalifs. Most important of all for the life of the Jews in Mohammedan lands was the fact that the new religion permitted the Jews to maintain their own communities and live in accordance with their own religious laws under the guidance of Exilarchs and heads of academies.

CHAPTER VI

GEONIC ACHIEVEMENTS

NEW CULTURAL INSTITUTIONS IN BABYLONIA AND PALES-
TINE MAINTAIN JEWISH UNITY AND CONTRIBUTE TO
JEWISH LITERATURE

The Torch of Learning—There have been periods of darkness in the history of mankind. At such times civilization
took several steps backward: the human mind ceased to function; superstition replaced thought; greed ruled instead of
kindliness; and brutality bestrode the world. Such a period in
the history of Europe was the one which started with the barbarian invasions and which has come to be known as the
Dark Ages (from about 500 to about 800). During a large
part of the same period eastern Asia and northern Africa
were also upset because of a bad political situation and the
disorders caused by the Mohammedan conquests.

The Jews found themselves in a particularly trying position. With the difficulties encountered by the European Jews
we shall deal later. Here it is necessary to point out that they
would have been lost completely if the Jews of Babylonia had
not come to their aid by providing them with the means for
rising above the conditions which surrounded them.

1. THE EBB OF JEWISH LIFE

Extent of the Diaspora—Nowadays an airplane can take a
man from Bagdad to Paris in a day, while people living in
these cities can talk to each other by telephone. In those days
it took many months to traverse that distance, and besides, it
was hazardous, subject to encounters with storms and pirates
by sea and with highwaymen by land. There were Jewish
communities in what is now France and Germany and Spain
as well as in all parts of North Africa, Italy, the islands of
the Mediterranean, and in what is today southern Russia. It

was exceedingly difficult for all of these to keep in touch with each other and with Babylonia and its academies, the center of Jewish life at that time. After the Mohammedans had conquered some of this territory from the Christians, the difficulties of communication were increased, since Christians and Mohammedans were nearly always at war.

Effects of Ignorance—Most of the lands in the western part of the world had at one time been part of the Roman empire and had been influenced by the culture of the Greeks and the Romans. All that, however, was a thing of the past. In the course of the centuries, barbarian nations invaded this territory, and Greek-Roman culture was all but forgotten. There were almost no schools for children, let alone for adults. The Jews who lived in these lands were influenced by these conditions. They had no incentive for study, since the little they knew about the Bible and Jewish life was far more than their neighbors knew about the Bible and Christian life. But, since Judaism is impossible without knowledge, there was grave danger that Judaism would be forgotten among the Jews as Greek-Roman culture had been forgotten among the Christians. Nevertheless, though reduced in numbers and living in the midst of the deepest ignorance, many Jews and Jewish communities scattered throughout the then known world survived, largely because of the moral courage and intellectual guidance given them from Babylonia and Palestine, where Jewish life and thought were active.

2. AID FROM BABYLONIA

The Revived Exilarchate—One source of such encouragement was pride in the Babylonian Exilarchate. Upon their conquest of the Persian empire, the Mohammedans restored to the House of David the power which it had enjoyed for centuries. Once more an Exilarch stood at the head of all the Jews of Babylonia and represented them at the court of the khalifs. He lived like a prince and was respected as such by Jews and Moslems alike. He appointed the judges in the Jewish communities in Babylonia, and had power to punish wrongdoers. He also collected the taxes from the Jews and turned them over to the Mohammedan government. In every sense he was an official of the king who appointed him. But he had to be chosen from the royal family of David, and was usually the oldest son of the previous Exilarch. The Jews who lived in distant places, where the Exilarch had no authority at all, also felt that they were not completely lost or disunited as long as a son of David held power somewhere in the world.

Geonim—More practical and definite aid to the Jews of the far-flung Diaspora, that enabled them to survive as Jews, was given by another institution which developed in Babylonia. Just how it came about is not yet known, but as the situation cleared after the Mohammedan conquest, we find that the *Rosh ha-Yeshiba* of amoraic and saboraic days had acquired a new title. He was now called "The Gaon." The word means "Excellency" and probably derives from a phrase which at first was applied to the academy as a whole, and later used for its head—"The *Excellency* of Jacob," or "The *Pride* of Jacob." Whatever the origin of the name, the fact is that the Geonim guided Jewish life for some four centuries and gave their name to that entire period of Jewish history—the Geonic Age. The Gaonate's powers and functions, therefore, deserve more detailed description.

The Restored Academies—When normal Jewish life was resumed after the Mohammedan conquest, first the academy at Sura and then that at Pumpeditha reopened its doors. In time students began to flock to them as they used to do in amoraic days. A great deal was made of the *Kalla* months, those two months of popular study which attracted the businessmen and farmers. More than ever these sessions became intellectual congresses and served to spread the knowledge of Jewish law and tradition. For the main subject of study was the Talmud. There was no further attempt to add to it. The task was to absorb it, clarify it and apply it to the problems which confronted the people.

Power of the Geonim—The Gaon of Sura was considered superior to the Gaon of Pumpeditha, though both were looked upon as the guides in religious life. All doubtful questions came before them, so that they acted as a kind of Supreme Court. Along with the Exilarch, they were the most distinguished Jews and had a host of officials under them who supervised the courts and the schools in all parts of the country. For, although each Jewish community still ruled itself through communal heads and trustees (*gabbaim*) of its own choosing, the actions of these communal leaders were subject to the criticism of the Geonim.

Geonic Correspondence—One of the most interesting methods used during this period for guiding Jewish life was an outgrowth of the general recognition of the authority of the Geonim to interpret the Talmud. The system was that of "responsa," and worked as follows. In a certain town, Dura, for example, if a difference of opinion arose about the application of a legal principle to, let us say, laws of inheritance, the judges of Dura decided that the matter was too difficult for them. They then sent a message with a question *(She-elah)* to the Gaon of Sura. He presented the question to the scholars of the academy. After a thorough discussion of all the statements in the Talmud bearing on the subject, the Gaon and the scholars arrived at a decision. This decision the Gaon then communicated in an answer *(Teshubah)* sent to the judges and the head of the community of Dura. Such correspondence resulted in the strengthening of Jewish unity. For, not only did the question recognize the supreme authority of the Gaon to interpret Jewish life, it also recorded in Dura the principles which the Gaon's answers established everywhere else, since an answer once given served as a precedent for the same and subsequent Geonim. These important questions and answers are known in Hebrew as *She-elot u-Teshubot,* and in English they are usually referred to as "responsa."

Responsa to the Diaspora—This method of keeping in touch with the center of Jewish life in Babylonia played a most important role in the survival of the Jews in other lands. Neither Jewish nor secular law gave the Geonim any authority over Jews outside of Babylonia. Nevertheless, the Jews of even the most distant lands soon learned to refer their problems to them. From North Africa, from Spain, even from cities of what is now France, questions were dispatched. It might take years before an answer arrived, and, if the messenger were lost on the journey, it might never arrive. But in the course of time the Jews of the entire then known world achieved a definite sense of unity in the feeling that religious guidance could come from one or another of the Geonim.

An Example of a Responsum—Let us take as an example the prayers in the synagogue. In a general way the arrangement of the prayers was very old. By this time every Jewish community knew the most important prayers that had to be said and the time for reciting them. But in the course of time various communities had added psalms and a variety of new poetic compositions for different occasions. Consequently, there was some confusion as to the order of the service and the permissibility of including the more recent additions.

Now it so happened that about the year 860, a certain community sought to clarify this situation by finding out once and for all what prayers to say and in what order to say them. The community had till then made the arrangement for itself, as had every other, until general confusion threatened. Now it turned with a question (*She-elah*) to the Gaon of Sura, at this time Rav Amram. He received the question and, in due time, composed the answer, detailing the arrangement of the prayers. This has become known as the *Seder* or *Siddur* (both words mean "arrangement") of Rav Amram. He did not compose a prayer book; he merely indicated, sometimes by the first sentence or phrase, what should be recited and in what order. It was a bulky answer of many pages. Copies of it were made by any number of communities which had also been looking for just such an authoritative statement. Thus, unity was attained once more through the aid of geonic authority. About sixty years later another Gaon, Rav Saadia, was asked a similar question, and, in response, gave another arrangement which did not differ substantially from that of Rav Amram. That is how it came about that till a hundred years ago, all Jews everywhere followed practically the same order of service in the synagogues and at home.

Spreading the Talmud—The responsa of the Geonim brought about something even more important for the strengthening of Judaism and the achievement of Jewish unity. In those days, many centuries before the invention of printing, books were few and difficult to obtain. It may have taken a century or more after the completion of the Talmud for the Jews in distant lands to become aware that such a series of books existed. Then came the responsa. The Geonim usually based their decisions on the discussions to be found in the Talmud. Thereby they indicated that the talmudic literature was fundamental to the guidance of Jewish life. Respect for and interest in the Talmud increased and, before long, the leaders among the Jews in the rest of the Diaspora sought to obtain copies and attempted to study them. Eventually, of course, the Talmud as a book became the basis for Jewish life in every part of the Diaspora and played a most important part in the preservation of the Jewish people.

Historical Source Material—One by-product of the responsa method has been of special importance to the study of history. The responsa naturally reflect the social and economic conditions prevailing at the time when the questions were asked and the answers given. They show the ethical standards of the questioners, the customs they practiced and the life they led. The responsa have therefore been among the most useful historical sources for the geonic age and the periods which followed. The rabbinic leaders of the Jews have adhered to the responsa method ever since.

The Academies' Messengers—In addition to the responsa
the Geonim also dispatched a rather unusual type of messenger. With every *She-elah* addressed to a Gaon there was sent
a contribution to the geonic treasury. But the income from
this was small. Consequently, the Geonim adopted the policy,
which had been followed centuries previously by the Palestinian patriarchs, of sending messengers to the communities in
the rest of the Diaspora to raise funds for the support of the
academies. These messengers (*Meshullahim*) were chosen
from among the scholars, in order that they might represent
the academies worthily. Coming to a community, they would
describe the work of the academy. They would speak about
the Talmud and about the Geonim as the interpreters of talmudic law. It is likely that they brought copies of the Talmud
to communities or individuals interested and willing to pay
for the laborious process of copying it. They might even have
given the first instructions in the use of the Talmud and its
method of presenting the principles of Jewish law and tradition. In this way these messengers tied the Jews to one another and to the Geonim, and enabled the Jewish group to
remain united after Babylonia ceased to be the center of Jewish life.

3. THE REVIVAL OF PALESTINE

Restored Opportunities—With the restoration of peace,
after the Mohammedan conquest, the Jewish population of
Palestine grew somewhat larger. The restrictions imposed by
the Mohammedans were not nearly so heavy as those under
which the Jews there had lived during the Christian period.
Galilee was the most populous district, with the city of Tiberias a center of culture. There, and in other places, schools
were opened and in the course of a few generations began to
make new contributions to Jewish life.

The Palestinian Mind—In some respects the interests of
the Jews of Palestine differed from those of Babylonia. The
latter were more concerned with the legal part of the Jewish
tradition; the Palestinians favored the poetic and imaginative.
This tendency, dating from very early times, had been
strengthened by the need of offering a Jewish interpretation
of the Bible in opposition to that which the Christians were
giving it. The Mohammedans, when they came, also showed
a love for poetry and the study of the Koran, and this further
encouraged the interest in poetry and Bible among the Jews.
That did not mean that the Palestinians were not interested in

Jewish law and in the Talmud. Only in looking back upon that period of Jewish history one realizes that the one community was strong in one aspect of Jewish culture and the other in a different aspect.

How Shall the Bible Be Read?—The Jews of Palestine contributed to a better understanding of the Bible. A Torah scroll, used for reading in the synagogue, contains only the consonants of the Hebrew words; there are no vowel indications such as are to be found in printed books. There are hardly even any paragraph divisions to be seen, and no sentence markings. How then did people know how to read and where to stop? They were in the same position as we would be if English had no vowels and we came across the letters "ct." Only the sense of the sentence would tell us whether to read it "cut," "cot" or "cat." A word of three Hebrew letters like שכל might be read *sachal*, "he acted cleverly;" or *sechel*, "good sense:" or *shikel*, "he lost his children;" or *she-kol*, "that all." The meaning depends upon the vowels, according to which the consonants are read. Until the period we are now discussing, people learned this from their teachers. That is to say, the reading of words, like the divisions into phrases, sentences, paragraphs and chapters, was handed down by tradition. But that certainly was not a satisfactory situation when troubles prevented people from studying, when the Jews were scattered all over the world and teachers were few, and when Hebrew had ceased to be the language spoken by any part of the people.

The Jews, both of Babylonia and Palestine, learned a lesson from the Mohammedans, and from certain Christian groups who lived near them. These people, confronted with the same problem in their Arabic and Aramaic languages, had invented little signs to indicate the vowels. Jewish scholars in Babylonia began to use a variety of lines and dots written above the letters of the Hebrew alphabet to show how they were to be read. Certain scholars in Palestine, at the same time, suggested another set of signs, written mostly below the line of letters. The Palestinian system turned out to be the easier and more efficient, and was soon adopted universally by all Jews. These scholars were very careful to follow the traditional pronunciation of the words, and then wrote under them the sign appropriate to indicate that tradition. They did more. They used another set of signs, below or above the words, to indicate the phrases and stops within the sentence. These are the signs now used for chanting. For the chanting, too, was traditional, and the new signs now fixed the chant for the future. Their most important use, however, was as commas, colons and periods rather than musical notes. Finally, the same Palestinians wrote footnotes to the words of the Bible into which mistakes had crept; they counted every word and letter, all with the object of handing the traditional readings of the sacred books down to the future exactly as they had been handed down to them from the past.

Masoretes and Grammarians—The people who were active in this work are known as Masoretes, from the Hebrew word which means "to hand down." This work of handing the past over to the future was neither simple nor quickly accomplished; it took a number of generations of scholars to do it. Moreover, these scholars thereby laid the foundation for the study of Hebrew grammar. For, as anyone can see, a discussion of words and how they are to be read in various connections was bound to lead to the fixing of grammatical rules. The Palestinian Masoretes, down to the tenth century, did not go that far; the real beginnings of Hebrew grammar were made by their followers in Babylonia and in distant Spain.

Midrash Agada—Palestinians far more than Babylonians indulged in haggadic, that is, imaginative, interpretations of the Bible. While the Jewish Commonwealth was still in existence, the students and the preachers had weighed the story of the past and glorified it, looked into the Jewish future and spoke of it in glowing terms, took every character of the Bible story and used it for lessons in morals and ethics. This sort of activity continued among the Jews century after century, until a vast mass of such interpretation and instruction came into being. Imaginative literature of this nature was called *Midrash*. It became more important after the destruction of the Jewish state than it had ever been before, since the Jews now needed the encouragement which could be derived from the knowledge that they had had a great past and were destined for an even greater future. How important this encouragement was can be seen from the fact that Emperor Justinian (about 550), upon the advice of the Christian clergy, forbade the Jewish preachers to make use of this manner of interpreting the Bible since it contradicted Christian interpretations. The prohibition was evaded in one way or another. With the coming of the Mohammedans, such restrictions were removed. Now actual collections of midrashic material began to appear in the form of a commentary on various books of the Bible, especially of the Torah portions read in the synagogue on Sabbaths and holidays.

Poetry and the Synagogue—At the same time, Palestine contributed to Jewish culture the beginnings of a type of poetry which in time, in other lands, became one of the noblest possessions of the Jewish people. The original motive for it was the desire to expand and beautify the synagogue service. Prayers for personal forgiveness, for the restoration of Zion, for the hastening of the day when God would reign over the whole world, were added to the usual ritual of the synagogue, especially on holidays. Some of these prayers were in simple and beautiful Hebrew. Others were not so much poetry as a clever arrangement of midrashic material applicable to the particular day for which the prayer was intended. Sometimes the poet arranged the poem in such a way that every line began with a succeeding letter of the alphabet; at other times, he cleverly worked his own name into the poem. This is known as an "acrostic." By means of such acrostics it is often possible to identify the author. Many of these poems may still be found in the prayer book for Rosh Hashanah and Yom Kippur, and some even in the Passover *Haggadah*.

The Influence of Palestine—From the above it can be seen that the influence of Palestine was far from ended with the close of the Second Commonwealth and the Patriarchate. The coming of the Mohammedans gave it a new lease on life. If we at the present time can read the Bible easily, if we can gain courage from Jewish idealism and hopefulness, if we can pour out our hearts in beautiful and instructive prayers, we owe it to the Jews of Palestine of the sixth to the tenth centuries. They did not add much to the development of Jewish law. In that field the Babylonians did more for the preservation of Jewish life. The Palestinians supplemented the work of the Babylonians. Both together built the spiritual bastions of Judaism.

CHAPTER VII

CULTURAL REBELLION

INTERNAL REVOLTS AGAINST JEWISH LIFE WEAKEN THE JEWISH PEOPLE AND ALMOST RESULT IN ITS EXTINCTION

The Greatest Danger—Jewish spiritual life did not always run smoothly during the centuries of geonic leadership, and the Jewish group, whose survival depended upon unity of mind and spirit, suffered from inner division of the kind more dangerous to it than external oppression. This lesson might have been learned from the catastrophic results of the dispute between the Sadducees and the Pharisees many centuries earlier; events during the geonic age were to teach the same lesson once more. Fortunately, an intellectual giant arose who stemmed the tide of disunion.

1. FALSE MESSIAHS

Mixed Ideas—Jews have always acquired new ideas from their neighbors. A Jew may sometimes be unable to tell whether one or another of the ideas which are part of his mental arsenal originated from his Jewish or from his non-Jewish surroundings. This we call assimilation. It is a natural and often desirable state of affairs. It becomes bad only when ideas acquired from the non-Jews begin to destroy valuable Jewish ideas or to weaken the spiritual unity of the Jewish group.

Persian Ideas and Judaism—One of the main tasks of Jewish leadership in Persia had been to guard important Jewish principles of life from being submerged by Persian influences. In view of the many centuries during which Jews and Persians lived in close proximity, it is remarkable that the Amoraim and Saboraim succeeded so well. Of course, they were considerably aided by the fact that the Jews formed a closely-knit community with its own leaders and laws and by the further fact that, during the pagan period, Persian thought was not of a high order. Nevertheless, in a great many respects the Jews were Persian, not only in dress, in food, in manner of living, but also in their thinking. When Persia became Mohammedan the problem for the Jews became more serious. For Mohammedanism stimulated Persian culture, while Jewish life had been weakened by more than a century of economic distress and comparative inactivity in the academies. The Geonim of the late seventh and eighth centuries faced a difficult situation.

Prophets and Redeemers—The influence of Mohammedanism became apparent in a crop of false messiahs. In the course of the centuries the old Jewish messianic idea had greatly developed in the popular imagination and in the haggadic-imaginative literature. The Messiah was now thought of, not as an ordinary human being, but as a man possessed of divine powers. His coming was to be preceded by the reappearance of the Prophet Elijah as well as by a subordinate messiah. From time to time, men would appear, in one land or another, and claim to be the Chosen Deliverer.

The story of Mohammed gave a new turn to the messianic idea. The biography of the Arab leader proved that such leadership could come from among the poorest and simplest people and that a popular movement need not have large numbers to start with. In all parts of the Jewish population, Mohammedanism increased the belief in miracles. The tremendously important events which had taken place in so short a time, involving the downfall of the old Persia and the expulsion of the Roman empire from Asia, seemed to give strength to the belief that the "End of Days" had come and with it the time for the Jewish Redeemer.

Abu-Issa and His Successors—About the year 700, miracle-working redeemers began to appear among the Jews more frequently than before. One of these was a tailor by the name of Abu-Issa of Ispahan. A surprisingly large number of the poorer elements of the Jewish population believed his promises to throw off the yoke of the khalif and lead the Jews back to Palestine. He gathered an army of Jews who, though poorly equipped, trusted in their leader's miracles. Rumor had it that, faced with an army of non-Jews, Abu-Issa had roped his followers off and announced that the enemy could not get inside the circle. The miracle, it was asserted, had worked. Nevertheless, a battle was finally fought and the Jews were badly defeated and scattered. Abu-Issa died by his own hand. But this did not discourage others from following his example. A man by the name of Judghan al-Rai, a shepherd, attempted the same thing and, in the end, was also defeated and killed. Almost at the same time, in Syria, a man named Serenus called upon the Jews to follow his leadership in the reconquest of Palestine. Jews flocked to him by the thousands only to be deeply disappointed when his promises came to naught.

The Attack on Authority—These messianic uprisings were based on a strange mixture of ideas. The desire of a fairly large number of Jews to throw off the yoke of their new Mohammedan masters was bound up, somehow, with rebelliousness against Jewish authority. Part of the program of these false messiahs was the relaxation of the laws of *kashrut* (dietary regulations). They advocated the increase to seven of the number of times a man must pray every day, and the recognition of both Mohammed and Jesus as prophets. We may well be astonished that such radical departures from Judaism should have found supporters among the common people. It merely proves that the influence of the ideas current among non-Jews was great among the Jews, and that the power of the Talmud was still weak, since the Geonim had not yet gained control over the spiritual life of the people. Thus the freedom of movement and of contact with their neighbors had served to weaken Jewish unity as long as Jewish knowledge and faith had not counterbalanced the influence of the environment. For generations after the downfall of the false prophets, a considerable number of Jews still believed in them and their principles. In the course of time their followers were either absorbed by the Mohammedans or returned to the Jewish fold. The net result was a loss in Jewish numbers.

2. KARAITES

Bible versus Talmud—Another and still more important rebellion was to follow. Although not led by a pretender to messianic authority, it, too, was directed against the Talmud and the Geonim and withdrew from Jewish life a large number of earnest and sincere men. Indeed, for a while it looked as though this movement would cause Judaism to disintegrate completely by destroying those unifying bonds which the Tannaim, Amoraim, Saboraim and Geonim had been forging for over seven hundred years. The Judaism which these teachers had developed was based on tradition. The new movement denied the value of their work and went back to the Bible alone as the guide of Jewish life. That is why they bear the name *Karaim,* "Scripturalists," believers in the Bible only, from the Hebrew word *mikra,* "Scripture."

Anan ben David—It happened around the year 760 that, upon the death of a certain childless Exilarch, a successor was to be chosen from among his closest relatives of the male line, as was the custom. In such matters the Geonim of Sura and Pumpeditha made the choice; the khalif merely acted on their advice. Now, the closest relatives of the deceased Exilarch were his two nephews, Anan and Hananiah. Anan was clearly the abler of the two. But the Geonim suspected him of two things. First, they were afraid that he would try to impose his authority on them to a greater extent than they desired. Secondly, they felt that he was not completely devoted to Jewish tradition and that, therefore, he might not enforce talmudic law as the Geonim and their predecessors interpreted it. Consequently, the Geonim urged the khalif to appoint the younger and weaker brother. Hananiah was appointed. Thereupon, Anan spoke his mind about the Geonim, the academies, the Talmud, and Jewish tradition in general. Such action, reported to the khalif, was interpreted as rebellion against the government. Anan was thrown into prison and was in danger of his life. At this time a number of conflicting sects had arisen within Mohammedanism. This gave Anan the idea of announcing that, far from being a rebel against Judaism, he was the founder of an entirely new religion. He owed no allegiance to the organized Jewish community because, so he claimed, he was not a member of that community. The khalif then freed Anan, who began in earnest to set forth his arguments against Judaism.

Principles of Karaism—The chief argument of Anan and his successors was that the rabbis had misinterpreted the Bible so that the original intentions of the Holy Book were lost in the numberless laws built on top of the biblical words. They realized, of course, that the statements of the Bible often needed explanation. Their belief was that each Jew had a right to explain these statements in accordance with his own views, without regard to the "official" explanation offered by the scribes or any of their followers. Consequently, the duty of the true Jew was to study the Bible with exceedingly great care in order to discover the meaning of its laws and commands. Each man was to be his own authority.

Karaism and Unity—Unfortunately for Karaism, it was based on two fallacies. In the first place, the Karaites did not realize that the traditions of the rabbis were based on careful study and on the need for adjusting Judaism to the life of the people of the time. For example, there is very little in the Bible on the question of the proper preparation of food, so that the Karaites themselves soon had to fall back upon many regulations worked out by the rabbis. On the other hand, in the matter of observance of the Sabbath, the statements of the Bible present no possible way out but to stop all work, to sit still at home, and not even to prepare food. On the surface it would seem that the rabbis had made numerous regulations which burdened life. Actually, however, they had made the observance of the Sabbath very much easier. The Karaites, for example, had no fire on the Sabbath so that their food and homes were cold; whereas the Jews permitted fire to burn if it had been kindled before the Sabbath began. The second mistake of Karaism lay in the assumption that every man has enough knowledge and experience to understand the full meaning of the Bible. Before long it became

clear that either the Karaites would have to substitute new
guides for the old, or see their type of Judaism degenerate
completely.

The Spread of Karaism—It took several generations for
the weaknesses of Karaism to become apparent. In the meantime it appealed to those Jews who had become critical of the
Geonim. The latter had not always been the finest type of
men. Some were more interested in their authority than in
being examples of Judaism at its best. In the course of the
century and a half since the arrival of Islam, the leadership
of Babylonian Jewry—Exilarchs, Geonim, chief scholars and
local authorities—had become hardened into an aristocracy.
The result was that many Karaites wrote better and more
persuasive books than the Rabbinites (as the believers in oral
tradition were called), led nobler and more self-sacrificing
lives, and often came closer to understanding the common
people. Many intelligent Jews became Karaites, and the
movement spread beyond the borders of Babylonia: into Persia, into Palestine and Egypt, into some parts of the near-by
Byzantine empire and, eventually, even farther. Karaism thus
presented a really serious danger to the survival of the Jewish
group.

3. PALESTINE AGAINST BABYLONIA

Claims to Leadership—The revival of Jewish life and
learning in Palestine brought another problem. A strange situation developed, in which Palestine actually threatened Jewish unity. The academies of Tiberias and other cities in Palestine organized themselves in a manner similar to those of Babylonia, sent messengers throughout the Diaspora to seek
financial support, and answered questions in much the same
way as the Babylonian Geonim. The Palestinian academies
had a great advantage because of the fact that the land was
the center of Jewish memories and hopes. Also its greater
proximity to Egypt and the rest of northern Africa, where
Jewish communities were growing, was important in making
Palestine's influence felt more easily than the influence of
Babylonia.

The Weaknesses of Palestine—The results, if Palestine had
succeeded in replacing Babylonia, would probably not have
been healthy. The culture of the non-Jews in Palestine was
not then the kind to inspire the Jews to great cultural efforts.
Moreover, a few centuries later the crusaders turned Pales-

tine into a battlefield and destroyed Jewish life completely. The immediate reason why Palestine lost in this rivalry was the smallness of the Jewish population. Its students were fewer, and its first-rate scholars were also less significant. The Jews of that day stood in greater need of the strength and unity which result from common law and tradition, in which the Babylonians were stronger, than the poetic creations of beauty and imagination which the Palestinians emphasized. Finally, there was going on at that time a constant emigration westward of Jews from Babylonia to northern Africa and to Spain. It was natural for these people to keep more closely in touch with their original home. All these causes combined to defeat the ambitions of the Palestinian scholars to be considered the more important. Nevertheless, Palestinian influence was especially strong upon the Jews of southern Italy and, through them, upon those of Central Europe.

4. MOHAMMEDAN CULTURE AND THE JEWS

The Lure of Culture—One of the great achievements of Mohammedanism was the cultural movement which it started in almost every land it conquered. The need of the desert faith to adjust and justify itself in the midst of older theologies and cultures spurred the Moslem mind to new activity. In Persia Mohammedanism came in contact with the cultures of East and West. This stimulated it and started a movement toward the study of the philosophies of ancient Greece and of India, which in turn gave the teachings of Islam a much more intellectual and literary foundation than they had in the Koran. Naturally, this cultural activity made a strong appeal to numerous intelligent Jews, who openly expressed the wish that Judaism, too, might be dignified and supported in the same way. They became critical of the Geonim for their exclusive devotion to law and tradition.

Jewish Contributions—The fact is that Jews took an active part in the cultural movement among the general population. A number of Jewish poets wrote in the Arabic language, and Jews were active as translators into Arabic of philosophical and scientific works originally written in Greek or in the languages of the East. These translations laid the foundations for further cultural growth. It is said, for example, that a Jew introduced the so-called Arabic numerals into the Persian khalifate. He had become acquainted with this system of numbering when on his commercial journeys to India. From Persia this system came into Europe, and thus laid the basis for scientific progress. This type of cooperation in promoting civilization involved, however, one element of danger, namely, that intellectual Jews began to think that only non-Jewish culture encourages philosophical and literary efforts.

5. SAADIA GAON

The Babylonian Crisis—Every once in a while the course of history is affected by the good or bad characteristics or ambitions of a single human being. All through Jewish history such individuals have played exceptional roles. A man of outstanding ability appeared among the Jews of Babylonia about the year 900 and helped defeat all the forces just mentioned which threatened the continued influence of that center of Jewish culture. He achieved this result through the richness of his knowledge, the depth of his learning, the keenness of his intellect and the ruggedness of his personal courage.

The Rise of Saadia—This man, strange to say, was not a Babylonian. Saadia was born and reared in Egypt, where he laid the foundations of his great learning, a fact which proves that the Jews of Egypt had developed an active and worthwhile Jewish life. While still in Egypt, Saadia attacked Karaism and exposed the weaknesses of that interpretation of Judaism. The Karaites sought to silence him by using their political influence. He was forced to abandon home and family and flee for safety to Palestine. Here he hoped to continue his studies and his association with scholars greater than those to be found in Egypt. After a number of years in Palestine, he went to Babylonia.

The Defeat of Karaism—The Karaite scholars had already found in Saadia a man who was more than a match for them. In his teaching and especially in his writings, Saadia had taken up the arguments of Karaism and showed that they were both illogical and destructive of Jewish life. He even poked fun at them for having developed traditions, the very thing which they had started out to abolish. He continued to point out that their traditions were inferior to the traditions developed and adhered to by the Rabbinite Jews. These were blows struck at Karaism from which it never recovered. It lived on, but it was never again a danger to Jewish life.

The Defeat of Palestine—Even before he became Gaon, Saadia took his stand on the side of Babylonian supremacy.

The Palestinian scholars had been pushing their claims to leadership. One of them, Aaron ben Meir by name, tried in an argument centering about calendrical calculations, to prove to the Jews of the Diaspora that the Babylonian leadership was unreliable. Saadia completely demolished the arguments of Ben Meir.

Appointment to the Gaonate—Soon after Saadia's arrival in Babylonia, the Gaon of Sura died. Ordinarily the Exilarch would have used his influence to appoint a member of the intellectual aristocracy of Babylonia. Fortunately, David ben Zakkai, the reigning Exilarch, realized that the time had come to restore the vitality of rabbinic Judaism by placing at its head the best man possible, no matter what his origin. From this point of view there was no doubt that Saadia was the best choice, although he was not even a Babylonian Jew, let alone a product of a Babylonian academy. David ben Zakkai was warned that Saadia held very strong opinions and was so fearless that the Exilarch might have trouble controlling him. For Exilarchs frequently dominated Geonim, and David ben Zakkai was a particularly imperious man. Nevertheless he appointed Saadia to be Gaon of Sura.

Expansion of Culture—It was not like Saadia to be satisfied with the re-establishment of Babylonian Judaism. He wanted to place Judaism on the highest possible intellectual and cultural level. This was necessary, in view of the ever-increasing number of Jews who had too much admiration for the poetry and philosophy of the Mohammedans. Saadia not only wrote poetry himself, he also prepared a rhyming dictionary of Hebrew to help other Jewish poets. Above all he wrote an important work on philosophy. He called it *Beliefs and opinions* (*Emunot ve-De'ot*). In it he tried to answer two questions which were troubling the thinking Jews of his time. On the one hand, he argued that religion and reason were not in conflict; the same truth which was taught by the one could be arrived at by using the other. On the other hand, he felt it necessary to indicate the depth of spiritual truth in Judaism when compared with Mohammedanism. He not only set at rest the intellectual doubts of his contemporaries, but restored their self-respect.

The Bible and the Hebrew Language—Saadia wrote his philosophical book in the Arabic language. Arabic had already become the language spoken by the Jews of the lands where Mohammedanism prevailed, the Hebrew tongue being reserved for prayer and for correspondence with scholars. Under these circumstances, the Bible became a closed book to a great many Jews. It was a situation parallel to that which had confronted the Jews in Alexandria many centuries before, when the Jewish population spoke Greek, and in Palestine, when the Jews translated the Bible into Aramaic. The problem was more serious in the days of Saadia, because upon a correct understanding of the Bible depended many of the arguments which the Rabbinite Jews used against the Karaites. Here, too, Saadia saw the problem and solved it. He translated the Bible into Arabic. He did more: he wrote explanations of many parts of the Bible, in other words, a commentary, also in Arabic. In this way, he literally opened the eyes of the Jews to the beauties of the Holy Scriptures as compared with the Koran, and to the truth of Jewish tradition as interpreted by the rabbis.

The Quarrel—It took a full lifetime to accomplish all the work described above. It was started long before Saadia was raised to the Gaonate, and a good deal of it was done during the period of bitter misfortune while he was deprived of his dignity and office. For Saadia's life was not an easy or a happy one. The warning given to the Exilarch David ben Zakkai, that Saadia was a man of stubborn principles, proved but too true and was the cause of a quarrel unfortunate in its results for Saadia, for the Exilarch and for the Exilarchate.

It started with a simple lawsuit in connection with a will which had been brought to the court of the Exilarch on appeal; it developed into a bitter struggle for supremacy between the Exilarchate and the Gaonate. Orders, threats and excommunications followed one another from both sides. The Exilarch, being a civil officer, had the police and the Moslem government on his side, and Saadia had to flee. The Jews of Babylonia and the scholars among them took sides. The situation became a public scandal not alone in Babylonia, but wherever Jews lived and looked for guidance from the leading Jewish community. But that did not help Saadia. For seven years he felt the bitterness of persecution. Finally the good sense of the leaders of Babylonian Jewry prevailed. A peace meeting was arranged between Saadia and David ben Zakkai, and the Gaon was restored to his place. He showed himself broad-minded and forgiving to such an extent that when David ben Zakkai died and his son soon after him, Saadia took in and lovingly reared his former enemy's grandson, the child who was to be the next Exilarch.

Results of Saadia's Work—Saadia's achievements were great. He removed the threat of Karaism and thus re-established the supremacy of Jewish tradition. He kept Palestine from reasserting its claims at an inopportune moment and thus saved Jewish unity. He struck a telling blow against the supremacy of a hereditary prince like an Exilarch and in favor of the purely religious leadership of a Gaon. He fought successful battles against the alluring influence of Mohammedan philosophy. He strengthened Judaism in many ways. Nevertheless, his life's work had one injurious result. By exposing the evils of the Exilarchate he caused the Jews to lose respect for that institution. The exalted Davidic dynasty was dealt a mortal blow by his pointing out the lack of scrupulous ethics on the part of its descendant, David ben Zakkai. This was an important consideration in the ultimate decline of Babylonian Jewry as the leading community among the Jews of the world. Ethically Saadia may have been justified. From a practical viewpoint, however, he undermined the one institution which offered a living, tangible symbol of the continuity and unity of the Jewish people.

CHAPTER VIII

THE END OF AN ERA

THE BABYLONIAN JEWISH COMMUNITY LOSES ITS INFLUENCE; BUT THAT NO LONGER MATTERS, SINCE THE FOUNDATIONS FOR CONTINUED JEWISH LIFE IN THE DIASPORA ARE ALREADY LAID

A Community Grown Old—From the days of Rav to the days of Saadia, Judaism had been guided by the thought and the spiritual vigor of the Jews of Babylonia. The achievements of Sura and Pumpeditha during those centuries have in fact continued to influence Jewish life to our own day. But from the time of Saadia's death, there was a progressive loosening of the bonds which tied the Jews of the West to those of Babylonia in the East, and after eight hundred years of almost continuous intellectual leadership, the reins of power slipped from the hands of this ruling center. The community continued to live; it never completely disappeared; but its influence was neither sought after nor needed by other, more vigorous, Jewish communities in the West who started to build a new Jewish life on the foundations laid by the Babylonians and Palestinians. Undoubtedly part of the explanation for this loss of influence may be found in the mistakes made by the Babylonian Jews themselves. Far more important were certain historical forces which changed the whole aspect of Eastern life, and with it Jewish life—forces over which the Jewish community could not possibly have had any control.

1. THE BREAKUP OF AN EMPIRE

Mohammedan Politics—The loss of influence by the Jews of Babylonia over the other Jews of the world was due, in large measure, to quarrels among the Moslem peoples. For over a century all the lands which the Mohammedans had conquered remained under the rule of one dynasty, united under one khalif. His empire stretched from beyond the easternmost boundary of Persia, across North Africa to the Pyrenees, the mountains which form the northern boundary of Spain. The western part of this vast empire then broke away and established a khalifate of its own, including modern Tunis, Algeria and Spain. The result of this for the Jews was that contacts became difficult between those who lived in the western lands and those in Babylonia.

Economic Problems—One difficulty was economic. The easy flow of commerce between East and West was interrupted for a time. Still worse, the khalifs of the East did not know how to maintain the prosperity of their subjects. They imposed heavy taxes upon non-Mohammedans and enforced other laws which weighed heavily upon them. Both agriculture and commerce ceased to flourish. The Jews of Babylonia became poor, and the academies and the Exilarchs could not obtain enough funds either from their supporters near by or from those faraway.

The East Goes to Sleep—The same loss of contact and the same economic troubles affected Mohammedan cultural life. Philosophical and theological discussions among the Mohammedans were not as numerous nor as important as they had been in Babylonia and Persia or as they were becoming in Spain. To be sure, this cultural decline did not occur at once. After Saadia's death it became noticeable that the Jews of Spain and southern Italy were making new contributions to Judaism, while those of Babylonia were for the most part standing still.

Jewish Emigration—The result of the economic and political situation was a steady increase in the number of Jews leaving Babylonia to settle in other lands. With the narrowing opportunities in Babylonia, merchants found their way to commerce and comfort elsewhere; they left for good. Farmers and workers were forced off the land by the heavy taxation and unfriendly laws. Students and scholars, learning of growing Jewish communities to the west which were anxious for Jewish guidance, found their way to those new and distant homes. The emigration was at no time extensive, but it continued over generations. Babylonia became a shadow of its former self.

2. IN DISTANT LANDS

Eldad the Danite—About the year 875 a very strange man appeared among the Jews of northern Africa and told a weird story. He spoke a peculiar kind of Hebrew mixed with Arabic, and introduced himself as a member of the tribe of Dan. He said that members of his tribe had escaped from the kingdom of Israel after Sennacherib had conquered it (719 B. C. E.), and that Israelites of other tribes likewise lived in that same distant land from which he came. They were all good warriors, quite able to defend their independence. Not far off, across an extraordinary river that flowed with sand and stone all week long but ceased on the Sabbath—hence its name Sambattion—lived the Children of Moses, a tribe of saintly Levites. He told of the laws followed by his people, who had received them by tradition from Joshua ben Nun, the successor of Moses. These laws were somewhat different from those developed in Palestine and Babylonia. About himself Eldad related exciting adventures of shipwreck and cannibals and hairbreadth escapes. The Jews who heard Eldad's story doubted it; they even suspected him at first of being a tricky Karaite in disguise. But in a responsum to their question the Gaon of that day assured them that most of the story might be believed. Some modern scholars argue that Eldad was an Ethiopian Jew, a descendant of the ancient colony which, in the days of Ezra, lived on the southern border of Egypt. Their religion would naturally not show any signs of the later developments in Palestine and Babylonia, and may well have spread among their Ethiopian neighbors. They would thus be the ancestors of the modern Falashas (black Jews of Africa). Others believe that he came from a country east of Persia and find in his story evidence of a visit to the Chinese Jews. In his own day Eldad's story was soon accepted literally, the Jews becoming convinced that mighty Jewish tribes lived in some far-off land. For centuries the story spread and developed both among Jews and Christians, and prepared them to believe another traveler from the same region who appeared in Europe seven hundred years later.*

The Khazars—An equally fascinating story, but carrying a greater measure of truth and dealing with the spread of Judaism during those days, occurred in another distant part of the world. Around the year 600, a belligerent tribe of half-

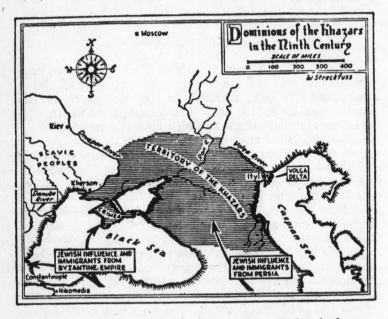

Mongolian people, similar to the modern Turks, had conquered the territory of what is now southern Russia. Before long the kingdom of the Khazars, as this tribe was known, stretched from the Caspian to the Black Sea. Its capital city, Ityl, was at the mouth of the Volga River. The Khazars mingled with the native Slavic population. Jewish, Christian and Mohammedan merchants visited them, and these contacts had a cultural result. Some time during the eighth century, the Khazar king and nobility became civilized enough to want to abandon their pagan worship and adopt a monotheis-

* See below, pp. 372 ff.

tic religion about which the visitors from neighboring lands to the south used to tell them. But which monotheistic religion was it to be? The merchants from the Byzantine (Eastern Roman) empire urged Christianity upon them. The merchants from Persia urged them to adopt Mohammedanism. Both of these were the religions of mighty, conquering kingdoms. Each argued that God was on its side. Apparently each of these religions won a large number of adherents among the Khazars. But the royal family and the largest number of the nobility were impressed with Judaism. That was the religion they adopted, though they did not force it upon others.

For several centuries, the Jewish kingdom of the Khazars continued to rule over southern Russia, and even the prince of Kiev paid them tribute. By the end of the tenth century, the strength of the Russians increased, especially after their king accepted the Greek Catholic faith and joined forces with the Byzantines. Though the Khazars' kingdom declined, recent investigation seems to indicate that they nevertheless maintained their rule over much of their former territory down to the Tatar invasion around 1240. Their state then came to an end, though a good many of them remained Jews. Some mingled with the Jews of the Byzantine empire; others remained as Jews within the Moscovite principality. But even those who adopted Christianity retained many Jewish observances. It is interesting to speculate whether the observance of the Sabbath among certain clans of Cossacks in the territory now known as the Ukraine, which the Russian Church was still attempting to stamp out as late as the eighteenth century, was an echo of the ancient Khazar influence.

Jews of the Byzantine Empire—A considerable Jewish population had existed within the territory of the Eastern Roman empire for many centuries. Long before the beginning of the Common Era, the cities of Asia Minor had many Jews, and the islands of the Greeks many more. From there they spread to the coast of the Black Sea. Generations before the destruction of the Second Commonwealth, Jews had penetrated and settled in the Crimea, and cities which now belong to Bulgaria, Yugoslavia and Hungary had Jewish communities when Herod ruled over Jerusalem. Trouble for these communities began with the triumph of Christianity in 325. But their numbers and their commercial power prevented the Christian emperors from accepting the advice of some bigoted counselors to destroy Judaism completely. The more violent among the clergy, however, began a systematic campaign to make life hard for the Jews. Eventually the discriminating laws and the hate-rousing oratory had their effect. The emperors Theodosius in the fifth century and Justinian in the sixth made the practice of Judaism very difficult. Attacks on synagogues became common occurrences. Some were destroyed and others were turned into churches. The local clergy took the stand that such synagogues, once converted, could not be restored to Jewish worship. The civil government accepted this view, though on occasions it decreed that the Jews be permitted to build new synagogues elsewhere. In general, the law prohibited the building of new synagogues and only permitted the repairing of old ones. Moreover, the Byzantine emperors, having solidified their alliance with the clergy, extended their anti-Jewish legislation into the political sphere. They forbade Jews from holding offices of honor and restricted Jewish rights in non-Jewish courts of law. Jews could not proselytize even among their slaves. At the same time, the government took care not to harm the economic position of the Jews, since that would have affected the imperial treasury. In the eighth and ninth centuries certain emperors, who were accused of being Christian heretics, tried to prove their orthodoxy by persecuting the Jews. Many Jews were then driven farther away from Constantinople, Asia Minor and the Greek Islands and toward the Crimea and the lands now called the Balkans as far as the Danube and to the north of it. Such remained the situation in Jewish life in the eastern half of Europe at the time when the Babylonian center was entering upon its decline.

India and China—From Babylonia and Persia Jews spread also to the northeast and southeast. India was near to Persia, and trade with the northern part of that land had been carried on for a long time. As more and more Babylonian and Persian Jews entered commerce, it was natural, after a while, when living conditions became difficult in the Persian-Mohammedan lands, for these merchants to settle down in the country with which they had become familiar through trading.

While the Jews of India managed to maintain relations with the Jews of Babylonia, those who had gone to the northeast, to China, were completely cut off from the rest of the Jews. Just as Persian Jews had always been active in the importation of spices from India and their export farther west into Europe, so other Persian Jews had been active in the importation and exportation of silk from China to Europe. This eventually led to the resettlement in China. In a later chapter, the history of the Indian and the Chinese Jews will be discussed at greater length.*

* See below, pp. 634–43.

3. BRIDGES TO THE WEST

The Bridge across Europe—The communities of Asia
Minor, the Crimea and the Balkans, described above, eventually moved to the north and west, across Russia or modern
Hungary. They laid the foundations for the great communities
that were later to grow up in Eastern Europe.

Kairawan—Of more immediate importance were the communities of northern Africa, chiefly that of the city of Kairawan. This city was located about forty miles from the site of
the ancient city of Carthage. After the Mohammedan conquest, it sprang into prominence as a trading center, and
within a century it held a community of Jews. Schools and
scholars soon developed there, and its leading men kept up a
constant correspondence with the academies of Babylonia.
Just as merchants would stop off at Kairawan before continuing toward Spain or before transferring their goods to ships
plying the narrow water-route which went to Sicily and
Southern Italy, so scholars and their cargo of knowledge used
this city as the halfway house between Babylonia, Egypt and
Palestine to the lands of Western Europe.

From Fez to Gibraltor—On the extreme western tip of
Africa, the East made its last stop before crossing over to the
West. Just below that point was the city of Fez which had
had a Jewish community even before the Mohammedans
extended their conquests that far. For, during the century
before the arrival of the Mohammedans, the Christians of
Spain had driven almost the entire Jewish population out
of their homeland, and many of them had sought refuge in
northern Africa. This story will have to be told on another
occasion.* For the present, it is sufficient to point out that in
North Africa these exiles waited for an opportunity to return
to Spain. That opportunity came when the Mohammedans
took the country. For a long time thereafter Fez was practically Spanish territory. Western Jewry and Eastern Jewry
mingled there; it was the last bridge from one to the other.

Sherira's Letter—A realistic, historical account of the transfer of learning from the East to the West is given in a letter
sent by Sherira, the last but one of the really great Geonim.
Towards the end of the tenth century the Jewish sages
of Kairawan became curious to learn just how the Talmud had come into being. Having accepted the work of the

* See below, pp. 272 f.

Tannaim and Amoraim as the source of Jewish tradition, they wanted to know about the individual men mentioned in the various treatises, the time when the treatises were written down, how the academies used to be conducted, and similar matters of interest. They turned to Sherira with these questions, and in time received his answer.

In his long answer, Sherira gave a fairly detailed explana-

Bridges to the West in the 10th century

tion of the origin of the Talmud. A great deal of our information about the periods of the Tannaim and Amoraim comes directly out of this responsum, which is considered, therefore, as a most valuable source of Jewish history. It is significant that this disclosure of the background of the Talmud's origin should have been given to the more Western Jewish communities just at the time when the place of its origin was retiring into obscurity.

4. OFF THE CENTER OF THE STAGE

The Final Act—By the year 1000 the Jewish community of

Babylonia had lost its hold on the Jewish mind. The deteriorating conditions of Jewish life in the East combined with the more liberal treatment of the Jews in Spain to draw leadership away from the old center. At the same time, the constant quarrels among the Geonim and between the Geonim and the Exilarchs gave the final blow to the respect which the rest of the Jews had for Babylonian leadership. Two more Geonim, Sherira (Pumpeditha, about 970–1000) and his son Hai (about 1000–1038), both outstanding and respected scholars, appeared and shed the last flicker of glory upon the ancient community. After them, Geonim continued to function in the academies, now removed to Baghdad, for several centuries. There were even Exilarchs for a time. But outside of their own country they had neither power, nor influence, nor much respect. It is sad, of course, to contemplate the decline of a once-flourishing center. This sort of thing, however, happened time and again in Jewish history, and it is much more useful to recall the great achievements of the community, those contributions to Jewish life and thought upon which succeeding communities built their life and influence.

Literary Heritage—The actual books written during the age when Eastern Jewry was supreme have been mentioned already. They all grew out of the Bible and fell into the following literary categories: Law, Midrash, Masorah (which proved to be the beginning of grammar), Poetry (which was mostly in the form of prayer), Stories and Parables, and Philosophy. Through them this first half of Jewish history bequeathed to its succeeding ages a number of important principles by which the Jews continued to be distinguished from other peoples.

Knowledge Is Supreme—One of the primary ideas which Eastern Jewry left as an inheritance to the Jews of the West is that learning is the foundation of Jewish life. They argued that an ignorant man cannot be a pious one, for such a man does not understand God's world or the bases of human behavior. They did not underestimate physical strength or wealth, but they considered them secondary to the good life. Leadership must rest in the hands of the scholar. Subsequent communities of Jews sometimes wandered away from this ideal, and the Jewishness of such communities was always in danger. The usual Jewish community, the self-respecting one, never failed to encourage study among adults as well as children and to show the utmost respect for the learned man. To study the Torah, which meant all of Jewish learning, became one of the foremost Jewish ideals.

Conduct and Character—A second idea transmitted by the East to the West was that man's whole life must be dedicated to God. It was not enough to *think* of Godliness; it was necessary to *act* in such a way as to devote every minute of the day to holy living. A man's character is developed by his actions. Consequently, the more exacting the actions he imposes on himself, the better his character will be. *Mitzvot,* religious commandments, became the bases of Jewish life.

Unity of Israel—"All Israelites are brothers." Other peoples might depend upon national territory to keep them united. But the Jewish people was considered a unique people in that its unity depended, not upon race or land, but upon a common devotion to the One God and to the laws and ideals developed throughout Jewish history. Saadia said: "Israel is a nation by reason of the Torah." The hope of restoring a Jewish nation to Palestine never died in Jewish hearts, but Jewish unity did not altogether depend upon the realization of this hope.

Community Life—The Palestinian and Babylonian Jews developed a form of community which was taken over and continued by the Jews of the West. The same officials and the same public institutions as existed in Sura were established in Rome, Toledo, Cologne or Cracow. In time they became modified to some extent, but till the nineteenth century the general forms remained unchanged. Every Jew was a member of the community; rich and poor had rights and duties which they could not be denied.

A Vision of the Future—Finally, Eastern Jewry bequeathed to the Jews of the West an ideal of a future world which inspired hope. They called it the Days of the Messiah. In His own good time God will redeem the world from oppression and wickedness. Humanity will then recognize the greatness of the Jewish contribution to civilization, and peace will reign supreme. That time will come when Israel deserves it; hence its coming or its delay depends upon the actions of each individual Jew.

Strength of the Jewish People—These ideas, and others which derived from them, gave the scattered Jews such spiritual strength that they were able to withstand and survive the many difficulties which faced them during the thousand years following the end of the supremacy of the East. The effect of these ideas is what has come to be known among the enemies of the Jewish people as "Jewish stubbornness" and, in friendlier and happier minds, as "The Miracle of Jewish Survival."

BOOK THREE

THE JEWS IN THE WEST

THE JEWS COOPERATE IN BUILDING THE CIVILIZATION OF WESTERN EUROPE AND, AT THE SAME TIME, HEROICALLY DEFEND THEIR IDENTITY AS JEWS

INTRODUCTION

The Role of the Jew—We turn now to the lands of the West where new nations were making their entrance into the arena of history. In several instances Jews had inhabited these lands long before the new tribes moved in. More Jews followed during subsequent centuries. The tribes which were displacing the Roman empire were just taking their stumbling first steps toward civilization. They had no history other than the tales of mighty deeds by their mythical heroes; they had no ambitions other than conquest. Slowly and imperfectly they were beginning to understand the ideas which the young Christian religion had previously taken from the Jews. By contrast, the Jews were an old people. They had already passed through a kind of national adolescence when the physical heroism of judge and king had been balanced by the spiritual heroism of prophet and poet. They were even then approaching the end of the student period begun by the scribes, developed by the Pharisees, and continued by the Tannaim, Amoraim and Geonim. The Jews already carried with them the wisdom of maturity which valued peace, freedom and the chance to search for truth. They could serve as cultural links to the civilizations of the past—their own and those of the peoples among whom they had lived for many centuries. Their mere presence among the new nations was a cultural stimulant. This period of Jewish history, therefore, may well be called the period of the Jew as culture-bearer and teacher. The Jew played that role without in the least being conscious of it, and for it he has received far too little credit.

Heroic Loyalty—There is a widespread, but erroneous impression that Jewish experience in Europe during the Middle Ages was one of continuous and unmitigated sorrow. There were, as a matter of fact, long periods when the Jews and their neighbors lived quietly and peacefully side by side. It is true, however, that for many centuries the relations between the Jews and the Gentiles were a blot on the name of humanity. The important thing during such periods is not that horrors were visited upon the Jews, but that they suffered them with dignity and heroism. It is this that makes Jewish history inspiring. The history of no other group can offer such examples of willingness to carry on an unpopular ideal for century after century, despite every temptation and in defiance of every force. Numerous explanations have been offered for this remarkable fact. The true explanation is probably the simplest, namely, that knowledge of Jewish teachings, thorough acquaintance with Jewish idealism, compel such admiration for Judaism as to make its abandonment shameful. Our history in Europe is a continuous illustration of this truth.

CHAPTER I

THE JEWS COME TO EUROPE

THE JEWS SETTLE IN VARIOUS PARTS OF WESTERN EUROPE AND HELP THE OCCUPANTS OF THESE LANDS TO ADVANCE THEIR CIVILIZATION

The End of a World and a New Beginning—In order properly to relate the story of the Jews of Europe, we shall have to go back about a thousand years so as to describe the beginnings of the Western states and their earliest contacts with the Jews. The Western Jews originally came from the East, bringing with them many of the cultural and all of the religious attitudes of their Eastern brothers. Their settlements were new, their neighbors were new, and the situations which they faced were quite different from those faced by the Jews of the East. But their memories, their traditions and their interpretation of life were the same. The first thousand years of Jewish life in Europe show how the new situation and the old attitudes affected one another. This period is, therefore, a necessary introduction to the history of the European Jews in the same way as the history of the Thirteen Colonies is a necessary introduction to the history of the United States.

1. THE EARLIEST SETTLEMENTS

The City of Rome—The earliest connection between the Jews and Western Europe was made in the city of Rome. We have already told how in response to a plea by Judah the Maccabee, about the year 160 B. C. E., for aid against the Syrians, the Roman Senate then declared the Jewish people friends and allies, though it did not send any help. During the following century, a number of Jews came to settle in Rome. Some came for reasons of trade, probably from Egypt and other diaspora lands. In the year 63 B.C.E., Pompey, the Roman general, conquered Palestine and carried off to Rome a large number of Jewish war captives whom he sold as slaves. Later, these people, or their children, were freed and remained in Rome. Similarly, every subsequent Jewish rebellion against Rome resulted, through captives of war who were enslaved and then freed, in an increase of Rome's Jewish population. It is estimated that by the time of the great Jewish war against Rome, in 66–71 of the Common Era, there were about fifty thousand Jews in the city. They had several synagogues and a community organization. Though there were prosperous merchants among them, the vast majority were very poor. For the most part they were artisans and peddlers. This Jewish population soon began to take part in the political and cultural life of the city. For example, no part of Rome's population expressed greater sorrow than the Jews over the death of the popular Julius Caesar. When Nero was emperor, the most noted actor in Rome was a Jew. Another Jew, Cecilius by name, was one of Italy's foremost literary critics.

From Rome North—The Roman armies pitched their camps in the interior of Gaul (France and western Germany) and along its frontier. Around these camps there developed the first cities of that part of the world. Close behind the armies came Jewish peddlers, trying to escape from the limited economic opportunities of overcrowded Rome and bringing with them the merchandise found in the Italian cities. Thus the Jews helped lay the foundations for the commerce of the new towns. For eventually the peddlers established themselves permanently in these places. This is how Paris and Lyons in the interior of Gaul, and Treves, Cologne and Mayence along the Rhine River, acquired the first Jewish settlements. This may have happened as early as the first, but certainly not later than the third century of the Common Era.

From Rome South—Jewish settlements in southern Italy and on the island of Sicily came into being even earlier than those in Gaul. The manner of these settlements was not much different from that of the Jewish community of Rome itself, that is, through Jewish slaves who, when freed, remained there. In addition, southern Italy and Sicily were on the sea-route both to Rome and to Spain from the more eastern parts of the empire and from northern Africa. Consequently, merchants and their agents were tempted to settle there.

Spain—The settlement of the Jews on the Iberian Peninsula, the land now occupied by Spain and Portugal, was likewise of ancient date. Jews used to maintain that their ancestors had come to Spain as early as the days of King Solomon. Though this is an assertion impossible to prove, it is not altogether incredible. In the biblical era that land had been colonized by the two important Phoenician cities, Tyre and Sidon, whose commercial expeditions used to go clear across the Mediterranean. King Solomon, as well as later Israelite kings, had entered into partnership with the kings of Tyre, and on several occasions sent Israelites to serve with their neighbors, the Phoenicians. Later on, Spain was ruled by Carthage, which had originally been a Phoenician colony and trading post. Thus the beginnings of Spain were, if not Jewish, at least Semitic. In any event, soon after Spain was taken by Rome, Jews must have begun to find their way there, attracted by the beauty and the fertility of the country.

2. FOUNDATIONS OF TRAGEDY

Rome's Tolerance—Paganism was usually a tolerant religion. Believing in the existence of more than one god, the
pagan readily granted his neighbor the right to worship a god
or gods other than his own. A slight degree of intolerance developed when the chief god of a country was identified with
that country's honor and interests. The religion of a country
then began to mean something like its patriotism, and all the
inhabitants were asked on certain occasions to pay divine
honors to the patron deity, no matter what other gods they
might worship. The arrangements entered into between Rome
and the Jews regarding the emperors' statues have already
been explained.* After Caligula, there was no further interference with the religion of the Jews.

Attractiveness of Judaism—Some difficulties arose because
the Jews criticized paganism. Judaism, as we have seen,
proved attractive to thoughtful pagans, many of whom, all
over the Roman empire, including Rome itself, visited the synagogues and followed certain Jewish observances, especially
the Sabbath. There was a good deal of intermarriage between
Jews and pagans. When a pagan woman married a Jew, she
almost always adopted his religion. But even when a Jewish
woman married a pagan man, the result was of advantage to
Judaism, since the wife often brought her children up as
Jews. This was particularly the case in the Roman provinces,
like Spain and Gaul. Much of the increase in Jewish population in these provinces is accounted for in this way. Not even
the destruction of the Jewish state, with the loss of prestige
which this brought upon the Jewish people, resulted in more
than a temporary setback to the spread of Judaism.

Christian Progress—In the meantime another danger arose
for paganism and turned the attention of the Roman government away from Judaism. Christianity made more rapid progress among the pagan population of the Roman empire than
Judaism. The first Christians were Jews, or sympathizers with
Judaism, and Judaism too began to look upon Christianity as
a competitor for converts among the pagans. Christianity had
two advantages over Judaism: it made fewer demands and it
held out greater rewards. Judaism imposed any number of
restrictions, prohibitions and commandments, not the least of

* See above, pp. 142–3, 146, 152, 157.

them the painful operation of circumcision. Christianity asked for no more than faith in God and Jesus. Christianity also emphasized far more than did Judaism the blissful eternal life that was to follow death. The pagan who, at no sacrifice, adopted the new religion could feel that he was part of the great tradition of monotheism. At the same time, Christianity, like Judaism, offered an escape from hopelessness. For the Roman empire was degenerating. All but a very small class of aristocrats were finding life increasingly hard, and the pagan gods offered nothing either in this world or the next. Among the poorer population, the artisans, the slaves, Christianity spread from day to day.

Judaism and the Christian Triumph—In the rivalry between Judaism and Christianity for the pagans of the Roman empire, Christianity won. The Jews had sown the seeds, and Christianity reaped a plentiful harvest. Pagans impressed by Jewish ideas were ready to abandon their old religion long before the Christian missionaries arrived. Among the missionaries of the first two centuries a great many were Jews who had accepted Christianity, and even more were pagans who had been considered candidates for Judaism.

Constantine's Edicts—By the year 311, Christianity had become so widespread that Constantine I, then emperor of Rome and engaged in a war with a rival, Maxentius, saw political advantage in proclaiming his favor of Christianity. He announced that Christianity was a "permitted religion," just as Judaism was permitted. This was a severe blow to paganism, which had till then been the favored religion of the empire. Later in his reign, Constantine took the next step and made Christianity the favored religion while paganism was merely "permitted."

Church and Synagogue—An important change now took place in the attitude of Christians toward the Jews. Until now the rivalry for converts had been between the *ideas* of Christianity and Judaism, and in this conflict Christianity had won. Now, however, the Christian Church, that is, the organization of the Christians, took up the fight and carried it on with the assistance of the government. It has been charged that when pagan Rome persecuted the Christians, the Jews were a party to the persecution. For this charge no real proof has been advanced. It is true that the Jews had driven the Christians out of their synagogues after the Christians had refused to support Bar Kochba, so that it looked as though they sympathized with the Romans in that struggle. It may also be true that the Jews would not have minded seeing Christianity disappear. But there is no proof that the Jewish people, or any individual Jews, instigated persecutions by the Roman emperors. In any event, churchmen of a later day justified their persecution of the Jews by the charge that the Jews of former days had helped to persecute the Christians.

The Policy of Separation—The fact is that Judaism still appealed to a great many people among pagans as well as among Christians. There were many Christians who respected the Synagogue and its traditions as institutions of the Mother Religion. The Jews were more learned than many of the Christian clergy in just those books which Christianity considered sacred. Moreover, since Christianity was a movement among the lower classes of the empire's society, the more cultured pagans had more respect for Judaism which had for centuries been a part of the Roman world.

The council of churchmen which met at Nicaea in 325 undertook to separate the Jews from the Christians. It forbade Christians to eat *matzah* on Passover, or to celebrate this holiday at the same time as the Jews. It prohibited Christians from visiting synagogues and listening to Jewish preachers. It also urged them not to observe the day of rest on Saturday, and instituted Sunday as the only Christian Sabbath. The bishops prevailed upon the emperor to prevent pagans from becoming converts to Judaism, and also to take away from the Jews some of the political privileges which they had long enjoyed.

Attacks by Word and Deed—Many of the Christian clergy, who now stood very close to the Roman government, urged the emperors to deal harshly with Judaism. Some were for prohibiting it entirely. But the Roman government had a great deal of respect for old Roman law, and the law had always permitted Judaism to be practiced. A material argument was found in the fact that the Jews were numerous and economically very important. Emperors occasionally did arise who added restrictions upon Jewish life, but none of them made the practice of Judaism illegal.

The Christian clergy, however, continued to express their desire to see Judaism disappear. They claimed that the Jews had always misunderstood the Bible. They pointed to the loss of the Palestinian state as a sign that God had rejected and abandoned the Jewish people. Worse still, the orators among them did not hesitate to incite the mob to riot against the synagogues of their locality. Thus the Church, as soon as it acquired power, began to use those unfair methods which have flagrantly contradicted the great ideals for which Christianity stands. Misunderstanding and hate were fostered which poisoned the relations between the Jews and the Christians.

3. THE JEWS AND THE BARBARIAN TRIBES

The Decay of Rome—The poverty and hopelessness of the common people, which brought victory to Christianity, resulted also in the decay of Rome's culture and the sapping of Rome's strength. The emperor and the aristocrats of Rome greedily continued to accumulate wealth and power. They did nothing to maintain independence of spirit and optimism in the masses. The population of the empire dwindled; cities grew smaller and disappeared; culture all but vanished. The Jews, of course, were affected by these social changes as much as the rest of the population. The city of Rome was itself a good example of what took place. Between the fourth and the sixth centuries the population of Rome decreased, its wealth disappeared, its nobility moved to Constantinople. Invasions and plagues added to Rome's ruin. By the year 550 it was almost a deserted city. Its Jewish population, like the other Romans, had scattered north and south.

The Barbarians and Their Religion—The growing weaknesses of the Roman empire had made it possible for barbarian tribes to invade its territory and establish themselves as rulers in several of its provinces where Jews had settled centuries before. By the year 500, Vandals ruled over North Africa, Visigoths over Spain, Franks over France, and Ostrogoths over Italy. They laid the foundations of the modern West-European states. With the exception of the Franks, these tribes had become converted to a type of Christianity, called Arian, containing pagan elements. Being different from the Roman Christians, they broke the relationship between the Church and the government. They permitted each religious group complete freedom of worship and took particular pains to protect the Jews against attacks by the mob. Since they themselves preferred to live under their own tribal laws, they saw no reason for interfering with the Jews who desired to regulate their life by Jewish law.

An Economic Change—During the period of Roman imperial greatness and decline, the Jews underwent an economic change of considerable importance to themselves and the world in which they lived. Many of them may have started out as small farmers in various parts of the empire. Others, perhaps after being freed from slavery or as poor immigrants, became artisans, peddlers and merchants. Through those Jews who had made their homes on the boundaries of the empire, the barbarians learned their first lessons in the comforts of civilization and were stirred to imitate civilized life. It may be that, like their descendants centuries later in America, the peddler's pack of these Jews carried more than knickknacks; it carried ideas about a wider and different world to which the peddler helped to unite the outlying districts which he served.

In those days the ownership of land was considered socially most desirable. The Jews, too, were agriculturally minded and, as soon as they could afford it, bought farms. Moreover, as the Roman empire of the West became less prosperous, as conditions grew more unsettled because of constant wars, as cities declined, there was less need for merchants and artisans. This increased the flow of Jews from commerce into farming. In Spain, southern France and Italy, Jews became owners of estates. The new rulers of these lands did not interfere with this development. This, of course, does not mean that there were no longer any Jewish merchants or artisans in the West, but only that their number had decreased.

A Cultural Change—The changes within the Roman empire resulted also in a cultural change among the Jews. As the Jews left the cities, they could not maintain their connections with the schools and other communal institutions which they had developed. The unsettled conditions of the time also prevented them from keeping in constant touch with one another and with the centers of learning in the East. The culture of the Romans and of the inhabitants of the empire having reached the vanishing point, the culture of the Jews also lost in extent and intensity. Among the Jews, however, it did not quite disappear. The need to read prayers and to know the Bible demanded a minimum of knowledge among them, and this, little as it was, far exceeded the knowledge among the Christians, whether laymen or clergy, Roman or barbarian. The Christians consequently had a great deal of respect for the Jews. The Christian farmer often called a Jew, and not a priest, to bless his soil or his crops, as was the custom of those days. No wonder the Christian clergy were upset by this situation and, in their meetings or councils, passed resolutions prohibiting Christians from calling Jews in to bless the soil, or to intermarry with Jews, or to have Jews settle disputes among them. But these things went on nevertheless.

4. CHURCH, POLITICS AND PERSECUTION

A Great Pope—As long as Christianity was divided and the ignorance among the Christians very great, the Church found it impossible to reduce the influence of the Jews. It also happened that during this period one of the most liberal and high-minded popes ruled over Roman Christendom. This was Gregory I, subsequently called Gregory the Great (590–604). He thought it wrong to force people into Christianity; the proper method was to persuade them or tempt them to adopt the religion. He protected the Jews against violence and urged the clergy to be just to them. He was therefore important not only for his own time, but for later times as well, since some of his successors followed his example in certain respects. Nevertheless, on one occasion he himself acted contrary to his noble principles, when he congratulated a king of Spain for initiating a violent persecution of the Jews.

Visigoths and Jews—In 412, the Visigoths (West Goths), a Germanic tribe, became the rulers of Spain. They found there a mixed population, consisting of Roman Catholics, pagans and Jews. The Visigoths themselves were Arians, that is, Christains not yet converted to Roman Catholicism. As a result, they granted the other elements of the population the right to follow whatever religion they desired. This continued for more than a century and a half. The Jews, important merchants in the cities and owners of large estates on the land, were respected and wielded considerable influence.

Trouble began because of a struggle for power within the ruling class. The Visigoth kings were kings only in name. Their nobles did not always obey them. Rebellions were frequent. In 589, Reccared was elected king and decided to strengthen his position. He turned Roman Catholic, thereby obtaining the help of the Catholic clergy. Through the clergy he also gained the support of the Catholic population against the unruly Visigothic nobility. The bishops, in turn, now saw their chance of destroying the respect which the Jews enjoyed among the common people. The king wanted to prevent the aid which the Jews might extend to the nobles who opposed him. Therefore, king and bishops joined hands to prohibit Judaism entirely. The Jews were ordered to become Catholics or leave the country.

The Jews met this new danger as best they could. Some

fled to North Africa or to southern France. Others feigned
Christianity but practiced Jewish ceremonies in secret. Still
others sought the protection of powerful nobles. The whole of
the next century was occupied in this struggle of Judaism to
survive in Spain. Help came once in a while when the nobility gained the upper hand and the king they elected did not
enforce the decrees against the Jews. Then the following ruler
would join the bishops in making the anti-Jewish laws even
stricter. The climax was reached around the year 700 when it
was decreed that anyone found practicing a Jewish ceremony
should be sold into slavery, and the children of people under
suspicion of being Jews should be taken from them and to be
brought up by the Christian clergy.

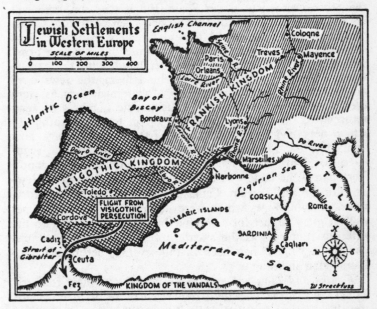

In this way a combination of secular and religious politics
succeeded in ruining the life of a peaceful minority of the
population. The fact that it took a hundred years for the enemies of the Jews to achieve their ruin proves that the people
of Spain were not easily persuaded to treat the Jews in this
manner. Besides, these political maneuverings did more than
ruin Jewish life; they also weakened the life of the entire
country. Indeed, some of the Visigothic nobles entered into
intrigues with outside powers and invited them to invade
Spain.

The Mohammedan Conquest of Spain—In the meantime, the Mohammedans completed the conquest of northern Africa. They were willing and ready to continue their march northward into Europe. Encouraged by the dissatisfied Visigothic nobles, the Mohammedans crossed the narrow straits below Gibraltar. With incredible ease they conquered Spain in the year 711. That they succeeded so easily in conquering the country and in converting so many of its inhabitants, proves that the Visigothic kings had failed to unite their people and that the hate which the bishops had succeeded in arousing against the Jews had not deepened loyalty to Christianity.

It is not known whether or not the Jews actually helped the Mohammedans conquer Spain. But if they did, who will blame them? Certainly, those who had been outwardly Christians now openly returned to Judaism. The Mohammedans could rely upon them not to rebel while the invading army was fighting elsewhere. On the other hand, with the experience of a century of resistance behind them, the Jews were not nearly as easily converted to Mohammedanism as were the Christians of Spain. Also, considerable numbers of Jews returned to their former homes in Spain from the refuge to which they had fled in northern Africa. The Moslems now applied to the Jews of Spain the Pact of Omar which regulated Moslem-Jewish relations in all Mohammedan lands. Fortunately the code was not interpreted too rigorously. Jewish life in the Iberian Peninsula recommenced, therefore, under circumstances which were destined to lead it to a period of glory to last for some five hundred years. Only in the fifteenth century was the situation destined to return almost exactly to what it had been in the seventh, before this Mohammedan invasion.

Franks and Jews—Events in France, the country formerly called Gaul, to some extent resembled those of Spain. Here, too, the Jews had settled while it was still a Roman province and the population was friendly to them. The Frankish conquerors, who were orthodox Roman Catholics from the start, and their kings nevertheless continued to be friendly. Some members of the clergy, however, were disturbed by the favorable position which the Jews held. For a long time their efforts to arouse the people were fruitless. While here and there the clergy succeeded in stirring up the populace so that the Jews were compelled to turn Christian, the loss was partly counterbalanced by intermarriages which resulted in a gain for Judaism or by the conversion to Judaism of slaves who thereupon became members of the Jewish household.

In 629, however, Dagobert ascended the Frankish throne. Ambitious to increase his power, he was more submissive to the influence of the clergy. A few years previously a council of the Church had passed a resolution urging that Jews be not appointed to civil or military office. Like so many similar resolutions, this one had been disregarded. Now the example of the Visigoths near-by was not lost upon Dagobert. He yielded to the urging of the clergy and expelled all Jews from his kingdom. Some went eastward to live along the Rhine; others turned southward to settle around the city of Narbonne, in the territory later to become famous as the Provence. For over a hundred years no Jews are heard of in the central part of France.

The Jews and the People of Europe—From all that has been said, it is possible to draw several conclusions. In the first place it is clear that the Jews, though originating in Asia, were inhabitants of Western Europe centuries before the new tribes conquered and settled in those lands. The fact is that to a considerable extent they became mingled racially with the local inhabitants and with the conquerors themselves. In the second place, it is evident that the Jews, along with the rest of the old population, helped keep alive, during the period which has come to be known as the Dark Ages, the remnants of civilization of the Roman empire which the barbarian invaders had helped to destroy. Finally, there can be no doubt that, in the early centuries of the Common Era, the Jews were living peacefully and harmoniously with the population of Western Europe. It took many years of zealous preaching and the political ambitions of the kings to stir the populace against them. The clergy justified their action by claiming that the Jews, left alone, were a danger to Christianity because they attracted pagans to Judaism and caused heresy among Christians. If that was so, then it is further proof that the general population found their Jewish neighbors friendly, helpful and deserving of respect. Anti-Jewish feeling seems to have been externally and artifically stimulated by individuals and classes who used it to advance their personal interests or the interests of their institutions.

CHAPTER II

ECONOMICS, SOCIETY AND RELIGION

AN ERA OF PEACE AND PROSPERITY MAKES IT POSSIBLE
FOR THE JEWS TO HELP DEVELOP MEDIEVAL SOCIETY AND
TRANSPLANT JEWISH TRADITION AND LEARNING TO WEST-
ERN EUROPE

Building Western Europe—The first thousand years of the Common Era were a period of turmoil and disorganization for Western Europe. Wars and invasions were constant. Most of the population was reduced to serfdom, a status little better than slavery. Those physical comforts and intellectual interests which we now identify with civilization did not exist then even among the nobility. Life was narrow, raw, hard and brutal. Nevertheless, toward the end of that period, a beginning was made in the direction of a better world. In this improvement the Jews naturally played a part: it affected them, and they affected it. And as the general level of civilization rose, their own peculiarly Jewish cultures also took an upward turn.

1. ECONOMIC FOUNDATION

Another Economic Change—When we last spoke of the economic activity of the Western European Jews, we saw many of them engaged in farming. This continued for about three centuries, from about 350 to 650. Then another change began to take place. Gradually, Jewish farmers and landowners became merchants. Since the Jews are now credited, rightly or wrongly, with an inborn ability to trade, it may be well to note the process by which they became identified with the trading occupation.

Slave-Owning Prohibited—There were several reasons which compelled the Jews to abandon farming. One of these was the attitude of the Christian Church toward the owning of slaves by Jews. In those days agricultural tools and methods were primitive, and farming required human labor by many hands. Such hard work was done by slaves. Slavery was then an accepted institution. The church, too, had slaves working on its lands. These were men and women captured in war whom their captors preferred to sell rather than kill. Now, slaves naturally adopt the customs and manners of the master's household. Slaves of Jews were particularly apt to adopt Judaism, since that insured their rapid attainment of freedom, Jews being religiously bound to free fellow Jews from slavery.

The Christian Church saw great danger in Jewish ownership of slaves. Though it had long ago forbidden Jews to convert a Christian to Judaism, the Church now further decreed that Jews must not keep Christian slaves for more than three months. Thereafter the Christian slave must be sold to a Christian. Even pagan slaves were ordered freed or sold three months after their conversion to Christianity. At the same time, the Church re-emphasized its old decree forbidding Jews to convert pagans to Judaism.

The effect of these Church laws, when the Church was finally able to enforce them, was to make it impossible for Jews to maintain themselves as farmers. In Spain Jewish owners of estates lost their lands during the century of Visigothic persecution. In France they held them a little longer, but in the end they had to give them up there as well as in Italy.

Beginnings of Feudalism—Another, equally important, reason made it impossible for Jews to retain their farm land. The turbulence and misrule which prevailed in Western Europe for several centuries helped to bring about the political and economic system known as feudalism. This involved joining a military defense association. To this day such associations demand an oath, more or less religious in nature. An oath in those days was surrounded with much impressive religious pageantry. A Jew, conscious of his Jewishness, could not possibly take it; yet without it he could not call upon anyone to help him defend himself and his lands from roving bands and land-greedy neighbors. The belligerent, undisciplined nobles of that age were quick to seize upon the difference in religion to squeeze the Jews out of the landowning class. No doubt a substantial part of the Jewish landowning population of Western Europe was lost to Judaism because of their unwillingness to give up their estates. The majority of

Jews held to it despite the attractions of ease and profit which conversion offered them.

International Commerce—At this very moment a change was taking place in the international situation which opened a new opportunity to the Jews. In spite of the fact that after the barbarian invasions commerce had dwindled to a small fraction of what it had been, there was always some interchange of goods between the East and the West. It was limited to those articles of luxury which the aristocracy and the higher Church dignitaries could afford. This commerce had fallen largely into the hands of Syrian Christians who had settled in the harbor towns of the West and from there carried on trade through their fellow Syrians in the eastern Mediterranean. The goods thus received from across the sea were then sent in boats along the rivers of Western Europe, the Rhone, the Rhine and the Danube, to the few remaining towns whence they were carried farther inland. The Syrians became very wealthy, and before long allied themselves with the West European landed aristocracy. But by the year 650 the Mohammedans had gained control of the eastern Mediterranean coast. Between them and the Christians there was constant warfare. The trade-routes of the Christian Syrian merchants were closed, and for a while the small but profitable trade in luxuries from the East stopped almost completely.

The Jews Become the Merchants—To the Jews of Western Europe, however, this situation opened up an excellent opportunity. The Mohammedans knew that the Jews were not involved in their quarrel with the Christians. The Christians, on the other hand, did not fear the Jews as they did the Mohammedans. Thus both sides permitted the Jews to come and go freely. Moreover, the Jews had another advantage: fellow Jews lived in every land and formed a chain of trading stations, a vast mercantile network which enabled trade to continue and develop. There were not many things which the West of those days could export to the East; furs and weapons were the most usual articles. On the way back, however, the merchants carried a fair variety of products: tapestries, valuable cloth and silk, and, above all, sugar and spice, which Western Europe lacked entirely. These journeys were not made quickly and easily. It took many months, if not years, for the Radanites (as a Moslem writer of those days called the Jewish merchants) to cover the distance between France and India or China. The roads were infested with robbers and many other perils. It required courage, daring and imagi-

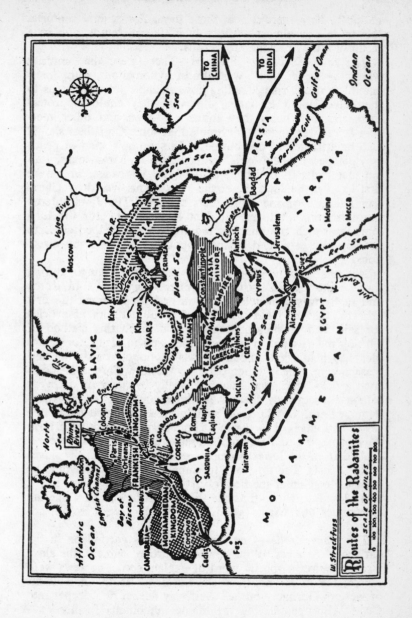

nation to be a merchant in those days. For several centuries this trade was almost exclusively in Jewish hands, and as a result of it they became prosperous.

The Jews Encourage Progress—Those were the centuries when the word "Jew" was almost synonymous with "merchant." Various rulers, noting how valuable this trade was to themselves and their lands, did what they could to protect them. In such cases they spoke of "Jews and other merchants." It was, indeed, inevitable that some Christians should also be attracted to this business. As soon as a kind of peace was patched up between Christians and Mohammedans, Italian merchants followed the lead of the Venetians, who were first to rival the Jews. Later the Jews themselves drew Christian fellow townsmen into their business. The Jews entered partnerships with them and lent them money for the long journeys which the business required. Trade helped cities to develop and expanded business opportunities in many directions.

Artisans and Jews—Another economic change during those centuries was destined to affect Jewish life. In Rome and in Rome's provinces the Jews had been among the first artisans, that is, handworkers and manufacturers of articles for sale, and they never entirely abandoned this method of earning their living. In southern Italy and in Sicily, for example, they held what amounted to a monopoly of dyeing and glassmaking. But in other parts of Western Europe all common articles were manufactured locally by the serfs on every estate; consequently there was almost no need for independent artisans. By the time such need arose once more, the Jews were engaged in the most important and profitable business of export and import. Moreover, the artisans were recruited from the lowest elements of the population, the slaves and the serfs. The time was to come when the Jews would be anxious to re-enter the field of artisanship, but by that time it was closed to them through the establishment of Christian fraternities of artisans (guilds) into which Jews were not admitted.

The Slave Trade—One type of business carried on in the early Middle Ages by the Jews of Europe, namely, the slave trade, requires a special word of explanation. The Jews were among the most important slave-dealers. As the inhabitants of western Germany pushed their way deeper and deeper into Central Europe, driving the Slavic inhabitants farther eastward and taking away their land, they brought back captives whom they sold to Jewish traders. The Jews, in turn, transported these slaves to other lands to be sold to Christian and Mohammedan masters. Everyone condemns this type of business nowadays, but it was a legitimate and, in view of the economic organization of society, a necessary business then. The Church objected to the Jews' retaining the slaves for themselves, but it had no objection to slavery or to slave trade.

2. THE JEWS AND MEDIEVAL SOCIETY

The Jews and the Nobility—One class in medieval society which most thoroughly appreciated the value of the Jews was the aristocracy. From the king down they made use of the Jews to meet their economic needs and sometimes also to help in the government. There were exceptions, of course, when greed or fanaticism turned one or another nobleman into an enemy. Generally speaking, however, the Jews received ample protection both at home and on their long journeys. Official laws were sometimes hostile because they were influenced by the Church, but the more important human relationships were not unfriendly even when a churchman was the ruler of a district.

Some Kings and Their Jews—Charlemagne (768–814) was one of the wisest and most important kings of the early Middle Ages. While his laws may have discriminated against the Jews, his actions did not. He, too, found it to his interest to protect them and their expanding commerce. In 797 he sent an embassy to the khalif of Bagdad, Harun al-Rashid, and with this embassy went, as interpreter and guide, a Jew by the name of Isaac. Isaac was, in fact, the only survivor of the difficult three-year journey. His return, in 802, to Charlemagne's court created a tremendous stir because he brought with him, as a gift from the Moselm king to the Christian emperor, an elephant, an animal till then unseen in the West. Charlemagne's son, Louis the Pious (814–840), showed an even more favorable attitude. Jews were so important economically at this period that the market day of Lyons was changed from Saturday to a weekday.

The Jews and the Cities—The Jews played a prominent part in the revival of town life. The old cities of Roman days woke slowly from their sleep of many centuries. New towns, surrounded by walls characteristic of the period, sprang up along rivers and other highways of commerce. Under the protection of kings and the local noblemen or monasteries,

Jews once more settled in towns, and carried on their business. From there they started on their long journeys and thither they brought the goods to be sold at the fairs. A Jewish community meant a prosperous town. As late as the year 1084, that is, only a few years before the First Crusade, the bishop of Speyer made an effort to get Jews to settle in his town. He started his famous edict with the following sentence: "Desiring to make a town out of the village of Speyer, I thought to raise its dignity many times by getting Jews to settle there."

The Jews and the Townsmen—The Christian inhabitants of the towns were also friendly. Jews and Christians visited one another and joined in each other's joys and sorrows. On occasions when the town was attacked by an enemy, the Jews did their share of the fighting. Even religious discussions were not uncommon. The Jews dressed and acted like their Christian neighbors and spoke the same language. In all but religion there was essentially no difference between the two elements of the population. And although religion held a very important place in the life of every man and woman during the Middle Ages, there were but few indications between the sixth and the twelfth centuries that the period of friendliness and goodwill would be brought to a violent close.

3. The Communal Foundation

The Jewish Street—Among the Jews of the towns life went on in accordance with well established traditions, modified to some extent by the needs of the time and place. The number of Jews in Western Europe was not large; but, then, the Gentile population also was comparatively small. An important city might have forty or fifty Jewish families among a few thousand Christian families. There were no restrictions requiring the Jews to live in any particular part of the town. Jews lived near Christians and Christians lived in streets which were otherwise predominantly Jewish. The natural tendency, however, for like-minded people to live close together, persisted and continued to be reinforced by Jewish religious needs.

Although almost all Jews lived in towns after the eighth century, some of them owned small parcels of tillable land. A good many Christians, too, had patches of land within or close to the city, plots large enough for the needs of the family. In wine-growing districts a Jew living in the town might own an extensive vineyard from which he could even draw his livelihood, as the famous teacher, Rashi, did in the eleventh century.

The Power to Punish—All Jews belonged to the Jewish community. Any other arrangement was impossible. A man was either a Jew or a Christian, and, if he were a Jew, the Jews and the Christians held him to certain duties and responsibilities. If he refused to accept the regulations imposed by the Jewish community, including Jewish religious observances, he could be punished. The Jews had the right to imprison a fellow Jew, punish him with stripes, that is, lashes not exceeding thirty-nine, or by excommunication. The last was the severest penalty, for it meant that no Jew, not even a member of his immediate family, would have anything to do with the excommunicated man or woman. If he moved to another town, the Jews there would usually also exclude him as soon as they found out about his past. There was nothing left for him but to become a Christian. In such an event, however, the Christian government, for reasons of its own, cooperated with the Jews by confiscating the man's property. Excommunication was thus a powerful weapon in the hands of the community leaders and enabled them to enforce their authority.

Community Leadership—Jewish communities were organized in very much the same way as those of Palestine had been toward the end of the Second Commonwealth. There was the Head of the Community, known as *Rosh ha-Keneset*. Among the Christians he was often known as the "Jewish Bishop," though of course he was nothing like a bishop of the Church in his manner of life or the duties he was called on to perform. Along with him were the *gabbaim*, overseers of the various communal institutions, collectors and distributors of charity, and assessors of the amount of taxes which each Jew had to pay. The usual number of *gabbaim* was seven, though this number varied in accordance with the size and the needs of the community. These officers were elected annually by the taxpaying members of the community.

Paid Officials—Certain duties in communal life had to be performed so regularly and were so burdensome or time-consuming that men had to be engaged to perform them. The office of *shammash*, for example, has a long and honorable history behind it. Its predecessor, in Palestine as well as in the early days of the Diaspora, had been called *hazzan*, which meant overseer. It used to be the duty of the *hazzan* to superintend the activities inside the synagogue. Then, two developments took place at the same time: the reciting of the prayers became more complicated by poetic additions and by changes in melody, and communal activities began to multiply. While the leading of ordinary daily services could still be done by any Jew, extraordinary or Sabbath services had to be led by an expert. The *hazzan* was the logical person to take this duty upon himself. While leading the service, he could not supervise the administration of the synagogue; nor was it any longer sufficiently dignified for him to act as general assistant to the *Rosh ha-Keneset* and the *gabbaim*. Thus, in time the *hazzan* became the prayer-leader, while other communal duties were performed by another paid official, the *shammash*, or "assistant."

Men of Learning—Most communal duties were performed without salary, since, according to rabbinic teaching, the Torah was not to be "used as a spade to dig with." Indeed, communal service was considered a high honor. In most instances even the *hazzan* led the services as a volunteer. The one thing required of many of these communal officers was a considerable degree of learning. Certainly the head of the community was almost always, at this time, chosen for his knowledge. Since there were as yet no rabbis in our sense of the word, the heads of the communities had to guide their Jewish fellow townsmen in matters of religion and tradition. Another man whose knowledge could frequently be relied on was the community teacher. His duty was to teach the children, and he was paid for his work by the parents, although his teaching was supervised by the communal officials. He sometimes had more knowledge than was needed for instructing the young, and, if so, this knowledge was also at the service of the community. Aside from *hazzan*, *Rosh ha-Keneset* and teacher, there were probably other men in each town whose knowledge of Jewish law and life could be relied on. There was, therefore, no difficulty in bringing together a Jewish court of law, consisting of three men, whenever some dispute made it necessary. Of course, in case of doubt they could consult the learned men of the next town, and there was always the possibility of sending a *she-elah* to the distant Gaon at the academy of Sura or Pumpeditha.

Communal Property—Every Jewish community had to have a certain amount of property. A synagogue-house was a necessity, for it was used not only for religious services, but also for many public occasions. In it meetings of the community would take place, and outside it, in the courtyard, weddings were celebrated. In many communities the *mikvah*, the ritual bath, was an annex to the synagogue. In most instances, a part of the synagogue building, or another annex, was used as a schoolhouse. In some way, too, a "hospice" was arranged for, where travelers could be accommodated. Finally, a plot of ground had to be acquired for a cemetery. Essentially, the same institutions continued throughout the later periods of Jewish history in Europe. From time to time, the institutions were modified because of changes in the position of the Jews, advances in Jewish culture, and the influence exerted by the Mohammedan or Christian environment.

4. Cultural Foundation

The Rise of Christian Culture—When the Jews enjoy freedom, Jewish and non-Jewish cultures benefit from one another. During the reign of the wise Emperor Charlemagne, around the year 800, dawn began to break over the dark mental horizon of Western Europe. Decrease in disorder, gradual growth of the towns and efforts of important leaders of the Church laid the foundations for a cultural revival. There were still to be many ups and downs—the real revival was not due till three centuries later—but in the ninth century ignorance began to be looked upon as something of which at least a clergyman ought to be ashamed. Many bishops and abbots were disturbed that so many of the friendly discussions on religion resulted in the Jews getting the better of the argument.

The Italian Cultural Bridge—An improvement in Christian culture worked in favor of Jewish culture as well. As conditions became more stable, the Jews became more prosperous; and as they became more prosperous, they had more leisure to study. The fact that most of them lived in towns made the spread of knowledge easier and more rapid. Moreover, the Jews were stimulated by their contacts with distant Jewish communities.

Ever since the heyday of the Roman empire, in the first century, Jews had been living in southern Italy and had always kept in touch with the Jews of Palestine. When the Palestinian academies revived under the Mohammedans, in the seventh and eighth centuries, the South Italian Jews benefited therefrom and for a while led in Jewish learning in Europe. Naturally, the Jews of North Italy were the first to take advantage of the learning of their neighbors, and invited scholars to come and settle among them. Several important books in Jewish literature were written by Italian Jews around the year 1000. The best example is the 'Aruch, a dictionary of the Talmud. The fact that such a dictionary was written proves that knowledge of talmudic literature was spreading, although it also proves that many students were finding the Talmud difficult. From the Italian city of Lucca came the learned Calonymos, who is said to have saved the life of Emperor Otto II in 982. The Calonymos family, settling in the German city of Mayence, is supposed to have brought with it the desire for learning which soon thereafter began to spread among the Jewish communities of the Rhineland.

The Cultural Bridge over the Provence—The Jews of Central Europe were encouraged at the same time from another direction. Jewish cultural activity had long been going on in the south of France in the Provence district. An academy had been established here perhaps by one of the itinerant geonic emissaries, perhaps by some young Jews who had gone to Babylonia to study and then returned home to teach. In any event, by the year 900 there were several important scholars in the Provence who attracted Jewish students from Central Europe. One of these, in the middle of the tenth century, was the famous Gershom of Mayence, who later returned to Central Europe to teach. He subsequently became so famous that he was called, not simply *Rabbi* Gershom, but by a higher title—*Rabbenu* (Our Teacher) Gershom, to which was added the phrase *Meor ha-Golah*, "Light of the Dispersion."

Gershom's Regulations—With Rabbenu Gershom's return home, the Jews of Central Europe became culturally independent. They no longer needed inspiration and guidance either from Italy or from the Provence. His academy now produced Jewish scholars able to interpret the Bible and Jewish tradition, and to guide Jewish life. Rabbenu Gershom himself made certain modifications which are of great importance to Judaism to this day. Jewish law gave him no authority to make changes except for his own community. But so great was the esteem in which he was held that other communities accepted his regulations. Later generations also adhered to them. Rabbenu Gershom did not really make the changes all by himself; he called a synod, that is, a conference, of the leaders of his community and perhaps of other communities as well, and they passed upon his regulations. In Hebrew these are called *takkanot*, or improvements.

The Takkanah against Polygamy—His most far-reaching *takkanah* dealt with the question of monogamy. The Bible permitted Jews to have more than one wife. As time went on, however, the Jews adopted monogamy as their rule, although, since the law on the subject had not been changed, there was a Jew now and then who married more than one woman. This gave their Christian neighbors a chance to speak ill of the Jews. It probably also resulted in quarrels within the family. It was time, therefore, that the willfulness of a few should be curbed for the sake of the reputation of the entire group. At the synod Rabbenu Gershom introduced a *takkanah* by which anyone who married more than one wife was to be excommunicated. His regulation was to be in force for only four hundred years; consequently it should have expired around 1350. But the good sense of the *takkanah* has kept it alive among Jews of the German tradition. Sephardi Jews and others, who came under Mohammedan influence, have never considered themselves bound by it. To this day cases of polygamy occur among the Yemenite Jews and the Sephardi Jews of the Near East.

Other Regulations—Others of Rabbenu Gershom's *takkanot* reflect Jewish life of a thousand years ago. One *takkanah* required the woman's assent to a divorce. Another threatened with excommunication anyone reading another person's letter. Since there was no postal system then, letters would be entrusted to people going in the general direction of the one to whom the letter was addressed. It was a courtesy people rendered one another. But there must have been travelers who yielded either to curiosity or to the temptation of whiling away some tedious hours by reading the letters entrusted to their care. They might thus learn too much about the private life and business of the sender and the recipient.

Another prohibition was aimed at those who made changes in a book. Printing was not destined to be invented for five hundred years, and books used to be copied by hand. A reader or a copyist, not understanding a sentence, might think it should read differently and make the change to suit his own thought. The next reader or copyist then ofttimes considered the change part of the original wording. In this way, truth would sometimes be changed into falsehood even in such important works as the Talmud. Rabbenu Gershom's *takkanah* was necessary to safeguard Jewish culture.

The Problem of Culture—The great problem of that day was not so much to get people interested in reading and study; that had already been achieved. It was not even to develop scholars from among the Jewish people. The academies of Italy, the Provence and the Rhineland were doing well in that respect. The real problem was how to make it possible for the ordinary person to understand the books fundamental to Jewish life, such as the Talmud or even the Bible, with all the profound ethical and social truths which they contain. The common people among the Jews no longer understood the Hebrew and Aramaic languages. Many of them could not follow the complicated explanations offered by previous commentators on the Bible. To even more of them the argumentation in the Talmud made of it a closed book. Yet all of them wanted to study and to understand. That this problem was solved, and that for many centuries thereafter knowledge was the rule and ignorance the exception among the Jews, was due to the genius of the scholar and teacher always referred to by the Jews as Rashi.

Life of a Sage—Among the very great names in the long history of the Jewish people that of Rabbi Solomon ben Isaac holds high place. For century after century since his death, every Jewish boy became acquainted with him on the very threshold of education. Adults, too, found him an indispensable intellectual companion. As in the case of every great Jewish name, the name of this man also was affectionately abbreviated, the *R* from Rabbi, the *Sh* from Shelomo and the *I* from his father's name being combined into Rashi.

He was born in 1040 into a scholarly and well-to-do family. He evidently enjoyed a fair income throughout his life, his earnings being derived from a vineyard which he inherited near his native city of Troyes, in the French district of Champagne. His teachers, including his father, had been directly or indirectly pupils of Rabbenu Gershom, so that Rashi was brought up in accordance with the finest traditions of Jewish scholarship. Sometime during his twenties he felt the need of going to Mayence and to Worms, then the seats of great academies. Upon his return home, he gathered some pupils about him and inspired them by his piety as much as by his learning. Even his daughters, for he had no sons, were brought up to a fair degree of Jewish learning. He led a quiet, simple life about which not much is known. There was probably little enough to tell about a man whose life was confined to his study.

The Commentaries—Rashi's great reputation rests upon his two commentaries: one explaining the Bible, the other the Talmud. His object was not to show how learned or clever he was, but rather to guide the student through difficult passages and enable him to understand the plain meaning of the two fundamental books of Jewish life. He wrote, therefore, in a clear, simple Hebrew, the sort that even a beginner could follow. When he came across a word in the text which was hard to explain, he gave its translation in the French language, the one which he spoke. Into his commentary on the *Humash* (Pentateuch—the Five Books of Moses) he put many of the most beautiful midrashic stories and ethical maxims, thus making it an inspiring textbook in the good Jewish life. His commentary on the Talmud turned it from a collection of discussions understood only by the scholar into a work which an intelligent Jew could read with comparative ease. Frequently a single word of his sheds light on an entire passage and makes a complicated argument perfectly clear. There have been many other commentaries on Bible and Talmud, but Rashi has remained the teacher of generation after generation of Jews.

Rise of the Rabbinate—A direct result of the increase in scholarship among the Jews of France and Germany was the development of the rabbinic office. The *Rosh ha-Keneset* had until then guided both the religious and the secular life of his community. That worked well enough as long as a community did not have a large number of men interested in learning. But when the situation changed for the better, it became necessary to have someone whose superiority in Jewish knowledge could not be disputed. If a lawsuit arose among Jews in a community, the judges had to be men who could support their opinions by a profound knowledge of the Talmud and other legal tradition. If, as was the case more and more often, the men of the community wanted to continue their studies, it was necessary to have someone capable of guiding them. Every fairly important Jewish community prided itself on maintaining an academy. What eventually happened, therefore, was that the head of the community and his *gabbaim*, or trustees, were left to carry on its civil business, whereas for guidance in religious and intellectual life someone noted for scholarship would be invited to take the helm and preside over the Jewish court of law. He still was not paid a salary. The office was purely honorary, and the man thus chosen had to earn his living through some other occupation; he might be *hazzan*, he might be a teacher, or he might be a businessman. The custom of paying him a salary began later, when the duties of religious guidance became so numerous and burdensome that he had time for nothing else.

The Fortified Spirit—It was well for the future of Jewish life that this cultural development took place during this period of comparative peace and prosperity. It strengthened the Jewish spirit and prepared it for the evil days which were lying ahead. For as the eleventh century drew to a close, when Rashi attained his fifty-fifth year, a storm broke out which shook the economic and social foundations of Jewish life, and only their religion and culture helped the Jews maintain an indomitable, unconquerable spirit.

CHAPTER III

THE GOLDEN AGE IN SPAIN

THE JEWS OF SPAIN LIVE THROUGH AN ERA OF PEACE AND FREEDOM DURING WHICH THEY ACHIEVE MUCH FOR THEM-SELVES AND FOR THE WORLD

An Ideal Age in the Diaspora (900–1200)—There is one period in the history of the Jews in Europe to which the Jews have always looked back with pride, which has served them as an example and inspiration and which they therefore call "the Golden Age." An age rich in poets and grammarians, moralists and philosophers, scientists and statesmen, it is comparable to the best produced by any people at any time. No mere accident caused so many great men to live at that particular time and place. Give any group a number of generations of peace and a stimulating environment, and it will yield the best that is in it. The Jews of North Africa and Spain enjoyed both these factors for several centuries after the Mohammedan conquest, and the results were remarkable for European culture, both Jewish and non-Jewish.

1. Spain's Promise

Mild Rule—In 711 the Jews of Spain sighed with relief.* After a dreadful century of physical and religious slavery under the last Visigoths, they were now free. The conquest of Spain by the Mohammedans meant the removal of barriers to living as Jews. Many of those who had fled their homes and

* See above, p. 274.

gone into exile in North Africa and the Provence now returned to their ancestral land. The Mohammedans, to be sure, also made efforts to convert the population. But there were no persecutions and the mild political rule of the new masters attracted Jewish immigrants from lands as far away as Babylonia and Persia.

Economic Opportunities—The Mohammedan conquest also reopened to the Jews the economic opportunities of a prosperous country. They could become farmers if they had the means to acquire land. But the previous century had impoverished them and they had to start from the very bottom. In time, there were a good many Jews who owned small estates near the larger towns, but the majority of Spain's Jews, like those of Christian Europe, became local or international merchants, and they made an important contribution to the wealth of Spain. For several centuries business was the more attractive because of the fact that Mohammedan territory stretched uninterruptedly from the shores of the Atlantic to the eastern boundary of Persia, and because the Mohammedans controlled the waters of the Mediterranean Sea.

Cities and Culture—Before long Spain became the wealthiest and the most cultured land in Europe. The Moors of Spain took over the interest in science, poetry and philosophy of the Mohammedans in Persia and of the other lands of the Near East. The Jews were influenced by the intellectual pursuits of their neighbors, and became zealous students of the same branches of learning, except that they substituted the Bible for the Koran, Hebrew for Arabic, and Jewish for Mohammedan theology. The very fact that so large a portion of the Jewish population of Spain lived in cities, made for the widest possible spread of cultural interests among them, since cities have always been the centers of culture.

Politics and Cultural Independence—Within a comparatively short time it became clear that the vast territory conquered by the Mohammedans could not be held together under one ruler. Spain and western North Africa broke away from the rule of Bagdad, and established a number of independent principalities. Striving to make their states the intellectual superiors of all Mohammedan territory, the rulers were wise enough to see the advantage of encouraging similar cultural independence among their non-Mohammedan subjects. The result was that the Jews cooperated with Mohammedans in scientific and philosophical studies as well as in teaching at the schools which the Spanish kings established. A Christian monk from France might come to study at a Mohammedan university in Spain, where he would be taught by a Jewish professor the learning acquired from books written by an ancient pagan from Greece or Alexandria. Important books originally written in Greek or even in the language of the Hindus made their way to Spain in Arabic translation. Here a Jew would translate them into Hebrew. The Hebrew translation, in its turn, made its way into the Christian Provence, where another Jew translated it into Latin, thus making it available to the rest of Europe. Any number of works fundamental to the development of European thought went through this process. Thus the Jews of Spain and the Provence acted as transmitters of ancient and Arabic culture to Christian Europe.

2. THE FOUNDERS OF SPANISH JEWISH CULTURE

The Great Hasdai—In addition to what they were doing for the revival of the European mind in general, the Jews were developing their own culture. The two centuries after 711 witnessed a slow but steady accumulation of knowledge. Then the Golden Age opened with one of its most remarkable men. Hasdai ibn* Shaprut (from about 925 to 975) started his career as a physician and always remained one, never giving up his interest in medical experiments, especially in drugs. In time, he became physician to the khalif, to whom he also rendered distinguished service as unofficial adviser on matters of state. He gained the reputation of being an excellent diplomat, and on several occasions helped maintain peace between the Mohammedans and the Christians. In the course of his diplomatic correspondence he established communication with the Jewish kingdom of the Khazars in southeastern Russia. But his chief claim to immortality among the Jews lay in the field of Jewish scholarship. He surrounded himself with Jewish men of learning, whom he encouraged and supported. He befriended Moses ben Hanoch, a messenger of the Babylonian academies, who laid the foundations of talmudic study in Spain.

From Grocer to Diplomat—Another important representative of the first generation of the Golden Age was one whose story reads like a fairy tale. Samuel ibn Naghdela (993–1056) started his career as the owner of a grocer's shop. He

* The word *ibn* is the Arabic for the Hebrew *ben*, which means "son of."

managed to acquire a remarkable amount of learning in languages, mathematics and philosophy. In 1012, a series of civil wars began among the Mohammedans of Spain. The unsettled times forced Samuel to move from Cordova to Malaga, where he opened his grocer's shop near the royal palace. The illiterate servants of the palace would come to him to read their letters and write their replies. Then, a letter written by Samuel fell into the hands of the grand vizier, who was astonished at its beautiful handwriting and fine style. The vizier invited Samuel to become his secretary, and in this position Samuel made excellent use of his knowledge and his wisdom. When the vizier died, Samuel succeeded him as adviser to the king of Granada. His duties placed him on several occasions at the head of Granada's armies.

Samuel ibn Naghdela was important as well in Jewish life. The king of Granada appointed him *Nagid*, that is, leader of the Jews, and he was given approximately the same authority that the Exilarch exercised in Babylonia. He, too, encouraged scholars and poets, and was himself an excellent poet. He established and conducted a talmudical academy, wrote an introduction to the Talmud and a dictionary of biblical Hebrew.

His son Joseph, however, was a different sort of man. He inherited some of his father's virtues and all his positions. Learned and clever, he followed his father as vizier of Granada and as *Nagid* of the kingdom's Jews. But he lacked his father's wisdom and humility. Loving authority and display, he aroused the envy and dislike of the Mohammedans, and thus brought misfortune upon the Jews. A riot broke out, during which Joseph and several thousand other Jews paid with their lives for the tactlessness of their leader. This was one of the temporary storms which passed over the Jewish people. Fortunately, it was over quickly and left no bad effects upon the Jews of Granada or the rest of the Mohammedan lands. But it was a warning that the mob is easily stirred, that the majority of a population never long remembers the service rendered by a member of a minority, and that one Jew may bring misfortune upon his entire group. These were the lessons Jews have learned time and again.

Foundations of Talmudic Study—In addition to the other fields of Jewish culture, there was being established in Spain a tradition of talmudic study destined to exert a great influence on Judaism. The first important academy was founded by Moses ben Hanoch in Cordova about 950, and there were other teachers of the Babylonian Talmud after him. But the real foundation of the Spanish talmudic tradition was laid by Isaac of Fez, or Alfasi, so called because he came from the North African city of Fez. At the very time that Rashi was preparing his great commentary in France, Isaac Alfasi was writing his work on the Talmud in Spain. Whereas Rashi was interested in making the entire contents of the Talmud clear to every student, Alfasi was interested only in talmudic law. His book was an abridgment of the Talmud, omitting material which had no relation to law; but legal discussions, especially such as were important for the Jews of the Diaspora, were plainly set forth. Rashi and his successors placed the emphasis on study; Alfasi and his successor emphasized practical observance.

3. THREE GREAT POETS

Poetry and the Jews—The Jews have always been interested in poetry. It could not be otherwise, since they were brought up with the poetry of the Bible upon their lips. The imagery and the deep feelings of the prophets and the psalmists were bound to sink into their hearts. They continued to write poetry, but the events of their history made them prefer folklore (Midrash) and legal discussion (Talmud). For poetry seemed to be a luxury, unless it were in connection with the liturgy, that is, the prayers. But the early liturgical poets, with a few exceptions like Rav, were more interested in clever historical allusions and in complicated poetical constructions than in beauty of language and imagery. The result was much poetry, but little that might be considered of the first order.

Arabic Influence The situation changed under the influence of the Mohammedans in Spain. In the first place, the Mohammedans brought with them the tradition of the original Arabs, who loved good poetry, whether religious or secular, and encouraged it. Secondly, the Mohammedan interest in the purity of the Arabic language brought about a revival of Jewish interest in Hebrew style and grammar. Finally, the greater freedom of thought and wider cultural interests which the Jews of Spain now enjoyed prepared them to read poetry and to appreciate it in Hebrew.

Solomon ibn Gabirol—The first and, in the opinion of some, the foremost of the Spanish Jewish poets was Solomon ibn Gabirol (1021–1069). He showed signs of his poetic gifts when he was but sixteen years old. Orphaned of both parents, he was supported and protected by wealthy men who were interested in his talents. Few men, however, could get along with Ibn Gabirol; he was too conceited and too quarrelsome. He said of himself:

> When my anger is roused,
> The heavens rumble with my thunder.

He expressed his contempt for other poets by saying: "Tiny little ants that they are, they venture to compare themselves with me." The result was that he could never stay in one place for any length of time. Lonely and disappointed with himself and his surroundings, he could express his emotions in incomparable imagery. He was primarily a lyric poet, and most of his writing was religious in nature. Many of his verses were subsequently included in the prayer book, especially that of the Sephardim. The following poem was written for the Passover service:

> Look up to thy Maker, O soul of mine,
>   Thy Creator remember whilst thou art young;
> Cry morning and night to His grace divine,
>   And in all thy songs let His name be sung.
>
> On earth the Lord is thy portion and cup,
>   And when from thy body thou goest lone,
> A place for thy rest He hath builded up
>   And made thee a nest underneath His throne.
> Wherefore morning and night I will bless my Lord,
>   And from all that hath breath let His praise be poured.

The language of Solomon ibn Gabirol was a superb Hebrew; his meter was flawless; his imagery apt; his sentences stirring; his thoughts exalting.*

Moses ibn Ezra—The second of the famous Spanish Jewish poets was Moses ibn Ezra (about 1080–1139). He came of a prominent and learned family; later he and several of his brothers lost their possessions during political disturbances in Spain. An unfortunate love affair is supposed to have saddened him deeply. The troubles which were beginning to overtake the Jewish people both in Christian and in Moslem countries gave rise to some of his most touching laments. One of his poems takes up the midrashic comparison of Israel to a dove:

* See *Selected Religious Poems of Solomon ibn Gabirol*, by Israel Zangwill and Israel Davidson. The quotations were drawn from this volume.

> O doves, by cruel foes beset,
>> Dispersed to every wind—
>> Sad ones, devoid of strength,
> And grieving in the snares of wretchedness—
> In quiet cotes, in houses safe and strong,
>> God give you to find rest!

His poetry, much of which is religious in nature, likewise found its way into the Sephardic liturgy.*

Judah ha-Levi—The third of the great poets, and in some respects the greatest of them, was Judah ha-Levi (1086–1145). He was a physician, happy in his family and his profession, a man of great personal charm and possessed of numerous friends. Nowadays we would call him a nationalist, for he expressed the hope of exiled Israel to be redeemed and restored to the home of their fathers where, he thought, they would inevitably become the religious guides of mankind. He said in his famous *Ode to Zion:*

> Zion, wilt thou not ask if peace's wing
>> Shadows the captives that ensue thy peace,
> Left lonely from thine ancient shepherding?

> Lo! west and east and north and south—world-wide—
>> All those from far and near, without surcease,
> Salute thee: Peace and peace from every side. . . .

> Happy is he that waiteth:—he shall go
>> To thee, and thine arising radiance see
> When over him shall break thy morning glow;

> And see rest for thy chosen; and sublime
>> Rejoicing find amid the joy of thee
> Returned unto thine olden youthful time.

He himself could not rest among the comforts of family and friends. Despite the dangers to travelers in those days and the risk involved in going to Palestine while the crusading movement was in progress, he went to spend the rest of his days in the Holy Land. His joy during the preparations for the departure were expressed in such verses as these:

> Beautiful height! O joy! The whole world's gladness!
>> O great King's city, mountain blest!

* See *Selected Poems of Moses ibn Ezra,* by Solomon Solis-Cohen and Heinrich Brody.

My soul is yearning unto thee—is yearning
   From limits of the west.
And who shall grant me, on the wings of eagles,
   To rise and seek thee through the years,
Until I mingle with thy dust beloved
   The waters of my tears?

The last Judah ha-Levi was heard of was in Egypt, where friends tried to persuade him not to venture into Palestine. Thereafter we lose track of him. A legend has therefore grown up that, at the very moment when he knelt to kiss the ground at the gate of Jerusalem, an Arab horseman hurled his spear at the prostrate figure and cut short the poet's life.

Judah ha-Levi was a nationalistic poet. Repeatedly he expressed his sense of the holiness of the Jewish people and his belief in its eternity. Thus, for example, he comforted the Jews for their exile by saying:

Let them not cry despairing, nay, nor say:
   Hope faileth and our strength is near to die.
Let them believe that they shall be alway,
   Nor cease until there be no night nor day.

Consequently, although Ibn Gabirol surpassed Judah ha-Levi in the power and grandeur of his verse, it was the latter who remained the beloved poet of Israel and their inspiration in days of evil.*

4. A COMMENTATOR, A TRAVELER AND A NUMBER OF PHILOSOPHERS

Abraham ibn Ezra—One of the most interesting characters of medieval Jewry was Abraham ibn Ezra (1092–1167), a contemporary and perhaps a relative of the poet Moses ibn Ezra. Abraham ibn Ezra also tried to write poetry; some is not bad, none is very good, and much is merely clever rhyme. He was as poor in worldly goods as he was rich in wit and learning. Wandering all over Western Europe, he stimulated scholarship wherever he spent any time, whether in Italy, the Provence or England. He wrote books on grammar, philosophy, religion and astrology. His chief work, however, was his commentary on the Pentateuch and many other

* See *Selected Poems of Jehudah Halevi*, by Nina Salaman and Heinrich Brody. The above translations were taken from this volume.

books of the Bible. The difference between his commentary and that of Rashi reflects not only the difference between the two authors, but also that between French Jewish culture and Spanish Jewish culture. Ibn Ezra lacked Rashi's simplicity, his piety and directness. But his commentary is more profound and philosophical; it goes into questions of grammar and rational interpretations. It is therefore more difficult and is not meant for the beginner in scriptural study. Its influence has been more limited than that of Rashi, but it has served to exemplify the attitudes of Spanish Jewish culture to the Jews of other Western lands, both in his own and later generations.

Benjamin the Traveler—Benjamin ben Jonah was a resident of Tudela in the northern part of the Spanish Peninsula. Having gathered a tidy sum as a merchant, Benjamin felt that he could indulge himself in the way he had always dreamed, and in 1160 he set out on a leisurely journey. He went across southern France into northern Italy and made his way south; then he went over to Greece and from there into Asia and then into North Africa. His trip consumed thirteen years, so that he returned home in 1173. It may well be that Benjamin was not the only Jewish traveler of his day; there must have been many Jews who still traveled eastward on business. What makes Benjamin's journey important is that he kept a diary. He did not include in it all the experiences he encountered—though in those days he must have met with many—but limited himself to giving the best information he could obtain on the Jews of the various places he visited: their number, their economic conditions, their learning or ignorance, and the manner in which they lived. It is this that makes his diary one of the most important sources of our knowledge about the Jews of his day.

Jewish Philosophy—The word *philosophy* means "love of wisdom." Its object is to explain life and its problems. During the Middle Ages, religion was considered the greatest wisdom: proof of the existence of God, the problems of the creation of the world, questions of the nature of good and evil, and demonstration that the writer's religion was better than any other—these were the most important subjects with which the philosophers of that day dealt. There had been Jewish philosophers before the Christian Middle Ages: Philo of Alexandria in the first century of the Common Era, and Saadia Gaon of Bagdad in the tenth century. Spain of the period we are now studying produced others.

Ibn Gabirol as a Philosopher—A close relationship existed between philosophy and poetry. Solomon ibn Gabirol, for example, wrote a work called *The Fountain of Life,* which was an excellent discussion of the fundamentals of religious faith. The work had a strange history. Ibn Gabirol wrote it in Arabic, and in it he discussed religion in general, not Judaism in particular. As a result the Jews of his day did not feel the need of translating it into Hebrew, and the non-Jews never recognized that a Jew had written it. Eventually it was translated into Latin and was studied by Christian monks as though it were a work of Christian authorship. In the course of time and of much recopying, the name of the author became corrupted from Ibn Gabirol to Avicebron. It was not till about 1850 that Solomon Munk, a French Jewish scholar, discovered the true authorship of the work. Through the centuries a Jew had been teaching religion to Christians.

Judah ha-Levi as Philosopher—Judah ha-Levi was another example of a poet who was also a philosopher. He named his book, *The Kuzari,* after the Khazars; for he used the story of their conversion to Judaism as the thread on which to hang his discussion of the merits of Judaism, Mohammedanism and Christianity. He introduced his book by giving each religion a spokesman who defends it against the criticism of the other two, the Khazar king and his court acting as judges. Naturally, it is the spokesman for Judaism who gets the best of the argument and finally wins the Khazar king over to the Jewish faith. Thereupon the Jew instructs the king in Jewish life and its meaning. This book was written in Arabic. Translated into Hebrew, it has enjoyed great popularity among the Jews, serving to bolster up faith in Judaism during days of trial and distress.

On the Duties of the Heart—There were other philosophers among the Jews of Spain. Bahya ibn Pakuda, for example, was a judge in a Spanish Jewish community during the first half of the twelfth century. We might have expected him to be interested in law; instead he was interested in what should be the foundation of law, that is, human attitudes. Judaism, he argued, is a religion which imposes a great many duties upon a human being. The mind has a duty to absorb knowledge; the tongue has a duty to speak truth; the hands have a duty to do charity, and so on. But the heart also has its duties, and these are more numerous and more important than those of any other part of the body. For unless the heart accompanies every act with the proper feeling and emotion, it becomes merely mechanical, and therefore religiously insufficient. He called his book *The Duties of the Heart*, and few books down to our own day have enjoyed greater popularity among the masses of the Jews.

5. A SECOND MOSES

The Foremost Jew of the Middle Ages—It is generally agreed that the foremost Jew of the Middle Ages was Moses ben Maimon, whom the Jews have known under the abbreviation RaMBaM (*R*abbenu *M*oshe *b*en *M*aimon) and the world under the name Maimonides. The path of his life was not smooth and even; misfortune often sought him out. He was born in the Spanish city of Cordova in 1135, his father being a local judge of the Jewish community. When Moses was but thirteen years old, troubles came upon the Jews of Spain which forced the entire family to flee along with other coreligionists to North Africa. Here Moses continued to study with his father, and in these somewhat hostile surroundings he laid the foundation for a degree and depth of knowledge which has been the marvel of the world.

About ten years later, what remained of the family took ship across the Mediterranean in order to settle in Palestine. But Palestine was in disorder because of the crusades, and the family had to make their home in Egypt's capital, Cairo (called Fostat at that time). Here Moses continued to study and to write while he and David, his younger brother, went into the business of importing gems from India and Ethiopia. By this enterprise the entire family was supported. But after only a few years of peaceful life, Moses again faced trouble. David died in a shipwreck, and the family's support devolved upon Moses. He became a physician, gaining, before long, such fame in this profession that the ruler of the country, the lieutenant of the famous Saladin, made him physician of his court and of Saladin's family. Moses, it is said, even received an invitation to become the physician of Richard the Lionhearted when he was in the midst of his crusade in the Holy Land. Moses refused the offer, for he wanted no more wandering. In addition to his medical duties, Moses was appointed head (though probably not *Nagid*) of the Jews of Egypt. This was an office for which he received no compensation, though it involved an enormous amount of work. That this man found time to write his remarkable books is further proof of his genius. He died in 1204, and legend tells of his burial in Palestine.

Maimonides' Writings—Even if he had not written his three great works, Maimonides would have had a place in the cultural history of the Jewish people. He was still a young man when his reputation for immense scholarship spread among the Jews east and west. Like one of the Geonim of several centuries previously, he was called upon to answer questions addressed to him by various Jewish communities. He wrote on medicine and other secular subjects. But his large works are such unusual contributions to Jewish thought that each one of us, whether we have known it or not, has been influenced by them.

The Luminary—He began on his first great book when he was only twenty-three years old, and he worked on it during the long and dangerous voyage to Egypt. It is an attempt to illuminate the construction and contents of the Mishna. That is why he called it *The Luminary*. But it shed light on other matters as well. One of the things Maimonides tried to do was to indicate that the best of human knowledge was not in conflict with Judaism. He did this with physics and astronomy and mathematics. Most important of all for us is the fact that he did this also with ethics. As an introduction to the Mishna tractate *Abot* (sometimes called Ethics of the Fathers), Maimonides presented a discussion of the ethical rules of Aristotle and of several important Arab philosophers. He showed that Jewish ethics, rising independently from Judaism's teaching, compared favorably with the best that Greek and Arab had to offer. This discussion has been one of the most widely read little books for it has been studied separately under the name *The Eight Chapters*.

In connection with another part of the Mishna he tried to answer the question: "What are the most important ideas which Judaism asks every Jew to believe?" The question had been asked before and various answers had been given. Maimonides believed that in his day it was necessary, not only to indicate the important principles of all religious life, but also to show where Judaism differed from Mohammedanism and Christianity, since so many Jews lived in the midst of these two religious communities. He, therefore, formulated the famous "Thirteen Dogmas," or thirteen beliefs. Each dogma is a simple statement either of a principle fundamental to all three monotheistic religions or of a principle by which Judaism may be distinguished from the other two. In later years, as we shall see, people disputed Maimonides' formulation; conditions in their day required a different statement of the basic beliefs and ideals of Judaism. Nevertheless, the

Thirteen Dogmas soon became, and have since remained, the most popular definition of Orthodox Judaism. They were even included in the prayer book and have formed a basis for religious hymns, such as *Yigdal,* which are sung to this day in many synagogues.

The Code—Since Judaism is a religion of active duties (*mitzvot*), it was not enough to set down the theories upon which it was based; it was also necessary to acquaint people with its laws. Until Maimonides' time, the laws of the rabbis had never been arranged topically. Numerous discussions by the Tannaim or Amoraim on various subjects lie scattered through the treatises of the Talmud. The need to coordinate and clarify Jewish law was consequently urgent; but the difficulties were great. Such work required, not only a mind full of knowledge, but one also capable of organizing this knowledge and choosing among conflicting tannaitic and amoraic opinions. Only a man like Maimonides could have done it. He prepared his work in clear, concise Hebrew and offered it to the Jewish people as a *Mishneh Torah,* a "Repetition of the Teaching," that is, something which can take its place. Of course, Maimonides did not escape criticism for his manner of deciding what was and what was not the law, and even for the proud name he gave his book. Nevertheless, it has remained the most distinguished code of Jewish law in spite of the fact that many codes came into being later.

The Philosophy—Maimonides' crowning achievement was his philosophical work, *Moreh Nebuchim* (The Guide of the Perplexed). Others, as we have seen, had written on philosophy, but none had succeeded in answering so well the questions which challenged the intelligent man of that day. What with the claims of the other religions and their constant criticism of Judaism, what with the growing interest in the work of the ancient Greek philosopher Aristotle and the seeming disagreement between his views and certain statements of the Bible, the intellectual Jews of Maimonides' time were troubled, perplexed. One of them, Joseph ibn Aknin, earlier a pupil of Maimonides and later a physician in Bagdad, wrote to him and presented some of these difficulties. The *Moreh Nebuchim,* written in Arabic, was his reply, a reply eagerly studied for centuries not by Jews alone, but by Christian theologians as well. For this book was not only a justification of Judaism, it also proved that Judaism could and should be acceptable to the most advanced thinkers of Maimonides' time.

The Hero of the Age—Because of the books which he

wrote to guide future generations, and because he stood out as fulfilling the innermost ambitions of the Jew for intellectual vigor, deep faith, profound understanding and wealth of knowledge, Maimonides was the greatest of the great men whose names shed luster upon the Golden Age and upon Jewish history in the Middle Ages. What made these people great? What gave them so high a place in our story? They were not conquerors; they were not statesmen for the Jewish people. They advanced the cause of truth; they used their own talents to sing of the hopes of the Jewish people; they dignified and purified Jewish life, giving it an inner beauty and strength. Their words, their thoughts, their hopes reechoed through Jewish life over many centuries.

CHAPTER IV

CRUSADES AND DEGRADATION

THE CRUSADING AGE STIMULATES PIETY AND COMMERCE
AMONG THE CHRISTIANS, AND BRINGS POVERTY AND HEROIC
MARTYRDOM TO THE JEWS

An Age of Iron—Why was there no Golden Age among the Jews of Europe outside Spain? During the tenth century there seemed to be as much chance for the Jews of France and Germany to develop a high culture as there was for the Jews of Spain. Yet the Jews of Christian Europe did not produce the philosophers or the grammarians, the poets or the scientists who made up the Golden Age of Spain. The fact that Christian culture was not as inspiring as that of the early Mohammedans was only one reason. A more important cause was that the Jews of Christian Europe did not have a few more generations of mental peace so essential for cultural maturity. For in those sections of Christian Europe where peace prevailed a little longer, in the Provence and in Italy, there was some cultural ripeness and glory. In the northern and central parts of France, however, and in Germany, physical suffering was too great to permit of cultural fruitage.

But if the Jews of Central Europe suffered a stunting of

their cultural possibilities, they yielded other fruits. They produced a hardy Jewish loyalty and a rich religious piety. For them the period was an age of martyrdom and self-sacrifice. They lived through an Age of Iron: iron in the sword raised against them, iron in their determination to maintain Jewish life. How this came about requires a lengthy explanation. It involves a description of changes in the Christian Church and in the position held by the non-Jewish city-dwellers. It calls also for a discussion of the important half-military and half-religious movement known as the crusades.

1. THE CROSS AND THE SWORD

The Church Finds Its Strength—After many centuries of internal weakness the Catholic Church finally established its unity and its power. By a slow process, the local clergy and the monks obtained a firm hold on the minds of the population of Western Europe. Through them the popes exercised stronger power than any ruler of their day. Toward the end of the eleventh century, Pope Urban II could undertake an international policy for the Church such as his predecessors might have dreamed of but could not have thought possible. He called for a crusade, an attempt by the Christians of the West to take Palestine away from the Mohammedans and to make of it a province of the Roman Catholic Church. He offered to forgive the sins of anyone becoming a soldier of the Cross and to guarantee admission into Paradise to anyone who fell in battle fighting for Christianity. The response was remarkable. Every parish church became a recruiting station, and every monk with a loud voice and the ability to stir the emotions of the populace urged the men to abandon mere earthly occupations and join the army of the Lord.

The Crusaders—They started a tremendous emotional movement. Even children enrolled and set out on the perilous journey, certain that God would guide them on the road. On the whole, it was as sincere a religious movement as was to be found anywhere. These people were horrified, now that it was insistently called to their attention, that the sepulcher of Jesus should be in the hands of unbelieving Mohammedans, and they were willing to sacrifice themselves for its redemption. But there were a great many who had other motives. Some of the nobility among the crusaders were nothing more than fortune hunters, looking for lands to rule over. Some of the ordinary crusaders were serfs, peasants of the lowest mental type, who sought a chance for adventure and for freedom from a dull and servile life. Even worse was the fact that the First Crusade was poorly organized. Armies of peasants marched off without proper leadership and without adequate provisions. Unrestrained, they were bound to become a danger where there was not enough force to hold them in check. The fact that many Jews had wealth which could be taken as booty was a constant temptation, and a reason for taking it away from them was not hard to find. Before long the crusaders began to argue that it was ridiculous to go forth to kill God's enemies in a distant land while the Jews close at hand, equally opposed to Christianity, were left behind unharmed. Soon the cry was heard, "Kill a Jew and save your soul!"

A Difference in Persecutions—Between the previous persecutions and those which now followed, there were several important differences. The former ones had been temporary and had been initiated usually by the man at the head of the state. They had therefore been executed with a minimum of cruelty, for those days, and were soon repented of. The storm over, the Jews could resume their life. The persecution during the First Crusade, in 1096, however, was the first of a long series. The emotion of hate upon which it was based was kept alive by generation after generation of priests and monks, either because of sincere but narrow religious zeal, or because attacking the Jews proved to be a sure means for self-advancement. The appeals of these agitators were directed, not so much to the nobility and the responsible rulers, but to the mobs in every land, whose cruelty, once aroused, could not easily be restrained.

Martyrs on the Rhine—The events of 1096 proclaim the bestial conduct of the attackers and the unmerited suffering of the attacked. They have also ever served as a heartening example of Jewish heroism, of the Jew's willingness to die for the "Sanctification of the Name," that is, for all he considered holy.

Secure in the favor of the princes of the land and on excellent terms with their Christian neighbors in the cities, the Jews of the German states which lay close to the river Rhine refused to believe the warning sent by the Jews of France that danger threatened. Nevertheless, as disquieting rumors of unruly crusaders on the march continued to reach them from across the Rhine, they asked the local nobility, the bishops and their fellow townsmen whether they could count on their help. This was freely promised. The Jews also decreed a fast day to invoke the aid of God. Towards the beginning of June, at the time when the Jews were preparing to celebrate Shabu'ot, the crusader hordes—for these were not really armies—approached the Rhine, which was on their line of march eastward. The Jews of Speyer, Worms, Mayence, Cologne and other neighboring towns sent their property for safekeeping to the homes of friendly Christian burghers; some went to hide in Christian homes, others in the palaces of the bishops; still others depended upon the promises of protection and stayed at home. In the end it was really all the same. For when the crusading bands arrived in any town, the mob there invariably joined them. The local burghers, that is, the middle-class Christians, though sincerely sorry to see their Jewish fellow citizens suffer, nevertheless refused to risk their lives in defending the Jews as they had promised, while the small forces of the resident bishops and local constables could not withstand the attack, and, besides, many sympathized with the attackers. The Jews defended themselves and sometimes temporarily beat back the attacks; but theirs was a hopeless struggle against great numbers of armed enemies. To be sure, they could save themselves by baptism, and in some few cases Jews did so. The vast majority preferred to die with the cry of *Shema' Yisrael* upon their lips. Altogether some ten thousand Jews lost their lives in Central Europe. Nor was this all. When the crusading army captured the city of Jerusalem, they drove the Jews who lived there into the synagogue and set fire to the building.

The Second Crusade and a Defender—This loss of life and property resulted in a permanent change in the position of the Jew. For the moment it was natural for everyone, Jew and non-Jew, to try to restore the situation to normal. The Jews were urged to return to their homes; the emperor permitted the return to Judaism of those who had been baptized by force. But the chief obstacle in the way of returning to former conditions was the fact that the mind of the common people had been so poisoned as to believe that it was pleasing to God to kill a Jew. When, therefore, a Second Crusade was preached in 1144, there could be no doubt that the events of 1096 would be repeated. It was then that the Jews found a defender in the most unexpected place. Bernard, abbot of Clairvaux, the most respected churchman of his day, came forward with a denunciation of those monks and priests who were urging the murder of the Jews. He did this not because he honored Jews and Judaism, but because of a deeper understanding of Christianity. To be sure, there were still many attacks upon Jews, both on individuals and on communities. But due to St. Bernard's intervention and the better organization of the forces during the Second Crusade, these attacks were comparatively mild.

The Third Crusade and England—In 1189 still another crusade was preached. By this time, attacks upon the Jews in France and Germany, as we shall see, did not require the frenzied emotions of a crusade to start them. They had become a frequent occurrence, requiring only a slight pretext. More directly connected with the crusade was the misfortune which overtook the Jews of York, in England. Jews had come to settle in England about the time of William the Conqueror, and for a century they had lived in peace. The trouble started on the day of the coronation of Richard the Lionhearted. London was full of men who had vowed to join the new king on the crusade which he had promised to lead right after his coronation. The rumor spread suddenly that the new king had ordered an attack on the Jews. Here was one order which the rabble promptly obeyed, and royal officers were hard put to it to stop the outrages. Richard had three of the ringleaders put to death and issued a proclamation forbidding anyone to molest the Jews.

A few days after Richard's departure from the country, the riots broke out afresh. This time the crusaders in the smaller towns were the instigators, and the entire population, including the wealthier citizens and the clergy, joined them. Most serious was the riot at York. Sensing trouble, the Jews, about five hundred of them, took refuge in the royal castle. First their homes were pillaged, then they were besieged. For several days they fought back bitterly from the castle walls. But with no food and few weapons, they could not hold out long. They decided on suicide, and when the enemy finally broke in, they found the castle a silent tomb. This time even the call to conversion had been a lie. Those few who, trusting the invitation to become baptized, had not submitted to self-slaughter, were also killed by the mob. The reason for this is significant. The ringleader of the attack and a number of his followers owed money to some of the Jews. They wanted no heirs or witnesses to survive; and when all the Jews were dead, many of the attackers lost no time in going to the cathedral and burning all the records of their debts which, as usual in those days, were in the church for safekeeping.

2. THE ROAD DOWN

The Transformation—The century of the three great crusades witnessed the transformation of the Jews of Christian Europe from a peaceful and quite prosperous group of people to one holding on to a bare semblance of comfort and never knowing what tragedy the next day might bring. A number of factors were involved, most of them having as little to do with the Jews directly as did the crusades, but all combining against their peace and their life.

The Jews Alone Refuse—One fact to remember is that by the time of the crusades Western and Central Europe, except Spain and a part of Italy, had become united under the Christian religion. The Jews remained the only ones who still continued to deny the claims of Christianity. For a time, as long as the churchmen were not quite sure of their real strength, they had been willing to argue with the Jews, and tried to convince them. It soon became evident that this was hopeless; the Jews insisted on remaining Jews. It seemed to the churchmen that to permit the Jews to continue unmolested in their favorable position would be to encourage doubt about fundamental Christian teachings. Every time a thoughtful Christian saw a Jew walk by, he might say to himself: "Here is a man who denies what my priest just told me, and yet he is not a bad sort, and, what is more, God seems to like him quite as much as He likes me. Maybe there is something to what he thinks." It followed that, if the Jews refused to admit the Christian argument, it was necessary to convince the average Christian that a Jew could not possibly be a "good man," and that God did not like him. Many of the clergy and the monks of that period persuaded themselves that, in reality, the Jews knew better than to disbelieve the Christian dogmas, but that they were in league with the Devil and were trying deliberately to corrupt innocent Christians. Others believed that the Jews were merely stubborn, "stiff-necked," or at the very least, that they were afflicted with a blindness of the spirit which kept them from seeing the truth of Christianity. The practical recommendations of the clergy varied in accordance with their attitudes. Some advocated preaching to the Jews. Others urged political and economic pressure. Still others wanted to expel them completely from Christian society.

The anti-Jewish attitude of the clergy was not new. Signs of it had appeared as early as the Council of Nicaea in the year 325.* Many churchmen, high and low, had given expression to it. The reason it had not worked before the twelfth century and was so successful after that period was due to new factors in the European situation.

The New Merchants—For one thing, the Jews were no longer indispensable as merchants. During the tenth century, the Venetians were especially active in pushing Jews out of commerce. One of their doges appealed to the Christians of Europe in the name of Christianity not to trade with and through Jews. The crusades completed the process of substituting Christian for Jewish merchants. On the one hand, the crusading spirit of the Christian population made it unsafe for Jews to be on the commercial highways and destroyed much Jewish capital. On the other hand, the Christians conquered for themselves a route to the East. The Jews were now reduced to the status of disliked competitors, and the Christian merchant did not particularly mind what was said about or what was done to his competitor.

Usurer or Banker—As the Christian merchant class developed in wealth and numbers, many Jews were driven to seek other sources of livelihood. Agriculture was closed to them because they could have no serfs and could own no slaves. Besides, the feudal system was now in full operation; and it was a Christian system. It was too late for them to become artisans, since by this time artisans were forming themselves into guilds which refused to admit Jews. In southern Italy, in the Provence and in various other Mediterranean lands, where the guilds were not so strong or so religious-minded, manual labor never ceased to be characteristic of the Jews. In France and Germany, too, the majority derived their livelihood from petty trades and whatever artisanship was still open to them.

There was one important field of economic activity which was thrown wide open to Jews—the lending of money at interest. For centuries after the barbarian invasions there had been no real need for money. Things not grown by a landowner on his own soil, and not manufactured by serfs or slaves, were obtained by barter. Extra money needed for building churches or castles or for waging wars used to be borrowed, at some interest, from wealthy monasteries. When European life became more settled, human wants increased and merchants needed capital. Many Jews, beginning to be crowded out of commerce by their Christian competitors used the wealth accumulated during years of mercantile ac-

* See above, pp. 269 f.

tivity for lending to princes or to Christian merchants. Even some churches and cathedrals were erected with money borrowed from Jews. It so happened, moreover, that about this time the Catholic Church began to proclaim the theory that any interest, no matter how small, was usury. It announced that a Christian dared not lend money to another Christian in the hope of gain; if he did so, he was guilty of a very great sin and deserved to be excommunicated. Of course, the Church did not succeed completely; there were always Christians, as there have always been Jews, willing to risk being called sinners, if only they could snatch some profit. In large measure, however, the field of lending money to Christians was left to the Jews to whom the Church's theories did not apply. It should be noted in passing that the Church had less objection to Christians lending money at interest to Jews, and that the rabbis objected to Jews lending money at interest to fellow Jews.

At the present time, in lands where economic life is based on capitalism, it is clear that the Jews of those days performed a highly useful economic service. They took the place of the modern bankers and fostered private and public undertakings. Now, banking has its faults. It charges high rates of interest where the risk is great, and it is frequently heartless in collecting the money it lends. The Jewish moneylenders of those days may have been no better; there is proof that certainly they were no worse than the average banker. Money in general was scarce then and the risk involved in lending it much greater than it is today, especially where a Jew was the lender. Consequently, the legal rates of interest were unbelievably high. But even if they had been lower, the Jews would have suffered. The Church seized upon this situation as proof that the Jews desired to bring misery upon the Christians. They thus added the natural dislike of a debtor for his creditor to the hate stirred up against the Jew as an opponent of Christianity. In time, when banking became a firmly established and highly respected business and its risks not nearly so great, Christian bankers displaced the Jews in moneylending just as Christians had previously displaced them in trading.

Serfs of the Treasury—The increased power of the kings and emperors of Christian Europe brought about another change in the position of the Jews. The Jews used to be free to move where they liked. Such freedom was necessary if they were to be merchants. The king of France or the emperor of the Holy Roman Empire extended them protection wherever they went. After the Jews became part of the rapidly growing towns where they lived as moneylenders, they, more directly than anyone else, remained under royal protection. The Jews sought it and were willing to pay for it. Since the feudal system, which prevailed at that time, required that every human being belong to a certain class and have a definite relationship to an immediate superior, the Jewish population was classified as approximately a serf population. But they were a peculiar kind of serf, not attached to the soil; they were more like wards of the royal or imperial treasury. Their economic uses and their traditional status made it impossible to deny them a position somewhere higher than an earth-bound peasant. Just as the ordinary serf was expected to give part of his labor to his overlord's field and was otherwise completely in his lord's hands, so the Jew was expected to give part of his financial labor to his overlord's treasury and was otherwise completely in his power. In France of the thirteenth century the rule was established that everything the Jew owned belonged to his lord, and consequently a Jew could never move, without permission, out of his lord's domain. The lord could impose upon the Jew a tax of any amount. The only consideration that might hold the lord back from confiscating his Jew's property was that the Jew might then not be able to make more money for the master to take away later. In this way emperors, kings and other nobles who "owned" Jews actually profited from the Jewish moneylending activity. The simile generally used is that the Jews were like a sponge which the nobility would dip into the purses of the general population and then squeeze dry into their own. Emperor's and kings gave protection, but in return the Jews lost their freedom of movement, their right to their own property and their status as free men. Had it not been for their ability to make money to pay the enormous taxes, they would have lost their right to live.

3. The Hunted and Downtrodden

The Spiritual Expulsion—The Church's fear of a different opinion, the Christian merchants' greed for the control of trade, the curse of being a defenseless creditor, and the nobility's greed—these were the general factors which, during the twelfth and thirteenth centuries, created a situation dangerous for the safety of the Jewish group. By the time the Third Crusade was over, at the end of the twelfth century, there was no more prosperity for nine tenths of the Jews and no more peace for any of them. The Jews had inhabited Western Europe longer than most of the peoples who lived there; yet they were more than ever considered aliens. They had contributed at least as much as any other group to Europe's civilization; yet they began to hear that they were the enemies of that civilization. Mentally the Christian population of Western and Central Europe was prepared, by the year 1200, to expel the Jews or to destroy them. The surprising thing is that this destruction or expulsion was delayed for about two centuries. The delay was due almost entirely to the fact that the rulers of the various parts of Europe still needed the Jews. What happened, therefore, is that the destruction and expulsion were slowed down from events to processes; that is, instead of being forced upon the Jews all at once, their elimination was achieved step by step over a long period of time.

Brandmarked—The most obvious indication of the manner in which hostility was leading to expulsion was the introduction of the Jewish Badge. Many years before this, a Mohammedan ruler had forced both Jews and Christians of his dominions to wear an outer mark by which they could be distinguished from Moslems. Some high church dignitaries thought that this was a good idea for them to use, and they almost succeeded in passing such a law at a church council in 1179. At that time the private financial adviser of the pope was a Jew by the name of Yehiel and he prevailed upon the pope not to permit this. In 1215, however, the reigning pope was Innocent III, a man of great ability and determination, zealous for the interests of the Church. In that year another important council was held, and this regulation was then adopted. Any Jew above the age of thirteen, or Jewish woman above eleven, was to wear a mark, usually a yellow patch, front and back, on the outer garment. The Church's order grew out of the circumstance that without such a Badge the Jews were not distinguishable from Christians, a fact which proves that the Jews were anything but aliens in the lands in which they lived. The Badge was to be a mark of shame, and drive them out of European society.

A number of revealing incidents followed. The Christian kings of Spain, who were making tremendous efforts to win more territory from the Mohammedans of the Iberian Peninsula, became frightened. The Jews of their kingdoms threatened to emigrate and go over to the Mohammedans if they were forced to wear the Badge. Now the Jews of Spain were still the backbone of Spanish economic life; to drive them out would mean to strengthen the Mohammedans. For this reason the Spanish Christian kingdoms were permitted to dispense with the Badge, at least until such time as the Jews would cease to be so important. To a lesser extent the same was true in other Christian lands. The Badge was not imposed upon them as long as the Jews had economic strength. Moreover, if a Jew paid enough to the royal treasury, he could obtain the privilege of going around without the Badge. In other words, the Church set the goal, to exclude the Jews, and suggested the means for attaining it; but, generally speaking, little was done as long as the rulers of the lands felt that they could ill afford it. The eventual enforcement of the law of the Badge merely serves as proof that the Jews had lost their economic importance.

Royal Officials—A similar situation existed in connection with officeholding by Jews. In earlier days, before the age of the crusades and the changes which it brought about, it was rather common for Jews to be appointed by rulers to help run the government, especially its financial department. Ever since the day of its victory, the Church had argued against this, claiming that no Jew ought to be in a position of authority over Christians. But no ruler who needed the services of a Jew hesitated to employ one despite the attitude of the Church. This was true in the case of the Spanish Christian kings down to the very end of Jewish life in Spain; it was true of the rulers of the Provence until that district lost its freedom in 1210; it was true of Austria and Hungary all during the thirteenth century; it was true even of the popes in Rome till the time of Innocent III. Frequently the Jews had charge of minting the money and collecting the taxes. This state of affairs lasted for centuries, until the Jews were impoverished, completely degraded and expelled.

Physicians—Even more to the point is the story of the Jews in medicine, for which Jews have always shown an aptitude. Some of the earliest books on how to identify and treat various diseases were written by Jews. A number of Jewish physicians have already been mentioned: Hasdai ibn Shaprut, Judah ha-Levi, Moses Maimonides. The Church had early begun to urge Christians not to employ Jewish doctors, on the ground that this involved danger to the patient's soul. This, however, did not stop the Christians from calling on Jewish medical experts. In the late Middle Ages the popes themselves used Jewish physicians. The very fact that the Jewish physicians were so skillful and popular made their Christian competitors the more anti-Jewish. Indeed, there was no group, with the possible exception of the monks, throughout the history of the Jews in Europe, more bitterly anti-Jewish than the Christian members of the medical profession. Eventually they succeeded in reducing the number of Jewish physicians to insignificance. Nevertheless, when a Jewish physician was available, he always found Christian patients, especially among the higher nobility and the upper ranks of the clergy.

Accusations of Ritual Murder—Among the lower elements of Christian society, suspicion of the Jews was fed by all kinds of stories which were spread with the double aim of proving the miraculous powers of the Christian religion and the debased, godless character of Judaism. For the first time the accusation was made in the twelfth century that Jews used the blood of Christians for ritual purposes. Long before, while Christianity was still being persecuted by paganism, Christians had been accused of exactly the same crime. Near the time of the Second Crusade the charge reappeared with the Jews as the guilty party. The story was told in a variety of forms, but its essential elements were the following: A Christian would disappear. The Jews would be accused of having kidnaped, tortured and crucified him in memory of the crucifixion of Jesus. They were said to have drawn off his blood and distributed it among the neighboring Jewish communities, where it was used in the preparation of *matzot* for Passover. But very frequently the Christian thus martyred "miraculously exposed" the crime. He was eventually raised to sainthood, while the "guilty" Jews were massacred. Incidentally (or perhaps this was no accident), the property of the Jews was taken away by those who destroyed them, and a poor local church became famous and wealthy through the fact that the remains of the martyr were buried there.

Only perverted, bloodthirsty minds could make such accusations, and only an incredibly deep ignorance and fear of Judaism can explain its spread among the population. The fact, however, is that it spread and became a part of the strange and fearful legend which the Jew has been to the Christian mind. It sealed the hostility which pursued the Jews throughout the second thousand years of Christian history, in marked contrast to the friendliness with their neighbors during so large a part of the first thousand years. The charge made its first appearance in 1144 in Norwich, England. It was still new when it caused the destruction of the Jewish community in Blois, France, in 1171. But it became an almost annual occurrence in Germany toward the end of the thirteenth century in spite of the attempts even of Christians to refute it. For in 1236, enlightened Emperor Frederick II called a conference of learned Jewish converts to Christianity, and these had the honesty to testify that the accusation was a lie. A few years later Pope Innocent IV issued a Bull (decree) in which he announced that the accusation was not to be believed. But it was all useless; the accusation continued to crop up. Geoffrey Chaucer, the great English poet of the fourteenth century, put one such story in the mouth of the lovable prioress in the *Canterbury Tales.*

Accusation of Desecrating the Host—Another charge, just as generally believed from the thirteenth century on, involved one of the sacred ceremonies of the Catholic Church. In the celebration of the Mass, a wafer is used, a small, flat, round piece of unleavened bread which, according to Catholic belief, becomes the body of Jesus. Quite illogically it was assumed the Jews also looked upon the wafer as representing Jesus. They were said to be very anxious to get hold of such wafers and to "torture" them by sticking pins into them, or putting them into boiling water, or pounding them in a mortar. On such occasions blood was said to flow from the wafer and other miracles were believed to occur which would lead Christians to discover the blasphemous actions of the Jews. For this, too, the Jews accused were killed, their property taken away and the miracle-working wafer made into a sacred relic.

The Defenseless German Jews—Events during the thirteenth century showed the growing dependence of the Jewish population upon the strength and interests of the rulers. In Germany, for example, there was a direct relationship between the power of the emperor and the safety of the Jews. Emperor Frederick II was a strong ruler and, on the whole, protected his Jewish subjects. His death (1250) and that of his son Conrad were followed by about twenty years during which Germany was without a king. These were among the cruelest years the Jews there had to endure. Dozens of towns, cities and provinces had their local Jewish persecutions. Sometimes the Jews succeeded in buying the protection of the baron or the bishop. Usually this meant further impoverishment and, consequently, greater weakening of their status. In 1273 a new emperor was finally chosen in the person of Rudolph I, a member of what had been the comparatively unimportant family of Hapsburg. He set for himself the goal of making his family rich and powerful. He needed money and therefore sold charters of protection to the Jews of various towns. His son, Albert I, had a more difficult time maintaining the power and lands which Rudolph had gathered. During the civil war which he had to fight with his rival, there was again confusion in Germany. A petty nobleman by the name of Rindfleisch (1298) gathered a band of cutthroats and went from city to city, killing and pillaging Jews in the name of God and for the sake of their pockets. Thus the fateful thirteenth century closed for the Jews of Germany on the cry of *Shema' Yisrael.*

French Piety and Greed—The motives behind the treatment of the Jews in France during the same period were no different from the motives in Germany, but the results were not exactly alike. The reason was that the French monarchy was stronger and could direct its policy to suit what it considered its own interests. The very shrewd Philip Augustus—he who eventually deprived the English kings of their vast possessions in France—needed a great deal of money for his schemes. He clothed himself in piety and in 1182 expelled the Jews from his territory, which at that time was still not very large. Of course, he first stripped them of all their worldly possessions. In 1198, realizing that he could use the income which he would derive from the moneylending Jews, he invited them to come back and settle in the places from which they had been driven.

Louis IX, grandson of Philip Augustus, was a really pious man. But part of a Christian's piety in those days was stern opposition to Judaism. Like his grandfather, Louis IX protected his Jews, in the same way as he protected his other property. He even made a pious gesture in trying to abolish usury. He ordered that henceforth Jews must not depend upon moneylending for their livelihood, but upon artisanship, that is, upon the work of their hands. Considering that such labor was largely closed to the Jews of France and that it would not have brought into the royal treasury a tenth of the taxes which the Jews were called upon to pay, it is obvious that Louis' order was merely hypocrisy, though perhaps unconscious. Still, the working of the order was useful to the treasury. Every so often the wealth of one or another Jew could be confiscated on the ground that it was gain ill-gotten from usury. Louis used such money for the support of the unsuccessful crusades which he led.

The Provence and Expulsion—In some respects the most important Jewish community in the twelfth century was that of the Provence. Altogether this district of southern France was one of the happiest and culturally the most productive in

Christian Europe. Its Jews could still own property and engage in trade at the beginning of the thirteenth century. Its Jewish physicians were famous and its Jewish financiers were frequently called upon to assist in the administration of the county of Toulouse, as the almost independent province was called.

The very liberalism and culture of the Provence was the cause of the disaster which befell it. The population was advanced enough to see the faults of the Church organization. They compared the simplicity and greatness of early Christian teaching with the complexity of the Church's teachings in their day and the corruption which had crept into its organization. As a result they denied the Catholic Church and established churches of their own, Albigenses or Waldenses. Naturally the capable Pope Innocent III was scandalized by all this and called for a holy war, a crusade, against the heretics. Here was further proof for him that heresy and freedom for Judaism went hand in hand. Consequently, the crusaders sought out Jews as much as Albigensians (1208–1215). The reformers lost their lands and their authority. Among other things, they had to admit that they had been wrong in employing Jews and to promise not to do so in the future. The entire province was attached to the French crown. Its period of cultural brilliance was over, and so was the cultural opportunity of its Jews.

Philip the Fair, called so because of his appearance and not because of his actions, was a grandson of Louis IX and had a character very much like his ancestor Philip Augustus. When he needed money he stopped at nothing, neither at causing the death of a pope nor at branding the Knights Templars as criminals and confiscating their property. He decided to lay hands on whatever wealth the Jews of his kingdom still possessed. In 1306 he ordered them out of his domain, where they and their ancestors had dwelt for at least a thousand years. Their homes, their valuables, the debts due them, their synagogues and even their cemeteries were confiscated.

Expulsion from England—The story of the Jews in England is briefer both in its days of comparative happiness and in its sorrows.* The greedy and despicable King John and his son, Henry III, were not slow to see in them a source of money. At one time the Jews sent a deputation begging permission to leave the country. It was refused, because they

* See above, p. 307.

were still too useful to the treasury. Slowly their wealth was drained out of them, until by the end of the century their financial value was nil. Besides, the Lombards, Italian bankers, had come to England and had taken the place of the Jews in England's economic life. Under the vigorous urging of the Church and because of an accusation of counterfeiting money—as though all sixteen thousand Jews were guilty of what a dozen might have done—the Jews were finally ordered to leave the country during the autumn of 1290. King Edward I was kind, relatively speaking. He let them take along whatever cash they had, though their homes and the debts still due them were confiscated by the treasury. The king provided them with ships for the crossing to the Continent, and it was not his fault that a number of the captains robbed some Jews and threw others into the Channel. The majority went back to France from which their ancestors had come two centuries earlier. Sixteen years later, as we have seen, the English refugees suffered another expulsion, this time from France, along with the Jews who had never left that country.

4. RESULTS FOR JEW AND CHRISTIAN

The Process of Degradation—The period from 1096 to 1306 established a definite mental attitude in the relations between Jew and Christian. At the beginning of these two hundred and ten years there was ample hope that Jew and Christian could live near one another in harmony, each contributing to the development of their common country. By the end of this period the Christians had learned to look upon the Jews as queer and suspicious, and the Jews to look upon the Christians as people who could be easily brutalized, whose friendship was not to be trusted. The Jews had fallen completely into the hands of the rulers whose sole interest in them was financial. The Jew's money was his only defense, as well as his greatest danger. Each side came to look upon the other as greedy for wealth.

The Wandering Jew—For the first time, about the middle of the thirteenth century, the legend appeared which has become famous under the name of "The Wandering Jew." The legend itself deals only with one man who had been cursed by Jesus to live and wander over the face of the earth until Jesus' second coming. But the story was generalized among the Christians to stand for the entire Jewish people. In a sense it became true; the Christians made it come true. In the thirteenth, and to an even greater extent during the fourteenth century, the Jew lost the sense of being at home in the various lands and provinces where his ancestors had lived and where his community had taken root. Clearly the legend that the Jew is by nature a wanderer is false; but a series of expulsions made his wanderings seem a true description of the conditions under which the Jews actually lived.

CHAPTER V

INNER PEACE AND CONFLICT

CULTURAL AND SPIRITUAL STRENGTH DERIVED FROM STUDY
AND EXAMPLE ENABLE THE JEWS OF CHRISTIAN EUROPE
TO WITHSTAND ALL ATTACKS

The Fortified Spirit—Stories of Jewish martyrdom hold an important place in the history of the Jewish people, but martyrdom is not all there is to Jewish history. More fundamental than self-sacrifice is that which gave the people the moral courage, the strength of will to continue their Jewish life despite the danger involved in remaining Jews and the temptations offered to become Christians. Unless we say that Jewish survival was a miracle defying explanation, we must assume that our people survived after centuries of grinding oppression because of the type of life they lived as Jews, the thoughts they thought, and the hopes which they cherished for the future. Their life, thoughts and hopes were recorded in the books they wrote and the exemplary life lived by great-souled individuals among them. Such writers and saints were abundant during the twelfth and thirteenth centuries. Consequently, if one would understand the real history of the Jews during the crusading age and thereafter, it is not enough for him to shed tears over Jewish suffering, or glow with pride at their heroic martyrdom; it is necessary to turn one's mind to the works of these men and their influence upon their fellow Jews.

1. CONVERTS AND CONVERSION

Losses and Gains—To start with, one must not assume that every Jew rejected the opportunity to become a Christian and thus save himself from death or expulsion or poverty. This was not so. There have always been some who, for one reason or another, became baptized and were thus lost to the Jewish fold. To use a common though unscientific expression, it is safe to say that there is a great deal of "Jewish blood" in the veins of the population of modern Europe. On the other hand, there were Christians, even during the ages of the crusades, who threw in their lot with the Jews. The Jews never dared to keep records of their proselytes, since converts to Judaism, as well as those who converted them, were subject to the death penalty. But there are enough veiled references to such proselytes to warrant the belief that there were some Christians who became Jews, though not nearly as many as Jews who became Christians.

Converts by Force—The majority of those who left the Jewish fold undoubtedly did so through force or fear. Every attack upon the Jews started with the proclamation that those would be spared who submitted to baptism. To be sure, the rule of the Church was against the use of force in conversion, but in actual fact this rule was interpreted very liberally in favor of Christianity. Only if a man still insisted on remaining a Jew though the sword was at his throat did the Church admit that he was baptized by force. It is easy to see that such cases would be few indeed. So, too, in the case of children, the theory was that no child could be baptized without the consent of its parents. In practice, however, even infants were baptized over the protests of their parents and then taken away to be brought up as Christians.

Secret Jews—Sometimes converts returned to Judaism as soon as the danger was over. At the very beginning of the era of great persecutions, men like Rabbenu Gershom and Rashi had advised that Jewish communities accept such persons back into the fold without punishing them for, or even reminding them of, their temporary treason. After the terrors of the First Crusade had subsided, Henry IV, emperor of the Holy Roman Empire, permitted forced Jewish converts to return to their old faith. The Church was opposed to such permission and this was, therefore, the only occasion when it was given. After subsequent persecutions, converts had to resort to secrecy if they wanted to continue to live as Jews. Outwardly Christians, but inwardly Jews, they observed what they had to observe of Christianity and what they could of Judaism. This was dangerous, for the local priests and bishops watched them closely and treated as heretics those caught reverting to their former faith. Those who could, would change their land of residence, though sometimes the long arm of the Church reached for them even in their new home. The majority of the forced converts, and certainly their children, who could not be brought up in Jewish tradition, undoubtedly were lost to Jewish life. But a smaller number succeeded in regaining and maintaining their Jewish associations, and thus brought to Judaism an even stronger loyalty. All this was a foretaste of what was to happen on a larger scale in Spain in the fifteenth and sixteenth centuries.

Willing Converts—Some individuals in all honesty preferred Christianity and became willing converts. These being honest people, one does not hear about them nearly as much as one hears about those willing converts who became Christians because they had something to gain from this step. The Jews were justified in doubting the motives of the great majority of the converts, since life as a Christian offered so many more worldly advantages over life as a Jew.

The Talmud on Trial—Nicholas Donin is an example of such a renegade Jew. A man of considerable knowledge and understanding, he realized that the study of Jewish lore and tradition was the mainstay of Jewish existence. He made the long journey from France to Rome and explained to the pope the importance of the Talmud and of its Rashi commentary for the Jewish religion. In 1239, Pope Gregory IX issued an order to the kings and the archbishops to confiscate all copies of the Talmud, investigate the work and, if they found that it contained anything insulting to Christianity, to condemn the book and all it commentaries. On a certain summer Saturday, while the Jews were in the synagogue, police surrounded their homes and carried off what books they could find. Then a trial was arranged in Paris: the prisoner was a book, the Talmud. The prosecution was led by Nicholas Donin; the defense by a group of rabbis, with Rabbi Yehiel of Paris as the chief spokesman. The judges were a number of bishops; and the queen-mother of France presided. Donin was given every opportunity to poke fun at the Talmud by pointing out the naive tales and legends which it contained, and to twist a number of its statements into attacks upon Christianity. Rabbi Yehiel did not have the right to point out equally naive ideas to be found in Christian literature. All he could do was to give a more truthful interpretation of the passages cited by Donin. He did his best. But even if Yehiel's arguments had been ever so strong, he could not have won the trial. The judges being what they were, his cause was lost from the start. The Talmud was condemned as a book dangerous to Christianity, and a few years later twenty-four cartloads of copies were burned in the public square in Paris. From that time on, the new kind of attack became fairly frequent; it was directed not only against Jews and Judaism, but also against Jewish literature, especially the Talmud.

The Disputation of Barcelona—A similar event took place scarcely a generation later in Barcelona, Spain. Again it was a converted Jew, Pablo Christiani, who instigated it and thought thereby to bring disgrace upon both the Talmud and its Jewish teachers. In 1263, Pablo persuaded the king of Aragon to compel the foremost Jewish scholar of Spain, Moses ben Nahman (Nahmanides), to join him in a public disputation. Pablo tried to prove that the midrashic statements of the Talmud indicated a belief in the messiahship of Jesus. In other words, he wanted to show that the rabbis were aware of the divine nature of Jesus, but deliberately misled the common people. Nahmanides had little difficulty in showing that Pablo misinterpreted the statements he quoted. But this did not prevent the disputation from having a tragic personal result. Nahmanides was exiled from Aragon for having dared to say that he had won this public debate. An old man, he had to leave his family and friends and undertake the dangerous journey to Palestine. Pablo, on the other hand, obtained from the pope the right to have Jewish books confiscated and to compel the Jews to admit him to their synagogues and to listen to his tirades against Judaism.

Conversionist Sermons—In the good old days before the age of the crusades, Jews and Christians, living side by side, used to discuss their religious beliefs in a friendly spirit. The Church succeeded in stopping such discussions, on the ground that the Jews used them to introduce doubts into the minds of the Christians. In the disputations of Paris and Barcelona just described, the Jewish representatives did not have and dared not employ full freedom of speech, while Nicholas Donin and Pablo Christiani did. But at least Rabbi Yehiel and Nahmanides could defend themselves. Toward the end of the thirteenth century, another kind of religious discussion was introduced, which was not a discussion at all. The Jews were commanded to listen to Christian sermons without having any opportunity whatever to reply. What made this worse was the fact that very often the Christian preachers were converted Jews who took delight in turning biblical and rabbinic statements against Judaism. It was a method of mental torture which we shall meet again.

2. STRENGTH THROUGH COMMUNAL LIFE

Social Influence—The fact that the Jews were prevented from engaging in agriculture increased their hardships, but it also resulted in making their Jewish life more secure. Had they continued to live on scattered farms they would not have been able to give one another that encouragement to persist in Judaism which was one of the most important results of their living in communities. The actual communal organization has already been described. It did not change much from previous centuries, and what change there was came in the direction of greater internal control. By forcing the Jews to pay their taxes in the form of a lump sum collected by themselves, the various governments helped to keep the Jewish communal organization powerful. By insisting that the non-Jews separate themselves from the Jews, the Church drove the Jews closer together. By their constant pressure, the Christians of medieval Europe induced the Jews to feel that they were dependent upon one another. Each Jewish community was like a town for itself. It received a charter defining its relations with the non-Jews and with the overlord of the town. It had the right to adjudicate lawsuits according to Jewish law in all but criminal matters. This helped to inspire respect for Jewish tradition and to encourage study. Though each community was independent, neighboring communities would sometimes send their leaders to take counsel together about necessary regulations of importance to all of them. The results were more conscious loyalty to one another, increased dignity of Jewish life, and deepened devotion to those principles upon which their life was based.

The Three Pillars—The Jewish world of the Middle Ages rested firmly upon study, worship and charity. Every community made education one of its most important activities. It supervised elementary education and supported a talmudic academy wherever the rabbi was sufficiently noted for his learning to attract pupils. For a man not to want to study was considered disgraceful and sinful. Worship, that is, prayer, was considered next in importance in Jewish life. The Jews never adopted the idea that one among them could pray for the rest. Each had to pray for himself, although the regular prayers of the day were conducted publicly. This had the effect of strengthening in each man his sense of religious responsibility, while at the same time he drew inspiration from the gatherings and ceremonies in the synagogue. The fruits of good Jewish training were expected to show themselves in deeds of charity. Quite apart from the charitable activities of each individual, there were well-organized public charities for resident as well as non-resident Jews. No Jew was ever abandoned to the charity of non-Jews. In this way the mind, the spirit and the heart were exercised through loyalty to the Jewish community.

The Rabbi—Among the most powerful factors enabling the Jews to survive was the example set by their rabbis. Judaism had long outgrown the need of a priestly class to perform religious ceremonies. Any Jew, if he knew enough, could perform the ceremonies prescribed by his religion. Only a very few activities, purely honorary in nature, were still associated with the descendants of the ancient priests (*Kohanim*). Religious leadership had definitely passed into the hands of the teacher.

The rabbinate, in the sense in which it is known to this day, came into being during the early Middle Ages in response to the need of the Jewish people to be guided in the observance of Jewish laws. The rabbi's influence, however, went beyond that. He became the model for piety and the source of religious inspiration. Down to the fourteenth century, most rabbis did not receive a salary for their rabbinic work; the rabbinate was considered an office of honor. In many cases the more affluent among the rabbis themselves maintained the pupils who came to study in their academies. But above all, the purity of their life, the profundity of their learning and their willingness to lead in self-sacrifice won them their influence over the people whom they led. In every instance of an attack upon a Jewish community, the rabbi was the first to suffer. Theirs was an inspiring example and, therefore, an effective one.

An Emperor's Prisoner—The story of Rabbi Meir of Rothenburg illustrates the leadership which the rabbis offered and the respect in which they were held. Towards the end of the thirteenth century Rabbi Meir was the foremost rabbi of western Germany. The constant pressure upon the Jews and his pious regard for the Holy Land impelled Rabbi Meir to decide to spend the last years of his life on the sacred soil of Palestine. On the way, somewhere in northern Italy, he was recognized by a convert to Christianity, who revealed to the authorities the identity of the traveler. Rabbi Meir was arrested. The reason given was that, as a Jew, the rabbi was a serf of the emperor's treasury; by leaving he was depriving the treasury of a source of income. Emperor Rudolph demanded a large sum from the Jews as ransom for their respected leader. The Jews were perfectly willing to pay any sum the emperor demanded, but Rabbi Meir refused to be ransomed. He argued that, if this trick of the emperor's succeeded, every prince would likewise arrest the rabbi of his territory each time he wanted to squeeze money out of the Jewish community. For years Rabbi Meir remained in prison. After the rabbi's death, the emperor refused to give up his body for Jewish burial unless the Jews paid him for it. Many years later a wealthy Jew of Frankfort, Alexander Suesskind Wimpfen, paid this money to the emperor on one condition. The condition which he made with the Jews was that, on his death, they would bury him by Rabbi Meir's side. The Jews fulfilled this condition, and in the cemetery at Worms one could see a double grave, with one tombstone over it marking the resting place of the two men.

3. BOOKS FOR THE STUDENT

Books and Survival—The rabbi of the community was only one source of inspiration and guidance. Another fountain of inspiration was books. In those days, long before the invention of printing, books had to be copied by hand. They were consequently so expensive that a library of a hundred volumes was considered a large one. Nevertheless, in every community there were one or more men who possessed books, and almost every community owned a number of such standard works as the Talmud and the Midrashim. Other books, too, began to make their appearance. People studied them, thought about them and discussed them. As a result their Jewishness became not alone a matter of deep faith, but also one of intellectual conviction. In order to understand this better it is necessary to have an idea of the sort of books written and read during this period.

Tosafists—One group of authors who exercised tremendous influence on the development of the Jewish mind has become known as "the Tosafists." The word comes from the Hebrew root "to add" for they added explanations to the Talmud, thus continuing the work begun by Rashi. As a matter of fact, the early and more important Tosafists were descendants of Rashi. Chief among them was his famous grandson, Rabbenu Tam. Actually what the Tosafists did was to write comments, not a commentary. Their work was not, like Rashi's, a direct, simple explanation of passages in the Talmud, but highly complex and difficult argumentation intended to shed light on its deeper meaning. The fact that this was considered necessary, and soon became an added study, indicates the progress in learning which had been made among the Jews of Christian Europe since Rashi's day.

Writers of Responsa—The feeling of unity among all Jews was further strengthened by the continuation of the method of exchanging questions and answers. There was a constant interchange of letters, the important results of which were similarity in observances and an increasing regard for scholars and scholarship in Judaism. Later the responsa of the greatest rabbis of that day were put together in books and became a separate subject of study. To this day people find in these collections of responsa evidence of the wisdom, the loyalty and the intellectual richness of the rabbis and leaders.

Compilers of Laws—Another type of literary activity began at this time among the Jews of Christian Europe. Until the twelfth century, legal codes, that is, books in which the various laws and customs of Judaism are arranged systematically according to subject, had been produced by scholars of Babylonia and Spain. Now the Jews of France and Germany also wrote a number of them. The importance of this lies not so much in the nature of the codes, but rather in the fact that they came into being at all. For they were written not for scholars but for the common folk. Everyone seemed to be anxious to find out exactly what his duties and obligations to Jewish life were. Persecutions had not frightened them; nothing had tempted them to weaken their Jewish loyalty. On the contrary, they devoutly consulted these codes and guided their life accordingly.

4. BOOKS FOR THE PIOUS AND THE MYSTICS

Books on Ethics—Jewish law and tradition were not the only studies in which the Jews of the period were interested. No study was more eagerly followed than that of the Midrash, the collection of folk tales and poetic interpretations of the Bible which largely emphasizes ethical and moral relations between man and man. The midrashic books always hold up the example of the patriarchs and sages as people who aimed to deal justly and lovingly with their fellowmen. On the other hand, the villains of the Jewish past, whether Jews or non-Jews, are always portrayed as men of violence and deceit. These midrashic works were studied by the common people and used as texts for popular lectures and sermons. There were many excellent preachers among the Jews of the Middle Ages, and numerous new midrashic books were written during that time. From these books and from the lessons based upon them the Jews were inspired to continue to think of themselves as a holy people in duty bound to emulate the noble ideals of their past.

Judah the Pious and His Book—Simple-minded people are not always satisfied with descriptions of laws and customs, sometimes not even with beautiful stories and sage advice. Often they are moved only by mysterious happenings and so become frightened into obeying laws by tales of terror of what would happen if they did not obey. Among the Gentiles and among the Jews of that day such wonder-tales and superstitions existed in abundance. It is surprising to what an extent the same stories and beliefs can be found among the adherents of the different religions. Among the Christians they were used to illustrate popular beliefs of Christianity, and among the Jews the same use was made of them for the sake of Judaism. There were many such books, but the one which proved most popular among the Jews was written by a man noted for his saintliness. Judah the Pious, or the Saint, lived in Regensburg about the year 1200. His book was called *Sefer Hasidim*, the "Book of the Devout." It is a collection of laws and customs of Judaism, sometimes illustrated by a story of a miraculous event. Angels, spirits, devils, wandering souls without bodies are encountered frequently. They punish people or protect them; they tell them secrets or warn them against missteps; they annoy and they amuse. These stories are not told merely for the sake of the telling, but in order to make the reader a more pious follower of the ways of Judaism.

Cabala—Intellectuals of those days were also interested in the mysteries of the universe. Religion must have a certain amount of mysticism, and Judaism had its normal share of it from the very beginning. The sixth chapter of Isaiah, the first chapter of Ezekiel, and parts of the Book of Daniel have been pointed to as evidence that even the Bible contains sections dealing with what is known as mysticism. The Tannaim, Amoraim and Geonim dealt with similar subjects: how the world was created, how the heavenly hosts are organized, how souls are lodged under the Throne of the Almighty, how judgment is rendered on the dead, and many other subjects upon which the human mind sometimes likes to dwell. Such speculation, known as *Cabala* (another word for tradition), never stopped among the Jews. French and German Jewish scholars at first wrote more extensively on it, though with considerably less system and profundity than did the Spaniards. The foremost book of Cabala, however, the one known as the *Zohar,** appeared in Spain around 1250.

5. Books for Entertainment

What People Read—For the most part the Jews of the Middle Ages concentrated their reading on religious literature. Life was harder in those days and there was little time or inclination for merely pleasurable reading. At the same time, it should not be imagined that the various types of book mentioned above did not afford pleasure. The scholars derived pleasure from the study of the Talmud and the commentaries; the people in general derived pleasure from the study of the midrashic books and the reading of such mystical works as the *Sefer Hasidim*. There were, however, books which were read chiefly for entertainment.

Stories and Fables—A popular kind of literature at that time, among Jews and Christians and Mohammedans, was stories and fables which ended with a moral lesson. One collection of stories, called *Sefer ha-Ma'asiot* (The Book of Adventures), had been compiled around 1050 by the famous Talmudist, Rabbi Nissim of Kairawan. It contained stories drawn from the Talmud and the Midrash as well as from Arabic sources. Berechiah ha-Nakdan, an English Jew of about 1200, compiled a collection of stories about animals, mostly the fox, based on Aesop's fables, sometimes modified to suit Jewish taste.

Example of a Discouraged Poet—The twelfth and thirteenth centuries produced many wandering minstrels, or troubadours. They composed the verses and music of love-poems and visited the palaces of the nobility to entertain them and their guests. Suesskind of Trimberg was this kind of poet. Being a Jew, however, he was kept out of many places and was shabbily treated in others. No wonder that in the end he

* See below, pp. 335–6.

expressed his disappointment in one of the few poems which have come down to us. In part it reads as follows:

Be silent, then, my lyre,
We sing 'fore lords in vain;
I'll leave the minstrels' choir
And roam a Jew again.

Under such circumstances, few Jews in Northern Europe turned to poetry. When they did, it was to write lamentations describing the terrors and misfortunes which befell their fellow Jews in their inhospitable motherlands.

Books of History and Travel—Knowledge of history in those days was not extensive. Authors wrote either stories of miracles or dry chronicles consisting of lists of events. The Jews did exactly the same thing. The most popular history book then current among them was the *Book of Yosippon*, which was an abbreviation of Josephus' historical works with a great many miraculous tales added. They also had chronicles, for the most part lists of names of the great teachers. The Jews of Germany and France possessed, in addition, accounts of events which took place during the crusades. This could hardly be called pleasurable literature, but it did serve to hold up before the eyes of the people the example of self-sacrifice which they themselves might be called upon to make. Finally, just as the Jews of Spain had their Benjamin of Tudela, so the Jews of Germany had a traveler in the person of Petahyah of Regensburg. Starting from his home-town, toward the end of the twelfth century, Petahyah traveled through southern Russia, Palestine, and as far as Babylonia and Persia. On his return home, he described his visit to the Jewish communities of these lands. Reading the account of his wanderings, the Jews of France and Germany must have felt a stronger sense of unity with their fellow Jews everywhere, who were studying the same holy books, worshipping God in the same fashion, and looking forward to the same promise of better days.

6. CRITICISM OF CHRISTIANITY

Fear of Christianity—In addition to the internal factors by which Judaism was strengthened, there were external factors by which they were repelled from Christianity and made more conscious of their common Judaism. For as time went on, the Christian Church began to appear in the role of an enemy. It was the Church which tried to impose complete separation between Jews and Christians; churchmen, like Bernard of Feltre and John Capistrano, frequently stirred up hostility, led riots and accused the Jews of the most horrible crimes. Naturally the Jews failed to distinguish between the essential teachings of Christianity and the brutality of those who called themselves Christians. Surrounded by hostility, the Jews drew closer to one another.

Criticism of the Christian Tradition—From the very beginning the Jews had, of course, criticized the fundamental basis of Christianity. The narrative of Jesus' birth and the idea of a Trinity violated the Jewish belief in the absolute Unity of God. In earlier ages, when friendliness prevailed, it had been possible to discuss this difference of view without bitterness. During and after the era of the crusades this was no longer possible. The Jews now could not understand how anyone could believe in Christianity, any more than the Christians could understand how anyone could still follow Judaism. A rather amusing illustration of this was the attempt of a certain mystically-minded Spanish Jew, Abraham Abulafia, who felt so certain that he could convince any Christian of the superiority of Judaism that he went to Rome in 1280 in order to convert the pope to Judaism. Upon his arrival in Rome, Abulafia was arrested and condemned to be burned. But the pope died soon thereafter, and the officials in Rome considered Abulafia crazy. After keeping him in prison for a month. they let him go his way.

Hope for the Messiah—The Jews strongly believed in the eventual coming of the Messiah to bring justice and peace to the world and re-establish them in Palestine. Naturally the Jews could not accept the view of the Christians that Jesus was the Messiah. How they felt about it was illustrated in a famous incident which took place during the disputation at Barcelona, mentioned above. In the course of the argument, the king asked Nahmanides why the Jews refused to believe that so noble a personality as Jesus was the Messiah they hoped for. In reply, the Jewish sage asked the king what he considered his greatest occupations. The king replied that these were to conduct war against his enemies and to watch over the courts of law. "You yourself have given me the proof," Nahmanides answered. "The coming of the Messiah was to be followed by peace and justice. As long as Christians themselves conduct wars and as long as there is so much injustice in the world, we cannot believe that the Messiah has already come."

CHAPTER VI

THE SILVER AGE

EXTERNAL EVENTS ADVERSELY AFFECT THE INTELLECTUAL
ACTIVITY OF THE JEWS IN SOUTHWESTERN EUROPE

Bases of Cultural Change—Jewish culture, like all other cultures, depends to a large extent upon external circumstances, social, economic and political. The thirteenth and fourteenth centuries witnessed many fundamental changes in southwestern Europe, and these in turn affected the life of the Jews. The two cultural traditions which had developed during the previous thousand years—that of northern and central Europe, the Ashkenazi, and that of southwestern Europe, the Sephardi—continued on their separate ways. The Sephardi tradition, however, no longer was to be characterized by that intellectual brilliance and that variety of cultural output which had given its previous period the name of the Golden Age.

1. THE CHANGES IN SOUTHWESTERN EUROPE

The New Spain—The Mohammedans maintained their hold on Spain for about three hundred years. But they had not remained united. Broken up into a number of small kingdoms, quarreling among themselves, further weakened by fanatically religious Mohammedans who invaded the peninsula from North Africa, they could not withstand the attacks of the Christians from the north and gradually yielded to them. After a great battle in 1212, only the kingdom of Granada, in the southeastern part of the peninsula, remained to the Moors. In the rest of the land the Christian kingdoms—Aragon, Castile, Leon, Portugal and Navarre—continued to grow in strength. Thus, by the beginning of the thirteenth century, the large majority of Spanish Jews lived in these Christian countries. They were now subject to all the anti-

Jewish prejudices and to many of the anti-Jewish laws which had been developing among the Christians in other parts of Europe. There could be no doubt that they faced an uncertain future.

Effect of Deteriorating Spanish Culture—The culture of the non-Jewish Spanish population was no longer as high as it had been. The invasions from the south and from the north weakened the intellectual interests of the Mohammedans. Unceasing wars with the Mohammedans and with one another left no time or energy for intellectual pursuits among the Christians. Several centuries were to pass before Spain could recover from the disorders which the wars left behind. Thus, the waning cultural activity about them reacted upon the Jews and was a reason why their poetry and philosophy were no longer of a high order.

The Kings and the Merchants—Another source of trouble for the Jews of the Christian kingdoms was the increasing influence of the merchants in the cities, who controlled much of the wealth and ruled the towns. The kings increasingly depended upon them for their income and for their political support. The Christian merchants looked upon the Jewish merchants and tradespeople as competitors. Consequently, they were always ready to support an anti-Jewish policy. They resented the fact that their kings frequently engaged Jews as advisers and financiers. Whenever possible they passed local laws against the Jews and persuaded the kings also to restrict the activities and the opportunities of their Jewish subjects. In this way the Jews, who had become accustomed to a considerable amount of freedom, found themselves more and more hedged about and hampered. Under such circumstances full development of cultural life was impossible.

The Plain People—The Jews of Spain, as of any country at any time, were not all rich merchants, physicians and financiers. Most of them, living in the cities and towns, were small shopkeepers and manual workers: blacksmiths and silversmiths, potters, shoemakers, tailors and followers of other trades. These simple people also felt the rising tide of anti-Jewishness. The prejudices of the upper classes of Christians seeped down to the lower, and they came to regard the Jews as economic rivals no less than did their superiors. Year by year and generation after generation the situation among these poorer Jews became more difficult. Nevertheless, they were the ones who adhered to their Judaism with marvelous fortitude, with greater courage, in fact, than was shown by the more prosperous.

2. FORTIFYING THE FAITH

Changing Interests—One of the most striking differences in Spanish Jewish life between the Golden Age and the Silver Age was reflected in the kind of books which the authors of the two periods produced. During the former age the literary products about which we hear most were poetry and philosophy; during the succeeding period they dealt with Talmud and Jewish law. To a large extent this difference may be explained by the fact that among the general population, now almost all Christian, a similar change had taken place. But among the Jews this change of emphasis in type of literature resulted also from the fact that, for the majority of them, poetry and philosophy were luxuries, and in time of danger and doubt they naturally turned to necessities. The Jews of the later days needed a stronger faith, firmer bonds of union and a better explanation of Judaism. The rabbinic literature of the time provided them with these.

Communities and Leadership—The same needs brought about a change in Jewish leadership. Externally the organization of the Jewish communities remained the same, but internally there was a profound difference. There were no Hasdai ibn Shapruts and Samuel ibn Naghdelas, who had combined in themselves civil and religious leadership during the earlier period. Now the civil heads of the communities were for the most part merely men of wealth and influence, sometimes favorites of the kings. They were chosen not for the depth of their Jewish culture or their loyalty to Judaism, but for their ability to represent the Jews before the government and to prevent the passage of anti-Jewish laws. Consequently, Jewish influence and inspiration had to be provided by others. This was done by the rabbis. The common people now looked to them for strength and encouragement to guide them through the terror and darkness which were fast approaching. The civil heads of the communities tried to stem the tide of evil; the religious heads tried to fortify the spirit within.

Rabbinic Authorities—Three distinguished religious leaders of the Spanish Jews will serve us as examples of the culture and spirit during the Silver Age. They showed by their personal activity and in the books they wrote, the change which was coming over the Jews.

Moses ben Nahman (Nahmanides, 1194–1270) has been mentioned already in connection with the disputation which took place in Barcelona in 1263. He was a great man, gentle and pious. Like Maimonides and Abraham ibn Ezra of the previous century, he was a man of wide erudition. Like Maimonides, he was interested in medicine as well as the Talmud, and like Abraham ibn Ezra he wrote a commentary on the Torah. But his differences from his two predecessors were equally important. Both the others emphasized reason and philosophy, and they wrote their books for the intellectuals among the Jews. Nahmanides was inclined to mysticism; he discouraged the study of philosophy; and his commentary was clear, simple and replete with pious instruction. Nahmanides was more interested in the religious attitude of the average Jew than in the depth of his thinking.

Solomon ibn Adret (1233–1310), a pupil of Nahmanides, was another important religious leader. His influence extended beyond the city of Barcelona, where he was rabbi, and even beyond Spain. Numerous questions were addressed to him, and his answers (responsa) show how greatly the interest of the Jews of his day turned to matters of religious observance and the faithful following of talmudic law. Equally significant is the fact that, like his teacher, Ibn Adret also opposed the study of philosophy by those unfortified by deep Jewish loyalties.

Rabbi Jacob ben Asher (died in 1340) was a third great teacher of that age. His father, Asher ben Yehiel, had come from Germany to serve as rabbi in Toledo, Castile, and brought with him the rigorous traditionalism and piety of his native land. Though the father was more famous, the son left a more lasting influence because of the series of books which he wrote. These books are a code of laws covering every aspect of a Jew's life. Through subsequent centuries this code formed the cornerstone of Jewish legislation. Rabbi Jacob called his entire series of four books *Turim*, "Rows," a reference to the four rows of jewels which the ancient high priest used to wear on his breastplate. Perhaps he meant to imply that the Jew, a member of the priest-people among the nations, must carry these laws close to his heart as though they were the jewels of the high priest.

3. MYSTICISM AND ITS BIBLE

Mysticism and Theology—There are two ways of dealing

with the problems of religion. One is the way of the philosophers, like Saadia and Maimonides, who use reason to arrive at whatever religious truth is humanly comprehensible. This method results in a system of religious thought which is called theology. Obviously, theology cannot appeal to everybody, for it is the product of fine-spun reasoning and systematic logic, requiring acute intellectual powers and large resources of knowledge. The masses of the people could not be interested in this method of describing their religion. Moreover, when difficult times come upon a religious group, it wants a warm faith, some assurance that God is near and friendly, not a theology which depends upon cold logic. The method of mysticism was, therefore, more suitable for the Jews of the thirteenth and fourteenth centuries. For to the mystics God was a matter of daily experience in direct and intimate contact. They had no objection to speaking of Him in human terms; they were sure that angels could be described as glorified and pure living beings; above all, they could encourage the people by the certainty that the divine powers were all about them, taking an intimate interest in their daily life. No wonder that mysticism grew among the Jews of Spain in direct proportion to the somber difficulties of their life as Jews.

The Bible of the Mystics—It is not surprising, therefore, that about the middle of the thirteenth century a book appeared which became the chief expression of mystical Judaism. Moses ben Shem-Tob de Leon announced that he had found a commentary on the Pentateuch which had been written by Simon ben Yohai, the famous Tanna of the second century who had lived alone for thirteen years, in hiding from the Roman government, after the unsuccessful Bar Kochba rebellion. During these years, legend has it, he was instructed by angels who revealed to him the profound divine meanings hidden within the seemingly clear words of the Bible. Rabbi Simon thereupon wrote a book, something like a commentary on the Pentateuch, in which he disclosed some of these mysteries. The book was known only to a select few until it fell into the hands of Moses de Leon who published it under the name of *Zohar* (Brilliance), as if to say that it revealed the divine light until then unseen by the usual reader of the Bible.

Views on the Zohar—Not all the Jews even of Moses de Leon's time accepted the *Zohar* for what he claimed it to be. On the other hand, many Jews have been deeply impressed by it. It has served, ever since its appearance, as the starting point for every mystical discussion of Judaism. Many mystical interpretations of the Pentateuch had been in existence for centuries, some of them ascribed, rightly or wrongly, to Rabbi Simon ben Yohai and others dating from the geonic period or even later. Probably what happened was that Moses de Leon put these interpretations together in book form. That this book became popular at once need cause no wonder. It contains some illuminating passages, rich with deep and satisfying religious inspiration. Above all, it appeared at a time when the Jews of Spain as well as of Central Europe needed the simple faith and definite assurance of God's interest which the *Zohar* inspired.

4. Cultural Efforts in the Age of Decline

Location and Character—The growing interest in rabbinic lore and in mysticism did not mean the end of poetry and philosophy among the Jews of southwestern Europe. There was still much of both, for literary traditions among the Jews never die. But the center of literary activity moved from Spain proper to the district north of Spain, across the Pyrenees, known as the Provence. Stimulated by the Spanish literature of the earlier period and by the free and liberal atmosphere which existed in that province, the Jews had a chance to develop their powers. Unfortunately, the Jews of the Provence had no sooner started on their literary career than they were overwhelmed by the tragedy of the Albigensian crusades (1208–1215) which the Catholic Church organized against the Christian heretics of southern France. Many Jewish communities were destroyed, their prosperity was undermined and the government which had protected them was replaced by one which was hostile. Nevertheless, the literary works of the Jews of the Provence during the thirteenth century as well as similar products in Spain of the same period contain much that is of value.

Translators and Linguists—The Provence was the bridge, physically and intellectually, between Spain and Central Europe. Many of the important literary products of the Jews of Spain were worked over by those of the Provence and thus found their way into the thoughts of the Jews of Northern and Central Europe. Two famous families were particularly important in this connection: the Kimhi family and the Ibn Tibbon family. Joseph Kimhi and his two sons, Moses and David, lived in the then important city of Narbonne and occupied themselves with Hebrew grammar and with exegesis, that is, explanations of the Bible. David Kimhi, especially, summarized the conclusions arrived at by the earlier Spanish grammarians and presented a scientific analysis of the Hebrew language which did much for its study later both by Jews and Christians. He also wrote a commentary on the greater part of the Bible which is considered next in importance to those of Rashi and Ibn Ezra.

The Ibn Tibbon family chose another sphere of labor. Judah and Samuel, father and son, became noted translators from Arabic into Hebrew. Judah ibn Tibbon translated the works of Saadia, Bahya and others. Samuel translated Maimonides' *Guide of the Perplexed* and also many philosophical works of non-Jewish authors. These translations achieved a number of results: they made important works available to non-Spanish Jews, they enriched the Hebrew language and they made it easier for Christian Europe to become acquainted with the great works of the Spanish Jews.

Storytellers—One of the most interesting types of literature during this age was the book of fables. The Jews had long been interested in stories with a moral lesson. Indeed, Jews were most active in carrying such stories from the places where they were originally told, India and Persia, to Western Europe. One such story was *The Prince and the Dervish,* by Abraham ibn Hisdai. It is the story of a prince who gave up a life of pleasure to become an ascetic and searcher after truth. Another book consisted of many short fables, known as *Kalila ve-Dimna,* and became very popular in the Middle Ages under the name *Fables of Bidpai.* The best known of these collections was the *Book of Delight,* by Joseph Zabara. The author tells of a journey which he undertook in the company of a giant who turned out to be a demon. That, however, was only the string on which he strung a long series of gemlike little stories, each told in rhyme and with a point to it. The title of the book was fully justified, for it made delightful reading.

Popular Poets—Equally characteristic of the time was its poetry. It did not measure up to the great poetry of the Golden Age; it had neither the same force, the rich style nor the powerful imagery. It was more simple, direct and storylike. Obviously it was intended for the wider public and the less intellectual class. Two famous poets and their books serve as illustrations.

Judah ben Solomon al-Harizi (about 1170–1230) did his work at the beginning of the thirteenth century. He was a traveler to lands as distant as Palestine, a translator of Maimonides' *Guide* and a poet who occasionally still showed some of the brilliance of the age which had just closed. The book which brought him lasting fame was a collection of stories and poems, fables and moral teachings, loosely tied together by means of a humorous description of a journey. Al-Harizi named his book *Tahkemoni* (He Who Makes Wise), for his object was to entertain and at the same time to bring practical and religious wisdom to his readers. In these objectives he was highly successful, since the Jews through the subsequent centuries read the *Tahkemoni* as avidly as we now read popular novels.

Almost a century after Al-Harizi, a Jewish poet of a somewhat different kind lived in Italy. Immanuel of Rome was a friend of the great Italian poet Dante. Frequently Immanuel preached in the synagogue, urging morality and serious study upon his hearers. This, however, did not prevent him from writing poetry containing secular reflections on life. The Jews of his day found some of these poems rather shocking, but they went on reading them just the same. Immanuel's most important book was also written in a light vein. Being a fervent admirer of Dante, he attempted to imitate Dante's immortal work, *The Divine Comedy*. He, too, tells of a journey through Heaven and Hell. His book was called *Ha-Tofet v'ha-Eden* (Hell and Paradise) and described in detail the various punishments meted out to sinful Jews of the past and more particularly of his own age. To be sure, Immanuel's book cannot be compared to that of Dante either in description or as poetry. It is written in rhymed prose and is entertaining rather than inspiring. Perhaps for that very reason it became popular.

5. THE BATTLE BETWEEN MIND AND HEART

The Opposing Forces—The new factors which entered into the life of the Jews in Southwestern Europe in the thirteenth century were the increasing danger of persecution and the growing cultural interests of the Jewish masses. These factors were bound to affect the answer to the ever-present question of Jewish education. What type of cultural preparation should be given to Jewish children in order to make sure of their loyalty to Jewish life? Two answers were given to this question. The intellectual, aristocratic Jews emphasized the need for the study of philosophy as being the best foundation for an understanding of Judaism. Bring up a child on the principles of Maimonides, they argued, and he will have a weapon to defend his faith against attack. Another group of Jews disagreed violently with this theory. They argued that it was not necessary to discuss Judaism, but to observe it and believe in it. Teach a child to keep all the commandments (*mitzvot*), let him follow the precepts of the rabbis, let him study the Talmud rather than theories about the Talmud, and his loyalty will be assured. What was needed was the heart with its ardent devotion, not the mind with its cold reasoning. Behind these differences of attitude lay similar arguments to be found among the Christians of that day. Deeper still were the social and economic differences between the wealthy Jewish aristocrats and the common people.

The Quarrel—The adherents of the opposing points of view soon broke out into open quarrel. Since Maimonides' *Guide of the Perplexed* was the most important philosophical work, it became the center of the conflict. Charges and countercharges of disloyalty to Judaism flew thick and fast; bitter letters were exchanged; excommunications were hurled from each camp at the other; important communities became divided within themselves; blows were exchanged and, even worse, tragedy followed. It started, as one would expect, in the Provence, in the city of Montpellier. There a learned Talmudist, Solomon ben Abraham, led off with an attack on philosophy, especially on the *Guide*. He easily obtained the support of the rabbis of France (1232) and of some important scholars of Spain. On the other hand, equally important men, like David Kimhi, did their utmost to defend the study of philosophy. Apparently the anti-philosophic party felt that it was the weaker side, for they committed the very serious mistake of appealing to the Catholic Church to help them destroy the study of philosophy among the Jews. The monks, ever willing to fight heresy, and even more willing to interfere in Jewish affairs, confiscated many Jewish books, especially copies of the *Guide*, and publicly burned them. When this happened, both sides among the Jews recognized what a calamity had befallen them, for now there would be no end to Church interference in Jewish life. Most of the supporters of the anti-philosophical group abandoned the fight. Even the compromise which seemed about to be accepted, that no one permit his children to study philosophy before the age of thirty, was given up. For a generation the quarrel subsided.

The Fears of the Orthodox—The traditionalists watched the continuing spread of philosophic study with ever-growing apprehension. To be a cultured Jew began to mean looking upon biblical stories as allegories and upon the talmudic laws and Jewish traditions as attempts to represent an ideal way of living. It was argued that if one believed in the ideal, it was unnecessary to practice the *mitzvah* which represented it. It was an argument which showed how much influence Christian ideas were having among the well-to-do Jews. The Jews who loved their traditions saw in all this a serious threat to the survival of the people, and continued to lay the blame for the situation on the study of philosophy.

The Quarrel Continued—Toward the end of the thirteenth century a number of traditionalists, this time too of the Provence, again started a movement aiming to prohibit the study of philosophy and science. Quickly the more liberal-minded men of the Provence and of Spain accepted the challenge, among them a member of the Ibn Tibbon family and the noted Hebrew poet Jedaiah of Beziers. Both of them exerted great influence among the liberals as well as the traditionalists. They pointed out the obvious fact that to prohibit the study of science and philosophy would be to subject Judaism and the Jews to great danger, since it would separate them from that which the rest of the world considered wisdom. This time the great rabbi of Barcelona, Solomon ibn Adret, took a hand in the controversy. He and many scholars of his city issued a decree of excommunication against anyone who studied or permitted his child to study philosophy and science before the age of twenty-five. Only philosophical and scientific works of Jewish authorship and the study of medicine were excluded from this prohibition. The liberal party now replied with a decree excommunicating the excommunicators. The situation was becoming intolerable, when an external calamity overtook the Jews which made them forget their internal quarrels. In 1306 the Jews were expelled from all of France, including the Provence, thus destroying the communities where lay the heart of the controversy.

Results for Jewish Culture—This expulsion of the Jews from France had results for Jewish culture far greater than the end of the quarrel about philosophy. It meant the complete discontinuance of literary activity in the one district of Europe where scientists, translators, grammarians and poets had been concentrated as almost nowhere else for two centuries. In view of what the Jews of the Provence had been contributing to literature, philosophy and science, European culture in general was also the loser. As to Jewish thought and tradition, in the Provence, if anywhere, the proper balance might have been found between the study of philosophy and science, and the study of Talmud and Jewish law, for there the majority of the Jewish population was truly liberal and sincerely loyal. With that community destroyed, the fate of Jewish culture was left to the Jews of Germany, Italy and Spain, and each of these Jewish communities was so situated as to be unable to attain the necessary balance between general culture and traditionalism.

CHAPTER VII

THE AGE OF TERROR

THE JEWS, DURING THE FOURTEENTH CENTURY, UNDERGO EVERY KIND OF MISFORTUNE BECAUSE CHRISTIAN EUROPE DOES NOT KNOW HOW TO PREVENT WAR, INJUSTICE AND DISEASE

Learning from Evil—The fourteenth century was one of the most disastrous periods in the history of Europe. Nature and man combined to show themselves at their worst. Plagues and social revolutions attacked country after country, and human society lay in chaos. Everyone suffered; and where there was general suffering, the Jews were fated to suffer most. They were powerless to do anything about social problems of that day. They could not be so far ahead of their time as to know how to cure economic difficulties or contagious disease. And Europe's masses had long since been persuaded that whatever misfortune came upon the world, the Jews were to blame for it.

Massacres and expulsions were the result. The greater part of the Jewish population of Western and Central Europe during this period was compelled to change its home. New, smaller and poorer communities were established as the old ones were destroyed. Only tradition and faith, the heritage of former generations, kept the Jewish spirit alive and brought inner triumph in the midst of external defeat. Reading the sad story of those days, one can only marvel at that triumph

and learn from it the greatest lesson that history can teach—
the human spirit is indestructible.

1. GREED AND NEED IN FRANCE

An Invitation to Return—When, in 1306, Philip the Fair
of France expelled the Jews from his entire country, they did
not go far beyond the borders of their native land. They settled in districts close to France and waited for an invitation
to return. Nine years later, in 1315, the invitation came.

Behind the Invitation—This action on the part of the rulers of France illustrates the prevalent attitude towards the
Jews of that time and proves that many of the reasons given
for persecuting and expelling them were sheer hypocrisy. In
expelling the Jews, Philip had given as his reason that they
were oppressing the common people by charging them high
rates of interest. But, having driven the Jews out, the king did
not free anyone from paying the debts owed to the Jews. On
the contrary, the king made every effort to collect these debts
and keep the money for his treasury, that is, for himself.
King Louis X, Philip's successor, and his advisers soon discovered that all the confiscated Jewish property did not make
up for the taxes which the Jews used to pay. The expulsion
proved to be bad business for the government. Christian moneylenders were taking the place of the Jews, and complaints
reached the government that these Christians were charging
higher rates than the Jews had charged. The Jews were then
asked to come back to the cities where they had lived, and
their communal property, such as synagogues and cemeteries,
was returned to them.

Shepherds, Lepers and Another Expulsion—The Jews
naively expected to resume their former life, even though on
a poorer and smaller scale. They quickly learned that such
was not to be their fate. Two submerged groups in the society
of that day broke loose from their miserable existence. One
of these was made up of shepherds and other peasants of
southern France. Treated practically as slaves, they possessed
little more intelligence than the animals they guarded. In
1320 they were stirred by one of their number who claimed
to have received a message directly from heaven to lead an
army on a crusade to the Holy Land. Actually these peasants
were rebelling against the social system which was holding
them in chains. But it was easier and safer to start by attacking the Jews, murdering them and taking their property. Be-

fore long the shepherd hordes attacked also the nobility and their property. Only then did the king and the aristocrats bestir themselves. Within a few months the shepherd armies were destroyed with merciless cruelty. But many Jews in southern France had already lost their lives.

One year later the lepers were the cause of misfortune. No human being, during the Middle Ages, was treated more inhumanly than the people afflicted with the disease known as leprosy. Fear and disgust pursued them. They were driven out of human settlements and treated worse than wild beasts. For some reason, the suspicion became current, in 1321, that the lepers were planning to spread their disease. The population in the towns and villages of southern France was terrified. Some lepers were put to torture. A "confession" was thus forced out of them to the effect that the Jews and the Mohammedans of Spain, in league to poison the Christian population of Europe, had bribed the lepers to spread disease by poisoning the wells from which people drew their water. The stupidity of this accusation should have been evident from the fact that the Jews drank the same water. Nevertheless, hundreds of Jews were tortured and killed. It was well understood by the more intelligent people that plunder, not self-protection, was the cause for these crimes. An enormous sum of money was extorted from the others by the king. Then, completely ruined economically, they were once more expelled from the entire country.

The Tragedy Continued—Even this was not the end of the connection between the Jews and France. About a generaton later, in 1359, the need of the French government for more income induced it to invite the Jews to return and settle in France once more. The first part of the Hundred Years' War had made France poor. When Jews were forced to set themselves up as moneylenders, it was possible to impose very heavy taxes upon them and later to confiscate whatever property they possessed. Thus the Jews were used in a coldly calculated manner to get more income for the government, and as a means of indirectly taxing the population. Why did the Jews lend themselves to such a scheme? In the first place, they hoped that their old homeland would be kinder to them than it had been. Secondly, the French government gave written promises of protection, at least for a period of twenty years. Finally, we shall see a little later that conditions in the German provinces into which the French exiles had moved were such as to make it necessary for them to go elsewhere.

Those who had fled from French into German territory now had to flee from German provinces back to France.

For a number of years Charles V and Charles VI of France protected them. But the general situation in France was bad; the population was restless, dissatisfied and disunited. Evils which had been generations in developing were now blamed on the newly-returned Jews. A demand arose to expel them, though it was hard to see how that would solve the internal and international problems which faced the country. This demand was strengthened when a certain Denis Machault, a Jew who had been baptized, returned to Judaism. In September, 1394, the Jews were expelled definitely from all of France, excepting a few districts in the southeastern part of the country which were not directly under the rule of the French king, and the district of Avignon which then belonged to the popes. Thus ended the connection between France and the Jews who had lived there for about twelve hundred years.

2. Black Lies and the Black Death

A People Libeled—While the Jews of France were being expelled, recalled and expelled again, those of Germany were suffering a similar fate in the various cities which they called their home. The events of the Rindfleisch persecution of 1298 were repeated in 1336–1338 by a group of ruffians under the leadership of two petty noblemen, called Armleder because of a piece of leather which they wore as an armband. They went about southwestern Germany spreading the usual accusations of ritual murder and the desecration of the Host, and massacring the Jews.

The Plague—Somehow the Jews of Germany escaped the serious consequences of the rumors which spread in 1321 as a result of the lepers' scare. But their lot was to be infinitely worse in 1349 and 1350. In 1348 a terrible, deadly plague began to spread through Europe. People died by the hundreds of thousands. No one was safe; rich and poor, bishop and peasant were struck down, sickening and dying within a few days. Modern medical science has analyzed the symptoms of those of the bubonic plague, brought by rats which must have been carried from the East to Europe. To us, therefore, there is nothing mysterious about the plague; we know it to be a very contagious disease. But the people of the fourteenth century knew nothing about fleas or rats as causes or carriers of contagious disease germs. They were merely terrified. By the thousands they abandoned their homes and moved from place to place on the excuse that, as pilgrims who scourged themselves near every sacred building, they would gain forgiveness from God and thus be spared from death. These flagellants, as they were called, thus actually helped to spread the disease.

It was natural for the people, in their terror and ignorance, to accept what the clergy had been dinning into their ears for centuries, that the Jews were in alliance with the Devil, and to assume that they were responsible for the prevailing death. The accusations of 1321 were revived; again rumors began to fly that the Jews had poisoned the wells of drinking water. The frenzied minds of the fear-crazed people did not consider that the Jews died of the same Black Death. To the ravages of death among the Jews were now added the murderous attacks of the lower classes in the towns and of the wandering flagellants.

Pope Clement VI sent letters urging the protection of the Jews and testifying to their innocence. Emperor Charles IV halfheartedly tried to prevent their slaughter. But nothing availed. Probably fifty per cent of the country's Jewish population perished.

3. THE TOWNS AND THE JEWS

"Their Wealth Is Their Poison"—One prominent man of those days put his finger on another important reason why the Jews suffered so much during the fourteenth century when he said that the wealth of the Jews was the poison which destroyed them. He was correct in more than one sense. The Jews, to be sure, were no longer as rich as they had been. Their property, however, was always an attraction —not only to the attacking mob, but also to the rulers, the members of the town councils and even the emperor. There were instances when the property of the Jews was divided up, by regular negotiations resulting in a treaty, long before the Jews were actually attacked and expelled.

Towns and Charters—By expelling the Jews, the towns of Germany achieved a still more important aim. From their beginning towns had developed within the territory of various nobles or bishops or of the emperor, who ruled the towns for their own profit. All through the thirteenth century the towns had tried to free themselves from this domination. In France they had failed, for a series of able kings had succeeded in creating a strong central government. In Germany, on the other hand, the central government had grown weaker, the power of the emperors having been reduced to a shadow. This fact encouraged the German townsmen to try for independence.

In this struggle the Jews were like pawns in a chess game. Their very existence had given the rulers an excuse to interfere in the internal affairs of the towns. The Jews were the serfs of the treasury; in other words, they were like the private property of the ruler. If this property were hurt or threatened, the ruler would issue prompt orders to the towns' councils, much to those councils' disgust. Besides, the towns felt that the taxes paid by the Jews ought to go to their treasury, instead of strengthening the power of the lord. Constant disputes between the towns and their overlords resulted. And the Jews were caught in the middle of these disputes; no matter with whom they sided, they were badly off.

Expulsion from the Towns—The Black Death gave the town councils an excellent opportunity to solve this problem. Until then, when the Jews were in danger, the rulers of the towns made an effort to protect them because they knew that their overlords would call them to account. The plague, however, unsettled all human and political relations, and no one could really be held responsible for what happened. Knowing very well that the Jews were in danger, the townsmen did nothing to protect them. Where the Jews were not completely destroyed in a day of bloodshed, the town council simply ordered their expulsion as "enemies of God" and a danger to public order. Thereby the towns rid themselves of the most important cause for interference in their affairs by emperors, lords and bishops. As to the Jews, those who escaped the massacre or were expelled either wandered farther east or were given an opportunity to settle in neighboring small towns and villages belonging to their original overlords.

New Masters—When the worst of the Black Plague was over, the rulers of Germany came together to reorganize the government, and they defined the powers of the emperor in a document called "The Golden Bull" (1356). The emperor, Charles IV, had to yield much of the power which his predecessors had exercised, including his authority over the Jews. From now on, they and their property were placed in the hands of the towns, or of the nobles in whose territory they lived. The town councils could admit them or exclude them as they pleased. They could also tax the Jews within their borders and subject them to any law they chose. There were only two exceptions to this arrangement. A few cities, like Frankfort on the Main, remained under the direct control of the emperor; they were called imperial cities. The second exception was in the matter of taxes. It was now agreed that wherever Jews still lived or were to live in the future in Germany, each one of them was to pay the emperor one "Golden Penny," representing more nearly our quarter of a dollar. In addition, the emperors could claim a sum of money from the Jews of each town as a coronation gift.

Invitations to Return—Under the changed circumstances, the town councils saw advantages in having the remaining Jews return to their former places. One after another the towns, which had sworn only a few years previously never to let "unbelieving Jews" reside in their midst, now invited them back. What could these unfortunates do but jump at the opportunity to return to where they and their ancestors had lived for generations and centuries? The cities, however, insisted on readmitting only a chosen few. They did not want poor Jews, but only such as still had money to lend out at interest or who had the ability to acquire such money. The town councils carefully examined the financial standing and ability of each Jew whom they admitted to residence. Then they imposed upon the reconstructed Jewish community a heavy annual tax. Moreover, the right of the Jews to live in the town was limited to a number of years, sometimes ten or twenty, sometimes as few as three. At the expiration of term, the agreement had to be renewed, and each renewal meant the payment of large sums of money to the town.

Beginnings of the Ghetto—One of the restrictions imposed upon the Jews at this time is interesting and important. There had been no legal objection to Jews living anywhere in a town, or to Christians living in the district inhabited by the Jews. All this was changed when the Jews were readmitted during the second half of the fourteenth century. One condition of permitting them to return was that they must live close together, in a section of the town shut off from the rest. Frequently the streets leading out of the Jewish district were barred. After nightfall Jews dared not be found outside of the district nor Christians inside it. Later on the name *ghetto* was applied to this district.*

An Economic Sponge—The establishment of a separate district for the Jews really represented the extent to which the Jews were excluded from general society. They were wanted

---

* See below, pp. 412 ff.

simply as a means for getting money, not as human beings. The enormous tax burden which was placed on them meant that they could never become wealthy. They had to work hard; they had to lend money at interest; but in the end it was taken away from them. What was even worse, their hard work and their moneylending aroused against them the hatred of the middle and working classes of the towns. For the patricians, that is, the upper classes of the towns, did not use the money obtained through the Jews to make life easier for the poor among the Christians, but only for the enrichment of those who were already rich. Between 1380 and 1390 the lower classes of the towns rebelled against the patrician town councils. The Jews were the first to be attacked, and many towns again witnessed massacres. The patricians of course blamed all the evils upon the Jews. It was agreed that debts due to the Jews were to be canceled; one-fourth of each debt owed by any townsman did not have to be paid at all, while the other three-quarters were to be paid to the city treasuries. A few years later, the emperor, Wenceslas, canceled all the debts owed by the nobility. Thus the Jews were impoverished once more. Many Jews wanted to leave. But the towns would not allow them to emigrate, since they hoped to start the process all over again.

Emotional Relief—Obviously, the masses of the people in the towns got nothing out of all these massacres and confiscations. They were no better off after it was all over than they had been before. They had merely given vent to their emotions and had brought punishment upon their leaders. This was a lesson which the upper classes were quick to learn. Thereafter another use was found for the Jews. They became a means for giving the oppressed lower classes some relief from their pent-up resentment against the patricians and nobility. Any internal or external difficulty which aroused the emotions of the common people was immediately blamed on the Jews.

The Jews and a Rebellion Against the Church—An example of this situation is the tragedy in Vienna in 1421. Jews are known to have lived in the Danube city in the ninth century, and probably even earlier. Down to the end of the fourteenth century they were well treated; the dukes repeatedly issued charters affording them protection and granting them privileges. A number of them acted as financial advisers to the Viennese court. As a result of the expulsions and persecutions in the more western portions of Germany, the Jewish community of Vienna increased in number. In the meantime, however, a Christian middle class had grown up in the city and had begun to look upon the Jews as competitors. At the same time the city council had the usual disagreements with the dukes of Austria. It is not surprising, therefore, to find the Jews being blamed, for example, for a year of drought which caused suffering to the Viennese population.

Trouble came in 1420 from an attempt to reform the Christian religion. A Bohemian by the name of John Huss had voiced strong criticism of the Roman Church, and for this he had been executed. The Bohemians thereupon broke out in rebellion and won some remarkable successes against the Catholic armies. The clergy naturally looked upon all this as the Devil's own work, and the rumor was spread that the Jews were behind the affair and were supplying the Hussites with arms and money. Further to divert the mind of the population and to make the charge against the Jews more real, they were accused of having bribed a Christian woman to steal a sacred wafer which they tortured and mocked. Who were the gainers from these nonsensical accusations? The poorer Jewish inhabitants of the city were deprived of all they had and were then set adrift in oarless boats on the Danube. The wealthier ones were killed, some being burned alive in a huge bonfire on the outskirts of the city. All the property of the Jews was taken over by the town council, though the king received a substantial share. The stones of the destroyed synagogue were presented to the university for a new building. This must have been a token of gratitude for the part the students had played in organizing the riots. For about a century there were no Jews in Vienna, and the Christian merchants had the trade of the city to themselves.

4. THE RESULTS OF TRAGEDY

Emphasis on Preservation—The most the leaders of Judaism could hope to achieve during this period was the preservation of what had been developed in the past. In France during the final period of residence, after their return in 1360, Rabbi Mattathiah ben Joseph concentrated all his energies on rebuilding the community life of his people. It so happened that the French king, Charles V, liked Mattathiah personally and gave him a free hand. The rabbi was thus able to breathe a spark of life into the small and fear-haunted French Jewish community and even to reopen a number of the old academies of Jewish learning. In Germany, which had been the home of talmudic study during the previous centuries, not a single important scholar remained. Away from the center of the German lands, in Vienna, there still were a few scholars. They occupied themselves with writing down the religious customs and traditions which were in danger of being neglected or forgotten because the majority of the Jews lacked the opportunity and the peace of mind to study.

Decay in the Rabbinate—One of the worst effects of the disorganized situation was that unworthy men were selected to act as the rabbinic heads of several communities. From the very beginning, every Jewish community was independent in its religious life; it could elect any man it pleased to guide its spiritual and educational activities. In the course of the thirteenth and fourteenth centuries it became necessary to pay men thus chosen as rabbis. The reason was that such men were called upon to spend so much of their time in teaching and judging that they had no time to earn a livelihood for themselves. Now men began to appear, attracted more by the salary than by the sacredness of the calling, and laid claim to knowledge and to qualities of character which they did not possess. The upheavals which Jewish life had just experienced made it impossible to check these claims, and many communities were victimized. Moreover, some of these seekers after the rabbinic office did not hesitate to ask for and to obtain the support of the non-Jewish authorities to help them secure the post over a rival candidate. City councils, lords, bishops and even kings saw an advantage to themselves in having as the rabbi of their communities a man who was in their debt. There was serious danger that the rabbinic office would degenerate into a political football and the rabbis become employees of the non-Jewish government rather than guides and interpreters of the Jewish spirit.

The New Ordination—How to raise the declining standards of spiritual leadership and to re-establish the independence of the rabbinic office were problems which the more earnest rabbis of that day tried to solve. The chief rabbi of Vienna, Meir ben Baruch ha-Levi (died in 1408), was the most widely respected teacher of his time, and he undertook to set matters right. With all his might he opposed the son of Mattathiah who, though a worthy enough man in other respects, claimed the right to succeed his father in the rabbinate of France by virtue of having had his position ratified by the French king. Even more important was Rabbi Meir's establishment of a new regulation. He urged various Jewish communities to refrain from accepting anyone as rabbi who did not show a written document from the hand of a well-known rabbinic authority testifying to the candidate's knowledge and character. In a measure this was a revival of the ordination (*Semichah*) practiced during the days of the Tannaim. To set a qualified man apart from any other learned Jew, and as a sign of his position as the rabbinic leader of a community, the man thus ordained was to have the title *Morenu*—our Teacher—whenever he was addressed officially. It is to the credit of that and of subsequent generations in Central Europe that this reform was accepted quickly and enthusiastically. The Jews were anxious to have their spiritual leadership as free of fault as was humanly possible.

Poverty—By the beginning of the fifteenth century the storm of persecutions and expulsions had subsided to some extent. The remaining Jews in the German cities, and those readmitted to some of them, were now faced with the problem of earning their livelihood under the serious restrictions imposed upon them. Merchants and artisans refused to have them as competitors; moneylending on a large scale, for business enterprises, was now wholly a monopoly of Christian bankers. Here and there a Jew could still be found with enough capital to lend to the city council when the city treasury was temporarily empty. It was a dangerous transaction, because a city could always find an excuse to expel all the Jews and thus avoid the need for repayment. The most available means for earning their livelihood, therefore, was peddling and making loans of very small sums to workmen or students. Out of the earnings from such petty business transactions the Jews had to pay the enormous taxes and imposts which were the condition of their continued stay in the towns. The vast majority of the Jews of Central Europe were reduced to abject poverty.

Eastward Migration—Where could the Jews turn when they found life in Western and Central Europe impossible? Beginning with the period of the crusades and down to the fifteenth century they could wander in only one direction—to the east. Slowly the lands lying east of the Elbe River entered the circle of European civilization. Ever since the twelfth century the Germans had been pushing their way into Hungary, Bohemia and Poland. At first the Germans made short shrift of the Slavic population, slaughtering and enslaving, and taking away the land from its owners. When that was no longer possible, Germans migrated into those territories and established themselves as merchants and artisans. Fleeing before their persecutors, the Jews found in these partially developed lands an opportunity to establish new homes and to found new communities. All this, however, is so important a story that we shall have to tell it later in greater detail.

CHAPTER VIII

TRAGEDY IN SPAIN

THE JEWS OF SPAIN, AFTER A CENTURY OF DEEPENING MIS-
FORTUNE, ARE EXPELLED FROM THE ENTIRE PENINSULA

A Climax in the Jewish Drama—Before going into the story of the new center of Jewish life in Eastern Europe, it is necessary to describe the great tragedy which overwhelmed the Jews of the Iberian Peninsula. No single happening in the eventful history of the Jews in Europe has so stirred the imagination of Jewish and non-Jewish students of history as has the expulsion from Spain. It overshadows the similar fate suffered at the same time by the Jews of the rest of the continent. Ordinarily one would have expected just the opposite. For, while in both cases tens of thousands willingly sacrificed everything for their faith, there were more weaklings and renegades among the Spanish Jews than among the German Jews of that day. The Spanish event, however, stands out as the more dramatic. The Spanish Jews had been more closely connected with Spanish culture and had produced a superb culture of their own. They had risen much higher; consequently their fall was more spectacular. Their contributions to the development and strengthening of the Spanish king-doms are more obvious; hence the ingratitude with which they were treated is the more striking. Moreover, the expul-sion from Spain did not affect a comparatively small group, like that of England two centuries previously; it was not done in stages, like that of France during the fourteenth century; it did not happen piecemeal, city by city, as was the case in Germany. The Spanish expulsion struck an entire population of hundreds of thousands, all at the same time, in the entire country.

The gigantic scale of the Spanish misfortune enables us the

better to see the effect of centuries of Jewish teaching. For
there is in all this a lesson more important than the mere
knowledge that our people suffered tragedy. The Jews of the
present day can certainly sympathize with the Spanish Jews
of the fifteenth century; we can understand the misery into
which they were plunged. At the same time, we can, and we
often do, feel strengthened and uplifted by the willing acceptance of their hard fate by the many thousands who, faced
with the greatest dangers and the hardest kind of exile, accepted everything for the sake of the religion dear to them
and to us.

This part of the Jewish story most closely resembles a
drama, with the Iberian Peninsula as a vast stage. The first
act, during the first part of the fourteenth century, shows the
Jews living in comparative peace. Like the rumbling of distant thunder while the sky is clear overhead, there are increasing signs of approaching danger. The second act opens
with the year 1391, beginning a century of rapid descent into
the abyss of disaster. The actual expulsion of 1492 is the climax of the drama; but it is not the end. The final act is the
struggle of Judaism, stretching over centuries, against the Inquisition—the Human Spirit against Brute Force. Comparatively few of the secret Jews survived this struggle; but the
Inquisition, too, was destroyed; and wherever men have
valued freedom they have been ashamed of the Inquisition
and its works.

1. THE GATHERING STORM

The Balance of Forces—In the background of the events
which led to the Jewish misfortunes in Spain were certain political and economic rivalries which the reader must keep in
mind. Within the rather small Iberian Peninsula there were,
in the fourteenth century, five different kingdoms. One of
these, the kingdom of Granada in the southeast, was Mohammedan in population and government. Two of the Christian kingdoms, Aragon and Castile, were divided internally
into a number of none too friendly provinces. The efforts of
the various Christian kings were directed to uniting their territories and extending their personal rule. In these ambitions
the kings were opposed by the nobility and by the middle
class in the cities, although these two classes of society were
suspicious of one another. The wiser among the kings saw an
advantage to themselves in gaining the favor of the towns-

men, so as to be able to curb the individualism of the proud
and quarrelsome nobles. In the course of time this policy
was successful. But part of the price which the kings paid for
this success was to sacrifice the lives and homes of the Jews
and the Moors.

The Jews and the Spanish Kings—For the fact is that
throughout the period when the Christian kingdoms were developing, the kings and the Jewish population found one another very helpful. In Spain, as elsewhere in Europe, although the Jewish population had inhabited the land at least
as early as the Christians, the latter, because they were in the
majority, brazenly assumed that the Jews were outsiders. The
merchants and artisans looked upon the Jews as competitors;
the nobles envied the wealth which some of the Jews had acquired. The Jews, therefore, could look only to the kings for
protection. The kings, on the other hand, found their position
strengthened by the taxes which the Jews paid directly into
the royal treasuries. Moreover, distrusting their nobles and
having little faith in the rich townsmen, the kings frequently
used Jews in administrative positions, especially as treasurers
and collectors of taxes. This intensified the hostility of the
other elements of the population.

Protection and Confiscation—The result was that every
once in a while the kings, feeling that their position was none
too strong, would shut their eyes to an attack upon the Jews
or would limit their rights in one way or another. Sometimes
the kings themselves would order the execution of their Jewish financiers and the confiscation of their property. On the
whole, however, they continued to protect the Jews of their
kingdoms. The economic influence of the Jews was still their
greatest strength as well as their source of danger.

The fate of the Jews was illustrated by the treatment which
they received during and after the civil war which afflicted
Castile in the 1360s. King Peter, who was quite properly surnamed "The Cruel," showed favor to the Jews. Consequently
his half-brother, Henry, who coveted Peter's throne, encouraged attacks upon them. Death and poverty were their lot
wherever Henry gained authority. When Peter was killed, in
1369, and Henry became king, the Jews expected no mercy.
That, however, is not what happened. Before long Henry
adopted the usual royal policy of protecting them from attack
and choosing his financial advisers from among them.

2. THE ATTACK

Steps Leading to Disaster—Step by step the danger moved closer. The hatreds which King Henry himself had fanned into flame compelled him to impose upon the Jews in general all those restrictions which had long been demanded by the clergy. The king was not anxious to enforce these laws, but they hung suspended like a sword over the heads of the people. Some years later, the Jews committed a serious blunder by bringing about the death of a Jew who was a royal favorite. This man, Joseph Pichon, probably deserved his fate. As foremost royal tax collector he had tried to win the favor of the Christians while acting unethically toward his fellow Jews. The Jews looked upon him as a spy in their midst. When, however, they used a trick to obtain his condemnation to death, they aroused against themselves the ill will of the king as well as of the Christian population. Soon thereafter a weak king came to power in Castile; and the enemies of the Jews saw their chance.

The Black Year—The year 1391 marked the beginning of the series of events which destroyed Jewish life in the entire Iberian Peninsula. Ferrand Martinez stands out as the Haman of that day. Possessing the prestige of being the queen-mother's father confessor, this monk used his great eloquence to stir up the population. Followed by a mob, he went from city to city, invaded the Jewish streets, often broke into synagogues, and offered the Jews a choice between death and the cross. The Jewish communities of Seville, Cordova, Toledo and dozens of other cities were almost annihilated. No efforts of the government, which in any case were probably only halfhearted, could hold the mobs in check. From Castile, Martinez went into Aragon, and many other communities were attacked in the same fashion. From there the murderous movement spread to the island of Majorca where, in the city of Palma, hundreds were killed.

Martyrs and Converts—For several months the vicious attacks continued without letup. Christian Spain was destroying the lives of thousands of its Jewish inhabitants and the peace and happiness of the rest. At length the authorities made an honest effort and succeeding in halting the massacres. An accounting could now be made of the results. It was clear that, as in Germany so in Spain, many thousands had preferred to die as Jews than to live as Christians, unwilling to be like those who were ready to kill them. But large numbers had sufficiently valued life and comfort to accept the terms offered by the mobs. Tens of thousands, especially among the Jews of the upper class, had accepted baptism. Even after the storm had quieted down, and those who had escaped the massacres by hiding or by fleeing had returned to their homes, the wave of conversions continued.

New Christians—Were these converts convinced of the truth of Christianity? Could anyone believe that force had opened their eyes to the greatness and nobility of the Church when arguments had failed during many generations? Obviously, the acceptance of baptism was in almost all cases merely a means of escaping violent death. They must have hoped that, the storm over, they would be able to return to the faith of their fathers. This, however, was not permitted them. The Spanish clergy raised their hands in horror at the mere thought that anyone who had once accepted baptism, no matter under what circumstances, should be permitted to leave the Christian fold. They made it perfectly clear that any convert refusing to follow Christian observances would be treated as a heretic. The converts were forced to remain Christians just as they had been compelled to become Christians. Certainly there were some among these New Christians who early gave up the struggle and tried to make the best of the situation. There were others, as we shall have occasion to see, who made up their minds to profit from the situation. Still others fled the country and sought a new home where they could worship God in accordance with the dictates of their conscience. But many, perhaps a majority of the New Christians, continued to hope and wait for a change of fortune, for the time when they could return to Judaism within the borders of their native land. In the meantime, they tried their best to observe in secret the religion which was forbidden them in public.

3. ATTACK THROUGH WORD AND FEAR

Failure of Rioting—The year 1411 saw another series of riots and another herd of unwilling converts who had succumbed to terror and despair. This time Vincent Ferrer, a Dominican monk, was the instigator, breaking into synagogues with a cross in one hand and a Torah scroll in the other. He offered a choice; but the mob at his heels came armed with other weapons and emphasized to the assembled

Jews what choice they really had. On the whole, however, this method of winning the Jews was found to be unsatisfactory. It destroyed a great deal of property. Besides, it brought into the Church too many halfhearted Christians. At last the government and the Church, if not the mob, began to look at the problem of converting the Jews as one requiring the destruction of Judaism rather than the destruction of more Jews.

Zealous Ex-Jews—In the intensified attack on Judaism a number of former Jews played an important role. The most prominent of these was Paul of Burgos. He had been known as Solomon ha-Levi, a wealthy and learned Jew who had acted as rabbi in the city of Burgos. In 1391 he became "convinced" that his future lay in Christianity. He went to Christian theological schools to study and then rose rapidly to the rank of archbishop. He became a member of the governing circle of Castile and a close friend of the anti-Pope Benedict XIII. He not only wrote and preached against Judaism, but he did his best to make life hard for the remaining Jews. A former admirer of his while they were both Jews, and now his apt pupil in Christianity, was Joshua Lorki, who also attacked his former religion. Together these two instigated the severest verbal attack which Judaism had ever suffered till then.

The Tortosa Disputation—This was a disputation, dramatically organized to settle the question of the relative merits of Judaism and Christianity. The order for the Jewish representatives to participate in this debate was issued by Benedict XIII. Now, Benedict was an anti-pope, that is, most Christians did not consider him the legitimate pope; only Spain recognized Benedict's claim to the papacy. Consequently, he thought he could add to his reputation by focusing the eyes of all Christians on an elaborate attempt which he would conduct to refute Judaism. Nowadays we would call it a propaganda trick to use anti-Jewishness for personal advancement. The Jews, of course, did not want to take part in anything of the kind. They knew that, far from being a free and open debate, in which they would have an equal right with their Christian opponents to speak their mind, this was but another attempt to humiliate Judaism. But there was no refusing the invitation; threatened with fines, imprisonment and expulsion, the most prominent scholars among the Jews of Spain were forced to appear. The disputation was conducted before a brilliant assembly in the city of Tortosa, in February 1413. The ex-Jew Joshua Lorki opened for the Christians, and the learned Vidal Benveniste for the Jews. The disputation, which, with many interruptions, dragged on for more than a year, degenerated into the usual interpretations and misinterpretations of biblical and talmudic passages. The Jewish representatives tried to present their attitude, though they knew how useless it was to do so. The verdict was, naturally, what had been expected from the very start. The Talmud was condemned and the Jews forbidden to study it. A variety of other hostile laws was announced by the anti-pope and by the government of Castile.

A Philosopher's Answer—The actual arguments of the Christian side in the disputation could not possibly have convinced the Jews, but the entire proceedings and its result served further to depress them. Something had to be done to fortify their spirit and strengthen their loyalty to Judaism. Even before the disputation several Jews had tried to do exactly that. Hasdai Crescas had written an important philosophical work, *Or Adonai* (The Light of the Lord) in which he pointed out the essential beliefs of Judaism, namely, faith in God's guidance and in Jewish destiny. After the disputation, Joseph Albo, a pupil of Crescas, who had participated in it as one of the Jewish representatives, wrote another book, more popular in tone and therefore more calculated to answer the needs of the hour. He called it *Sefer ha-'Ikkarim* (The Book of Root Principles), for his object was to show that all religion grows out of the same ideas; only after they grow out of these roots do various religions begin to differ from one another. Albo tried to point out that Judaism is superior to Christianity as a religion. The branch principles which make up Judaism are purer and more in harmony with philosophy than the branch principles which compose Christianity. Thus Albo sought to refute the fundamental claims of Christianity and bolster Jewish morale.

4. THE INQUISITION

Jews and New Christians—As the fifteenth century continued, the Christian clergy realized that much still remained to be done before Judaism in Spain could be considered completely defeated. The number of conversions was decreasing, since those Jews who had remained Jews, having withstood the threats during the period of rioting, were evidently the more loyal and devoted adherents of the old faith. Even worse than that, from the point of view of the clergy, was the obvious disloyalty to the new faith on the part of many New

Christians who were less than halfhearted in the observance of Christian ceremonies. From the Jews living near by, the New Christians were receiving instruction and assistance in their efforts to observe as much of Judaism as was possible. The Christian clergy considered this a scandalous situation. They tried to get the Jewish communities to cooperate with them by threatening the rabbis with dire punishments if they did not reveal the names of those New Christians who kept in touch with the Jews. But the rabbis refused to be party to such betrayals; and the clergy began to devise other means to keep the New Christians in line.

Religion and Politics—In the meantime there was growing dissatisfaction with the New Christians in another direction. One would have supposed that the Christian population of Spain, which had clamored for the conversion of the Jews and had taken such an active part in forcing them into Christianity, would now receive them with joy. Quite the contrary happened; the New Christians were resented by the Old Christians. Within a few years an ugly name began to be applied to the converts; they were called Marranos, which meant "pigs." The reason given for this attitude was that they were not loyal Christians, but secret Jews. The real reason for the dislike, however, must have been quite different. As long as the New Christians had been Jews, the Old Christians could discriminate against them and complain about their competition. Now that they were equal Christians, all the opportunities which had formerly been closed to them were opened. The New Christians rapidly rose in the fields of politics and economics. The very fact that so enormous a number of Jews became Christians worked against the interests of many less capable Old Christians. No wonder that the New Christians met with almost the same hostility they had suffered when Jews. During the fifteenth century bloody riots broke out in many important cities, not against the Jews, but against the New Christians. The true reason for these riots becomes clear when one notes that the rich Marranos suffered more than the poor. Moreover, the government was forced to promise that it would not permit the Marranos to hold public office, a promise which the pope soon nullified on the ground that it involved persecution of Christians by Christians. Limitations, however, were imposed upon them which, in the past, had been imposed only upon Jews. The problem of economic rivalry remained unsolved.

The Threat of Inquisition—Unfortunately, zealous churchmen saw only one way of turning insincere Christians into sincere ones. Theirs was not the way of mercy and kindness, by which people converted under the threat of death might gradually have gained respect for their new faith; theirs was the way of fear and force. Loudly various churchmen, especially members of the religious orders of monks, began to advocate the introduction of the Inquisition into Spain. The Inquisition had long been an office of the Catholic Church dedicated to the special task of finding and punishing heresy, which was interpreted to mean any violation of the laws and beliefs of the Church. Nobody had ever liked the Inquisition. People feared it because it pried into their private lives, because its investigations were secret and because most of the inquisitors were stern and relentless persecutors of anyone who differed from the official religion. The civil governments disliked it because the Inquisition acted with complete independence and disregarded the country's legal system. Besides, punishment by the Inquisition always meant confiscation of property, which made the so-called Holy Office that much richer while depriving the royal treasury of taxable wealth. The clergy, especially the bishops, were also generally opposed to the Inquisition, for its establishment anywhere deprived the local bishop of much of his authority. Thus, not only the Marranos, but all liberal-minded citizens as well as the heads of the government and the Church, objected to the plan of introducing the Office of the Inquisition into Spain. Against these objections must be set the desire of pious Christians to exterminate heresy, the interest of the townsmen to destroy competition, the eagerness of the aristocracy to remove or, at least, cast suspicion on capable rivals, and the greed of King Ferdinand to enrich the royal treasury if he could arrange the matter of confiscations.

The Inquisition Begins Its Work. Events played into the hands of those in favor of the Inquisition. The secret Jews could not hope to keep their secret forever. In 1480 a number of prominent New Christians were caught celebrating the *seder* on the first night of Passover. Queen Isabella of Castile, a very pious Christian, was so shocked by this that she agreed to have the Inquisition establish itself in her country. The pope had already reluctantly consented. The Marranos now became frantic and attempted to stop the Inquisition by force. But all their plots and plans came to naught. A few years later the Inquisition was introduced also into Aragon, after an agreement had been reached with King Ferdinand on the division of the confiscated property. Thus were established the torture-chambers in which thousands were made to suffer; thus were kindled the fires in which other thousands were burned alive. For the Inquisition continued to function in Spain down to the end of the eighteenth century.

An Auto-da-Fé—Auto-da-Fé, or Act of Faith, was the name given to the public executions of the Inquisition's punishment. It was held in the public square of the town, made gay with decorations. Since it was the occasion for a popular holiday, spectators crowded every roof and window. Royalty and nobility, in gala attire, sat on seats especially provided for them. A scaffold and a pulpit occupied the center of the square. As the church bells tolled, the procession filed in: helmeted soldiers carried their halberds; hooded monks and priests chanted praises to God; and the servants of the Inquisition shepherded the condemned prisoners. The prisoners were arrayed facing the pulpit. They looked gaunt after months of confinement, hunger and terror; some were ill and crippled by the torture they had suffered. Each prisoner carried a candle; each wore a tunic from which the spectators could judge the degree of blasphemy or heresy for which he, or she, had been convicted. A preacher delivered a long sermon. Then the chief inquisitor announced the punishments: penance, stripes, confiscation, imprisonment or death. Those destined to die were handed over to the civil government, since the Church followed the letter of the Divine Law against the taking of life. The inquisitor addressed a final exhortation to those condemned to the scaffold; he urged on them a last-minute repentance. Those who confessed that they had practiced Judaism secretly, but now recognized the Roman Church as the sole source of salvation, were first strangled by the executioners. Their bodies were laid on the scaffold beside the living men and women already bound there. A prominent dignitary, sometimes the king himself, set fire to the faggots. The tolling of the bells and the cheers of the spectators mingled with the shrieks of the dying. Sometimes, above the agonized tumult, floated the defiant cry: *Shema' Yisrael, Adonai Elohenu, Adonai Ehod!*

A tragic story—it is also a story of triumph. The tragedy is not one-sided, for it arouses pity not alone for those thousands who suffered torture and death, but also for the Christian religion, all of whose lofty ideals thus went up in flames. The triumph, on the other hand, is one-sided, for despite all its efforts the Inquisition failed to destroy Judaism, even in the Iberian Peninsula. Once more it afforded proof that force cannot prevail against the human spirit.

5. Expulsion from Spain

Delay of the Final Blow—The Inquisition, it must be re-membered, did not have any authority over the Jews, but only over those who had been converted to Christianity. Nevertheless, the inquisitors and others of the Christian clergy were convinced that it was impossible to hold the Marranos in line unless all associations with their former relatives and friends were cut off. If all the rest of the Jews could be forced out of the country or into the Church, it would be another triumph and it would also be much easier to keep watch over the New Christians. Consequently, the clergy continually urged King Ferdinand and Queen Isabella to clear their lands of Jews and Mohammedans. But the royal couple hesitated. Not only were Jews still prominent in the government, and not only did influential Marranos and their friends oppose such a move, but the country still needed the Jews. At the time, Ferdinand and Isabella were planning to conquer the kingdom of Granada, the last bit of territory still held in the Iberian Peninsula by the Mohammedans. It would have weakened them for the great effort if they had caused the economic upheaval involved in the departure of thousands of businessmen and artisans.

The Edict of Expulsion—On January 2, 1492, Granada surrendered to the army of Ferdinand and Isabella. For the first time since the Mohammedan conquest in 711 the Iberian Peninsula was entirely in the hands of Christians. The way was now clear for the Spanish rulers to rid themselves of the Jews. On March 31, in one of the halls of the beautiful Alhambra, the palace of the kings of Granada, Ferdinand and Isabella signed the decree expelling the Jews from Castile and Aragon. The reason given was that they corrupted the Marranos by secretly encouraging them in disloyalty to Christianity. The Jews had till August 1, 1492, to make arrangements for their departure. In theory they could take their wealth with them. Since, however, the export of gold, silver or any other precious metal was forbidden them, they were reduced practically to loading themselves with whatever goods they could purchase and carry, which obviously could not be much. To the Jews the edict meant something very much worse than poverty.

The Final Plea and Its Rejection—The edict of 1492 meant homelessness, physical and mental suffering for all, and death for those too sick, too old or too young to travel as traveling had to be done in those days. Spain had been the home of these Jews in every possible sense from earliest times. The mere prospect of leaving Spain, never to return, was unmitigated tragedy. Besides, where were they to go? Who would receive them? No wonder they were willing to give up all their worldly goods, to suffer the worst humiliations, for the chance of remaining in the land of their fathers.

A delegation went to see Ferdinand and Isabella, perhaps in the hope that the king and queen would be touched, as human beings, by the tragedy they were imposing upon so many of their faithful subjects; they also hoped that an offer of money could persuade them to recall the cruel edict. The delegation consisted of Abraham Senior and Isaac Abrabanel, who for years had faithfully labored to set the finances of the country in order and to make the victory over Granada possible. Senior was the "Chief Rabbi" of Castile, that is, the secular head of the Jews, entrusted with the supervision over the Jewish communities. Isaac Abrabanel, possessed of much more Jewish knowledge and loyalty, was adviser on matters of state finance. Both royal favorites could well feel that Ferdinand and Isabella were indebted to them for services competently performed. The appeared before the royal couple and made an eloquent plea. To reinforce their arguments, they laid on the table a bag full of money. A story relates that at that very moment, when Isabella was wavering because of the force of the arguments and Ferdinand because of the sight of the gold, Grand Inquisitor Torquemada strode into the room. Eyes ablaze with anger, a cross in his hand, he approached the table, placed the cross near the bag of gold and said, pointing to the figure of Jesus on the cross: "Here he is; sell him." Isabella could never withstand religious zeal. The plea of the delegation was rejected; the edict remained in force. Abraham Senior, like so many others of his kind, unwilling to make the final sacrifice for the sake of his religion, thereupon became converted to Christianity. Isaac Abrabanel chose to cast his lot with his people and joined them in their exile, even though the king and queen were willing to make an exception of him and let him remain in Spain as a Jew.

The Departure—August 1 was the day set for the final departure of the Jews from Castile and Aragon; actually, the last groups left on August 2. By another of those strange coincidences of which Jewish history is full, that day was the

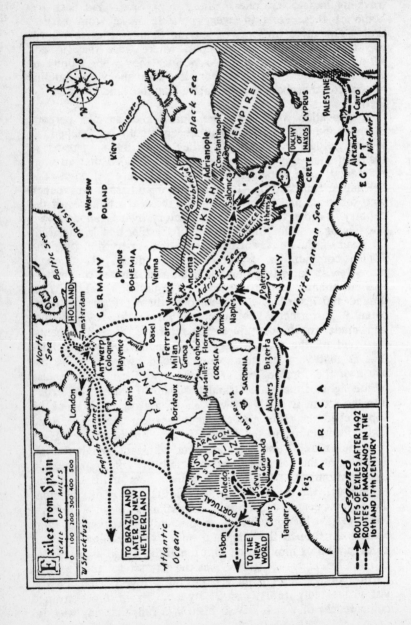

9th of Ab, the fast day which recalls the destruction of the First as well as of the Second Temple.

A Note in Columbus' Diary—On that August 2, in 1492, three little vessels sailed out of the harbor near Seville, past the ships upon which Jewish exiles were embarking. It was Christopher Columbus starting on his epoch-making voyage of discovery. As his ships moved past the others, he noted the fact in his diary. One may well wonder what Columbus would have thought if it had been revealed to him that he was on the way to discover a new world in which the descendants of these exiles would find a haven of refuge. As a matter of fact, Columbus' voyage was more closely connected with the expulsion of the Jews, and with the events leading up to it, than he was ready to admit. As we shall see when we discuss America, Columbus' plans were aided by a number of prominent ex-Jews; his ships were fitted out with money confiscated from Jews; and his sailors were, to some extent, former Jews, now turned Marranos, fleeing from a land made inhospitable by the Inquisition.

6. PERFIDY IN PORTUGAL

The Price of Admission—It is understandable why most exiles from Castile and Aragon wanted to go to Portugal in preference to any other land. Portugal was near by and required no exhausting and dangerous journey. In language and culture, moreover, it was not much different from the land they had called their home. The king of Portugal was willing to admit them only temporarily. To be sure, the wealthier Jews, who could pay a considerable sum as the price of admission, and the artisans who could be used in the manufacture of munitions of war, were granted leave to stay indefinitely. But the poorer ones were permitted to stay only upon the payment of a smaller sum, and then only for a few months, until they could find some other place to go to. Naturally, the very poor were thus completely excluded. It is doubtful, however, that they were any worse off than the hundred thousand temporarily admitted. Perhaps intentionally, not enough ships were provided for the latter when the time came to leave the country, and those thus left behind were sold into slavery unless they adopted Christianity.

A Sly King—By 1495 there still remained in Portugal the original Jews of that country and some thousands of the wealthier exiles from Spain. At this time a new king, Manoel I, ascended the Portuguese throne. He recognized the impor-

tance of his Jewish subjects for the economic prosperity of
his country. But he had ambitions of a personal nature. He
wanted to marry a daughter of Ferdinand and Isabella and
thus possibly become heir to their kingdoms. These monarchs
refused their consent to the marriage unless Manoel's kingdom, like theirs, was completely free of non-Christians. Thereupon, Manoel, while ordering the Jews to leave Portugal, issued secret orders to the police. On the first day of Passover,
1497, all Jewish children were dragged out of their homes
and forcibly baptized. Manoel hoped in this way to retain the
parents. No doubt many families were thus forced to remain.
The majority, however, still insisted on leaving the country
on the date set for the expulsion. Manoel, therefore, resorted
to still another trick. He detained them beyond the date he
himself had set for their departure, herded them together like
cattle, refused to give them food and drink for several days,
and sent converted Jews to preach to them. That, too, having
failed with most of them, they were converted against their
will. Only a small number of the twenty thousand who
suffered this treatment succeeded in escaping the country.

Marranos in Portugal—Even the pope, Alexander VI, recognized that it would be unwise to establish an Inquisition in
Portugal in order to compel people converted in this fashion
to adhere strictly to the religion into which they had been
forced. Year after year a number of them managed, in spite
of obstacles, to leave the country and seek homes elsewhere,
in lands where they could return to Judaism. Emigration was
finally forbidden and the Inquisition was established in Portugal as in Spain. No wonder that the Portuguese Inquisition
found more to do than the Spanish one, for the Marranos
with whom it had to deal came of stock which had made
greater sacrifices to retain their ancestral faith.

Uncertain Numbers—If we knew how many Jews there
were in Spain and Portugal when the trouble started in 1391,
we could tell how many remained as Marranos and how
many fled to other countries as Jews. We do know that after
1492 thousands of Jews searched for homes in lands bordering on the Mediterranean. But these could have been only a
small portion of the population which had lived as Jews in
their original homes. Many thousands had suffered death, and
perhaps ten or twenty times as many had been forced or
frightened into the Church. The most prosperous and populous Jewish community in Europe, a community of at least a
quarter of a million people, a large number for that age, was

completely destroyed. But their epic story was not ended; the scattered remnants were destined to establish other communities in various parts of the world.

CHAPTER IX

HOPES AND DISAPPOINTMENTS

THE AGE OF THE RENAISSANCE OFFERS HOPES FOR AN IM-
PROVEMENT IN RELATIONS BETWEEN THE JEWS AND THE
CHRISTIANS OF WESTERN EUROPE, BUT THESE HOPES ARE
DISAPPOINTED

A Fleeting Spark of Hope—Despite the events in Spain and Portugal, the period covering the late fifteenth and early sixteenth centuries was really a time of great promise from which the Jews had every right to expect an improvement in their lot. A new spirit began to sweep over Western and Central Europe; it was the spirit of the Renaissance, that is, the Rebirth. Reborn were the culture, the desire for freedom and the love for beauty which had prevailed in the ancient world at its best. Intellectuals began to study the classical languages —Greek, Latin and Hebrew—and the wisdom and poetry written in those languages. The upper classes of West European society abandoned the crudities and cruelties of feudal life, and a new, critical spirit awakened that tested current ideas, values and institutions. It was an age of great intellectual and cultural achievement.

Unfortunately, that movement suffered from a number of weaknesses which destroyed most of its value and postponed the realization of its promise. The Renaissance was limited to the upper classes. Workers and peasants who caught some of its spirit, and tried to gain some freedom and beauty for themselves, were suppressed. The movement, moreover, did not satisfy the desire of the people for a deeper and more spiritual religion. On the contrary, the most obvious result of the Renaissance, as the common people saw it, was a growing looseness in morals and ethics. Consequently, the Renaissance gave way, all too soon, to reaction and bloodshed. Artists and poets, students and philosophers continued here and there to work in the spirit of this hopeful age; but Western Europe as a whole was plunged into wars in which religion and politics were hopelessly confused.

The fate of the Jews was bound up with the history of the Renaissance. The revival of culture affords another illustration of the close connection between Jewish life and general civilization. Common sense and knowledge seemed to be raising human beings above prejudice. When, however, the Renaissance gave way to reaction, Jewish hope for a better world was extinguished along with the flame of enlightenment which, for an historical moment, had lighted up the somber horizon of European civilization.

1. JEWS AND THE RENAISSANCE

The Broadening Mind—The slow labor of many men over many centuries finally lifted the clouds which had descended upon the human mind with the disintegration of the Roman empire. Italy was once more the center of European culture. Italian high society became polite and learned, and the strenuous knightly tournaments gave way to discussions of philosophical and cultural problems. The Jews, especially in Mohammedan Spain and in the Provence, had done their share in bringing this change about through their translations and original works. In the fifteenth and early sixteenth centuries, their activity became even more direct. Some of the most important men in the Renaissance movement had Jewish teachers and encouraged Jewish scholars. Elijah del Medigo, for example, was a familiar figure in the court of Lorenzo the Magnificent of Florence, a court which, for a whole generation, formed the very heart of the Renaissance. There Elijah spread the knowledge and interpretation of the philosophy of Aristotle.

The Expanding World—The age of the Renaissance was remarkable also for its discovery of new lands and new routes to old lands. The great voyages of Portuguese and Spanish navigators laid the foundations for the modern world. Jews had long been interested in astronomy, and from that science a number of them turned to the science of navigation. Among the important contributors to this science was the philosopher Levi ben Gershom (Gersonides), who lived in the first half of the fourteenth century. His discussion of astronomy was considered so important that Pope Clement

VI (1342–1352) ordered this part of his book translated from Hebrew into Latin. This led to the construction of a nautical instrument, Jacob's Staff, by which sailors could more easily chart their position. The preparation of maps became the specialty of a family of Jews in the island of Majorca. The name of Abraham Zacuto, the scientist who prepared the astronomical tables which Columbus used on his voyage, is another of many notable names in this field. A story has come down of a remarkable Polish Jew whom Vasco da Gama met in India, which this Jew had already explored. The important part which the Jews played in the discovery and early settlement of the American continent will be discussed later.

Medicine and Other Sciences—The age of science had not yet begun, but it is clear from the above that its early manifestations greatly interested the Jews. The study of mathematics had always attracted them, and they continued to devote themselves to it. Their favorite study, however, was medicine. Its combination of knowledge and humaneness has ever appealed to the Jewish mind. During the period of the Renaissance this was especially the case.

The Jewish Bible and the Christians—The most profound Jewish influence on European civilization has been exercised through the Bible. The clergy studied it, and, through them, its ideas penetrated into the minds of the people. From the beginning of the Christian era, lessons were drawn from the Bible and commentaries were written on it as regularly by Christian as by Jewish scholars. European law and morals, theological beliefs and hopes for the future derived largely from what the Christians called the Old Testament. Many Christian reformers of the Middle Ages based their views on interpretations of the Bible text. Frequently, when the Church opposed such reforms, it called them Jewishly inspired, that is, based on Jewish views of the Scriptures. In numerous instances the charge was true. Nevertheless, the extent to which early Christian Bible students were directly affected by Jewish interpretations is still a subject of investigation. During the first thousand years of the Christian era, when relationships between Jews and Christians were friendly and direct, such influences came through personal contact and, therefore, have been left unrecorded. Later, Christian scholars used actual Jewish writings. Nicolas de Lyra, of the early fourteenth century, is the outstanding example. His Bible commentary was admittedly influenced by that of Rashi three centuries earlier. He quoted Rashi constantly, either in approval or refutation. Lyra, in turn, exerted a profound influence upon all succeeding Christian commentators. When Martin Luther translated the Bible, as part of his religious reform movement, he leaned heavily upon Lyra's commentary and thus, indirectly, upon Rashi.

The Study of Hebrew—In the fourteenth century, the study of Hebrew was made part of the curriculum in a number of European universities. The frankly stated object was to use the knowledge of Hebrew—that is, of works written in Hebrew—as an aid in converting Jews to Christianity. At first, the new subject appealed to very few; teachers and pupils were mostly converted Jews. The Renaissance made the study of Hebrew more popular, and this resulted in an increasingly sympathetic attitude on the part of cultured Europeans toward the literary treasures of the Jews. The life and work of Elias Levitas illustrated the new situation. He was a German Jew who immersed himself deeply in the study of Hebrew grammar and Masorah, that is, the Bible text as it was handed down by Jewish tradition.* At first he wrote only for Jews. In fact, he was among the early writers in Yiddish-German. At the beginning of the sixteenth century, Cardinal Egidio of Viterbo invited Levitas to become his teacher of Hebrew, and presently other noted Christians became his pupils or studied his grammatical works.

A Pope's Sympathies—An illustration of the attitude toward the Jews which prevailed in the upper circles of Christians is to be seen in the behavior of many of them toward the exiles from Spain. Most of the nobility and the churchmen of Italy recognized the cruelty of the expulsion and freely admitted the exiles into their lands. A considerable number of exiles sought admittance into the city of Rome. It is understandable that the Jews already resident in the city feared having the refugees join them. They were concerned lest so large an addition to their number might arouse further anti-Jewishness. Pope Alexander VI, however, was outraged by the attitude of Rome's Jewish population. He not only permitted the exiles to enter, but he also punished the Roman Jews by imposing a fine upon them.

2. A CONTROVERSY ABOUT JEWISH BOOKS

Revival of an Old Charge—In the year 1509 a controversy

* See above, pp. 241–2.

began over Jewish literature which, though it affected the Jews, had an even greater effect upon the Christians. A Jew by the name of Joseph (John) Pfefferkorn ran into difficulties with both the Jewish and non-Jewish authorities. To avoid further trouble with the state, he turned Christian and sought the protection of the clergy. Eager to avenge himself upon the Jews he revived the old accusation that Jewish literature, especially the Talmud, was full of blasphemies against all that Christians considered holy. Pfefferkorn was far from being a man of learning, but among the monks he posed as such. The Dominicans at Cologne aided him in writing his books and in slandering the Talmud and its commentaries. What they did was to retell all the stories and charges which had been current ever since the days of Nicholas Donin in 1239. Pfefferkorn and his assistants received the emperor's permission to confiscate all copies of the Talmud and other Jewish books, including prayer books, and to burn them. Frantically the Jews did all they could by arguing and bribing. One year later, the emperor himself restored the confiscated books, after a number of Frankfort Jews extended the time limit on a debt which one of his favorites owed them.

A Christian Scholar—This, however, was not the end of the matter. Pfefferkorn and the other opponents of the Jews continued their hostile propaganda. The emperor had established a commission to investigate the Jewish books. One of its members was John Reuchlin, foremost Christian scholar of Hebrew in Germany. Reuchlin expressed himself as opposed to the destruction of the books, arguing that through the study of their mystical literature the Jews could be brought closer to Christianity. He appealed to the emperor and to all intelligent Christians not to permit this crime against human knowledge.

A Battle of Words and Wits—Jewish literature now became the center of a controversy which raged for a number of years. There was not a liberal Christian in Europe, nor a single critic of the forces of bigotry within the Church, who failed to range himself on the side of Reuchlin in defense of the Jewish books. The upper churchmen, especially in Italy, and the pope himself sympathized with Reuchlin. Everyone who was not a peasant in Europe was thus ranged on one or the other side in the controversy. The only people who were forced to stand aside and not participate were the ones most directly concerned—the Jews.

Results of the Controversy—After a few years, the quarrel died down. It was forgotten because of other discussions which began to shake the foundations of the Church and of the Western world. For at that very time, Martin Luther came forward with a series of devastating criticisms of the Catholic organization. The Reuchlin-Pfefferkorn controversy had helped to bring to public notice some of the weaknesses of the religious society of that day, and Luther took full advantage of this situation. From the Jewish point of view, the controversy proved once more that the growth of liberalism has always tended to make Jewish life more tolerable. Unfortunately, this broad-minded era was soon to end.

3. Two Strange Men

False Hopes—Before describing the change that came over Europe after 1520 and its effect on the Jews, we must speak of two of the strangest characters in Jewish history. They left no permanent effect on Jewish life, yet the mere fact of their existence sheds a peculiar light on the Jews of that day, on their hopes and on their fate.

David Reubeni—Around 1525 there appeared in Rome a short, stocky, swarthy man who announced that he was the emissary of his brother, king of a Jewish kingdom somewhere near Arabia, a kingdom whose population was descended from "the lost Ten Tribes." His object was to obtain enough ammunition to arm a Jewish force for an attack on the Mohammedans from the east while the Christians attacked them from the west. At that time the Turks were triumphant over their enemies and were carrying everything before them, having captured almost the entire territory of the Balkans. Reubeni's plan was just the kind which would appeal to the Christians of that day. The pope did not doubt the truth of Reubeni's identity, received him as befitted an ambassador, and gave him letters of recommendation to the king of Portugal. The Jews of Italy and the Marranos of Spain and Portugal were enthusiastic. The idea that a powerful Jewish kingdom existed somewhere raised their self-respect. They believed that when a Jewish ambassador entered into negotiations with European powers, the Jewish state which he represented might persuade Christendom to improve the lot of its Jews, whose defenselessness accounted in large part for their miseries. It may be that they also hoped for a Jewish restoration to Palestine once that land was conquered with the aid of Jewish arms.

Solomon Molcho—Among the Marranos of Portugal was

Diego Pires, a young man who had been brought up as a Christian and had obtained a good post in the government. Apparently he tried to persuade Reubeni to take him along to the Jewish kingdom where Diego could become a Jew. When Reubeni refused to have anything to do with him, Diego escaped from Portugal, became a Jew and adopted the name Solomon Molcho. This was only the beginning of his strange career. After a brief stay in Palestine, he went to Rome, managed to make the acquaintance of the pope, predicted an overflow of the Tiber and an earthquake in Portugal, both of which events actually happened, and thus established a reputation as a man of mystical powers. The Inquisition sought him as a heretic, but the pope himself aided him to escape. Solomon Molcho built up a following for himself as a messiah.

Adventurers or Visionaries—To this day it has been impossible to decide what the motives of these two men were. Were they merely notoriety seekers, or did they have a plan in mind to aid the Jewish people? Some have supposed that David Reubeni was an impostor, and Solomon Molcho a man half-crazed with religious fanaticism. Others have of late come around to a different view, namely, that Reubeni came from one of those long forgotten settlements of Jews around Persia who, with some justice, claim descent from the ancient Israelites; or perhaps from Ethiopia where the ancestors of the modern Falashas actually did have, in those days, an independent kingdom.* Thus, at least a part of his story was true. Molcho may have been a visionary. His plans may have involved a mass migration of Jews to Palestine. Without preparation or leadership such a migration would have ended in disaster. Yet, remaining where they were also brought misfortune to the Jews. Not Molcho's ideas, but his actions and his methods made him seem an adventurer.

Their Tragic End—Reubeni and Molcho eventually joined forces and tried to persuade Charles V, emperor of the Holy Roman Empire, that they could help defeat the Turks. Charles and his advisers refused to listen. Moreover, there were Jews who feared that these two men were endangering the slight measure of security which the Jews still enjoyed in Italy and Germany, for they thought Reubeni was lying and they knew that Molcho was sought by the Inquisition. Emperor Charles had them arrested. Molcho was eventually burned at the stake. Reubeni's fate is not known, though in

* See below, pp. 627–8.

all likelihood he suffered the same fate. Thus ended the career of two men who, for a number of years, had raised the hopes of the Jews and the Marranos.

4. MARTIN LUTHER AND THE JEWS

In Defense of the Jews—Europe in the meantime had witnessed the rise of a rebellion within the Roman Catholic Church. Martin Luther, an Augustinian monk and an ordained priest, had started out to preach reform and found an unexpectedly large following among the people and the nobility of Germany. Before long, his movement broke completely with the traditions and organization of Catholicism. One of Luther's charges against the Church and its methods was its harsh treatment of the Jews. He used very strong language to describe the attacks and the persecutions by which priests and monks sought to obtain the conversion of the Jews to Christianity. The proper way, he argued, was the way suggested by the best among the ancient fathers of the Church, the way of kindness and consideration.

What the Jews Thought—To the Jews these words of the leader of the new movement came as a great relief. They were overjoyed that at last a famous Christian teacher spoke of them as human beings. They did not stop to consider Luther's real aim, which was their conversion to Christianity as he understood it; they could grasp only the fact of his speaking and writing against the expulsions and oppressions to which they had been subjected. A few enthusiasts among the Jews of Germany went so far in their misunderstanding of Luther that they actually congratulated him on the steps he was taking to come closer to Judaism. The majority of the Jews looked merely for a lightening of their burdens.

Luther's Disappointment—Luther had thought that he could win the Jews with a few kind words. When this did not happen, he was bitterly disappointed. He now attributed everything to the stubbornness of the Jews and to what he chose to call "the falsehoods" contained in Jewish literature. He outdid the Catholic clergy in the vile terms which he heaped on the Jews and Judaism, and advised their complete extermination. Once more, a movement, hopeful in its beginnings for the Jews, ended in utter disillusionment.

5. THE RETURN OF REACTION

End of the Renaissance—As the sixteenth century moved into its third decade, it became clear that the liberal promises of the revival in art and learning were not to be fulfilled. The energies of the peoples of Europe were spent in wars in Italy, in the suppression of the peasant revolts in Germany and in conflicts between Protestant and Catholic. The emperor, Charles V, was attempting to spread Spanish dominion and influence, and the Catholic Church was trying hard to regain the power it had lost. There was not time for the cultivation of the mind. Under such circumstances, it is not surprising that the position of the Jews did not improve; it even degenerated.

More Expulsions—Of all European lands, Italy had been most favorably disposed toward its Jews. In the various half-independent and independent provinces they had lived comparatively unmolested from the earliest days. During the period of the Renaissance, a good many Jews, expelled from Spain, Portugal and portions of Germany, as well as many Marranos, came to settle in Naples, the Papal State, and the cities of the north. But as the spirit of reaction supplanted liberalism, the situation changed for the worse. About 1540, Charles V, to whom the kingdom of Naples now belonged, ordered the complete expulsion of the Jews. Some years previously, a hostile government in Venice had expelled the Jews from that city, but then permitted them to return. A reactionary pope, zealous to re-establish the Church's reputation for piety, saw no better way to do this than by expelling the Jews from the entire Papal State, that is, the central part of Italy. He made only two exceptions: the cities of Rome and Ancona. The reason for these exceptions, significantly, was that the papal treasury would have suffered too much from their total expulsion. There were expulsions from other parts of Italy also, although, on the whole, the northern part of the Italian Peninsula still remained open to them.

The Refuge in Turkey—There were few places to which the exiles from the various parts of Europe could now turn for refuge. The most important of these was the expanding Turkish empire. One sultan is supposed to have remarked that the expulsion of the Jews from Spain helped him to build and strengthen his empire, and that Ferdinand and Isabella were fools to drive their most industrious citizens out of their lands. Salonika and Constantinople and other portions of Turkey developed large Jewish communities and some Jews gained high posts in the Turkish government.

6. SOME HEROES IN A CHANGING AGE

The Abrabanel Family—The chain of events which overwhelmed the Jews of Spain before and after their exile finds its best illustration in the life and experience of Isaac Abrabanel who claimed descent from the Davidic dynasty. His grandfather, a distinguished man in Castile before 1391, had fled to Portugal in that year of calamity. There he and his son rose high in royal favor. Isaac, too, became an important financier in the employ of the Portuguese government. In 1483 he was accused of participating in a conspiracy of the Portuguese nobles against the king. His property was confiscated and he fled to Castile where he started life all over again. His financial ability was immediately recognized by Ferdinand and Isabella, so that before long he was employed by them. Isaac Abrabanel was not merely a financier. Throughout his life he was a student, especially of philosophy and the Bible. His richly endowed mind and his social station attracted Jews of the upper class around him and he tried to strengthen their loyalty to Judaism. Spurning every inducement to remain in Spain after 1492, he preferred to join his fellow Jews in their bitter exile. He went to Naples and settled down to continue his commentary on the Bible and to write a book on theology. Once more the government called him into service. A few years later he had to move to Venice, where he died in 1508.

Abrabanel's Children—The same combination of learning and public service characterized Abrabanel's children. The Spanish exile had disrupted the family, so that thereafter they remained scattered in Portugal and various sections of Italy, where two became teachers in princely households. Isaac's son, Judah, is particularly interesting. His young son had been kidnapped by the Church in Portugal and brought up as a Christian while his parents searched for refuge in Italy. Judah Abrabanel earned his living as a physician and in time gained fame as a philosopher. His best known work bears the name *Dialogues of Love* and is an explanation of the essential unity of the universe, held together by the power of love. It is a revealing sentiment in one who throughout his life met ple. A number of Jewish writers tried to satisfy this curiosity. Abraham Farissol, who lived in Italy, wrote a book [on] geography, wherein he described the divisions of the [wo]rld and the peoples who inhabited them. Joseph ha-Kohen, [wh]o also lived in Italy, found that men's minds were agitated [no]t only by the discovery of new parts of the world, but also [by] the great conflicts which went on about them between [Ch]ristianity and Mohammedanism. The Turks were extend[in]g their sway over southeastern Europe and no Christian [po]wer seemed able to stop them. Consequently Joseph ha-Ko[he]n described the history of France, representing Christian[ity], on the one hand, and the history of the Ottoman Turks, [on] the other.

Histories of Tragedy—At the same time, the Jews recog[n]ized that the destruction of the great Jewish communities in [S]pain and Portugal marked the end of an important period in [J]ewish life. There was need to analyze why this calamity had [b]efallen the Jewish people and, if possible, to strengthen and [c]onsole them. Only a few years after the Spanish expulsion, [A]braham Zacuto, the famous astronomer who was himself an [e]xile, wrote a book called *Sefer Yuhasin* (The Book of Genealogies) in which he noted the chain of great men who had [c]ontributed to Jewish life and glory. About half a century [l]ater the famous *Shebet Yehudah* (The Rod of Judah) appeared, in which the original author, Judah ibn Verga, and [s]everal successive members of his family, gathered all the accounts of the persecutions which the Jews had suffered during the centuries preceding his own. It was not really a history, but an attempt to indicate that, sometimes through their own fault and at other times through the fault of others, the Jews had undergone many persecutions and had, with the aid of God, survived them. He called attention to pride, social climbing and neglect of Jewish life, but also to the ill will and bigotry which surrounded the Jewish people. A similar work was written by Joseph ha-Kohen, who was mentioned above. He called it *Emek ha-Bachah* (The Vale of Weeping) and made it much more of a history than was the work of Ibn Verga. Still another book of the same kind was the *Tzemach David* (The Shoot of David), written by David Ganz. All these books are not only chronicles of Jewish tragedies, but also monuments to Jewish endurance and hopefulness in the face of hostility.

The Art of Printing—The invention of printing in the second half of the fifteenth century counterbalanced, to some extent, the intellectual and economic losses of the Jews of

with so much hate. Perhaps in this respect, too, Abrabanel mirrored the life and thought of the entire Jewish group.

The Nasi Family—Another family of Spanish-Portuguese exiles reflected, in its equally romantic career, not so much the fortunes of the exiled Jews as those of the freedom-seeking Marranos. The compulsory baptisms in Portugal in 1497 left the Mendez family residing in Lisbon as Christians. They were bankers with wide connections, with branch offices in Holland and debts due them from the kings of France. For years the members of this family looked for an opportunity to escape to a land where they might revert openly to Judaism. Before this could be achieved, the two brothers who were at the head of the banking firm died. The rest, the womenfolk, their children and several nephews, however, found an opportunity to change their residence to Antwerp, which was then also under the rule of the king of Spain. The headship of the firm and of the family now devolved upon the beautiful, clever and gracious Doña Beatrice. Her daughter, Reyna, was sought after in marriage by every high-placed bachelor noble in the Netherlands, and her refusals began to cast suspicions on the Christian loyalty of the entire family. At the same time, João Migues, Doña Beatrice's relative, attracted to himself the favorable attention of the diplomats at court and the consequent envy of ambitious young nobles.

Doña Beatrice sensed danger. Without much warning and preparation, she and her family departed for Venice, where she announced that they planned to stay. Venice, however, was a Christian state, and the arm of the Inquisition could reach them there. Moreover, it was a usual stopping-off place for Marranos on their way to Mohammedan Turkey. This flight to Venice, therefore, confirmed the general suspicion of the family's secret Jewishness. The Venetian government imprisoned Doña Beatrice, on the charge of attempting to leave Christianity, and confiscated what wealth she had with her, while the king of France announced that considerations of piety would prevent him from repaying the debts which he owed to her banking firm.

Joseph the Diplomat—João Migues escaped from Venice and went to Turkey. There he lost no time in persuading the sultan to give aid to Doña Beatrice by pointing out the benefit which Turkey would derive from having the wealth of the Mendez family transferred there. The sultan was then one of the most powerful rulers in Europe, and neighboring Venice especially feared him. When, therefore, the sultan declared that Doña Beatrice was under his protection, Venice had to release her and her property. At last the dream of the family was realized. Once in Turkey, they openly returned to Judaism. Beatrice changed her name to Gracia, perhaps a translation of her Jewish name Hannah; João adopted his Jewish name, Joseph Nasi, and married his cousin Reyna. Gracia spent the rest of her life in works of charity and in encouraging Jewish learning. Reyna followed her example, while Joseph rose high in the favor of the sultan, who eventually created him duke of Naxos and made it possible for him to plan a Jewish settlement in Palestine. In this connection we shall meet him again.

Joseph of Rosheim—There was still another man who lived through this period of hope and disappointment and spent the better part of his life in trying to ward off the troubles which were descending upon the Jewish people. His life's story shows what the Jews of Germany faced during the sixteenth century. Joseph, or Yossel as he was called in his own land, lived in the little town of Rosheim in western Germany. Resourceful and an able diplomat, he early learned how to deal with manifestations of anti-Jewishness in his immediate neighborhood. As his reputation spread, all the Jewish communities of Germany turned to him whenever there was trouble, and the governments looked upon him as the representative of the Jews. He attempted, sometimes successfully, to prevent expulsions; he tried to persuade Martin Luther to discontinue his literary attacks on the Jews and, when Luther refused, to persuade the imperial government to stop the circulation of Luther's anti-Jewish writings.

In 1539 Yossel stood before the gathered princes of the Holy Roman Empire and pleaded against the proposed expulsions of the Jews, especially the threats of such action in Brandenburg (Prussia) and Saxony. Yossel furthermore did not hesitate to enter into a disputation, at this same gathering, with Protestant preachers and scholars on the question whether the Jewish Bible could more easily be interpreted in favor of Catholicism or Protestantism. Yossel favored the Catholic side of the great dispute then raging in Europe. This may have been due to his personal conservatism, or to the fact that Luther and his followers were becoming violently anti-Jewish. In any case, his stand won for his cause the favor of the gathered nobility. The privileges of the Jews in the empire were renewed and, for the time being, the Jews were not expelled from Brandenburg. In Saxony, however, Luther's influence was too strong and the Jews were expelled a few years later. Thus Yossel was the unofficial diplomat

(*shtadlan*) of the German Jews. It was cha... man and his time that he left behind a pra... by a Jew about to be martyred for his religion...

7. BOOKS AND AUTHORS

Conflicting Influences—Books are to a larg... growth of the experiences of their authors. It... fore, that books written during the period of t... and the Reaction showed signs of both the... Jewish experience, however, lay under the s... tragedy of the Spanish and Portuguese expu... search for new homes and the need for new... That is why scientific and historical works in th... Renaissance were outnumbered by chronicles... strengthen faith and hope, and by works wh... unity and new adjustment. The last type belong... period of Jewish history, but the first two deserv... this point.

New Knowledge—The scientific contributions... to the period of the Renaissance continued ev... breadth of view which had existed at the beginnin... teenth century gave way to the narrowness alrea... in its middle years. Amatus Lusitanus, who was b... (1511) of Marrano parents and succeeded in e... Inquisition, became one of the most noted physic... century. David Ganz, who lived in Prague, con... important work on astronomy. Judah Abraban... mentioned, wrote of love as a universal principle i... of philosophy. There were others who worked in... related branches of human knowledge.

One of the foremost fields of study among the... history. The Jews as a group had always been co... history, from the Bible through a fairly large number... er or longer chronicles during the Middle Ages.... teenth century, however, stands out as the one wh... duced the most varied and most interesting histor... Josephus wrote his *Jewish Antiquities* at the end of... century of the Common Era.

World Histories—The voyages of discovery toward... of the fifteenth century had stirred men's minds, so... desire for more knowledge about the world and its... tants was as keen among the Jews as among other int...

Western Europe and enabled them to continue an active cultural life. Printing made books cheap and easily available, so
that wider circles could derive strength and inspiration from
the written word. The Jews, therefore, saw the value of printing almost immediately and spoke of it as "sacred labor."
David Kimhi's commentary, the commentary of Rashi, legal
books, the Talmud, prayer books and ethical works were
printed even before the Spanish expulsion. Italy became the
Jewish printing center. Christian printers, knowing the interest of the Jews in Hebrew books, made a specialty of producing them. They employed learned Jews, like Elias Levitas, to
find the best manuscripts and to arrange them in the best
manner. Incidentally, this was the time when different types
of Hebrew letters were set to different uses. Variations in size
and form of letter were made to indicate what was text and
what was commentary, as well as to separate one commentary from another. Thus the Rashi alphabet gained its name,
not because Rashi invented it, but because the early printers
adopted this particular form of letter for use in his commentary. A glance at a rabbinic Bible will make this clear.

A Critical Historian and What Might Have Been—It seems
safe enough to assume that the Jews of Western Europe
would have contributed greatly to science and learning, both
Jewish and non-Jewish, if the spirit of reaction and intolerance had not thrust them into poverty and distress. An example of what might have been is the work of Azariah dei Rossi
(1513–1578). Brought up in Italy in the midst of the Renaissance spirit, he learned many languages, including Latin and
Greek. He became a physician and scientist. Above all, he
learned to look behind the haze of legend and prejudice surrounding the events of the past and thus discover what actually happened. His book on Jewish history and literature,
Me'or 'Enayyim (Light of the Eyes), could have been written
by an historian of the nineteenth century. But men like Azariah dei Rossi, David Ganz, Amatus Lusitanus and others
needed a free atmosphere to rear a generation of pupils
equally devoted to scientific labor; and this was not to be.
The wave of reaction which overwhelmed Western Europe
during the sixteenth century broke the chain of progress and
prevented it from resuming its normal course until two and a
half centuries later. Only here and there, beneath the surface
of an age whose stream of life seemed to have become frozen
into immobility, did the spirit of scientific inquiry continue to

stir. On the outside, however, hope and courage faced tremendous odds.

8. SUMMARY OF AN EPOCH

An Age of Slow Transition—The middle of the sixteenth century brought to a close another period in the history of the Jewish people. It saw the degradation of the little that was left of the old communities and the uncertain, halting beginnings of new ones. Before entering upon the new period, it may be well to cast a glance backward over the fifteen hundred years of Jewish life on the European continent.

The Jews and the Nations of Europe—We have seen Europe become the home of a substantial number of Jews. They came into Italy even before the beginning of the Common Era. They spread into Gaul and Spain where they established communities long before the ancestors of the modern inhabitants of these lands occupied their territory. They gained numbers by conversion, and lost more by assimilation. There is not a nation in Europe, excepting the Scandinavians, in whose formative period the Jews did not play a part.

The Jews and European Civilization—The Jews contributed substantially to the development of European civilization. In the economic field they were in the vanguard. They moved from farming to trading, and from trading to banking, as these activities answered the needs of the society in which they lived. In the field of science the Jews aided substantially in transferring the knowledge of the East to the peoples of the West. Medicine and mathematics, astronomy and philosophy especially owe much to the Jews of the early Middle Ages.

The Expulsion from Christian Society—Christianity is a development out of Judaism. Much of Christian thought and ceremony is the same as Jewish thought and ceremony. In theory, Christianity and Judaism should have lived together in friendly spirit. But the Church and the Synagogue are human institutions, and they looked upon one another as rivals. The Church was stronger, and, unfortunately, too many churchmen resented the insistence of the Jews upon holding to their religion. They implanted suspicion of the Jews in the minds of the common people. Eventually, the economic rivals of the Jews made use of this suspicion to turn it into fear and dislike and thus rid themselves of competitors. Little by little Jewish life was restricted. The Jews were subjected to attack and degradation. Large numbers were killed. Then, when deprived of opportunity and of no further economic use, they were expelled and made to wander in search of new homelands. All the lands bordering on the Atlantic Ocean expelled the Jews. In Germany and Italy they were compelled to live apart in ghettos.

Inner Life—All these difficulties affected Jewish life. As life in general became easier and more cultivated, Jewish life developed, so that the Jews of Europe took over the intellectual and spiritual leadership when the Jewry of Babylonia fell from its high estate. Teachers arose and books were written whose inspiration has continued to our own day. The history of the Jews during the period just discussed offers proof to all humanity that no force and terror can destroy hope and faith when these are founded on truth.

Exhaustion—Nevertheless, the brutal force and conscienceless terror exercised against the Jews for several centuries in Western Europe decreased their numbers and exhausted their resources. They were no longer capable of providing that spiritual leadership which they had enjoyed. Jewish communities in other lands might have been left without that guidance which Jewish life, like all other cultures, needs in order to survive. But these other Jewish communities quickly learned to assume this task of leadership. We must now turn our attention to the efforts in this direction made by Jews in several newer settlements.

BOOK FOUR

RETREAT AND PROGRESS

THE JEWS OF CENTRAL AND EASTERN EUROPE WITHDRAW
INTO THEMSELVES, WHILE OTHER, SMALLER GROUPS SET-
TLE IN LANDS OF GREATER PROMISE, UNTIL A CHANGE IN
EUROPEAN THOUGHT BRINGS FORTH NEW HOPE FOR THE
ATTAINMENT BY THE JEWS OF THEIR RIGHTS AS MEN

INTRODUCTION

Experiments in Cooperation—Thus far we have taken the
Jewish people through three major experiments in cooperation, not only among themselves, but also between them and
the people about them. The first experiment was carried
through when the Jews lived as an independent, or semi-inde-
pendent, community in Palestine. The second took place in
Babylonia and Persia during the first thousand years of the
Christian era. The third was in Western Europe down to the
period of the Renaissance. The experiments terminated in
each case, not because they were unsuccessful—on the contrary, they redounded to the benefit of civilization in general
—but largely because of external interference, or the deterio-
ration of the environment, or the misunderstanding of cooperation to mean uniformity.

The Rise of East European Jewry—The major interest of

the next three centuries, from the sixteenth to the nineteenth, lies in a fourth attempt at cooperation between the Jews and their environment—the one made in Eastern Europe, especially Poland. Talmudism and pietism flourished and new movements arose testifying to the vitality and spirituality of the Jewish way of life.

New Communities—In the meantime, smaller groups of Jews tried to achieve a personal solution of their problems by settling in newly discovered lands or in territories reopened to them. Communities were established in various parts of America and in Holland, England and France, and prepared the way for the new world which was to emerge after the French Revolution.

Freedom and the Jews—When one speaks of the sufferings of the Jews and the restrictions on Jewish life in the sixteenth and seventeenth centuries, as well as in the preceding ones, one must not forget that the Jews were not the only people who found life difficult and whose future seemed hopeless. The common people of Europe were to some extent in the same situation. Wars were frequent and tyranny was then in full control. The peasants were still little more than serfs, and the workers in the towns enjoyed few privileges. None but the nobility and the rich guildsmen had any rights. The essential difference between the lower classes of the general population and the Jews was that the Jews were a cultured people and therefore more sensitive to their hurts and to the restrictions imposed upon them. They knew that in respect to what was most important for civilization, intellect and idealism, they were at least the equals of those upper classes who led in oppressing them. It was this that made the Jewish situation more tragic than that of the lower classes of general society. But apart from this it is one of the lessons of history that where the Jews suffer, they are not alone; the common people suffer with them. It is bound to be so. For oppression of the Jews is based on unjust social systems which produce greed, intolerance, narrowness and lack of reason. These forces do not and cannot stop with the Jews. We shall see any number of illustrations of this principle in the part of the story which we are about to tell. A nation's treatment of the Jews is an unfailing test of the strength or weakness of the human values within its society.

CHAPTER I

JEWISH ORIGINS IN EASTERN EUROPE

THE JEWS OF EASTERN EUROPE MAKE READY TO ASSUME
LEADERSHIP OF JEWISH LIFE AT THE VERY TIME THOSE OF
WESTERN AND CENTRAL EUROPE ARE BEING EXPELLED

Another Providential Development—We have now reached
the point in our story when another such change took place
as happened when Babylonian Jewish life was built up while
Palestine was growing weak, and as happened again when,
centuries later, Spanish Jewry and the communities along the
Rhine came into the foreground just as leadership was slipping out of the hands of Babylonia. Spanish Jewry had been
dissolved through forced conversions and expulsion; German
Jewry was reduced by sword and terror to a shadow of its
former self. It then became apparent that for a number of
centuries a new community had been in the process of developing in Poland and was about ready to act as the home of
Jewish culture. To this community we must now turn and
trace its rise from insignificance to prominence To do so. we
have to go back to an earlier time and, beginning there, bring
the story down to the sixteenth century.

1. THE SOURCES OF THE COMMUNITY

The Black Sea Region—During the first century before the
Common Era, there were Jewish settlements all along the
coast of Asia Minor and on the Greek mainland.* Before
long, and for several centuries thereafter, there were fairly
large and prosperous Jewish communities in the lands which
we now call the Balkans and, especially, on the Crimean Peninsula. During the eighth century of the Common Era, persecutions by the emperors of the Eastern Roman Empire drove

* See above, pp. 257–8.

more Jews to settle farther along the Danube River and deeper in the Crimea. From there they carried on trade with the inhabitants of the lands to the north of them, the still pagan barbarians known as Slavs.

The Khazars—This was the time when the Khazars entered upon the scene. They have already been mentioned on several occasions,* so that the story of their conversion need not be repeated here, except to emphasize that at first only the royal family and many of their upper class adopted the Jewish faith. In time, Judaism no doubt spread among the Khazar population, but there were Christians and pagans among them to the end, for their government believed in religious tolerance. When the Khazar kingdom was defeated by the Moscovite Russians, many Jews among them joined such others as had already penetrated Russia. Kiev especially profited from this migration, remaining the most prosperous and progressive Russian town down to the thirteenth century. Vague references to Jews, whose native language was Russian and who read their Bible in Russian, are to be found in the responsa of the rabbis in Germany in the twelfth and thirteenth centuries. Whether these were the descendants of the Khazars or of the Crimean Jews it is impossible to say. Probably they were a mixture of both. Nor does it make any difference, except to those who are more interested in fanciful theories of race than in matters of religion and humanity.

The Tatar Invasion—About the middle of the thirteenth century the steppes of Russia were overrun by hordes of Tatars. The territory now called the Ukraine was given over to fire and sword. Much of the population fled westward, into the Carpathian mountains and beyond. Many Jews settled in the territory which, at that time, was being organized into a new state, Poland. Here they were to meet other Jews who were coming into Poland from Western Europe.

From West to East—For centuries the territory north of the Danube and east of the Elbe River had been inhabited by half-barbarian Slavic tribes. The merchant Jews of the early Middle Ages had made their way across these lands, and a few may have settled there. Coins dating from that early period in Polish history bear inscriptions in Hebrew letters and are evidence of the economic importance of the Jews in that country. Polish rulers apparently entrusted the minting of their money to Jews, whose peaceful penetration aided Poland in its first efforts at national organization. Slowly Ger-

* See above, pp. 256–7, 292, 299.

man settlers also seeped into these provinces. Some of the
German nobles, moreover, organized regular marauding expeditions, though they called them crusades against the pagans, to wipe out the Slavs and take their land. That is how
Prussia came into being, ruled by German settlers who absorbed the Slavs or drove them farther east. The need to fight
the German invaders brought about organization among the
Slavs themselves. At that time the crusades against the Moslems in Palestine were bringing misfortune upon the Jews of
the lands in the west and the south. The Jewish population

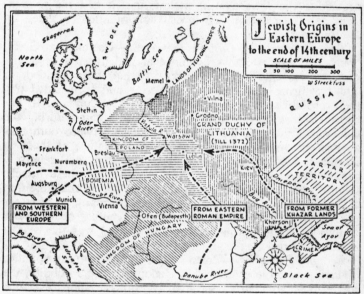

from the shores of the Rhine and the Danube rivers sought
greater safety, and the Jewish migration began from Central
Europe into Bohemia and the principalities into which Poland
was divided. Thus, the two migrations, one from the east and
the other from the west, laid the foundations for what was to
become the Jewry of Eastern Europe. Apparently the one
from the west was numerically the larger, as it certainly was
culturally the more important. For the Western Jews set the
tone for and gave the language to the new community.

2. LAYING THE FOUNDATIONS

An Invitation to Come and Stay—The immigrant Jews

were welcome in the lands of the Slavs. They constituted the active population and the middle class of the towns, and they drew the rude noble class nearer to the civilization of the more western lands. Recognizing the advantages which the Jews brought to his country, Boleslav the Pious, ruler of the province called Great Poland, sought in 1264 to encourage the coming of more Jews. He issued a highly favorable charter of privileges to the Jews already within his domain, in which he regulated the relations of the Jews with the government, with the Christians and with each other. In addition to protecting the Jews against molestation, it laid the foundations for the existence of Jewish communities regulated by Jewish law.

The Protection of Casimir the Great—Casimir the Great, one of the noblest kings Poland ever had, ruler over all the principalities into which the country had been divided, in 1344 reaffirmed the charter of Boleslav and even added further regulations to safeguard the Jewish population. It was fortunate that he did this, for a few years later, during the epidemic known as the Black Death, there were outbreaks against the Jews of Poland of the same nature as those in Germany. Royal protection, provided by this relatively progressive social code, apparently prevented these attacks from becoming too serious. Moreover, it was at this time that a further immigration took place from Germany, even larger than the previous ones. For this was the century of numerous expulsions from German cities, and Poland was the nearest place of refuge.

Economic Activity—Poland was an agricultural country, divided into large estates which belonged to the nobility, the soil being cultivated by serfs. It had not developed as much commerce as existed in Germany in the twelfth and thirteenth centuries. The Christian German immigrants, who quickly organized themselves into guilds, tried to monopolize artisanship. The Jews were thus, from the very beginning, unable to enter agriculture and had to wage a constant struggle for their right to engage in most trades. Very few of them had the chance to acquire wealth, unless it was through tax-farming or commerce. Nevertheless, despite the efforts of their competitors to limit their activities, they were indispensable to the economic life of the country.

Foundations of Jewish Culture—Polish culture in those days had not caught up with the culture of the peoples to the West. The Jews, on the other hand, had come from communities in which learning had been a tradition for a number of centuries. Although the generations of terror which preceded their departure from Germany had given a decided setback to their intellectual activity, those who wandered into Poland during the thirteenth and fourteenth centuries were, nevertheless, on a higher cultural level than the Poles. This situation remained unchanged for several centuries and had an extraordinary influence on the history of the Jewish people.

3. The Jews and Their Polish Neighbors

The Opposition—Two types of people, neither altogether native to Poland, objected to the presence of Jews and Judaism. On the one hand, the German merchants and artisans, who had also been introduced into the land for the purpose of establishing a middle class, saw in the Jews challenging competitors. As a matter of fact, it was partly to protect the Jews against attack by these German settlers that Boleslav issued his charter. On the other hand, the Church found the privileges granted to the Jews distasteful. In reply to the charter, a Church council was held at Breslau in 1267, and there a number of resolutions were adopted. The attempt was made to introduce into Poland, whose population had been Roman Catholic for only about a century, all the restrictions on Jewish life which had developed in Western Europe during the previous thousand years.

Clergy and Townsmen—In the first battle for restricting Jewish rights the clergy and the Christian merchants in the towns had been defeated by the broad-minded policy of Casimir the Great. But these two orders of Polish society continued their bitter and relentless fight to win the government over to their views and to prejudice the lower classes against their Jewish neighbors. To achieve the second part of their program they used the familiar method of arousing the fears of the ignorant. An avalanche of accusations was let loose by the clergy. Jews were "discovered" blaspheming against Christianity, desecrating the Host, and murdering children in order to use their blood for Jewish ritual purposes. The townsmen, for their part, gladly joined in riots which resulted from these charges.

Poland and Its Kings—Much of the fate of the Jews of Poland was tied up with the nature of the Polish government. Early in the fourteenth century the various provinces into which the land was divided were joined under one king. These kings, being strong, were able to withstand the pressure from the enemies of the Jews. Toward the end of the fourteenth century Jagello, grand duke of Lithuania, married the heiress to the Polish throne, became a Catholic and started a new dynasty. Thus Lithuania and Poland were united. In order to establish himself more firmly, Jagello yielded to some extent to the clamor of the clergy against the Jews. His successors were less willing to restrict Jewish activity; they did so only when they were politically weak.

Lithuania and Its Jews—An example of such vacillation is the temporary nature of the misfortune which befell the Lithuanian Jews in 1496. Jews had migrated into Lithuania at the same time as into Poland, though in smaller numbers. The only difference may have been that the Lithuanian Jews consisted of a greater proportion, though by no means a majority, of Jews of Crimean origin. In 1496 the grand duke of Lithuania, brother and heir of the king of Poland, suddenly decided to expel the Jews from his land. In all likelihood he committed this act because the clergy held up before him the similar action, on a grander scale, of the greatest rulers of that day, Ferdinand and Isabella of Spain. Within a few years, however, this same grand duke became king of Poland and Lithuania. Perhaps because he was no longer so dependent upon the clergy, or because from the higher point of vantage he had a broader view of the entire situation, he recognized how helpful the Jews were to Polish economic life. He realized that Lithuania needed them, and he therefore granted the Jews permission to return to their former homes.

Enemies and Politics—Two factors strengthened the forces opposed to the Jews during the sixteenth century. In the first place, the spread of Protestantism from near-by Prussia frightened the clergy. They responded by arguing that Protestants and Jews were one and the same and by intensifying their accusations against Judaism. In the second place, concentration of land in the hands of the wealthier nobles had brought an impoverished noble class into being. These noblemen, having nothing left but their pride, resented the economic security of the Jews. It made them feel better to blame the Jews for their own poverty and incapacity. In the Upper House of the Polish parliament the dissatisfied nobles could exercise a certain amount of political influence. Combined with the clergy and with the envious townsmen, they threatened the foundations of Jewish existence.

4. SPIRITUAL MATURITY

Taking Up the Task—Against this background the Polish Jews took up the task of Jewish living. The centuries from the thirteenth to the sixteenth were the period of adjustment and growth; in the sixteenth century Polish Jewry attained a full-grown life and a character of its own.

The Community—The Jewish community was called the *Kahal*. Its basic organization was the same as in the Jewish communities of the countries already discussed. It had its president, the *Rosh ha-Kahal*, and its trustees, the *gabbaim;* it had its charity funds, its synagogue, its ritual bath, and its combined hospital and home for the aged, or as many of these institutions as the community's size warranted. The Polish government had reasons of its own for seeing that the *Kahal* was strong enough to manage its affairs, for it relied upon the Jews to collect their own taxes. This system was not an unmixed blessing. If, on the one hand, it kept the government from interfering in the affairs of the Jewish community, it led, on the other, to the rule of the *Kahal* by an aristocracy of wealth. For, since the wealthy people paid most of the taxes, it seemed only fair that they should stand at the head of the community. But these taxes were levied upon the Jews of any city in a lump sum, and those who headed the community had the power to decide how much each member of the *Kahal* should pay. The temptation to shift some of the burden of taxation from their own shoulders to those of less wealthy members was too great to resist. As a result, community life was not always peaceful.

The System of Control—It must not be imagined that the Jews lived in a physically closed community, that is, a ghetto such as came into being in Europe outside of Poland. The Jews preferred to live near one another, but generally speaking, they were not compelled to do so. They were united, not by ghetto walls but by their Judaism, by their desire to live in accordance with Jewish tradition. The charters granted them by various Polish kings gave them the right to regulate even their business life by talmudic law. Consequently, they followed their own judicial system and appointed their own judges, *dayyanim,* who were communal officials. The heads of the community enforced the decisions of the judges. In case of necessity, they could call upon the Polish government to help in the enforcement, though they did not like to do this. It was within the *Kahal's* power to impose and execute flogging, imprisonment and, as a last resort, excommunication. They had no right to impose the death sentence, for they had no authority over cases involving such a penalty. In general, cases of lawlessness were remarkably few among the Jews. This was due, not to the strict enforcement of the law, but to the willing submission of the Jews to the traditions and ideals of their religious life.

Jewish Learning—During the sixteenth century there arose in Poland a number of great rabbinic authorities, who laid foundations for the learning which was to characterize Polish Jewry. In the twelfth and thirteenth centuries Russian and Polish Jewish students had gone to Austria and Germany and even to Spain to study. Thereafter, because of the calamities which were falling thick and fast upon the heads of the Western Jews, Polish Jewry had to become increasingly self-reliant. It was aided in this by the large immigration from Germany and by internal conditions. One such condition was the fact, already referred to, that talmudic law was the basis of Jewish individual and communal life. The Talmud was thus alive and functioning, not a purely theoretical study as it is today. Secondly, the Jews retained the respect they had always felt for learning. To be a man of learning raised a man's social standing, and in this respect rich and poor were alike. The three great names connected with the rise of Jewish learning in Poland are: Shalom Shakhna (1500–1558), rabbi of Lublin and later of that entire province; Moses Isserles (1530–1572), head of the *yeshibah* in Cracow and famous rabbinic authority throughout the Jewish world; and Solomon Luria (1510–1573) of Posen, who wrote a very important commentary on a number of talmudic tractates. These three men began to rear the intellectual structure of Polish Jewry.

The Academies—By the sixteenth century few talmudical academies could be found in Germany, where two or three centuries previously there had been hardly an important town without one. Now it was the Slavic lands, especially Poland, that could boast of the most famous ones. Study was carried on with complete self-sacrifice. The *yeshibot* were not schools to train rabbis; most of the students never sought any such professional career. The ordinary young man, whether the son of poor or of wealthy parents, attended them because it was expected of him. Naturally the sons of poor parents could not stay as long as they might desire. But if they showed the slightest inclination toward study, there was no reason for them to discontinue, since every community which harbored a *yeshibah* was so proud of it and of the sacred privilege of fostering religious study, that it gladly maintained whatever students needed support. In this way, a most extraordinary situation developed wherein almost the entire population was raised to a high intellectual level. Neither medieval Germany nor Mohammedan Spain had witnessed the like.

Pilpulism: A Method of Study—This hunger for knowledge on the part of the Polish Jews might have overflowed the bounds of talmudic study and branched out into other fields, as Jewish culture once had done in Mohammedan Spain. Unfortunately, the culture of the general Polish community was then of a rather low order. Nor did the culture of the German Jews, their closest neighbors, have anything to offer. Jewish culture was an intellectual oasis in a cultural desert.

The study of the Talmud became not only a search for knowledge, but also a means of satisfying the people's intellectual hunger. That is why *pilpul*,* used already to some extent in the Babylonian *yeshibot*, became the popular method of studying the Talmud in Poland. It was a method based on the assumption that the ancient sages, whether those mentioned in the Talmud or those who had written commentaries on it, could not be wrong. If they disagreed, it was only a seeming disagreement. The aim of the student was to find a means of arguing this disagreement away. The basic assumption was doubtful, and most of those who made use of *pilpul* knew that it was a questionable assumption. Actually the object was not so much to argue away the disagreements as to sharpen the mind of the student so that he might see deeper into the difficult arguments of the actual talmudic text. *Pilpul* enabled a man to display his knowledge and keenness of mind. As a matter of fact, many of the notable rabbis of Poland, including Solomon Luria, objected to extreme *pilpulism*, and the abler heads of the academies knew how to keep it within bounds. Nevertheless, it became the characteristic method of study in Polish *yeshibot*. The mental alertness of the Polish Jew, as well as his tendency toward argumentativeness, has sometimes been attributed to it.

The Lower Schools—Before a young man could enter upon his studies at a *yeshibah*, he had to possess a considerable amount of knowledge. For *yeshibot* of any period of Jew-

---

* The word *pilpul* means "pepper," therefore "sharpness," and therefore "sharpness of mind."

ish history did not teach the reading of the Talmud text, but rather its understanding along with the numerous commentaries which had developed around it. The ability to read the text intelligently had to be acquired in the lower schools (*heder—hadarim*). Every village with a number of Jewish inhabitants made certain to engage a teacher for the children. The schools were one communal activity which was never neglected. Parents felt obligated to pay for the education of their children; but if they could not do so, the community provided a free school. Besides, all schools were under communal supervision and all teachers, whether paid by their pupils' parents or by the community, had to be acceptable in character and attainments to the local rabbi and to the *gabbaim* in charge of schools. Under such circumstances, illiteracy was rare among Poland's Jewish male population.

Method and Content—Parents considered nothing in the life of their child more important than the acquisition of a Jewish education. Beautiful ceremonies developed around the occasions when the boy began to study the alphabet and again when he began the Pentateuch. He was wrapped in a prayer-shawl (*tallit*), given sweet cookies and in general made to feel that something of the utmost significance was happening in his life. And this was true. For the child was setting out on an intellectual and spiritual search for what the world he was to live in considered of the highest value. The aims of the education which a boy was given are illustrated by the fact that, as soon as he was able to read, he was taught the biblical book Leviticus, a dull and difficult book, full of descriptions of sacrifices which used to be offered in ancient days in the Temple. For Leviticus prepared the child for the study of Jewish Law. The other books of the Pentateuch, consisting mainly of stories, were considered too easy for the mind of a Jewish boy. Altogether, the methods used in these schools were not such as we would use now, but the aims were loftier and the demands greater, so that, in the end, the system was effective. Long hours of study, frequent reviews and examinations and, above all, the encouragement received at home and everywhere else in the child's environment made the *heder* as successful an institution as any school ever was.

Printing and Jewish Culture—Beginning with the sixteenth century, the Jews of Eastern Europe had an additional advantage over previous centers of Jewish life. In earlier periods only the rich person could afford a copy of the Talmud or of the other rabbinic works: books copied by hand were expensive. The Jews had tried to overcome this difficulty by making the lending of books a high virtue and a religious obligation. The situation, nevertheless, had set bounds to the spread of knowledge. The art of printing now placed books within the reach of almost everyone. Ordinary people could possess a library. Synagogues and houses of study (*Batte Midrash*) set up public libraries, open to use by anyone. Above all, the numerous Jewish families scattered among the tiny settlements of Poland and the Ukraine, far from the cultural stimulations of a city, now took books along with them and had the fountains of Jewish knowledge on a shelf at home.

A United People—Thus the Polish Jews of the sixteenth and seventeenth centuries presented an unusual aspect. A group, whose economic opportunities were limited, learned to disregard economics and emphasize intellect. Surrounded by enemies of their religion, they developed their religious life and clung to it more tenaciously than had Jews of other lands under better conditions. Living under the uncertain protection of nobles who were interested only in the income they could derive from them, they learned to cooperate among themselves and establish a stimulating communal life. In the midst of a population almost completely lacking in culture, they engaged in an amazing literary and cultural activity. The most ignorant of them could recite portions of the Bible by heart, and an astonishingly high percentage was at home in the difficult field of talmudic legislation. Only the Babylonian Jewish community at the height of the Amoraic Age produced anything resembling Polish Jewry around the year 1600.

5. A LANGUAGE FOR THE MASSES

Yiddish as a Language—The language spoken by the Polish Jews, the Yiddish language, has also had a strange history. It developed like other languages, as a result of social and political conditions. Like any other language, it has been a source of unity among the people who spoke it and, sometimes, of misunderstanding with the neighbors who did not speak it. Again, like many other languages—indeed, more than a good many—it has developed an excellent literature. Yet, more than other languages, it was long despised by the very people who spoke it, and certainly by those ignorant of it.

How Yiddish Came to Be—Jews always spoke the language of the land which was their home. Maimonides spoke and wrote most of his works in Arabic; Rashi spoke French; the rabbis of the Middle Ages in the provinces of Germany spoke German. All these people were, at the same time, also thoroughly familiar with Hebrew and Aramaic, the languages of the Bible, of the prayer book and of many other writings sacred to them and constantly in use by them. While they spoke a pure Arabic or French or German with their non-Jewish neighbors, it was natural that, in their conversation among themselves, they should occasionally mix an expressive Hebrew word or phrase. In discussions centering in religious life this was necessary; for how else was one to refer to a religious ceremony or symbol? But it was carried over also into secular discussions, where it might have been considered clever or a sign of superior education. Just so, a person nowadays will display his knowledge of Latin or French by inserting a phrase from these languages into his conversation or writing. When expulsions and persecutions eventually brought about a wider separation between the Jews and the non-Jews, the result was a growing dissimilarity between the intimate languages spoken by each group. Then came the migration of the German Jews eastward. In Bohemia, Poland and Lithuania the Jews were completely separated from German-speaking people. They were no longer aware of the changes which were taking place in the language within Germany. They were thrown back more and more upon the Hebrew. Also Slavic words became mixed with the language in daily use among them. By the sixteenth century, as a result of all these movements and changes, the Jews of Eastern Europe spoke a Yiddish whose Germanic content varied from province to province almost in direct ratio to its proximity to Germany. The comparatively few Jews who were still in Germany spoke Judaeo-German, a language which, while not exactly the same as that spoken by the Polish Jews, was nevertheless not quite the German which was being spoken by the non-Jews.

Early Yiddish Literature—The fact that the Jews have ever been people who like to read has also had an effect on the development of Yiddish. The males, all through Jewish history, received some instruction from early childhood. Most of them could read the sacred literature or the writings of the rabbis in Hebrew or Aramaic. The women, however, were taught only enough to enable them to read the prayer books. Their life was, therefore, comparatively empty of intellectual interests, although they lived in an atmosphere in which culture based on books was prized beyond anything else. The men could find in their studies spiritual instruction as well as entertainment. The women were compelled to seek these elsewhere. It became apparent that, for lack of any other source, the women might turn to the romantic stories of knightly deeds and affairs of love which were so common among the Christians. This was considered dangerous for the high moral standards of Jewish home life. Consequently, a literature for women began to develop, probably as early as the fourteenth century. It consisted mainly of poetic translations of Bible books. These were not really translations of the text, but rather a mixture of the Bible stories and elaborations provided by the Midrash. In their deeds and their love affairs, the heroes of the Bible were made to rival and excel the heroes common in the non-Jewish romances. Piety, Jewish loyalty and religious fervor were their most prominent themes. All of these books were written in Judaeo-German or in Yiddish. Such literary products, if they originated in Germany and were later republished in the countries farther east, underwent a linguistic transformation in the process.

The Bible for Women—For the longest time one book, the *Tze'enah u-Re'enah* (Come Forth and Behold), proved to be most popular with the women of Eastern Europe. It was not the first book of its nature to be written. Several attempts to paraphrase the Pentateuch had preceded the efforts of a certain Jacob Janow, of Cracow or Lublin, around 1600. In the course of time, however, his book assumed a sacredness which the others, more thrilling and more poetic, did not have. The *Tze'enah u-Re'enah* is really an ethical and midrashic commentary on the Five Books of Moses. Divided into the same sections as were read in the synagogue every Saturday, it enabled the women to keep step with at least part of the intellectual activity of the men. Generation after generation of Jewish women was brought up on this mental food.

Struggles of a Language—The peculiar situation of the Jews in Poland—the compactness of their settlements and their consciousness of cultural superiority—kept them from adopting the language of the land and made the Judaeo-German or Yiddish speech a permanent feature of their life. But, although they used it for everything, including their studies, they never looked upon it as deserving of attention. Differing in vocabulary, and especially in pronunciation, from province to province, even from town to town, it did not develop fixed forms, let alone a grammar. As to using it for writing, the more scholarly the man, the more he disdained to use Yiddish even in a letter, except perhaps to his wife. Hebrew was still the accepted language even for business documents. Hebrew was and remained "the holy tongue." Not till the middle of the ninteenth century, hardly one hundred years ago, did Yiddish gain the recognition it deserved.

CHAPTER II

EXPERIMENTS IN PALESTINE

SPANISH EXILES IN AND OUT OF PALESTINE MAKE AN EFFORT TO MEET THE NEEDS OF JEWISH LIFE IN THE SIXTEENTH CENTURY

New Communities and New Hopes—The communities and organizations, the scholars and academies of the Jews in Poland in the sixteenth century were as yet hardly known among most of the Jews in the rest of Europe or wherever they were scattered. These Jews were overwhelmed with problems of their own. The recent tragedy of the Spanish and Portuguese expulsions, the heartbreaking search of these exiles for new homes and the threatening storms which resulted from the wars between Catholics and Protestants obscured from their view the rising new center in Eastern Europe.

Of all the communities which the Spanish-Portuguese exiles established, the small community in Palestine proved to be the most interesting. These men were stirred by the memories and the hopes which the Holy Land aroused. They saw themselves as the redeemers of Israel and the instruments by which the ancient Homeland could reclaim its place of supremacy among the Jews. They failed; but even in their failure some of the spiritual activities which they initiated had important results for later generations.

1. NEW HOMES FOR OLD

The Turkish Refuge—In Southeastern Europe Jewish refugees could be completely beyond Christian control. In the last-named place a new empire had just been established. For, after the fall of Constantinople in 1453, the Turks extended their sway over the land of ancient Greece (Byzantium) and across all the countries which we now call the Balkans, even into Hungary. This expanding empire, not completely tolerant of non-Mohammedans, was more tolerant than Christian states of that day were of non-Christians. They welcomed the Jews in their hour of supreme need.

The New Communities—The first to arrive in Constantinople and Salonika and other cities of the Turkish state were Jews from Germany. Jews from Spain, from Portugal, from Sicily and Naples came a generation or so later, as each of these countries expelled them. Then, during the sixteenth century, began the steady flow of Marranos, as one by one, or family by family, they succeeded in escaping from the watchful eye of the Inquisition. These people, coming from different lands, speaking different languages, accustomed to following somewhat different traditions, formed themselves into a number of different groups, the Jews of Salonika alone having thirteen congregations. Until time and their common environment brought the descendants of these immigrants closer together, they presented a disheartening spectacle of internal dissension, quarrelsomeness and the shirking of obligations. All this did not prevent them, however, from making progress either materially or Jewishly.

Adjustment and Prosperity—The Turkish empire was not the loser by its tolerance. The Jews did their best to restore the commerce of the land to what it had been before Venice defeated the decaying empire of Byzantium three centuries before. They built up the handicrafts of Turkey and manufactured leather, cloth and garments. They also taught the Turks the secret of the manufacture of gunpowder and cannon. Jewish merchants penetrated into the vast Balkan agricultural lands, where they bought hides and wool and grain. The ports of the country, especially Salonika, teemed with activity.

Cultural Contributions—The cultural life of the new communities began at once upon their establishment. The immigrants tried hard to resume in their new homes the activities in which they had participated in the old. Especially those who hailed from Spain, but also any number of German Jews, were men of high intellectual standing. The famous physician, Amatus Lusitanus (1511–1568), illustrates the fate of the Jews and the part they continued to play in the diffusion of human knowledge. He was a Marrano and his early years were spent in his native Portugal. There and in the still famous University of Salamanca in Spain, he acquired great medical skill and knowledge. But the Inquisition had already begun to suspect him. He therefore went to the slightly freer atmosphere of Belgium, and from there to Italy. The highest nobility and clergy, as well as the pope, were his patients. He taught medicine at universities. Still he could not shake off the suspicious Inquisition. Again he was forced to wander, and he seized the first opportunity to escape to Salonika, where he practiced Judaism openly. Here he continued to publish his important works which were contributions to various departments of medical science.

Jewish Culture—It was in furtherance of Jewish culture that these communities made the contribution of greatest interest to us. A number of very important talmudic scholars settled in Constantinople and Salonika, the two foremost Turkish communities. Jacob ibn Habib, for example, compiled there the famous and long-popular work known as *'Ain Ya'acob* (Well of Jacob), which does for the Agada of the Talmud, that is, its narrative and ethical portions, what Alfasi had done about five centuries previously for the Halacha, or its legal portions. Active Jewish printing presses were established there and provided books for the entire Jewish world. For a while it looked as though the Turkish empire, and not Poland, would foster the leading Jewish community in the world. Turkish Jewry was, during the sixteenth century, broader, if not deeper, in its outlook and cultural interests. Its failure to retain an influential position in Jewish life was due, not only to the growing preference of the Turkish Jews for mysticism, but also to the incredibly rapid loss of energy and common sense among the rulers of Turkey. Moreover, the Turks, unlike the Mohammedan Arabs seven hundred years previously, did not succeed in developing a cultural life which might have served as a stimulus to the Jewish inhabitants.

Jewish Statesmen—The Jews who immigrated into the new Turkish empire provided it with a succession of statesmen. Two men, Joseph and Moses Hamon, father and son, were physicians to the early sultans; and they used their influence in matters of foreign policy as well as for the protection of the Jews. Solomon Ashkenazi, a skilled Jewish physician of German origin, rose equally high in Turkish diplomacy. He once used his position in the Turkish court to save the Jews of the neighboring republic of Venice from expulsion by the Christians. Esther Kiera was still another interesting personality of that period. Her charm gained for her the favor of the sultana, and her philanthropies and interest in the furtherance of Jewish culture won the admiration and gratitude of the Jews. Greater than the influence of any of them was that of Joseph Nasi, the nephew of Doña Gracia Mendez whose story has already been told. He exerted great influence on the foreign affairs of the Turkish empire at its height. Defeating the intrigues carried on against him by the representatives of France and Venice, he rose high in the favor of the sultan and was created duke of Naxos, an island in the Aegean Sea which was given to him as a fieff. For a while, he was among the most powerful statesmen in Europe. From the Jewish point of view, however, his most interesting activity was his attempt to redeem Palestine.

2. A Plan of Redemption

A Land Without a People—Ever since the crusades Palestine had remained a land all but deserted. Its non-Jewish population was small and lacking in energy. Too many wars had passed over their heads and the country had changed hands too often for the natives to be anything but discouraged and dispirited. A prey to greedy petty nobles, without incentive to progress, they lived on the border of a Bedouin existence. The number of Palestinian Jews was insignificant and their condition miserable. Toward the end of the fifteenth century a famous Italian Jewish scholar, Obadiah of Bertinoro, went to settle there, and his letters indicate his grieved astonishment that Jewish life in the land of their ancestors should have become so weak. He described his approach to Jerusalem in the following terms: "Its (Jerusalem's) inhabitants, I am told, number about 4,000 families. As for Jews, about seventy families of the poorest class have remained; there is scarcely a family that is not in want of the commonest necessities; one who has bread for a year is called rich."

A Land for Pilgrims—Palestine still held an important place in the minds of the people; for Christians as well as Jews it had ceased to be just another country and had become "the Holy Land." The Christians especially built churches and shrines, monasteries and nunneries in various parts of the country. It was an act of piety to undertake the long journey to the Holy Land to pray at the spots sanctified in the biblical stories, both Jewish and Christian, and thereby atone for sins committed. Both Judaism and Christianity looked forward to a time when the Land would once more

404 RETREAT AND PROGRESS

form the center of God's Kingdom. But that was to be only after the miraculous appearance of the Messiah. In the meantime, Palestine's condition added to its picturesqueness. Many people already felt that for Palestine to become active and populous would disturb the legends that had grown up about it. They had convinced themselves that the Holy Land was meant to sleep until God, in His own good time, would awaken it.

Symbol and Hope—This was true of the Jews as much as of the Christians, except that among the Jews the symbolism and the hope were deeper and more personal. The actual state of Palestine somehow had come to stand for the miserable state of the Jewish people. Both were desolate; both were in hostile hands; both awaited God's redemption. Fervent prayers were uttered daily for Palestine's restoration, but few, if any, Jews thought of practical plans to achieve it. They no doubt sensed that neither Christians nor Mohammedans would allow them to settle in the Holy Land in any appreciable numbers. At any rate, they never made the effort. They went there on pilgrimages, or to die and be buried in the sacred soil, but never with the hope of reviving the country.

The Dream of Another Joseph—Joseph Nasi, duke of Naxos, was the first man in centuries to produce a practical plan. He realized that many Jews were still in urgent need of a secure home and he knew from personal experience how many Marranos were willing to make the greatest sacrifices for a place of refuge. Palestine was now under the rule of a friendly sultan. It was fairly easy for Joseph Nasi to obtain complete rights over the Tiberias section of the country; the more difficult task was to find a practical way for settling there a large enough number of Jews. He used his great wealth and powerful influence to solve this problem too. Knowing the difficulty that Europeans had in obtaining silk, he arranged to introduce into Tiberias the cultivation of the silk worm, so that the manufacture of silk might be the means for the incoming Jews to earn a livelihood. He also arranged for a number of ships to convey refugees from various parts of Italy. It looked like a good, workable arrangement.

Failure—The plan was never tried. War broke out between Turkey and Venice, so that Joseph's ships could not sail for their Italian ports. Moreover, this war and other difficulties within the Turkish empire caused a cooling in friendship between the new sultan and Joseph. He fell from favor. The

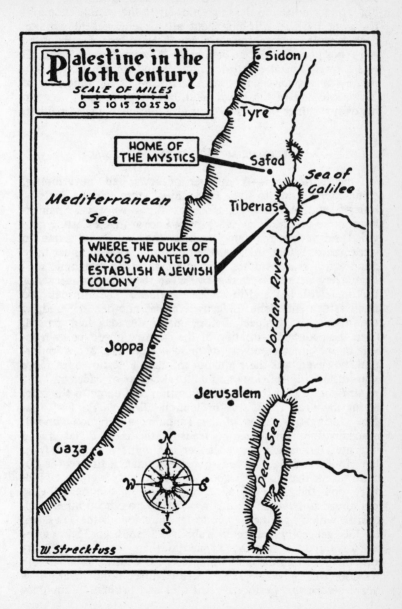

Palestine in the 16th Century

SCALE OF MILES
0 5 10 15 20 25 30

Sidon

Tyre

HOME OF THE MYSTICS

Safad

Sea of Galilee

Mediterranean Sea

Tiberias

WHERE THE DUKE OF NAXOS WANTED TO ESTABLISH A JEWISH COLONY

Jordan River

Joppa

Jerusalem

Dead Sea

Gaza

W. Streckfuss

Arabs around Tiberias proved troublesome. Instead of retiring from politics and devoting himself to the grand scheme of restoring Palestine, Joseph bent all his energies to winning back his place at the sultan's court. His plans for Palestine were postponed until he would be powerful once again. It was a tragic mistake both for himself and for the Jewish people. He might have gone down in history as the redeemer of his people and of the Holy Land, but he preferred to recoup his own fortunes first. The result was that he achieved neither.

3. PALESTINE AND CULTURAL SUPREMACY

New Settlements—A number of Jews had, nevertheless, come to Palestine to live. They hailed from various parts of Europe and Africa, but most of them were of Spanish-Portuguese origin. Since it was well known that Palestine provided few economic opportunities, the Jews who came to settle there, rather than in other parts of Turkey, must have done so for reasons other than interest in their economic welfare. They were interested above all in the religious aspects of life, in Jewish law and in Jewish mysticism. They formed two main settlements: one in Jerusalem and another in Safed, in the district of Galilee. Before many decades had passed, even the economic situation of the country improved as a result of the greater activity of these newcomers. More important, however, was their attempt to make Palestine once more the outstanding religious and cultural center of Judaism.

Ordination and Unity—The question that came to the fore, about the year 1540, was ordination (*Semichah*). Long before, during the period of the Tannaim, a ceremony known as ordination had served to transmit the right to teach and interpret Jewish law from teacher to pupil.* Separation from the Holy Land had caused religious guidance to become decentralized; decisions of rabbis in one locality were not binding upon the Jews of another. If Jewish life nevertheless continued to have unity, this was due to no official human authority which had the power to legislate for all the Jews, but to the generally respected rabbinic literature. Maimonides had deplored the fact that in his day there was no longer any system of ordination and, therefore, no central authority. In his code, the *Mishneh Torah*, written three hundred and fifty years before this period, he had said that ordination could be

* See above, pp. 189, 194–5.

revived in Palestine if a sufficiently large number of scholars unanimously ordained one of themselves as head, and if he in turn then ordained them. Thus the ancient Sanhedrin would be re-established and Jewish unity restored.

Attempts and Ambitions—It was natural for the scholars in the new Palestinian communities to turn their attention to this problem. Not for many centuries past had so many men learned in Jewish law lived in the Holy Land at the same time; nor since the days of Johanan ben Zakkai had there been a time when, with the centers of Jewish life destroyed, Jewish unity seemed so threatened. The new settlers in Palestine were not acquainted with and had no respect for the new center of Judaism in Poland. Jacob Berab, the highly honored head of the Jewish community at Safed, thereupon gathered about himself some thirty recognized Jewish scholars and had them ordain him. He then ordained several of them. Their next step was to write to the head of the Jerusalem scholars, Levi, son of that Jacob ibn Habib who was the author of the *'Ain Ya'acob*, to inform him of their action. Levi ibn Habib, however, resented the act of the scholars of Safed. He considered himself superior to Jacob Berab and his colleagues, if for no other reason than that Jerusalem was superior in Jewish tradition to Safed. He claimed that he should have been the first to be ordained. A bitter quarrel followed, with accusations and counteraccusations. Instead of unity in the Jewish world, there was greater disunity in Palestine itself. The entire plan had to be abandoned.

The Shulhan 'Aruch—Nevertheless, the Palestinian Jewish community did make an important contribution to Jewish unity. It was not in the form of organization, but in the more characteristic Jewish method of unity through literature. Joseph Karo (Toledo, 1488–Safed, 1575) was among the scholars of Safed, one of those ordained by Berab. He spent many years writing a commentary on the *Arba'ah Turim* (Four Rows) of Jacob ben Asher, which for two centuries had been the most useful code of Jewish law. Having completed that, he turned his attention to preparing a popular code, one meant for the ordinary person rather than the scholar. Man, especially the Jew, so Karo believed, was created for the service of God. What the Jew needed, therefore, was an outline of his duties for every moment of the day, or, to use Karo's own metaphor, a "Prepared Table" upon which all the *mitzvot* appear in set order, like a feast upon which the human soul can thrive. That is why Karo called his book the *Shulhan 'Aruch*. It became popular immediately, for it consists of simple, straightforward statements, without arguments or other complicating additions. Since Karo was of Spanish origin, he followed the customs of the Sephardi Jews, which differed somewhat from those of the German, or Ashkenazi, customs. This drawback to the use of the code by all Jews was overcome when the famous Polish rabbi, Moses Isserles (1530–1572), pointed out in detail wherein Ashkenazi tradition differed from the regulations set forth by Karo. Isserles thereby suited Karo's work to the needs of his own people. Adherence to this code thereafter became the test of orthodoxy.

4. THE NEW MYSTICISM

Cabala in the Renaissance World—Mysticism was the other development in the Jewish life of that period in which Palestine took a leading part and which, carried to an extreme, became the source of much good and not a little evil. The *Zohar*, that famous work of the thirteenth century in Spain,* had by the sixteenth century become the source book of the mystic. The book was filled with veiled, puzzling, ambiguous statements, as well as with occasional profound reflections on the universe, and many deeply religious ideas. The *Zohar* therefore attracted all who sought an answer to the problems of God and man, who searched for the causes of things that were and for the shape of things to come. Even Christian scholars believed in the great antiquity of the *Zohar* and in the possibility of using it to solve many mysteries, if only it were rightly understood. The term "Cabala"—by which is meant all of Jewish mysticism, including the teachings of the *Zohar*—became popular. It entered the vocabulary of the educated man, of the pseudo-scientist and of the Christian magician. One need not wonder, therefore, that the *Zohar*, and Cabala in general, came to hold an important place among certain Jews, who steeped their thought in mysticism.

Theoretical Cabala—The Jews considered the Cabala one section of their traditional, theoretical teaching—hopeful, revealing, inspiring, but not calling for action other than deeper piety. Yet one result of the situation in which the Jews found themselves in the sixteenth century was a change in attitude toward Cabala. This change was the more remarkable because it occurred among the Spanish Jews. Until the thir-

---

* See above, pp. 335–6.

teenth century they had differed from the German and French Jews in that the latter were more interested in Cabala, while the Spaniards were more rationalistic and philosophical. When, however, misfortunes began to overwhelm the Jews of Spain, as life became more troubled, as the future grew more dark, cabalistic teachings gained in popularity among them. The expulsion of 1492 completed the victory of mysticism. Thereafter the Jews of Spanish origin became the leaders in the study of Cabala. They sought in it the reason for the suffering they had to endure as well as an indication of the time and the conditions for their redemption.

Safed and Its Cabalists—As might have been expected, the thought of redemption was more prominent in the minds of the new settlers in Palestine than among the other Jews. Jewish tradition taught that the Messiah would appear in Palestine. In cabalistic belief Palestine was nearest the gateway by which human prayers ascend to heaven. Mystically speaking, therefore, the Jews of Palestine had the opportunity and the responsibility of persuading the Almighty to speed the end of evil and hurry the coming of His Kingdom. For some reason the Jews of Safed, not those of Jerusalem, took the lead in this movement. It may have been due to the accidental gathering there of mystically-minded students, or to the location of Safed in especially impressive surroundings, in the midst of awe-inspiring hills and their reverberating echoes. The fact is that the study of the Cabala became entrenched in that place and was pursued with extraordinary zeal. Before long, the object became not merely the theoretical understanding of God's mysteries, but the practical use of this mystical knowledge in order to redeem the world.

Practical Cabala—These people were not superstitious. Superstition, fundamentally, is based on fear that some supernatural power may do harm to one's person. The superstitious man does not try to improve himself, but to protect himself. The cabalists of Safed and their successors were moved not by fear, but by hope; they were interested not in themselves, but in the Jewish people and, through this people, in the world; they believed that no magical formula or prayer could achieve the slightest good unless the person who uttered it was free from sin. Their methods depended upon study, prayer, fasting and the strict observance of every detail of Jewish law and ethics. They viewed life as a struggle to fulfill God's hopes for mankind. The forces of evil, Satan and his hordes, were busy persuading people to act contrary to God's commands, so that God might remain unwilling to send the

Redeemer. The cabalists' task, therefore, was to defeat the forces of evil and to gain the assistance of the forces of good: the angels, the patriarchs and the other saintly souls near to God's throne. The Jewish people, in the opinion of the cabalists, was the very center of the battle which Satan was waging for the control of the world, for to this people was given the Torah, God's clearest message for human guidance. Every effort was bent to defeat Evil by calling upon the angels for assistance, and to support Good by calling upon Israel to obey God's Law. Once this was achieved, the Messiah would appear. The saintliness of the cabalists of Safed became famous throughout the world, wherever Jews lived.

Cabala and Poetry—With its emphasis upon the human spirit, with its constant appeal to the imagination, with its personification of the forces of nature as well as of good and evil, mysticism is very close to poetry. Indeed, poetry sometimes becomes the garment of mysticism. An example of this was the cabalists' attitude toward the Sabbath. Ancient mystics had personified the holy day of rest and looked upon it as the Bride which God sent to Israel. Late every Friday afternoon, the men of Safed, dressed in white, would leave the city in a body and march eastward across the fields to meet the approaching night which ushered in the Sabbath. As dusk fell on the countryside, they stopped and, still singing hymns and psalms, returned to the synagogue and recited the evening service. For this occasion of going out to meet the Sabbath Bride, Solomon Alkabetz, a cabalistic poet of that period, wrote the beautiful hymn *L'chah Dodi*, with its refrain, "Go forth, my beloved, to meet the Bride; let us welcome the Sabbath." A curious indication of the influence exerted by the cabalists of Safed is the custom, still observed in orthodox synagogues, of turning to the door when reciting the last verse of *L'chah Dodi*. It is a symbol of the walk to meet the Sabbath Bride.

Cabala Carried to Extremes—The society of Safed mystics inevitably moved farther and farther away from the real world to live in the world of imagination. The leader in the extremist movement was Isaac Luria (1534–1572), a man of German ancestry. He settled in Safed, attracted to it by his interest in Cabala. His name was abbreviated to ARI by using the initials of the words *ha-Ashkenazi Rabbi Isaac* (the German Rabbi Isaac). The word *Ari*, which means "lion," seemed to his new disciples to fit the man who was so thorough a cabalist. Isaac Luria took seriously the doctrine of the transmigration of souls, the belief that a soul may be born again and again, sometimes in a human and sometimes in an animal body. Also, he looked upon himself as the Messiah son of Joseph, who, according to Jewish legend would precede the real Messiah, the son of David. Through Luria and his most prominent disciple, Hayyim Vital, the teachings of practical Cabala became diffused throughout the Jewish communities of Europe.

The Land of Dreams—Palestine thus made, during the sixteenth century, a number of attempts to become once more the center of Jewish life. All it succeeded in achieving, however, was to strengthen its place as the land of miracles, the land of hopes, to which the dreams of future peace and glory were directed. The Messiah, it was firmly believed, would some day appear there. In the meantime, its small Jewish population drew to itself the charitable offerings of the rest of the world.

CHAPTER III

PRISON OR REFUGE

A WALL IS BUILT AROUND THE JEWS OF ITALY AND GERMANY WITHIN WHICH THEY SUFFER MANY HARDSHIPS AND HAVE FEW JOYS

Social Outcasts—While East European Jewry was assuming the religious leadership of Jewish life and the Jews of Palestine traveled the path of mysticism, the Jews still left in Germany and Italy were subjected to new regulations which had profound effects on later Jewish life. Many Jews were compelled to live in ghettos. The Jews will never forget the period of the ghetto, not because they want to remember the evils they were made to suffer, but because it provides another illustration of the strength in adversity of the Jewish soul and the life-sustaining power of Judaism.

That period, however, seared the spirit of many an individual Jew. For, as generation after generation spent its life under degrading circumstances such as the ghetto system imposed upon them, the Jews began to show the effects of being harassed and constantly threatened. There were actually not many sharply defined ghettos, with walls and gates and guards, but everywhere contempt and disabilities were heaped upon the Jews and the boundaries of their lives were narrowed. Timidity, self-consciousness, suspicion of their neighbors became characteristic of the ghetto Jew. The term "ghetto" came to represent a mental attitude. This attitude spread to the Jews of other lands as ghetto conditions, though no actual ghettos, spread beyond Italy and Germany into other parts of Europe.

1. Origin of the Ghetto

The Term Ghetto—The Jews of former days explained the meaning of the word "ghetto" with bitter humor by tracing its origin to the Hebrew word for divorce, *get*. It looked as though the peoples with whom the Jews had cooperated in the building of the world they lived in had decided to divorce them and send them forth from their common household. Actually, the most likely explanation for the word "ghetto," as applied to a special place assigned to the Jews, is that the one such district, set up in the city of Venice around 1516, was located near an iron-foundry which was called *geto* in the Venetian dialect. Jews have always preferred to live near one another, as do all people who have something important in common. What made a ghetto, where it was established, different from other Jewish streets or districts where no ghetto existed was the fact that it was compulsory. Jews could live nowhere else, while Christians could live anywhere but there. The ghetto was fixed by law as the exclusively legal district for Jewish residence.

Why the Ghetto Was Established—For a thousand years the Church had been urging Christians to have as little as possible to do with Jews. Until the sixteenth century it had been only partly successful. There were several reasons why the ghetto came into being just at that time. 1) The expulsion from Spain and Portugal, considered the most advanced European states of that day, spread the idea that Jews ought not to be permitted to live in Christian society. Spain's example bore fruit in a land as distant as Lithuania. 2) The middle of the sixteenth century witnessed a revival of bigotry. Protestantism came into existence, and Luther, in his later years, went to extremes in advising the extermination of the Jews. At the same time, Catholicism was fighting the new Protestant heresies with might and main. Part of its method was to brand the new religious movements as born under Jewish influence. Thus both parts of Christianity made the treatment of the Jews as social undesirables a test of religious zeal. 3) Moreover, the old economic source of trouble for the Jews gained in intensity. Many Christians had long desired that their Jewish competitors be expelled; and in many instances this desire was now gratified. In other instances, however, Christian princes or the patricians who ruled over many important cities felt that they could ill afford to deprive themselves of the income which the presence of Jews brought into the treasury. Since in Germany and Italy each city or district could follow an independent policy, some of their rulers yielded to the popular and ecclesiastical pressure to expel the Jews, while others compromised by putting their Jewish subjects into a ghetto.

Expulsion or Ghetto—Jewish life from the fifteenth century on was the result of the interplay of these forces. The important Jewish community of Regensburg was finally expelled in 1519, fundamentally because a number of rival princes could not agree as to who was entitled to the income from the Jews and, therefore, all of them surrendered to the will of the greedy or misled populace. In Florence the ruling Medici family considered it advantageous to itself to permit a number of Jews to settle in that city. In Venice the question whether the Jews should be expelled or permitted to stay was debated for a long time. The ghetto established there was an obvious compromise between these two possibilities. Nevertheless, during the sixteenth century there were several occasions when it looked as though the Jewish population would be told to go. But Venice was a commercial city and its rulers saw the advantages which the Jews of near-by Turkey brought to that land. The Jews were, therefore, permitted to stay under fewer restrictions than anywhere else. Frankfort's Jews were under the protection of the German emperor; consequently they were not expelled, but placed within the walls of a ghetto.

The Roman Ghetto—The origin of the ghetto in the city of Rome is particularly interesting. The fate of the Jews of Rome depended largely on the character of the reigning pope. On the whole, they had lived in comparative peace in this capital of Christendom. During the fifteenth century and the age of humanism they had been especially well off. Then came the period of the Counter Reformation and the election of a number of popes who reacted to the rising tide of Prot-

estantism by showing a great zeal for the authority of the
Roman Catholic Church. Paul IV was an exceptionally zealous churchman, and he considered it his duty to lead in making Jewish life as difficult as possible. In July 1555 he issued
a decree which, for ferocious anti-Jewishness, was not
equaled until the coming of Hitler to modern Germany. No
amount of effort on the part of its Jews could save the community from imprisonment within a ghetto.

2. INSIDE THE GHETTO

What a Ghetto Looked Like—The very appearance of a
ghetto district was enough to depress the spirits of its inhabitants. The worst section of the town was usually the one set
apart for Jewish habitation. In Rome, for example, it was
near the river which overflowed very frequently, leaving a
layer of filth and causing perpetually unhealthful conditions.
Everywhere the ghetto was too small for the number of people confined in it. Houses had to be close to one another and
several stories taller than in other parts of the town. The
streets were narrow, and the tall houses prevented the sun
from penetrating the dark, unsanitary alleys.

Some Ghetto Rules—The few streets or alleys which constituted the ghetto were walled up to prevent free entry or
exit, and the windows of Jewish homes which looked out on
streets outside the ghetto were boarded up. One or more
gates at the ends of the Jewish streets permitted the inmates
to leave their district. These were locked at night and
guarded by non-Jewish watchmen. After a definite hour in
the evening no Jew was permitted to remain outside the
ghetto and no Christian within it. The gates and guards presumably protected the ghetto against attack, but certainly the
clothes which the Jews were compelled to wear could serve
no such purpose. For the Jews were not only forbidden to
put on expensive clothes or ornaments, but were ordered to
wear peculiar, peaked hats and yellow badges, so that, as
soon as anyone of them ventured outside the ghetto, he might
become the butt for the ridicule and assault of the town's ruffians. In practice, however, the ghetto regulations about exit
and entrance were not always strictly enforced. Italian Jews,
especially, enjoyed some freedom; and on Saturday afternoon
they might be seen taking a walk along the river bank or the
less crowded avenues of the city.

Ghetto Economics—The descendants of those who had

been Europe's merchants and then its bankers were now reduced to the lowest possible economic level. Christians had by this time taken over the profitable occupations of trade and moneylending. As a result, only two occupations now became characteristic of the Jews: trade in secondhand goods, and the lending of small sums of money in exchange for a pledge of an article (pawnbroking). Into the ghetto wandered spendthrift students who had exhausted their allowance or manual laborers who, because of some personal misfortune, had need of ready cash. They brought with them personal or household articles which they sold or left in pawn with the Jews. Out of the ghetto went the Jews with packs on their backs to sell the articles which they had thus acquired or to buy castoff clothes from the wealthier homes. Within the ghetto, the rooms used for sleeping at night became workshops during the day. There the women repaired the old clothes and other articles bought by the men, who then sold them at a very low profit. Even this was objectionable to the merchant guilds, since the Jews sold their secondhand articles more cheaply than the guildsmen charged for new ones. The presence of Jews was, of course, beneficial to the poorer people of the town. These, however, were not permitted to see this benefit; for they were, as they still are, subject to the influence exerted by their social and economic superiors.

Wealth in the Ghetto—Every ghetto had a number of families who managed to escape the grinding poverty of the rest of the inhabitants. One or two might be physicians; for well-to-do Christians persisted, despite the prohibitions of the Church, in calling Jewish doctors in case of need. A small number of Jews rose, through their business ability, to become the financial advisers of the local prince or bishop. Still others might, with luck, have amassed enough ready funds to be able to lend larger sums of money to various Christians of the upper class. An example of this type is Mordecai Meisel of Prague. His financial ability brought him to the attention of the emperor, who did him the honor of borrowing money from him. But when, in 1601, Meisel died childless, the emperor simply confiscated all his wealth. For wealth was never safe in the ghetto. These few well-to-do people were, however, the ones who enabled the ghetto to survive at all. If it had not been for them, the Jews could not have paid the taxes imposed upon them and so, having become useless to the rulers, would certainly have been expelled.

Community Life—The Jews recognized their dependence upon the few wealthy families and entrusted them with the rule over the community. The structure of the ghetto community was, on the whole, the same as during the Middle Ages. There was a community head (*parnas*) and a community council (*gabbaim*) who were elected. But the votes which elected them were limited to those who could afford to pay taxes. Usually these voters elected a committee which, in turn, selected the members of the council. This indirect method of election enabled a number of families to perpetuate their rule over the community. The council supervised the functioning of the communal institutions—synagogue, school, the charities, court of law—and enforced whatever rules were adopted for the government of the ghetto and the relations between the ghetto and the outside world. The council had the power to decide how much each individual should pay in taxes, since the ghetto had to pay its major taxes to the government in a lump sum.

3. LIFE IN THE GHETTO

Religion in the Ghetto—The sordid district and the miserable houses which were their home, their precarious life on the edge of poverty, the grinding burden of heavy taxes, the constant threat of expulsion or attack made the inhabitants of the ghetto ever conscious of the utter hopelessness of improving their lot. Their religion was all they could turn to for a measure of comfort. In the study of Talmud and Midrash men could forget time and place. Though physically they resided in Frankfort, or Vienna, or Rome, mentally they dwelt in the Palestine of kings and prophets, or in the academies of Sura and Pumpeditha. Their hopes were centered not upon any earthly rulers who, as far as they were concerned, were hostile or greedy, but on the promise made to their ancestors of a Messiah who would come to redeem them. In the meantime, they could only hope and pray, study and observe, labor for their families and derive what joy they could out of the simple round of life.

Jewish life in the Middle Ages was not without its lighter and more joyous aspects. Celebrations in the close communal quarters of the ghetto were associated necessarily with the social events that clustered about the Sabbath, the holidays and important occasions in the life of the individual. The religious spirit was strong in that age and holidays among the Christians also were fervently observed. Among the Jews, moreover, the holidays played the additional role of making it possible to throw off the oppressive mood of ordinary days. Holidays are fortunately frequent in the Jewish year. The awe-inspiring Rosh ha-Shanah and Yom Kippur, the gay festivals of Passover, Shabu'ot and Sukkot, the optimistic half-holidays of Purim and Hanukkah were welcomed eagerly and observed in every detail. Each holiday had its distinctive games for the children, its appropriate foods and dishes to vary the occupation of the women, its fitting synagogue melodies and ceremonies to entertain and absorb the men. The synagogue service occupied a considerable part of the celebration of a holiday. The *hazzan* (cantor) satisfied their artistic and aesthetic needs and he, therefore, assumed during the ghetto period an importance far out of proportion to his place in Judaism. Apart from the religious services, the day was spent in visiting.

The joyous mood of the occasion, more than the actual activities, refreshed and strengthened their spirit. Heinrich Heine, the German poet who knew the ghetto atmosphere in his childhood, caught its meaning for the ghetto Jew in his poem called *Princess Sabbath*. He told the fairy tale of the prince whom magic had cruelly transformed into a dog destined to live all week long in the midst of mire and hostility. With the approach of the Sabbath he became a prince again:

> And his father's halls he enters
> As a man, with man's emotions,
> Head and heart alike uplifted,
> Clad in pure and festal raiment.

His surroundings became transformed and he led a life of glory till nightfall of the Sabbath day:

> But the lovely day flits onward,
> And with long swift-legs of shadow
> Comes the evil hour of magic—
> And the prince begins to sigh.

Marriage in the Ghetto—Personal and family events were other occasions for festivities. A marriage, for example, was cause for celebration in the entire community, especially in the smaller ghettos. The young people concerned were, by modern standards, hardly ready for marriage. The parents, rather than the boy or girl, made the choice. In fact, the *shadchan* (marriage broker) ofttimes planned the prospective marriage even before the parents knew about it. For the *shadchan,* under the circumstances which prevailed, was an essential functionary. He suggested a possible match; through him the two families concerned carried on their negotiations over matters of dowry and other arrangements. The affair was sealed with the signing of a betrothal pact (*tena'im*). The actual marriage ceremony might be delayed for months or years, until the groom completed his studies at the *yeshibah* and the bride the preparation of her trousseau. Occasionally the prospective bride and groom saw one another for the first time at their wedding.

The marriage ceremony was performed under the *huppah* (canopy) in the open air, usually in the synagogue courtyard. Jewish musicians were fairly common during the ghetto period; they were employed frequently even on non-Jewish occasions. The wedding ceremony provided them with their great opportunity, for they accompanied the bride on her march from her parents' home to the synagogue. The ceremony was followed by a feast. For this occasion a local poet might write a poem extolling the groom's learning or the bride's charm. In some instances, where prominent families were involved, a play, teaching a moral lesson, might be presented. Entertainment was provided also by the master of ceremonies, the *marshallik* ("the little marshal," as he was called in Germany), or *badhan* ("the jester," as he was called in Eastern Europe). Sometimes the groom himself delivered a learned address either at the synagogue on the Sabbath before the wedding, or at the banquet-table. The wedding gifts, which the guests there and then presented, therefore acquired the name *derashah-geschenk*, "the gift for the speech," as though the groom's learning had inspired them to make their liberal presents to the couple. The wedding celebration was not confined to one feast. It sometimes lasted for seven days and attained its climax when the bride and groom attended the synagogue services on the Sabbath following the wedding.

Despite outer gloom, the Jews succeeded in retaining their optimism regarding their own and mankind's future. It might truly be said in the words of the modern scholar, Israel Abrahams, "A merry spirit smiled on Jewish life in the Middle Ages, joyousness forming, in the Jewish conception, the coping stone of piety."

4. FRIENDS AND ENEMIES OF THE GHETTO

Preaching to the Ghetto—As though life were not difficult

enough for the Jews of the ghetto, repeated efforts were made to add insult to injury by invading the synagogue and heaping abuse upon the Jewish religion. Ambitious or zealous monks refused to permit the Christian population to forget the presence of Jews behind the ghetto walls. Often with a mob at their heels, they would make their way into the Jewish district, sometimes into the synagogue itself, and hurl threats and curses upon the Jewish population for stiffneckedly holding to the faith of their fathers. To answer the preacher was to invite bloodshed. The best the Jews could do was to let the monk have his say and then complain to the city authorities against the invasion of their district.

The Roman ghetto was worse off, for there the pope felt in duty bound to institute regular preaching to the Jews. Every Saturday afternoon one third of the ghetto's population of men, women and children had to appear at a church located at the very edge of their district. Fines were imposed if the proper number failed to show up, and punishment was meted out to any inattentive person. The preacher, frequently an apostate Jew, would take his text from the portion of the Torah read in the synagogue that morning, and his message sought to win converts to Christianity by casting contempt upon Judaism. This went on for centuries.

The House of Catechumens—How many of the inhabitants of the ghetto were converted by the sermons is hard to tell. Some were no doubt honestly convinced by the arguments which the preachers presented. Ordinarily, however, human nature would and did call forth the very opposite reaction. Nevertheless, there were converts during the ghetto period in considerable numbers. Some succumbed to the lure of a freer life and opportunities. Others were forced into conversion by a variety of less savory methods. For the slightest pretext was employed to bring Jews to baptism against their will. A father or a husband, having become a convert, could call upon the Church authorities to compel the rest of his family to follow suit. Even a word dropped carelessly and overheard by someone who interpreted it as expressing a desire for baptism sufficed to bring the Church's officials to the door. Perhaps the most common convert was the one who could not stand the grinding poverty of the ghetto and was willing to be supported at public expense. For the Church maintained homes in which converts were fed and housed, sometimes for the rest of their lives. These were known as Houses of Catechumens, that is, for the newly converted. In line with the general policy, these houses were maintained by a special tax imposed upon the synagogues of the Papal State.

Danger and Favor in Prague—A ghetto which enjoyed a great measure of peace, comparatively speaking, was the one in the Bohemian city of Prague. This may have been due to the fact that it was under the direct rule of the emperor of the Holy Roman Empire, who was also king of Bohemia. Sometimes, on the other hand, this very fact was a source of danger. In 1561, for example, Emperor Ferdinand I suddenly, for some petty reason, took an oath to expel the Jews from Prague. They were saved by the heroic efforts of Mordecai Zemah, a prominent member of the Prague community, who hurriedly journeyed to Rome and in some manner succeeded in persuading the pope to free the emperor from his vow. Another important personality in Prague, who had the respect of the emperor was Rabbi Judah-Loew ben Bezalel. Besides being a great Talmudist, he was a mathematician and astronomer. The people of Prague still point to a tower where, they say, Emperor Rudolph II would watch Rabbi Judah-Loew scan the skies. After the rabbi's death (1609), numerous legends began to develop about him. The most famous one was the story of the giant body *(golam)* which he had fashioned out of earth and into which he had placed the name of God, thus bringing it to life and making it obedient to his will.

The Frankfort Purim—The nature of Jewish life during the first century of the ghetto is further illustrated by an event which took place in Frankfort on the Main between 1612 and 1616. A period of unemployment among the lower elements of the city had been causing much unrest. The patricians who ruled the town could not or would not do anything about it, thus giving the demagogues who sought to attain power a chance to stir up trouble. They found it easy to blame all the people's woes upon the Jews and to demand of the patricians that the inhabitants of the ghetto be expelled. The ringleader was a baker with the appropriate name of Fettmilch, whose sole gift was an ability to deliver rabble-rousing speeches. The ghetto was stormed. For a while the Jews defended themselves, but the mob set their homes on fire. Fettmilch's followers, fearing the emperor's punishment, prevailed upon their leader to let the Jews leave the city, though with nothing but their lives. The Frankfort Jews scattered through the neighboring towns and villages and, for two years, were supported by the charity of other Jews.

The patricians of Frankfort, certain that the mob would

turn upon them now that the Jews were no longer there to bear the blame for the general poverty, sought aid from the emperor. The Jews were his property and he had derived from them considerable sums annually. The emperor sent troops to restore order in the city. Fettmilch and some of his fellows were condemned to die as rebels, and the Jews were invited to return to an enlarged ghetto. A parade of imperial soldiers led them, to the accompaniment of music, under the gate of the city which was decorated with Fettmilch's head. The patricians returned to power and the masses of the Christian population to their miserable existence. For even their just complaints had been completely forgotten in the unnecessary struggle about the Jews. The Frankfort Jews then established two fast days and one special Purim to commemorate the days of misfortune and the day when another Haman received his merited punishment.

Balance in Vienna—The delicate political and economic balance by which ghettos survived or perished is excellently exemplified in Vienna. Almost immediately after the expulsion of the Viennese Jews in 1421, the dukes of Austria, who were frequently also emperors of Germany, showed eagerness to have the Jews return; for no one really believed the charge of host desecration which had caused their expulsion. The best the rulers of Austria could do, against the stubborn resistance of the townsmen, was to grant one or more Jews the right to stay in Vienna for a specified period to transact business for the court. Consequently, though there were Jews in Vienna almost at all times, it was only in 1582 that an organized community of some thirty families could be found in the city. Since they were a source of enormous profit to the imperial treasury, repeated objections by the Viennese Christians could not dislodge them. On two points, however, the emperor had to yield: in 1625 the Jews were forced to move into the district called Leopoldstadt which was made into a ghetto; and, after 1630, they were forced to listen to Christian sermons. As long as imperial need outweighed the power of the townsmen, due to the Thirty Years' War, the position of the Jews in Vienna was fairly secure. After that war ended in 1648, the influence of the townsmen increased along with that of the Church. When the empress, a Spanish princess, joined the ranks of its enemies, the fate of the Viennese ghetto was sealed. The poorer Jews were the first to go; the wealthier ones followed soon after. In 1670 the second settlement of Jews in the Austrian capital came to an end.

Business and Culture in Venice—The island ghetto of Ven-

422 RETREAT AND PROGRESS

ice was hedged in with numerous annoying restrictions, but it was permitted to rule itself and nothing was done to limit its commercial activity. The Jews had to negotiate a new contract with the doge and council of the city every ten or twenty years, and every such contract involved the payment of a large sum of money over and above the regular taxes. Thereafter, the ghetto met, on the whole, with little interference. Not being separated from the outside world as strictly as were the Jews of other ghettos, the cultural interests of the Venetian Jews were wider than those of the others. There were even Jewish women poets, who wrote both in Hebrew and in Italian. Enterprising Christian businessmen established printing presses in Venice and, in cooperation with Jews, published a number of basic rabbinic texts, among them the Bible and the Talmud with commentaries.

Christian Scholars—Among those who came closely in touch with the Jews and Judaism were Christian scholars who studied Hebrew and the Jewish religion. Unfortunately, most of these students were connected with the Church, and their chief aim was the conversion of the Jews. Consequently, they were critics even more than students. There were a few who nevertheless displayed a different spirit.

Johann Christoph Wagenseil, for example, a Protestant, was a student of Judaism. For a while he resided in Vienna and was a frequent visitor at the synagogue. He acquired a good knowledge of Hebrew and some knowledge of the Talmud. He then published (1681) a collection of Jewish writings in which Jews, writing in Hebrew, refuted the claims of Christianity in order to strengthen Jewish resistance to conversion. Wagenseil's intention was not to advance the Jewish side of the argument among Christians. On the contrary, his motive was to protest and to express horror that Jews were permitted to say such things about Christianity. He urged Christian princes to stop the Jews from "insulting" Christianity and to make greater efforts to convert them. At the same time, Wagenseil protested against the shameful methods employed by Christians to degrade the Jews. Greater kindness, he felt, would produce better results. For this reason Wagenseil must be numbered among the friendly Christians of that day. Another such scholar, by the name of Eisenmenger, was a person of greedy mercenary motives. He made a collection of all the statements in the Talmud and other works of Jewish literature which he sought, by the wildest stretch of his perverted imagination, to interpret as hostile to Christianity. He offered not to publish his work if the Jews would pay him a large sum of money. The Jews would not pay that much, but they bribed the authorities not to permit the publication of the book. In 1711, however, it was published and, thereafter, to this day, Eisenmenger's *Judaism Unmasked* has served as the source-book for anti-Jewish writings.

5. WAR AND EPIDEMICS

The Thirty Years' War—Between 1618 and 1648 Central Europe was made to suffer from one of the most destructive wars which that unhappy part of the world ever experienced. For a century before, Protestant and Catholic in various parts of Europe had been at one another's throats. In 1618 a struggle began in Germany which was meant to decide into which religious camp Central Europe would go. Before the war had lasted many years, the purpose of the fighting changed from religion to questions of political domination, the unity of the German states, the power of the emperor of the Holy Roman Empire, and other matters of purely political and economic importance. There were invasions and sieges and betrayals and massacres. The common people and the peasants suffered indescribably; the war was accompanied by a terrible plague; the population of Germany was considerably reduced. And when it was all over, the only decision reached was that Germany would remain disunited religiously and politically. A struggle so prolonged and bloody was bound to have unhappy effects on the Jews of Central Europe.

Effect on Jewish Life—The general disruption of Jewish life, the number of ghettos sacked by soldiers, the enormous fines and forced contributions imposed on Jewish communities by the generals of one side or the other, would take too long to relate and, besides, can be readily imagined. The Jews did not participate in the fighting—no one expected them to —but they suffered from both sides. It was easy enough for the general occupying a town to threaten the Jews with punishment unless they contributed to his own treasury or that of his cause, on trumped-up charges that they had shown sympathy for the rival army. Generally speaking, the Jews of Germany were affected by the Thirty Years' War at least as much as the rest of the population.

Court Purveyors—At the same time a small number of Jews profited considerably from the Thirty Years' War. In those days there had not yet developed any commissary department to provide for the needs of an army. The equipment and the food for men and animals were supplied by private individuals on a contract basis. The rulers, from the emperor down, frequently entrusted the job of finding the supplies and sending them where necessary to any Jew who had shown financial skill in other matters. Such Jews now became the official purveyors for the courts. An equally important reason for choosing Jews for this purpose was the fact that the Jews, neutral in a war with an avowed religious motivation, could conduct business with fellow Jews on the other side of the line. In this way, a small number of Jews became wealthy and influential. They could help pay the fines and contributions imposed upon their home communities, and often their influence in high quarters protected the very lives of their fellow Jews. The best example of a court purveyor during the Thirty Years' War was Samuel Bassevi, a Jew of Prague to whom the emperor gave a title of nobility for his services to the state. He was, thus, among the first Jews to be honored in this way.

What happened to a few individuals could not, of course, affect the economic situation of the Jews in general during or after the war. As a result, many Jews left Germany and, this time, turned toward the more promising land to the northwest.

CHAPTER IV

REOPENED DOORS AND A NEW HOME

HOLLAND AND ENGLAND ARE THE FIRST LANDS IN MODERN EUROPE TO TREAT THE JEWS KINDLY; AND AMERICA BEGINS TO SERVE AS A REFUGE FOR MARR NC 3

Where Hope Revived—We turn now to the lands whose people broke with the medieval past and were the first to lead the way to a new Europe. Through years of struggle the Dutch people learned the value of freedom; and they were not narrow in applying this lesson. Soon the English started on the road to progress which made freedom a necessity. As a result, while the Jews of Germany and Italy remained in their ghetto-prison for another century and a half, and while the Jews of Poland drew deeper into themselves, new communities came into being in Holland and England which, enjoying comparative freedom, helped these countries to grow in prosperity and culture.

Another land, moreover, completely new to the world, had no traditions of the past to break with. America offered the best possible refuge for the Marranos and still another opportunity for the Jews to help build a new civilization. Unfortunately, the southern half of the New World was compelled to accept the intolerance of the Middle Ages, so that the Jews were driven to the northern part, where they participated in the forward march of freedom.

1. THE DUTCH REFUGE

Holland's Fight for Independence—In the late Middle Ages, when countries and provinces of Europe were being lost and won through war and diplomacy, the Netherlands fell into the hands of the Hapsburg family. Emperor Charles V (1500–1558) ruled over these provinces as he did over Spain, Germany and Austria. The Dutch did not at all like being under Spanish domination, especially since many Netherlanders were sympathetic to Protestantism. The attempt of the Spanish administration to uproot the new religion and to introduce the Inquisition into their land was too much for the Dutch. Under the great-hearted leadership of William of Orange, they began a struggle against tremendous odds and emerged victorious. This victory for freedom in Holland was of great importance to the Jews.

Marranos Seeking Refuge—A small number of Jews had lived in Holland some centuries earlier, but they had been expelled. After 1492, however, the Marranos of Spain and Portugal, desperately in need of a way to avoid the Inquisition and to return to the faith of their fathers, used Holland as a way-station on their road to freedom. In order to avoid suspicion, they would move from Spain to Holland, then one of Spain's provinces; from Holland they would go to Italy, and from Italy they were within fairly easy reach of Turkey. Even after Holland broke away from Spain, a thin but constant stream of Marrano refugees continued to flow there from lands dominated by the Inquisition. They did not dare to throw off the cloak of Christianity, but they were at least out of the Inquisition's reach.

The Double Community—Around 1600 the Dutch permitted the Marranos to observe Judaism. The complete victory did not come all at once. Attempts to prevent open practice of Judaism took place during the first half of the seventeenth century, but these were merely temporary setbacks. Early in the seventeenth century a synagogue was established in Amsterdam and ground was acquired for a cemetery. Freed from external pressure and unaccustomed to united Jewish action, the small group of Jews began to quarrel among themselves and for a while there was more than one congregation. This, however, was remedied before long, especially because of the influx of German Jews (Ashkenazim), to whom the Spanish-Portuguese Jews (Sephardim) wanted to present a united front. For, while Marrano refugees from the Iberian Peninsula made Holland their goal, the Thirty Years' War induced also a number of Jews from Germany to migrate to this land of freedom. Amsterdam, the largest city in Holland, thereafter had two distinct Jewish communities: the Sephardi and the Ashkenazi, each with its rabbi, its school, its cemetery and its communal officials. They cooperated only in the larger Jewish matters. Otherwise the Sephardim kept the Ashkenazim at a distance, looked down on them and went so far as to consider it a disgrace to intermarry with them. Ridiculous as one may consider such an attitude, it has appeared on several occasions in Jewish history. In this particular instance it was an understandable reaction. The Sephardim of Holland were descendants of families which for some generations had been counted among the nobility of Spain and Portugal, and they found it hard to forget their coats-of-arms. Besides, the Sephardim retained a tradition of general culture. The German Jews, while more deeply steeped in Jewish learning, did not enjoy the grand manners nor display the self-possession of the Sephardim. Moreover, there was an important economic difference.

Holland and Prosperity—The Sephardi Jews, on escaping from Spain or Portugal, had been able to bring along a portion of their family wealth. The Ashkenazi Jews, impoverished by ghetto conditions and fleeing before armed enemies during a war, arrived in Holland penniless. Consequently, the Sephardim were able to take part almost at once in the improving economic conditions of Holland. For the Dutch had begun to trade far and wide over the seas; they had given up the cramping guild system; they recognized that general prosperity demanded the free and unhampered activity of every able human being. The Sephardi Jews joined in the growing colonial trade and became so important in the diamond industry that for centuries they had all but a monopoly of it. The rise of the Ashkenazim was necessarily slower. Within a short time it became perfectly clear that the Jews of both types were contributing materially to the general prosperity of Holland. As a result, even those Netherlanders who disliked Jews and Judaism did not attempt to impose restrictions on Jewish life.

2. RELIGIOUS CONFLICT AND ADJUSTMENT

Judaism Among the Ex-Marranos—The former Marranos, having obtained the right to practice Judaism openly, became strict observers of tradition. After all, these were the customs and ceremonies for the sake of which they and their forefathers for over a century had lived in constant dread of the Inquisition. Moreover, Catholicism, with which the first generation of Dutch Jews had been familiar since their birth, also insisted on religious piety expressed through observances. Unfortunately, this first generation could not attain to the more profound understanding of the traditions of Jewish life. Jewish literature and thought were too wide and too deep for any newcomer to Judaism to acquire quickly. The Dutch Jews of German origin, no matter how inferior otherwise, had the advantage in this respect. They had never broken, willingly or unwillingly, with the chain of Jewish thought; their loyalty was fortified by knowledge. The Sephardi Jews tried hard to remove this defect in their Jewishness by establishing schools. They were, indeed, remarkably successful; for, within a single generation they had rabbis reared and trained in their own community. To their own Judaism, however, the first generation could bring little more than loyalty; and for an inquiring mind loyalty alone is not enough. Therefore an individual here and there found himself dissatisfied with the Judaism he had but recently assumed because he was unsatisfied by the ill-understood reasoning which backed it.

Uriel da Costa—The outstanding example of this unfortunate situation was Uriel da Costa. In Portugal, where he was born and brought up for a career in the Church, he had studied a great deal of theology. Dissatisfied with Christianity, he secretly turned to Judaism and idealized the faith of his ancestors. He succeeded in making his way to Amsterdam, where he openly adopted Judaism. But instead of discovering a faith which was to transform human beings by its pure idealism, all Uriel could see was an endless series of observances whose importance in the preservation of Jewish life he could not appreciate. His writings in criticism of Judaism brought down upon him the wrath of the Jews, and he was excommunicated. This left Uriel spiritually and physically alone in the world, for he would not return to Christianity and he could not accept Judaism as it was practiced. He tried to become reconciled with the Jews by submitting to the humiliating penance imposed upon him. Finally, unable to adjust himself to the situation, he committed suicide (1640).

Baruch Spinoza—No sooner had the scandal of Uriel da Costa been forgotten than a new scandal shook the Amsterdam community: that of Spinoza (1632–1677). But there was a difference between the two men. Uriel da Costa broke with Judaism because of inadequate early training and insufficient knowledge; Baruch (Benedict) Spinoza left Jewish life because he was an individualist who could find no place in any organized religion. The Jewish community of Amsterdam had had high hope for young Baruch Spinoza. In the schools of that Sephardi community he had shown early promise of becoming an excellent rabbinic scholar. His study of the Jewish philosophers of former days, however, led him to turn to the study of philosophy in general. At that time, philosophy was abandoning its interest in theology, which had been its main concern during the Middle Ages, and was turning to the study of the natural sciences and the human mind. Young Spinoza associated with a number of freethinking Christian friends and teachers. Soon the Jews were horrified to note that he was not observing the Jewish ceremonial laws. There was danger in this for the newly established Jewish community, whose enemies might now point out that Judaism was fostering irreligion and a disbelief in God. The Sephardi community of Amsterdam consequently placed Baruch Spinoza under the ban of excommunication. Spinoza did not mind. In the free environment of Holland he could live peacefully without being a member of any religious group. He earned his meager livelihood by grinding lenses, and spent his time in writing on ethics and philosophy.

Spinoza's Jewish Writings—Spinoza cannot be considered a Jew in religion, although he never joined the Christian faith. In his writings, however, there is ample evidence of his Jewish training and turn of mind. He wrote a book about Judaism, or rather about religion, which the Christians liked as little as did the Jews. He denied that Jewish laws had any divine origin, and asserted that they were meant to strengthen Jewish solidarity and had, in fact, succeeded in preserving the

Jewish people. He denied that the books of the Bible had actually been written by the men to whom they were ascribed, and in this he was far ahead of his time. But even his purely philosophical works showed how much he had acquired from the Jewish philosophers of former days. He never questioned the unity of God, and believed that everything in the world showed God's presence. His very emphasis on ethics is proof of his essential Jewishness.

The Fruits of Freedom—These two exceptions, Uriel da Costa and Baruch Spinoza, indicate that otherwise the Sephardi community of Amsterdam was thoroughly and loyally Jewish. Here, moreover, for the first time in a good many centuries, was a Jewish life voluntarily accepted and possessing the opportunity for free development. The Sephardim of Holland, their sense of human dignity not crushed by ghetto treatment, associated with their Christian neighbors on terms of equality without feeling the need of any modification in their Jewish institutions.

3. MENASSEH BEN ISRAEL (1604–1657)

Rabbi and Scholar—A good illustration of the type of Jew developed in the Sephardi community of Amsterdam was Rabbi Menasseh ben Israel. Born into a Marrano family, he received his training in Amsterdam. Many of the liberals and philosophers all over Western and Northern Europe were among his correspondents. He was at first a teacher in the Jewish school and then a rabbi of the Sephardi community. Menasseh ben Israel also tried his fortune at the business of printing. He published his own works, in Latin and Spanish, and thereby widened his reputation even though he did not increase his wealth. At one point in his career he wanted to emigrate to the new Jewish community established in South America.

America and the Lost Ten Tribes—One of Menasseh's works dealt with America and led him to the effort which has earned for him, more than anything else he ever did, a place in the history of the Jews. Over a century and a half after the discovery of America, the New World was still a land of mystery. All sorts of stories were believed about it in Europe. For instance, about the middle of the seventeenth century a Jewish traveler, Antonio de Montezinos, returned from America and spread the fantastic story that the American Indians were descendants of the Lost Ten Tribes. The proof he

offered was naive. Menasseh ben Israel, however, was convinced and referred to the subject in his book, *The Hope of
Israel,* which he published in Spanish (1650). He believed
that these Israelites, exiled from their homeland by Sennacherib (719 B. C. E.), had wandered across Asia and into
North America, whence they spread over the newly-discov-
ered continent. The existence of Hebrews in far-off America
interested him because this seemed to be a fulfillment of various biblical prophecies then interpreted by the Christians to
mean that the Messiah would come only after Israel had been
scattered to every corner of the world. The finding of Hebrews in America meant that the coming of the Messiah was
that much nearer at hand. *The Hope of Israel* was therefore
hailed by learned Christians even more than by Jews.

Menasseh and England—His theory turned Menasseh's attention to the land across the narrow channel from Holland,
to England, which seemed to be the only country where Jews
could not be found. Thereupon Menasseh began to nurture a
plan whereby England, too, might be persuaded to readmit
the Jews. Whether or not the Messiah idea was his only reason one cannot tell, but Menasseh emphasized it. He translated his little book into Latin and dedicated it to the English
Parliament.

4. ENGLAND AND THE JEWS

Four Blank Centuries—England had had no Jews since the
expulsion in 1290. After the expulsion from Spain, a number
of Marrano refugees ventured into the island, but they never
professed Judaism openly. During the reign of Elizabeth, one
of these Marranos was suspected of having plotted against
the queen's life so as to make it easier for Spain to conquer
England. He was executed, though he was quite innocent, as
has now been definitely established. (Incidentally, it follows
from all this that neither Marlowe nor Shakespeare could have
been acquainted with a Jew and that Shylock was therefore a
purely imaginary character.) The fact that in the sixteenth
century England definitely broke with the Roman Church removed one possible source of objection to their readmittance.
Two factors, furthermore, drew the attention of the English
to the desirability of letting Jews settle among them: one was
the obvious economic advantages which the presence of Jews
had brought to Holland; the second was the religious arguments advanced by Menasseh ben Israel.

Cromwell and Menasseh—Oliver Cromwell ruled over England at that time. England and Holland were then rivals for overseas trade, and it seemed to Cromwell that the Jews had done a great deal to make Holland as powerful as it was. In 1652 Cromwell invited Menasseh to cross the Channel for the purpose of discussing the possibility of reopening England to Jewish settlement. Wars and other difficulties prevented Menasseh from accepting the invitation at once; he did not arrive until 1655.

Debate and Arguments—Powerful as he was in the country, Cromwell did not dare make a favorable decision all by himself. The question of readmitting the Jews had been a subject of discussion in England for a number of years even before Menasseh ben Israel entered his plea for it. It became intensified after 1650, when pamphlets by the hundreds were devoted to the subject. Those opposed to the readmission raked up all the arguments against the Jews which they could think of—from bad manners to the danger of their turning St. Paul's Cathedral into a synagogue. Those in favor of readmission denied some of the charges and refuted others. They pointed out that countries like Holland and Turkey, which had Jewish populations, had made rapid economic progress and asserted that the opposition came from certain merchants who feared Jewish competition. Jews, they said, were kindly people, hard-working, clever. Some even argued that, after coming in contact with the superior Christianity of England, the Jews would be converted. These public and private debates reached their climax at the time of Menasseh's arrival. Cromwell now called a national conference to discuss the matter. The lawyers present agreed that there was no real legal obstacle to the resettlement of the Jews; no new law specifically permitting them to return to England was necessary. As to the advisability of letting them return, the conference could come to no decision. It had become obvious, moreover, that there was more politics than sincerity in the discussion, and that those secretly opposed to Cromwell were using the issue to hurt him. That is why Cromwell thought it wiser to dismiss the conference and let the entire subject be forgotten.

Readmission by Silence—Menasseh ben Israel was deeply disappointed. Personally he had been treated very well; he had even received a pension from the English government. But he felt that his mission had been a failure, and he died shortly after his return to Holland. Actually, however, he had succeeded far better than he had hoped. For, if England had passed a law admitting the Jews, their return would certainly have been hedged in by a number of social and economic restrictions. As it was, nothing was officially stated except the decision of the lawyers that there was no legal obstacle in the way of their return. The seemingly heated debate during Cromwell's time proved to be mostly talk. Already in 1655 a number of Marrano merchants, long resident in England, openly declared themselves Jews. Singly, or in very small groups, Marranos and Dutch Jews classified as merchants entered the country without any hindrance. When Charles Stuart was restored to the throne of England in 1660, the situation underwent no change. Charles II's government was as anxious as Cromwell had been to outrival Holland in commerce. The presence of Jews was considered to be, and really proved to be, useful for this purpose. For a while Jews undertook no open public worship, but before many years passed a synagogue was opened. The Jews could not participate in the government or in any other part of official English life because an oath was required which only a Christian could take. But in economic life and even in society they soon began to play an important part.

5. New World, New Hope

Opening a Continent—At the very time when a Jewish congregation was being established in London, another Jewish congregation was being formed in a newly-acquired English colony across the Atlantic Ocean, in territory recently renamed New York. Nor was this the first Jewish congregation founded in the New World. In the year 1667 the Jews already had a history in America of one hundred and seventy-five years, reaching back to Columbus when he was laying his plans for his voyage westward. Jewish history since the discovery of the New World touched in turn the various nations connected with its colonization: Spain and Portugal, France, Holland and England.

Jews in the Story of Columbus—The life of Christopher Columbus is, in some respects, still a mystery. Certain of his actions, such as hiding his ancestry and using strange symbols in his letters to his son, seem to point to a possible Marrano origin. But whether or not he was himself of Jewish origin, it is a fact that those who helped him carry his plan through successfully were either recent and probably unwilling converts from Judaism or men of Jewish descent. Luis de Santangel, members of whose immediate family were condemned by the Inquisition as "Judaizers," helped Columbus persuade Queen Isabella to permit the voyage of discovery and raised for her some of the money needed to outfit his vessels. To him Columbus sent the first report of his discoveries. Columbus used, in his navigation, the charts prepared by Abraham Zacuto. Some of Columbus' sailors have been identified with certainty as Marranos, who joined him perhaps in the hope that he would really land in China where they might remain to live far away from the Inquisition. Moreover, Luis de Torres, who went along as interpreter because of his knowledge of oriental languages, was baptized just before going on board Columbus' ship. He was the first to set foot on the soil of the New World and the first white man to settle there.

Marranos in the New World—As soon as it became clear that Columbus had discovered new lands, Marranos of Portugal and Spain sought an opportunity to settle there and return to their religion. But the Inquisition was not slow in placing obstacles in their way. Prospective emigrants to the New World were investigated, while the clergy sent from the homeland to the New World were ordered to keep their eyes open for any manifestations of Judaism. As early as 1520 a Spanish soldier in Mexico was executed on suspicion of practicing Judaism in secret. As the sixteenth century went on, the number of such suspects increased. Some were sent back to Spain for trial and punishment; others were imprisoned and executed in America. A famous auto-da-fé was the one of 1593 in which the family of Luis de Caravajal, governor of northern Mexico, went to their death confessing Judaism; another auto-da-fé took place in 1639 in Peru, where the gifted Francisco Maldonado de Silva along with ten others were burned at the stake for Judaizing.

Religious Liberty in Brazil—The first struggle for religious liberty in the New World was thus the one begun by the Jews. The most successful attempt by Marranos to return to their ancestral faith was the one made in the Portuguese colony at Pernambuco, or Recife, on the Brazilian coast, to which a considerable number of them had come. The Inquisition kept a watchful eye on them, and they long observed their Judaism in secret. About 1620, however, a war between Spain and Holland resulted in the conquest of the colony by the Dutch. Immediately the Marranos threw off the mask and established a Jewish community, which went so far as to invite a rabbi from Amsterdam. It was to this community that Menasseh ben Israel wanted to go, and was disappointed when the Americans preferred his rival, Isaac Aboab da Fonseca, who became the first rabbi on American soil. Unfortunately the Dutch could not hold the colony. It fell back into the hands of Portugal in January 1654. Despite the efforts of the Dutch to obtain favorable terms for the Jews who had defended the colony for them, it was obvious that Jewish life could not survive the reintroduction of Portuguese rule and the inevitable Inquisition. The Jewish community of Recife fell apart and scattered, some returning to Holland, others making their peace with the Catholic Church and continuing to live as Marranos, still others abandoning most of their possessions and fleeing to the islands in the Caribbean. Before long, Jewish plantation owners and Jewish communities made their appearance in Jamaica, the Barbados, and other French and English islands of the West Indies. The same thing happened in the Dutch colony of Surinam (Dutch Guiana) on the South American mainland.

Arrivals in New Amsterdam—A small number of refugees from Brazil, instead of staying in the West Indies, took ship for the colony in North America which the Dutch West India Company had recently established under the name of New Netherland. After an eventful journey, during which they lost all but a few personal belongings, twenty-three of them arrived at the port of New Amsterdam in September 1654. But they were unable to pay in full for their passage, even after everything they had with them had been sold at auction. The angry captain of the *Saint Charles,* the ship which had brought them, haled them before the Dutch governor and court. He insisted that the Jews, or at least some of them, be imprisoned until they obtained enough money from their coreligionists in the Indies to pay for their journey. The Dutch agreed to imprison two of the Jews. When, however, the Jews pleaded for the right to remain in New Amsterdam permanently, even after their debt had been paid, Peter Stuyvesant, governor of New Netherland, made it perfectly clear that he would permit nothing of the kind.

A Problem for Stuyvesant—Peter Stuyvesant was not really an official of the Dutch government: he represented the Dutch West India Company which held the charter to exploit the resources of the colony. He was efficient, but narrow-minded, and permitted religious worship only to members of the Dutch and Presbyterian Churches. Lutherans, too, had their difficulties with him; as to Catholics and Quakers, they were not permitted to set foot on the territory under his charge. Naturally, therefore, he was violently opposed to the admission of Jews despite the colony's need for more settlers. The Dutch population and its pastor also did not like Jews, but they at least sympathized with their poverty, helped them with food, and seemed willing enough to let them stay. As a matter of fact, one Jew, a certain Jacob Barsimson, apparently of German origin, had preceded by about half a year the twenty-three who arrived on the *Saint Charles*. He was there, it seems, as the local representative of a group of Jewish fur-traders in Europe. He, however, presented no problem. He had probably made it perfectly clear that he had no intention of remaining permanently. It was the idea of a permanent settlement by a group that aroused Stuyvesant's opposition.

A few days after the arrival of the Jews, the governor wrote to his company in Holland, expressing himself in most vigorous terms about Jews in general and these Jews in particular. Confidently he awaited the answer of his employers, permitting him to expel these applicants for settlement in the colony. The answer came some four months later, and its contents shocked Governor Stuyvesant. It told him frankly that the Jews in America deserved consideration because a number of Jews in European Amsterdam had become stockholders in the Dutch West India Company and because the people now seeking admittance to New Netherland had fought for Holland in South America. As a result the directors were forced to order their governor to permit the Jews to stay. Stuyvesant was dumbfounded. Again he tried to expel the Jews; again he wrote to his directors, this time with the approval and assistance of the pastor and the population. In reply he received an impatient command to obey his instructions. The Jews were to have in New Netherland the same rights which they enjoyed in old Netherland. The condition was made, however, that they were not to become a burden on the non-Jewish population, but were to take care of their own poor. Stuyvesant was forced to swallow his prejudices and let the Jews remain.

The Struggle for Human Rights—This was not the end of the problem for Stuyvesant, for these Jews were not meek and submissive. They refused to be treated as second-rate residents. Some of them had been citizens in Amsterdam; they knew their rights and had the courage to fight for them. First came the struggle for religious freedom. Stuyvesant was correct in his fear that to grant the Jews the right of public worship would entail granting the same right to various Christian sects until then prevented from having churches of their own.

A compromise was reached. While the Jews were not granted the right to have a synagogue, they did obtain from the directors of the company the right to conduct worship in a private home.

Asser Levy—The second struggle was for personal freedom. The need had arisen for doing guard duty on New Amsterdam's fortifications. Every citizen was liable to such duty, but the authorities took it for granted that Jews should not perform military service by the side of Christians. Nevertheless, they followed European tradition in asking the Jews to pay for their exemption. Asser Levy came forward in this struggle as a valiant defender of Jewish rights. Asser Levy van Swellem, to give him his full Dutch name, was one of the original arrivals. A young man of energy and self-confidence, he insisted that he, unless physically disqualified, would bear arms and would not pay the tax. In the end, Asser Levy had his way; he, and presumably the other Jews, stood guard along with the Christian residents of New Amsterdam.

The third struggle was for economic freedom. In European Holland the Jews were kept out of certain trades, and the same restrictions were placed on them in New Netherland. Again it was Asser Levy who fought the measure and won for himself the right to open a butcher-shop. It took a longer time and another appeal to the directors of the Dutch company to obtain for the Jews the right to trade in fur, whether in the lower part of the colony, now New Jersey, or the upper part, as far as Albany. Finally, in 1657, the last step was taken when, in the face of opposition from Stuyvesant and many others, the Jews won the right to be considered burghers on equal footing with everyone else, at least from the political and economic points of view.

New Amsterdam to New York—During the first ten years of Jewish life on the North American continent the Jews thus made considerable progress. By 1664 they were, if not well-to-do, at least firmly established. More important was the fact that here, in far-off America, they first began to win for themselves those elementary rights and freedoms which were still denied them in most progressive lands of the Old World. At this time the English took over the colony and renamed it New York. During the next century this colony, along with the others on the Atlantic coast, witnessed the rise of new ideas which were to form the foundations for the Land of the Free.

CHAPTER V

REALITIES AND DREAMS

THE JEWS OF EASTERN EUROPE GO THROUGH A PERIOD OF
FIRE AND SWORD, AND THE JEWS OF ALL EUROPE FALL
VICTIM TO THEIR OWN DREAMS

A Tired Generation—The Jewish populations of Germany, Eastern Europe, North Africa and Palestine could not foresee, in the seventeenth century, the promise of a better future contained in the new developments in Holland, England and distant America. Oppression was too real for them to imagine that a day would come when the chains which bound them would be removed as the result of new conditions and new ideas that were soon to emerge. In Eastern Europe, the Jews no sooner developed a remarkable system of self-government than calamity overwhelmed them. The situation became so hopeless that, when a leader and dreamer arose who promised them the sort of miracles they hoped for, they turned to him out of sheer despair. Impostor or victim of self-delusion, Sabbetai Zevi failed them. That the Jews survived this added disappointment proved once more their spiritual vitality.

1. A COUNCIL OF FOUR LANDS

Bases of Self-Government—While the Marranos were still looking for means of evading the Inquisition and while the small community of Palestine was trying to establish its supremacy in Jewish life, the Jews of Poland attained intellectual maturity and formed for themselves a well organized government. The Polish state encouraged them to do this, primarily because it made the collection of taxes easier. The Jews found further advantages for themselves in a union of all their communities. They needed unity in order to safeguard their common interests against their enemies. Moreover, the rabbinic leaders of Polish Jewry saw cultural advantages and an opportunity for the wider application of Jewish law.

Organization—Probably Shalom Shakhna, rabbi of Lublin, gave definite form to the idea of intercommunal union about 1530. The lands under Polish rule were divided into three districts: Poland proper, Polish Russia (Ruthenia) and Lithuania. The Jews of these provinces joined together in a Council. A little less than a century later, in 1623, the Jews of Lithuania withdrew to form a Council of their own, since the government had begun to impose a separate tax on them. The Polish Jewish Council was then reorganized into four "lands," or provinces (*Va'ad Arba' Aratzot*): Great Poland, Little Poland (Cracow), Ruthenia, and Volhynia. Each province had a separate council and chose its representatives to the Council of Four Lands. The general Council consisted usually of thirty men and it met semi-annually, unless an emergency demanded an extra session. In order to make sure that matters of business and finance remained in experienced hands, the number of rabbis in the Council was limited to six. The head of the Council was always a layman. His was a position much sought after, because it meant being the head of

the entire Jewry of Poland. There were two standing committees: one, headed by a rabbi, dealing with matters of culture
and law; another, headed by a layman, concerned with problems of taxation. Special committees dealt with other matters
of interest to all Polish Jewry.

Shtadlanim—One result of this nation-wide unity and of
the peculiar position of the Jewish group within the Polish
state was the appearance of the *shtadlan* (one who tries). He
was an official ambassador of the Jews, appointed by the
Council and responsible to it, without having any official
standing at the Polish court. Knowing well that powerful enemies were ready to seize every opportunity to hurt Jewish interests, the Council would engage the services of a Jew whose
duty it was to live in the capital and guard the welfare of his
people. He had to possess definite qualifications: good manners, thorough knowledge of the Polish language, wide ac-
quaintanceship among the Polish nobility, ability to judge
human nature and to use the art of diplomacy. Every meeting
of the Polish parliament was a critical time for the Jews of
that country. The combination of the lesser nobility, the middle class and the lower clergy was too powerful to be disregarded. At such times the *shtadlan* had to be on hand to visit
people privately and, by an appeal to reason and justice, to
turn them from enemies into good, if temporary, friends.
When he failed to prevent the passage of an anti-Jewish
measure, he would exert himself to persuade the Polish king
to temper its severity. If every effort failed, he could at least
warn the Jewish community of the dangers which lay ahead.
Thus he was a backdoor diplomat—in American political language, a lobbyist.

Courts and Taxes—The fact that the Jews were united in a
Council does not mean that life among them was always
peaceful. Disputes between individuals could be settled in
local Jewish courts. Appeals could be taken to other courts
recognized by the disputants and by the community as
higher courts because they consisted of men more learned in
Jewish law. Disagreements between individuals and communities, however, and quarrels between two communities, had
to be taken directly to the Council. The most common
causes for such lawsuits were the taxes imposed upon various
individuals or communities and the jurisdiction over smaller
communities. Every large community desired to extend its
power over as many smaller ones in its neighborhood as possible, since this gave the community a larger number of individuals among whom its quota of the tax could be divided. In

such matters the judicial committee of the Council was the final court. In case of necessity, the Polish government enforced the Council's decisions, although they were arrived at according to Jewish, not Polish, law.

Culture and Education—The Polish Jews actually lived in accordance with talmudic law and were consequently deeply interested in its study as more than an intellectual exercise. Nor did the Jewish community, and its leadership in the Council, make any distinction between civil and religious law. They realized that the life of the Jewish group depended on both aspects of Judaism and that behind everything else lay the necessity for Jewish education. The Council made it its business to encourage, even to insist upon, the establishment of schools and talmudical academies in every town. They laid down rules for instruction. They ordered the strict enforcement of the moral law, so that the Jewish population might not descend to the level of the masses of ignorant peasants among whom so many of them lived. Naturally, they also enforced the government's laws regarding the Jews, even though some of these laws were anti-Jewish. Such, for example, was the law forbidding the Jews to dress in expensive clothes. The Councils, whether of Poland or of Lithuania, were thus strong central governments under which the Jews realized a considerable measure of cultural and religious autonomy. Unfortunately, their effectiveness was undermined by an avalanche of misfortunes which overwhelmed the Jews of Poland in the middle of the seventeenth century.

2. WITH FIRE AND SWORD

Poland's Calamity—The old law of Jewish history, that the Jewish population suffers doubly for the social and political mistakes of the society in which it lives, was exemplified once more in the case of Poland. When the Jagello dynasty died out, in 1572, the more powerful nobles refused to permit another family to establish itself as hereditary rulers. They preferred to "elect" a king. Before electing one, they made sure that he would have as little power as possible. As a result, each one of the great Polish landowners became in reality almost independent in his own territory, while the king became merely a figurehead. The Polish state became weak and defenseless, with no permanent central authority, a prey to the jealousies and rivalries of its important families. The Polish parliament, moreover, suffered from a peculiar distortion of democracy—any member could veto a project even if everyone else voted for it. Worst of all was the terrible injustice done to the peasants of the southeastern province, the one known as the Ukraine, situated between the Dniester and the Dnieper rivers. The population of this territory was Greek Catholic, while Poland was Roman Catholic; the Ukrainians considered themselves Russians and looked upon their Polish landlords as conquerors; they loved the freedom of the steppes, while the Poles held them as serfs tied to the soil. Frequent rumblings of rebellion were heard, which the Poles put down with great cruelty. Sooner or later trouble was bound to come.

The Jews of the Ukraine—Each of these factors in the condition of the Polish state affected the Jews. As the central government became weaker, the Jews were left to the mercy of the propaganda carried on by the lower clergy and to the malice of the townsmen. The Jews of the towns in Poland proper found it increasingly difficult to earn their livelihood. The large landowners, on the other hand, were able and willing to protect the Jews who settled in their territory. A system developed whereby the Jews would either rent the vast farms of the landlords or become resident overseers. The Polish noble, immersed in politics or pleasure, would go to Warsaw or Paris, living on the money squeezed out of the peasant by means of the Jewish overseer. The noble was interested only in his income; the Jewish population, scattered over the Ukraine, was left exposed to the hate of the peasant. The Jew may have sympathized with the Ukrainian peasant more than with his pleasure-loving landowner, but he had to do what his employer demanded. It stands to reason that the Ukrainian peasant associated the Jews with the hated Poles.

Chmelnitzki's Revolt—A petty officer of the local Ukrainian forces, named Chmelnitzki, seeking revenge for a personal injury by a Polish noble, did what many Ukrainian peasants would do when they grew tired of the oppression of the Poles—he ran away across the Dnieper River into the land as yet unconquered by the Poles. There he was welcomed by the free-roaming, hardriding, quarrelsome Ukrainians, known as Cossacks, who were always ready to go on a marauding expedition into Poland. Chmelnitzki was able to unite their quarreling clans. He succeeded, moreover, in entering into an alliance with the Tatars who ruled over the Crimea and some territory between the Black and the Caspian Seas. Chmelnitzki announced that he would invade Poland in order to free the Ukrainians and avenge their cause against the Poles and Jews.

The Black Years—The decade beginning in 1648 was for the Jews of Poland what the fourteenth century had been for those of Germany, except that Poland now held more Jews than Germany two centuries before and that the Jews of Poland had fewer protectors. Because of the weakness of its central government, many months passed before Poland could put an army in the field, and even then treachery and disunion were rampant. The Chmelnitzki hordes and his Tatar allies penetrated deep into Polish territory before they were stopped and turned back. In the meantime the slaughter of the Jews went on in southern and eastern Poland. The first to meet their death were those living as overseers on Polish estates, for they were alone and cut off from escape. Best able to protect themselves were the Jews living in larger communities. By the side of the Poles they fought off Chmelnitzki as long as they could. But without military aid, the civil population could not withstand the siege and attack. Then the slaughter would begin, and it was usually indiscriminate of Poles or Jews. Sometimes the Christians of the town thought they could purchase their own safety with the blood of their Jewish neighbor. But the treacherous Polish population was spared no more than they had spared the Jews. Many Jews preferred to surrender to the Tatars, who were infinitely less cruel than the Cossacks and were satisfied to sell their captives into slavery. Three years passed before comparative peace was restored to the ravaged Ukraine, and the Jews who had fled were able to return.

Russians and Swedes—Poland's difficulties, moreover, did not end with the retirement of Chmelnitzki across the Dnieper; the weakness of the country attracted other conquerors. The provinces which had escaped the Chmelnitzki horrors, because they did not lie in the path of his march, now had their turn of terror and martyrdom. Lithuania was invaded by the Russians, so that the rising Jewish community of Vilna, for example, was temporarily scattered. The Swedes, on the other hand, who attacked from the north, acted as much like civilized beings as the nature of war permits. They even protected the Jews against the "gangster" elements within the Polish population. The result was that when, some years later, peace was re-established, the Poles accused the Jews of having been in league with Sweden. The pogroms from which they had been saved by the Swedes were loosed upon them by the Poles, their own neighbors.

Counting the Losses—When, after ten years of war, Poland had expelled all its enemies, it had an opportunity to take stock of its losses and make sure that its enemies would not again be attracted by its weakness. The Poles unfortunately did not learn much from the period of national horror and at once fell back into the internal disunity which was to cost Poland its life about a century later. At the end of these ten years the Jewish community of Poland also re-established itself; but the Jews could not possibly hope to attain the strength which had been theirs before the hurricane struck them. At the very least, one hundred thousand of them had been killed and almost all the rest impoverished.

The Council of Four Lands could hardly raise the taxes imposed by the government, let alone help the homeless and starving to resume a normal life. The number of orphans who had to be fed by the various communities alone presented an appalling task. The Council had to borrow money in the name of the Jewish community. It continued to borrow for the next hundred years. Large numbers sought refuge in Western lands, going as far as Holland, England and Alsace. Gloom and a sense of hopelessness weighed down the next generation in Poland, exceeding similar feelings of the German Jews of that age who had just gone through the Thirty Years' War. No wonder that the study of Cabala and of its practical applications, as taught by Rabbi Isaac Luria (Ari) in Palestine two generations before, seized hold of the Jewish mind everywhere, but particularly in southeastern Europe and Poland.

3. SABBETAI ZEVI

The Vision-Seeing Generation—Not only the Jews, but also a good many Christians to whom mysticism appealed, looked for the coming of the Messiah during that generation. Cabalists among the Jews had calculated that the messianic year would be 1648; Christians had fixed on the year 1666. All the misfortunes which came upon Central and Eastern Europe in that period served as so much proof that the messianic era was approaching, since the Messiah's arrival was to be preceded by war and pestilence. Men's minds were prepared for something unusual, especially the minds of the Jewish cabalists. Ready to be deluded, they fell victim to the most deluded among them.

The Makings of a Messiah—On the 9th of Ab of the year

RETREAT AND PROGRESS

1626, in the city of Smyrna, a son was born to a family of Spanish-Jewish origin, and he was named Sabbetai Zevi. The date is significant, for, according to an ancient Jewish legend, the Messiah's birth is connected with the date of the destruction of the Temple. The child was given the usual Jewish education. He had an exceptionally keen and receptive mind; but, on emerging from boyhood, he found less interest in talmudic study and more in the *Zohar* and its cabalistic commentaries. He had other personal gifts which proved to be important: he was handsome and he was a born leader. Before long, a group of young men crowded about him and he secretly initiated them into the mysteries of the Cabala. He looked upon himself and was looked upon by others as destined for very great things. He considered his thoughts too deep and his life too pure for marriage. Finally, when the year 1648 came, he boldly took the step which he had long been plotting and which was to mark him as being on terms of unusual familiarity with God. Standing before the Torah in the synagogue, Sabbetai Zevi pronounced the name of God as it is written, not as it is always spoken by Jews.

Years of Exile—Probably counting on the widespread expectations for the year 1648, Sabbetai Zevi meant this act to symbolize the opening of his messianic career. Shocked by the blasphemy, the leaders of the Smyrna community excommunicated him, and he was compelled to go elsewhere. Far from discrediting him, his bold actions and his claims, supported by evidence from cabalistic writings, won for him adherents wherever he went. Most of these were honest men anxious to believe; some were no doubt adventurers ready to take advantage of the credulity of the masses. Ever conscious of the value of dramatic actions, Sabbetai Zevi himself lost no opportunity to advance his cause. In the presence of learned men and cabalists in Salonika, he suddenly produced a marriage canopy and a scroll of the Torah, and went through a marriage ceremony with the Torah as his bride. Again his audience was more shocked than impressed, and Sabbetai Zevi was forced to wander further. For years he moved from place to place, looking for adherents, but biding his time till the next open stroke. In Cairo he finally found an environment fitted for his purpose.

The Revelation—The wealthy Raphael Joseph Chelebi supported in his home a number of pious followers of the teachings of the Ari. Sabbetai Zevi found a place among them and soon showed his personal and cabalistic superiority over them all. When Chelebi sent a mission to Jerusalem for the purpose of distributing charity, he picked Sabbetai Zevi. To the starving mystics of the Holy City, he appeared as literally a divine messenger. At this point in his life Sabbetai Zevi met Nathan of Gaza, a young man who claimed and was generally credited with possessing prophetic powers. Nathan, it is believed, actually suggested a messianic career to Sabbetai Zevi, who might otherwise have remained merely a dreamer. Nathan undertook to announce himself as a reincarnation of the Prophet Elijah and to spread the propaganda of Sabbetai Zevi as the messiah. The pious people of the Holy Land fell in with the idea, and this in turn corresponded to the mystical belief that the Messiah must first appear in Jerusalem. Upon Sabbetai Zevi's return to Cairo, Chelebi's group of mystics also supported his claims. At the same time another bold, dramatic stroke spread the news of the messiah's revelation. For several years the Jews of Europe had been hearing the story of a girl, named Sarah, whose parents had been murdered by the Chmelnitzki barbarians. She related that subsequently her dead father had kidnapped her from the nunnery where she was being brought up and had told her she was destined to be the bride of the Messiah. She wandered from one Jewish community to another, everywhere arousing the sympathy and obtaining the aid of the Jews. It was not surprising that Sabbetai Zevi, hearing of her, should invite Sarah to become his wife. The wedding was celebrated with great pomp at the home of Chelebi.

Hailing the Messiah—Provided with a rich patron in the person of Chelebi, with a wife who had predicted that she would marry the Messiah, with followers who represented the most respected mystics and the residents of Jerusalem, and even with a prophet, Nathan of Gaza, Sabbetai Zevi now entered upon his real activity. As the news spread among the downtrodden, helpless, miracle-hungry Jews of Europe, it was greeted with a frenzy of enthusiasm. At last the age of misery was coming to an end! People danced in wild exaltation; hysterical women prophesied, even the Sephardim of Amsterdam and Hamburg indulged in boundless joy. Many practical men of affairs hastily disposed of their possessions and laid in supplies for the journey to Palestine which, they believed, the Messiah would soon order them to undertake. One after another even Talmudists and former opponents of Sabbetai Zevi joined the ranks of his followers. The Christians of Europe stood by watching in wonder, by no means sure that it was all a delusion. After all, their own mystics had predicted messianic revelations for the year 1666.

Prison or Court—As the fateful year approached, Sabbetai Zevi was compelled to take some action. He announced that he was going to Constantinople where, at the mere sight of him, the sultan would give up his throne and Sabbetai Zevi would become king of kings. But when his ship, crowded with his followers, arrived at the Turkish port, Sabbetai Zevi was arrested and placed in a fortress at Abydus. The visit to the sultan would come later, Sabbetai Zevi announced. In the meantime he held regular court in the fortress within which he was free to move about. It looked as though the Turkish authorities themselves had put a castle at his command. Jews from Europe, Asia and Africa arrived in crowds to pay homage to the messiah. Sabbetai Zevi and his prophets issued commands and proclamations to the Jews all over the world.

The Sudden Fall—Among Sabbetai Zevi's proclamations was one directed to the Jews of Poland in which he promised them a great future and an end to their sorrows, and ordered them to send him a certain Nehemiah Cohen. This man was himself regarded as the prophet of a messiah who was still to come. Sabbetai Zevi wanted to convince him that there was no need for waiting; that he was that messiah. Nehemiah Cohen came to Abydus; he talked at length to Sabbetai Zevi; and he emerged from these discussions more sure than ever that Sabbetai Zevi was not the Messiah. For this disbelief Nehemiah's life was threatened by the zealous Sabbetians, and the Polish prophet could save himself only by running away to the Mohammedans and promising to join their religion. Upon Nehemiah Cohen's advice to the Turkish authorities, Sabbetai Zevi was finally taken before the sultan. The end came quickly. Challenged to prove his boast or suffer the death penalty, the would-be messiah abandoned all his claims and promises and, accepting a petty post in the sultan's court, even consented to become a Mohammedan.

Disillusionment—The event was a stunning blow to those Jews who had put all their faith and hope in the promise of miraculous deliverance. Not only were their hopes disappointed, but the one who had aroused them had gone over to another religion. Sabbetai Zevi and his immediate followers offered an explanation, of a piece with all of Sabbetai Zevi's attitudes and teachings. It claimed that, at the last moment, God had revealed to the messiah that the time was not yet ripe for redemption; there were still too many unbelievers, too many sins for which atonement had yet to be made. The messiah, therefore, had himself volunteered to go into exile among the Ishmaelites as a means of atoning for the people's sins and hastening the end of the exile. Some of Sabbetai Zevi's prophets argued further that the one who had become a Mohammedan was not Sabbetai Zevi at all, but a human image of him, whereas he himself had ascended to heaven to wait for a more opportune time. This mixture of Judaism, Mohammedanism and Christianity was actually accepted by a number of Sabbetai Zevi's followers. Indeed, they were so anxious to help him atone for the sins of the Jewish people as quickly as possible that they chose to follow him into "exile." They, too, joined Mohammedanism, not for the sake of Mohammedanism, but for the sake of Judaism. Eventually these converted Jews and their descendants, waiting for generations for the return of Sabbetai Zevi from exile, became a sect within the Mohammedan religion called the Donmeh. This, however, involved but a small portion of the disillusioned followers of the messiah. The rest turned sadly back to their ordinary tasks, angered and chagrined at the mystics who had misled them, and more ready to follow the level-headed Talmudists who had warned them against their enthusiasm.

Idealist or Charlatan—Jews have been trying ever since then to decide what kind of person Sabbetai Zevi had really been. It is easy to say that he was a scoundrel, willing to play on the needs and the hopes of his people in order to enjoy a brief period of glory. Certainly the cowardly end of his career lends color to such a view of him. But this is not necessarily the true interpretation of his character, for others incline to believe that he was the most misled of all his generation. His deep study of the Cabala and other mystical writings had caused him to find in himself the qualities needed for the mystical personality of the Messiah. A more recent view describes Sabbetai Zevi as a man of great charm and ability but suffering from a psychological ailment which subjected him to periods of depression and exaltation. Nathan of Gaza is represented as the one who, recognizing Sabbetai Zevi's weakness, used him as a tool. Whichever view of Sabbetai Zevi one takes, it must be admitted that the influence of his career was enormous. We must recognize the fact that, if only for one or two years, he gave hope and self-esteem to a most unfortunate generation. At the same time, he left among the Jews certain attitudes, for good as well as for evil, which are inseparable from the history of the Jews in the generations which followed.

4. A LEGACY OF DREAMS AND FEARS

Sabbetianism—With his conversion Sabbetai Zevi disappeared from the scene of Jewish life. It was too much to expect, however, that the hopes he had stirred should be soon forgotten or that fears should not arise lest other false messiahs awaken similar hopes and again disrupt and confuse Jewish life. The leaders of Jewish life, therefore, undertook to guard the talmudical and legal ramparts of Judaism and to suppress any further manifestation of overemphasized mysticism. These defenders of Judaism did not realize that Sabbetai Zevi would never have risen so high if Jewish fortunes had not previously sunk so low. The next century witnessed a tug of war between Rabbinism and Mysticism, until, Sabbetianism having been eradicated, both forgot their differences in the need to fight a new, common danger.

Misguiders and Misguided—For the next two generations a crop of false prophets and men who claimed to be successors to Sabbetai Zevi wandered through Europe, North Africa and Palestine, each with a message more bizarre than the others. Each would obtain a hearing among the Jewish people, until someone recognized the destructive implications of his teachings. The prophet or messiah would then be excommunicated and, frequently thereupon, would lead his followers either to Mohammedanism or Christianity. The most rascally of these was one named Jacob Querido, who proclaimed himself the son of Sabbetai Zevi. He announced that in him Sabbetai Zevi's soul continued its messianic career. Excommunicated in various Jewish communities, he and his followers joined Mohammedanism. Nehemiah Hiyya Hayun, a good scholar and persuasive preacher, was even more dangerous. He traveled through Western Europe advocating a type of Judaism very close to Christianity.

Moses Hayyim Luzzatto—Unfortunately the rabbis who fought the danger of Sabbetian heresy were unable to distinguish between proper and improper types of mysticism. Deeply concerned with the survival of the Jewish group, they struck at everyone who made Cabala rather than Talmud the basis of his study. Moses Hayyim Luzzatto was the innocent victim of this suspicious attitude. He was born in 1707 in Padua, Italy, where the Jews had never been quite as completely separated from the Christians as in other parts of Europe. He was given a good talmudical training, with greater emphasis placed on the Bible. Moses Hayyim early showed inclinations to poetry. Even as a very young man, at the age of sixteen, he began writing secular verse in pure, biblical Hebrew, something which had not been done for many generations. His themes were moralizing dramas in which the human virtues and vices were personified. The poet in him soon saw deeper meaning in Judaism as set forth in the *Zohar* and in the writings of Ari than in the writings of the Talmudists. A group of young men gathered around him and he expounded to them his theories on the mystical effects of good and evil actions and on the part assigned by God to the Jewish people in the redemption of the world. His teachings were so attractive that some of his pupil-friends could not hide their enthusiasm. As a result, the overcautious rabbis took him to task. He tried to prove that his teachings had nothing to do with Sabbetianism, but were grounded in good Jewish doctrine. But the rabbis refused to take chances with a young man, attractive and convincing, a natural leader of religious thought, who dealt in mystical terms. They forbade him to write and eventually they burned those of his writings which he had left with them. He moved with his family to Amsterdam where he earned his livelihood by teaching. Though continuing to write and to correspond with his friends, Moses Hayyim Luzzatto no longer had the opportunity to exert any great influence. He hoped to regain his importance when he resumed his mystical writings and teaching, after settling in Palestine upon reaching the age of forty. But he died soon after his arrival in the Holy Land in 1747.

A Lost Opportunity—This personal tragedy proved also a misfortune for Jewish life. Judaism needed a mystical revival, especially an explanation of Jewish suffering, so as to provide hope and fortitude to those whom intellectualism alone did not satisfy. Luzzatto might have led such a movement, and his leadership might have stamped the revival with the richness of his own wide culture and deep spirituality. With him gone, the revival took place anyway, but on a lower plane and devoid of cultural foundations. What Moses Hayyim Luzzatto did leave behind proved, nevertheless, to be of great importance. In the first place, he revived the use of the Hebrew language for purposes of secular literature, such as drama. Secondly, he left behind a most charming ethical work, called *Mesillat Yesharim* (The Path of the Righteous). Good conduct, Luzzatto thought, is the road to God; but, in order to find out what good conduct is, one must study and then try to follow the guidance offered by sage and saint. This was good Jewish doctrine and it was no wonder that it became popular among the Jews. Unfortunately the living personality of the author was no longer there to expound it further and to spread it.

The Frankist Heresy—The yearning for an emotional interpretation of Judaism was illustrated anew by the success of an adventurer who almost brought misfortune upon all the Jews of Poland. About 1740 Jacob Frank appeared in southern Poland, after having wandered through southeastern Europe and absorbed some of the peculiar doctrines of the secret Sabbetian heretics still to be found there. He claimed to be the reincarnation of Sabbetai Zevi, and announced that the time of redemption would come after the people had sated all the evil within them, so that they could no longer be tempted. By such strange doctrines Jacob Frank reversed the demands of all religion. Reports spread about wild and immoral orgies indulged in by his followers. Naturally, the Jewish population was shocked and drove him and his followers from one town after another. Frank and his group, in revenge, became converts to Catholicism and revived the ancient accusations against the Talmud. Eventually Frank was forced to leave Poland, not because of the Jews, but because the Catholics doubted his Christian orthodoxy. For years he and his daughter lived in lordly style in a small German town. All his crimes and impostures failed to deprive him of sympathy among some Jews in southeastern Europe. He, however, was the last one to meet with some success by invoking the name of Sabbetai Zevi. Another movement arose to answer the spiritual needs of the people.

CHAPTER VI

TWO GIANTS OF THE SPIRIT

TWO GREAT MEN ATTEMPT TO RESTORE BALANCE TO JEWISH LIFE

Reason and Emotion—The Jews of Europe, at the end of the seventeenth century and the beginning of the eighteenth, still labored under the effects of the misfortunes they had suffered. Their prolonged imprisonment in the ghettos of Central Europe would alone have been enough to cause their spirit to break; the devastation during the Thirty Years' War depressed them further. In the lands farther east, the ten years during which fire and sword had ravaged the Jews were followed by generations which could foresee no escape from the hate and poverty around them. The Jew of the eighteenth century felt that the Judaism to which he had fallen heir was not giving him the same spiritual strength and comfort which it had given his ancestors. He did not, of course, admit this feeling openly, but the criticism was implied in his willingness to follow teachers with strange ideas and stranger promises, in his adoption of new religious cults and in his grumbling against the communal leadership. Intellectually and emotionally the Jews of that day were sorely bewildered.

About the middle of the eighteenth century two religious leaders arose among the Jews of Eastern Europe who attempted to restore equilibrium to the mass of their people. The two men were as different from one another as two people could possibly be; but both were earnest, saintly and devoted to their people and its faith. Each one saw the problem facing his generation from a point of view characteristic of himself. One of them, the Gaon Elijah of Vilna, tried to restore vigor and balance to Jewish intellectual activity. The other, Israel of the Good Name, tried to redirect the flow of emotion toward deeper and purer religious worship. Each of the two left an important spiritual legacy which their followers, unfortunately, did not always keep untarnished.

1. Escaping a Hard Life

The Background—At the bottom of all the problems which beset the Jews was the determined and persistent hatred which surrounded them. The Polish state, due to its internal weaknesses, was in dissolution. Its kings could obtain no power; its parliament could arrive at no decision; many of its princes were in the pay of Poland's enemies; its peasants were oppressed. At such a time the middle class and the clergy found nothing better to do than indulge in persecutions of the Jews, then desperately trying to heal the wounds inflicted upon them during the terrible decade between 1648 and 1658. The Jews sought to re-establish an economic basis for their life, to reorganize their communities, to revive their schools. At every turn their enemies thwarted them. The

Christian middle class envied every morsel of bread won by
the Jewish merchant or artisan, and it succeeded in obtaining
laws restricting Jewish trade and industry. The result was un-
imaginable poverty among the Jews, a poverty which ground
down their bodies and depressed their spirits.

Allied with the middle class was the lower clergy, who
used the unreligious method of inventing cases of ritual murder in order to arouse the religious frenzy of their people.
Never was this inhuman accusation made so frequently as in
Poland during the first half of the eighteenth century. Things
reached such a pass that the Council of Four Lands dispatched a special *shtadlan*, Jacob Zelig, to Rome to complain
to the pope. Somehow Jacob Zelig succeeded in reaching the
ear of Pope Benedict XIV, who appointed Cardinal Ganganelli to investigate the matter. Several years later Ganganelli
made his report. He called the ritual murder charge un-
proved, foolish and vicious. The Polish clergy did not cease
making the accusation, nevertheless, even after Ganganelli
himself became pope, as Clement XIV. The atmosphere
around the Jews continued to be charged with hate and violence.

In the Land of Books—Such was the world in which the
Polish Jew had to seek ordinary human happiness; obviously
he could not find it there. For the Jew, however, this was not
a fatal situation since there was another world into which he
could retire and where his happiness was assured, namely, the
world of the spirit, the realm of Jewish literature. Consequently, it is not surprising that in the northern part of Poland, and more particularly in Lithuania, where economic life
was hardest, the ideal of Jewish learning developed to its full-
est. Every man's ambition was to become a thorough student
of the Talmud and its complex and difficult commentaries.
Every moment of leisure from the intense struggle for a bare
living was spent in the acquisition of knowledge and in endless friendly disputation over the ancient books. Such study,
in fact, not only brought forgetfulness of pain and sorrow,
but also restored to the Jew the dignity of which his persecutors sought to rob him.

Learning in South Poland—Obviously, not everybody even
in these districts was able to maintain the necessary mental
pace. In the southern part of the country there was less intellectualism, except among the rabbis. The Jews of the south,
more joyful by temperament, were not so given to sustained
study. Yet their situation, too, was by no means a happy one.
They also lived under conditions of economic restriction and

social ostracism. A good many lived scattered through the estates of the nobles, feeling themselves to be a foreign element among the antagonistic population and longing for greater contact with Jewish life. Among these inhabitants of farm districts—*yishuvniks*, as they were called—Jewish knowledge was slight. The emphasis was upon ritual rather than study, on imagination rather than information.

In the Land of the Imagination—For this reason two personalities, apart from the rabbis, became prominent in the life of the Jewish population: the *maggid* and the *ba'al shem*. The official preachers, or *maggidim*, expounded the teachings of Judaism on morals and ethics. Many of them were men of extensive knowledge; others, especially those who traveled from small town to small town, were not far above the common people in their attitudes. Their sermons were based on emotion and mysticism rather than on learning. Even more influential than the *maggidim* were the exorcisers of evil spirits. Claiming knowledge of the manners and habits of the demons and the wandering souls, these men, and sometimes women, distributed amulets, offered up magic prayers, healed sickness by the laying on of hands, and even attempted to predict the future. Such a dealer in practical magic was known as a "master of the name," in Hebrew *ba'al shem*, for by his acquaintance with the names of angels and demons he could force them to do his will.

2. Reaching for God

Education of a Saint—In Okop, province of Podolia, about the year 1700, a son was born to a certain Eliezer and his wife. The child was named Israel. Within a few years both parents died and the boy was brought up as the ward of the small Jewish community. While Israel acquired some knowledge of Hebrew and Judaism, he was not of the studious type; he preferred to wander through the neighboring fields and forests. Eventually, the community felt that it had done its duty by him and that the boy would have to shift for himself. He went to the larger town near by and became assistant to a teacher of young children, guiding them to and from *heder* and rehearsing the alphabet with them. In time he set himself up independently as a teacher of beginners. While he never had any reputation for scholarship, he was distinguished for his quiet manners and pious life. He married a woman of good family, sister of a prominent scholar of those parts. But his brother-in-law was ashamed of Israel, whom he considered an ignoramus. This, together with the inner urge to be close to nature, prompted Israel to move to a lonely hut somewhere in the Carpathian mountains. He and his wife earned a bare livelihood from the sale of lime which they dug from the mountainside. Israel, however, now had time to delve deep into the literature of mysticism to which he had always been drawn. After a number of years spent in this way, Israel and his wife returned to a settled community. With the financial assistance of her brother, she opened a small inn; Israel resumed teaching Jewish children. Gradually he acquired a reputation as a *ba'al shem,* a "master of the name."

The Fame of the Master—Israel was thirty-six years old when he began to minister to the emotional needs of the Jews in his neighborhood. People would come to him, as to other *ba'alei shem,* for amulets and benedictions, for advice and cheering prophecies in times of personal trouble. Probably his ministrations were no better and no worse than those of similar mystics. The people, however, felt the piety and simplicity of the man. He had deeper faith and therefore inspired greater confidence. Soon it became known far and wide that a real mystic had revealed himself, and he was called Master of a Good Name, or *Ba'al Shem Tov.* Now people began to revere him and to flock to him and to hang on his words. The greatness of the man is evident from the fact that his rise from obscurity to fame did not spoil him. On the contrary, he made use of his opportunity to teach, no longer the elements of Hebrew, but the elements of religious faith; and to minister, no longer to individuals, but to the entire, sorely tried Jewish community.

Teachings of the Master—Israel possessed extraordinary gifts of speech and imagination. He would gather friends and visitors about him and quietly discourse on the subject of the relations between God and man. He did not possess the arts of the orator nor the subtleties of the scholar. He did possess the power of illustrating his ideas with simple examples from everyday life. What he taught was Judaism; but what he emphasized were the heart and the hopes of man. The first duty of man was to seek God and to identify himself with God's purposes. This he argued was not too difficult, because God was everywhere in the universe and the pious man need only learn to break through the coarse externals of the world in order to find its Soul. For this, great learning is not needed nor a multiplicity of prayers. Simple prayers, uttered with one's whole heart, are enough. Moreover, self-affliction and gloom are not the ways to come closer to the Divine; joy and lightness of heart are more effective stimulants to prayer. Most people, however, are incapable of approaching God in this way; their earthly life weighs them down. They need an example and a guide. Now there are men in every generation who are capable of just such spiritual leadership and these righteous men *(tzaddikim)* must be recognized and highly treasured. Thus Israel's teachings may be summarized as the search for God, the effectiveness of prayer, joyful living and spiritual leadership.

3. The Rise of Hasidism

Israel's Legacy—Nothing in what Israel of the Good Name taught was new to Judaism; he merely gave added emphasis to ideas which had been current for centuries, especially among Jewish mystics. His teachings, however, now took hold of the Jewish population of southeastern Europe and spread with remarkable speed. For he offered the lower middle class and the masses of Jews a means of escaping from the inferior position in which they had been held by their wealthy or learned fellow Jews. He emphasized humility on the part of the student and an all-embracing sense of brotherhood on the part of the men of means. Moreover, he tried to dispel the gloom which had descended upon Jewish life during the previous trouble-filled century. His followers therefore glorified Rabbi Israel and told stories about the miracles he performed. His name, *Ba'al Shem Tov,* was abbreviated into *Besht;* his every word was remembered and treasured; he was thought to be in direct communication with the heavenly powers, the defender of the Jewish people before the Throne of God.

The Besht's Biography—The Besht left no writings. His ideas were preserved in the minds of those who had come in contact with him and in notes jotted down by some of them. One of these, Rabbi Jacob Joseph, gave currency to many of the Besht's teachings in a book which he published after the death of the Besht (about 1760). Other admirers related miraculous tales about him which became magnified and multiplied with each telling by subsequent biographers. Nevertheless, the Besht's personality and the essentials of his doctrine shine through this mass of material. A heroic and legendary figure was thus created, a source of inspiration to succeeding generations.

The Maggid of Meseritch—One of the disciples won by the Besht in his late years was Rabbi Ber, a learned man who had been a maggid, or itinerant public preacher. While Jacob Joseph spread the tales of wonder and piety connected with the Besht's life, the Maggid continued the Besht's religious instruction. He became the center of a group similar to that which the master had gathered about himself. Being more scholarly than the Besht had been, the Maggid was able to provide the Besht's religious teachings with a firmer foundation in traditional Jewish learning and in the writings of former mystics. His chief contribution was the training of a number of men who carried on the idea and became the leaders of the next generation.

Tzaddikism—The weakest spot in the teachings of the Besht and the Maggid turned out to be their advocacy of a personal leadership. Judaism had never known of an intermediary between God and man. Neither learning nor official position qualified a man to claim that he could bring salvation to another. A rabbi might be a teacher or serve as an example, but was not regarded as an instrument or a favorite of the Almighty. The masses of southeastern Europe, however, were so troubled and so humble, so anxious to be near God and so convinced of the ability of some people to prophesy and work miracles, that they grasped at this notion of spiritual leadership as expounded by the Besht and the Maggid. The pupils of the Maggid and the descendants of the Besht were therefore accepted as leaders in various Jewish communities and districts, where they actually replaced the rabbis or at least received greater loyalty. Such men came to be known as *tzaddikim* (singular—*tzaddik*), or "righteous men." They held court and gave personal advice. They offered religious instruction and guidance in piety. They formed the center of the people's social life. The spacious home of the *tzaddik*, visits to which were encouraged, provided an opportunity for comradeship for which the common people, at least the men, had long hungered and which they had been unable to find in the rather austere atmosphere of the house of study. The next step was for the people to assume that the special favor which a *tzaddik* enjoyed with God was due, not so much to his learning and piety, as to his person. A *tzaddik*, moreover, was considered able to transmit his standing and ability to his son or another member of his family; and, as a result, regular dynasties of *tzaddikim* came into being, some of them lasting to this day.

Hasidim and Hasidism—The followers of the *tzaddikim* were known as *hasidim* (singular—*hasid*). The word *hasid* means "pious man," and was probably assumed by these people because they claimed that theirs was the true interpretation of Judaism, and that the way of those Jews who refused to follow a *tzaddik* and who laid greater emphasis on study than on prayer, on intellect than on emotion, was lacking in piety. The Jews in Eastern Europe thus became divided into two groups, Hasidim and Mithnagdim (opponents), which grew more hostile to each other from day to day. Hasidism's appeal to the masses caused it to spread rapidly, especially in the southern provinces of Poland. The northern provinces, on the other hand, with their stronger tradition of intellectualism, remained loyal to Rabbinism of the traditional type. Yet even here this loyalty was retained only after a struggle; for the masses would have succumbed to the attractive features of Hasidism had not the powerful personality of Elijah, Gaon of Vilna, stemmed the tide.

4. The Gaon

An Extraordinary Personality—Around the year 1700 the Jewish community of the Lithuanian city of Vilna stood in the forefront of learning and saintliness. Nowhere was knowledge so highly prized and piety and scholarship so widespread. A son was born in 1720 to one of the distinguished families in this distinguished community. He was named Elijah and turned out to be a prodigy. At the age of six he had completed the study of the Bible and was deep in the Talmud. By thirteen he had mastered most rabbinic and mystical literature. As he grew older, various opportunities presented themselves to occupy important rabbinic posts, including that of his native city. But he steadfastly refused to undertake the responsibilities of the active rabbinate. He preferred to live on a meager stipend left him in a relative's will, so that he might have more time for study. His reputation, however, grew despite his seclusion and before long he was recognized as the unofficial spiritual head of all the communities of Eastern Europe. He came to be referred to as "the Gaon." Long ago, in Babylonia, the word had been applied to the heads of the academies; here it was used to describe a man who, in intellect and piety, towered above his fellows.

The Gaon's Views—The Goan Elijah recognized that all was not well with the Jewish life of his day, but he considered the remedy offered by the Besht unworthy of Judaism. Faith, hope and the joy of worship, which seemed all-important to Hasidism, he took for granted as by-products of Jewish study and of living as a Jew. The real problem was to remove from the Jewish mind whatever hindered its complete development, so that the joy of study and pious observance might counterbalance all the evils which the outside world imposed upon the Jews. The Gaon was an intellectual aristocrat. He would not modify traditional Judaism's attitude toward study in order to suit the masses and their needs; rather he demanded that the masses change themselves so as to find an answer to their needs in living the traditional Jewish life.

The Reforms—There were, nevertheless, three aspects of Jewish life in his day which the Gaon did attempt to modify. He tried to simplify the prayers by the removal of many *piyyutim*. Poems almost unintelligible to the majority of the people, distinguished for their cleverness rather than their spirituality, had long filled the holiday prayer books. The Gaon established a synagogue in which such *piyyutim* were eliminated. The study of the Talmud had, as we have seen, become characterized by argumentation which shed little light on the actual text. The Gaon taught the few students who gathered about him to avoid such useless show of mental agility and to concentrate on the true meaning and applicability of rabbinic statements. Later, Rabbi Hayyim, one of these pupils, established the famous *yeshibah* of Volozhin, where teaching was done according to the ideas of the Gaon. Finally, the Gaon felt that Jewish learning had excluded too much of the secular knowledge which could be helpful in understanding the world as well as Judaism. He had no objection to the acquisition of general information, provided such information could be used to dignify life and broaden understanding, especially if it helped in the study of Jewish lore. The Gaon urged one of his pupils, who apparently knew German, to translate Euclid's *Geometry,* for example, which he felt ought to be studied by Jews.

The Gaon's Influence—There can be no doubt that, if there had been time for the Gaon's influence to penetrate the life of the people, many problems would have been avoided which subsequently plagued the Jews of Eastern Europe. His influence was not as spectacular as that of the Besht. Moreover, it came too late. During his lifetime forces were already at work which were destined to transform the world and profoundly affect the life of the Jews. In one respect, however, his influence was powerful and immediate. He saw danger in the spread of Hasidism and he set bounds to it which it was not able to overcome.

5. THE CONFLICT WITH HASIDISM

Hasidic Rebellion—The Gaon looked upon the hasidic movement as heresy. To minimize the value of Jewish learning, for common people to make changes in Jewish prayer, for men whose scholarship was second-rate, like the Maggid and his pupils to set themselves up as *tzaddikim* and claim the reverence of the people—all these were breaches of tradition which the Gaon believed had to be suppressed. The Mithnagdim failed to see that Hasidism was an expression of the need of the masses for a simple religion of warmth and feeling which they could understand despite their comparative lack of education. The Mithnagdim saw only that Hasidism was destroying learning, dignity and tradition, and mixed public worship with shocking exhibitions of frivolity. It derided talmudic study, but considered the most childish expressions of mysticism holy. At the same time, some of the *tzaddikim*, who were thrusting the ordained rabbis into the background, brought shame upon the entire movement by scheming for lucrative positions. Many of these faults did not become apparent till later. It was clear, however, even before the death of the Maggid, that Hasidism was a movement against the aristocracy of learning as well as of wealth, a rebellion against the constituted authorities of both the community and the *yeshibah*.

The War of the Sects—Elijah Gaon was shocked by reports from the southern provinces. Moreover, before long the movement spread into Lithuania, the stronghold of Rabbinism. In the city of Minsk, and even in Vilna, the Hasidim organized secret synagogues where they followed the ritual of the new sect and expressed sentiments hostile to the communal leaders, the rabbis and the Gaon himself. When this was found out, the leading Hasidim of Vilna were compelled to undergo public penance and see their writings burned. Immediately thereafter, in the spring of 1772, a meeting of rabbis was held and a resolution adopted excommunicating the entire sect.

The Battle of Words—The chief result of the decree of excommunication was to increase bitterness. In the southern provinces of Poland, where Hasidism was strongest, the Mithnagdim suffered the same social and economic persecution which the Hasidim were experiencing in the northern provinces. Pamphlets and accusations began to circulate thick and fast. In Lithuania the spread of the movement was arrested, but it continued to live in secret. The climax was reached at the time of the Gaon's death, in 1796. It became known that, at the very time when his decease was being mourned by Jews everywhere, a group of Hasidim in Vilna had indulged in a celebration. This enraged the Mithnagdim. At the grave of the Gaon they vowed not to rest until they exterminated the new sect. A second and even stricter excommunication was now pronounced against the Hasidim and all their friends. It looked as though East European Jewry had suffered an irreparable breach.

Attempts at Peace—Among the Hasidim there were a number of men who recognized the danger in the situation and, while adhering to the general principles of the Besht, tried to guide Hasidism back into the ways of traditional Judaism. The Maggid himself had been pained by the antics of his more extreme followers. At his death, which occurred soon after the first excommunication, one of his foremost pupils tried hard to make peace between the two groups. Rabbi Shneor-Zalman of Ladi had received a thorough rabbinic training before coming under the Maggid's influence. Since he possessed profound talmudic knowledge and a wide acquaintance with mystical literature, he could appreciate the attitudes of both factions. Joy in the service of God was essential, Shneor-Zalman argued on the side of Hasidism; but he pointed out the obvious fact that such joy was derived by men who devote themselves to study. A religious leader ought to be an expert in Jewish law and a teacher of rabbinic literature, he argued in agreement with the Mithnagdim; but he ought not keep aloof from people in a personal way, even if they are ignorant, since it is his task to bring all Jews closer to God. In pursuing a middle-of-the-road policy, Rabbi Shneor-Zalman urged the modification of hasidic ideas by saying that Hasidism should be based on Wisdom (*Hokmah*), Understanding (*Binah*) and Knowledge (*Deah*). Since not all Hasidim adopted his attitude, his group became known by the combined first letters of these three requirements, *HaBaD*, and was looked upon as the intellectual group in

Hasidism. In his main effort, however, to restore peace, Rabbi Shneor-Zalman failed.

Unfriendly Peace—Though hostility between the Hasidim and the Mithnagdim did not cease, the bitterness of the conflict gradually wore off. It became apparent to the Mithnagdim that Hasidism was not aiming at the destruction of Judaism; and it became clear to the Hasidim that the Mithnagdim were not sinners and oppressors. Actual conflict stopped when both groups recognized, early in the nineteenth century, that a common enemy was threatening them equally. This common enemy was the so-called Enlightenment *(Haskalah)* which was beginning to gain adherents among the youth of both camps. A purely external fact also contributed to the cessation of hostilities. While the war of words was at its height, the kingdom of Poland disappeared. Many of the strongly hasidic provinces were taken over by Austria, while the districts where Mithnagdim prevailed went to Russia. Divided between two governments and two different cultures, faced with internal political and economic problems of a dissimilar nature, the two groups continued to look askance at one another, but with ever decreasing hostility.

The Legacy of Hasidism—Even while the conflict was at its height Hasidism continued to expand. Among the *tzaddikim* were men, like Levi Yitzhak of Berditchev, of such saintly character and profound homely wisdom that their very existence added spirituallity to hasidic life and luster to Judaism in general. Others, like Rabbi Nahman of Bratzlav, possessed a remarkable gift for telling stories and parables which became the spiritual heritage of all Israel. To be sure, there were among the *tzaddikim,* or *rebbes*—as they came to be known to distinguish them from the rabbis—some whose chief function was "miracle-working." They developed a court about themselves and lived off the fat of the land from the contributions of their poor adherents. These were the men who gave Hasidism a bad reputation and who were the butt of jokes by the Mithnagdim. Actually, however, such *rebbes* were a small minority. Generally speaking, the *rebbes* were pious men and inspiring leaders, who kept alive the hopes of Israel and the beauties of Jewish life at a time when these were endangered by the new currents of the nineteenth century.

CHAPTER VII

PRIVILEGED AND DISDAINED

THE JEWS OF CENTRAL EUROPE SLOWLY REBUILD THEIR
OWN LIFE AND ALSO HELP TO IMPROVE THE ECONOMIC
SITUATION OF THE LANDS IN WHICH THEY LIVE

New Hopes Within the Ghetto—While Hasidism was rising in Eastern Europe and causing a rift within the large Jewish population living there, the Jews of Central Europe were gradually finding a place in the economic life of their homelands. They were being called out of the ghetto-prisons to help rebuild the lands ravaged by the Thirty Years' War. In return a few of them received the thanks of the rulers, and many others obtained some slight relief from poverty and restriction; but of complete freedom there was as yet no sign. The Christian population continued in its accustomed hostility, despite the new ideas which were slowly spreading among the more cultured classes. Then, even while the ideas of the Besht and the Gaon were answering the needs of the Jews of Eastern Europe, Moses Mendelssohn advanced a plan which he believed corresponded to the needs of those of Central Europe. He, too, sought to revive and restore the Jewish spirit, weighted down by evils and benumbed by the cold hostility which surrounded it. Unfortunately, his methods failed. For his plans depended more than he imagined upon the cooperation of the non-Jews, and such cooperation was not forthcoming in sufficient measure.

1. JEWS AS AN ECONOMIC INSTRUMENT

The Germanies of 1650—Central Europe emerged from the calamity of the Thirty Years' War greatly diminished in population, badly disorganized economically and more than ever broken up into tiny political states. The largest of these states was Austria, whose king was usually also emperor of the so-called Holy Roman Empire, though his powers as emperor were purely nominal. The next in size was Prussia, whose ruler, about 1700, changed his title of elector to that of king. Then there were literally hundreds of almost independent principalities, cities, bishoprics. The head of each of these, or its group of ruling patricians, exercised authority with few limitations, the common people having no say whatever in the government. Few of the rulers, moreover, had any idea of how to improve the economic situation of their people. Their interests were confined to taxing, conducting war and living in as grand a style as possible. Against this background profound changes were imperceptibly affecting the life of the Jews.

New Economic Methods—The rulers were not the only ones blindly interested in their own authority and income; the burghers were equally bound to the old ways of doing things and feared the slightest change in the methods of commerce and industry. Their guilds regulated everything, from the price of the smallest article to the rights of succession in any business enterprise, whether it was to be the older son or younger son or son-in-law of the owner. Whatever advantages such a closed system offered were more than offset by the impossibility for trade to make any progress. England and Holland had broken with these old-fashioned methods and were rising rapidly in wealth and power, while the rest of Europe was standing still. Alone among the princes of the Continent, Frederick William, elector of Prussia (1640–1688), saw the need for reforming the economic conditions of his country by breaking the stranglehold of the guilds. Strong and capable, also brutal, cunning and ruthless, this man gained for himself the title of "Great Elector" because he started Prussia on the road to military and political power. This power derived from the changes he forced in the economic order of his lands.

Guilds and Jews—As one of the means to achieve his ends, the Great Elector made use of the Jews. Despite the destructive results of the Thirty Years' War, the burghers did not slacken their vigilance and, whenever there was the slightest suspicion of competition by Jews, the guilds bestirred themselves to force the Jews out of the occupation involved. In this situation the Great Elector now began to play a shrewd game. He granted the Jews certain trading privileges, now in one locality, now in another. The guilds, on behalf of the burghers, reacted by making vigorous protest. Then the elector would use the privileges of the Jews to bargain with the burghers, either to gain greater authority for himself or to make some change in the general economic situation. That this giving and taking back of privileges caused hardship for the Jews was apparently the least of his concerns; their protests went completely unheeded. Nevertheless, the elector's effort to strengthen the economic position of his state did have a beneficial effect on the Jews. They became increasingly interested in international commerce, in the trade among the various small German states, in the many opportunities for wholesale trading and in the manufacturing of new articles which the guilds, in their unprogressiveness, had been neglecting. The Jews of the late seventeenth century did for the economic welfare of the Germany of their day what their ancestors had done for the same part of the world a thousand years before. Their commerce and industry made life easier for the masses of the population and helped Germany recover from the destructive effects of the Thirty Years' War.

Regulating Jewry—The people however, refused to see any connection between the improved situation and the economic activity of the Jews. They preferred to listen to the complaints of the burghers that the Jews were taking away profits which would otherwise have gone into the pockets of Christians. Such accusations were wholly false and economically unjustified. Nevertheless, no improvement was made in the conditions under which the Jews lived; and, in this respect, the Great Elector was not ahead of his people. The ghetto regulations were continued in force and many localities stood on their old privilege of excluding Jews altogether. The right of residence was restricted in many towns to the oldest son, while the remaining children had to seek homes elsewhere as they came of age. Jews could not cross any of the numerous boundaries within Germany without paying a degrading tax, as though they were so many head of cattle. Taxes were as heavy as ever. Some slight opportunity was given to Jews to participate in the cultural advances being made by a small portion of the general population by opening to them the University of Frankfort on the Oder.

2. THEY WHO PUT THEIR TRUST IN PRINCES

Privileged Jews—A small number of Jews played, during this period, a particularly interesting and significant role. It became customary for the princes of Germany to make use of a Jew as private financial adviser.* The very helplessness

* See above, pp. 423–4.

of the Jew made him more trustworthy. The emperor, king or duke well knew that the Jew was always in his personal power, the Jew's life and property depending on the caprice of the ruler. For any one or for all of these reasons there was hardly a ruler without his court Jew. To this one Jew and his family a number of privileges were usually granted. He had rights of residence anywhere within the state and the right to travel without being hampered by restrictions which were imposed on other Jews. He was free from interference by any guild regulations. What is more, his family and employees enjoyed some of these privileges, so that in this way a number of towns where Jews had long been forbidden to reside now saw the beginnings of new Jewish communities. Berlin was one such city. When the Jews were expelled from Vienna in 1670, the Great Elector picked from among the refugees the most capable financially and invited them to settle in his capital, where Jews had not been permitted to set foot in more than a century.

Samuel Oppenheimer—The life of a court Jew is best portrayed in the dramatic story of Samuel Oppenheimer of Vienna. Only a few years after the Jews had been expelled from the city, on the ground that their presence was harmful to Christianity, the emperor invited Samuel Oppenheimer to come and settle there. Throughout the costly wars which Austria was then carrying on against Turkey, Oppenheimer provided the supplies for the army. He proved so efficient as to be praised by the generals and by the emperor himself. Around him his retainers built up a new Jewish community, for Samuel came of a prominent and loyal Jewish family. But his very success and honesty soon stirred up against him the ill will of the leading churchmen. Their attempts to dislodge him proved vain, not only because the emperor was deeply in debt to Oppenheimer, but also because no Christian could be found with equal ability and an equal willingness to take risks. In the end, however, the patience of Oppenheimer's enemies was rewarded. A minor riot broke out around Oppenheimer's home in 1701. Was it mere accident that his house was set on fire, destroying most of the financier's business records? Thereupon the churchman who was acting for the emperor called upon the Oppenheimers to produce proof of the debts due them from the state. Since this could no longer be done, the state produced its records of money paid to Oppenheimer. It was thus "proved" that Oppenheimer had been overpaid. All the services he had performed for the emperor and the state were forgotten and the Jew was rewarded by being thrown into prison while his family was left penniless.

Other Grandees—This was not an isolated instance of ingratitude. A distant relative of Samuel Oppenheimer's, Joseph Suess Oppenheimer, suffered a similar fate a generation later. For several years he had been court Jew to the Duke of Wuerttemberg. But upon the duke's death, Joseph's enemies gained the upper hand and had him hanged. Other court Jews were more fortunate. Some years after Samuel Oppenheimer's death, a nephew of his, Samson Wertheimer, became the foremost banker in Austria and Hungary. He was a great favorite at the Austrian court and was appointed chief rabbi of Hungary, which meant that all Jewish affairs of that kingdom were under his control.

Jews and Court Jews—The court Jew's position gave him enormous influence over the Jews of his state or city. Sometimes such a man became the leader of the Jewish community, though he may not have had the necessary intellectual or spiritual qualities. Frequently the influence of the court Jew helped to protect his less fortunate brethren against attack and accusation. On the other hand, when such favorites lost the political game, their private misfortunes had a disastrous effect on their fellow Jews who were in no way involved with them. Thus the Jewish communities always shared the evil even though they may never have shared the good. Sometimes the selfish interests of a court Jew prompted him to work against the interests of other Jews. Israel Aron of Berlin, for example, court Jew of the Great Elector, at first tried to stop the admittance of the Viennese exiles. Later he warned the elector against "bad Jews," meaning no doubt Jews likely to compete with him in business. Still later, he and other privileged Jews of Prussia stood out against permission for Polish Jews to enter the country. On the other hand, Baron Diego d'Aguilar, a favorite at the Viennese court and the organizer of the Austrian tobacco monopoly, used his influence to establish a Sephardi community in Vienna and to save the Jews of the city from expulsion by Empress Maria Theresa.

3. Cultural Barrenness

Germans and German Jewish Culture—One of the worst results of the Thirty Years' War was the setback German culture suffered for at least a century. In neighboring France, literature and philosophy flourished; in Germany there was little evidence of such cultural activity till the second half of the eighteenth century. The like was true of Jewish culture. The days when the German rabbinate stood at the forefront of Jewish intellectual life were over. The ghetto imprisonment, the impoverishment, the terrors of war had not only destroyed schools, but also crushed the independence of spirit necessary for cultural progress. In Poland of that day there were at least large communities of Jews and the very numbers stimulated intellectual activity. In Germany the Jews were so small a minority as to have neither incentive nor opportunity for cultural development.

Rabbinic Learning—Most of the rabbis of German Jewish communities were men who had gained knowledge and reputation in Polish academies. This situation was partly due to the large number of Jews who had fled from Poland as a result of the Chmelnitzki uprising and the other Polish wars. Indirectly these wars thus helped spread the intense talmudic study which had become characteristic of Polish Jewry. This does not mean that there were no native Jewish scholars in Germany. One such scholar deserves mention, not so much because of his rabbinic learning, though that was extensive, as because of the library of books of Jewish interest which he collected. David Oppenheimer (1664–1736), nephew of the Viennese court Jew, Samuel Oppenheimer, was chief rabbi of Prague and a man of considerable wealth. He managed to gather a large library of rare Jewish books and manuscripts. Early in the nineteenth century this collection of books was purchased by the Oxford University of England, where, as part of the Bodleian Collection, it helped form what was for a long time the greatest single Jewish library in the world.

Inadequate Leadership—The lay (that is, non-rabbinic) leadership being in the hands of men of wealth whose personal interests were outside the Jewish community, Jewish culture and internal religious affairs became matters of secondary importance. They made sure that the rabbis did not exert too strong an influence on communal life. A rabbi of strong personality was not as acceptable to these communal leaders as was one more likely to limit his interests to the interpretation of civil and ritual law. Under these circumstances the rabbis of Central Europe found an outlet for their energies and for their religious zeal in hunting out every suspect of heresy. The story of their persecution of the gentle and gifted Moses Hayyim Luzzatto has already been told.* About the middle of the eighteenth century another quarrel

* See above, pp. 448–9.

broke out between two important rabbinic authorities and their friends on both sides. This quarrel showed how widespread cabalistic doctrines still were among the people; but even more important was the proof it offered that the rabbinic leadership did not appreciate the changes which were taking place in the world.

Emden vs. Eybeschuetz—Jonathan Eybeschuetz was one of the foremost rabbinic scholars and preachers of his day. From the rabbinate of Prague he was called to become the chief rabbi of the combined communities of Altona, Hamburg and Wansbeck. Jacob Emden was an equally famous rabbinic scholar and showed great zeal in fighting against every manifestation of Sabbetianism. Eybeschuetz, it seems, was prevailed upon by some of the common people under his charge to give amulets which were suspected of containing charms and prayers used by Sabbetian heretics. Emden, who apparently was jealous of Eybeschuetz, raised a loud cry against him. Before long there was not a rabbi in Germany who had not taken sides with one or the other. Who was right is less important than the fact of the quarrel itself. While the world outside was beginning to discuss the rights of man and to awaken to the needs of spreading human culture, the Jews, whom these problems affected most closely, plunged into a dispute about amulets. No one felt more distressed about this than a certain Jew then residing in Berlin who already exerted an increasing influence upon cultured Jews and Christians alike.

4. Moses Mendelssohn

The Education of a Philosopher—Moses, son of the Torah-scribe Mendel of Dessau, was born in 1729. He was thus a contemporary of the Besht and the Gaon. His life was lived, however, in an altogether different environment; his education differed from theirs and, as a result, his view of the needs of the Jewish people also turned out to be different. He started life very much like any other bright young Jew of the day; he studied the Talmud. But in David Fraenkel, the rabbi of Dessau, he had a teacher who appreciated young Moses's keen mind and introduced him to the study of Maimonides' works. When Fraenkel was called to the rabbinate of Berlin, Moses, aged fourteen, left Dessau and walked to the Prussian capital. Years of material struggle followed; at times the boy had nothing more than a single loaf of bread for a whole week's rations. He was, moreover, jealous for his every moment. He spent only what time he had to spend in giving private lessons and, later, in acting as bookkeeper. Every other moment he devoted to study and to reading the works of philosophers. Moses Mendelssohn emerged from this period of labor and study with a thorough knowledge of ancient and modern languages and a profound acquaintance with the thinkers of the past; but also with poor health. He became hunchbacked, so that his beautiful soul lived in an ugly body. When he became famous, people referred to him as the modern Socrates.

Philosophical Beginnings—At that time men of culture were beginning to speak in more liberal terms. A young German aristocrat by the name of Gotthold Ephraim Lessing even dared to publish a play, *The Jews,* in which a Jew possessed of fine human qualities was the hero. For the most part, however, the cultured men only talked liberalism; their prejudices were still too strong, and Lessing's play was condemned as being contrary to fact. Soon thereafter, Lessing made the acquaintance of Moses Mendelssohn and was deeply attracted by his remarkable mind and spirit. In the shy but high-minded Jew, Lessing saw the image of the hero of his play and he determined to have the cultured world become acquainted with Mendelssohn. Without asking the latter's consent, Lessing published a number of philosophical essays about which Mendelssohn had solicited his opinion. They were received with acclaim and, thereafter, Mendelssohn became recognized in cultured circles in Berlin. His literary and philosophical criticisms were highly valued, and his fame was firmly established with the publication of a philosophical work, *Phaedon,* on the question of the soul and immortality.

Destroying the Mental Walls—Mendelssohn analyzed the situation of the Jews and offered a remedy. The Jews had erected about themselves a mental ghetto to balance the physical ghetto around them. Quite naturally, even though perhaps mistakenly, the Jews had long ago decided that a civilization which had excluded them and treated them with such cruelty could have nothing worth while for them. Consequently, they had limited themselves to their own cultural heritage. Mendelssohn's object (not unlike that of Elijah Gaon, whom he did not know) was to lead them out of this mental ghetto into the wide world of general culture without, however, doing harm to their specifically Jewish culture. As a first step in this direction he considered it necessary to teach the Jews the use of the German language, so that it might serve as a key to cultural treasures with which they were not acquainted. With this in view he undertook a translation of the Pentateuch into German and eventually published it in Hebrew letters by the side of the original text. Moreover, he cooperated with two of his younger friends, Solomon Dubno and Naphtali Hertz Wessley, in the preparation in good Hebrew of a common-sense commentary on the Bible. In addition, he encouraged Wessley and other Hebrew scholars to begin issuing a magazine, under the title *Ha-Meassef* (The Gatherer), wherein the fruits of general culture were transmitted to the Hebrew-reading population. Finally, he had some of his wealthy Jewish friends sponsor a school for Jewish children in Berlin where German was taught in addition to the traditional Jewish subjects and where the boys were trained in manual occupations. Mild as such a program sounds to us today, it seemed revolutionary to Mendelssohn's contemporaries.

Judaism and Emancipation—Many Jews of that day believed that Mendelssohn was destroying Judaism. They were particularly angry about the translation of the Bible, for they feared, with reason, that the knowledge of the German thus acquired would lead the youth of Israel away from Jewish studies. The translation was therefore placed under the ban in many communities, that is, its study was forbidden. Yet Mendelssohn himself had no desire to destroy Judaism. His views on the subject were explained in a book which he wrote under the title, *Jerusalem, or the Civil Emancipation of the Jews*. He criticized the organization of Jewish life and asserted that the rabbis had too much power. He argued, however, for the observance by Jews of all the traditions of Judaism, which he considered of divine origin. Mendelssohn was a firm believer in freedom of conscience; no man had a right to impose his own beliefs or preferences on another. Consequently, it was just as wrong for a Jewish community to punish a Jew for his refusal to obey Jewish tradition as it was for the civil government to refuse to grant civil rights to the Jews because they did obey Jewish tradition. Matters of religion must be left to each man's private conscience. Fine thinker though he was, Mendelssohn failed to see that religion, especially Judaism, had also social aspects for which communal organization was indispensable.

Mendelssohn and Christian Liberals—While trying to break down the ghetto wall from the Jewish side, Mendelssohn tried to get the Christians to break it down from their side too. His home had become the meeting-place of cultured men of every religion and nation, all of whom admired him. Lessing, for example, published his famous play, *Nathan the Wise*, obviously with Moses Mendelssohn in mind. Like Lessing, others came to see the senselessness of treating as inferiors a group of people which counted a Mendelssohn among them. Christian Wilhelm Dohm, a Prussian officeholder and aristocrat, was induced by Mendelssohn to write a work on the subject of Jewish civil emancipation. Describing how the Jews had been mistreated and how valuable they could be if given equal rights, Dohm's book exerted considerable influence on the liberals of his day. The trouble was that these liberals had but slight influence on the policies of the various states. In Prussia itself not even Mendelssohn could obtain the right to live as a free man. Again and again the king refused to grant this fighter for German culture the right to consider himself a permanent resident of Berlin.

Mendelssohn's Achievements—Moses Mendelssohn died in 1786, on the eve of tremendous changes in general and in Jewish life. How much he contributed to the transformation which then began in the internal and external conditions of his fellow Jews has been a subject of much debate, as has also been the question whether his influence was for good or evil in the next generation. Long after his death, orthodox Jewish circles continued to look upon him as a destructive influence. For his plan to draw young Jews away from talmudic study into the study of general European culture bore considerable fruit, not only among the youth of Germany, but to some extent in Eastern Europe as well. While orthodox Jews considered this an evil, the fact is that Mendelssohn's plan prepared Jews for the period of greater personal freedom which was soon to come. Mendelssohn also turned the mind of his followers to criticism of Judaism as it was represented by the rabbis of his day, and in this way laid the foundation for the internal religious adjustments of the next generation. Finally, his own life and his influence brought forward a number of influential Christians who subsequently stood at the side of the Jews in their fight for human rights. On the whole, therefore, his influence was on the positive side. The real difficulty was not at all of his doing. It was due to the fact that the Jews caught his spirit of eagerness to re-enter European society much more quickly than the Christians were willing to permit them to enter. The Jews destroyed their intellectual protective walls before the Christians removed the prison walls of the ghetto.

5. Price of Admittance to Society

Eighteenth-Century Liberals—The liberal Christians who desired to have the Jews emancipated from the restrictions which had long rested upon them were of several kinds. There were the economic liberals, who saw an economic advantage to the state rising from the grant of greater freedom to the Jews. There were the political liberals, who realized that all restriction was part of the same system of privilege and oppression which they wished to abolish. Then there were the few intellectual liberals, who saw the ghetto as the embodiment of the prejudices of the Middle Ages. But all of these liberals combined represented a tiny proportion of the general population. The rest of the people continued to regard the Jews as they had been taught to view them for centuries, as something strange and evil.

The assumption even among the liberals was that the Jews would have to transform themselves before emancipation could be granted them, and by such transformation they meant anything from learning to speak the language of the land to giving up Judaism completely. At best the liberalism of that day was strongly tinged with smugness; at worst it was mixed with a strong dose of ignorance and prejudice. Some examples from the more important European countries outside of Prussia reveal this situation.

Liberalism in England—The Jews who had been drifting into England since the days of Cromwell met with little opposition in society or economic life. They participated fully in the commercial rise of the country and were granted considerable freedom in financial transactions so as not to put them at a disadvantage in relation to non-Jewish financiers. Nevertheless, there were certain aspects of life in which the Jews of England were held in an inferior state. Chief among these was the requirement for an oath of a Christian character. Jews were thus excluded from any position of an official nature; politics was closed to them and even the opportunity to obtain a university degree. By 1753 those who guided the government of England were ready to recognize the contribution of the English Jews to the commercial expansion and financial stability of the country. Prime Minister Pelham had a bill passed by Parliament granting the Jews complete equality. He soon discovered, however, that he was far ahead of his countrymen. Such a storm of objection was raised by the populace, purely on grounds of religious prejudice, that the law had to be repealed a few months later. Another century passed before emancipation was actually achieved.

Enlightened Prejudice in Austria—Another example of the price demanded for the grant of human rights may be seen in the so-called Edict of Toleration granted by Joseph II of Austria in 1782. The decree removed some of the restrictions on Jewish movements and occupations. At the same time, it insisted that the Jews reform their school system and their communal organization. Behind this apparently harmless demand lay the assumption of the emperor that the Jews had to be "civilized" before they could be accepted into full partnership with the rest of the population. Naturally, most of the Jews of his eastern provinces preferred to get along without Emperor Joseph's favors if these meant giving up what they considered sacred. But Joseph's Christian subjects were equally opposed to his edict. They objected to the slightest improvement in the conditions of the Jews. If a man was not a Christian he deserved no consideration. The Edict of Toleration was practically abandoned when Joseph died a few years later.

CHAPTER VIII

THE BIRTH OF AMERICANISM

JEWS TAKE PART IN THE SETTLEMENT AND DEVELOP-
MENT OF THE ENGLISH COLONIES ALONG THE ATLANTIC
COAST OF AMERICA AND IN THE ESTABLISHMENT OF THE
AMERICAN IDEAL

The World's Western Frontier—With a sense of relief one leaves the deep prejudices, political tyrannies and outworn economic traditions of the Old World in the eighteenth century in order to enter the fresh and forward-looking environment of the New World then being built on the American continent. A vast, uncharted land lay before the men and women who came in small groups from across the sea, a land of overpowering majestic beauty and of obvious unmeasured wealth. It was almost untouched land, as though God had been keeping it in reserve against the day when humanity would make a new start. It therefore needed men and women of spirit and enterprise, not only adventurous colonizers, but such as would be willing to forget the errors which mankind had previously made, and begin another experiment in human cooperation. The people who came to colonize the new land were well suited to meet the adventure of subduing a wilderness and to seize the opportunity of starting life anew. They consisted of the hardiest sons and daughters of older countries and of many peoples. They were men and women for whom the old homes had been too cramped physically and too restricted spiritually. Some of them, and their descendants for a generation or two, could not rid themselves of the notions of intolerance which they had learned in Europe. But, given their character and the condition of the new environment, such narrowness and prejudice could not long survive. Before they knew it they were living the American ideal.

The Jews were among the early settlers in the New World. Even more than the others, they appreciated the wider opportunities and the possibilities for greater political and religious freedom which were becoming part of America. Their share in laying the foundations for the great new nation and the relations they established with their neighbors constitute an integral part of American history.

1. SETTLEMENT

Origin and Character—Part of the story of Jewish settlement along the American coast has already been related in connection with the opening up of England and Holland for settlement by Marranos.* Not only New Amsterdam but the entire eastern coast of North America attracted people of the Jewish faith who could find no rest or chance for a livelihood in the Europe of the seventeenth and eighteenth centuries. Wandering Marranos, German Jews unable to find a legal home in their native land and some Polish Jews, driven forth by poverty and persecution, braved the uncertainties of the long and dangerous voyage across the sea. In most cases they came by way of Holland or of England; sometimes they arrived directly from Portugal. All of them came inspired by

* See above, pp. 432–6.

the hope of finding religious freedom in the New World and the chance of shaking off the social and political oppression to which the Old World's prejudices had condemned them.

Welcome in New England—The Massachusetts colony was, at first, not a particularly hospitable place for any but Puritans. Since members of other Protestant sects were excluded, it could hardly be expected that the Puritans would permit the settlement of Jews. The first mention of a Jew in the Massachusetts records is the appropriation of a small sum for the expense of getting rid of a man named Solomon Franco. Nevertheless, by 1674, Rowland Gideon is mentioned as a permanent settler. It may be that Gideon's wealth and his trade connections with the islands of the Caribbean made him more welcome among the Puritans than were poor Jews, but thereafter there seem to have been no attempts to

keep Jews from settling in the colony. Connecticut was more hospitable. Best of all was the situation of the Jews in Rhode

Island. Founded by the courageous and broad-minded Roger Williams, who had broken with the authorities of Massachusetts on the question of religious freedom for everybody, this colony made no distinctions among the settlers it admitted. Fifteen Jewish families settled there in 1658; more came later. Before long, Newport had an active Jewish community. By the beginning of the eighteenth century there were no restrictions anywhere in New England on the settlement of Jews.

The Middle Atlantic Colonies—Outside of New York, Maryland had at least one Jewish inhabitant before 1660. This man, Jacob Lumbroso, was a physician and apparently a man of some skill and education. For a while he was in trouble there because of too vigorous a defense of Judaism, but he was soon accepted as an equal in all but matters of politics. Others came in small numbers. As early as 1680, before William Penn took it over, there were Jews in Pennsylvania. They may have been newcomers from distant lands, or Jews who had wandered down from New York after they had won the right to trade along the shores of the Delaware. Names like Aaron, Franks, Marks and Levy occur among the residents of Philadelphia around 1700. Within a generation they had wandered westward to Lancaster and Easton which were then the farthest outposts of civilization.

Georgia and the Carolinas—When, in 1669, John Locke, the English philosopher, prepared a constitution for a proposed settlement of the territory called Carolina, he included in it a statement granting religious freedom to anyone desiring to go there. Locke, of course, was far ahead of his time and complete equality for members of all religious groups was not attained in Carolina during the colonial period. Enough of his spirit prevailed, however, so that Jews could settle in that territory without interference. But their coming was delayed until after the territory to the south had been opened. The most southern colony, Georgia, was not started until 1730 by James Oglethorpe, one of the most interesting persons of that age. For Georgia was settled in order to give certain types of Englishmen, who could not make a place for themselves at home, a chance to start life all over again in a new country. One would have supposed that such people would be sympathetic to others equally unfortunate and equally eager for new opportunities. Such was not the case. The second vessel to arrive at Georgia brought with it a number of Jewish families. Oglethorpe was willing to let the Jews have a share in the land, but the men he had brought over raised a loud protest. Neverthless, Oglethorpe had his way. A few years later, some of the Jews preferred to leave Georgia and make their way northward into the Carolinas.

2. BUILDING A COUNTRY

Variety of Occupations—At first the Jews had some difficulty in finding occupations to which there would be no objection from the majority of the settlers. Whether they wanted to open a shop or to join in the profitable trade with the Indians, there were always some Christians who resented the new competition. But, after all, in those days there was enough for everybody. Besides, the stockholders of the colony back in the mother country always felt that to impose restrictions on any colonist would be to limit their profits. Consequently, the Jews soon gained the right to enter whatever business they pleased.* Before long these opportunities were broadened, so that during the rest of the seventeenth and eighteenth centuries their occupations showed great variety. Engaged for the most part in manual trades, there were among them tailors, watchmakers, saddle-makers, distillers and the like. They engaged, also, in some special occupations about which a word must be said separately.

Commerce—When Jews could no longer be excluded from trade with the Indians, a number of them pioneered as far west as the Mississippi. Next came a general store in the town along the coast; and this in turn was sometimes followed by contacts with the West Indies or with England. These are the steps by which the brothers Barnard and Michael Gratz became prominent merchants in Philadelphia before and during the Revolutionary War. Other Jews limited themselves to the export and import part of the business. Early in colonial history, the Gideons gained great wealth in this fashion. The like was true of David Franks immediately before the Revolution. The best example is afforded by the Jews of Newport, Rhode Island, where the colony's liberal policy encouraged Jews to settle and where the port offered excellent shipping facilities. They had a considerable share in the growth of the whaling industry and in the manufacture of articles derived from whale oil, such as candles and soap. Distilling and sugar manufacturing were by-products of their

* See the story of Asser Levy, above, p. 436.

trade with the West Indies. Aaron Lopez, one of the Newport Jews, became exceptionally prominent in shipping.

Farmers and Planters—Farther south along the Atlantic coast the Jews entered with equal thoroughness into occupations characteristic of that environment; they acquired land and became farmers and planters. Jacob Lumbroso in Maryland and Samuel Nunez in Georgia divided their time between healing the sick and attending to their farms. A certain Moses Lindo came to Carolina with the specific object of developing indigo. In Georgia, Abraham de Lyon was a successful winegrower. Francis Salvador of South Carolina owned a very large plantation. (He was one of the first to be killed by Indians after the outbreak of the Revolution.) Clearly the Jews in every part of colonial America were doing their share in developing the new land and preparing it for the great future which was in store for it.

3. JUDAISM IN THE COLONIES

The First Synagogues—Soon after they arrived, the Jews of New Amsterdam asked permission to establish religious services. They were refused the right to have a synagogue, but they were allowed to meet in one or another private home and there carry on Jewish worship. Although in theory the English were more liberal, it was not until 1685 that the Jews set aside a house which they called their synagogue. Even this was unofficial for the next ten years. But by 1700 the Shearith Israel congregation was already established and the existence of a synagogue taken for granted by the entire population. A minister was designated: Saul Brown, a merchant, being honorary minister during the early period and Abraham Hayyim de Lucena taking over the duties later on. A similar procedure was followed in both Philadelphia and Newport. In the Pennsylvania city the unofficial place of worship was made official in 1740, when the Mikveh Israel congregation came into being, though a building was not erected till the time of the Revolution. In Newport a synagogue was built around 1760, although here, too, a congregation had been in existence for decades. At about the same time a congregation was organized in Charleston, South Carolina, under the name of Beth Elohim (House of God).

Religion and Education—The Jews who came to America during colonial times were not blessed with much Jewish knowledge. Whether they were of Spanish-Portuguese ancestry, that is, Sephardim, or of German ancestry, that is, Ashkenazim, they were with few exceptions energetic men of daring and courage rather than such as could sit quietly and lead a studious life. Prayer books and Bibles were all that their physical and mental baggage could hold. Since the majority of them, during the early colonial period, were Sephardim, the Sephardi ritual prevailed, and the Jews of German ancestry quickly adjusted themselves to it.

More serious was the problem of educating the young. At first, some new arrival, still struggling to establish himself commercially, would take over the task of teaching Jewish children to read the prayer book. Before long the Jewish colonists began to send to the better established Jewish communities of Jamaica or London or Amsterdam for men willing to migrate to the distant land and become the official teachers for Jewish youth. The difficulty was increased by the fact that there were as yet no public schools, so that many Jewish parents sent their children to various non-Jewish private schools, with the result that there was no time or opportunity for Jewish studies.

The situation was saved to some extent by regular attendance at synagogue services, which was considered a duty, whereby the child learned to read and take part in the ritual. Besides, the Jewish communities, like all other groups in the colonies, watched carefully over the actions of their adherents. Punishment for the violation of Jewish tradition took the form of exclusion from synagogue honors or, for a greater or lesser time, from the synagogue itself. In this way, discipline maintained unity even where knowledge was not plentiful. On the other hand, as generation followed generation, this lack of knowledge and the constant influence of the environment weakened loyalty to tradition.

A Rabbi and a Clergyman—Both knowledge and loyalty might have been greater if the early American Jewish communities had been able to obtain religious guidance. In important problems of Jewish law they turned for advice to the communities of Jamaica or London. Otherwise, whether for reading the service in the synagogue or for decisions on matters of lesser weight, they would call upon their own members. All the greater was the general interest aroused whenever an itinerant preacher arrived in America. Such preachers were the *meshullahim,* or emissaries, sent by *yeshibot* or other institutions in Europe or Palestine to collect funds. Frequently to be met with in Europe, a few of these men came as far as the New World. Rabbi Hayyim Isaac Karrigal was such a *meshullah* who hailed from Palestine. After passing through Philadelphia and New York, he reached Newport in 1773 and was induced to stay there for a while and guide the congregation. On special occasions he delivered sermons. His language was Spanish, as the majority of Newport's Jews still understood the language. This was practically the first series of real sermons delivered by a rabbi on North American soil. They were fervent and stimulating, and the Newport Jews were delighted with them. Nor were they the only ones to be pleased. In the Newport of that day there was a clergyman by the name of Ezra Stiles, who was later to become president of Yale University. He and Karrigal became friendly and exchanged frequent visits. Stiles became a visitor in the synagogue where he followed the service closely, and Karrigal helped him with his study of Hebrew. Here was another example of the new spirit which the American environment encouraged.

4. THE JEWS AND THEIR NEIGHBORS

Religious Friction and Tolerance—The broad-mindedness of Ezra Stiles did not mean that he was not critical of Jews and Judaism; he was still readier to find fault with them than with his own coreligionists; but it does show the spirit of cooperation and mutual respect which had come into being during the previous century. The desire to convert Jews to Christianity was still in evidence. The noted Massachusetts clergyman, Cotton Mather (died in 1728), prayed for the privilege of converting at least one Jew and even wrote a book of arguments by which conversion might be achieved. But the zeal eventually cooled off. By the time of the Revolution, Jews had been contributing to the building of churches and Christians to the building funds of synagogues. The best example of this spirit of neighborliness was in connection with the Mikveh Israel synagogue, erected in Philadelphia, to which a number of prominent Christians subscribed, among them Benjamin Franklin.

Jews and Colonial Colleges—The study of Hebrew was considered of the utmost importance in the colleges of colonial days and was compulsory at Yale and Harvard. From 1720 to 1760 the professor of Hebrew at Harvard was Judah Monis, who became a convert to Christianity presumably in order to obtain this position. Neither he nor his subject was popular with the students. Obviously, Jews could not be students in such colleges as long as the sole object of the institution was training for the Christian ministry. Toward the end of the colonial period, however, a change in attitude became noticeable. It started with Benjamin Franklin, who, in founding the academy which is now the University of Pennsylvania, introduced non-theological subjects. King's College, now Columbia, followed this example. A small number of Jews was graduated from these two institutions even before the Revolutionary War, thereby symbolizing the broadening of the educational ideal in America. In 1770 Brown University opened its doors to Jewish students.

Friendships and Partnerships—In view of the small population of colonial America, Jews and Christians were frequently thrown together and learned to cooperate in business, to establish friendships and to visit one another. It is said that Jews introduced Masonry into the colonies. Men like the Gratz brothers of Philadelphia and the Franks of Philadelphia and New York had many Christian business associates who became their friends. While conversions to Christianity were few, there were instances of intermarriage. The attitude fostered by American life is expressed in the questions formulated by Franklin as tests for membership in the intellectual society, the *Junto,* which he founded: "Do you sincerely declare that you love mankind in general of what profession or religion soever? Do you think any person ought to be harmed in his body, name, or goods for mere speculative opinions or his external way of worship?"

Political Rights—The attitude toward Jews in political matters followed closely upon the liberalization of the general attitude with respect to them. The need for settlers at the beginning had been the motive for protecting their persons and their property and eventually for granting them freedom of religious worship. This did not mean that they could be appointed or elected to office, or that they could vote in elections. Throughout the colonial period, almost all the colonies required the oath which contained the words "upon the true faith of a Christian." As a matter of fact, in some of the colonies Catholics were even worse off, from this point of view, than Jews. This was probably the reason why James II of England, with his Catholic sympathies, favored complete political and religious equality in New York. Their interest in overseas commerce also made for an improvement in the Jewish status. English law granted Letters of Denization to merchants who applied for them. Since such documents afforded greater protection to trade, a number of Jews applied for and received them.

By 1730 the restrictions against political activity by Jews were so far forgotten that Jews voted for the members of the colonial legislature in New York. Then, in 1737, a political dispute resulted in a lawsuit in which one side challenged the election of the other by claiming that the Jews who had voted for the latter had had no right to vote. The politically-minded court thereupon decided that the Jews had no right even to be witnesses, and the colonial legislature passed a resolution to this effect. But in the atmosphere of colonial New York, such restrictions could not be long enforced. In the other colonies, too, the strict letter of the law kept Jews from office and probably also from voting. That this was no longer in line with the sentiments of the population is proved by the ease with which such laws were abolished in almost every state when the Revolution asserted the spirit of America that "all men are created equal."

5. THE REVOLUTIONARY WAR

Americanism Against European Tradition—Many factors combined to bring about a desire among the colonies to break away from England. These involved the Jews of America as much as the non-Jews. There was one factor, however, the most important of all, which concerned the Jews more deeply and more immediately than others. This was the difference in mind and spirit between Europe and America. Europe was weighted down by traditions which kept men apart; America was impelled onward by opportunities which united men. During the century of colonial life most Americans learned through daily experience that a man could be valuable no matter what his racial or religious background; Europe needed philosophers and encyclopedists to achieve only temporary and halfhearted results in learning the same truth. Consequently, when on July 4, 1776, the Continental Congress adopted the Declaration of Independence, asserting the rights and the dignity of all men alike, it was giving voice to the spirit of America. It was also justifying the stand long taken by the Jews everywhere in the world when, for centuries, they had refused to yield their personality and surrender their religious convictions, while their wanderings and their life in ghettos were silent protests against oppression and compulsion. By far the largest proportion of the Jews of America hailed the Declaration with delight.

Jewish Patriots—Every Jewish merchant of consequence in the colonies had signed the Non-Importation Agreement which aimed at persuading England to change its policy towards its American possessions. When that failed and war broke out, Jews joined the ranks as soldiers and officers in numbers out of all proportion to the 2,500 Jews who were in America at that time. Jewish merchants turned their ships into privateers. The community of Newport suffered such heavy losses that it never revived after the war was over. Aaron Lopez, its wealthiest citizen, lost practically all he had gained in decades of successful trade. A number gave their lives or were wounded in action. On the other hand, there were also some Tories among the Jews, that is, people who objected to the break with England. The most prominent among these was the wealthy Philadelphia merchant David Franks who supplied the British army with much material. Other Jewish Tories suffered considerable persecution for their sympathies.

A Rabbi and a Broker—Two names among the Jewish patriots deserve special mention: Gershom Mendes Seixas (1745–1816) and Haym Salomon (died 1785). The former was the first native Jew to become a rabbi. Seixas acted in this capacity at the Shearith Israel synagogue in New York. He was so ardent in his patriotism that, when the city was about to be occupied by the British, he refused to continue holding services there. Taking the Torah and other sacred objects, he went to Philadelphia, deposited the objects with the Mikveh Israel synagogue and took up the duties of *hazzan* in that congregation. When the war was over, he went back to his duties in New York. Haym Salomon, of Polish Jewish origin, had come to America shortly before the Revolution. His remarkable financial ability brought him considerable wealth from a brokerage business which he opened in New York. He put himself and his wealth at the disposal of the patriot cause. Captured by the British, he succeeded in making his escape and came to Philadelphia. Here he again set himself up in business; and Robert Morris repeatedly testified to the liberality with which Salomon assisted the treasury of the struggling republic. Others were no less liberal according to their means. Among these were the Gratz brothers of Philadelphia, Jacob Hart of Baltimore, Isaac Moses of New York and many more.

Prejudice Dies Hard—While the war was being fought on

the field of battle, the principles which underlay the conflict were asserting themselves in the legislatures of the states. As individuals the members of these bodies were willing enough to recognize the equality of other religious groups, but they found it very difficult to visualize a situation in which their type of Christianity would be no more privileged than any other type and especially than Judaism. The conflict in Virginia was particularly interesting because that state provided the country with outstanding leadership. Patrick Henry, for example, fought hard for continuing an established Church, that is, for the state to subsidize Christianity. On the opposite side was James Madison, who pointed out the injustice of taxing Jews for the support of Christian churches or Catholics for the support of Protestant churches. Thomas Jefferson was out of the country at the time of this debate and for that reason it may have lasted longer than it would had he personally added the great weight of his influence to Madison's side. In the end, the American attitude won, and the Jews were given the complete freedom and equality which one now takes for granted. Other states had similar debates at about the same time. In each case fears were expressed that to grant equality to non-Christians would destroy Christianity. Eventually, when all the states had adopted constitutions, it was found that three actually did limit officeholding to Christians: Maryland, North Carolina and New Hampshire. It took several generations for these to fall in line.

The Federal Constitution—The actual temper of the common people was better expressed in connection with the movement to overcome all local loyalties and establish a strong, united nation. The great leaders who gathered at Philadelphia to frame a federal government took these fundamentals of Americanism so much for granted that they did not include freedom of religion in the original Constitution. Then, as is well known, popular demand arose for specific guarantees of the freedoms for which the Revolution was fought. As a result the Bill of Rights was adopted, the very first article of which reads in part: "Congress shall make no law respecting an establishment of religion, or prohibiting the free exercise thereof."

George Washington Teaches a Lesson—As commander-in-chief during the War, Washington had had occasion to watch and work with Jewish soldiers and officers. A number of Jews had been with him also at Valley Forge. When he was elected president of the United States, several congregations sent him their congratulations and good wishes. The congregations of New York, Philadelphia, Richmond and Charleston joined in sending one letter; that of Savannah, Georgia, sent another; that of Newport, Rhode Island, sent a third. While the letters sent by the Jews were dignified, there was within them an undertone of concern lest the good fortune of freedom be but temporary. Thus the Jews of Newport wrote in their letter, dispatched on the occasion of Washington's visit to that city in August, 1790:

> Deprived as we heretofore have been of the invaluable rights of free Citizens, we now, with a deep sense of gratitude to the Almighty Disposer of all events, behold a Government, erected by the Majesty of the People—a Government, which to bigotry gives no Sanction, to persecution no assistance—but generously affording to All liberty of conscience, and immunities of Citizenship:—deeming every one, of whatever Nation, tongue, or language, equal parts of the great governmental Machine.

With the fight which had but recently been waged in his native Virginia still fresh in his mind and sensing the mixed feelings of thankfulness and uncertainty in the minds of the writers of the letter, Washington expressed his faith in the America of which he was the chief, in these immortal words:

> The Citizens of the United States of America have a right to applaud themselves for having given to mankind examples of an enlarged and liberal policy: a policy worthy of imitation. All possess alike liberty of conscience and immunities of citizenship. It is now no more that toleration is spoken of as if it was by the indulgence of one class of people, that another enjoyed the exercise of their inherent natural rights. For happily the Government of the United States, which gives to bigotry no sanction, to persecution no assistance, requires only that they who live under its protection, should demean themselves as good citizens, in giving it on all occasions their effectual support.

This was the real America speaking; and Washington was equally correct and prophetic in expressing elsewhere the hope that the example given by America would be followed in other, older lands. For already events were taking place in Europe which gave promise of better days everywhere for the Jewish people.

BOOK FIVE

THE SEARCH FOR A FRIENDLY HOME

THE STRIVINGS, DISAPPOINTMENTS, MIGRATIONS AND HOPES
OF THE JEWS DURING THE PAST ONE HUNDRED AND FIFTY
YEARS AND THE PROBLEMS, OLD AND NEW, WHICH ARE
STILL WITH US

INTRODUCTION

The Modern World—The past leads into the present; and
Jewish history to the end of the eighteenth century is, in this
sense, but an introduction to the story of the Jewish people in
the modern world. By "modern" we mean the time closest to
us, the age in which the past four or five generations, as well
as our own, have been sharing the destiny of mankind and, in
the case of the Jews, also the destiny of the Jewish people.
We have seen how the Jews of previous ages acted in the
face of crises and how they maintained the heritage transmitted to them. Now we shall see how those of the most recent
period have been meeting the problems of Jewish life during
the past one hundred and fifty years.

An Age of Revolutions—Modern history began with two
revolutions—one in America and the other in France—followed by a series of world-shaking wars, those of Napoleon.
Each revolution helped spread the ideals of democracy and

freedom and therefore had a tremendous effect on Jewish life. The modern period has been climaxed with another revolution, in Russia, and two world wars which have brought a modification of democracy and freedom in many parts of the world. The full consequences of the last revolution and of World War II cannot yet be foreseen, but up to the present they have undone for the Jews much of what the Jews had achieved during the previous century. The modern period has also experienced revolutions in commerce and industry, in faith and habits.

The period between the early and the latest wars and revolutions has been an era of unceasing change for the Jews of the world. Their numbers, their habits and their relations to the non-Jews never remained the same for a single decade during the nineteenth and twentieth centuries. Thus, the modern period started with an expansion of their economic and political opportunities, but brought a reversal of the process after two or three generations. It saw the Jewish population of the world rise from two to about fifteen millions; and in more recent years witnessed half this number either destroyed or subjected to pressures tending to make them forget their Jewishness. More than twice as many Jews met an untimely death between 1933 and 1945 as had been alive in 1790. It has been a period of extensive migration, of religious transformation, of progress as well as retrogression in Jewish literature, of assimilation and nationalism flourishing side by side.

The Search for a Home—The modern period has been characterized, furthermore, by a heartbreaking yearning among the Jews for a sense of being at home. During the nineteenth century the Jew became a full citizen of his native land, especially in Western Europe and America. But it became clear, when the nineteenth century was two-thirds over, that the advances of the Jews were being spurned and their cooperation rejected by a substantial number of the very people and classes from whom they had expected understanding. A new theory of anti-Jewishness was invented and given a high-sounding name—antisemitism. This was a terrific blow to the Jews who were just beginning to feel at home in the lands of their birth.

Spiritual Nationalism—The new hatreds helped create Zionism, another characteristic of Jewish history in the modern period. The patriotic emotions which swept over the world during the nineteenth century also affected the Jews. Since many of their neighbors refused to permit the Jews to identify themselves fully with them, there was reawakened among the Jews the dream of a restored Jewish national life in Palestine. But Jewish life had emphasized culture and religion far too long and far too strongly for this Jewish nationalism to be mere territorial patriotism. The Zionist movement is as much cultural and spiritual as it is political.

The Land of the Free—The phenomenal growth of the United States of America has been of the utmost importance during the modern period. When the thirteen colonies established themselves as a new nation "conceived in liberty and dedicated to the proposition that all men are created equal," they began an experiment in human freedom which has served as proof that all races and religions can adjust themselves to one another and live at peace. The rise of the Jewish community in the United States is a glorious epic within the larger story of America. Unfortunately, some prejudices of the old world have been imported also into the new. As ever, the Jews form the strategic point around which is being fought the battle for and against the broad spirit of Americanism. If we make certain that Americanism triumphs, the next generation of Jews will have an opportunity to face with wisdom and courage its problem of adjustment to the expanding life in this Land of the Free.

CHAPTER I

THE BATTLE CRY OF FREEDOM

THE REVOLUTION IN FRANCE BRINGS ABOUT REVOLUTION-
ARY CHANGES ALSO IN THE LIFE OF THE JEWS IN OTHER
LANDS

Uncertain Fatherlands—In the year that Washington assumed the presidency of the United States, France experienced its great social and political revolution. France had for some centuries been the intellectual leader of Europe. French philosophers of the eighteenth century—Voltaire, Rousseau and many others—had spread their humanitarian ideas among all middle-class Europeans. The revolutionary events in France consequently found an echo in most other countries. The slogan "Liberty, Equality, Fraternity," the cry of the French Revolution, caused the ancient regime to totter everywhere.

The Jews of Europe heard that battle cry and wondered. Would they, too, be liberated and henceforth be treated as equals and brothers by the men who had kept them in ghettos and restricted their every movement? Some were sure that the day of deliverance had come; others suspected the sincerity of men who suddenly mouthed lofty and stirring ideals. Both the optimists and the doubters, it turned out, were to some extent correct. In most lands of Western and Central Europe freedom was half-heartedly granted the Jews, only to be withdrawn as soon as the revolutionary ardor cooled and reactionary forces reasserted themselves. Nevertheless, the French Revolution started Europe and its Jews on a course from which a complete turning back was not possible.

1. STRANGERS OR CITIZENS

Jews in Eighteenth Century France—France, it will be recalled, had decreed the expulsion of its Jews in 1394. Yet there were, in the eighteenth century, three French districts where Jews lived legally: the district of Avignon which, from the fourteenth century to the French Revolution, was under the rule of the popes; the provinces of Alsace and Lorraine which had been annexed to France after the Thirty Years' War (1648) and from which, therefore, the Jews had never been expelled; and the city and district of Bordeaux whither Marranos had fled from Spain early in the sixteenth century. Members of each of these three groups managed to establish themselves in Paris, where most of them lived without rights or comforts. When this and the condition of the Jews in Alsace came to the attention of King Louis XVI and his ministers, the government planned an improvement in their status. It was to have been part of the reform program by which the more liberal French ministers hoped to remedy the faults from which the country was suffering. But years passed and no more was done about the Jews than about any of the other pressing problems which were driving France to revolution.

Friends and Enemies—The fall of the Bastille, on July 14, 1789, marked the visible beginning of the French Revolution. A National Assembly was called to reorganize every phase of

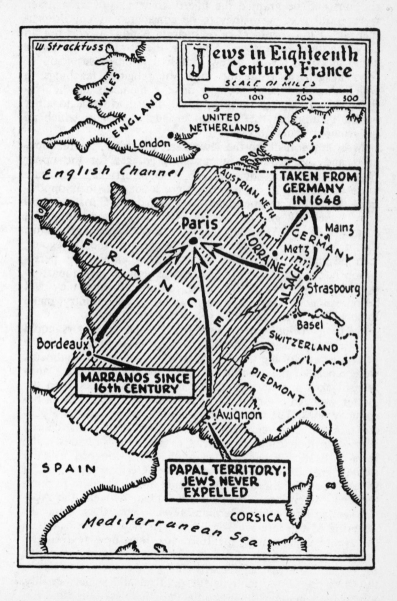

French life. Among the topics on the program was the question of the Jews. Were they to be freed from medieval restrictions and be granted the liberty to which all Frenchmen were entitled, or were they to be considered as not Frenchmen at all but members of a separate nation? It was not an easy question to answer. Most of the deputies had never come in contact with a Jew, but had imbibed suspicion of Jews in general from the medieval religious teachings in which they had been brought up. As members of the National Assembly, on the other hand, they had come together on the assumption that all men had definite rights which no government could abrogate.

Most antagonistic to the Jews were, of course, the reactionaries and the believers in special privileges for the upper classes. The representatives of Alsace-Lorraine, especially those of the city of Strasbourg, were loudest in their opposition. According to them, all Jews hated all Christians and were hopelessly given to usury. The liberal and thoughtful members of the Assembly, led by the statesman and orator, Count Mirabeau, and the saintly clergyman, Abbé Grégoire, asserted that the Jews were what Christian enmity and persecution had made them. Treat them as equals, give them opportunities to earn a livelihood respectably, and they will become as good men and citizens as any in the country; make them feel at home and they will never be strangers.

Division Among the Jews—The French legislators could not make up their minds. Every once in a while a session was devoted to the Jewish question. The same arguments were repeated; the reactionaries told the age-old vulgar anti-Jewish jokes and resorted to the old political tricks; then the matter was again tabled. Months rolled by and the Jews became anxious. The various communities had organized a general committee to represent them. Fear of defeat now caused a break in their ranks. A quarter of a century previously, the Jews of Bordeaux had written to the sharp-tongued Voltaire disclaiming all connection with the German Jews. In a statement as childish as it was untrue, they laid claim to pure-blooded descent from the tribe of Judah, whereas the Alsatian Jews, like other German Jews, were, they said, the offspring of the inferior Ten Tribes. In view of the delays in the National Assembly, the Bordeaux Jews now revived this argument and requested that the National Assembly separate their case from that of the Alsatians. This was not to be the last time that Jews, anxious for political and social equality, joined their enemies in branding their fellows. This time disloyalty was rewarded. Many members of the National Assembly felt less guilty for excluding the numerous, poor Alsatian Jews from the enjoyment of the Rights of Man, while they admitted the few but rich Jews of Bordeaux to French citizenship (1790). The Jews of Alsace were left to fight alone.

Revolution and Victory—The French Revolution, in the meantime, moved towards greater liberalism. The strength of the aristocracy and the clergy waned, while the masses gained control. The Jews, especially those of Paris, actively participated in the mass movement and soon persuaded the Parisian leaders that the logic of the Revolution demanded equality for all Frenchmen. In September, 1791, more than two years after the outbreak of the Revolution, all Jews, whatever their origin, were admitted to French citizenship. One statement made to justify the final resolution is especially interesting. "The Jews," said one of the leading revolutionaries, "conscious of the error of their ways, have felt the need for a fatherland; we have offered them ours."

2. French Arms and Jewish Emancipation

Personal Freedom and Its Price—The 40,000 Jews of France, and particularly the 500 Jews of Paris, hailed their new-found freedom with joy. Some were soon to be found in the National Guard; others enlisted in the citizen armies to defend the Revolution. But within a short time a new danger arose. Extremists among the revolutionaries attempted to abolish all established religions. Churches, synagogues and religious schools were ordered closed and the Catholic and Jewish clergy were commanded to worship the "Goddess of Reason." A few Jews made a public show of their abandonment of Judaism for the new religion, but, for the most part, religion was simply driven underground and observances were adhered to in secret. Fortunately, the period of religious oppression did not last long. But the Jews had been forewarned of the high price which political and economic freedom demand.

Freedom in Holland—The French armies carried the slogans of the Revolution to other parts of Europe and established new republics on the principles of liberty and equality. A considerable number of the Dutch Jews were not at all sure that they liked the new regime. They had found in Holland religious freedom and an opportunity to live in comfort and in peace. Conservative in every respect and devoted to the house of Orange which had given them protection, the older men were willing to forego the privilege of voting and of sitting in legislative halls. The younger Jews, however, were already imbued with the doctrines of the French and eagerly accepted political emancipation, paying for it by the surrender of the rights of autonomy which the Jewish communities had enjoyed.

In the Roman Ghetto—The Jews of Rome were in a different situation. The eighteenth century had, on the whole, been a very depressing period for them. Compulsory attendance at sermons aimed to convert them, the kidnaping of children and sometimes of adults to be forced into Christianity, the restrictions on their social and economic activities and the heavy burden of taxation made the ghetto a prison of tortured souls. In addition to all this, in 1775, Pope Pius VI issued a bull in which he emphasized and re-enforced all the restrictions on the Jews as part of his plan to suppress the spirit of liberalism which was then sweeping Europe and which had penetrated Rome itself. In January, 1793, a number of Romans staged an attempt at revolution. It was defeated, and the mob attacked the ghetto on the ground that hostility to the Old Order was rooted there. Later the same year, the mob was again permitted to attack the Jews. As everywhere and at all times, the reactionaries tried to discredit the spirit of freedom by branding it an invention of the Jews.

Out of the Ghetto—Conditions in Rome changed only after the arrival of the French armies in 1798. Their entry into the city was the signal for the Roman Jews to take off the Badge which they had been compelled to wear for centuries and to open the gates of their ghetto prison. Yet it was all for naught. Within a few months the French were driven out of Rome by the soldiers of Naples and out of other Italian cities by native reactionaries. In many places this was followed by serious rioting; everywhere the Jews had to pay heavy fines and return within the walls of the ghettos, there to remain until the next change in the situation a few years later.

3. NAPOLEON'S PLANS FOR ASSIMILATION

Napoleon's Jewish Contacts—In time the French Revolution destroyed itself. Within a few years, little was left of it except pride and patriotism of the sort that a clever general-politician like Napoleon could use to make himself master of the country, first as military dictator and then as emperor. Having diverted the French Revolution to serve his own ends, Napoleon tried to do the like with Jewish emancipation. He had never met any Jews and understood nothing about Judaism. During his unsuccessful campaign in Palestine in 1799, he had invited the Jews to accept him as their defender and so win Palestine for themselves. But that had been merely political propaganda and was soon forgotten. His attitude toward them continued to be based on the suspicions and prejudices of that day. As not infrequently, the actions of some Jews, reflecting anything but glory on the rest, helped to confirm these prejudices. When Napoleon visited the provinces of Alsace and Lorraine, he found the peasants complaining that the usury of the Jews was making it difficult for them to retain control of much of the land which, during the Revolution, had been distributed to the peasants. What the Jews had done was altogether legal: they had loaned money to peasants who unfortunately did not know how to manage farms. Now the peasants found it hard to pay the interest on their debts. Because Jews were involved, such financial operations were considered criminal. Napoleon, who had just stolen the liberties of all Frenchmen, was horrified by the activities of the Jews.

The Notables—The Jews, Napoleon was sure, had to be treated differently from other portions of the population. A policy had to be found for them, partly of persuasion and partly of compulsion, by which one could break down their resistance to assimilation with the rest of the population. Such a policy had to be based on some arresting act. Napoleon knew the value of being dramatic. In 1806, as emperor of France, he issued a call to the Jewish communities of France, and of the provinces most closely attached to it, for representatives of the Jews to appear at a meeting, a sort of parliament, to consult with him on the relations between them and the French empire.

Tricky Questions—The convocation, known as the Assembly of Notables, was organized with great pomp and ceremony and met in Paris. The first session was deliberately called on a Saturday to see whether the Jews had enough spirit to object. There were no open objections; the Jewish representatives simply arranged to avoid traveling and writing on the Sabbath. There was little that the Notables were permitted to do other than vote "yes" or "no" on a list of questions which was put to them by one of Napoleon's ministers. The questions themselves suggest the prejudices which surrounded the Jews. Did the Jews consider themselves Frenchmen? Could they engage in manual labor or did they insist on living by usury? Could Jews marry more than one wife at the same time? Was it not possible to encourage intermarriage between Jews and Christians? Some of these questions could be easily answered. A proper answer to others would have required a long historical essay. Of course the Jews considered themselves Frenchmen; and of course they had no objection to manual labor. But how was one to explain that money-lending had been forced upon them by their historical situation and that few could be called usurers? How was one to make clear the difference between proper assimilation and the type of self-destruction which would follow intermarriage? In any case, the answers which the Notables gave showed sufficient subserviency to satisfy Napoleon.

The Grand Sanhedrin—Nevertheless, the emperor was not yet satisfied. He wanted to make the pledge of Jewish loyalty and the admission of Jewish subordination even more dramatic and more binding. In characteristic fashion, therefore, he tried to revive the most dignified legislative institution of the Jewish past, the Sanhedrin. Again orders went forth to the various provincial governors to select Jewish representatives, this time a majority, forty-six, being rabbis. Napoleon now took care that most of those selected would not oppose the decisions of the Notables. The "Sanhedrin" was organized according to tradition: with seventy-one members, a *Nasi* and all the cermonials that could be devised. They reaffirmed the decisions of the Notables, declaring themselves Frenchmen of the Jewish faith, on whom the laws of the state were as binding as on any citizen. They even freed soldiers in the French army from religious obligations, and they declared usury illegal. They refused, however, to have rabbis officiate at mixed marriages. As far as Napoleon was concerned the entire matter was just a propaganda trick; but it worked so well that to this day Napoleon is believed by many to have been a friend of the Jews.

The Infamous Decrees—Actually he was nothing of the kind. He was not an enemy in the sense of being a persecutor, but, like so many other intolerant non-Jews, he was impatient with Jewish persistence. He saw no point in the survival of the Jewish group and, in his ignorance of it, felt that Judaism was harmful. He was going to cure the Jews of their "faults" even if he had to do it by force. As though the Grand Sanhedrin had given him the authority to do so, he now published a number of edicts which became known as

"Infamous Decrees." They suspended the repayment of debts to Jews for a period of ten years. They denied Jews the right to settle in certain parts of France unless they became farmers. They imposed restrictions on Jews wanting to go into business. They insisted that Jews conscripted into the army could offer no substitute for themselves as Christian conscripts were permitted to do. Napoleon thus took away from the Jews of France and its conquered territories much of what they had hailed with such joy as the fruits of the Revolution.

The Consistorial System—One part of these decrees lasted for a century: this was the organization of Jewish religious life more or less on the same model as that of Catholics and Protestants. All local congregations were joined into one body directed by a board of laymen and rabbis, which was called "a consistory" and which had complete authority over synagogue ritual and property. The local consistories were joined together under a national consistory. The difference between Jewish and non-Jewish consistories was that in the case of the Christians the state contributed toward the salaries of the clergy, whereas the rabbis were to be paid by the Jews without state aid.

4. EMANCIPATION AND REACTION

Effect of the Revolution on Germany—In the German states, the hopes of the Jews for emancipation, during the era of the Revolution and of Napoleon, depended on a number of factors which now came into play. The economic conditions and opportunities of each state and the degree of liberalism to be found among its rulers were two such factors. Of more importance was the proximity of a state to France. The near-by kingdoms of Baden and Westphalia granted the Jews complete equality. The city of Cologne, from which Jews had been expelled some centuries previously, now readmitted them. Luebeck and Bremen, farther away from French influence, permitted Jews to settle within their borders, more because of enlarged commercial opportunities than because of a broadening spirit. Of great interest is the course events took in Frankfort on the Main, where one of the famous medieval ghettos was located. After much haggling, the patrician rulers of the city freed the Jews from most of the old restrictions, but made them pay an enormous sum of money for this grant of ordinary human rights. One general gain was the abolition, by 1810, of the degrading, discriminatory taxes which the Jews had had to pay in German-speaking countries.

Discussion in Prussia—The course of emancipation in the kingdom of Prussia was of the utmost importance. During the last decade of the eighteenth century the king of Prussia debated with his advisers the desirability of granting the Jews some measure of freedom. A commission was appointed and in due time reported that the Jews were not yet worthy of the honor of Prussian citizenship. The Jews, the commissioners said, were still outlandish in religion and occupation and, through their community organization, constituted "a state within the Prussian State." The commission failed to indicate how the Jews could transform themselves as long as they were burdened with onerous restrictions and taxes. In the course of the next decade a few insignificant restrictions were removed. In 1812, however, after Prussia had been disastrously defeated and when it needed every ounce of energy to prepare for its war of liberation from France, the Jews were granted partial emancipation. Civil disabilities were removed; Jews could be elected to city councils, but they still could not hold any state office.

Reactionary Hapsburgs—The empire of Austria-Hungary not only adopted no measures towards emancipating the Jews, but even took some steps backward. The number of special taxes was increased, a tax being imposed on the candles used in Jewish homes on Sabbaths and holidays. Jewish books were strictly censored. Petty police regulations made life miserable for the Jewish inhabitants of the city of Vienna. The object evidently was to make living as Jews so difficult as to drive them into baptism. Curiously, the reactionary government of the Hapsburgs had a sense of guilt about its treatment of the Jews. The rulers, from the emperor down, persuaded themselves that Napoleon's friendly words and his revival of the Sanhedrin would have the effect of attracting the Jews of Austria and Hungary to France. The police redoubled their watchfulness lest the Jews turn to revolution.

Russian Liberalism—The widening influence of French revolutionary ideals beat also on the borders of Russia. Consequently, fears similar to those of the Hapsburgs lay behind the relations of the government of the czars with the Jews of what had been Poland. When Poland was divided up among its neighbors, some districts thickly populated with Jews fell to Russia. The Russian government appointed a commission, during the last years of the eighteenth century, to find a "so-lution" to the Jewish problem. The investigators arrived at the conclusion that the Jews had to be civilized by force, so that they might recognize the superiority of the Russian type of Christianity. One of their suggestions, adopted by Czar Alex-ander I, was to drive the Jews out of the villages and into the towns. As long as there was danger from Napoleon this measure was not put into effect. When that danger seemed past, the expulsion was begun. A few years later, when Napo-leon invaded Russia and fear was revived that the Jewish population might sympathize with the French, liberal prom-ises were once more held out to them. Actually the Jews had no more intention of siding with the French than they had of becoming converts to Christianity; the governors of the var-ious provinces testified to their loyalty. As might have been expected, the czar and his government forgot their generous promises as soon as the Napoleonic danger passed away.

5. Betrayal at Vienna

Turning Back the Clock—After Napoleon's defeat, the Eu-ropean states, large and small, sent representatives to a con-gress which met at Vienna to reconstruct the map and to see what each might grab for itself. With few exceptions, the princes and princelings, soldiers and burghers who repre-sented their governments hoped to re-establish the old, pre-revolutionary order, including their former attitude toward the Jews. The Prussian representatives were willing enough to let the Jews enjoy the slight gains they had made towards eman-cipation. Austria and the smaller states, however, especially those which had been occupied by the French, saw in the freedom of the Jews the most provoking reminder of the Revolution, the memory of which they wanted to erase. One of the prominent Austrian diplomats was even convinced, or so he said, that Jews had been responsible for Napoleon! Every once in a while the question of the Jews would come up before the delegates to the congress, and before long the reactionary tendency of the discussions became clear.

Ineffective Charm—Several Jewish communities, recogniz-ing the danger to their few, hard-won rights, sent unofficial delegates of their own to the Congress of Vienna. These were Jews or non-Jews who could exert pressure or use persuasion against a return to medieval conditions. The influence of these lobbyists did not prove effective. On the other hand, another type of Jewish effort was more influential. Vienna boasted a number of Jewish homes, like those of the two financiers, Nathan von Arnstein and Bernhard von Eskeles, to which invitations were eagerly sought. The foremost intellectuals and statesmen used to gather there, less because of the practical abilities of the men than because of the charm and high culture of the women of these households. Over cups of tea, all sorts of subjects were discussed, including presumably the future of the Jews. The mere enjoyment of their visits at these homes should have proved to the diplomats the desirability of granting greater economic and social rights to the Jews of their countries. The visitors, however, enjoyed Jewish hospitality in the afternoon and voted against Jewish emancipation in the evening. Their attitude clearly depended not on practical accomplishments but on prejudice, not on a desire for the Jews to become what they called "useful citizens," but on a wish to keep them in an inferior position.

Tricky Resolutions—The committee in charge of the matter at the Congress of Vienna eventually brought in a resolution on the subject of the Jews. Its original wording permitted the Jews to continue to enjoy the rights already granted them. But a slight change was made in one word, so that on closer analysis the resolution said exactly the opposite. It limited the Jews to the continuance of the rights granted by the various governments in existence at the moment of the voting. Since rights had been granted the Jews by former governments, such as had been under revolutionary influence, any existing government could withdraw every shred of emancipation acquired by the Jews during the previous twenty-five years.

The New "Hep, Hep!"—Thus it was proved once more that reaction in politics and economics brought with it reaction in the treatment of the Jews. The great states of Europe, after the Congress of Vienna, organized themselves for the purpose of keeping their own populations in subjection and of lording it over the smaller states. Russia, Austria and Prussia, who formed a "Holy Alliance," used every unholy means to uproot the slightest suspicion of liberalism. In numerous anti-Jewish pamphlets and articles and in statements by the reactionary governments, it was asserted that Christian society could not grant equality or economic opportunity to Jews. Many of the smaller states of Germany now went back on their promises to the Jews. Some places, into which the Jews had but recently been admitted, expelled them again. The city of Frankfort, which had accepted cash payment for the grant of limited rights, kept the money but not its promise.

Throughout the lands where German was spoken, a derisive cry greeted the Jews—"Hep! Hep!"—a cry which recalled the darkest moments of the dark Middle Ages. Whatever its origin, this cry, sometimes accompanied by violence, indicated that the work of the Revolution in freeing the human mind from enslaving prejudice would have to be done all over again.

Remnants of Freedom—The old order, nevertheless, could not be re-established as thoroughly as the reactionaries desired. Europe's middle classes had tasted freedom and liked it; sooner or later, they were bound to demand it again. Above all, reaction could not be re-established in France, where the memory of the Revolution was too strong and where the middle class would not be denied its new opportunities. While the Jews there were deprived of the absolute equality they thought they had gained in 1791, they were not treated with anything like the indignity which Jews suffered in German lands or in the territory of the restored popes in Rome. In England, too, where the situation had not been at all bad even during the eighteenth century, there were definite signs of further improvement. The example of these countries was sure to affect the rest of the European continent and to spur the Jews of Germany to ask and work for the equality which was their human right.

CHAPTER II

PLEADING FOR RIGHTS

THE JEWS OF GERMANY TRY FLATTERY, ARGUMENT AND RELIGIOUS REFORM IN ORDER TO PERSUADE THEIR NEIGH-BORS TO TREAT THEM AS EQUALS

Yearning to be Equal—For two generations after the French Revolution the Jews of Europe were given explanations why full emancipation from medieval restrictions could not be granted them. They took these so-called reasons seriously and did all they could to make the adjustments required of them, sometimes sacrificing their dignity as men in order to attain the dignity of citizens. Too many of them failed to see that the pretentious arguments of their opponents were little more than excuses for prejudice and envy. Nevertheless, the struggle resulted indirectly in considerable good. It revived investigation among the Jews into the nature and history of Judaism and of the Jewish group. In society generally, it brought greater cooperation between the Jews and the forces of honest liberalism, thus enlisting added strength in the struggle for the rights of man and for greater human freedom. The struggle for adjustment and emancipation was, therefore, an important event in the story of the modern Jew.

1. FREEDOM THROUGH RELIGIOUS REFORM

Mendelssohn's Heritage—While Mendelssohn, orthodox in his Jewish observances, had advised adding general culture to the Jewish, without abandoning the latter, his followers found little time and sympathy for the Jewish manner of life. They accepted every criticism of Judaism but made no effort to acquire an appreciation of its virtues. They fell an easy prey to the ridicule of Judaism current among the Christians with whom they associated, so that they began to chafe under the restraints of Jewish life. Some years after Mendelssohn's death, several of his own children and grandchildren became converts to Christianity.

The Desire to Feel at Home—Ignorance of Jewish teaching was only one cause for this treason to the Jewish way of life. Another cause was the failure of society to recognize the Jews as equals. Following the Congress of Vienna, the liberals among the Christians lost their influence. The result was a terrific blow to the hopes of the upper-class Jews. Physically, spiritually, and economically outside the ghetto, they were now told that their very Jewishness constituted a ghetto, so that politically and to some extent socially a Christian state must keep them within one. A wave of conversions therefore set in, many members of the wealthiest and most aristocratic Jewish families flocking to the churches to be baptized. Such Jews, in acquiring Western culture, clearly had lost that spiritual stamina which had kept the Jewish group alive through many darker ages. Something had to be done to revive self-knowledge and self-respect in large sections of the people.

External Reform—The Jews of Germany took very seriously the argument that they were too different in manners and customs to be considered the equals of Christian Germans. The terms applied to Jewish life were "queer" and "outlandish," and Judaism was called a relic of a dead Asiatic civilization. The deserters from Judaism gave the same justification for their action. A number of the more loyal Jews thereby became convinced that the stigma of outlandishness must be removed from Judaism, both to put an end to the conversions and to refute the specious arguments against emancipation. A start was made early in the nineteenth century in the Western German province of Westphalia while it was still under French domination. Israel Jacobson, the most prominent Jew of that province and the leader of its consistory, introduced a number of changes into the synagogue ritual. A few of the Hebrew prayers were to be recited in German; a mixed choir and instrumental music were to accompany the services; a sermon in German was to be part of the ritual. These were rather mild reforms, but they represented a break with the traditions of many centuries and therefore horrified the mass of German Jews to whom their traditions were still dear.

Temples—When conditions in Westphalia changed, Jacobson moved to Berlin and carried his ideas with him. Since the established synagogues could not be used to introduce reforms, a group of the wealthy Jews organized services in private homes—one was in the home of Jacob Herz Beer, father of the composer Meyerbeer. This was the period when reaction was at its height; when all change, religious as well as political, was under suspicion. Some fanatics among the Jews resorted to the ugly method of calling the government of Prussia to their aid to compel the discontinuance of the new service. But once begun, the movement could not so easily be stopped. In the freer atmosphere of Hamburg, a building was put up and two men, with rabbinic training and modern culture, were engaged as preachers (1816). The service was organized on the model of the Berlin service, with an organ, with a few German prayers and with some changes in the Hebrew prayers to modify the expressions of hope for the Messiah and the restoration of Palestine. As good an indication as any of the spirit which underlay the changes was the fact that the name synagogue was given up in favor of the name temple. The word "synagogue" stirred ghetto memories and stood for all that Christianity had bitterly combated; with the word "temple" the Jews, who sought forgetfulness of the age-old conflict, thought that they could make a new start.

Opposition and Progress—The storm of protest which arose among the opponents of Reform served merely to solidify the ranks on both sides. Undaunted by the outcry against them, the Reformers continued to spread their views with missionary fervor. They organized a model Reform service in Leipzig, so that the Jews who came there twice a year to attend the famous fair might be inspired to emulate this example when they returned home. The Reformers also exerted more polite but just as effective influence on various local governments. Thus the government of Saxe-Weimar was induced to insist on the introduction of German into the synagogue service. In fact, the influence of the Reformers spread far and wide beyond the borders of Germany. Echoes of Reform were soon heard in England and in France, and even in the small Jewish community of the United States. In 1824 a group of Jews in Charleston, South Carolina, petitioned the board of their congregation to introduce the German reforms into the service. When their petition was rejected, they seceded and organized a Reform congregation of their own. While this particular experiment did not last long, the United States eventually proved fruitful soil for the new ideas.

New Justifications—The violent quarrels and the name-calling which accompanied the spread of the Reform ideas during the first generation of the movement could not continue without each side developing justifications for its actions. The practical consideration of meeting the Christian charge that the Jews were too different was bound to give way among the Reformers to more worthy and more mature explanations of the need for change within Judaism. The leadership of the second generation of Reformers saw their problems in religious and philosophical terms. The Orthodox, thus put on the intellectual defensive, also brought forward arguments more worthy of Judaism than excommunications and appeals to reactionary governments. Altogether, Reform after 1830 produced on both sides men and ideas which lifted the level of the discussion to a higher plane and, therefore, profoundly affected Jewish life from that day to this.

Rabbinic Conferences—The new ideas themselves created a problem. Each rabbi, whether he leaned towards Orthodoxy or towards Reform, advocated his own ideas on Judaism and drew from them his own conclusions for changes which he considered necessary. This threatened chaos in Jewish life where previously there had been close unity. Consequently, it was thought desirable to call a conference of the so-called "modern" rabbis in order to discover whether some measure of common action could be achieved. But the conferences, called between 1844 and 1846, did not attain the desired unity. From the very beginning of the discussions it became clear that the new religious leadership of the German Jews contained four distinct points of view.

Two Extremes—Farthest apart in their attitudes were two interesting and influential men: Samuel Holdheim and Samson Raphael Hirsch. Holdheim, who had received a thorough rabbinic training in an East European *yeshibah* and who subsequently became the rabbi of the Reform congregation of Berlin, was in favor of the most extreme reforms. Religion, he argued, was an instrument developed by man for the purpose of improving the nature of mankind and human society and, like all instruments, it required constant adjustment to new conditions. The traditions of Judaism, its theology and practices, might have been suitable to situations in the past, but were outgrown and ostmoded. Judaism must be modified and recast completely to fit the new age. Man's intelligence, not tradition, must rule.

Hirsch held quite the opposite point of view. He argued that God's revelation of the Torah on Mount Sinai was a fact, and that without Torah there was no Israel. Until a new divine revelation was granted Israel, no change dared be made. Man's intelligence could not measure itself against the divine, and it was bold presumption for any generation to set itself up as the possessor of perfect wisdom and as superior to God's expressed will. Hirsch, therefore, argued against the slightest change in Jewish tradition and for the retention in their minutest details of the beliefs and customs of Israel. He was so powerful a writer, preacher and leader of men, that he won back to Orthodoxy not only the important Jewish community of Frankfort on the Main, which in the 1840s was a stronghold of radical Reform, but also many other individuals and communities. Holdheim, on the other hand, had but a meager following in his own day and in later Germany. The influence of his ideas turned out to be much stronger in the newer environment of the United States a generation later.

Two Moderates—Between these extremes stood two men, Abraham Geiger and Zechariah Frankel, whose influence on Judaism has been tremendous. Abraham Geiger laid the intellectual foundations for Reform Judaism, especially as it has been known in Europe. Judaism, he argued, was a living institution, not a mere dead instrument such as Holdheim imagined, nor an unchangeable fossil as Hirsch represented it to be. Its spirit was sacred and not to be tampered with; but, like all living things, its form was subject to change. Consequently, the Jews of any generation had a double duty; to search deeply into the nature of the Jewish spirit and to modify the forms, namely, the customs and ceremonies, so as to express the spirit most clearly and truthfully for any given period.

Zechariah Frankel accepted the first part of this view. Judaism, he agreed, was a living spirit and, the more one studied it, the more he recognized how very much alive it was. Forms, he felt, were not something to be put on externally like clothes, but were outgrowths of the spirit itself. Judaism had undergone many changes during its long history, but no one deliberately made these changes. They came into being of themselves, because any living thing adjusted itself to its surroundings through the process of life, that is, of history. Consequently, Frankel objected to making changes in Jewish tradition. These changes, he said, would come of themselves, naturally, and would then be in conformity with the spirit of Judaism as well as with the environment. Frankel's view came to be known as "Historical Judaism" and in America found the largest following among those who style themselves Conservative Jews.

The Period of Consolidation—The conferences in which these differences were debated served to clarify the issues, even if they did not result in unity. Other conferences were to have been called. The decade between 1840 and 1850, however, witnessed another struggle, political in nature, in which the Jews became deeply involved, and attention was drawn away from religious controversy. In any case, attempts at religious reform seemed to get the Jews nowhere from the point of view either of reconciling internal differences or of bringing nearer that complete emancipation at which, to some extent, the Reform movement had aimed. Nevertheless, the various attitudes continued to be discussed and written about, and produced scientific works of the utmost importance.

2. FREEDOM THROUGH DEMOCRACY

The Struggle for Freedom—All the youthful and progressive forces during the first half of the nineteenth century were absorbed in the struggle for political democracy. The reactionary governments which, ever since the Congress of Vienna, had attempted to keep the world from making the slightest progress were meeting with increasing opposition. Revolutionary agitation flourished underground. Secret societies and able journalists managed to spread the ideals of democracy and the hatred of tyranny in ways which were the despair of the police and the admiration of the common people. What the reactionary governments failed to see was that the day of a privileged nobility and a landed aristocracy was over and that, since economic power was already in the hands of the middle class, that class ought to have a voice in the political guidance of the state. While the reactionaries appealed to the divine right of kings, the progressives appealed to the divine rights of man, to liberty, equality and fraternity and all the other ideals made popular by the French Revolution. Since the Jews were, economically speaking, members of the middle class, and since it was impossible to exclude them from these broad ideals, the struggle for democracy involved also the political emancipation of the Jews.

The New Nationalism—The progressives of that day had still another ideal, that of nationalism. As a result of the French Revolution and the Napoleonic wars, the peoples of Europe became conscious of belonging to national states. They no longer fought the kings' wars and they no longer felt that they were the kings' subjects; they now pursued national policies, adopted national ambitions and, in the case of Germany and Italy, sought for national unity. From then on the nationalist spirit became an important factor in Jewish life as well. Indeed, the Jews adopted the national ideal of the nation into which they were born and became more zealous in advocating the nationalism of Germany, France, England, Italy, or any other country, than many of the Christians of these states.

Crémieux and Democracy in France—Throughout the nineteenth century France continued in its role of liberal political leadership. What happened there found an echo in other lands of Europe. The government which was established in Paris after Napoleon's fall tried to be as reactionary as that of Austria or Russia, but the French people, among whom the ideals of the Revolution had been born, would not easily yield them. One of the most important among those who continued to fight for their realization was Adolphe Crémieux, who made an illustrious name for himself as a defender of the ideals of the Revolution and of the French nation. At the same time, he boldly and skillfully claimed for his fellow

Jews all the rights which any other Frenchman enjoyed. His first important victory for the rights of the Jews was the abolition of the long, ugly and insulting oath which a Jew had to take in a court of law. Crémieux called this not a victory for the Jews alone, but for all Frenchmen to whom the equality of man was dear and medieval discrimination abhorrent. The fall of the Bourbons in 1830 insured for the French Jews the possession of every right of citizenship won early in the revolutionary era. His fervid oratory and shining courage in the fight for freedom soon made Crémieux famous and honored throughout France. He moved to Paris where he played a prominent part. As a member of the Chamber of Deputies, he fought the increasingly reactionary policies of the next king, Louis Philippe. When the revolution of 1848 broke out, Crémieux was made a member of the provisional government. Heartbroken over Napoleon III's betrayal of his trust, when this adventurer declared himself emperor, Crémieux became the center of the opposition. To the end he fought the restrictions on individual liberty which became more and more characteristic of Napoleon III's policy. When Napoleon resigned his throne, Crémieux was once more entrusted with a share in the provisional government of 1870.

Throughout this life of loyalty to France and its ideals, Crémieux never failed to defend the position of the Jews in whatever part of the world they were threatened. He thus became the outstanding example of the emancipated Jew to whom the welfare of his country and of the Jewish people were equally dear and who saw in the treatment of the Jew, with all his differences from the majority, an expression and a test of the civilization and idealism of his nation. Long before his death, in 1880, Crémieux saw the Jews of France and even of Algeria, one of the French colonies in North Africa, fully recognized as French citizens.

Emancipation in England—The Jews of England, who grew in economic importance with England's industrial and commerical rise, had as much difficulty as those of France in attaining equality with their fellow Englishmen. Obstacles in the way of their commercial and financial activity had long been removed (around 1700), and, even after the defeat of their political emancipation in 1753,* liberal Englishmen continued to raise their voices in behalf of the Jews. The Jews did what they could to help abolish political discrimination against English Catholics, but when that was achieved in 1828

* See above, p. 472.

they found that their own cause was not much farther advanced. The struggle continued, and, though a bill removing their disabilities passed the House of Commons on several occasions (1833, 1834, 1836), it failed in the House of Lords. Nevertheless, that same decade saw the English universities open their doors to them and an act passed permitting Jews to hold the local office of sheriff. David Salomons was elected sheriff of London in 1835, and two years later Moses Montefiore was elected to the same office, whereupon Queen Victoria knighted him. In 1855, David Salomons was elected lord mayor of London, and the only remaining step was for Jews to be permitted to enter Parliament. On this point a long and dramatic struggle ensued, Lionel Rothschild and David Salomons being repeatedly elected to the House of Commons and as often prevented by the reactionaries from taking their seats. This last shred of discrimination was abolished in 1858.

Social Equality in England—Even before the final victory the Jews had enjoyed social equality, especially among the upper class of English society. Sir Moses Montefiore, possessed of wealth and dignity, exerted a profound influence in behalf of Jews wherever they were oppressed. Sir Nathaniel Rothschild was created a peer of England in 1885 and took his seat in the House of Lords, where others followed him. Although the spectacular and exotic Benjamin Disraeli cannot be counted among the Jews who rose high to public office, since he had been converted to Christianity as a child, he deserves mention in this connection because he spoke and wrote with pride about his Jewish ancestry, while his enemies used his Jewish origin as a reason for opposing him.

Gabriel Riesser and Revolution in Germany—Emancipation in France and England had thus been obtained with comparative ease; in Germany there was a different story to tell. Year by year the tide of sentiment in favor of greater democracy was rising in every German-speaking land, and in this tide the Jews became increasingly influential. Ludwig Boerne and Heinrich Heine exercised, through their poetry and journalism, a tremendous influence in favor of liberal, democratic action. Though both had become converts to Christianity in the hope of being accepted into the social and cultural life of Germany, they were still looked upon as Jews and denied equality.

Gabriel Riesser was a different sort of person. The grandson of an Orthodox rabbi, he, like so many other cultured German Jews of his generation, had lost interest in Judaism. He steadfastly refused, however, to become a convert to

Christianity even though this step would have won him the professorship of law which he desired and deserved. To take such a step, he asserted, would be cowardice and a betrayal of the high ideals which he identified with the German spirit. He published a newspaper which he challengingly named *The Jew,* and in which he advocated political emancipation for all Germans, the Jews included. Like all liberals of his day, he sought to bring about a union of the German states. When the revolution of 1848 broke out and the various peoples of the German states and communities sent deputations to a national assembly at Frankfort, Riesser was honored by election to a vice-presidency of that body. Even there, among these liberals, the question of Jewish equality was coolly received. But Riesser and the other Jews did not consider this reception of too great importance. The cause of German unity and democracy came first and their own cause second, and they felt that the one would bring the other. The revolution, however, failed of its most important objectives. Many Jews and liberals, in their despair of progress in Germany, thereupon migrated to the United States.

It was to take twenty years longer, two wars and the cleverness of Bismarck, for the Jews to obtain some measure of political equality. For Bismarck recognized that the Jews would be enthusiastic in support of a German nation and he imposed both unity and emancipation upon the German people. Thus out of economic and political advantage the Jews were given what they had been unable to obtain either by appeals to idealism or by deliberately setting out to abolish differences between themselves and the Christian Germans. Gabriel Riesser, the symbol of this struggle, died in 1863, long before the final attainment of the reforms for which he had fought.

Emancipation in Austria and Hungary—The empire of the Hapsburg dynasty was at first the leader in reaction. The revolution of 1848 in its lands actually turned into a war between the dynasty and the people. In Vienna, a young Jewish medical student, Adolf Fischhof, was entrusted by the revolutionaries with governing power. Other Jews were active in the nationalist movements in Austria, Bohemia and Hungary. Those who had fallen in the first encounter between people and soldiers were buried in a common grave, Christians and Jews together, and Rabbi Isak Noah Mannheimer participated in the funeral. While the revolutionary movement was defeated, wider democracy and with it a greater degree of emancipation resulted during the twenty years which followed. The Jews of the various provinces achieved the gradual removal of the medieval restrictions upon them in trades and professions and on their rights to own land. Finally, the Constitution of 1867 granted the Jews complete citizenship.

The Fall of the Roman Ghetto—Events in the city of Rome were symbolic of the conflict of forces which in Western and Central Europe marked the end of the era of reaction. Immediately after the Congress of Vienna, the popes returned in every detail to the medieval policy in government and religion. The ghetto of Rome once more stood as evidence of the desire of the reactionary forces to keep the Jews separate. The people of Italy, however, divided among many masters, began to clamor for unity and liberalism. The Jews of northern Italy at any rate, having long enjoyed more freedom than most other Jews of Europe, freely participated in these movements. A change in the direction of progress was anticipated when Pius IX ascended the papal throne in 1846. Himself of liberal inclination, he surprised the Jews, on the night of Passover, 1848, by permitting the removal of the ghetto's gates as evidence of his willingness to improve their lot. But the revolutionary movement among the Italians, quite apart from the Jews, could not be arrested by the pope's policy of gradual liberalization. Some weeks after his friendly gesture to the Jews, the pope was compelled to flee Rome and from his exile witness the establishment of a Roman republic, in which Jews participated. He was so embittered by this that when he returned to Rome, after the revolution had been crushed, he displayed an intense hatred for everything liberal. He now blamed the Jews for the revolutionary movements, for liberalism's growing strength in Europe and for the decreasing influence of the Catholic Church. Consequently he re-established the ghetto, although its existence was already foreign to the spirit of most of the population. For twenty years this situation continued, until, in 1870, Italy was united under the king of Savoy and the Jews were granted complete equality.

3. THE KNOWLEDGE OF JUDAISM

A Young People's Club—In 1819, while Reform was still in its early stages and democracy little more than a hope, a small group of young Jews met in Berlin and founded an organization which they called "A Society for the Culture and (Scientific) Knowledge of Judaism." Their program was as long and as ambitious as their name. They intended to establish a magazine in which Judaism would be shown to be a religion of rich culture and profound significance. They planned to encourage improved education among the Jews and hoped to establish branches of their club everywhere. In brief, they sought to bring about a renaissance of Jewish life. The originators of the idea were carried away by their youthful enthusiasm. Yet, how urgently such work was needed was proved when the president of the organization left Judaism shortly after in order to obtain a professorship of law in a German university, and when one of its most gifted members, Hayyim Herz (or Heinrich) Heine, likewise became outwardly a convert because he hoped to obtain a professorship in German literature. One member, however, Leopold Zunz, remained loyal to the principles of the organization and helped achieve the most important of its aims.

Zunz and Jewish Scholarship—Leopold Zunz (1794–1886) received an excellent Jewish and general education. As early as 1818, he published a little book in which he pleaded for the recognition of research into the Jewish past as an indispensable study. To the cause of such research he devoted himself wholeheartedly, earning his livelihood in the meantime from tutoring and acting as rabbi. Eventually he became the principal of a teachers' seminary established by the Jews of Berlin in 1840. By this time he had already produced important works and this position gave him more leisure for further research.

The great discussion between Orthodoxy and Reform raged at that time and it set Zunz's mind thinking in the direction of the controversy. His foremost work was called *The Religious Discourses of the Jews,* wherein he undertook to show the part that preaching had played in Judaism. In reality it turned out to be a heavy but highly significant volume dealing with the elements of instruction and prayer in Jewish life. It proved that Judaism had never stood still, but had undergone changes in accordance with requirements of time and place; it changed itself even when there were no reformers advocating change. Zunz's many other books on the history of Jewish culture and religion tended to prove the same theory, while showing that the cultural level among the Jews had always been exceptionally high. On the whole, Zunz offered scientific proof of the historical correctness of Zechariah Frankel's attitude. In a letter to Geiger, Zunz said: "It is ourselves that we must reform, not our religion. We should attack the evil usages which exist within and without, not our sacred heritage."

Geiger and Frankel—Two other men, who made highly important contributions to the revival of Jewish knowledge on a scientific, historical basis, have already been mentioned in connection with the Reform controversy. Abraham Geiger's (1810–1874) most important work was on the Bible in the original and in its translations; it was actually a history of the Bible as a book. It was characteristic of Geiger that he subjected the Bible and Jewish tradition to cold criticism. The very tone and attitude of the work aroused the anger of some of the Orthodox Jews. Yet Geiger was very proud of Judaism and its contribution to the culture of the world and showed his pride, along with his critical ability, in a large number of books and articles. Looked up to as the founder of the Reform movement, Geiger provided a foundation of knowledge and an example of learning for the Reform leadership of Germany.

To an even greater extent the same can be said of Zechariah Frankel. He was less interested in criticizing the traditions of the past than in making them and their causes clear. Through a number of works on the Talmud and other rabbinic sources, Frankel made possible a modern approach to the study of this type of literature. Both Frankel and Geiger edited scientific journals and both became the heads of rabbinical seminaries: Geiger of the one in Berlin, and Frankel of the one in Breslau.

An Intellectual Awakening—These men, and others of every shade of religious opinion among the Jews of Germany, began one of the most remarkable movements of our time. Working in the midst of a comparatively small population which, at the beginning of the nineteenth century, had shown every sign of dissolution, they revived interest in and knowledge of Judaism and inspired pride where there had been self-contempt. It is all the more remarkable that they succeeded in achieving this by means of rather heavy, scientific works. There were a number of reasons for their success. Cultured Germans of that day laid great stress on reading and on scientific knowledge. This general attitude strengthened the tradition of learning among the Jews, whose hunger for knowledge had ever been strong. Besides, the controversy about Reform had stirred interest in the question of Jewish tradition and literature, and intelligent people sought the facts behind the arguments which each side presented. Finally, the Jews were then still hopeful that truth would overcome prejudice among the Christians. They therefore encouraged the search for truth about themselves so as to bolster their own self-respect and to make their neighbors respect them. But whatever the reasons, the Science of Judaism, as this movement of searching for knowledge has come to be known, profoundly affected Jewish life and thought in every part of the world to this day.

Graetz the Historian—In a sense Heinrich Graetz (1817–1891) and his work round out and summarize the age and the movement. Graetz was professor of history at the Breslau Seminary and wrote a complete history of the Jews in the modern scientific spirit. Another Jewish scholar, Isaac Marcus Jost, had completed a similar work in 1828. But Graetz possessed a better understanding of history and was better equipped to write about the Jews. He had the immense energy necessary to search for and evaluate the thousands of source documents which till then had remained untouched. He was able not only to recognize a fact but also to see the causes which lay behind it, and he could fit the events of Jewish history into the background of general events. Moreover, quite unlike the majority of Jewish scholars of that age, he could write movingly and interestingly.

Two factors in the Jewish past emerged as most prominent in the story as he told it: Jewish suffering and Jewish thought. In spite of this suffering, the Jewish mind never stopped functioning; the Jewish spirit never ceased contributing to the culture of humanity; and Jewish hope never died. It took Graetz twenty years to tell this story in eleven rather long volumes; and when it was told the Jews the world over hailed it with enthusiasm. Among many Christians, however, it aroused resentment, because Graetz, not interested in the social and economic motivations of human society, had laid the blame for the persecution of the Jews on the narrowness and bigotry which had characterized Christianity during the Middle Ages. Graetz, in addition to writing a history book, had thus written a justification of Jewish life and, in a sense, given a pledge of Jewish continuity. The *History of the Jews* appeared at an opportune moment. Forces were already in motion in Germany which were opposed to that spirit of freedom and democracy which had brought emancipation to the Jews.

Graetz and East European Jewry—Heinrich Graetz, gifted though he was as an historian, could not overcome at least one of the prejudices of the German Jews of his day—the inclination to think poorly of the East European Jews. He disparaged their study of the Talmud as vain and useless pilpulism, and looked down on Hasidism, which was so widespread among them, as pure superstition. He failed to see the beautiful piety which prevailed in Eastern Europe despite hostility and poverty. Had he taken the trouble to learn more about the living Jews of Russia, Poland and Rumania, Graetz would have found among them that very loyalty to Jewish life which he admired so much in the Jews of the Middle Ages and which he was trying to revive among the Jews of Germany.

CHAPTER III

STRUGGLE FOR ADJUSTMENT IN EASTERN EUROPE

THE JEWS OF RUSSIA, OPPRESSED BY CZARIST AUTOCRACY,
FACE A NUMBER OF CULTURAL AND POLITICAL PROBLEMS
WITHIN AND WITHOUT THE JEWISH COMMUNITY

Contrasting Populations—In some respects the Jews of Russian Poland and of the other lands of Eastern Europe at the beginning of the nineteenth century faced a much more difficult problem than did their fellow Jews of Germany; in other respects their problem was considerably easier. Their difficulty was that they lived under a government and in the midst of a population infinitely more benighted than the government and population of Germany. There was absolutely no point in talking to the czarist regime in terms of idealism or the rights of man. Russia was only just beginning to develop a literature. Some kind of culture could be found only among extremely few of the Polish and Russian upper classes who had received their training in Western Europe. There was thus nothing in their environment to stimulate the Jews to emulate the non-Jewish population, as was the case in Germany. This resulted in throwing the East European Jews back upon their own cultural resources. Fortunately, the Jewish population of Eastern Europe was large and it possessed a

tradition of learning. The masses of the Jews were not lonely
and lost as were the comparatively small number of German
Jews; consequently the desire to be adopted by the Christians
as equals was confined to a very few.

Nevertheless, a number of factors made for change among
the East European Jews, too, so that their life also became
transformed inside of two or three generations. This transformation in turn eventually brought new ideas and attitudes
which, fusing with the ideas developed among the Jews of
Germany, have affected our life to the present.

1. Czarist Methods of "Solving a Problem"

Rejection in Poland—The large Jewish population which
Russia took over from Poland, after joining its neighbors to
destroy that state, was supposed to present a problem. That
problem, as the Russian and Polish governing classes saw it,
was not how to improve the economic conditions of this poverty-stricken population and thereby improve the economic
conditions of the entire country; it was rather how most
effectively to destroy Jewish life. Both Poles and Russians
agreed on treating the Jews as a hostile population. The Poles
wanted them to become Poles. Fighting for Polish freedom
was not considered sufficient. The Jews had done just that in
1794, to prevent the last partition of Poland, and they were
to do so again in 1830, in the Polish uprising against Russia.
But all this made no difference in the attitude of the Polish
Christians. The Jewish fellow fighters themselves and their
families received scant and grudging recognition. There was,
indeed, a small number of Jews who took seriously the usual
arguments that the Jews were too "different" to deserve
equality of treatment. Such Jews spoke slightingly of the Talmud and deplored the distinctive customs of the Jewish population; they called themselves "Poles of the Mosaic Persuasion." The vast majority of the Jews were depressed by the
action of the government and scandalized by the words and
actions of the "assimilationists;" they would not yield to either.

The Pale of Settlement—Interior Russia suffered from the
lack of an energetic middle class to develop its rich resources.
The Jews suffered from living in crowded cities with limited
economic opportunities. For the benefit of the Russian state
the Jews should have been encouraged to spread more thinly
throughout Russia and thereby serve its economic needs.

That, however, was not the way of the czarist government. The command was given for the Jews to move out of the few rural districts which were still open to them and out of the territory which had not been part of the old Polish state. Thus, with some slight modifications of boundary now and then, was established the so-called Pale of Settlement, that is, the district in which Jews were permitted to reside. It was really a large-scale ghetto.

Czarist Civilizing Efforts—The czars made up their minds to "civilize" their Jews. To Czar Nicholas I, one of the cruelest and most unimaginative tyrants that ever lived, this meant nothing more than issuing orders, some sensible, others ridiculous, but the largest number cruel in their attempt to change people by decree. An example of a sensible one was the order that each Jew adopt a family name. Western Jews had had family names for centuries; those of Germany for at least a generation. The Jews of Russia were enrolled now either under the name of the place from which they came or the occupation they followed, or under some personal peculiarity. To this the Jews submitted willingly enough, though they did not consider it important. An example of the ridiculous was the attempt to force the Jews to wear clothes on the Western model. The wearing of long overgarments *(capotte)* had become traditional among the Polish Jews. Actually this garment and the long beard that Jewish men wore were survivals of the fashion of the Polish and Russian nobility of a century or two previously. To the czar the failure to follow the majority in such externals was evidence of disobedience. He commanded the Jews to wear short coats and to trim their beards. When the Jews failed to obey this command, ridiculous scenes became common in every city where Jews lived. One could see a policeman give chase to a bearded and long-robed Jew and, catching him, pull out a long scissors and there and then proceed to make him stylish.

The Cantonists—Tragic beyond description was the order of Nicholas I establishing military service for Jewish children. For the Jews to be permitted to serve in the army was considered a privilege in other countries. The Jews themselves accepted it as such. In 1827, Nicholas opened his army's ranks to the Russian Jews. His avowed purpose was to "Russify" the Jewish soldiers so that, upon their homecoming, they might in turn influence the other Jews with what they had learned. The length of service for all soldiers in the Russian conscript army was set at twenty-five years, begin-

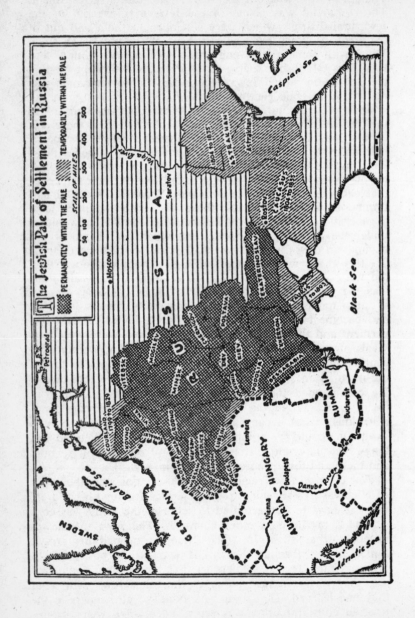

ning at the age of eighteen. Jewish conscripts, however, could be taken as young as twelve years of age, thus giving them an extra six years of preparation for army life. Such conscripted children were placed in special army camps, or cantons, in charge of a peasant sergeant whose business it was to break them of such "bad" habits as refusing to eat pork or to make the sign of the cross. The cruelties practiced on these children made it certain that few would survive. A great many others could not endure the struggle and became converts to Christianity. Under these circumstances, the Jews made every effort to keep their children from being taken into the Russian army. The government, therefore, imposed upon each *kahal,* or Jewish community council, the obligation to produce a certain quota, for the filling of which the members of the *kahal* board were held personally responsible. The *kahal* boards, under such compulsion, often employed official kidnapers in order to fill the ranks of the cantonists.

An Educational Plot—Becoming disgusted with the failure of the Jews to respond to its efforts, the czarist government, in 1840, undertook to achieve by subtlety what it had failed to win by force. The Jews were to be persuaded this time, to establish Jewish schools in which the Russian language and other secular subjects would be taught along with the Jewish subjects. The government intended later to make sure that the study of the Talmud and of Jewish tradition would become so subordinate to the secular subjects as to destroy the religious and cultural basis of Jewish loyalty. This second part of the plan was naturally not revealed. Max Lilienthal, a young German-trained rabbi, with mild Reform sympathies, was prevailed upon to head the proposed school system. Lilienthal, not suspecting the perfidy involved, visited the Jewish communities and tried to persuade them to fall in with the plan. The Russian Jews, knowing their government, warned him that somewhere in this attractive proposal there lurked a sinister plot. Lilienthal took a public oath that, should he discover any such hidden scheme, he would immediately resign. On this basis the Jews promised cooperation. Work on the new school system had hardly begun, when suddenly Lilienthal left Russia and went to America. He had discovered that the real object of the czarist government was to lure the pupils into the Christian fold.

Western Intercession—These were only the more spectacular methods used by the Russian government to ill-treat the Jews. The daily oppressions and petty annoyances were numberless and increasing. The authority of the internal Jewish organization, the *kahal*, was reduced almost to the point of non-existence. Taxes were increased at the same time that economic opportunities were further restricted. Even ritual murder accusations were not unknown. Medievalism was in full swing in Russia even while liberalism was making obvious progress in lands to the west. In 1846, Moses Montefiore tried to persuade the Russian government to modify its policy. He was received with all honor, but, when he pleaded that Russian Jewry be granted a measure of the freedom which Jews were beginning to enjoy in the West, he was told that Russian Jewry was different, that it did not deserve the consideration which Western Jews were receiving.

2. THE FALSE DAWN

The Liberal Era—The death of the tyrannical Nicholas I and the accession of Alexander II (1855) were hailed with delight by the entire Russian population. Much was expected from the new czar who was considered a man of liberal tendencies. He started by curbing the corrupt officialdom which had long held the country in its grip and by planning the liberation of the peasants from the serfdom which had been their lot for centuries. The Russian press began to speak, hesitantly to be sure, about freedom and popular government. Russian literature began to flower and signs of progress appeared in the country's educational institutions. In this happy atmosphere the progressives took it for granted that the hoped-for emancipation would include the Jews as well.

Pro-Jewish Reforms—The Jews had good reason to join in the general spirit of hopefulness. On the day of his coronation, Alexander II ordered the discontinuance of the canton system instituted by his predecessor. The children who were being held by the military, excepting those who had become baptized, were sent home. Discussions were initiated on the subject of removing some of the restrictions which hemmed in Jewish life in the Pale of Settlement. Before long, Jews were again permitted to reside in the border provinces from which they had been barred, and the city of Kiev was opened to them. After prolonged discussion the government permitted three classes of Jews to settle in the interior of the country: the merchants who carried on a volume of business enabling them to pay a sufficiently high tax; the graduates of universities; and artisans recommended by the police of the

Pale as "well behaved." The poverty and the crowding within the Pale were thus to be alleviated, while the interior of Russia would gain from the presence of this new and enterprising population. The Jews, furthermore, were encouraged to enter Russian schools by being offered exemption from military service in return for a diploma from a secondary school. The oath imposed upon the Jews in the Russian law courts was modified by the elimination of its insulting features.

The Response of the Jews—Jews of all classes considered these reforms an excellent beginning. They looked to further expansion of their economic opportunities. Industry within the Pale was somewhat encouraged to expand; but, above all, a number of Jewish capitalists outside the Pale were now enabled materially to aid in the development of Russian resources. Samuel and Lazar Poliakoff, for example, greatly extended the railroads of which Russia was in need; the Geunzburg family of St. Petersburg expanded their banking business; and other Jews established factories far in the interior of the country. There was glowing enthusiasm among this class of Jews for the Russia of the future. A petition to the czar urged the granting of emancipation to the Jews of the upper class so that the rest might be stimulated to abandon their ways and manners in order eventually to gain similar consideration. Above all, the promise of liberalism marked a turning-point in an internal cultural movement which had been gaining ground among the Jews of Eastern Europe for three generations.

3. FOUNDATIONS OF HASKALAH

Two Types of Enlightenment—Had the czarist government really understood what was going on within Jewish circles, it would have shown greater appreciation of the movement towards the modernization of Jewish thought and culture of which Russia and Russian Jewry could well be proud. The movement has received the name *Haskalah*, a word derived from the Hebrew *sechel* which means "intelligence" or "understanding." It represented an effort on the part of Jewish intellectuals (*maskilim*) to "enlighten" the masses of Russian Jewry. *Haskalah* was therefore parallel to *Aufklaerung*, a movement of the same nature in Germany at that time. But there were several basic and significant differences between the two. Whereas the German movement grew up in and for a German-speaking and German-thinking population, *Haska-*

lah was rooted in Hebrew language and thought. *Aufklaerung* emphasized history and theology, while *Haskalah* manifested itself most strikingly in Hebrew literature.

The Beginnings of Haskalah—As in Germany so in Eastern Europe, the movement for enlightenment traced its origin to the intellectual impetus given the group about him by Moses Mendelssohn. Several of his co-workers started publishing *Ha-Meassef*, the magazine whose contributors aimed to transmit to the Yiddish-speaking but Hebrew-reading Jews the thought and literature of the non-Jewish world. They carried on their propaganda in other works as well, in plays, essays and poems. The Hebrew language, however, which they used exclusively, sounded artificial after so many centuries of disuse for ordinary literary purposes; and the subjects with which these authors dealt were for the most part foreign to the spirit of the people for whom they were intended. But at least these originators of *Haskalah* made a valiant effort towards the integration of Hebrew culture with the culture of Western Europe.

A Scholar and a Philosopher—The next step in the development of *Haskalah* was taken by men who were interested in more specifically Jewish cultural values. One of them was Solomon Judah Rapoport (1790–1867), rabbi in Tarnopol (Galicia) and later in Prague. In a series of biographies of great Jews of the past, like Rashi and Saadia, he proved that Judaism had always been a living, growing, expanding religion. Nahman Krochmal (1785–1840), his contemporary, set forth the same idea in a famous philosophical work. Possessed of profound Jewish knowledge, widely read in Western philosophy and keenly sympathetic to the questions which troubled the Jewish intellectuals of his period, he exercised great influence among them. His book, which was published after his death, was appropriately named *The Guide for the Perplexed of the Time*, since it offered a much needed explanation of Jewish life and destiny. The persistent question among those who were coming in contact with Christian thought was: Were Judaism and the Jewish people dying, or were they gifted with that eternal life in which Jewish tradition believed? Krochmal's answer was that the Jewish group could not be compared to the nations of the world. Every nation had its period of growth, maturity and decay. The Jews, however, had experienced several such cycles. On a number of occasions the Jewish people seemed about to disappear, but revived and went through the living process again. The reason for this ability of the Jews to overcome the forces of decay and death was that Judaism was an eternal spirit and knew the secret of self-rejuvenation. In other groups the physical body, or the national territory, dominated the group-soul; in the case of the Jews the group-soul was the all-important element, for it molded and revived the nation. In this way, Krochmal offered a message of hope and what seemed to his contemporaries a plausible solution to the mystery of Jewish survival.

An Italian Sage—The influence of the new enlightenment spread southward as well as eastward. Samuel David Luzzatto (1800–1865) was professor at the rabbinical seminary which had been opened in Padua, Italy. In a series of books and articles he did much for the revival of the Bible as a branch of study among the Jews. But his attitude to Jewish culture in general was also important. European civilization, he believed, paid altogether too much attention to what it had inherited from Greek philosophy and art and altogether too little to what it had acquired from Hebrew ethics and religion. Human happiness and progress have little to hope for from Grecian emphasis on the externals of life, but they have everything to gain from greater attention to the sense of justice and the development of character which the prophets had tried to instill. Luzzatto called to the Jews not to be submerged by the civilizations about them; they had more to give to than obtain from their environment.

4. HASKALAH IN EASTERN EUROPE

Culture and Politics—In Eastern Europe, especially in the Russian empire, the *Haskalah* movement was affected not only by the inner urge to self-understanding and enlightenment, but also by the external political situation. As long as czarist reaction reigned supreme, the *maskilim* were on the defensive. They could hold out no incentive for the Jews to cast away ancient and respected ways in order to mingle with a hostile population and adopt the culture of a backward civilization. It was therefore only in the first part of Alexander II's reign that *Haskalah* took the offensive and, changing its tone and its approach, openly advocated a transformation of Jewish life. The traditionalists, on the other hand, whether Hasidim or Mithnagdim, used parental and communal authority in favor of the existing conditions, though in the second period they were obviously on the defensive.

The Russian Mendelssohn—The most influential of the early advocates of *Haskalah* in Russia was Isaac Baer Levinsohn (1788–1860). His contemporaries saw in him a parallel to Moses Mendelssohn because he too adopted the method of reason, urging the Jews to interest themselves in general culture while defending Judaism against external attack. In simple, unaffected Hebrew, he pointed out how the East European Jews might reconstruct their lives by broadening their intellectual and economic bases. Jewish education had been a broad education and many great Jews of the past had seen no objection to the study of foreign languages and non-Jewish philosophies. At the same time, Levinsohn wrote with mild regret about the inhuman charge of the blood libel which was spreading in Russia. His work had little effect on the enemies of Israel, but made a considerable impression on the traditionalist Jewish population.

Poets and Novelists of the First Period—The Hebrew language had developed sufficiently, by the second quarter of the nineteenth century, to produce a crop of poets and novelists. None of them reached the heights of the Spanish poets during the Golden Age, though they did show that not only was Hebrew a living language, but that the Jewish people was a living group. First among these were the Lebensohns: Abraham Dov (1794–1878), the father, and Micah Joseph (1828–1852), the son. The latter, in his brief career, proved to be the better poet. Judah Loeb Gordon (1830–1892) in his first period, also belonged to this group, and so did the novelist, Abraham Mapu (1808–1867). A characteristic of the last three was their use of Bible incidents and characters, by means of which they expressed the longing of their generation for the idyllic life of ancient Judea, the simplicity of the farmer's life, the heroism of combat, the freedom, the naturalness, the optimism which they found in the ancient past of the Jewish people. Mapu's *Ahabat Tziyon* (The Love of Zion, 1853), for example, exercised a tremendous influence upon his and subsequent generations. In excellent imitation of biblical style, Mapu here told the story of a love affair in the days of King Hezekiah. Many a *yeshibah* student was attracted by these works, which he read clandestinely—for to read them openly meant expulsion from the *yeshibah*—and eventually became sympathetic to the social and cultural reforms for which *Haskalah* stood.

Haskalah on the Offensive—The spirit of optimism which took hold of Russian Jewry as a result of Alexander II's reforms is evident in the changed tempers of these very authors.

From romantic portrayers of the ancient past, they now turned into sharp, merciless critics of their own age and its leaders. Gordon came forward with a number of long stories in verse, in which he blamed devotion to the letter of Jewish law and dry, lifeless Talmudism for personal unhappiness and social ills to be found among the Jews of that day. From treating themes of ancient times, Mapu turned to an outright exposé of his contemporaries. In a long and complicated story, ʻAyit Tsabuʻa (The Hypocrite, literally, The Painted Hawk) he tried to lay bare the prevalent hypocrisy and stupidity. Critics and satirists of Jewish life abounded. Even Shalom Jacob Abramowitch (1835–1917), whom we shall meet later in a more sympathetic role, wrote a Hebrew novel directed against the presumed evils about him. All these had become too deeply conscious of the charges directed against their Jewish contemporaries to point to the abstract virtues of Judaism, too anxious to leave the ghetto spirit and ghetto narrowness to speak critically of their non-Jewish neighbors whose ways they wanted the Jews to emulate. It is therefore not surprising that some well-meaning wealthy Jews and intellectuals organized a Society for the Promotion of Culture among the Jews (1863), with headquarters in St. Petersburg, whose object was to encourage Jews in the pursuit of secular knowledge. There were Jews who went even farther and urged the complete abandonment of Yiddish and Hebrew and the rapid acquisition of Russian, presumably with all that this implied for Jewish custom and tradition. The attitude of the more moderate was best expressed in Gordon's notorious phrase advising the Jew of his day to "be a Jew at home and a man abroad," as though Jewishness fell short of humanity.

5. The Spirit Within

Critics and Reality—One may well stop to inquire to what extent the harsh criticisms of the *maskilim* were justified. Was Jewish leadership in Eastern Europe as corrupt and the Jewish population as superstitious as these men maintained? One must remember that these men were special pleaders for the cause of Jewish emancipation. They had convinced themselves that the czarist government was sincere in its promise to grant the Jews equality if they surrendered their distinctiveness and cured themselves of internal evils. They therefore exaggerated one side of the situation. Like Mendelssohn and his followers in Germany almost a hundred years before, they failed to see that to destroy the inner fortifications of Jewish life, under an illiberal government and in the midst of a prejudiced population, was to endanger the very existence of the Jewish group. No doubt corruption, hypocrisy and superstition existed among the Jews—such evils exist among all groups—but it was simply not true that these vices dominated Jewish life in Eastern Europe. The *maskilim* emphasized the exceptions; that was why the *Haskalah* movement had comparatively slight effect on the inner life of the people, while it had tremendous influence on the revival of the Hebrew language and literature. People read Gordon and Mapu and were impressed by the style and the fervor; but they were left unimpressed by their accusations. They knew better.

Life and Piety—As a matter of fact, it would be hard to find a period in the history of the Jews in Europe which produced more beautiful living, more pious souls, more happy homes and, indeed, greater sympathy even for their persecutors, than the nineteenth century in Eastern Europe. Jewish life went its accustomed way regardless of events in the world about it. Hasidism continued to function in southeastern Europe and, with all its encouragement of naive belief in the supernatural powers of the *rebbes,* made life as livable as economic and social restrictions permitted. In the north, even in Lithuania, Hasidism had adjusted itself so thoroughly to the prevalent Rabbinism that, while Hasidim and Mithnagdim continued to poke fun at each other, the bitterness of the previous generations was gone. There was essentially little difference between them. Both sent their children to *heder* at an early age; both established *yeshibot* and observed the traditions of Jewish life in their minutest details. To be sure, the Jewish women of the period in Eastern Europe did not know French and could not play the piano; the men were more interested in the opinions of Rav Ashi than in those of Metternich or Bismarck. Instead of beautifully bound sets of Shakespeare, their shelves were decorated with tattered and worn copies of Maimonides' Code. Decidedly, the East European Jew of the mid-nineteenth century did not measure up to the accepted standards of Western Europe's middle class. To some extent that was indeed a pity; for it is not at all impossible to have Shakespeare as well as Maimonides If, however, the measure of a culture's success is the development of beautiful character, these poverty-stricken, socially degraded and politically rightless people shed a brilliant luster on their culture and religion.

Musar—A number of rabbis sensed danger, but it was not

danger from too much Judaism. On the contrary, they were afraid of too much worldliness. They, consequently, undertook to correct what they considered to be a wrong emphasis in their contemporary Jewish life. Rabbi Israel Salanter was the central figure among the religious leaders of that day. Though a contemporary of Zunz and of Levinsohn, he knew nothing of the scientific method and cared less about setting the Russian government right regarding the rites and customs of the Jews. His problems were Jewish living and Jewish character, and he thought these ought to be strengthened by adding to the curriculum of the *yeshibah* the study of ethical works (*musar*). He did not disparage talmudic learning; on the contrary, he wanted the Talmud and Jewish law to continue to hold the central place in the curriculum. But he feared that external influences might leave the traditional observances unfortified by emotion and thus make piety something mechanical, and talmudic study a matter of personal vanity rather than a sign of religious devotion. The attitude of this nineteenth-century Lithuanian Jew paralleled that of the twelfth-century Spaniard, Bahya ibn Pakudah. To study Jewish ethical literature, to preach occasionally about the fervor and sacrifice which must accompany Jewish living, above all to be an example of the purest ethical conduct—these were the bases of the school which he founded at Kovno, and which soon began to exert a wide influence.

Community and Government—To make matters worse in the relationship between Jew and Christian, the Russian government weakened the internal authority of the communal councils (*kahal*). The czarist government for some reason believed that it could Russify the Jews more easily without a strong autonomous authority controlling them. Besides, the government wanted to tax the Jews as individuals, not as communities. By thus removing the financial powers of the *kahal* board and depriving it of much other authority, such as the power to judge and to punish, Russia merely weakened external control without actually weakening the moral and religious bases of community life. While it was no longer possible for the Jews to punish their own people for moral and religious laxity, while the community lost control of education, the Jew, accustomed by centuries to community living, went to Jewish courts of his free will and submitted to taxation for communal purposes in addition to the taxes paid directly to the government. The salary of the rabbis and judges, the maintenance of *yeshibot* and synagogues, the support of charitable foundations, all came out of the taxes imposed, and willingly paid, on kosher meat and other articles of food for use among Jews exclusively. They went on electing community officers, whose limited powers the government watched with an eagle eye. When, however, the government needed the assistance of the *kahal,* it imposed obligations upon the members of the board, such as the recruiting of Jewish soldiers or the occasional interference in the Jewish schools.

Balance and Despair—The mood prevalent among the Jews of Russia and Poland in the 1870s was one of misgivings about the future. The *maskilim* had won a good many adherents, but their victory turned out to be purely negative. They had proved that the old fashions in life and education were not good enough; they had failed to produce anything, short of complete assimilation, that Russia would accept as an admission price into its society. The young *maskil* hungered for secular education; but the czarist government would not open the doors of the universities to Jews.

The traditionally-minded Jews were equally disappointed. It had become clear that persecution of the *maskilim* was not enough. More and more of the promising young people turned to secular studies. The old ways and the old homes were breaking up and the Orthodox did not know what to substitute for the ideal of personal behavior and Talmud study which had been sufficient till then. A sense of doom hung over the five million Jews who inhabited the narrow area permitted them. This premonition of catastrophe was destined to be fulfilled; the prospect of Russia as a home was soon to vanish. New ideals were to take the place of Orthodoxy as well as of *Haskalah,* and homes were to be sought in more hospitable lands.

CHAPTER IV

LAND OF THE FREE

AMERICA, CONSCIOUSLY ACCEPTING ITS ROLE AS HAVEN OF REFUGE FOR THOSE ESCAPING EUROPE'S TYRANNIES, WELCOMES JEWISH NEWCOMERS, GIVING THEM A CHANCE TO CALL AMERICA THEIR HOME

Opportunities and Problems—The United States, alone among the nations of the Western world, had no need to spend the first half of the nineteenth century in fighting against reactionaries and safeguarding the fruits of its Revolution. Thus favored, Americans were able to strengthen and deepen the principles of the rights of man and of equality of opportunity. The leaders of the new country, brought up in the free atmosphere of the New World, found the philosophy of liberalism and human rights exactly to their liking. Jefferson and his followers fought for religious freedom and against any connection between Church and State and they won without too much difficulty. The land was vast; opportunities were limitless; the ideals of the founders held firm. Here was a brave new world, with high hopes and a sense of brotherhood. Liberty, Equality and Fraternity had found their real home.

The small number of Jews who were part of the generation of the Revolution were accepted as equals almost everywhere, even in those states which did not immediately adopt the principle of separation of Church and State. As Jews, however, the old settlers and the new faced problems of their own. Their adjustment to the new environment from the Jewish point of view was not an easy matter. The new situation rather overwhelmed them. Moreover, their leadership was neither strong nor united.

1. Adjustment and Disintegration

Economic and Social Stability—About 2,500 Jews lived in the United States in the year 1800, in a total population of about seven and a half millions. The largest number lived in Philadelphia and New York, where they had established themselves in business. While few of them were wealthy, they were not among the poorest in the land. They did not suffer from discrimination. When, after the Revolution, King's College in New York reorganized itself as Columbia College, Gershom Mendes Seixas, then *hazzan* of the Shearith Israel congregation, was made a trustee. Jews and Christians formed bonds of friendship and visited one another without condescension or suspicion on either side. The real problem of that day was not the exclusion of Jews from general society, but the inability of the Jews to build and maintain a society of their own. Too few Jewish contacts among Jews, rather than too many, were proving a danger to Jewish life.

Education and Marriage—The basic difficulty was that the

Jewish population was so small and so widely scattered that no system of Jewish education could be established. The public school system was not yet in existence and the children were sent to private schools, under Christian supervision. Time and again Jewish congregations made efforts to establish schools, for general as well as Jewish education. Trained Jewish teachers, however, were very few even in the larger communities of the United States. Frequently the rabbi was the only teacher for all subjects; sometimes he taught the Jewish subjects—Hebrew and the fundamentals of Judaism—while Christians were employed to teach English, mathematics and whatever else the schools of that day taught. But such experiments did not work out satisfactorily. The wealthier parents insisted on sending their children to better organized and socially more acceptable schools, while the poorer people found it necessary to keep their children at home to aid in earning a livelihood. Jews who lived in small communities were completely cut off from Jewish educational opportunities. The surprising thing, therefore, was that early in the nineteenth century many Jews could still follow the Hebrew prayer book and that they still remained loyal to Jewish life. For, sooner or later, diminishing knowledge, combined with the limited social contacts with Jewish men or women eligible for marriage, made the growing number of intermarriages a matter of deep concern. There were, indeed, comparatively few outright conversions; the free religious atmosphere made that unnecessary. But the net result was the same, since the children of a mixed marriage, even if unconverted, were likely to follow the majority rather than the minority religion. Many Jewish men and women whose loyalties were somewhat stronger did not marry at all. Thus Rebecca Gratz remained a spinster, while many of her immediate family crossed the boundary into Christian society.

Judah Touro—An example of the mixed influences exerted by Jewish loyalty and Christian society was the eccentric and interesting Judah Touro. He was born in Newport, Rhode Island, in 1775, while his father, Isaac Touro, was *hazzan* of the synagogue there. After his father's death, Judah and his brother Abraham were brought up by their uncle, Moses Michael Hays, who refused consent to the marriage of his daughter with her cousin Judah. The latter went to the then little town of New Orleans, where he opened a small dry-goods store. Wounded in the Battle of New Orleans, in the War of 1812, he was rescued by a Christian fellow soldier who became his closest friend. Judah Touro's business increased in size until he became one of the wealthy men of the country. As his wealth increased so did his philanthropy. There was not a worthy cause, Jewish or Christian, to which he did not contribute liberally. He gave $10,000, an enormous sum in those days, for the erection of a monument at Bunker Hill, matching the gift of a Christian patriot. He never married, and at his death, in 1854, most of his wealth was distributed to charitable and religious foundations all over the country. A substantial sum was entrusted to Sir Moses Montefiore for distribution to the poor in the Holy Land.

Mordecai Manuel Noah—An illustration of a different career was the life of Mordecai Manuel Noah. Born in Philadelphia in 1785, Noah early developed an ambition for public life. In 1813, President Madison appointed him consul to Tunis, a rather difficult position because the Berber states of North Africa were then making a business of piracy. Noah represented the United States with dignity and force, but he was too generous with government funds in the redemption of captured Americans and thus barely avoided a scandal. Back in America, Noah settled in New York City and became a politician, one of the early leaders of Tammany Hall, and was appointed sheriff. These, however, were not his chief contributions to American life. As editor of *The Enquirer,* he was among the first to liven up the newspaper of his day so as to make it appeal to the ordinary reader. He published interesting articles instead of the staid and dull ones with which the news sheets of that period were filled. Above all, Noah was a playwright. His plays, now quite forgotten, were of the thrilling, melodramatic kind, full of villainous villains, and of fair damsels who had to be rescued: for example, *She Would Be a Soldier, The Grecian Captive, The Castle of Olival.* But they were popular and were among the first plays written by a native American. Florid in oratory, clever in repartee, generous and good-natured at all times, Noah, toward the end of his life, was one of the notable characters of New York.

Noah the Dreamer—Noah never forgot his Jewishness. There was hardly a Jewish cause in New York City or in the country in which his interest could not be aroused. He was the official Jewish orator of the day, at the dedication of synagogues or at public gatherings. Yet his one act which, because of subsequent events, aroused most comment was his attempt to found a refuge for the Jews. Moved by the conditions in which the Jews of Germany and of Eastern Europe found themselves, Noah's fertile mind hit upon the plan of establishing, under the flag of the United States, a colony in which the oppressed Jews might found a state of their own. He made it clear that this was in no way to affect Jewish hopes for the restoration of an independent state in Palestine whenever in God's good time this became possible. For his American place of refuge he picked Grand Island, above the falls of the Niagara River. With his usual ceremoniousness and love of drama, Noah proclaimed himself a Judge in Israel, on the model of Gideon and Jephthah of ancient days. He issued proclamations to the Jewish communities of Europe, inviting them to settle in this new city, which he called Ararat—suggested by the biblical story of Noah. He even adopted for this purpose the old myth that the Indians were the Lost Ten Tribes and invited them too. The Jews of Germany, of course, poked fun at Noah's plan, and those of Russia paid no attention to it. Noah nevertheless organized an impressive ceremony of dedication, with a long and pompous speech by himself. The dedication over, his numerous other plans completely occupied Noah's mind and nothing further was done about Ararat.

Commodore Levy—Uriah P. Levy also deserves mention as an example of the part Jews played in the growth of America. Born in Philadelphia in 1792, he ran away from home to become a cabin boy in the Navy at the age of eleven. His ability was soon evident and his promotions were rapid. His was really what one would call a checkered career of the dime-novel variety, with mutinies, duels, courts-martial and reinstatements. Some of his troubles were probably due, as he believed, to his Jewish origin. Nevertheless, at his death, in 1862, he was among the highest ranking officers in the United States Navy, though too old to fight in the Civil War. His proudest boast toward the end of his life was that he had helped abolish corporal punishment for sailors. He bought Thomas Jefferson's home, Monticello, which his heirs eventually sold to the United States.

2. The German-Jewish Migration

Three Stages—From the very beginning, in colonial America, a large number of the Jewish settlers were German and East European Jews, perhaps to the extent of forty per cent of the total. Nevertheless, the Jews of Spanish-Portuguese origin dominated the scene for two generations even after the Revolution. They organized the communities; their ritual prevailed in the synagogues. But particularly after the Napoleonic wars, events in Germany made life so much more difficult for the Jews of Central Europe that they began migrating from Germany, Bohemia and Hungary to freer lands. Really considerable numbers, however, arrived only after the failure of the German revolution of 1848 seemed to deprive German Jewry of any hope of freedom in their homeland. By the year 1860, there were more than fifty thousand Jews in the United States.

The Welcome—Jews were not the only ones to migrate to America during that period. Thousands of Christian Germans and Hungarians were equally anxious to find freedom and a chance for a better life away from the reactionary governments which were once more in the saddle, and thousands more fled from the famine and misrule in Ireland. On the whole, the population of the United States welcomed the newcomers. Only the Catholics, especially the Irish, met with a certain amount of ill will and suspicion. The attitude toward the Jews, on the other hand, was quite friendly. Liberty-loving Americans were shocked at the treatment of the Jews in various European countries and on a number of public occasions before the Civil War there were expressions of hope that Jews would come to settle in the United States.

The Break in Jewish Unity—The older Jewish settlers found the newcomers something of a nuisance. Feeling themselves part of the country in language, manners and attitudes, and conscious of the fact that complete religious equality had been won but recently, the Spanish-Portuguese Jews were both irritated and apprehensive. The German immigrants were poor and spoke English with annoying accent. They were at the same time ambitious to establish themselves quickly and thereby gave the impression of being aggressive. The older settlers forgot that their own ancestors, a few generations back, had probably been charged with similar "faults." On their part, the German Jews felt uncomfortable with the Sephardic ritual of the existing synagogues. Had the older settlers accepted them socially and permitted them to participate in the service on a basis of equality, the complaints of the Germans might not have been so loud. But they were treated with disdain, and when, as a result, they requested permission to organize a service of their own with their own ritual, permission was refused. Under the circumstances, there was nothing left for the German Jews but to secede completely from the organized congregation and to establish synagogues of their own. As early as 1796 a German congregation, Rodeph Shalom, was organized in Philadelphia. In New York a simi-

lar situation developed about thirty years later, with the establishment of B'nai Jeshurun in 1824.

The Problem of Unity—Thus came about the first breach
in the communal and religious unity of the American Jewish
population. Once the breach had been made, there was no
stopping it. Every group that came over from a different
town or province of Europe permitted its natural inclination
—to be among its own—to take precedence over the more
sensible and desirable method of cooperating for religious
and communal purposes with other congregations. With every
passing year, therefore, the number of congregations in the
larger cities multiplied and each was forced to face the same
problems for itself. Not even such common religious problems
as *kashrut, shehitah,* Passover food or Jewish burial brought
any appreciable number of the congregations together for any
length of time.

Jews and the Opening Up of the West—Long before these
internal problems became pressing, the German Jewish immigrants had taken up the task which was to be their major
contribution to the growth of America. The dramatic story of
their rise is an integral part of the romance of the American
West, and recalls the cooperation of the Jews in the founding
of civilization in other lands and continents. The earliest Jewish settlers, during the colonial period, had done a considerable amount of trading with the Indians, venturing into Indian
territory and helping the constant movement westward of the
American frontier. The first half of the nineteenth century
was the period of "the covered wagon." Natives and immigrants went to the Mississippi and beyond, clearing the forests and bringing more land under cultivation. It was the
heroic period of fighting against natural obstacles and of laying
the foundations of national strength. With a pack on his back
or in a covered wagon laden with trinkets and household
goods, the Jewish peddler followed close behind the agricultural pioneer. Everything, from needles to axes, from cheap
jewelry to pots and pans, was his stock in trade. He was practically the sole contact between the distant settler and the
world, bringing news along with the manufactured products
and helping to weave the bonds which tied the country together. Many of the settlers saw a Jew for the first time in the
peddler who came to their door and, their prejudices weakened by their own independence and the Jew's helpfulness,
accepted him as a welcome visitor and frequently became his
friends. As the settlement grew thicker, the peddler of a district as well as his customers found it advantageous for him

to move the center of his operations to their midst. The fortunes of the Jew and the steady progress of his neighbors were thus firmly bound together. The settlement grew into a village and the peddler's wagon stopped roving and became a depot; the village became a town and the peddler's depot became a dry-goods store; the town grew into a city and a department store occupied the very center of its Main Street.

Jewish Communities and Jewish Life—Not all Jewish communities developed in just that fashion. Often the first Jewish settler in a town was not a peddler but an artisan. On the Pacific coast there were many Jews among the forty-niners who joined the earliest gold rush and stayed to help bring order out of the chaos, a number being among the respected citizens and judges who controlled the turbulence of the adventurers. Whether as peddlers or artisans, Jewish immigrants from all parts of Europe settled in almost every one of the budding towns which sprang into life between the Alleghenies and the Pacific from 1820 to 1860. In the course of a decade or two after the arrival of the first Jewish settler, others came and, before long, organized a congregation. No social or economic difficulties stood in their way. Work was hard but plentiful and the future held great promise. Their only problems were the internal ones, incidental to maintaining the semblance of a Jewish life. There was less time and opportunity than ever to give the children a Jewish education. The first generation still remained sentimentally attached to the ways and traditions brought with them from across the sea, although even for them the continuance of *kashrut* was exceptionally difficult. But the new generation had neither knowledge of nor sympathy for a way of life which struck them as utterly different from that followed by the vast majority of their neighbors. They retained little more than a filial attachment to old traditions and a vague pride in Jewish survival, the methods and reasons of which they did not know.

3. LEESER AND JUDAISM IN AMERICA

A Rabbi's Ambition—It became apparent very soon that the central problem of American Israel was the revival of Jewish knowledge. Upon the scene of American Jewish life there now appeared a lovable character who, profoundly sensitive to this need, devoted his life with rare unselfishness to the revival of Judaism in the land of his adoption.

In his native Germany, Isaac Leeser (1806–1868) had received a fair Jewish education and some training in the German and ancient classics. He came to Richmond, Virginia, as a very young man to clerk in his uncle's store. There he identified himself with the only existing congregation, a Sephardic one, where he eventually aided in the conduct of worship. The Mikveh Israel congregation of Philadelphia some years later invited him to become its minister. He accepted the call and for twenty-one years he stayed with this congregation. Leeser regarded his ministry as an opportunity to serve the Jewish people, to interpret Judaism and to foster Jewish loyalty. Fortunately, the congregation did not stand in the way of his numerous outside activities.

Preacher, Translator and Journalist—Leeser was gifted with a clear and straightforward English style, and he made good use of it. The warmth of his Jewishness made him a traditionalist. He would not enter into the subtle theological discussions in which the rabbis of Germany were then engaged. Although he followed the progress of the Reform movement in Germany, the only change he actually made was to introduce the sermon in English as part of the service. It was years before he prevailed on his own congregation to let him preach at regular intervals, but he became a popular visiting preacher in other congregations all over the United States. In addition, he translated both the Sephardi and Ashkenazi prayer books into English. He is best known for his work on the Bible. He saw the need for revising the King James translation of the Bible by eliminating from it all Christian interpretations of the text. It was a difficult task, but Leeser accomplished it with astonishing skill. He undertook, at the same time, the publication of a magazine, *The Occident*, which served as a medium for the discussion of Jewish problems and for the creation of a sense of Jewish unity among the widely scattered Jewish population. By these means Leeser became the foremost disseminator of Jewish knowledge, the leading exponent in America of Jewish life and culture.

The Quest for Religious Unity—Isaac Leeser was pained to see the transplantation to America of all the varying rituals of the Jews in Europe. There might be historical justification for such differences, but, once Jews came to the United States, he felt they ought to drop all that made them Rhenish Jews or Galician Jews or Polish Jews and join together as American Jews with an American ritual. He hoped that this American ritual would be the Sephardic, since that was the

oldest in the United States. He also considered it historically
the most distinguished. He thought that all congregations
should unite in order to avoid' the ugly quarrels which frequently developed among rival groups and to aid the newly
established ones. There were few rabbis in the United States
at the time. Leeser suggested that they organize themselves,
to preserve Jewish values. He hoped that a school for higher
Jewish education could be established in the country to train
American youth for Jewish leadership in the land of their
birth. Many leaders of American Israel agreed with Leeser in
the desirability of all his plans, with the possible exception of
his suggestion regarding the ritual. Among these was also
Isaac Mayer Wise, a young Bohemian rabbi who arrived in
the United States in 1846. Yet nothing came of Leeser's
plans. The Jews of America at this time were too busy establishing themselves, too poor and too scattered to have the
time, the energy and the practical foresight to devote themselves to problems which did not contribute directly to their
all-important task of taking root in the new land. Another
generation was to pass before circumstances became favorable
for the achievement of Leeser's aims.

Sunday Schools and Maimonides College—Among those
who seconded Leeser's hopes for improving religious education was the pious and cultivated Rebecca Gratz. A member
of the famous Jewish family of Philadelphia, she retained a
strong devotion to Judaism. It is said that she was the proto-
type for Rebecca in Sir Walter Scott's *Ivanhoe*, the English
author having heard about her from Washington Irving. Miss
Gratz realized that the growing Jewish child population in
Philadelphia needed very much more religious training than
it was receiving. Leeser's efforts to establish a private school
for children had proved completely unsuccessful. Rebecca
Gratz thereupon took as her model the type of religious education given to the Protestant children on Sundays. With a
number of assistants from among the young women of the
Mikveh Israel congregation, she established a school which
was to meet on Sunday mornings. The amount of information imparted to the children obviously could not be great.
Instruction was limited to the broad principles of Judaism.
Leeser prepared a catechism, that is, a series of questions and
answers, on religious subjects for pupils to learn by heart.
There was, however, little time for the study of Hebrew or of
Jewish history, a fact which Leeser deplored.

This Sunday School system was decidedly better than no
education at all. It was vastly different from the thorough

Jewish education which had characterized Jewish life in the past and which was still dominant in various parts of the world. Yet it succeeded in implanting deep Jewish loyalties. Some years later, Lesser made efforts to open more advanced schools. The establishment of the Hebrew Education Society was encouraged by him (1848) as a Jewish all-day school. The Maimonides College, which he opened toward the very end of his life (1867), was meant to give more extensive as well as intensive information and possibly serve as the beginning of a rabbinical academy. The Maimonides College closed, after an existence of six years, but the Sunday school system spread over the country and has survived.

4. JEWS AND THE CIVIL WAR

The Government and the Jews—Between 1800 and 1860, the last vestiges of discrimination against Jews were removed. In 1825, Maryland voted complete political equality for its Jews. In North Carolina a similar step was taken some time later. The discriminations had been largely theoretical anyway. Jews had been elected to state legislatures and to the United States Congress and had been appointed to public office, despite the objection of a few bigots.

The most spectacular evidence of the prevailing attitude toward the Jews was the manner in which the federal government and the general population reacted toward acts of persecution in foreign lands. President Van Buren instructed the American consul at Alexandria, Egypt, and the minister to Turkey to indicate to the governments there that the sympathies of the United States were thoroughly on the side of the persecuted Jews in Damascus (1840). At public meetings in protest against the horrors perpetrated against the Jews of that city, prominent Christians willingly joined the Jews in expressing the sentiments of America. The federal government likewise took action on the anti-Jewish attitude of certain cantons of Switzerland which persisted in the medieval attitude of not permitting Jews to reside within their borders, thus preventing American Jews from taking up residence there to conduct their business affairs. President Millard Fillmore (1850), Daniel Webster as secretary of state (1852) and Henry Clay expressed official indignation over this situation, and the Senate refused to ratify a treaty which contained a discriminatory clause. The matter dragged on for years and was not finally solved until Switzerland cured itself of prejudice. In such ways did the United States bear testimony to the belief in human freedom which lay at the base of its character as a nation.

On the Question of Slavery—All the more remarkable was the fact that a civil war had to be fought in order to win freedom for other human beings, and all the more tragic that the Jews of America were not absolutely unanimous in their opposition to slavery as an institution. Some Jewish residents in the South refrained from slave-holding, and others, like Judah Touro, took care to free their slaves. But the majority of southern Jews had become so much a part of the prevailing social and economic system that there was little distinction between them and their Christian neighbors. David Yulee, for example, one of the first senators from the state of Florida and the first Jew in the United States Senate, owned a plantation in that state and was a defender of the slave system. Less comprehensible was the attitude of Rabbi Morris J. Raphall of New York. He preached and wrote on the subject of slavery, following the strange line of argument that, since the Bible recognized the existence of slavery, therefore slavery was an institution blessed by God. But the majority of Jews and the majority of rabbis were unmistakably opposed to human slavery. Rabbi David Einhorn dared to oppose slavery even though he lived in Baltimore, a city with southern sympathies, at a time when the secession movement was in full swing in Maryland (1861). As a result he was compelled to leave the city. The scholarly Michael Heilprin, of Polish origin, a veteran of the European struggle for human freedom, expressed anti-slavery sentiments; and Sabato Morais, Leeser's successor in Philadelphia, fresh from the revolutionary struggle in Italy, took a similar stand. The newly established Republican Party had many adherents among the Jewish population in the northern and western parts of the country.

In the Civil War—It followed, therefore, that there were Jews on both sides in the conflict, participating in the fighting on all the battlefronts. Judah P. Benjamin is frequently mentioned in connection with the Confederacy, of which he was successively attorney-general, secretary of war and secretary of state. He was not much of a Jew in private life, but this did not prevent many southerners from sneering at him during and after the war and from blaming him for all the misfortunes of the South. Of soldiers on the field of battle there were thousands of Jews, a good many officers among them, both in the Confederate and in the Union armies.

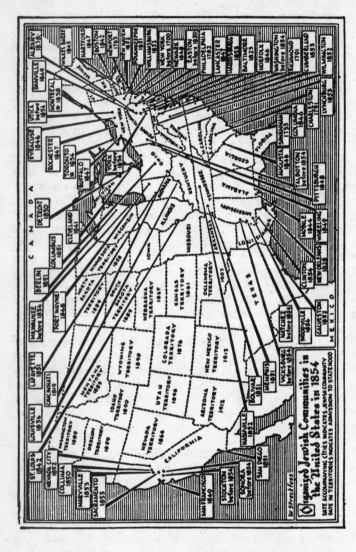

Organized Jewish Communities in the United States in 1854.

This map is based on the List of Jewish Institutions in A Jewish Calendar for Fifty Years, by J. J. Lyons and Abraham, de Sola, Montreal, 1854.

5. Consolidation and Reform

The New Generation—With the end of the Civil War, the United States entered upon a new phase in its history. The era of spectacular land expansion was almost over and the age of equally spectacular industrial expansion began. A Jewish population of 275,000 Jews was spread far and wide over the country. Almost without effort they were being drawn into the industrial progress of the country. Above all, a new generation of native American Jews was rising to face the new problem of American Jewish life to the best of its abilities.

Organization—The attainment of economic security was accompanied by a spurt in internal organization. The Independent Order B'nai B'rith was founded in 1843 with the object of uniting for social, cultural and philanthropic purposes those Jews who already differed widely in their religious views, and it spread rapidly. A number of other charitable organizations and hospitals made their appearance in the larger cities. But the chief interest in Jewish life continued to show itself in the field of religion.

Growth of Reform Sentiment—There were individuals as early as 1820, in various parts of the country, who advocated reforms in synagogue ritual of the sort being tried in Germany.* The number of sympathizers with Reform increased with the arrival of large numbers from Central Europe in the decade of 1840. With its founding, in 1845, Congregation Emanu-El of New York began to serve as a focus for Reform sentiment and an inspiration for Reformers in other cities. The movement then made rapid progress, starting with the introduction of a few prayers in English or in German and continuing before long to the removal of the hat and the abolition of the second days of holidays.

Leaders of Reform—The Sephardi congregations of the United States kept aloof from this movement, and most of the German congregations opposed the introduction of these innovations, though some yielded by introducing moderate modifications of the ritual. Much depended upon the leadership of their rabbis, almost all of whom were German trained. David Einhorn (1809–1879), for example, had been an advocate of Reform while yet in Germany and, coming to

* See above, pp. 505–6.

the United States in 1855, ardently continued to promote the movement, first in Baltimore and later in New York. Leo Merzbacher (1810–1856) and Samuel Adler (1809–1891), successively rabbis of Emanu-El in New York, were somewhat milder in their Reform views, though both permitted the more radical element in their congregation to override them. Even more conservative were Benjamin Szold (1829–1902) of Baltimore and Marcus Jastrow (1829–1903) of Philadelphia. Both these rabbis also believed in making changes in the Jewish ritual; but they believed, too, in the sacredness of Jewish tradition. The observance of the Sabbath and adherence to the dietary laws seemed to them indispensable to the survival of Judaism. There were also other rabbis who advocated every degree of Orthodoxy and Reform.

Isaac Mayer Wise and Early Reform—The man who left the most lasting impression upon Reform Judaism in the United States was the strong-willed and energetic Isaac Mayer Wise. For some years after his arrival in the United States (1846), he showed rather conservative inclinations and cooperated with Isaac Leeser in a number of projects. Like Leeser, Wise deplored the weakness and disunity of American Judaism. Even better than Leeser he saw among the rising generation of American Jews, thinly scattered through the growing towns of the country, great bewilderment regarding the faith of their fathers and mounting ignorance of its essential message. As rabbi in Albany, New York, his first pulpit in the United States, he advocated mild reforms; and in this spirit he later published a prayer book which he called *Minhag America* (The American Rite). This name indicated his hope for unity among the rabbis of the United States for which he pleaded also in his periodicals: *The American Israelite* (English) and *Die Deborah* (German). At his urging a number of rabbinical conferences were called, but they resulted in little more than further emphasizing the differences of opinion existing among the religious guides of American Israel.

Reform Institutions—After 1854, Wise continued his activity in Cincinnati, Ohio, and the new congregations in the Middle West and the South responded to his leadership much more readily than had those of the East. In 1873 he succeeded in forming an organization of congregations which was to survive as the Union of American Hebrew Congregations. The next step in Wise's program was the creation of a college for the training of rabbis. As president of the Hebrew

Union College for the remaining twenty-five years of his life, Wise trained an entire generation of rabbis who carried on his influence for many decades thereafter. Individually as well as through the Central Conference of American Rabbis, which Wise organized in 1889, his pupils have played an important role in Jewish life in America.

The Pittsburgh Platform—As time went on Wise inclined towards more radical reforms in Judaism. The policies of the institutions founded by him were set forth at a meeting of rabbis which took place in Pittsburgh in 1885, and the principles there adopted have become known as the Pittsburgh Platform. It emphasized the prophetic ideals of the Bible as against the regulations of the Talmud. It declared some of the Mosaic legislation no longer applicable, among these the dietary laws. It rejected a return to Palestine. It denied the expectation of a Messiah and substituted the hope for a messianic era, that is, an era of peace and perfection which would come to the world through cultural and scientific progress. It argued that the Jews were a group with a mission of spreading godliness among the peoples of the world. In many ways American Reform Judaism thus went much farther than European Reform, farther, in fact, than a great many American Jews were willing to go. A reaction against it was sure to come in the next period of American Jewish history.*

CHAPTER V

THE RENEWAL OF HATE

THE OLD FEELINGS OF ANTI-JEWISHNESS ARE REVIVED IN
WESTERN EUROPE AND DIGNIFIED BY A NEW AND PSEUDO-
SCIENTIFIC NAME—ANTISEMITISM

Old Hates and New Reasons—So much of what happened in the United States since the Civil War has been the result of events in Europe that it is well to postpone further discussion of American Jewish history in order to note develop-

* See below, p. 596, and p. 667.

ments across the Atlantic. For three quarters of a century the
Jews of Europe had struggled for the principles of democracy, human rights and national unity in their native lands.
By 1870 these objectives seemed within sight. Germany and
Italy were united; France was again functioning under a republic based on the ideals of its glorious Revolution. Everywhere the Jews saw the day coming when the spread of
knowledge would free men from prejudice and permit cooperation between them and their fellow citizens for the common good. Even in Spain, whose expulsion of the Jews in
1492 has ever stood out as the mark of greatest intolerance, a
temporary government in 1869 revoked that infamous decree
and invited Jews to return. Only the benighted eastern part of
the continent seemed unwilling to free itself from the heritage
of its dark past, though there too liberal voices were beginning to be heard. The influence and example of Western Europe were expected in time to compel East European lands
to change their attitude.

Suddenly the forces of darkness emerged once more in the
progressive Europe of the West. Some of the causes for this
reappearance of anti-Jewish sentiments were those which had
operated in previous centuries; there were also newer reasons.
They combined during the last quarter of the nineteenth century to lay the foundations for the most serious social and
economic problems facing the Jews and for the fundamental
problem of justice facing all humanity. Ever since then Jews
and Christians have been discussing antisemitism, whether to
justify or to refute it.

1. Intercession of the West

The Damascus Affair—In 1840 an event occurred in
which the Jews of the Near East were concerned directly,
and all the Jews indirectly. In the city of Damascus, in Syria,
a Christian monk disappeared. Ordinarily it would not have
required much investigation to conclude that the monk had
been murdered by a Mohammedan with whom he was known
to have quarreled violently. Suspicion, however, was deliberately directed by the other monks to the poor Jews of the
town. It might have been dangerous for these monks to
arouse the resentment of the Mohammedans by accusing one
of them, but to accuse the Jews of having murdered a Christian for ritual purposes seemed safe enough. A number of
Jewish artisans were arrested and "confessions" obtained

from some of them by means of torture. To make matters worse, the consul of France involved himself in the affair by supporting the monks; for France, too, was interested in maintaining peace between the Catholics and the Mohammedans. It wanted the support of both in its ambitions to become the dominant power in the Near East in preference to England, on the one hand, and Russia on the other. The accusation, and the support of it by the representative of the government of so liberal a nation as France, astonished and pained the Jews. Nor were they alone; the liberal elements of every country were equally shocked. There were protest meetings all over the Western world and a number of governments, including that of the United States, sent messages to Mehemet Ali, Pasha of Egypt, who controlled Syria at the time. For political reasons of its own, Russia also took the Jewish side in this instance. In France itself Adolphe Crémieux raised his eloquent voice against the crime being committed with the aid of his motherland. But the imperialist ambitions of its government kept France from doing anything to right the wrong committed in its name. Thereupon, Sir Moses Montefiore and Crémieux went to Egypt and finally prevailed on Mehemet Ali to issue an order freeing the prisoners who were still alive—some had died as a result of the torture—and to announce that he did not believe the charge of ritual murder. It was a victory against prejudice; but the efforts it took to win it should have served as a warning of how superficial the belief in freedom and justice still was even in France, the cultural leader of the nineteenth century. The Jews, of course, hailed the victory with delight and were more than ever convinced that better days were coming.

The Mortara Affair—A somewhat similar incident, much nearer home, gave the Jews of Europe another shock. In Bologna, Italy, a Jewish infant by the name of Edgar Mortara was secretly baptized at the instance of his pious Catholic nurse, who thought thereby to save the child's life during an illness. Subsequently, in 1858, the Church authorities forcibly took the child away from its parents and ordered him brought up as a Christian. It was as clear a case of official kidnapping as had ever been perpetrated. To the Jews it was a reminder of the complete lack of human rights which had been their lot till but recently. Again protests were made all over the civilized world. Most governments, including those of Catholic states, tried to use their influence with the pope. But Pius IX, now a thorough reactionary, rejected all protests and justified the action by an appeal to canon law which claimed that the effect of baptism cannot be erased. Once more the Jews saw that, on the one hand, medievalism was not dead and that, on the other, liberal forces could be attracted to their side.

The Alliance—These two "Affairs" had a unifying effect upon the Jews. On his return home from the Damascus Affair, Crémieux spoke of the need to establish schools among the Jews of North Africa and the Near East in order to improve their cultural and economic conditions. He felt, moreover, that the spirit of cooperation displayed by all Jews, of all lands, in the fight against medievalism ought not be allowed to remain unused. It also seemed desirable to create some permanent body to defend the human rights of the Jews wherever they were threatened. Combining the two aims of education and defense, he created the Alliance Israélite Universelle (1860), with headquarters in Paris and with local branches in all countries of Western Europe and America. Appropriately, Adolphe Crémieux was its president as long as he lived. Down to the fall of France in 1940 the Alliance continued to be active. Its schools in North Africa and as far east as Bagdad, not only spread Western culture but its technological schools also provided many young people with a trade. At a central school in Paris young men were trained and then returned to their native lands as teachers. Moreover, on a number of occasions the Alliance performed useful service in defending Jewish rights. Sometimes it was too timid. Sometimes its central office in Paris was too patriotically French and did not assert the rights of Jews when French diplomacy advised them against it. On the whole, however, the Alliance proved very helpful.

Perfidy in Rumania—An opportunity for the Alliance to act came in 1878 when the European powers met in Berlin to discuss the future of Turkey and of the Balkan states. Bulgaria, Serbia and Rumania had won their independence with Russian help. Rumania in particular presented a problem. Its backward population had long been led by a group of greedy landowners who taught their people to blame the Jews for the poverty which these landowners themselves caused. At the Congress of Berlin, the Balkan states tried to persuade the great European powers to recognize their complete independence. Thereupon, the Jews through the Alliance exerted themselves to have England, France, Germany, Russia and Austria insist upon the inclusion of equality of rights for Jews in the constitutions of the new states. The atrocities committed upon the Jews of Rumania had been so disgraceful that even Bismarck saw the need for such a constitutional guarantee. With the aid of Russia, the Rumanian representatives struggled against making any promise regarding the Jews, but finally had to yield. Yet the rejoicing of the Jews in their victory proved premature. The Rumanian government had not the slightest intention of living up to the constitutional promise. All sorts of subterfuges and brazen lies were used to deny the Jews equality of rights. None of the powers of Europe showed the slightest inclination to compel Rumania to keep its word.

2. EASTERN EUROPE

Hostile Poland—The Polish nobility and middle class had always prided themselves on being civilized. Yet the territory of Poland, where the largest number of Jews was concentrated, had to suffer from both Polish patriotism and Russian reaction. The Poles, ever hopeful for a restoration of their independence, never seemed to learn the need for organization and unity. Another instance of their old hostility occurred in 1860, when a new insurrection broke out. The rabbis of Warsaw and Cracow stirred their people to active cooperation. When, due to poor leadership, the insurrection failed (1863), the Jews had to suffer from the vengeance of the Russians and from the revival of anti-Jewishness among the Poles.

Incurable Reaction in Russia—Actually Czar Alexander II had never been as liberal as his subjects supposed.* He had yielded in the first half of his reign to his more progressive advisers, but turned in the second to the reactionary policies of others. The reforms of the Jewish status, as it turned out, had been motivated, not by a desire to right the wrongs from which the Jewish population suffered, but rather by the old aim of hastening their Russification and by the newer aim of stimulating the commerce and industry of Russia's interior provinces. The new governors of the western provinces, sent there to liquidate the Polish insurrection, urged a return to the old system of oppression, and their point of view now gained ground in government circles. The officials became suspicious; the press more hostile. The privileges granted in the previous decade were now hedged in by restrictions. In 1871 a pogrom broke out in Odessa, stimulated by the Chris-

* See above, pp. 520, 524–5.

tian merchants who were competitors of the Jews. A mob rioted and looted for two days, though it was easily stopped when the police interfered on the third. Nevertheless, the government and the press made it seem that the Jews were somehow at fault. Quickly the old atmosphere of hostility on the one side and despair on the other was re-established. When, in 1881, Alexander II was assassinated by a group of revolutionists, his son, Alexander III, became more than ever convinced that Russia must be purged of Western liberal influences.

Pogroms and May Laws—Russian policy was expressed openly by Pobiedonostsev, head of the Russian Church. This nineteenth-century Torquemada now declared that the way to deal with the Jews was to let one third die, force one third to emigrate and compel the last third to join the Russian Church. Deliberately the government set about executing this plan. In 1881 a number of riots (pogroms) broke out in the southern provinces of the country. Several hundred Jews were murdered, and tens of thousands saw their property destroyed. It was obvious that these riots were organized with the aid of the government, for the police stood idly by watching the murder and pillage. Among the civilized nations these events aroused horror and indignation. In London a great meeting was held, in which the English aristocracy and the intellectuals spoke their mind about Russia. From the United States, President Harrison, on the basis of his ambassador's report, expressed his disapproval to the Russian government. To the flood of protests from every part of the civilized world the Russian government replied that the pogroms were the spontaneous expression of the population's protest against exploitation by the Jews. Just how the small Jewish shopkeepers were "exploiting" the people was never explained, but the government undertook to stop the "exploitation" by passing a number of laws, in May 1882, whereby the Jews were forced out of the smaller towns into the larger ones within the Pale of Settlement. It meant that thousands of Jews were forced into starvation, since the towns to which they had to go were already overcrowded with small shopkeepers and artisans. The hopes of the *maskilim* suffered a shattering blow. Even those Jews who had believed in assimilation were compelled to admit that the Russian government aimed at extermination.

Nationalism and Austria-Hungary—The Hapsburg empire was troubled by the problem of conflicting national loyalties. The Poles in Galicia, the Czechs in Bohemia, the Magyars in

Hungary and the Germans in Austria clamored for supremacy over the rest of the population of these provinces, although these latter often constituted a majority. Each national group wanted to organize the political and economic life of the province so as to profit its own members. The only unanimity which existed among them was that of blaming the Jews for whatever was wrong. On the whole, the Jews tended to ally themselves with the group which held cultural supremacy. In Hungary, they fought for Hungarian independence. When that movement was temporarily successful, complete economic emancipation was not granted to Hungary's Jews. But when the movement failed, the Jews were punished and many had to flee the country along with the leading Magyar patriots. In Bohemia the Jews sided with the German part of the population, which, though a minority, was at that time culturally superior. For this they gained the enmity of the Czechs and received no gratitude from the Germans. In the Polish provinces of Austria, the Poles were no different from those in Russia. It would seem that the Jews of Slovakia were wisest in refusing cooperation to any of the antagonistic nationalities, not caring much for vague promises from any quarter. They remained apart in their old-fashioned Jewish existence, poor but at least self-respecting.

The Viennese Side Show—All these conflicts came into the foreground in the Hapsburg empire's capital, Vienna. The gay population of the city consisted of a mixture of all the nationalities. It was therefore in constant political uproar. Its Jews had ever been advocates of German supremacy in Austria and in the rest of the empire. They had advocated union with the Germans of Germany long before Prussia assumed the leadership of the German confederation. Now the Germans of Austria turned on them and called them foreigners, to be eliminated from every phase of life. Antisemitism became a game, political as well as social, to hound the Jews. And yet, in no city of Europe was intellectual and scientific leadership so much in Jewish hands as in Vienna. Emperor Francis Joseph was frankly grieved by the antisemites and insisted on fair treatment for Jews in the army, where several rose to high rank. The Austrian parliament and the Viennese streets became the scenes of anti-Jewish outbreaks. At the university the Jewish students were frequently attacked. For Vienna had a great many Jewish students from Russia and Rumania and other lands where educational opportunities were denied them. The only thing that saved these Jewish students from humiliation and expulsion was the respect which they gained for themselves by organizing their own clubs and fighting a series of duels. Slowly it dawned upon the Jews of Vienna, and especially on its students, that they were fighting against deep-seated prejudices which they could not hope to overcome in the seeable future. The time had come to reconsider the status of the Jews of Europe and find a practical solution to their problem.

3. GERMAN POLITICS AND THE JEWS

Assimilation and Industry—No group had hailed the unification of their country as much as had the Jews of Germany. Their emancipation was bearing fruit; for they were making tremendous strides forward in industry and commerce, in the professions and the arts. Their native ability, sharpened by the desire to take their place in a free society, had brought the Jews, in almost one leap, to the forefront of expanding Germany. Nor had the Jews permitted their Jewishness to stand in the way. In no land was there so obvious a desire on the part of the Jews to merge with the general population. In many instances this desire led to conversion and intermarriage; but even among the ultra-orthodox Jews there was no question but that German nationality came first.

Liberalism and the Jews—The triumph of liberalism meant the complete emancipation of the Jews along with the coming to political power of the middle class. Prince Otto von Bismarck, the shrewd and able chancellor of Prussia, had been willing to make use of the Liberals to attain German unity and Prussian supremacy. Liberalism having served his purpose to make Germany a great power, he had no further use for it. When, therefore, the Liberal Party objected to big appropriations for the army, Bismarck was ready to abandon this party and to lure away its supporters. He looked about for an issue which would confuse the Liberal voters and enable him to smuggle in his army plans under a smoke screen of emotionalism. First he tried accusing the Catholics of endangering the newly acquired unity of the German people. He thought this would gain for him the loyalty of the Protestants and frighten the Catholics into rallying to his cause. But it did not work; the Catholics stood firm, and they fought back. Then it occurred to Bismarck that the Jews would be an easier instrument. As though by magic, therefore, anti-Jewishness returned to life in Germany.

The Background—That the Jews of Germany were intensely proud of their achievements was understandable. Within a single generation they had moved from rightlessness to positions of influence. It seemed obvious to them, and they thought it was obvious to everybody, that their own rise had been accompanied by considerable benefits for their fatherland. Characteristically, they took their place in the new society very seriously and were more German than the German Christians in their efforts to guide their country on what they considered to be its road of high destiny. Naturally it did not occur to them that the Christian Germans looked upon their success with surprise and envy and upon their well-meant criticism with annoyance. Resentment easily flared into hate when the rapid economic rise of many Jews was interpreted as something bad in itself.

In 1873 the stock market slumped and many people lost their investments. Disregarding the fact that the very act of investing in speculative schemes was clear evidence of everyone's desire for easy gain—the stock market craze was a common disease of that generation—the Christian losers blamed the Jews for the financial crisis as though only they were the speculators. As a matter of fact, Eduard Lasker, a Jew and a leader of the Liberal Party, had issued repeated warnings against speculation; but when money-making seemed easy his warnings had gone unheeded. After the slump, however, every Christian who lost money was a potential hater of the Jews.

The Assault—Bismarck and his reactionary associates were perfectly willing to see the Catholics blame Jewish influence in the Liberal Party for the attack upon Catholicism which had failed so completely. Adolf Stoecker, chaplain to the kaiser, attacked the Jews and thus gave the hint that anti-Jewishness was looked upon with favor in the highest circles. A journalist by the name of Wilhelm Marr, himself said to be of Jewish ancestry, spread far and wide the idea that Jewish penetration into every phase of German life was something wicked. Germany must be saved from becoming completely Judaized. Richard Wagner, likewise said to be of Jewish descent, the great composer who had frequently accepted aid from Jews interested in the development of music in Germany, spoke out, with all the conceit and bitterness of which his soul was full, against the Jews and their influence on German music. Heinrich von Treitschke, of mixed German and Slavic origin and the author of a history glorifying the German people, gave a slogan to the new movement—"The Jews are our misfortune!"

The New Justification—Not even Stoecker or Marr wanted to place their anti-Jewishness on a religious basis. The day for a religious motivation of anti-Jewishness had passed. And yet it was necessary to find some high-sounding reason to justify these indiscriminate attacks upon an entire group; so a new word was coined—antisemitism. The Jew-haters took advantage of the most respected intellectual movement of the nineteenth century—scientific research. Besides, the new spirit of ardent nationalism had produced much interest in historical writing. False science and distorted history were now combined to erect a new intellectual refuge for the old hates. A Frenchman named Gobineau had attempted to "prove," some years previously, that everything worth while in the world was the work of the French. From this he concluded that France was the greatest nation on earth. Other nations would not, of course, let such a claim go unchallenged. In each land some ambitious pseudo-scientific publicist undertook to prove, by means of even greater distortions of history, that his particular racial mixture was the natural ruler of the world.

All of them, however, agreed that the Semites, who by definition were called non-Europeans, had contributed nothing to civilization. The Jewish contributions to the civilization of Europe during the Middles Ages were unknown, the Jews themselves having as yet done little to investigate the subject. As to Christianity, which would in itself seem to be an obviously substantial Jewish contribution, much ingenuity was used to prove that whatever in the Christian religion had come from Judaism was inferior to what had been derived from Greece or Rome. Indeed, Jesus himself was denied his Jewish origin and his Jewish background; his greatness was ascribed to a theoretical non-Semitic racial influence. Going to even farther extremes, historians of civilization and of the Bible made valiant intellectual efforts to prove that whatever had been good in the religion of the ancient Hebrews and Jews had been borrowed—they all but said "stolen"—from the surrounding peoples. The undeniable contributions to current civilization by certain individual Jews still remained. But these were easily explained away on the ground that such men were exceptions who had been influenced by their non-Jewish environment. Here then was a theory of the Jewish share in human progress which appealed to smugness and conceit of every European people, and sugar-coated the dislike of the Jews even for liberals and intellectuals who might otherwise have found it unpalatable. All of this pseudo-science was summed up, toward the end of the nineteenth century, by Houston Stewart Chamberlain, a renegade Englishman, in his notorious book, *Foundations of the Nineteenth Century*.

The Protests—A great many Germans and other Europeans did not succumb to this type of intellectual camouflage, and some of them made their protest heard. Prince Frederick, heir to the German throne, called antisemitism "the disgrace of the century." Both in Germany and in Austria leagues against antisemitism were founded by Christians to counteract the societies which antisemites were founding. Theodor Mommsen, a German historian as highly regarded as Treitschke, issued a statement in refutation of the latter's attack. Hermann Strack, a Christian student of the Talmud, wrote a book to disprove some of the more gruesome theories about the Jews and their life. Antisemitism may have become widespread, but liberalism was not dead.

The Results—No matter how different the justification for anti-Jewishness, the expression of it was the same as in days gone by. Any number of adventurers took advantage of the ease with which popular emotions could be aroused by an appeal to antisemitism. In many instances the rascals were exposed; in others they reaped a rich reward. There were several widely advertised ritual murder trials, which showed better than anything else that the populace did not discriminate between religious and racial theories. In every case malicious and lying witnesses against the Jews were not lacking; but respectable and scholarly Christians were also on hand to defend them. In one such case, Thomas G. Masaryk, years later the first president of Czechoslovakia, offered to defend the accused Jew. Nor was there any lack of poisonous and ignorant attacks on the Talmud, quite on the order of the Middle Ages. One attacker of the Talmud, Rohling, a professor of theology at the German university of Prague, was challenged by Rabbi Joseph S. Bloch of Vienna to prove his assertions in court. The trial was about to begin when the cowardly ignoramus withdrew from the case. The most obvious result of the antisemitic movement was experienced naturally in the reduction of political rights only recently gained. An army career was impossible for a Jew and even an appointment to civil office was out of the question. Few were the unconverted Jews who attained a professorship in a German university and these had to be men of quite extraordinary ability in their chosen field.

4. FRANCE AND THE DREYFUS CASE

Jews, Economics and Politics—The Jews of France, fewer in number and possessing freedom earlier than the German Jews, identified themselves completely with the French people. As in Germany, so in France, industrial and commercial activity was in the hands of Jews to a considerable extent. In the professions and in politics they were represented beyond their proportion. But all of this did not prevent the rise of antisemitism which, again as in Germany, was intimately bound up with politics and economics. France, in fact, provided the history of antisemitism with its most spectacular case which, outside of czarist Russia and until the rise of Hitler, was the best example of the sinister uses to which antisemitism could be put.

The Rothschilds—The Rothschilds offer an illustration of the manner in which useful business activity was twisted into a cause for antisemitism. The Rothschild family began its rise in Frankfort on the Main, during the ghetto period, when Anschel Rothschild was the financial adviser of several German princes. In the Napoleonic wars the Rothschilds gave substantial support to the cause of the allies against France. The age of vast commercial expansion which followed these wars afforded them their greatest opportunity. With important branches in Austria, France and England, the next generation of the family participated in the building of railroads and the development of mines and other industries. They made extensive loans to the various governments, to whom they appealed occasionally, though not always successfully, in the defense of Jewish rights. They were, of course, not the only bankers; but they were the most important and brilliant ones during the middle part of the nineteenth century, so that antisemites have ever since then used the Rothschilds as proof of the international character of Jewish business, as though that were in itself criminal. The fact is that even in the nineteenth century Jewish bankers were a very small proportion of the banking interests with international contacts. Furthermore, the Rothschilds of the various countries were very ardent in their patriotism to their respective lands. The English Rothschilds, for example, helped materially in the acquisition by England of the control of the Suez Canal, just as Bleichröder of Berlin, also a Jewish banker, advanced Bismarck the money for the war in 1870 which resulted in the establishment of the German empire. Since, however, antisemitism deals not in facts but in hates, the Rothschild interests, and other successful Jewish bankers, were pictured as a danger to Christian society and were used everywhere in Europe as an example of an evil influence which must be destroyed.

Corrupt Finance and Corrupt Ambition—The craze for speculation grew to great proportions in France toward the end of the nineteenth century. It resulted in a number of scandals, but none so great as that which followed the bankruptcy of the original plans to build the Panama Canal. The government of the Third Republic had permitted itself to be used by the backers of a Panama scheme to mislead the French public and encourage it to invest large sums of money, although many deputies in the French parliament knew that the plan could not be carried through. Unfortunately, a number of Jews were involved in the bribery of members of the government. The antisemitic newspapers lost no time in pointing out the corrupt influence of these Jews; but, as one might expect, they generalized their charge to include all Jews. The antisemites had a purpose in mind much larger than the destruction of the social and economic gains of the French Jewry. The antisemitic press was the same French press which sought the destruction of the Third Republic and the restoration of the monarchy. These political reactionaries had the support of the nobility, which wanted to regain its social and political prestige; the army officers, who resented being under the control of a civilian government; and many political-minded churchmen, who saw much of their influence gone with the ascendancy of a liberal republic. All of these combined to plot the overthrow of the republic and it suited their purpose admirably to be able to show how corrupt a democratically-elected parliament can be. Republicanism, they argued, was controlled by corrupt Jewish financiers.

The Arrest of Dreyfus—Before the Panama scandal was well over, an event occurred which played into the hands of the anti-democratic forces. Among the few Jewish officers in the French army was Captain Alfred Dreyfus, who had risen to a post on the general staff. He belonged to a prominent and wealthy family of Alsatian origin whose Jewishness was of the thinnest kind. On October 15, 1894, Captain Dreyfus was arrested on the charge of selling French military plans to the German government. The antisemitic press and other reactionaries lost no time in pointing to this as further proof of the dangerous influence of the Jews. In January 1895,

Dreyfus was publicly degraded and sent off to prison, while the mob shouted "Death to the Jews!" But there were people in France who had serious doubts about Dreyfus' guilt. An intense struggle now began in every department of French life. The army maintained that every expression of doubt was a slur on its honor. The Catholic clergy was loud in its attack on Jewish influence. A variety of reactionaries appeared to stir the mob, so that anyone daring to defend Dreyfus was exposed to the danger of physical attack.

Nevertheless, the agitation for a retrial went on. Émile Zola, at the risk of his life, published a pamphlet, *J'Accuse*, in which he openly charged the army with falsifying evidence. Colonel Henri Picquart, who discovered proof of the falsehood of the charge against Dreyfus, was commanded to be silent and sent off to a difficult colonial post. Thus, there were people in France who, whether or not they liked Jews personally, believed in the principle of justice strongly enough to fight for it. In the end, they forced a reopening of the case. Thereupon it was discovered that the real spy on the general staff was a certain Major Esterhazy, who fled to England, and that a number of accusing documents tending to throw the guilt on Dreyfus had been forged by Lieutenant-Colonel Henri, who committed suicide rather than face trial. Eventually Dreyfus was freed (1901), pardoned, and later declared innocent and restored to his rank.

The Enemy—The Dreyfus case stirred the civilized world; for ten years it formed the most important topic of political conversation. Its result was therefore all the more influential. Dreyfus' victory, it was perfectly clear, was a defeat for the enemies of democracy and saved the life of the French republic. To the Jews of the world it meant even more. Even if Dreyfus had been proved guilty, an unprejudiced person would not, for this reason, have drawn any conclusions about all Jews. But Dreyfus had become a symbol of the admission of the Jews into European society. The Jews realized, in the discussion of Dreyfus' guilt or innocence, how close they were to losing the civil rights they had recently acquired at such great pains. Clearing Dreyfus' name also meant re-establishing the honor of the Jewish people, not only in France, but wherever Jews lived.

The Dreyfus case performed one other service for the Jews —it pointed out their enemy, about whose identity there could no longer be any mistake. The real enemy of the Jews in the late nineteenth century was neither the lower class nor the middle class, but, in each country, a group with an economic and political ax to grind, using antisemitism to bewilder the rest of the population in order to hide their own selfish aims. In Russia and Rumania it was a feudal nobility and a corrupt bureaucracy; in Germany it was a scheming, strutting, militaristic Junker class headed by the cynical statesman Bismarck who, personally, did not believe the charges he helped spread about the Jews; in France it was the enemies of the republic and of democracy. Everywhere the real enemy at that time were those who sought to institute a reactionary movement against the gains made by the popular revolutions of the previous era, or to stop them from making further gains. This enemy was able to hire or delude journalists and politicians and sometimes obtain the support even of intellectuals and men of letters who lent dignity to its schemes.

There were Jews who recognized the true situation and there were many who did not; but all alike began a frantic search for means to defend themselves.

CHAPTER VI

THE RESPONSE

THE JEWS OF EUROPE REACT IN A VARIETY OF WAYS TO THE ATTACKS OF ANTISEMITISM

The Effect on the Accused—The Jews of Europe had fought hard against medieval prejudices; yet here it was crawling back, its ugly face hidden under a new mask, its raucous voice drowning out the Jewish plea for brotherhood. The physical effects of the new antisemitism need not be exaggerated. In the last quarter of the nineteenth century, antisemitism in Western Europe was still in its talking stage. It was making the participation of Jews in the world's work more difficult but not impossible in the West. As to the eastern parts of Europe, the Jews of Russia and Rumania would have been oppressed even if antisemitism had not been used to revive old hatreds among the more progressive peoples. Perhaps the force of the oppression in Eastern Europe would have been weaker if respect for the rights of man in the West had been stronger. But Russia and Rumania were still too medieval in organization and sentiment for anyone to have expected a change in their attitudes towards their Jewish citizens. The really important results of antisemitism at the end of the nineteenth century were not so much practical and physical as mental and emotional. Apart from its effect upon cooperation between Christian and Jew, it stunned the Jews. It was a blow to their hopes and to their self-respect. They had stretched forth the hand of sincere friendliness, willing to forget and forgive the past; they saw the world turn away from them with a humiliating gesture. They, not their persecutors, were being called before the bar of public opinion on charges which in their very nature could not be disproved. For it is impossible to answer arguments which either have no basis in fact or are founded on generalizations drawn from a few actual instances. The Jews felt that they must do something to counter the new movement; but what?

During the Middle Ages the Jews had been everywhere similarly oppressed. Then, however, a practical unanimity of response had been possible. In nineteenth-century Europe the situation was much more complicated. The democracy which the Jews had themselves helped to bring about served to make the middle class supreme. Antisemitism bribed and flattered the Christian population, especially the middle class. It bribed them by holding down their Jewish competitors, and it flattered them by asserting that they were racially superior, that they were better merely by being themselves. Besides, one of the first results of emancipation had been to weaken inner Jewish life. The Jews suffered from national divisions, class divisions and wide religious disagreements. There could not be a concentrated, unanimous response. The Jews made many answers to antisemitism. Some tried to reason with their enemies; others turned to self-education. Some preferred flight from Jewish contacts; others, generalizing the injustice done to themselves, sought to reform the world.

1. THE APPEAL TO REASON

External Aid—A number of liberal and high-minded Christians undertook the defense of the Jews because they considered antisemitism a blot on civilization. Books and articles from the pens of highly respected authors and scientists appeared in every country. The gratitude of the Jews was deep and lasting. But the Jews could not depend upon Christian defenders alone. It was unhealthy and unnatural for an accused group not to raise its voice in protest against insult. Some of the Christian defenders, moreover, pleaded too hard. Though antisemites might portray the Jews as devils, it was neither true nor wise to answer by presenting them as saints and supermen. The Christian defenders, and all too often the Jews themselves, missed the point because they misunderstood the nature of the antisemitic movement. It was not so much the Jews who needed defense, but truth, honor and justice as well as the newly-born rights of man that needed protection from the antisemite.

Refutations—It was natural for the Jews to undertake to refute the most common charges made against them. They answered the accusation that Jews were interested only in wealth by pointing out that the vast majority of Jews were poverty-stricken. It was not difficult to prove that at all times there were Christians, as well as Jews, who considered the acquisition of wealth evidence of wisdom and character. Statistics were cited which easily disproved the common charge that Jews had a disproportionately large number of lawbreakers. The arts and the sciences were summoned and used to show that the Jews were creative contributors to the culture of every land. The Jews defended their patriotism by counting the number of Jewish soldiers who fought in every war. The Jews wrote thousands of books and articles to prove the malice and falsehood of the accusations against them, but to no avail. Any number of learned men arrayed arguments in defense of the Talmud, and in every country of Western and Central Europe the Jews organized societies to aid in the publication of such material; but falsehoods regarding the nature and the contents of the Talmud continued to appear. In every country they also organized committees to help defend Jewish rights where these were threatened. Such committees usually followed the model of the Alliance Israélite Universelle; but now, unfortunately, not so much for the defense of Jews in far-off, uncivilized countries, but of those nearer home.

Self-Understanding—The most tragic result of antisemitism was its effect upon some of the Jews themselves. A considerable number of Jews, lacking the foundation of Jewish knowledge, were ready to accept the criticisms of the antisemites. They quite properly wanted to make their own group perfect; yet according to the antisemites everything about Jewish life was wrong, and the Jewish self-reformers fell into despair. In addition to refuting the antisemitic charges among the non-Jews, it seemed necessary to refute these same charges among the Jews. Without self-respect no group can go on living. Appreciation of this fact resulted in another type of activity. Attempts were made through literature to give the adult Jew that knowledge of Jewish life which in previous generations had been acquired almost automatically by every Jewish child. Newspapers for Jews were established; essays and books were written; lecture platforms were organized in England, France, Germany and Austria, in order to acquaint adult Jews with their past and give them back their self-respect. The scholarly publications which were begun during this period were on a higher level: *The Jewish Quarterly Review* in England (later transferred to the United States), the *Revue des Études Juives* in France and the *Monatsschrift für Geschichte und Wissenschaft des Judentums*, founded long ago by Frankel, and others devoted themselves to presenting before Jew and Christian alike the results of scientific research into the Jewish past.

Dignified Secession—Some Jews, during the last two decades of the century, learned quickly that appealing to reason in the face of prejudice would get them nowhere. Socially they continued to be ostracized. It was then that a number of German Jews invited the B'nai B'rith of America to organize a lodge in Europe. No doubt the very people who had excluded them, as Jews, from general organizations now joined in the cry that Jews were clannish. That being always part of the game played by antisemitism, the originators of the European B'nai B'rith disregarded the cry. The European branch of B'nai B'rith spread quickly and became a force in many communities, since the lodges were open to Jews of every religious attitude.

A tendency now appeared for Jews to defend themselves also politically, by refusing to vote for parties who countenaced antisemitism. A similar dignified self-assertion became visible even among the students of various universities. Refused admittance to Christian fraternities, a number of Jewish students organized their own and bravely adopted insignia which announced their Jewishness. They challenged to a duel any member of another fraternity who expressed himself in antisemitic fashion. There was to be no more groveling; and the Christian student, while he may not have ceased being an antisemite, at least gained respect for the Jew. Unfortunately such youths and adults were in the minority.

The New Literature—Unplanned but natural and welcome

allies in stirring the modern Jew's self-respect and healthy self-criticism were novels about Jews in various European languages. Jews as well as non-Jews were among the authors. The old-fashioned stereotyped picture of the Jew as evil and repellent was gradually giving place, in the best writings of the late nineteenth century, to treatment of Jews as both good and bad. England, with its sense of liberalism more deeply implanted, had more of this kind of literature written by Christian authors than any nation on the Continent. Charles Dickens, for example, portrayed a good Jew in Riah, of *Our Mutual Friend*, in order to make up for the evil Fagin of *Oliver Twist*. George Eliot's *Daniel Deronda* exercised an especially profound influence on the Jews. There were similar novelists, and also dramatists, in the rest of Europe.

The Jewish novelists, for the most part, were men who had gained a reputation in the field of general literature, especially in Germany. Leopold Kompert, with his beautiful sketches of Jewish life in Bohemia; Karl Emil Franzos, with his thrilling short stories entitled *The Jews of Barnow;* and a number of others did much to awaken sympathy for the same Jewish past which antisemites were deriding. The best work of this kind began to come, toward the end of the century, from the pen of the English Jew, Israel Zangwill. Unfortunately, however, neither these nor the scholarly or explanatory writings ever reached the masses of the people. Antisemites certainly did not permit themselves to be influenced by what the Jews wrote. Even among the Jews, the very ones who most needed to learn the lessons of self-respect paid least attention to what their fellow Jews offered in defense of Jewish life.

2. The Answer Through Religious Reorganization

Spiritual Hunger—For those Jews who looked upon their Jewish birth as a misfortune, one way out of the difficulty still existed. Despite the statement of the antisemites of that day that religion was not the basis for their anti-Jewishness, a convert to Christianity still could have any position which had been refused him as a Jew. Those who were ambitious to rise socially or academically often yielded to the temptation. Others remained on the boundary line, not taking part in Jewish life but holding back from conversion because it seemed cowardly to forsake a weaker group. These last, and the even more self-respecting and courageous Jews who never wavered in their attachment to Jewish life, did not consider mere answers to antisemitic accusations as sufficient evidence of their Jewish loyalty. There was need for a vibrant, stirring justification for continued adherence to Judaism despite all difficulties. Here was a challenge which the Synagogue might have been expected to meet, as it had done generations and centuries before. That it did not do so was due to a number of causes.

Religious Organization—The powerful, coordinated Jewish community of the Middle Ages had disappeared under the influence of emancipation. Nevertheless, fairly well organized community life existed. In France the consistorial system imposed by Napoleon worked efficiently to maintain religious unity. England, too, had a nationwide organization in the United Synagogue, with a chief rabbi whose office and position were modeled upon those of a bishop of the Church and whose duties included supervision over every aspect of religious life. In Germany and Austria each city had its communal organization in which Orthodox and Reform Jews cooperated. Unless a Jew publicly declared himself an unbeliever, he was compelled by the government to pay a tax for the support of Jewish religious institutions, the money being turned over to the community board. In all these cases, the community boards were elected more or less democratically and they, in turn, elected the rabbis. Naturally the most respected Jews of the community were chosen to control its affairs, though they were not necessarily the most devoted to Jewish life. These community organizations, however, no longer had any disciplinary power over their people; they no longer applied Jewish law to civil life; they represented little more than philanthropic, statistical and synagogal cooperation. They gave an impression of unity which they could actually do nothing to enforce.

Jewish Education—One of the clearest signs of the transformation in Jewish life was the change in Jewish education. Gone were the days, especially in the West, when the Jewish boy was sent to a Jewish school and then to a *yeshibah*. The desire to provide one's child with general culture and to prepare it for a career predominated over the desire to prepare the child for Jewish living. Here and there, private teaching and synagogue schools helped redress the balance to some extent, but on the whole Jewish education became at best a secondary activity and frequently no time was found for it at all. In Germany religious education was required by law and the Jewish communities participated in the selection of a teacher of Judaism in the public schools. But the time allotted this subject was far from adequate for the absorption of the barest fundamentals of the Jewish cultural heritage. In lands other than Germany the situation was far more chaotic, the community boards making less than halfhearted attempts to solve this most important problem.

Advanced education also underwent a change. The need for religious leadership was apparent, yet the old-fashioned *yeshibot* could no longer serve as the only training schools for rabbis. In the course of the nineteenth century, every country in Western Europe established at least one theological school, while Germany had several, representing various religious attitudes. These rabbinical seminaries largely subordinated the study of the Talmud to subjects better calculated to prepare rabbis for leadership among men and women whose interests were centered in current life and secular culture. They produced scholarly rabbis and excellent preachers, who compared favorably with the religious leaders of other faiths. But no matter how the Jewish theological curriculum was modernized, there were two factors which it could not overcome: the lack of a Jewish cultural background among the modern Jews, and the spirit of the age. This was the period when beautiful synagogue buildings were erected and when Jewish scholarship made great progress. But the problems of Jewish life could not be solved by these; both synagogue and scholarship were cold, formal, hence insufficient.

The Spirit of the Age—In the second half of the nineteenth century Western Europe gave up the religious interpretation of life. It was the age when strong attacks were made by science on religion, and in intellectual circles the Church was treated with open contempt. The very fact that the Jews were studious and book-loving brought them under the influence of this movement to a larger extent than other groups. Since everything in Jewish life had been based on religion, the general anti-religious attitude was certain to prove much more harmful to Judaism than to Christianity. Christian customs and traditions had become so much part of the ordinary life of a Christian, that his failure to attend church or to give his child a religious education was not fatal to Christianity. In the case of Judaism, the more the Jews mingled in general life and society the greater was the need for emphasizing Jewish education and religious ceremonies. A minority must always be clear about the distinctions between itself and the majority, and it was just such clarification which was made difficult by the spirit of the age. Reform Ju-

daism was no more successful than Orthodoxy. The struggle
for and against Reform, during the first half of the nineteenth
century, while it had stirred bitter controversy, had been a
sign of deep interest. The struggle died down afterwards, not
because agreement had been reached on matters of principle
and practice, but because Jews had lost interest in the entire
subject. The hopes of Reform Judaism had evidently not
been justified by developments. It had removed some of the
customs accumulated through the ages; it had modified the
prayer book, revived the sermon in the vernacular and introduced the organ into the service. It had made Jewish life easier, but it did not stop the trend away from religious loyalty.
For their part, the Orthodox continued to struggle for observances and traditions, but did not succeed in justifying them to
the mind of a man of that day. The spirit of the times was
inimical to both. As a result, Judaism could not serve to relieve the hurt inflicted upon the Jews by the new antisemitic
attacks.

3. RESPONSE BY FLIGHT

The New Exodus—The Western Jews suffered bitter disappointment over the rise of antisemitism, but as yet they had
no reason to despair. In Eastern Europe, on the other hand,
the trickery of Rumania and the persecutions of 1881–2 in
Russia shattered their every hope. Nevertheless, the liberals
of both countries, ever optimistic, as well as the revolutionists
among the Russian Jews frowned upon emigration. The former were afraid lest it be cited as proof of the Jews' lack of
attachment to the fatherland. The revolutionists wanted the
Jews to stay and help fight the czarist system. But the Jewish
masses, driven from their homes, haunted by the threat of
pogroms, were faced with the problem of maintaining life itself. It was obvious beyond the slightest doubt that the country in which they had lived for centuries, and which they as
much as anyone else had developed, denied them the sense of
being at home as long as they refused baptism. To most of
them, as well as to many kindhearted Jews and Christians
outside of Russia, it seemed that the Russian Jews must emigrate. They now began an exodus from Russia greater in extent than they or any other group had ever experienced.

Brothers in Need—Some 30,000 Russian Jews crossed the
sea during the decade of 1870. This, however, was a mere
trickle compared to the flood which sought new homes after

1881. The refugees, streaming over the Russian border, were stranded in the town of Brody, most of them without funds, all of them without guidance, some of them without any clear destination. Again the Alliance came to their rescue, aided substantially by committees and funds from Jews of other European lands. Far from being alleviated, the problem of caring for, sifting and directing the emigrants became aggravated in the next year, after the decree of the May Laws. About 25,000 entered the United States alone in the two years, 1881–2. Nor did the flight from Russia, and Rumania as well, stop during the 1880s, although it was considerably reduced in numbers. It was, in fact, resumed in 1891, after further harsh decrees, so that committees of assistance had to be organized again and more huge sums spent for personal aid and transportation. It was the West European Jews who at this time provided the funds.

Immigrants Create Problems—Many European Jews were afraid that the settlement of these refugees among them would react unfavorably upon their own status. They solved the problem by directing all but a tiny number of the fugitives to lands across the sea, mostly to the United States. Though a few American Jews were also not happy about the avalanche of immigrants, the vast majority—and most of the Christian population as well—sympathized with the unfortunates and tried to be helpful. But the American Jewish community was as yet not sufficiently well organized to cope with the problem. The Hebrew Emigrant Aid Society, which was established in 1881, along with other charitable foundations, had neither the efficiency nor the funds to care for the needy and help them adjust themselves to the new environment.

The Russian emigrants preferred to go to the United States, which had been portrayed to them, not only as a haven of peace, but as the land of opportunity. England, too, in proportion to its size and population, received a considerable number. The very extent of the immigration into these countries created social and economic problems. By choice as well as necessity, most of the immigrants settled in the large, industrialized cities. New York, Philadelphia, Chicago and other cities in the United States, and London and Leeds in England, saw their slum districts expanding with fearful rapidity. The working classes of both countries became concerned about the possible competition of the newcomers, whose presence depressed the wage scale. In England, where antisemitism had been almost unknown, the Jewish communities did their utmost to take care of the immigrants and thus prevent the development of serious antagonisms. But the demand for restricting immigration could not be stopped. A parliamentary commission was appointed to investigate the problem. While the commission reported that the Jewish immigrants were sober, hard-working and law-abiding, it nevertheless recommended a law to restrict the number of those permitted to enter.

Baron de Hirsch—Another approach to the solution of the immigrants' problem was made by Baron Maurice de Hirsch (1831–1896), one of the most remarkable personalities produced by the Jews during this period. A descendant of Jewish court-bankers in Bavaria, he lived in Brussels and directed the construction of railroads in the Balkans and Turkey, succeeding in these projects where others before him had failed. His philanthropy had always been broad and, after the death of his only son, he devoted his entire vast fortune to alleviating human distress. He at first believed that the Russian government was in earnest about its desire to make the Jews more "useful," and he offered to finance schools to train Russian Jews in handicrafts. The government refused his offer. He then wanted to pay for the settlement of Jews as farmers in Russia; but this, too, was rejected. The flight of the Jews from Russia in the 1880s moved him deeply and, at the call of American Jews for assistance in solving the problem of the immigrants, he established the Baron de Hirsch Fund of New York, in 1891. Its purposes were to aid in the transportation of properly qualified Jewish immigrants to such places in the United States where their labor might earn them a dignified livelihood, to teach them new trades and help in their education.

The ICA—At the same time Baron de Hirsch embarked upon a far more ambitious project. He had become convinced that the Jews of Russia and Rumania must be taken out of these countries and established as farmers in whatever part of the world land could be found for them. He set aside $10,000,000—a huge sum for those days, subsequently increased by his wife—for the creation of a Jewish Colonization Association (abbreviated into ICA). The Argentine republic in South America seemed to offer the greatest promise. In time seventeen colonies were established there, and a number of others in Brazil, Canada and the United States. To be sure, Hirsch's dream of transporting vast numbers of Jews and establishing them in agriculture was not realized, and even some of the colonists, lacking the necessary skills, abandoned the farms and turned to industry and commerce; yet

ICA has continued its labors in various parts of the world, from the Argentine to Palestine, down to this day and produced results which have influenced Jewish life.*

The New Diaspora—Almost 600,000 Jews came to the United States alone between 1881 and 1900. Tens of thousands of others sought homes in various parts of South America, South Africa and Australia. New Jewish communities were developing in the most widely scattered parts of the world.

4. THE ANSWER THROUGH LIBERALISM AND REVOLUTION

Karl Marx and his Effect on the Jews—Before the revolutions of 1848, liberals talked of the new world which was soon to be established after the forces of reaction had been defeated. Some liberals wanted more than a political change; they looked also for an economic revolution which would deprive the rising middle class of its control of socially essential property just as the old aristocracy was being deprived of its control of government. The philosopher of this movement was Karl Marx (1818–1883). In a number of ponderous volumes he laid the foundations for what has come to be known as socialism. Marx was of Jewish ancestry; in fact, both his father and his mother were descended from a long line of rabbis; but he was brought up as a Christian. He knew about Jews and Judaism only the little he might have picked up at home during self-justifying and therefore unfavorable discussions by his converted parents.

Karl Marx possessed brilliant intellectual gifts and an enormous power of concentration. He spent his life studying economic and social problems and developed in his writings the theory of economic determinism. By this he meant that the way people make their living colored and affected every other aspect of their lives. Not their culture nor their religion, not their political nor their intellectual ideas, but their activities dealing with the attainment of economic power and security molded all else and constituted the principal force in shaping the history of a group or a nation. He viewed the problems confronting the Jews as mainly economic problems. He saw no reason why Judaism should survive and he knew nothing of Jewish cultural values. Indeed, he was severer towards Judaism than towards Christianity. The struggle between anti-

* See below, pp. 575, 646 f.

semites and Jews, he argued in an essay which he wrote on
the subject, was a struggle for material wealth between two
groups of the middle class. It was, therefore, a struggle in
which the workers could have no interest. The conflict would
end when the classless socialist state came into being. He
could see in the Jewish situation no conflict between justice
and injustice.

The Labor Movement—The extension of the right to vote
made it possible for labor to exert political influence. The
foremost leader of labor in Germany who was conscious of
this potential power was Ferdinand Lassalle (1825–1864).
He was a Jew who, though never converted, had as little interest in Judaism as Karl Marx. He might have put labor on
the road to political power in Germany, for even Bismarck at
one time negotiated with him for labor support. But nothing
came of labor's power. The reactionary elements in Europe
were quick to recognize the danger from a self-conscious
labor movement. They also saw the possibility of using the
individual laborer's vote for their own purposes. The new politicians seized their chance to divert the attention of the poor
and the workers away from the class struggle as explained by
Marx; and their villainous instrument was antisemitism. The
Jew, they argued, not imperialistic politics and greedy economics, must be destroyed before everybody could be happy
and satisfied. No wonder an honest labor leader called antisemitism "the socialism of fools." Antisemitism spread among
the lower classes. Labor caused riots in Germany. Labor objected to the competition of the immigrant Jews in England.
Labor and its leaders even in France saw no reason for opposing the condemnation of Dreyfus. Only after the reactionary plot became clear and all the hard-won gains of the
republic were obviously threatened, did French labor swing its
influence to the side of justice. Consequently, Jewish labor
leaders saw more clearly than others how the masses were
being misled.

Origin of the Bund—Because of the small size and ignorance of the Russian working class in the second half of the
nineteenth century, it exerted almost no influence. The Jewish
artisans were intellectually better prepared to follow events
and showed an appreciation of united action long before they
heard of Marxist theories. But they lacked leadership, both in
politics and economics. The children of the *maskilim* of the
previous generation had so immersed themselves in general
Russian life and culture as to find no interest in Jewish life at
all. During the 1860s and 1870s they identified themselves

with the movement among the Russian intellectuals which idealized the peasant and strove to improve his lot. In the 1880s, disappointed in the response of the peasants, they, like their Christian colleagues, turned to socialism. A long list of Jewish fugitives from czarist wrath and of exiles to Siberia testified to the important part which Jews played in the struggle for progress and emancipation in Russia. They failed, however, to recognize the existence of specifically Jewish problems. They either knew nothing of Judaism or, if they came from ardently Jewish communities like Vilna or Minsk, accepted the materialistic interpretation current among the Marxists of their day. Jewish religion, culture or group survival had no part in their plans for the future.

Yet the Jewish workers were there, a growing, idealistic, potentially important mass which, because of its obvious difference from the Russian workers of peasant origin, required a different approach. In the early 1890s a number of Jewish radicals recognized this fact, although it was not till 1897 that they took definite action. In that year they laid the foundations for the Jewish Labor Alliance of Russia, Poland and Lithuania, subsequently to become important under the abbreviation *Bund* ("Alliance"). The Bund remained a branch of the underground Russian socialist movement, differing at first only in the use of Yiddish as a means of propaganda. In the course of the next few years, however, the Bund leadership, despite opposition from their colleagues, arrived at the conclusion that Russian Jewry, like similar national groups, deserved national recognition within the Russian state. This development was due, to a large extent, to the rise of Zionism and its appeal to the masses.

Jews and Politics—In every European country Jews could be found in every political party. Their individual economic interests motivated the party affiliation of most, exactly as was the case with other elements of the population. In addition to self-interest there was one other factor which affected the Jews: antisemitism. Other groups invariably abandoned any party which became tainted with hostility to them. Not so the Jews. The antisemities in Germany and Austria, for example, in line with their usual trickery, tried to discredit the liberal parties by identifying them with the Jews. The parties in question, instead of accepting the challenge and openly arguing for the rights of the Jews, thereupon showed their embarrassment over the presence of Jews in their leadership and even over the support of Jews in elections. They took the cowardly line of denying the influence of Jews upon their policies and such denials were frequently fortified by outright anti-Jewish expressions. If ever there was a case of insult being added to injury, this was one. Nevertheless, the Jews showed more understanding of other people's problems than of their own. While withdrawing from the leadership of these political groups, they continued to vote for them, thereby weakening their own cries for justice. Even when they had a chance to exchange their votes for protection by another political group, the liberal Jews refused to do so, although other religious and national groups never hesitated to play this type of political game. The Jews, as a result, forfeited the protection of all parties.

Some Jews of the middle class, moreover, disregarded their economic interests by actively struggling for economic reforms. Their sense of justice was outraged by the bad conditions and exceedingly low wage scales in many industries. Not only did this arouse further hostility to all Jews on the part of the anti-socialist forces, but it also split the Jewish group itself. Finally, the Jews further weakened their influence by permitting religious differences to divide them politically. Some of the Hasidim in Austria, for example, refused to vote for a Jewish candidate if they did not like his religious views. Later came the question of Zionism which added still more involvements to an already overcomplicated situation.

Intellectually, socially, religiously and politically, the Jews failed to find a successful response to the attacks of the antisemites.

CHAPTER VII

A HOMELAND OF THEIR OWN

A CONSIDERABLE NUMBER OF JEWS, DISAPPOINTED IN THEIR SEARCH FOR A HOME AMONG THE NATIONS, GIVE NEW MEANING TO THE ANCIENT HOPE FOR A RESTORATION OF ZION

The Nationalist Answer—By the end of the nineteenth century it was apparent that the Jewish hope for immediate acceptance by the nations of the world was not being realized. The Jews discovered, to their amazement, that the removal of economic restrictions and the grant of the right to vote did not constitute recognition of human equality. Important as it was for the Jews to be ready for political and social equality, it was even more important for their fellow citizens to be ready to grant it. If the masses had been left alone or had permitted themselves to be guided by the finer spirits among the Christian population, Jew and Christian might have become accustomed to living together as partners in the national life. This, unfortunately, was not the case. The masses of almost every European nation fell a prey to the spiritual marauders who went by the name of antisemites. The ease with which the antisemites won their victories forced the Jews to consider seriously whether the land of their birth could ever be anything more than merely their birthplace.

1. FORERUNNERS OF ZIONISM

Nationalism and the Jews—In the nineteenth century nationalism became a mighty force in the world. It meant the love of the people for their nation, their land, their institutions, folkways and customs, language and literature. Unfortunately, it sometimes also expressed itself in wars of conquest and imperialism and in intolerance of differences within a nation. The Jews were naturally under the influence of the nationalist spirit of their respective countries. There were no prouder Germans than the German Jews; there were no more enthusiastic Frenchmen than the French Jews. This was true of the Jews of every nation. At the same time, the spirit of nationalism affected the hopes of many of these very Jews for the future of the Jewish people. The Jews of those countries which denied them the sense of being at home revived the long dormant ideal of Jewish nationhood. Many Jews of more friendly lands, moreover, became sympathetic to Jewish nationalism because of the well-founded fear that the Jewish spiritual heritage was endangered by the pressure, both peaceful and hostile, of their non-Jewish environment. The Jewish nationalism of both these groups was unlike the usual type of nationalism rampant in Europe. It emphasized religon and culture; it lacked completely any conquering ambitions; its chief aim was to solve the heartbreaking search of the Jew for a friendly home.

Palestine in the Jewish Past—Jewish nationalist thinking could not fail to include Palestine. While Palestine had never for a moment been forgotten by the Jews, it had assumed, since the Middle Ages, the character of a Holy Land and, in the late nineteenth century, it still retained that character among larger segments of the Jewish population. Pilgrimages continued to be made to it and religious hopes were bound up with it. In fact, among most East European Jews, a restoration was conceived of only in messianic terms. The Messiah, they believed, would miraculously restore the Jews to Zion at the same time that the whole world would, equally miraculously, be turned into the Kingdom of God. Now and then an individual had arisen to agitate for immediate action without waiting for miracles. Such men received respectful attention, but no practical response from the people. In spirit the land was theirs no matter who was in actual control of it nor how distant they were from it. It could not well be otherwise as long as the Jew studied the Bible and permitted his religion to inspire him with hope, and as long as practical methods were not set forth by an inspiring leader to give direction to their vague aspirations.

Moses Hess—It was inevitable that the nineteenth century, full as it was of both practical-mindedness and revolutionary thought, should have started people thinking in more concrete fashion on the subject of Palestine and the Jews. Among the first of these thinkers was Moses Hess (1812–1875), advocate of a league of nations and an interpreter of socialism from the ethical point of view. The same ethical attitude made him defend the rights of small peoples. He argued that every people has a right to live and must be encouraged to do so, provided it has something to contribute to the sum total of human culture. From this he drew the conclusion, in his book, *Rome and Jerusalem* (1862), that the Jews certainly ought to be aided by mankind to re-establish their nation. Jewish culture, represented by Jerusalem and Christian culture, represented by Rome, need not be in conflict. Because he had great faith in the liberalism and the culture of the French, Hess advocated that Palestine be placed under the supervision of France and gradually turned into a Jewish homeland.

Hirsch Kalischer and Agricultural Self-Help—Another expression of hope for the rebuilding of a Jewish Palestine, *Derishat Zion* (The Loving Quest for Zion), was published, strangely enough that very same year (1862), by Zevi-Hirsch Kalischer, an Orthodox rabbi in Posen. Unlike his colleagues,

he argued that belief in the Messiah did not obligate the Jews
to a do-nothing policy towards Palestine. He thought the time
ripe for resettlement because the Jews of Eastern Europe
were in great need of a home and because the Jews of Western Europe possessed enough wealth and political influence to
make the attempt feasible. Far more practical than Hess,
Kalischer advocated the establishment of agricultural colonies
in Palestine out of which in time might grow a large and influential community.

The emphasis placed on agriculture was not accidental,
since a back-to-the-soil movement already existed among the
Jews of Russia. Hebrew poets and novelists, and *maskilim* in
general from Levinsohn down through Mapu and Gordon,
had for decades been glorifying the farmers of ancient Judea
and condemning their own contemporaries for their seeming
preference for urban life. The czarist government, too, repeatedly throughout the nineteenth century blamed the Jews
for their supposed unwillingness to become farmers. In actual
fact, the government interposed all kinds of annoyances and
discriminations, and by the inefficiency and heartlessness of
its bureaucrats turned the official offers of land into a cruel
jest. Nevertheless, more than 10,000 Jews, persuaded by the
crowded conditions in the Pale as much as by the arguments
of the *maskilim,* were settled on the land. But, in 1866, the
czarist government decided to stop the Jewish agricultural
movement ostensibly because the provinces involved in their
settlement did not need any more colonizers.*

Kalischer's proposal of agricultural colonization in Palestine
therefore fell on ready ears. His zeal and earnestness, moreover, won the support of such Western Jews as Crémieux,
Rothschild and Montefiore. As a result, the first colony was
founded in Palestine by the Alliance Israélite Universelle in
1869 and given the name Mikveh Yisrael (The Hope of Israel). Nor was this all. Kalischer traveled far and wide
through Europe to organize societies for the promotion of
Palestinian colonization. He thus laid the foundations for a
movement soon to become popular under the name *Hoveve
Zion* (Lovers of Zion).

Peretz Smolenskin—A third contributor to the idea of
Jewish national revival was the Hebrew author and journalist
Peretz Smolenskin (1842–1885). Beginning as a firm believer
in the renaissance of Jewish culture along modern lines, he
traveled and observed Jewish life in Central and Western Eu-

* Consider also the plans of Baron de Hirsch, p. 566.

rope. As a result, he became convinced that the *Haskalah*
movement was endangering the future of the Jews. In
Vienna, Smolenskin founded the monthly magazine *Ha-Sha-
har* (The Dawn) and made it his instrument for carrying on
an unceasing fight against the self-destructive forces in Jewish
life. Assimilation, he argued, was a failure; the search for
equality a mirage. The Jews must recognize themselves once
more as a nation. The Greeks, the Rumanians and other
small peoples had been able to restore themselves; why not
the Jews? They have all the attributes of nationhood; why not
the reality? Jewish nationhood, he held, is a progressive
force, and to surrender its culture is to hurt humanity. Smolenskin spoke of Palestine as the natural Jewish homeland;
but until the Russian pogroms of 1881–2 he did not consider
it essential. He placed greater emphasis on the awakening of
the Jewish national consciousness in the diaspora lands. The
fiery phrases of his books and articles made a deep impression upon the youth of his generation.

Christian Advocates—Jews were not the only ones who
thought of a Jewish restoration to Palestine. Thoughtful
Christians had come forward from time to time throughout
the centuries to suggest the return of the Jews to the Holy
Land as a step towards the realization of the world-wide messianic dream. During the nineteenth century, when the Turkish empire was showing signs of crumbling and portions of it
were falling into the hands of various powers, a number of
Englishmen proposed that England establish a protectorate
over Palestine and revive the land by letting Jews settle there.
Among these was Lawrence Oliphant, who visited Palestine
in 1879 and offered a practical plan for settling Jews in the
region of ancient Gilead. In the latter part of the nineteenth
century the importance of the Suez Canal for the maintenace
of British imperial communications was already recognized.
The occupation of Palestine by a friendly population became
of great importance to England and the possibility of its colonization by Jews a matter of practical interest. The most
earnest and thrilling presentation of this proposal was made
not by a statesman but by a novelist. In 1876 George Eliot
published *Daniel Deronda* and her fervid vision of a Jewish
Palestine made a tremendous impression. With mystical faith
in the Jewish future and an exalted conception of Jewish nationhood, she spoke, in eloquence worthy of a biblical prophet, of a Jewish rebirth in Palestine.

2. LOVERS OF ZION

Leo Pinsker—The inner foundations for a Jewish national
revival were thus already largely in existence, primarily in
Eastern Europe, even before the new antisemitism manifested
itself in the 1870s: the reinterpretation of Jewish group life
in line with the nationalistic tendencies of the age; the revival
of the Hebrew language and of Jewish culture; and the recognition of the desirability of establishing Jewish agricultural
colonies in Palestine. One step more had to be taken; one
more idea had to be expressed; and that was done by Leo
Pinsker, a Russian Jewish physician. Pinsker had believed in
the assimilation of the Jews to Russian culture; but the pogroms and May Laws of 1881–2 completely disillusioned
him. His pamphlet, *Auto-Emancipation* (that is, gaining
freedom through one's own efforts), was the result. As one
would expect from a man who had been in favor of assimilation, Pinsker's starting point was antisemitism. It could be
dissipated either by complete assimilation or by complete recognition of the Jews as a nation. In other words, the position of the Jews must be made normal. No one could do this
for the Jews, Pinsker declared; they must do it for themselves. Having openly declared themselves a nation, the Jews
would then be able to approach the other nations and ask
them for political recognition and for a homeland. Pinsker at
first cared little whether this homeland was Palestine or some
other territory. The important thing was for the Jews to free
themselves from their self-imposed servitude to other nations;
the rest would follow naturally. In ringing phrases he called
to the Jews: "Let 'Now or Never!' be our watchword. Woe to
our descendants, woe to the memory of our Jewish contemporaries, if we let this moment pass by!"

The Hoveve Zion—Pinsker's call to action electrified a
large number of Jews, especially the members of the societies
Hoveve Zion which had been organized under the inspiration
of Rabbi Kalischer's leadership. There were branches of the
Hoveve Zion in various countries. Their members proposed
to further the national idea among the Jews, to work for the
revival of Jewish culture and, above all, to foster Jewish colonization in Palestine. At the same time, in order to avoid
any misunderstanding of their motives, they made it clear
that their goals as Lovers of Zion did not constitute any compromise of their loyalty to the lands in which they lived.

Then, in 1884, under pressure of the migration from Russia, representatives of the various societies met at Kattowitz, in Germany, and formed a federation. Pinsker himself undertook to travel throughout Europe in order to organize more societies and to raise funds for colonization. Baron Edmond de Rothschild agreed to pay the expense of establishing six colonies in Palestine, and the Alliance Israélite became interested once more. By 1893 thousands of Jews in every part of the world had become Lovers of Zion.

The BILU—Under these influences the colonization of Palestine by Jews moved from dream to actuality. Not far from Mikveh Yisrael, the colony and agricultural school established by the Alliance, a number of Jews some years later (1878) established a colony with the equally expressive name of Petah Tikvah (Gate of Hope). They were soon joined by a group of Russian Jewish students who, translating the *Hoveve Zion* idea into action, had adopted for themselves the slogan BILU, a word made up of the first letters of the Hebrew words in which the prophet Isaiah had called out, "House of Jacob, come, let us go!" Answering this rallying cry, others soon followed and settled in four colonies started by Baron Edmond de Rothschild in 1882. One of these was Rishon le-Zion (First to Zion) where, hopeful of success in the ancient Palestinian industry of vine culture, the baron built a spacious cellar for the storage and aging of wine.

Other colonies came into being. Idealism and antisemitism, however, rather than the example of success in colonization, brought these newer ventures about. For the experience of the early colonies was anything but encouraging. Their knowledge of agriculture did not equal the colonists' love for Zion. Unused to the climate, suffering from malaria because of the swampy nature of the land, harassed by hostile Arabs, annoyed and overtaxed by a corrupt Turkish officialdom, even a hardier population than these ex-Europeans would have become discouraged. The Jews, however, had their ideals to sustain them and the liberality of Rothschild, and later of the ICA, to keep them from starvation. They held on during the critical years and then became the symbols of expanding Jewish hope.

3. THEODORE HERZL

Education of a European—While calls for national revival were being issued and settlements were established on Palestine's barren soil, the future leader of the back-to-Palestine movement was growing to maturity, though he was mentally still far removed from Jewish nationalism and Palestinian colonization. Born in Budapest in 1860, Theodore Herzl and his parents moved to Vienna while he was still a boy. He early showed the literary interest, the personal charm, the qualities of leadership and the powers of imagination which were to characterize his whole career. The logical profession for an aspiring young Jew of Herzl's social position was the law; but its practice interfered with his literary ambitions. He therefore soon abandoned the profession and concentrated his efforts on writing light, entertaining plays, several of which proved highly successful. At the same time he began contributing to newspapers brief, half-humorous reflections on current affairs. Herzl's temper and approach suited Viennese society perfectly and, before long, his contributions became a regular feature of the *Neue Freie Presse*, the most important journal of the city. When, in 1891, this newspaper appointed Herzl its correspondent in Paris, the cultural capital of Europe, he was well on his way to the highest literary and journalistic fame.

Education of a Jew—Throughout this period of successful achievement, Theodore Herzl's Jewishness remained far in the background. During his childhood his parents used to take him to the Reform temple in Budapest, where he became *bar-mitzvah*. Subsequently, he had no time for continuing his Jewish education. His mental life developed outside the circle then being stirred by the revival of Hebrew culture and Palestinian hopes. He could not, however, avoid taking notice of the rising antisemitic spirit all about him. What answer could one give to the hateful accusations cropping up in books and plays as well as in political contests? In reviewing such books, Herzl took the usual attitude of offering historical justifications for Jewish faults and arguing that a longer period of freedom from the ghetto was needed to eradicate them. Slowly it began to dawn on him that such an answer was beside the point, that antisemitism was not a religious nor a cultural problem, but rather one involving the economic and political transformations through which Europe was passing. Just as he was beginning to think more deeply on the subject, an event took place under his very eyes in Paris which revolutionized his entire life—the trial of Captain Alfred Dreyfus.

The Discovery of Jewish Nationalism—It was not the injustice being done to Dreyfus himself that stirred Herzl; as a matter of fact, at the beginning he considered the possibility that Dreyfus might be guilty; what affected him was the attitude of the French populace toward the Jews. Here was, presumably, the most civilized portion of humanity. Yet, these free citizens of a state which had been the first in Europe to grant the Jews complete emancipation took Dreyfus' guilt for granted, because he was a Jew, and held all Jews equally guilty. The cry "Death to the Jews!" which rang through the streets of Paris at the time of Dreyfus' public degradation, echoed in Herzl's ears and gave him no rest. He arrived at the conclusion that there could be only one answer to the problem which faced his people—removal from their hostile surroundings. He looked deeper into the situation and discovered that the Jewish people were a cultural entity, possessing enough of a common background to constitute themselves a nation. Herzl was completely ignorant of the writings of Hess and Pinsker; he thought he had made a discovery for which the world, Jewish and Christian, was waiting. In a fever of inspiration, Herzl set his ideas down on paper. The result was his famous pamphlet called *Der Judenstaat* (The Jewish State). The Jews were a nation, he argued, and should organize themselves into a Jewish society for the purpose of obtaining a land, preferably Palestine, in which their national life might be taken up anew. The other nations of the world would do well to provide such a territory for the Jews, since they would thereby solve the economic and political problems which otherwise manifested themselves in ugly antisemitism. The Jews should also organize a Jewish company to raise the money needed for the migration of hundreds of thousands to the national home. Herzl did not doubt that all this could be done. Once created, he believed the Jewish State could bring peace and happiness also to the Jewish people who remained where they were.

Friends and Critics—To his great astonishment, Herzl found that his friends refused to take his plan seriously. They would not grant his basic assumption that the Jews were a nation. They doubted that any such plan was at all practicable. Some even feared that Herzl had lost his mental balance. The editor of the newspaper for which Herzl worked, the *Neue Freie Presse* of Vienna, feared the effect which the publication of Herzl's ideas would have upon his paper and tried to dissuade Herzl from publishing the pamphlet. Herzl published it nevertheless. A flood of adverse criticism ensued. Surprising to Herzl was the amount of criticism which came from the Jews themselves. Half-assimilated Jews who worked on various European newspapers were caustic in their comments; Reform Jews editing Jewish periodicals condemned Jewish nationalism in vigorous terms. Orthodox Jews paid less attention to the dreams of Herzl than they had paid to the pleas of Kalischer. Jews who had for several decades lived for the idea of a national revival wondered whether this newspaper columnist, this writer of amusing social dramas, was not merely toying with an idea which he would soon tire of and abandon.

4. CONGRESSES AND POLITICAL ZIONISM

The Supporters—Herzl would have abandoned his plans for a Jewish state in view of the almost unanimous opposition of the Jewish circles of the West, the only Jews with whom he was acquainted. But there were other Jewish circles: the large mass of East European Jews; and those West European Jews who, like Herzl himself, saw in Jewish nationalism the only effective answer to anti-Jewishness. The Viennese student society *Kadimah* hailed Herzl enthusiastically and invited him to lead them. Jews from lands of Eastern Europe promised adherence to his plan. The *Hoveve Zion*, even those of England, responded with mild approval. There were, moreover, certain individuals who quickly told him of their adherence to any nationalist movement he might care to start. Three such men proved particularly encouraging and helpful: Israel Zangwill, who had already gained literary fame in England and America; Max Nordau, physician, critic and sociologist with a world-wide reputation; and David Wolffsohn, a businessman from Cologne, though of East European origin. Thus encouraged, Herzl issued a call for a congress of Jews at which the first steps might be taken to bring his plans to realization.

The First Congress—One hundred and ninety-seven delegates, representing almost every country where Jews lived, were called to order by Theodore Herzl in the Swiss city of Basle, on Sunday, August 29, 1897. It was the first step towards reconstituting the Jewish nation which had been destroyed by Roman arms some eighteen hundred and twenty-five years previously. One of the delegates arose and pronounced the ancient Hebrew benediction for first occasions, "Blessed art Thou, O Lord our God, King of the Universe, for keeping us alive, preserving us and permitting us to attain this day." Herzl's dignity and manner added to the thrilling mood of the situation. Everyone was conscious of the historic nature of the occasion and of the eyes of the world focused upon them. The Congress heard speeches by Herzl and Nordau and reports on the various aspects of Jewish life, and then took up the task of organizing a Zionist movement. It decided to set up an organization in every land. It further voted to revive the ancient Jewish tax of the *shekel*, now fixed at the sum of fifty cents, whatever its value may have been in biblical days. Above all, the Congress agreed upon a declaration of Zionist aims which has since then been known as the Basle Program: "Zionism seeks to establish for the Jewish people a publicly recognized, legally secured home in Palestine." The Congress, after deciding to meet again the next year, adjourned amid great enthusiasm.

Organization and Diplomacy—The Zionists met, during the following years, in annual congresses, each of which brought more clarity, greater enthusiasm and better organization. The real work, however, was done by Herzl himself, at the cost of great labor and heartache, and despite mounting opposition outside and growing criticism within Zionist ranks. Herzl refused to lose sight of his major aim—the obtaining of a national territory. He turned first to the German emperor, whose relations with the Turkish sultan were then very close. The plan to have Jews immigrate into Palestine and establish a Jewish commonwealth, under German protection, appealed to the romantic and imperialistic William II. Herzl had three interviews with the kaiser, one under Palestine's sky, on the road to Mikveh Yisrael. Zionists, of course, hoped for much from these dramatic interviews, for here was the most ambitious and powerful ruler on the Continent apparently taking an interest in the revival of the Jewish nation. They did not quite see the obstacles. William II was not a stable person; the sultan was opposed to Jewish resettlement in Palestine; and the German foreign office, for reasons for its own, was not above stabbing the scheme in the back.

Herzl, thereupon, centered his attention on the sultan himself. He held out the inducement of financial aid to the hard-pressed Turkish government if he could obtain a charter for Jewish settlement in Palestine. Herzl subsequently maintained that, if he actually had had the money at that crucial moment, his diplomacy with the sultan would have succeeded. But despite his repeated appeals to the rich Jews of Western Europe, the money was not forthcoming. Consequently the negotiations between Herzl and the sultan dragged along and became meaningless. Herzl visited foreign ministers and kings, in frantic efforts to obtain their support and influence with the Turkish government. Everywhere he was received with respect and cordiality, perhaps because of his Zionist leadership, perhaps because of his journalistic reputation. Actual progress, however, toward the obtaining of a charter was practically nil.

The Practical Dreamer—In those days of high hope and slight political achievement toward his goal, Herzl wrote another book on the Jewish state of the future. He called it *Altneuland* (Old-New Land). It was not a plea for Zionism, but rather the expression of the dreams which Herzl cherished for the new community to be established in the old land. In twenty years after his time, that is, in 1925, Herzl hoped a visitor would see in Palestine a united population, an intelligent government and an active cultural life creating a model community, whose progressive, idealistic citizens showed the way to human cooperation for the rest of the world to follow. Most interesting was the social and economic setup which Herzl envisioned for Jewish Palestine. He saw prosperous agricultural settlements, active industry and labor laws far ahead of his time. He predicted not only a seven-hour workday, but also the airplane and the radio. Nowhere did Herzl show his practical sense of what was possible better than in this dream which his contemporaries dismissed with an indulgent smile.

5. OPPOSITION AND HEARTBREAK

The Mass Response—Before long, federations of Zionists were established in every land, including England and the United States. But nowhere was the response to Zionism as enthusiastic as in Eastern Europe. Herzl himself was astonished and exultant at the reception which he received among the masses of Jews in Russia when he visited there in August 1903 to attempt to explain Zionism to the czarist government. The streets of every city visited by Herzl were crowded with young and old anxious to see and cheer. His experience in Russia added to Herzl's sense of vast responsibility.

The Uganda Project—Herzl was deeply grieved over the lack of progress in his negotiations for a charter from Turkey. He turned, in his disappointment, to the English government. Joseph Chamberlain, England's secretary for colonies, then suggested the possibility of establishing a Jewish commonwealth in some part of the British empire. He mentioned the island of Cyprus in the Mediterranean or a habitable portion of the Sinaitic Peninsula. Herzl was quite willing to accept a land in that part of the world because it was so close to Palestine; the English, for their part, were interested in having the Jews settle there because they wanted a friendly population near the Suez Canal. But there were objections to each of these places. Finally, Joseph Chamberlain suggested Uganda, in Central Africa below Ethiopia. Herzl agreed without enthusiasm to present this project to the forthcoming (sixth) Zionist Congress, which was to be held in Basle on August 23, 1903.

Even while submitting the English offer to the Zionists, Herzl pointed out that this was in no way a substitute for Palestine; it was to be rather an "asylum for the night," a place where the Jews might find refuge until the opportunity offered itself to settle in Palestine. Herzl felt that he was thus helping to solve the problem for the East European Jews, especially those of Russia who had just been through the terrors of a pogrom. Yet the Russian Jews were the very ones who raised the loudest objections to the Uganda plan: they saw in it an end to their hopes of Jewish revival. A bitter debate on Uganda followed. It revealed to Herzl how much more profoundly than he had imagined the Jews identified themselves with Zion. What to him had been an answer to a political problem was to them part of life itself. He was awed by the demonstration and yielded to it.

Herzl's Death—Few of those who attacked him at the sixth Congress, very few even of his close friends, knew that Herzl was suffering from a serious heart ailment. The debate, the subsequent arguments within Zionist ranks, the continued lack of diplomatic progress helped to aggravate his condition. On July 3, 1904, Zionists the world over were stunned by the news that their leader and hero had died. It was a terrific blow to national hopes, and the masses of Jews in Eastern Europe wept for him as though he had been a descendant of David. Only now did the Jews themselves and the world in general recognize the essential greatness of the man. Having abandoned a most promising personal career, he had given himself body and soul to the cause of his oppressed brethren. Practically singlehanded, he had come closer than any of his predecessors in eighteen hundred years to the restoration of a people long considered hopelessly disintegrated. The ease with which he moved among the highest political and diplomatic circles was evidence of his personal charm and skill, as well as of the fact that his approach to the problem of the

Jews was understandable and practical. Who knows what he might have achieved had more time been granted him to impress himself and his suggestions upon the statesmen of Europe! From this point of view, his untimely death at the age of forty-four, after barely eight years of Zionist activity, was an unmitigated tragedy. In these eight years he had created a movement, established institutions to carry on its activities and stirred within Jewish life dormant energies which were to keep Jewish hopes alive. Though not with the same vigor and intensity, Zionism nevertheless continued to take root, grow and spread throughout the Jewish world.

6. VIEWPOINTS ON ZIONISM

Zionism as an Issue in Jewish Life—Herzl's appearance on the scene of Jewish life made Zionism so crucial an issue that there was hardly a Jew who could avoid taking sides for or against it. A number of groups appeared within and without Zionists ranks, each representing a different attitude towards Jewish nationalism. Zionism became, next to antisemitism, the chief topic of discussion wherever Jews gathered.

Ahad Ha'am and the Primacy of Culture—Ahad Ha'am, meaning "One of the People," was the pen name of Asher Ginzberg (1856–1927) who had exerted an influence upon Jewish thought before Herzl's assumption of leadership. In 1891 he had begun a series of philosophical and sociological essays in a Hebrew style remarkable for its purity and strength. The Jews, he argued, were indeed a nation, but one which depended much less on race and territory than on bonds of culture forged through the ages. Colonization in order to alleviate poverty and persecution was not enough, since this assumed that the Jews were no more than an economic group. A search for national territory only was equally insufficient, since it implied that Jewish nationalism was no different from any other. The first requirement for Jewish nationalism, according to Ahad Ha'am, was the revival of Jewish spiritual values in the Diaspora, that is, the development in every country of a Jewish group strong in mind, character and idealism based on the values created by Jewish thought and experience. Only after that was achieved could a select group be established in Palestine to continue the work of Jewish national creativeness.

In Ahad Ha'am's teachings was found a combination of *Haskalah* at its best and Jewish nationalism in its most idealistic form. The Jews of Eastern Europe were deeply moved, since these ideas came closest to their conception of Jewish loyalty. While his followers were swept into the Zionist movement, Ahad Ha'am preferred to remain on the side lines. He was convinced that Herzl's political emphasis was mistaken, that a cultural renaissance must precede the obtaining of a charter. The relationship between Jewish culture and Zionism was discussed at several congresses and an educational program was adopted. But as long as Herzl lived diplomacy took precedence.

Opposition on the Basis of Religion—The loudest objection to Zionism in its earlier years came from many Reform Jews in the West and many Orthodox Jews in Western and Central Europe. The objection of the Reformers was based on their fear lest Judaism's claim to being a universal religion be compromised by the revival of Jewish nationalism. Moreover, they insisted that a Jew differed from his fellow citizen anywhere only in his religious beliefs and observances. An American Reform rabbi proclaimed that Washington was his Zion and that the Jewish mission needed no national territory. The aged Isaac M. Wise called upon the Jews of America to fight Zionism with all their energy.

At the opposite extreme of Jewish religious life, a group of Orthodox Jews opposed Zionism because it tried to achieve Jewish nationhood by ordinary human methods. Although an actual organization, named *Agudat Yisrael*, was not established till 1919, the basis for it was laid much earlier. Some of the most famous rabbis of Europe constituted its leadership, and the members too were by no means exclusively East European. Their fundamental principle was that the life of the Jewish people depended on Torah, which they interpreted as Judaism in the sense of religious study and observance; everything else being worldly, inconsequential and transitory. The latter also applied to Zionism.

Some Orthodox Jews, on the other hand, had been among Herzl's ardent followers. Among them were Rabbi Isaac Jacob Reines and the highly respected Rabbi Samuel Mohilever, aged head of Bialystok Jewry. But while they believed that work for the restoration of Zion was essential to Jewish survival, they soon (1902) organized a separate group within the Zionist ranks in order to advocate a more intimate relationship between Zionism and religious life. They called themselves the *Mizrahi*, perhaps "Eastern," in the sense in which a religious Jew faces east at prayer, or as an abbreviation of *Merkaz Ruhani*—Spiritual Center. They established branches in every part of the world.

Opposition on the Basis of Nationalism—There were Jews in all countries, especially in Western and Central Europe, who opposed Zionism because of their desire to see assimilation triumph. Whether they thought well or ill of the Jewish past and of Jewish idealism, they were convinced that there was no longer any reason or purpose in the revival of a Jewish nation. Others in Western Europe and America, while opposed to assimilation, nevertheless objected to Jewish nationalism on the ground that substantial progress had been made towards emancipation. Political equality and economic opportunity had, after all, been granted them, while antisemitism seemed to be losing its sting in the early years of the twentieth century. Moreover, these people also felt that Zionism was encouraging divided loyalties and thereby endangering their hard-won rights. They failed to realize that the fearsomeness implied in their second argument belied the optimism expressed in the first.

The Theory of Diaspora Nationalism—To many Jews these hopes and fears seemed utterly unreal. They could find no abatement of antisemitism among the ruling classes of Europe; nor could they discover in themselves any disloyalty to their respective nations in working for a restoration of the Jewish people. They did, however, see the assimilationist results of social and economic pressure. Nevertheless, many of them doubted that Zionism was the only answer to their problem of Jewish survival.

One solution, other than Zionism, was offered by Simon Dubnow (1860–1944), the most influential Jewish historian since Graetz. Dubnow came to the conclusion that the Jewish people had retained throughout its history an essential unity which did not depend upon a national territory or an independent state. The core of Jewish existence was not culture and religion alone, as Graetz had taught, but also communal organization which enabled the spiritual powers of the people to function. Such communities, whether civic or nation-wide, kept Jewish unity alive so that, on a higher level, the Jews were still a people, a cultural nation. Dubnow saw no objection to the revival of Palestine as a Jewish state, but he did not think it as indispensable as some Zionists supposed. The Jewish people could continue to function, as it had done for more than two thousand years, on the basis of diaspora nationalism. Now one community and now another might take the lead; but in the end, despite such shifting of the territorial center the virility of Jewish community life, especially in the realm of culture, would keep the Jewish people from sinking into insignificance and decay.

Socialism and Nationalism—Similar opinions developed among the Jewish socialists in Russia. They, too, had their assimilationists, who refused to grant that the Jews constituted a nation in any sense; and they also had those who believed that Russian Jewry was a nationality, like the Poles or Ukrainians or the hundred other national groups of which Russia was made up. This was the point of view of the Bund, best represented by Vladimir Medem (1879–1923), one of the most interesting men produced by that age. Medem, the son of assimilated parents and himself baptized in infancy, found his way back to the Jewish people. Coming close to the Jewish masses in the Pale of Settlement, he concluded that for them especially socialism was more than an effort at liberating themselves economically; they also sought cultural liberation. The Jews, he thought, were already a nation in Russia and did not need the special effort of restoring Palestine. He argued, however, that the national aspect of Jewish life will take care of itself, as it does with all nations, but that the primary task was to struggle for the establishment of socialism.

Other Russian Jewish socialists disagreed with Medem and adopted a more generally accepted definition of nationalism as a group bound together by history, culture and purpose. Of these, Hayim Zhitlovsky (1865–1940) was the most influential. He, too, was a diaspora nationalist. But, though a socialist, he stressed culture as an element in Jewish survival to a far greater extent than Medem. Jewish culture had to be based, however, on the Yiddish language. Zhitlovsky thus was the founder of the socialist-Yiddishist movement in Jewish life.

Finally, there were the outright Zionist socialists. They minimized, if they did not deny, diaspora nationalism and considered Hebrew the Jewish language of the future. Out of them came the Labor Zionist party (*Po'ale Zion*), organized in 1901 by Nachman Syrkin (1868–1924) and further developed by Beer Boruchov (1881–1917). They maintained that the economic difficulties experienced by the Jews in the Diaspora would keep them forever in an abnormal state, in the same way as their social and cultural differences from the majority population of every country were making abnormal their life as a people. Palestine would solve both these problems. Therefore, Po'ale Zionists argued, Palestine must be built as a socialist state from the very start, since only then would the result be worth the effort. Their viewpoint gained considerably through the teaching of A. D. Gordon (1856–1922), who expounded the idea that to labor on the sacred soil was to be religiously active. Arriving in Palestine at the age of forty-eight, he by his own life exemplified his Religion of Labor. The Halutz ("Pioneer") movement has been in large measure traced to his influence.

Opposition on the Basis of Territorialism—When the Uganda offer divided the Zionists and that offer was finally rejected, Israel Zangwill led a group out of Zionism and formed the Jewish Territorial Organization (ITO) with the object of settling Jews in any territory that might be available. Most of them believed that a Jewish nation should be revived; they did not oppose Palestine; but since the Jews of Eastern Europe were facing an emergency, there was no time for prolonged political maneuvering such as Zionist hopes involved.

After Herzl's Death—Herzl's death raised the question whether the Zionist movement could maintain itself at all. The leadership of the movement fell into the hands of those who were interested less in political than in colonizing activity. The most that could be expected was for the Zionist organizations in the various countries to strengthen themselves, carry on an active propaganda, collect money for the purchase of more land in Palestine, and start new colonies there. Between 1897, the year of the first Zionist Congress, and 1914, when World War I broke out, the Jewish population of Palestine increased from about 50,000 to about 90,000. The president of the World Zionist Organization, after Herzl, was David Wolffsohn (1856–1914), a quiet, hard-working man, with a good business sense, excellently suited for the plodding and unspectacular work that now had to be done. Zionists continued to pay their annual *shekel* and to hold congresses, biennially now. The Jewish National Fund (JNF), under the guidance of a directing board, gathered fairly large sums and bought more land in Palestine. For the rest, Zionists listened to speeches and sang songs, hoping for the day, apparently distant, when by dint of hard work Palestine would really become *Eretz Yisrael*.

They little knew that a terrible holocaust was about to break upon the world, and that one of the few positive results of the war of 1914–18 would be the very charter of which Herzl had dreamed. Nor could they have possibly foreseen to what extent the next step in the development of the Zionist movement would depend upon the Jews of America. These distant relatives of Europe's Jews had been left until then almost completely out of their calculations regarding the future of Palestine and of Jewish culture in general. When the proper moment came, however, the Jews of America were to find voice and make their influence felt.

CHAPTER VIII

THE ROAD TO MATURITY

JEWISH LIFE IN AMERICA UNDERGOES A PROFOUND
CHANGE AS A RESULT OF THE NEW IMMIGRATION AND
OF THE FORCES PREVALENT IN THE LAND

A Community in the Making—Jewish life in America also was entering upon a new phase of its development. As the arrival of the Jews from Germany had made important changes in American Jewish life earlier in the nineteenth century, so the arrival of Jews from Eastern Europe brought about a transformation at its end. New social and economic problems confronted both the old and the more recent members of the Jewish community. The old Jewish Americans and the newcomers did not understand each other. The descendants of the old settlers did not altogether appreciate the immensity of the difficulties facing the immigrants. The East Europeans, on their part, did not stop to consider the mind and motives of the so-called German Jews. This caused friction and delayed communal unity. America itself, moreover, was in the process of economic and cultural expansion. Adjustment to American life was no longer the simple matter that it had been. Neither the Sephardi Jews nor the Germans had met with the obstacles which the East European Jews now encountered. America was becoming industrialized; its western frontiers were disappearing; its cities were growing without social plan or direction. Coming from an environment almost medieval in nature, the East European Jews were bewildered by the language, the politics, the working conditions and the manner of living of their new neighbors, both Jews and Christians.

1. THE NEW IMMIGRANTS

Their Number—Over half a million Jews entered the United States between 1881 and 1898, in a total of eight million immigrants. The number rose to 700,000 between 1899 and 1907, in a total immigration of some seven millions. Between 1908 and 1914 about 600,000 Jews entered the country, while the total immigration was 6,700,000. Thus, the number of non-Jewish immigrants was ten times greater than the Jewish. In absolute numbers, however, the Jewish population of the United States grew very rapidly. Whereas there were only about 2,500 Jews in the country in 1800, 50,000 in 1850, 250,000 in 1875, their number had risen to almost three millions by 1914. One result of the large Jewish immigration was that only the Jewish community of Russia was larger than the American Jewish community in 1914, and the Russian Jewish center was soon to disintegrate.

Reception of the Immigrants—The spiritual return to her people of Emma Lazarus (1849–1887) serves as an example of the sympathy and brotherliness aroused for the unfortunates who were fleeing their persecuting fatherland. She had already gained an enviable reputation as an American poet. Now her admiration was stirred by the strength of character of the poor refugees, who had defied the czars and had resisted the tempting offers of ease if they would abandon the faith of their fathers. Poor, bedraggled, but in search of freedom, they appeared to her as worthy successors to the Maccabees. Under such inspiration she wrote some stirring poems on Judaism and the Jews. The republic of France at that time (1886) presented to the republic of the United States a statue to symbolize the love of liberty in both countries. Erected at the entrance to New York harbor, the Statue of Liberty became the first welcome sign that an immigrant beheld. It was most appropriate, therefore, that the United States government had one of Emma Lazarus' poems inscribed on the statue's pedestal (1903):

> "Keep, ancient lands, your storied pomp!" cries she
> With silent lips. "Give me your tired, your poor,
> Your huddled masses yearning to breathe free,
> The wretched refuse of your teeming shore.
> Send these, the homeless, tempest-tost, to me.
> I lift my lamp beside the golden door!"

The Problem of Distribution—The enormous number of the arrivals overwhelmed the existing agencies which were organized to help them across the threshold of the new world. The more recent immigrants themselves established societies to aid those who came later. But the chief problem, the distribution of the immigrants throughout the entire United States, was not solved despite earnest efforts. Fully seventy per cent of the Jewish immigrants settled in New York City, and ninety-four per cent preferred to remain along the Atlantic coast. In the 1880s the ICA urged them to take up farming, but with only fair success. In 1901 the Industrial Removal Office was established in order to hold out to them the advantages of more rapid economic adjustment away from the northeastern cities, and by 1906 it had succeeded in transferring about 40,000. A few years later the philanthropist, Jacob H. Schiff, initiated the Galveston Project, whereby the immigrant aid groups in Europe and several steamship companies cooperated to persuade immigrants to sail for that southern port. It was hoped that from there they would spread to the sparsely settled communities in the south. The plan began to work in 1907 and might have achieved a good deal had not World War I completely changed the situation. Human nature and circumstances were against all these plans. Most immigrants already had relatives in one or another eastern city and they naturally gravitated to the place where they could find aid in adjusting themselves to the new environment.

Their Economic Problem—Immediately upon his arrival the immigrant had to look about for a way to earn his livelihood. He was usually the more anxious to find employment as he had to send money for the support of that part of his family which had been left behind in the old home, and to save sufficient money for them to join him as soon as possible. But finding employment during this period was not what it had been when the Sephardi and the German Jews had arrived. At the height of the German Jewish migration the country was expanding westward and rising commercially, whereas after the Civil War the United States was growing industrially. It was, of course, still possible to peddle, and about twenty-one per cent of the gainfully occupied East European immigrants were peddlers in 1900. But this was no longer carried on among outlying farms, as had been the case a generation or two earlier, the peddler's pack or cart being a veritable department store. It was now carried on mostly within the city, from door to door, small articles like matches and pins being the stock in trade and a day's profits a matter of pennies. Most immigrants consequently preferred to go into industry. In 1900, forty-five per cent worked in factories manufacturing cigars, leather, metal goods and various other articles, but above all clothing.

The Sweatshops—In the previous half century the German Jews had helped bring revolutionary changes in the manufacture of garments, shoes, hats and shirts. They now took full advantage of the flood of immigrants. Not only did the East European Jews displace the former workers, but they substantially reduced the wage scale. Labor legislation of any kind was as yet almost unknown in the United States. Conditions were therefore bad enough in the regular factories; they were beyond all belief in the so-called "sweatshops." These were run by contractors who, with very little financial outlay, took cloth or unfinished garments out of the regular factories and completed them in their improvised shops, which were located in dimly-lighted, unsanitary, overcrowded stores, tenement flats or basements. The wages they paid were pitifully low, amounting in the 1880s and 1890s to between $4 and $8 per week. They could not guarantee steady employment, but they worked their "hands" sixteen or more hours a day during the busy season. In time, moreover, they used more and more girls, who thus displaced the men and further reduced the wage scale. To be sure, other immigrant groups were subject to the same economic conditions; the vast majority of these laborers, however, were recruited from the Jewish group.

Their Religious and Cultural Problems—The spiritual life of the immigrant also underwent a radical transformation. Often these peddlers and the workers in the sweatshops were men who in their old homes had set great value on intellectual activity and had grown up in surroundings where respect for human personality was one of the bases of religious life. No time could now be spared from the grind of labor for the observance of the religious traditions. The prayers three times a day, the holidays and even the Sabbath had to be abandoned, or, in some instances, paid for by agreeing to a reduction in one's meager pay. In the "Old Home" even the less educated had been accustomed to spending a little time each day in studying the sacred literature. In the "New Home" this was quite impossible; working hours were much too long and the labor too exhausting.

The problem of giving a Jewish education to children was still more difficult. Older boys and girls were put to work, since the family budget required their earnings and as yet no child labor laws compelled attendance at school beyond the age of twelve or fourteen. No organized Jewish community was in existence to establish and supervise adequate religious education. The Sephardi and German Jews had failed to solve the educational problem for their own children and therefore offered no model for the newcomers. The immigrants, on their own part, could not transport the East European *heder* to America, for the public school took up the major portion of the child's day. Deeply prejudiced against ignorance, the only thing the immigrants could do was to entrust the Jewish education of their children to men who may have possessed piety and knowledge, but who had no pedagogical or personal qualifications for teaching. A man too old or too weak to find a place in a factory would equip himself with a Hebrew prayer book and, for a few pennies per half hour, undertake to introduce a Jewish child into the rich traditional lore of his ancient people. The child was certain to sense the difference between the bright new world into which his public school teacher introduced him and the seemingly far-off, unreal and gloomy world which his Hebrew teacher represented. Add to this the pull and the promise of the environment, the prevalent materialism and secularism, and it becomes clear why the effect of Jewish knowledge upon that generation was so slight. The teacher with his strange and seemingly meaningless subjects, and the parents with their real and unending economic problems, destroyed the beauty of Jewish home life and offered little of that inspiration which had been the outstanding characteristic of East European Jewry. They represented, on the contrary, a state of affairs from which the child vowed to escape. Before long, parents realized with dismay that their children were wandering away from them, breaking down the intellectual and spiritual bridges which had bound previous generations together.

2. STRUGGLE FOR A BETTER LIFE

Labor Unions—Fundamental to life in the new homeland were the efforts to improve conditions of labor and to raise the standards of living. During the 1870s repeated efforts were made to organize the workers in the needle trades and among other employers of immigrant labor. The masses of East European Jews at first failed to grasp the significance of unionism. Strikes occurred at the beginning of almost every busy season, but their gains were as short-lived as the organizations which called them. Nevertheless, unionization in the needle trades was attained more quickly and proved more effective than in most other industries in the country. This was due in part to the fact that the immigrant Jewish workers constituted a like-minded group to begin with. The garment industry, moreover, was concentrated in the large cities and this simplified the process of organization. Besides, the leaders of the Jewish workers soon learned to appeal to them on the basis of broad political and economic ideas which the Jews, essentially a bookish group, could appreciate as more fundamental than simple trade unionism. For some time, to be sure, this very ideological interest was a cause of weakness, since the differences in theory caused all kinds of rifts within the ranks. As a result, though the process of unionization was in full swing already in 1886, it was not until the 1900s that the needle trade unions became instruments for the permanent improvement of industrial conditions. During that decade ideologies were softened and gave way to union statesmanship which won victory after victory for efficient, intelligent labor unionism.

From Factory to Shop—A large number of immigrants, discouraged by the long struggle to improve industrial conditions, stayed within the factory only until they could find a better opportunity. Some, by dint of enormous effort, succeeded in establishing small factories of their own, gradually expanding these as the market developed and as their fruitful imagination devised new styles and methods. Indeed, the time came, during the decade between 1900 and 1910, when the East European Jew gradually displaced the German Jew in the control of the garment industry. Others spent decades in rigid economy until they could establish themselves as petty merchants, in a candy-shop perhaps, or in the sale of dry goods, even though the income from these sources might not equal the wages of the factory. With hard work and luck the tiny shop might grow in size and affluence. The majority of the small shops remained small, providing their owners with barely enough to live decently and give their children an education which, it was hoped, would save them from bitter struggles such as their parents had had to undergo.

Social Adjustment—The neighborhoods in which the immigrants settled presented many broad social problems, but they solved the immediate social problem for the immigrants themselves. Teeming tenements and crowded streets, whatever their faults in sanitation, made for mutual helpfulness. On the other hand, there were also social differences within the new neighborhoods. Men and women coming from different parts of Europe discovered that they were after all not exactly alike. Each group looked down upon the other almost as much as the descendants of earlier settlers looked down upon them all. The intimacy and fellowship to which the immigrants had been accustomed in the towns and villages from which they came were lacking. To make up for this lack they adopted the method, common in the United States, of organizing lodges. These were mutual help associations of people who, hailing from the same town or province in Eastern Europe, could recreate among themselves that sense of at-homeness which they missed in the vast, strange, bitterly competitive world outside. Hence these lodges were called *Landsmannschaften*. The pomp and ceremony of their meetings gave color to the otherwise drab existence of the members; the "benefits" paid to the sick and the bereaved tided many a family over a difficult period; the discussions at the meetings answered the needs of the social consciousness of the "brothers." Through the celebration of American holidays, moreover, which was usually part of the lodges' program, and through the speeches of the local politicians, who found a useful forum in the lodge, the members were introduced to the political life of the country and given a deeper understanding of the part they were free to play in it.

The Yiddish Press—As important as any of the changes which an immigrant had to make upon his arrival on American shores was the change in his intellectual interests. The Jewish immigrant especially was not satisfied to live in a land without understanding it, and for this he needed reading material. Two periodicals—I. K. Buchner's *Die Yiddishe Zeitung* and Z. H. Bernstein's *Die Post*—made their appearance as early as 1870. But both appeared irregularly and both used a Germanized Yiddish, as though in apology for the language spoken by the people who were to be their readers. Actually the Yiddish-reading public was as yet not sufficiently large to make even such periodicals successful, so that these and subsequent experiments enjoyed but a brief existence. The situation improved in the 1880s. The *Tageblatt* began as a daily in 1885, and thereafter periodicals and dailies multiplied. The nascent Jewish labor movement made several journalistic efforts in the 1890s. Out of them *The Jewish Forward* emerged in 1897 as a Yiddish daily and within a decade became very influential. Other dailies, weeklies and monthlies, of all political tints and social and literary tendencies, came and went in New York and in other large cities, and by

1914 the Yiddish-reading Jews of the United States were amply supplied.

The New Literature—At the same time the Yiddish newspapers greatly helped to develop a Yiddish literary movement of a high order. The New York newspapers especially attached to their staffs poets and novelists of merit. Morris Rosenfeld (1862–1923) may serve as an example. As a young man he had left his native Lithuania and worked in the clothing sweatshops of London and later of New York. He found in the "shop" the main theme of his poetic work, so that already in the 1890s he was hailed as the "Poet of Labor." Humanitarianism rather than socialism was reflected in his verse: the sorrows of the immigrants, their struggles for a better life, their bewilderment and their hunger for crumbs of happiness. The Jewish immigrants responded to Rosenfeld's poetry. Several of his poems were set to music and sung in every Jewish neighborhood. His reputation later reached even non-Jewish circles. Solomon Bloomgarden, better known under his pen name Yehoash (1870–1927), also enriched the Yiddish language in poetry and prose. He spent the last ten years of his life in making a Yiddish translation of the Bible, remarkable for its easy and charming style.

The Yiddish-speaking population of the United States encouraged the development of drama. Abraham Goldfaden, Jacob Gordin, David Pinski and Perez Hirschbein wrote dramas of merit, while actors like Jacob P. Adler, David Kessler, Mrs. K. Liptzin, Bertha Kalisch, Boris Tomashefsky and Maurice Schwartz were consummate artists. What is more, the audiences warmly admired the talents of their dramatists and actors.

3. CULTURAL INSTITUTIONS AND RELIGIOUS STRIFE

Americanization—The general public and the native Jews did not quite understand the cultural progress which the newcomers were making in their crowded Yiddish-speaking neighborhoods. They brushed it all aside as a hindrance in the way of the immigrants' acquisition of the English language. Some of them accused the Yiddish newspapers, theaters and books of fortifying the immigrants in their seemingly stubborn adherence to the manners and customs of Eastern Europe. The Americanized Jews had reason to fear that they would be identified with these hordes of strange-mannered people inhabiting squalid neighborhoods, and that this identification would damage their social and even their economic position. It was not until some twenty or thirty years after the first wave of immigration that writers in English, from among the children of the immigrants as well as from among Christian social workers and authors, undertook to interpret the "American ghetto" to the rest of America. Israel Zangwill's stories, though they dealt with conditions among immigrants in England, applied almost as fully to conditions among the Jewish immigrants in America. During the first decade of the twentieth century a number of works on this theme presented the immigrants in a sympathetic light, explained their background and called favorable attention to their cultural standing.

In the earlier years, however, certainly down to the end of the nineteenth century, the opposition between the two groups of Jews was rather sharp. The Jews of German ancestry, impatient for the Americanization of the immigrants, contributed liberally to the establishment of classes, social centers and clubs. The immigrants gladly availed themselves of these institutions, though not with the best grace. They resented the snobbishness and condescension with which much of this work was done; they were hurt by the criticism implied in the desire to change them. Economic conflict likewise kept the two groups apart. The East European Jews looked upon all Jews of German ancestry as in a class with the factory owners. There were, besides, fundamental religious differences which did not further mutual understanding.

Opposition to Reform—If the Pittsburgh Platform* served as a rallying point for Reformers, it also solidified the opposition to Reform and thus destroyed whatever hope there had been of uniting American Judaism. Sabato Morais (1823–1897), successor to Leeser as minister of the Mikveh Israel congregation in Philadelphia, had given his support to the Hebrew Union College. But when it became clear that radicalism rather than moderation would be in control, Morais began to plan a new institution for the training of rabbis. His plans resulted in the foundation of the Jewish Theological Seminary of America. The new school opened in New York in 1886, with Sabato Morais as president. Its main support came from the English-speaking Orthodox element, that is, from the Spanish-Portuguese congregations, from the Hungarian and from some German second-generation Jews. This represented rather meager support. The growing masses

* See above, p. 543.

of East European Jews were as yet not ready to face the problem at all. Consequently, the Jewish Theological Seminary did no more than struggle along until it received new life with the coming, in 1902, of Solomon Schechter to assume the presidency of its faculty.

Solomon Schechter—Schechter's world-wide reputation for scholarship and his strong religious leadership not only revitalized the Jewish Theological seminary, but drew to it the attention of American Jewry. Schechter, no more than Morais, wanted to create platforms to define the type of Judaism which he represented. Differences of opinion were possible in Judaism and have always existed, but they have been and should be differences built on the basis of a fundamental unity. Unity in Judaism must exist not only within the present, but also between the present and the past. Judaism, in other words, must emphasize tradition; it dare not break with its past. This, however, presupposed knowledge of the past as well as understanding of the present, that is, culture and scholarship. Unity, tradition and scholarship were, according to Schechter, enough of a program for "Catholic Israel," that is, "Universal Israel." Given these, the rest could take care of itself. Such, in brief, was the attitude of Solomon Schechter, and in many respects it contrasted sharply with the Pittsburgh Platform.

To carry out his plans, Dr. Schechter gathered a faculty for the Seminary consisting of young scholars of exceptional promise, and impressed upon the graduates the need for study and teaching. In 1912 he called together a number of congregations who thereupon banded themselves into the United Synagogue of America. Unfortunately, Dr. Schechter died (1915) just as the influence of his vibrant personality began to bear fruit. The Jewish Theological Seminary, however, contined to grow in influence under his successor, Cyrus Adler (1863–1940), particularly during the next period, when the American-born children of the East European Jews attained maturity.

Experiments in Orthodoxy—Though the founders of the Jewish Theological Seminary considered themselves Orthodox Jews, the new immigrant population nevertheless held aloof from them. Unable to follow the English sermon and insistent upon the continuation of the local traditions to which they had been accustomed, they refused to join the Seminary movement. At the same time, they could not help recognizing that evils were developing in their religious situation. The number of tiny congregations multiplied with every passing

598   THE SEARCH FOR A FRIENDLY HOME

year, each a law unto itself and some with no greater object
than the vanity or profit of some ambitious individual. Men
posed as rabbis who in character and knowledge deserved no
such recognition. The preparation of kosher food was ineffec-
tively supervised, if at all. To the radicalism which resulted
from the economic situation among the immigrants was
added a disdain for religion due, in some measure, to the lack
of dignity and to inadequate leadership within the congregations.

In 1888 a number of congregational leaders in New York
jointly invited Rabbi Jacob Joseph, a noted preacher and
scholar of Vilna, in Lithuania, to become the chief rabbi of
the city's Orthodox community. A tax on kosher meat was to
pay for the extra expense of this and other communal undertakings. But the Jews concerned were not ready to submit to
either discipline or taxation. Any number of other rabbis
loudly expressed their resentment at having a chief placed over
them; each proclaimed his own qualifications for the office.
The pious old Rabbi Jacob Joseph had come from Vilna
quite unaware of the difficulties he would encounter and was
not equipped to cope with such opposition. Neither colleagues nor masses came to his support.

Philanthropic Organizations—Despite religious differences
and communal disorganization, the period from 1870 to 1914
was highly productive of Jewish institutions which showed
the basic unity of Jewish life. Charitable societies had been
among the earliest to be established in every Jewish community ever since the days of Sephardi ascendancy. Their number was increased and their work made more efficient with
the rise of the German Jewish population. In 1860 the
United Hebrew Charities of New York was established
through a union of the Hebrew Benevolent Society (organized in 1822) and the German Hebrew Benevolent Society
(organized in 1844). This did not take account of numerous
other types of philanthropy—the aid of immigrants, the care
of orphans, hospitals, free loan societies, and numerous other
institutions existing in the large cities. For it had ever been a
matter of pride with the Jews to take care of their own poor.
Before long the East European immigrants, objecting to dependence upon the bounty of the Jews of German descent,
and, in the case of hospitals, wanting institutions where the
dietary laws were observed, began establishing institutions of
their own. The Jews responded to appeals from all of these
and there was considerable duplication and waste. By the end
of the nineteenth century it became evident that combined

efforts to raise the necessary funds for all these institutions would be more productive of good results than the scattered and competing efforts of the individual charity foundations. The first attempt at federation was made in Boston in 1895, and the idea spread rapidly. Before long, every small and large community had its Federation of Jewish Charities, which soon began planning and administrative agencies in addition to being joint collectors of funds. In fact, the Christians in many cities learned to follow this Jewish example and also coordinated their charitable activities.

Social and Educational Institutions—The same period witnessed the rapid growth of the Young Men's Hebrew Association and, somewhat later, the Young Women's Hebrew Association. The main purpose of these organizations was to provide social contacts and cultural opportunities for young Jewish men and women. For it had become apparent already in the 1870s that the coming generation of Jews, having received but slight Jewish education in childhood and having entered wholeheartedly into the rising general culture of America, knew far too little about their Jewish heritage and the problems facing the Jewish people. Further to correct this situation, several attempts were made to found a society for the publication and distribution of Jewish books in English. The third attempt succeeded when, in 1888, the Jewish Publication Society of America was founded in Philadelphia as a non-profit publishing house. These were the fairly successful beginnings to lay the groundwork for an American Jewish culture. Other efforts, more strictly scholastic in nature, followed during the same period. In 1897 the Gratz College was opened in Philadelphia as a training school for American Jewish teachers. This institution, representing a distinct advance in the solution of the educational problem, found imitators at a later date in New York (The Teachers' Institute of the Jewish Theological Seminary; Bet Midrash l'Morim of the Yeshivah, the Herzliah Academy), Boston (Hebrew Teachers' College), Baltimore (Hebrew College), and Chicago (College for Jewish Studies). The Dropsie College for Hebrew and Cognate Learning was founded in 1907, in Philadelphia, under the presidency of Cyrus Adler, as a non-sectarian graduate research institute in Jewish and Semitic studies. The *Jewish Quarterly Review* became the scientific organ of the college.

4. THE POSITION OF THE JEWS IN THE UNITED STATES

Jews in American Life—Whether a descendant of many generations of American Sephardim or an immigrant still reading a Yiddish newspaper, a Jew felt a deep affection for the traditions of Americanism. Already by the end of the nineteenth century, the Jews were proud of their long and worthy history in the United States. Through the decades an increasing number of them had been entering American public life. Many were elected to local office in various parts of the country. Others were sent to Congress or appointed to federal posts. Oscar S. Straus, after having been several times ambassador to Turkey, became a member of Theodore Roosevelt's cabinet as secretary of commerce and labor. It was easy to see why the Jews of the United States were justified in feeling that here at last they had found a friendly home. In order to record the history of the Jews in America and to make it serve as a further stimulus to patriotism, the American Jewish Historical Society was founded in 1892.

Immigration and Americanism—Evidences of a new spirit unfortunately began to show themselves in the country during the last quarter of the nineteenth century. A great many immigrants from various parts of Europe were bringing their prejudices with them. These prejudices were sharpened by the economic rivalries which developed between the Christian and the Jewish immigrant. Moreover, the arrival of so many immigrants also had an effect upon the native population. Many of the latter felt that they were being swamped by outsiders and they, consequently, drew more closely together by emphasizing distinctions between old and new Americans in a manner never done before. Anglo-Saxon descent, Mayflower ancestry and Revolutionary parentage began to be spoken of as tests of the true American, quite apart from adherence to the spiritual bases, that is, essential Americanism, of the New World. The new antisemitism of Western Europe began to seep into American life. The spirit of America was, indeed, still too strong for these prejudices and distinctions to make any considerable headway. The country was as yet expanding too rapidly and economic opportunities were too abundant for anti-Jewishness to take root in the land. Here and there, however, there were signs of an attitude reminding one of European conditions.

The Hilton-Seligman Affair—The event which symbolized

the changed attitude of some Americans towards Jews was an
act of social discrimination which in itself was of no importance. Joseph Seligman was the most prominent Jew in the
United States in the days immediately following the Civil
War. His Jewish interests were rather slight; his social contacts were primarily with Christians. Nevertheless, he was refused admittance to a fashionable hotel at Saratoga Springs,
in 1877, solely on the ground that he was a Jew. The entire
press of the country followed the bitter quarrel which developed between Seligman and Judge Henry Hilton, a minor politician in New York, who was the executor for the estate to
which the hotel in question belonged. Hilton argued that it
was bad for business to have Jewish residents at the hotel,
since Christian "society" resented their presence. Thus the
matter was put on the basis of the undesirability of Jews altogether and represented the first frankly anti-Jewish act in the
United States. Equally significant, however, was the fact that
the better elements of the country deprecated Hilton's attitude. Henry Ward Beecher, the most popular preacher of the
day, openly and forcefully took the liberal side of the issue.
But the fact remained that the issue had been joined and that,
thereafter, certain Christian social and business circles became more shameless than ever in their clannish exclusion of
Jews, no matter how high their cultural or economic position.

Defending Jewish Rights—Neither before nor after this
affair did the Jews feel that their rights under the American
Constitution were in danger. In fact, American Christians
and the government itself expressed sympathy and gave active cooperation in the defense of Jewish rights when these
were attacked in Europe or elsewhere. This was the case with
Switzerland before it liberalized its government; this was likewise so in the case of the Damascus Affair and of the outrages in Russia and Rumania. The Jews of the United States
had early realized the interdependence of the Jews all over
the world, that, in other words, when Jews in any part of the
world were harmed, those of America were bound by duty
and self-interest to lend aid. For this reason, and that it might
be on hand whenever matters of interest to Jews and Judaism
came up, representatives of a number of congregations organized a Jewish defense committee (1859), and gave it the name
"Board of Delegates of American Israelites." Later (1878)
this Board merged into the Union of American Hebrew
Congegations. Simon Wolf (1836–1923), a prominent Washington lawyer, a friend of several presidents of the United
States, acted for the Board whenever matters of Jewish inter-

est required attention. This, however, was in no sense an attempt to organize the Jews of the country. It was a mistake to connect the Board with one religious group. The Jews, in fact, felt that Jewish interests required a more democratic and more effective method of representing the American Jewish population.

The American Jewish Committee—Although the internal disunity of the Jewish population continued to prevent a democratic expression of its will, there was no doubt that all Jews felt alike regarding one problem which came to the fore at the beginning of the twentieth century. The entire Jewish community wished to give voice to its pain over the Kishineff pogrom and the others which followed it in Russia in 1904 and 1905. Protest meetings were held in various cities, in which the Christian population participated, and the United States Congress passed a resolution of sympathy with the Jews (1906). At this time a group of prominent Jews, including Judge Mayer Sulzberger, Louis Marshall, a prominent lawyer, Jacob H. Schiff, the philanthropist, and Cyrus Adler, decided to establish a nation-wide organization of Jews to represent Jewish interests before the American public. They invited selected individuals from every important community of Jews to join them in an American Jewish Committee having as its aim the defense of Jewish rights whenever they were threatened.

The Abrogation of the Russian Treaty—Since the persecutions of the Jews in Russia continued, the Jews of America sought for forceful means of bringing the conscience of civilization to bear upon the Russian government. Ever since the United States and Russia had signed a treaty of commerce and friendship in 1832, Russia had consistently refused to recognize passports granted by the United States to its Jewish citizens. The very fact that the United States tolerated this indignity to its Jewish citizens was an insult to its Jewish population and to America in general. Repeated protests by Jews had time and again caused Washington to argue the point with Russia, but without effect. The volume of protests now rose so that the United States government could no longer disregard it, and the American Jewish Committee at this point played a significant role. At hearings before congressional committees in Washington, Louis Marshall argued the case as a matter of American honor and the constitutional rights of American Jews. As a result, the treaty with Russia was abrogated in 1911. Before a new one could be negotiated, the world underwent a world war and Russia became radically transformed. As for the Jews, they now had another reason to recognize that on American soil they could live their lives in freedom and dignity.

The Kehillah Experiment—An external event likewise stimulated the Jews to attempt community organization, first in New York and then in several other cities. In 1908 the police commissioner of New York City made the unwarranted assertion that the Jews accounted for fifty per cent of the criminals. Statistics easily disproved this charge, but as a result the Jews once more realized the need for a democratically elected representative body which might turn its attention to the solution of the many vexing problems which faced the Jews of the city and bring some order out of the chaotic religious, educational and social conditions. Such organizations had existed and were still functioning in various parts of Europe; why not in the United States? Representatives of various Jewish organizations, *Landsmannschaften* and synagogues met in 1909 under the inspiring leadership of Dr. Judah L. Magnes and formed themselves into a *Kehillah* (community). During its first years the Kehillah established a court of arbitration for religious disputes, a bureau for the furtherance of Jewish education, and a welfare bureau for the solution of social problems; it also attempted to regulate matters of *kashrut*. After a few years, however, the Kehillah movement petered out and failed. Internal conflicts weakened it; it had no authority to enforce its decisions or even to hold its organization together. The like was true in the other cities, like Philadelphia, where the experiment was tried. The Jews of the United States were obviously not yet ready for united action in local affairs. The only tangible result in New York City was the Bureau of Jewish Education which had been established under the guidance of Dr. Samson Benderly, and which continued to function after the Kehillah itself had become no more than a name. One of the chief reasons for the failure of the Kehillah, moreover, was the outbreak of the war in Europe, which drew the attention of the Jews to the problems of suffering across the sea.

CHAPTER IX

VICTIMS OF WAR AND PEACE

WAR AND REVOLUTION BRING MISERY TO MANY JEWISH
COMMUNITIES IN EASTERN EUROPE AND A TREATY OF
PEACE TRIES TO SOLVE SEVERAL PROBLEMS FOR THE JEWS

The World's Tragedy—The year 1914 brought a seemingly happy period of human history to a tragic end. Despite the lofty ideals and the shining hopes for peace and progress upon which the Western world had prided itself for several generations, a spirit of nationalism had been fostered in every country, so that it combined with economic rivalries in the West and with social and political reaction in Eastern Europe to bring about a furious war which raged for four years. Millions of lives were lost in fighting and through starvation. But this was not all. The war was followed by tremendous upheavals in Eastern Europe, equally costly in human life and happiness. When the fighting came to an end, negotiations were begun for a treaty of peace. The peace proved to be still another tragedy. Thoughtful people had hoped that the international congress of statesmen at Versailles would be wise enough to see how the mistakes of the past might be avoided. But there were others who were contemptuous of idealists. The men of little faith and narrow vision won. Consequently, the treaty which was signed at Versailles solved few problems and brought no real peace.

All this was of great importance to the Jews. In accordance with the invariable rule of history that, if wrong and evil exist, the Jews suffer for it more than any other part of humanity, the tragedy of the war and the tragedy of the peace fell doubly hard on the Jewish population. The peace negotiators made an effort to remove a number of evils in the Jewish situation. Since, however, they left many basic problems unsolved for humanity in general, their solution of Jewish problems, which were closely interwoven with the others, could not remain permanent.

1. The Jews on the Eve of World War I

England and France—The outstanding features of Jewish life in the two westernmost countries of Europe in the decade before World War I were the decreasing influence of anti-semitism upon the population and the comparatively large immigration of East European Jews. In France the victory of the liberal forces in the Dreyfus case strengthened the republic and freed the educational system from reactionary control. In England, too, society, culture and politics were open to Jews, while the small remaining forces of political and social reaction, which were synonymous with those of anti-Jewishness in both these countries, carried on a feeble and seemingly ineffective propaganda. Their most persuasive arguments were directed against the large number of fugitives from the persecutions in Russia and Rumania. By 1911 fifty per cent of the 100,000 Jews in France and about thirty-five per cent of the 250,000 Jews in England were recent arrivals. There was some restriction of immigration, especially in England; but fortunately this came to little. Moreover, before long the economic problem of the immigrants' competition with native labor also adjusted itself.

The immigrants brought new life to the declining religious spirit. Synagogue attendance and traditional observances had fallen off and voices were heard in England as well as in France in favor of rapid assimilation. To be sure, the old Jewish community life in France was reorganized (1905–6), with a chief rabbi of France at its head, and a few slight reforms were adopted; but this had little effect on the old population. The newcomers, hailing from the Jewishly vital milieu of Eastern Europe, organized independent congregations and schools for their children. Both in England and in France it was for the most part this group which responded to the call of Zionism.

The Jews in the Scandinavian Countries—The Scandinavian countries, the most progressive and cultured nations in Europe, had a very small Jewish population. Around 1910 Denmark had about 5,000; Norway about 1,000; and Sweden about 4,000. Their history was brief and their life untroubled. Sephardi Jews had begun to come to these countries in the seventeenth century, but only Denmark permitted the establishment of an organized community before 1700, although even there the Jews lived under some economic and political restrictions down to 1814. Sweden, where Jews were not permitted to settle until the end of the eighteenth century, withheld full emancipation till 1870, while Norway admitted them in 1851 and saw the establishment of their first synagogue in 1892. Since these dates, however, the Jews of the Scandinavian lands suffered from few onerous disabilities and almost no social ostracism. Religious life, on the other hand, was always exceedingly weak. Immigration from Eastern Europe was too slight to make up for the losses due to the very high rate of intermarriage. In each one of these countries, Jews and the descendants of Jews contributed enormously to general culture.

In Germany—The Jews of Germany during the first fourteen years of the twentieth century lived in an entirely different atmosphere. They continued to rise economically and to integrate themselves wholeheartedly with the culture of the fatherland. But any satisfaction they may have derived from their progress was more than counterbalanced by the equally obvious progress which the theories of antisemitism were making among the Christian population, especially among the upper classes. The Jews were pained by the government's disregard of their constitutional rights, its failure to appoint Jews to political and judicial posts, the practical impossibility of a Jew's attaining a professorship in a university and the utter impossibility of his getting a commission in the army. The German Jew failed to see that German antisemitism was in reality an aspect of blatant German nationalism, a composite of racial arrogance and a hunger for economic imperialism. Civilized themselves, the Jews assumed that their opponents could be reached by civilized methods: calm protests, appeals to logic, the publication of books correcting misconceptions of Jews and Judaism, and the piling up of evidence of their devotion to Germany and German culture.

The effect of these defensive efforts upon the antisemites was nil; the psychological effect of antisemitism upon the Jews, however, was in many cases destructive. Over 400 Jews annually became converts to Christianity, and almost twelve per cent of the marriages between 1900 and 1910 were intermarriages. The hold of Judaism upon Jewish youth was growing weaker despite the modernization of synagogue worship and the valiant efforts to maintain Jewish education in the face of the cultural pull of the environment. This does not mean that research in Jewish studies stopped in Germany. On the contrary, the very questioning of Judaism, which this situation implied, called forth, during the first quarter of the century, a number of attempts to restate the principles of Jewish thought in modern terms. Hermann Cohen (1842–1918), one of the foremost professors of philosophy in Germany in the past generation, re-emphasized Judaism's insistence on the doctrine of the absolute unity of God. This unity, he taught, is not merely a theological belief, but embraces also the unity of mankind and expresses itself in the Jewish system of morals and ethics which aims at the perfection of the individual. As against Cohen's rationalism was Martin Buber's (1878–1965) mysticism which drew upon the old hasidic movement, emphasizing fervent worship and man's eternal quest for God.

Jewish scholarship also flourished during this period in Germany. Moritz Steinschneider (1816–1907) founded the science of Jewish bibliography; David Hoffmann (1843–1921) was a profound student of rabbinic literature and a pioneer in the study of the geonic period; and Ignaz Goldziher (1850–1921) was a noted orientalist and a leader in Islamic studies. These were but three among a host of scholars in the field of Jewish and general Semitic research. On the more popular level, Jewish cultural associations were formed, Jewish libraries established, fundamental books of Jewish information published. The German Jews, moreover, extended sympathy and aid to the Jews of Eastern Europe. The Hilfsverein der deutschen Juden (1901) paralleled the activities of the Alliance Israélite and spent considerable sums at the time of the pogroms in Russia. But their German nationalism stood out above every other characteristic.

In the Czar's Empire—For the six million Jews in the Russian empire the decade and a half before World War I was a period of oppression and heroism. Russia was in the midst of its long overdue struggle for general emancipation and constitutionalism, and the Jews naturally aligned themselves with the forces of liberalism. The tottering czarist system and its reactionary supporters resorted to the old game of identifying the revolutionaries with the Jews and attempting to turn attention away from the existing abuses by stirring up anti-Jewish feeling. A wave of pogroms swept over Russia. The massacre in Kishineff at Easter 1903 saw dozens killed, hundreds wounded and thousands of homes sacked. The cry of horror which went up all over the civilized world and among the liberal elements in Russia itself did not stop the government from instigating similar pogroms in the city of Homel and elsewhere. The only police interference was with the efforts of the Jews to defend themselves. Not even the preoccupation of the country with the war against Japan (1904–5), welcomed by the czarist government as a means of distracting popular attention from the constitutional movement, stopped pogromist activity.

In 1905, reactionary czarism, defeated in war and despised by every progressive in and out of Russia, grudgingly granted a limited constitution which provided for the election of a representative assembly (Duma). This very announcement was at once followed by a series of pogroms. Yet the election, though hedged about by restrictions and interfered with by the government, indicated that the Russian people was, generally speaking, not antisemitic. Jew and Christian were united to free Russia from the curse of czarism. The liberal constitutionalist party in the Duma was led by Paul Milyukov, the foremost Russian historian, a Christian, and by Maxim Vinaver (1863–1926), noted jurist, a Jew. The first Duma was dispersed by the czar only three months after it met. Several Dumas followed it, each more reactionary than the previous as a result of the changes which the government made in the electoral laws to insure the choice of deputies who sympathized with it. The whip and the hangman continued to reign supreme in Russia, and as a direct result of reaction the Jews of the country were hounded and restricted in every possible way.

An example of the utter bankruptcy of the Russian government was afforded by the notorious Beilis trial. In September 1911, the body of a murdered child was found in Kiev, near a brickyard run by a Jew named Menahem Beilis. Although it was clear that the child had been killed by a gang of thieves to whom its mother belonged, the government brought Beilis to trial on the charge of ritual murder. The czarist minister of justice stopped at nothing to prove the charge; but he failed, even his handpicked judge and jury being unable to find Beilis guilty. The affair brought ridicule upon Russia and made the czarist reactionaries more than ever determined in their anti-Jewish policy. The outbreak of the war interfered with their plans.

Russian Jewish Culture—Assimilationist tendencies, such as had existed in Russian Jewry in the 1870s, were now quite dead. Any hope for cultural fusion between the Jews and the Christians of Russia which may have lingered on after the events of 1881–3 were dissipated by the pogrom period following 1903, when it became obvious that nothing short of the extermination of the Jews was the aim of the czarist government. Russian Jewry thereupon turned its cultural energies inward, and the result was a decade of cultural productivity which promised to outdo anything the Western Jewish communities had to offer. Literary clubs existed in every city with a fair Jewish population; Hebrew and Yiddish periodicals and newspapers came into being; also Russian Jewish publications made their appearance. There was no lack of literary talent. Ahad Ha'am, the essayist (1856–1927), and Hayyim Nahman Bialik (1873–1934), the poet, remained unique in their respective fields, but by no means alone. Joseph Klausner (1874–1958), Ahad Ha'am's successor in the editorship of the highly influential monthly, *Ha-Shiloah,* the militant essayist Micah Joseph Berdiczevsky (1865–19621), Joseph Brenner (1881–1921) the novelist, Zalman Schneor (born 1887) the poet, and a host of others, either attained maturity in this decade or laid the foundations for their literary careers in Hebrew. By their side, other poets and novelists, journalists and essayists worked in the Yiddish language. Mendele Mocher Sefarim continued to produce those delightful and critical stories which had been stirring the Jews into self-respect; Sholom Aleichem (Solomon Rabinowitch, 1859–1916) wrote his humorous and tender sketches of Jewish life; Isaac Loeb Peretz (1852–1915) added to his reputation with stories and novelettes dealing mainly with the Hasidim, and Sholem Asch (1880–1957) then entered upon his literary career with poignant, realistic novels. Historical research, too, was not neglected; in Eastern Europe Jewish scholarship was far from being dry as dust; it was characterized by a warm attitude toward the past as well as toward the present. Baron David Guenzburg (1857–1910) opened an academy for Jewish studies in St. Petersburg, where Simon Dubnow was among the teachers. Abraham Harkavy (1839–1919), the noted orientalist and historian of the geonic period, stimulated Jewish scholarship. Russian Jewry had become the throbbing, hopeful heart of the Jewish people and was about to assume the cultural leadership to which its numbers and its history entitled it.

In the Balkans—Brutal, arrogant nationalism was the enemy of the half million Jews scattered among the Balkan states. More than half of them lived in Rumania, which had never lived up to its promise of emancipation just as it had never lived up to its vaunted civilization. Economic reaction and diplomatic deceit were the foundations of its policy. Deprived of political rights, mercilessly taxed, ever in danger of violence, the Rumanian Jews emigrated as soon as they could, 55,000 entering the United States between 1899 and

1910 and other thousands going to South Africa. The Jews of the other Balkan states, including Turkey, were much better off. The latter, largely Sephardim, hoped for much from the revolution which occurred in 1908. But the revolution resulted in an intensification of Turkish nationalism, with no improvement in the Jewish status. Worse still, the Balkans were convulsed by a number of wars after each of which the Jewish position deteriorated. Salonika was conquered by Greece, which began a sytematic oppression of the city's large Jewish population, not only because of the religious difference, but also because of the accusation that they retained their Turkish loyalty.

The Balkans, however, a byword for national hatreds and conflicts, merely offered a preview of what all of Europe was to become soon thereafter. Out of these states came the spark which in 1914 set the entire world aflame.

2. World War I, 1914–1918

Jews in the Armies—In every one of the huge armies which faced one another, Jews were to be found in considerable numbers. Some of the armies, in fact, contained more Jews than the size of the Jewish population of the countries from which they were drawn would have led one to expect. Germany, for example, had a Jewish population of at most 600,000; yet it had about 100,000 Jewish soldiers in the fighting ranks during the war, an unusually high proportion. Moreover, during the course of the war, one third of these were decorated for bravery. In England and the English dominions, Jews flocked to the colors even before the draft was instituted. The Jews in France had always shown superlative patriotism. All this is worth noting, not because it is surprising, but because even in the midst of the war the antisemites of every land did not stop circulating their usual lies about the Jews' lack of patriotism. The accusation was made in Germany and Austria that the Jews were represented in the armies by insufficient numbers. The antisemites in England and France seized upon the fact that some Russian emigrants were not fighting for their native land, Russia, which had actually forced them to emigrate. Eventually many Russian-born Jews joined the armed forces of their adopted countries. Others organized the Zion Mule Corps, under Trumpeldor and Jabotinsky, which fought against Turkey under English command. Subsequently there was a Jewish Legion fighting for the liberation of Palestine.

Jews on the Eastern Battlefront—Casualties on the battlefield were not the only casualties suffered by the Jews. More heartrending were the sufferings of the civilian Jewish population in Lithuania, Poland, Galicia and Rumania, territories over which the tides of battle flowed back and forth. No sooner had the war broken out, than the guilty conscience of the czarist leaders convinced them that the Jews wanted a German victory; and they used such accusations as an alibi for their own defeats. The Jews were forced to evacuate their homes near the battlefront. They were driven inland, without any provision having been made even for food and shelter. What was still worse, as cities changed hands, each side treated the Jews as enemies, while the native Polish or Rumanian population took advantage of the political disorganization to attack the Jews physically or at least to slander them. Thus, death, misery and starvation overtook the Jewish population of those very sections of the world where it was most numerous.

Revolution and Civil Wars—This, however, was only the beginning. In 1917 the czarist government collapsed and the Russian empire began to disintegrate. After a brief attempt at democracy, Russia entered on its experiment in communism. The Bolsheviks looked upon the communal and religious leaders of the Jews, and of other religious and national groups, as members of the middle class and therefore to be exterminated. The opponents of the Bolsheviks, the remnants of the czarist army who started a civil war to destroy communism, by tradition considered the Jews their legitimate plunder. The worse their defeat at the hands of the Bolsheviks, the greater the fury with which these defenders of czarism fell on the defenseless Jews of the territory they were being forced to abandon. Most terrible of all were the recruited armies of the newly-formed states, struggling to rise out of the ruins of several empires. Poland, trying to establish an independent state, claimed portions of Russia, Germany and Austria. Hungary, seeking to feed its national appetite at the expense of the Slavic peoples, fought bitterly against the independence of populations long subject to its rule. The Western powers, who feared to see Bolshevist Russia grow strong, encouraged the Ukrainians to declare their independence. Eastern Europe, already in ruins as a result of four years of war, became the cockpit of numberless armies uncontrolled by any government authority. There was little difference between soldiers and highwaymen. Under such circumstances it is easy to imagine what happened to the Jews. Between 1919 and 1921 there are said to have been over twelve hundred pogroms in the Ukraine alone. To this must be added similar events, in equal proportion, in Poland, Hungary, Rumania and elsewhere.

The Divided Russian Jewry—Some years later, when a certain amount of stability was established in that part of the world, the position of the Jews was found to have changed profoundly. The large Russian Jewish community of pre-war days, the most numerous and the most Jewishly conscious community in the world, had been broken up. The Jews who remained in Soviet Russia, though treated as equals of all Russians socially, economically and politically, were cut off from contacts with the rest of the Jews. The other Jews of the former Russian empire, divided among the half dozen small states along the Baltic Sea and in the Balkans, tried desperately to recover their spiritual and economic balance. Perhaps worst of all for the future were the scars left upon the minds and characters of the non-Jewish population. For years they had given vent to their lowest passions against their Jewish neighbors. They had become used to blaming them for every conceivable ill. Patriotism had become identified for many with antisemitism. Every scoundrel and office-seeker knew exactly how to gain popularity cheaply. They were not required to make the least effort to solve the social and economic problems which were burdening their people. All they needed to do was to urge violence against the Jews.

The Great Forgery—Consequent on the prevailing chaos, therefore, the period after the war saw the spread of one of the most obvious lies ever invented. A certain group of Russian exiles plotted to discredit the Bolsheviks and re-establish the czarist regime. They produced a document alleged to be the minutes (Protocols) of the "Elders of Zion," an international committee of prominent Jews whose existence they invented. These elders were supposed to have met toward the end of the nineteenth century and devised schemes for the destruction of Christian civilization, so that the Jews might seize complete control of the world. The forgers pointed to the Bolshevist revolution as the first step in the realization of the fantastic Jewish "plot." They offered as proof of their charges the fact that a number of the communist leaders were of Jewish origin, among them Leon Trotsky in Russia and Bela Kun in Hungary. The apparent weakness of the Jews and the equally obvious divisions within their ranks were said by the antisemites to be attempts to hide the truth, namely, that a secret, world-wide Jewish government existed and was forever plotting mischief.

With remarkable rapidity the *Protocols* spread to every part of the world. Even though the falsity of the "discovered" document was clear from every page, millions of people took it seriously. Some years later the original model of the *Protocols* was found. It was an attack written in 1865 by a Frenchman named Maurice Joly upon Napoleon III, which represented him as plotting secretly against the safety of the rest of Europe. The Jews, of course, had no place in Joly's work. In 1904 the secret police of the czar had revised this old little book, and put the Jews in place of Napoleon III, in the hope thereby of drawing the attention of the Russian public away from the need for constitutional reforms. Even the czar had considered the forgery utterly improbable and unworthy of his consideration. After the war, however, people were less discriminating. No amount of effort to present the truth could cure the minds of men and women who were anxious to find someone to blame for the upset state of the world. Unfortunately, the United States also provided a fruitful field for this low type of propaganda.

3. THE NEW RESPONSIBILITIES

The Joint Distribution Committee—The cries of anguish which rose from Eastern Europe, ravaged by war and hate, touched the heartstrings of the Jews of America. As city after city was affected by the war, Jews in America recognized their birthplaces or the homes of their parents or relatives. Jews who no longer had any relatives in that part of the world wanted to help those whose misfortunes were doubled merely because they were Jews. At first several independent committees were organized. The *Landsmannschaften* had relief committees of their own; the workmen one for themselves; and the wealthier members of the American Jewish community organized still another. All of these came together before long and established a joint board, called the American Jewish Joint Distribution Committee (abbreviated into JDC). Campaigns for funds were started in every Jewish community in the United States and millions of dollars were raised annually for the relief of the distressed in foreign lands. No more astounding example exists of the charitable spirit of the Jewish people and of the possibility of uniting them for a noble cause than the response which the appeals of the JDC have met from that day on.

The Jewish Welfare Board—When the United States entered World War I, in 1917, it became necessary to care for the social and religious life of the tens of thousands of Jewish soldiers and sailors. The Jewish communities of the country thereupon readily joined in the formation of the Jewish Welfare Board (abbreviated into JWB), which performed outstanding service during the war period. Instead of disbanding when the war was over, the Jewish Welfare Board became the central organization for the numerous Young Men's and Young Women's Hebrew Associations and for the community centers which had come into being during the previous generation and which continued to be organized all over the country.

The New Sense of Unity—The events since 1914 thus brought a new realization of unity to the Jews of America. The rising generation of Jews became conscious of the fact that their common American patriotism united them more than the differences in their parental origin kept them apart. The stoppage of immigration gave greater opportunity for the unification of the Jews already in the United States. East European Jews and their children had risen by this time sufficiently high economically and professionally to blur some of the social distinctions between them and the descendants of German or Sephardi Jews, especially when their ability and liberality brought them to the fore in communal activity. But while unity was achieved in the various branches of philanthropy, religious and social differences still remained more or less sharp and most Jews continued to consider communal organization undesirable in the free environment of the United States.

4. Progress in Zionism

Zionism and the Balfour Declaration—One of the subjects on which there was much disagreement among the Jews of America was Zionism. When Europe was plunged into war, the responsibility for progress in Zionism came to rest upon the Jews of America. This, in turn, meant a revival of Zionist activity in the United States. The Jews of America followed the progress of England's battle against the Turks with keen interest. England's statesmen, it was recalled, had shown much interest in Herzl's plans. Might not England now be helpful in realizing Herzl's dream if the British army succeeded in wresting Palestine from Turkish hands? Consequently, a wave of joy swept over the Jews of the Allied countries when, on November 2, 1917, Arthur James Balfour, Britain's secretary for foreign affairs, issued the famous declaration wherein his government indicated its support of the Zionist cause. Known thereafter as the Balfour Declaration, the statement ran as follows: "His Majesty's Government view with favour the establishment in Palestine of a national home for the Jewish people, and will use their best endeavours to facilitate the achievement of this object, it being clearly understood that nothing shall be done which may prejudice the civil and religious rights of existing non-Jewish communities in Palestine or the rights and political status enjoyed by Jews in any other country." Credit for the attainment of this Declaration properly went to Dr. Chaim Weizmann who had been an ardent Zionist ever since Herzl's days and who at this time taught chemistry in the University of Manchester. Much negotiation had preceded the publication of this statement, which reminded the Jewish world so strongly of the Cyrus Declaration in the year 539 B. C. E.

When the British troops under General Allenby finally marched into Jerusalem, on December 11, 1917, a few weeks after the Declaration, it seemed as though the long exile of the Jews from their homeland had come to an end. It was highly significant that the first act of the Jews after the Declaration was the laying of the cornerstone for a Hebrew University, on July 24, 1918. The act was meant to symbolize the return to its homeland of the spirit of Judaism. The university was to be built on Mount Scopus, the place where Titus, besieging Jerusalem in the year 69 C. E., had given the orders which aimed to destroy the Jewish state forever.

Zionists and Anti-Zionists—Few thoughtful Jews and Christians failed to be thrilled by these dramatic, historical events. The Zionists, of course, rejoiced at the opportunity given the Jewish people to revive the Jewish nation. Most Jews of the world, even though they had never been members of a Zionist organization, were equally happy that Jewish spiritual homelessness was about to end. There were, however, Jews in Western Europe and in America who viewed the new situation differently. They feared the effect that the restoration of a Jewish national home might have upon the standing of the Jews as citizens of the lands in which they lived. To quiet their fears the Balfour Declaration had included the phrase safeguarding Jewish rights in every land.

But the anti-Zionists thought they knew the nature of anti-semitism and they refused to trust such promises. The result was a three-cornered debate: among the Zionists, the anti-Zionists and a group of men who, while not interested in Zionism, foresaw much good from the development of Palestine as a cultural center for —Judaism and as a refuge for persecuted Jews. The last group, under the leadership of Louis Marshall and Dr. Cyrus Adler in America and of Lord Rothschild in England, called themselves non-Zionists.

5. THE PEACE CONFERENCE AT VERSAILLES

Congress and Committee—When the war ended, preparations were being made for the peace conference which was to meet at Versailles. It was clear that the terms of peace would create new states and make considerable changes in the political and economic structure of the world. The Jews of the Allied nations felt that this presented an opportunity to settle once and for all the status of the Jews in the lands where they had long been rightless and oppressed. There was, therefore, general agreement that a Jewish delegation should meet in Paris at the same time as the international peace conference in order to set forth the desires of the Jews of the world. A movement was started for the election of an American Jewish Congress which was to select the delegates to the peace conference. The chief supporters of the Congress idea were the Zionists and those masses of American Jews who felt that the American Jewish Committee did not represent them. After some hesitation, the Committee went along with the Congress movement. Among the men chosen to go to Paris as representatives of the American Jews were Louis Marshall, president of the American Jewish Committee, Rabbi Stephen S. Wise, Judge Julian W. Mack, then president of the American Jewish Congress.

There were in Paris representatives of the Jews of the United States, England, France, and of the East European countries. It seemed logical for the various Jewish delegations to unite so as to present a common front and joint demands. Thus a *Comité des Délégations Juives* came into being, with Judge Mack, and later Louis Marshall of America, as chairman and Dr. Leo Motzkin, Zionist and publicist, as secretary. This body of representatives showed the complex varieties of thought and background into which the Jews of the world were divided. They ranged from religious universalism to the intense nationalism of Nahum Sokolow. The more extreme opponents of Jewish nationalism, like Claude G. Montefiore, did not join the Committee.

Minority Rights—It was finally agreed that no group of Jews had any right to deny another group what the latter thought necessary for its survival and happiness in its part of the world. The representatives of the East European Jews thereupon presented their plan which originally contained a request for "national rights." President Wilson advised against this, and this term was dropped. What was left was the request that Jews within each country be granted the right to organize themselves as a community with distinct cultural rights, while remaining an integral part of the political state wherein they lived. Some Western members of the *Délégations Juives* expressed the fear that even such a separation of Jews might result in an accusation of their being a state within a state. But the Jews of the new Eastern states were tired of being the political playthings of their Christian fellow citizens; they wanted control of their own destiny, especially in the field of culture; they argued, with some reason, that the same accusations would be made against them no matter how they were organized. Under the system of minority rights they would have at least some international safeguards and, when trouble came, a method for continuing their own cultural life, which was more important to them than doubtful political rights.

The peace conference accepted this plan, and thus the system of minority rights came into being. Under this system minorities of any country could run their own schools, speak their own language, and, nevertheless, remain part of the nation in which the group lived. Poland, Lithuania, Austria, Czechoslovakia, Yugoslavia, Bulgaria, Rumania and Greece, not only promised to treat them justly, but bound themselves to grant complete citizenship to members of their minorities and help in the maintenance of their cultural life. To make sure that minorities were not cheated of these rights, the newly-created League of Nations guaranteed them, so that a national government was answerable to the League for a violation of the minority provisions. It is significant that the Jews, fighting for their own survival as a cultural group, thus won similar rights for all other minorities. The minority system might, indeed, have worked if other problems had been solved successfully.

6. CONFLICTS IN PALESTINE

Mandates and Palestine—Palestine, too, figured in the peace discussions at Versailles. The Allied nations were faced with the problem of what to do with the territories taken away from the Germans and their friends. It was not considered advisable to annex these territories outright. The Allied nations, except the United States, were therefore appointed (mandated) as trustees for such territories and made responsible for their government to a Mandates Commission set up by the League of Nations. The mandate for Palestine, it was generally assumed, would go to Great Britain. The Jews enthusiastically supported this plan. Since all the Allied nations had subscribed to the Balfour Declaration, there seemed little doubt in anybody's mind that England would hold the mandate for Palestine as a trustee for the Jewish Commonwealth which would be established in the Holy Land. The Jews had sent a commission to Palestine even before the war was over. Its object was to bring food and medical supplies to the population and to lay the foundations of the homeland. Difficulties arose at once.

England, Jews and Arabs—Even as in the days following the Cyrus Declaration twenty-five centuries ago, both the Jewish people and the Land encountered difficulties from officials of the ruling government as well as from those inhabitants who refused to recognize the rights of the returning diaspora Jews. Some of the difficulties seemed to be due to British diplomacy during the war. In persuading the Arabs to join them against Turkey, England's diplomats had deliberately left vague the extent of the territory which they promised to make into an Arab state when the war was over. Nationalistic Arabs claimed that Palestine had been included in the territory promised. Britain denied this. Emir Feisal, the Arab prince who established (1919–1920) a kingdom comprising Syria and Transjordania, publicly agreed with Dr. Weizmann that Palestine was to be the homeland of the Jews. But the Arab nationalists in and out of Palestine itself were not to be silenced.

Economic ambitions as much as nationalism lay behind the Arabs' objections. Until now Palestine had been dominated by a small number of landowners (effendi). The peasants (fellaheen) were ignorant, poor and rightless. The landowners were convinced at first that England was in earnest about establishing the Jews in Palestine and they therefore gladly sold their lands to the Jews. The coming of the Jews was bound to bring a decrease in their power and a rise in the influence and independence of the Arab peasants. Then the effendis discovered that the situation was not quite so definite. Consequently they decided that, if they were going to stay in this land, they might as well hold on to their positions of authority. The opposition of some of the Christian missionaries was not so open, but was at least as influential both within and outside of Palestine. They, for reasons of their own, feared a growth of Jewish influence in the Near East. The result was that the Arabs, both Mohammedan and Christian, raised an outcry against the establishment of the Jews and began to spread propaganda among the peasants to the effect that the Jews were going to deprive them of their holy places and destroy the Mohammedan religion.

Unfortunately, these Arabs found allies among the colonial officials and the military officers whom England sent to govern the country. The British administrators had no interest in the country except as a colony of England and as a place from which the Suez Canal, on England's route to India, could be better defended. They deplored the prospect of the Jews taking over the country because it complicated the situation; they resented the claim of the Jewish commission to participate in the government. Some of the English officials had always been antisemitic; others now became anti-Jewish because they found it hard to get along with the Jews. The Jews could not be treated like backward colonials upon whom these officers were accustomed to look down. Some of the Jewish leaders, conscious that they were at least the cultural equals of the officials and fortified by humanity's promise that this would be their home, may have spoken and acted tactlessly. Hostility was on the increase.

Riots in Palestine—It took several years for the Allied nations to agree on the details of the Palestine mandate. In the meantime the government of the country was in the hands of persons who had no real interest in it, while the upper-class Arabs were encouraged to hope that, if they objected strongly enough, the idea of a Jewish homeland would be given up. Such Arabs resorted to two methods: protests and pogroms. They sent delegations to the British government and to the League of Nations. Not meeting with success, they thought to improve their argument by stirring the peasant Arabs to violence. Riots broke out in Jerusalem in April 1920 and, on a larger scale, in Jaffa in May 1921. On both occasions some of the outlying Jewish settlements were also attacked. Many Jews were wounded and some Jewish lives were lost. If the Arab plotters thought they could frighten the Jews, they soon discovered their mistake. The Jews in Palestine fought back; indeed, they fought back heroically, against odds, and inflicted more casualties than they suffered. In 1920, the defenders of Tel Hai, a Jewish village far up in Galilee, fought with especial bravery. Tel Hai has remained the symbol of Palestine's spirit under attack, and the colony's leader, Captain Joseph Trumpeldor, who was killed in the battle, became a Jewish hero. The English government, however, was frightened.

A Jewish High Commissioner—In the summer of 1920 a high commissioner was appointed to take over the civil administration of the country. The man chosen was Sir Herbert Samuel, a man of lofty ideals and great experience in government. The choice of a Jew apparently was meant to achieve a double purpose: to reassure the Jews regarding the intentions of England, and to make it possible to yield to the Arabs in certain respects without arousing too many Jewish objections, since it would be a respected Jew who would do the yielding. There was no doubt that Sir Herbert Samuel was devoted to the cause of the Jewish homeland, but he was naturally horrified by the bloodshed and hoped to quiet the Arabs by being more than fair to them. Government land, which everyone had expected would go to the Jews, was distributed among Arabs. The civil government to be established was planned with the Arabs having an equal share. As might have been expected, the effect was the very opposite of the one hoped for. The Arab upper classes drew the conclusion that their methods were proving successful. They greedily accepted the lands given them, but continued to insist that the government must be completely in their hands and the idea of a Jewish homeland entirely abandoned. That these events did not affect the progress made in the building of the Jewish homeland was evidence of the strength of Jewish hope and spirit.

7. PEACE AND ITS CONSEQUENCES

Summary of Jewish Gains—From the Versailles Peace Conference the Jews had emerged with several gains. The Jews of Eastern Europe gained the right to organize themselves as legally protected minorities. In this way the continuance of their cultural life could be assured, presumably without danger of political oppression by the majority populations. They at once set about establishing their own institutions. Self-governing councils were set up in various countries. Schools were established in every large city, where instruction was given either in Hebrew or in Yiddish. The Jews of the new states could look forward to an era of peace and progress. The second great gain was the universal recognition that the Jews had an historic and actual right to return to Palestine, if they so desired, and there in time set up a Jewish state. In addition, the various countries showed a disposition to greater democracy. Germany, too, now a republic under a supposedly socialist government, gave the Jews full political rights. Yet all these gains were short-lived, not because there was anything inherently wrong with them, but because the peace in general was not destined to last.

Failures of the Peace—Before the peace was more than a few years old, its faults revealed themselves, especially as they affected the Jews. Small states in Eastern and southeastern Europe, covetous of their neighbors' territory, disregarded the territorial arrangements of the peace treaty and took what they wanted by force. Local wars or, at least, local international hatreds were now worse than they had ever been. During such conflicts the petty politicians of each side accused the Jews of disloyal scheming. Murder and treachery and highhanded robbery were thus justified on the grounds of patriotism. The League of Nations, which had been created at Versailles, had no power and was not used with anything like the impartiality and justice which President Wilson had visioned. The great powers played their own political game with it. Worst of all, the makers of the peace had paid little attention to the economic problems of the countries whose fate they were deciding. Tariff restrictions were permitted to grow alongside of narrow patriotism, in order to destroy the industry and commerce of neighbors. No help was given to the defeated nations so that they might again return to normal economic existence. Consequently, poverty and hunger, bitterness and hate grew from day to day, and with them antisemitism.

Danger Signals in Germany—The most obvious illustration was what happened in Germany. The republic which was established in Germany after the army's defeat was forced to sign a treaty of peace whose terms were not so much harsh as humiliating. The militarists naturally tried to make the Germans forget the defeat which they had brought upon the country by attacking the new republican regime for signing the treaty. By the usual queer, illogical reasoning, the Jews were said to have been behind every calamity. The foremost and the wisest political leader of the Germany of that day was Walter Rathenau (1867–1922), a great industrialist and a profound thinker on social problems. He was far more German than Jew and had expressed the hope that the German Jews would soon become assimilated without leaving a trace. During the war he had helped in the reorganization of German industry; after the war, as a member of the cabinet, he urged that some method be found to establish real peace with France, so that Germany might be able to resume its economic life. For the German reactionaries and militarists it was enough that Rathenau was a Jew and a republican who sought peace with France. In June 1922, Rathenau was assassinated by several young Germans. The murder horrified the world. It led directly to the occupation of part of Germany by French troops and to the enormous increase of misery in Germany itself. This, in turn, led to more intense antisemitism. Thus the evils which the Treaty of Versailles had failed to abolish showed themselves first in their effect on the Jews, long before these same evils led to another and more destructive war.

CHAPTER X

STRANGE TRIBES AND THE NEWEST DIASPORA

ABOUT JEWISH GROUPS WHICH HAVE SURVIVED IN OUT-OF-THE-WAY PLACES IN SOME OF WHICH JEWISH HOME-SEEKERS AND EXILES FROM EUROPE MADE THEIR HOME

Off the World's Highways—Our story thus far has dealt mainly with the Jewish communities most intimately connected with the Western world in which we live. This has been done intentionally, because the primary purpose of studying Jewish history is to help us understand Jewish life in our own surroundings. Nevertheless, we ought not lose sight of the fact that for many centuries other Jewish communities existed beyond our horizons and developed in ways quite different from our own. Moreover, Jews escaping from parts of

Western Europe have recently begun to establish new communities alongside these old ones. As had so often happened before in Jewish history, a crisis once more brought about a crossing of paths which had separated in the distant, almost forgotten past.

Several factors in recent world affairs helped to discover some of these communities and to bring others closer to us. Colonial rivalry among the great European powers and the improvement in methods of transportation, which characterized the nineteenth and twentieth centuries, brought hitherto unexplored areas of the globe into the seething international life of our time. Peoples of strange languages and peculiar modes of life suddenly became themes of daily conversation and objects of economic interest. As might have been expected, forgotten fragments of the Jewish Diaspora were also rediscovered. Western Jews became curious about their newly-found fellow Jews; they were intrigued by their exotic customs and traditions; they began to speculate about their origin; they even tried, in some instances, to westernize them. Now that we have more information about these forgotten communities, we find that their histories offer us invaluable aid to a better understanding of Judaism and of Jewish survival everywhere. We learn from a study of their origins how every crisis both in world history and in Jewish history left its mark on the Jewish people, how their peculiar customs and traditions became local modifications of the Jewish heritage, and how well Judaism adapted itself to every kind of environment.

The Jewish Diaspora has always been wide; and it is now wider than ever. In the course of the vast migration of the past one hundred years, Jews have sought homes in every continent and on almost every island. Turning the globe of the earth, as we shall do in this chapter, we shall find that between old communities newly discovered and new communities recently established, there is hardly a spot on it but that a remnant of Israel lifts there its voice to God.

1. THE JEWS OF NORTH AFRICA

The Varied Population—Excluding Egypt, about 350,000 Jews lived in North Africa before World War II. Many of them were recent settlers from various parts of Europe. They had sought a new home there under the flags of the European powers who, in the nineteenth century, had carved colonial empires for themselves. Most of the Jewish inhabitants of the North African kingdoms, however, were ancient settlers there. The Jews of Europe at best knew only those who inhabited the cities along the northern fringe of the continent and who differed but little from their fellow Jews of Sephardi origin in Southern Europe. Few Europeans knew about the many strange vicissitudes which North African Jewry as a whole had undergone, or of the great antiquity of the Jews who lived in the continent's interior, or the varied and peculiar forms of their Jewish life. To almost this day Jews were found there who lived in oases in the desert, and others who dwelt in caves in the mountains. There were wandering Jews who loved their freedom in the desert so much that they could not settle in inhabited places, and others who served as slaves of the Moslem noblemen nearest their village. A number of Mohammedan tribes, in various parts of the continent, prided themselves on the tradition that their ancestors, not many centuries ago, had been Jews. There were, in North Africa, Jews who treasured every detail of Jewish learning and tradition; and others, even among the cave-dwellers, who still spoke Hebrew somewhat modified by the local Arabic dialect; while still others practiced a Judaism whose main elements consisted of strange superstitions. These very diversities indicated that the Jewish population of North Africa must have had a long and eventful history.

Under Mohammedan Power—The origins of North African Jewry before the Mohammedan conquest have been discussed in an earlier chapter.* The Jews fared well, on the whole, under Moslem rule till the middle of the eleventh century. Trouble began in 1056 and did not stop for two centuries. Many important Jewish centers were destroyed. Towns, famous for their large and learned Jewish populations, were left desolate. When, finally, a semblance of peace was established in the lands of North Africa, toward the end of the thirteenth century, the position of the Jews was no longer what it had been. The entire territory was sinking to lower economic and cultural levels, and the Jews were drawn down with it. Ghettos (*Mellah* or *Hara*), with all that they imply of social and cultural stagnation, were imposed upon the Jews, and the earlier Moslem anti-Jewish restrictions were revived.

The Spanish Exiles—From 1391 to 1492 Spanish Jews, and a few years later Portuguese Jews, fleeing compulsory

* See above, pp. 232–3.

conversion, found a measure of peace and religious freedom in the countries south of the Mediterranean. The native Jews in every part of North Africa welcomed the refugees and tried to obtain for them permanent rights of settlement. The newcomers, once settled, disdained the Berber Jews because of their lower cultural level, and it must be admitted that most of the religious leadership and talmudic erudition which existed in portions of North Africa until our own time were to be found among Jews of Spanish descent.

North Africa on the Downgrade—Their common misfortunes, if nothing more, should have brought these Jewish groups together. The North African kingdoms during the past four centuries have been weakened by misrule and shaken by civil uprisings. Unfortunately, the fate of the Jews in Tripoli, Tunisia, Algeria and Morocco depended, as in the darkest period of the Middle Ages in Europe, upon the whim or wisdom of the temporary ruler. Time and again the *mellah* was sacked, and its population massacred or forcibly converted to Mohammedanism. Thus, for example, the Spanish Jewish community of Fez was destroyed so completely, in the sixteenth century, that when resettlement was possible the new community consisted only of a small number of Berber Jews. The ancient Jewish community of Tripoli instituted two additional Purims in commemoration of last-minute deliverances from certain destruction which threatened the Jews in 1705 and 1792. Every internal disorder brought persecution; every new tyrant exacted the last possible penny, and yet the Jews filled important economic needs in the various countries of North Africa. They constituted a large portion of the artisan and heavy-labor class; they made important contributions to leather and jewelry manufactures; they participated extensively in what commerce there was between North Africa and Italy and between North Africa and the Sudan. But the poverty within the ghetto was appalling, and the houses were holes rather than homes. The ghetto of North Africa was, in fact, not a district in a city, but an independent town. In matters of law, a Jew had no rights at all in a Moslem court.

The Influence of Europe—When European imperialism in the nineteenth century found in the misgovernment of the North African kingdoms an excuse for imposing its rule upon them, the Jews were not sorry, for they were saved from the arrogant cruelty of their Moslem masters. Now they could go to European law-courts for protection. After 1870 the Jews of the French provinces, Algeria, Tunis and part of Morocco, gratefully exercised their right to become French citizens.

The Alliance Israélite Universelle established schools in various parts of North Africa, and within a generation the Jews became the bearers of European civilization. Their manners and customs were transformed. Their language and their interests, like their dress, were modeled upon what they thought was the style in Paris. Their transformation was made too rapidly, causing, unfortunately, their abandonment not only of Jewish traditions but also of Jewish knowledge. This was true of the Jewish communities located in the cities along the coast; but farther south, closer to or in the desert, where European influence could penetrate but feebly, life among the Jews continued as it had gone on for centuries before.

The Recent Years—European influences brought with them antisemitism, the European spiritual disease of the late nineteenth century. The French settlers in North Africa, who carved out for themselves huge agricultural estates and turned the commerce of the countries to their own benefit, encountered the Moslems' resentment against economic exploitation and their opposition to foreign rule. The Frenchmen followed the favorite European example and blamed the Jews, whom the Moslems had been accustomed to oppress and whom they now found legally beyond their reach. Antisemitic sentiments could not be expressed in action so long as liberalism and democracy prevailed in Europe. But as Hitler's doctrines gained currency in the 1930s, the position of the Jews grew worse. The Italians in Libya began active discrimination against them; and farther west, after France fell in 1940, the French eagerly seized the opportunity to deprive the Jews of their rights. After the armies of the allied nations had driven the Germans and the fascists out of North Africa, the former legal situation was restored (1943); but nothing could restore the lives lost and the communities destroyed, especially in Italian North Africa which had come more directly under German control. Benghazi, Derna and other towns along the coast saw their Jewish populations deported to do hard labor for the armies or to perish in concentratioin camps. Very few subsequently returned. The ancient Jewish communities along the African coast had to start life anew.

The Jews of Egypt—The more important part of the very long story of the Jews in Egypt has already been told.* The happy era in which Moses Maimonides lived continued through the lifetime of his son Abraham, who followed his

* See above, pp. 54 ff., 139, 145 ff., 173, 231 f., 301 f.; and below, pp. 695 f.

father as head of Egyptian Jewry. But it came to an end in 1250. The Mamelukes, those mercenary slave-soldiers who became masters of the Egyptian state, drove Egypt into a long period of decline. One or another Mameluke ruler had a Jewish favorite, but in general they compelled the Jews to live under constant threat of extortion, repression and even massacre. A Mohammedan Marrano life became fairly common among the Jews as well as among the Christians of Egypt. Nevertheless, Jewish religious loyalty and intellectual activity did not entirely disappear. Consequently, when oppressive economic and political restrictions were removed, as a result of the conquest of Egypt by the Turks in 1517, Jewish life quickly revived. The revival was fortified by the immigration, early in the sixteenth century, of exiles from Portugal and Spain. Occasional difficulties arose because the central government of the Turkish state was growing weaker and the Jews had to bear the brunt of the resultant unsettled conditions. Peace and prosperity came to Egypt and its Jews when England gained practical control of the Egyptian state in the second half of the nineteenth century. A considerable immigration of European Jews strengthened the Jewish communities of Alexandria and Cairo and made them of cultural centers in the Near East. In 1940 there were about 70,000 Jews in Egypt. In addition, there were small groups of Karaites with whom the Jews maintained friendly relations.

2. THE BLACK JEWS OF ABYSSINIA

The Falashas—Professor Joseph Halevi (1827–1917), a French Jewish scholar interested in oriental civilizations, announced in 1867 that he had made an unusual discovery while exploring Abyssinia, a country in Africa below Egypt —the land of the Ethiopians. There he found a population of some 50,000 black-skinned people who called themselves *Beta Israel* (House of Israel). They claimed descent from the ancient Israelites and observed a peculiar type of Judaism. The king of Abyssinia himself, though a Christian, boasts among his titles that he is the "Lion of Judah," and claims King Solomon and the Queen of Sheba as his family's ancestors. Their child, named Menelik, eventually succeeded his mother as ruler over Abyssinia. At this point the Jews of Abyssinia take up the story. Solomon, they maintain, sent priests and wise men to advise his son. They brought a rep-

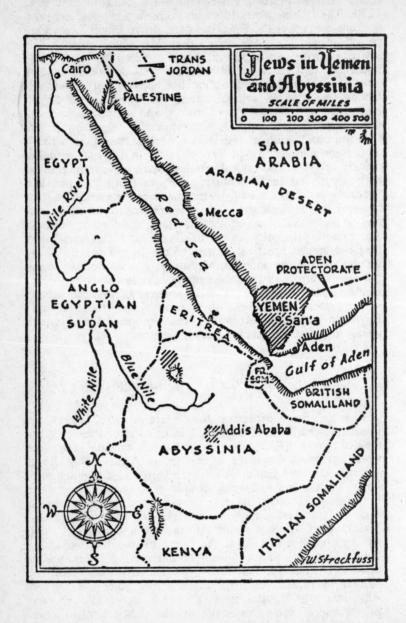

Jews in Yemen and Abyssinia

lica of the sacred ark and so established Judaism in the land
of the Ethiopians.

Who are the Falashas?—Professor Halevi did not carry his
investigations far enough into the history of the Abyssinian
Jews to offer an answer to the riddle of their origin. It was
left to his pupil, Jacques Faitlovitch (1880–1955), to spend
many years with these Jews and to piece their history together from various sources. It is generally agreed that their
remote ancestors were those guardians of the south Egyptian
border whose correspondence was found at Assuan.* Other
Jews came to Abyssinia during the Second Commonwealth
and after the Diaspora Rebellion of 115–7. These Jews intermarried with the natives, as the black skin of the modern
Falashas indicates. Judaism spread rapidly among the Abyssin-
ians. It spread more rapidly than Christianity, so that for a
long time, down to the sixteenth century, much of Abyssinia
was ruled by Jews. A series of destructive wars followed and
the Jews lost their power. The population became predominantly Christian and, to some extent, Mohammedan.
The victors then called the Jews "Falashas," which means
"strangers."

The Judaism of the Falashas—Defeated, and separated
from Jews elsewhere, the Falashas nevertheless loyally held to
their Jewish traditions. They lived as artisans and farmers far
inland in villages of their own. They knew no Hebrew; even
their Torah is written in an old Abyssinian dialect. *Kohanim*
(priests) lead them in religious service. At the approach of
the Sabbath, they bathe and dress in white, and the entire
community unites in prayer and shares in a common meal. Of
course, they do no work on the Sabbath. Their laws of *kashrut*
are somewhat different from those of other Jews. In general,
the Falashas show no evidence of having been influenced by
the rabbinical Judaism of the Talmud.

Dr. Faitlovitch's arrival among them, early in this century,
caused an upheaval in their thinking. They discovered that
there were other Jews in the world. Faitlovitch succeeded in
persuading the Falashas to permit the teaching of Hebrew to
their children so as to bring them culturally closer to the
other Jewish communities. But he found it more difficult to
persuade the Jews of Europe and America to contribute
funds for the support of these plans, although a Pro-Falasha
Committee long functioned in the United States. With the
limited funds gathered, Faitlovitch brought a number of

* See above, p. 46.

young Falashas to Europe and placed them in various universities. These students, after completing their studies, returned to Abyssinia to teach their brethren. Chief among the native teachers was the charming and cultured Taamarat Emmanuel.

The Promise of Ethiopia—When Abyssinia was conquered by the Italian fascists, in 1935–6, Faitlovitch's work had to be suspended. But in 1940–1 the foreign invader was expelled and Haile Selassie returned to his throne. Not only could Jewish work be resumed, but refugees from European oppression found their way to Ethiopia. They brought with them technical skills of which the country was in great need to develop its resources. The nearness of Palestine, where Haile Selassie spent part of his exile, also had its effect. He brought back some Jewish advisers, and they have been helping him modernize his state both economically and culturally. New industries and a port were developed. Commerce with Palestine increased. Abyssinia, till recently a forgotten land, may come to the foreground of a revived Near East. The impact of these events upon the Falashas is certain to be enormous.

3. THE JEWS OF YEMEN

How Jews Came to Yemen—The southern tip of the Arabian Peninsula lies on the Red Sea, directly across from Abyssinia. There Yemen is located. It is an ancient country, marvelous in climate and vegetation. Yemen, rather than Ethiopia, was probably the kingdom of Sheba whose queen visited King Solomon. A pious Jewish population of some 30,000 lived in Yemen for many centuries. Their tradition relates that the first Hebrews came there in the days of the Prophet Jeremiah, just before the destruction of the First Temple. They found their surroundings so congenial—so their story continues—that when Ezra invited them to return to Judea and aid in its rebuilding, they refused. Therefore, their ancestors were visited by God's punishment, and ever since then Yemenite Jews have remained poor.

The converts to Judaism who survived the Christian sword in the days of Dhu Nowas* no doubt merged with the original Jewish population of the country. The Jews of Yemen, unlike those of Ethiopia, never lost touch with the Jews far-

* See above, p. 225.

ther north, in Palestine and in Babylonia, or with those to the northwest in Egypt. They remained strict observers of the Jewish tradition and, in fact, had their share in the development of Jewish literature.

Life Among the Yemenite Jews—Almost all the Yemenite Jews were artisans. They used to have a practical monopoly of manual labor, but in more recent years imports began to compete with their products and forced some of them into trade. Even the rabbi of a settlement, the *Mori*, as they call him, earned his livelihood by manual labor. His rabbinic duties, which included serving as teacher, preacher, slaughterer (*shohet*), circumciser, judge and ritual guide, were purely honorary. Jewish law permitted Yemenite Jews to have more than one wife, since the edict of Rabbenu Gershom applies only to Ashkenazi Jews. Few Yemenite Jews, however, practiced polygamy, and their home life was exemplary. They considered the education of their children in Hebrew and in Jewish tradition a sacred task. A man called to the Torah was disgraced if he failed to read his portion faultlessly; for he had to read it himself, there being no official reader to help him.

Persecutions and Migration—The religious bigotry of the Moslems imposed many restrictions upon Jewish life. In 1677, an edict went forth expelling the Jews entirely. Their books were burned and many of them perished during their search for a new home. One of their number, however, had in the meantime exerted his great influence to have the edict revoked. His name was Mori Salim Shebesi, a poet, musician and author of a cabalistic work. The Jews were permitted to return to their former homes, except in San'a, the capital. But the conditions of their life thereafter became more difficult than ever. Early in the 20th century, Yemenite Jewry began a steady migration to Palestine. After World War II, Israel organized a total emigration of the Jews from Yemen and Aden, carrying the entire remaining population by plane to Israel. Yemenite Jews have always been among the most interesting Jews in the Holy Land—pious, naive, and artistically gifted.

4. THE JEWS OF PERSIA AND ITS NEIGHBORS

Origin and History of Persian Jewry—The Jewish community of Persia was one of the oldest in the world. Its origins date back to the days of Cyrus, the conqueror of Babylonia

and the restorer of Judea. The early story of the Persian Jewish community was indistinguishable for many centuries from
the Jews of neighboring Mesopotamia, whose Exilarchs and
Genonim exercised authority over the Persian Jews as well.*
The conquest of Persia by the Mongols (Hulegu Khan), in
the thirteenth century, changed very much for the better the
conditions under which the Jews of Persia had been living.
The Mongol rulers even appointed Jews to office. Despite
frequent political upheavals during the next few centuries,
Jewish life went on with fair smoothness. A definite change for
the worse occurred in the seventeenth century, when Moslem
clergy of the sect of Shiites gained the upper hand. Two rules
were adopted whose purpose was to undermine Jewish existence. 1) The Shiites declared that all non-Moslems were a
source of impurity. Very pious members of this Moslem sect
even washed their eyes if by chance they saw a non-believer.
This necessitated a separation of the Jews (as well as of
Christians and others) by means of a badge. 2) The Shiite
clergy, moreover, had the Persian government adopt a law
whereby a convert to Mohammedanism became the sole heir
to the property of all his Jewish relatives. Physical attacks
also became more frequent. In 1838, the entire community of
Jews in the city of Meshed was compelled to adopt Mohammedanism. But it retained its Jewishness in secret, with all the
embitterment of life and the danger which such a marrano
existence involved.

European Assistance—Sir Moses Montefiore and the Anglo-
Jewish Association along with Adolphe Crémieux and the
Alliance Israélite Universelle bestirred themselves. But their
protests and the pressure they exerted through diplomatic
channels availed nothing. The situation reached such a pass,
in 1871, that the Persian Jews appealed to their Western coreligionists to help them escape to the Holy Land or to emigrate to some other, friendlier country. In 1873 and in 1889,
Nasr-ed-Din, the shah, toured Europe. The Jews of Berlin,
Paris and London seized upon the occasions to try to impress
him with their interest in his Jewish subjects. He made promises which, as it turned out, he was unable to keep. The
only result of this interest on the part of the Jews of Western
Europe was the establishment in Persia of schools run by the
Alliance. Even the occasional intervention of diplomatic
representatives of Western powers, including the representatives of the United States, did little good. There were anti-

* See above, p. 245.

Jewish riots as late as 1907–9. By that time, however, European influences began to penetrate the country, and a better spirit manifested itself. Yet the power of the bigoted clergy was not finally broken until the establishment of a new dynasty under Riza Khan Pahlavi (1925–40) who made strenuous and fairly successful efforts to modernize Persia.

Fighting for Survival—Living under such oppressive circumstances, the Jews of Persia, during the last four centuries, could not rise to the cultural heights of their ancestors. Worse still, the very foundations of their Jewishness became shaky. While the results of Christian missionary activity were exceedingly meager, another religious movement, native to Persia, met with greater success. This movement was called Bahaism and represented a mixture of Mohammedanism and the messianic hopes of Christianity and Judaism as well. Its

mysticism and vague idealism appealed also to some Jews, not so much because of the claims made by the mystical leaders of the sect, as because it offered an opportunity to abandon the persecuted Jewish group without abandoning completely that belief in monotheism and those human ideals with which Judaism is identified.

Fortunately, it was at this point that the cultural situation began to change for the better. A number of Persian Jews migrated into Palestine and there started a literary revival.

They established a printing press for the Jewish-Persian dialect; they prepared translations of Hebrew books; they even wrote textbooks for the study of Hebrew. All this material was transported to Persia and, in turn, effected a revival of Jewish culture in that country. Once more, as many centuries ago, the dormant Jewish community of Persia gave promise of coming into its own.

In the Neighborhood of Persia—Several little-known Jewish communities existed in the provinces and states on every side of the Persian kingdom. Between 20,000 and 30,000 Jews were to be found in Kurdistan in the northwestern corner of Persia. About 50,000 had their homes in the region between the Black and the Caspian seas (Daghestan and Georgia) in the territory of the Soviet Union. Some 10,000 or more lived in Turkestan and Bokhara, on Persia's northeastern border and partly in Russian territory, and about 5,000 in Afghanistan to the east of Persia. The Kurdish and Daghestan Jews were for the most part farmers; the others had a higher proportion of merchants and artisans. All these Jews claimed descent from the Lost Ten Tribes of Israel, apparently with some justice, though neither they nor anyone else could give details of their history, except that their ancestors lived in these lands long before Mohammedan times. They observed varying social and religious customs. Those of Kurdistan, for example, practiced child marriage, wife purchase and the reciting of incantations on the presumed graves of ancient prophets. Their contacts with other Jews in the past depended on the infrequent visits of emissaries from the charitable and rabbinic institutions of Palestine. The Jews of Bokhara had, in fact, for centuries been unaware of the existence of other Jews. In 1802, they learned by accident that there were Jews in Russia, and a correspondence followed with some Jews in the town of Shklov. In view of their isolation, the Jews of all these provinces possessed exceedingly little Jewish knowledge; but this did not affect their loyalty to Judaism. In recent years thousands of these Jews migrated to Palestine, especially from Bokhara, and became a colorful and pious segment of Israel's population.

5. A LESSON FROM INDIA

Experiments in Survival—Two separate communities of Jews have survived from the dim past in the vast subcontinent of India. One was located in Cochin, near the southern-

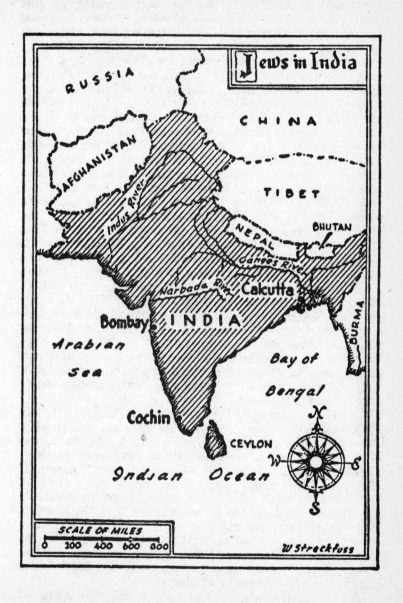

most tip of India; the other was farther north, near the western coast, in and around Bombay. Both communities were for centuries separated from contact with other Jews and nevertheless maintained their Jewishness. Both yielded in many respects to their Hindu environment, living and looking like their neighbors, yet remained Jews in every essential element of life. Neither suffered persecution, and they therefore showed the inherent strength and vitality of Judaism.

The Original Jews of Cochin—It may well be that individual Jews lived in Cochin even before the destruction of the Temple. Commercial relations between India and the numerous Jewish merchants of Alexandria in Egypt are known to have existed, so that the Alexandrians may have had representatives there. The chances are, however, that the first Jewish settlement was made by Jews who came from Babylonia and Persia as a result of the occasional difficulties during the amoraic and geonic periods, sometime between the fifth and the eighth centuries. The first actual record of these Jews dates from the year 1020, when the Rajah Bhaskira Ravivarman of the Malabar coast granted a charter of nobility and considerable estates to a Jew named Joseph Rabban. Through him the Jews of his community gained in prestige and influence. Rabbi Benjamin of Tudela heard of them a century and a half later; and a century after that Marco Polo mentioned these Jews. At that time they lived at Cranganore. Soon thereafter most of them removed to Cochin. They became well-to-do and influential. They even formed an important element in the armies of the local princes, who occasionally postponed a battle because their Jewish soldiers would not violate the Sabbath.

Arrival of Europeans—A revolutionary change in the life of Cochin Jewry occurred early in the sixteenth century when Europeans began to sail the Indian waters. The Portuguese were first on the scene and established their power in India. That, moreover, was the time when Jewish and Marrano exiles from Spain and Portugal were seeking some place on earth out of reach of the Inquisition. Some thousands of them arrived in India and settled near the Jews who had long lived there. Thereupon the Portuguese imported the tribunal of the Inquisition. Eventually their Dutch rivals expelled the Portuguese from India and thereafter the Jews were not molested. A small number of Jews from Persia and Bagdad later joined the new settlement of Europeans.

Jewish Castes—In matters of religion and culture the old settlement of Jews in India benefited from the arrival of the

European Jews. Their knowledge of Hebrew was revived; they adopted the Sephardi ritual; they emulated their fellow Jews in studying the sacred literature. Socially, however, the new settlement brought a problem which has afflicted Cochin Jewry to this day. The newer arrivals insisted on keeping aloof from the others. Their reasons were the ignorance of the Hindu Jews and the supposed racial impurity indicated by their color. For the old Cochin Jews are dark-skinned, like the other inhabitants of India. Their color is probably a result of intermarriage between the original settlers in India and Hindu natives who became converts to Judaism. Such converts may have been slaves, since slavery in a mild form was recognized in India. The Spanish Jews argued that they could not permit their own racial purity to be sullied by intermarriage or even by social contact with such "inferior" stock. On several occasions questions were forwarded to noted rabbis in Egypt and Palestine requesting a decision as to the legality of this conduct, and the rabbis replied (*teshubot*) that the conduct of the Sephardi Jews had no legal basis. But discrimination continued. The conflict, in fact, was sharpened. For a third division came into being through the slaves whom the Sephardi Jews converted from time to time and, temporarily at least, made part of the white family. These last still carried on a struggle for acceptance into the white community.

Life among the Cochin Jews—Before the establishment of the State of Israel, there were altogether about 2,000 Jews of all kinds in Cochin. The "white" community consisted of only 125 individuals. They lived close to one another, in a voluntary ghetto; their contacts, however, were few and very formal. All the groups were equally Orthodox, observing the same rites, although the "whites" and the older "blacks" worshipped in synagogues of their own. The synagogue was the center of each community's life and the worship was followed meticulously. While Hebrew was generally known and studied, the language of the Cochin Jews was the dialect of their environment. Economically the "white" Jews were not necessarily better off than the "blacks." The "whites" were engaged in what might be called white-collar occupations, whereas the others were merchants on a small scale and artisans. No doubt changed conditions in India and the growing influences of the outside world affected the Jews of Cochin. They have already proved, however, that given a friendly environment and some contacts with Jews outside, Judaism can survive no matter how small the number of its adherents and how different the religion of their neighbors.

Bene Israel—The other Hindu Jews, likewise brown of skin, who lived in and around the province of Bombay, called themselves Bene Israel, "Sons of Israel." The origin of their settlement and the reason for their color are as much matters of dispute as among the Jews of Cochin. As was to be expected, the theory of the Lost Ten Tribes has been advanced to explain them. The most plausible theory, however, is that the original settlers came from the north, or possibly as captives of war by a Roman slave galley of the sixth century.

Hindu and Moslem religious influences and especially the lack of contacts with Jews outside brought about fundamental changes in their life as Jews. They forgot the Hebrew language, so that only *Shema' Yisrael* remained with them. Through ignorance, they modified and neglected many observances and holidays of Judaism. But they scrupulously observed the Sabbath, circumcision and some of the basic dietary laws. Their traditions relate that a man named David Rahabi, a Cochin Jew, happened into their midst in the tenth century and brought about a revival of Judaism. Another such visitor, Samuel Divakar, performed a like service for them at the end of the eighteenth century. The result was that their Jewish religion was entirely restored, and they observed it in orthodox fashion, according to the Spanish rite.

The Modern Bene Israel—The coming of the English to India resulted in many changes in the life of the Bene Israel. They had been mostly farmers and oil-pressers, as many of them still are, but the English attracted them to the army, and many of them rose to comparatively high military rank and occupied important posts in the native civil service. Some also turned to commerce and others became skilled artisans. There were about 15,000 of the Bene Israel in the 1950s. A small number of these were descendants of intermarriages with Hindus in modern times. Such members of the community faced the same discrimination as similar mixed types faced among the Jews of Cochin. Moreover, relations have grown strained between the Bene Israel and the European Jews who have been coming to India in more recent years. Here, too, a caste system was in process of developing, even though the Sephardi rabbinate of England and of Israel hesitated to countenance it. The Jews of India may in time be fused with the rest of the Jews all over the world.

Jews in Modern India—As India opened up to the expanding commerce of Europe, a number of Jews came to live there. Their presence, as already indicated, sometimes added to the social confusion of the older Jewish groups. At the same time some of the newcomers contributed much to the welfare of its Jews as well as to the general welfare of India. The Sassoon family, originally from Bagdad, settled in Bombay early in the nineteenth century and, after making a considerable fortune in various branches of business, became very influential in the Jewish life of the country. Toward the end of the century, Waldemar Mordecai Haffkine (1860–1930), a Russian Jew and a noted scientist, saved the Hindu population from serious plagues which had been afflicting the country. Events in Germany and in Eastern Europe after World War I brought more Jews into India. During the 1930s, Nazi Germany, in its desire to create difficulties for Britain, resorted to its usual tactics of starting anti-Jewish agitation. The results were not impressive by the time World War II broke out. After the war and the establishment of Israel, the Indian Jews sought migration to the new state.

6. THE JEWS OF CHINA

Modern Settlements—The vast Chinese empire was a land of mystery to the Western world almost to the end of the nineteenth century. Marco Polo, around 1290, was the first Christian European to visit it. A small number of adventurous Christian missionaries came as far as China during the next centuries and brought back interesting descriptions of an incredibly strange civilization. Even they, however, rarely succeeded in penetrating beyond the coast cities, for China was suspicious of foreigners. A change came about the middle of the nineteenth century, when the energetic commercial activity of the Western peoples broke through China's isolation. Jews, too, were among the merchants who knocked on China's door. Members of the Kadoorie and Sassoon families and their employees, for example, penetrated into China with their mercantile interests which were centered in Persia and India. Others followed hard upon their footsteps. By 1900 there were colonies of Jews in Hong Kong, Shanghai and Tientsin. A considerable settlement of Jews was built up also in Harbin, the city nearest Russia. Jewish fugitives from Russia, after World War I and the Bolshevist revolution, increased the size of all these settlements and intensified their religious and cultural activity. Harbin in 1921 had about 10,000 Jews with an organized community and a school for their children. Shanghai Jewry, though smaller, also had a community with charitable institutions and two synagogues, one for Sephardi and another for Ashkenazi Jews. The Jews were, on the whole, far from wealthy. The more recent arrivals from Russia were quite poor. The German refugees, who began to come in the 1930s, further complicated the economic problems of the communities. Many refugees turned to manual labor and more would have liked to do so, but the standards of life among the native Chinese were so low that a Westerner could hardly expect to survive on wages derived from this source. American Jews and Jews of Western Europe consequently contributed to the support of the refugees in China, even after World War II broke out, so long as the situation permitted it.

Ancient Settlements—At the very time when these new Jewish settlements were coming to life in the coast cities of China, an ancient Jewish community was breathing its last in the country's interior. The two communities touched each other, as though to shake hands and symbolize the unending chain of Jewish history, and then the older settlement disappeared from view. Fortunately, the broad outlines of its history can be pieced together.

The traditions of the old Chinese Jews placed their earliest settlement in the first two centuries of the Common Era. Why the Jews of that day made the long journey across the broad continent of Asia to settle among the Chinese people can only be guessed at. Perhaps they were connected with the traffic in silk of the ancient world, for silk was in great demand in the Roman empire and China was the only source for it. The traffic caused enterprising Jews to establish trading posts in China, and trading posts tend to become permanent homes.

The Mohammedan invasion of Persia in the seventh century of the Common Era may have been the event which disrupted communication between the Jews of China and those of Persia. Occasional contacts there may have been, but they were too rare and probably also too brief to leave any lasting impression. The Talmud and the usual prayer book, for example, which gained currency among the other Jews during the geonic age, were not known among the Jews of China. They remained completely out of touch with the stream of Jewish life and thought.

Adjustment to the Chinese Environment—A process of physical and religious adjustment went on in China similar to processes that took place in other lands. Chinese dress and language were quickly adopted, and even religious adjustment was not particularly difficult. The Jews found in Chinese culture profound similarities to their own humane ideals. Moreover, the Chinese, peaceful by nature and possessed of a philosophic religion, never carried on religious propaganda. Jewish convictions on the subject of monotheism were, on the other hand, too strong to make their voluntary abandonment of Judaism at all likely. Jews did intermarry, and their wives certainly adopted the Jewish religion. Such intermarriage, practiced over centuries, made the Jews indistinguishable from the other Chinese. There were periods when the Jews were so wholly a part of their environment that they participated fully in Chinese politics and culture. Some of them became governors of provinces and ministers of state. The situation changed somewhat for the worse when Mohammedanism came into China. Whereas Judaism, like Chinese paganism, refrained from making proselytes even by persuasion, Mohammedanism at first was spread by force. In time the Mohammedans became more pacific and also less intolerant. Jewish life was, nevertheless, no longer without obstacle in those districts where Mohammedans were in the majority.

Chinese Judaism—Chinese Jews worshipped in a synagogue which consisted of a number of buildings surrounding open courts. The worshippers in the main synagogue building faced west, in the direction of Jerusalem. The westernmost compartment of the main synagogue hall contained thirteen arks, in each of which was a scroll of the Torah, one for Moses and twelve for the sons of Jacob. Closets on either side of the ark-compartment held the sacred books, handwritten but vocalized. Most of these books were copies of the *sidras* (portions of the week) of the Torah. They also had most of the Prophets and the Sacred Writings and some books of the Apocrypha. When the Torah was read, it was placed on a large throne, known as the Chair of Moses, which stood in the center of the synagogue hall. The same hall contained the *Shema'Yisrael* inscribed in Hebrew. A special place was also reserved for the name of the ruling dynasty and for a prayer in its behalf.

Another building had a ritual bath *(mikvah)*, and still another was a house for the ritual slaughtering of animals. A separate hall in the main synagogue building especially revealed the Chinese influence. This was the ancestors' hall and was used at times when all Chinese conducted memorial services. The largest of the many bowls of incense which it contained was in memory of Abraham. Around it were other bowls dedicated to Isaac and Jacob, the sons of Jacob, and to Moses, Aaron, Joshua and Ezra.

The Chinese Jews observed the usual Jewish holidays. In addition they had special observances on the first day of the moon (*Rosh Hodesh*) and on the day of the full moon. They believed in purgatory and in paradise, in angels and in resurrection. One of the curious things connected with their life as Jews was a little book which described Judaism and was kept for a special purpose. When the mandarin ruling in their district looked upon them and their customs with suspicion, they would let him read this book so that he might learn how harmless they and their traditions actually were. The pity is that this little book has disappeared along with almost everything else representing Chinese Judaism.

Death of a Jewish Community—Many Jewish communities, in various parts of the world, have risen and disappeared in the course of the long history of the Jewish people. Some were destroyed by external force. Others disintegrated because of the lure of personal advancement which the surrounding population held out. The Chinese Jews disappeared because of their isolation. For more than a thousand years they maintained their differences and traditions in the face of the criticism and perhaps the ridicule of their Mohammedan neighbors who were in the majority where the Jews lived. But they lacked the life-giving power of Jewish culture, including the Hebrew language and its literature. They missed the fortifying example of other Jewish communities. Furthermore, the Mohammedans could not be considered pagans by the Jews. For these reasons Judaism in China succumbed to Mohammedanism. Even through the little that is known of the history of the Chinese Jews, one can almost watch the process of decay.

Renewed Contacts—Christian missionaries in China around the year 1600 were the first to report to Europe that there were Chinese Jews living in several cities in the interior of China. Kai-feng Fu, in the province of Honan, had the most important Jewish settlement. It was still flourishing, while the settlements in the other towns were already disintegrating. The Chinese Jews were rapidly forgetting their Jewishness, but they knew enough to reject the statement of a missionary that the Messiah had already come. Some of them could still read their Hebrew books. They continued to worship in their synagogue in the manner described above. By 1850, when the interior of China could be visited more frequently, the Jews of Kai-feng Fu had been without any religious leadership for a generation. Their synagogue was falling into ruins and they were willing to sell their books and scrolls.

Rumors about the existence of Chinese Jews reached the Jews of Europe and America at the end of the eighteenth century. Out of curiosity, the Jews of England made two attempts in the first half of the nineteenth century to correspond with the Jews of Kai-feng Fu. About 1850 they finally received an answer through the British consul. The Chinese Jews expressed in this letter their joy that Jews were still found outside of China and asserted that they prayed daily, with tears in their eyes, for the restoration of their religion. Although a society for reclaiming the Chinese Jews was founded in America (1853), and Judah Touro gave money to it in his lifetime and left money to it in his will, nothing of a practical nature was done for them by Western Jews until, in 1900, European and American Jews living in Shanghai organized a Society for the Rescue of Chinese Jews. But this, too, had no results.

Again it was Christian missionaries who tried to do something effective. In 1919 they invited all known Jews of Kai-feng Fu to a social gathering. The heads of thirty-two families presented themselves and they estimated that many more were aware of their Jewishness. In 1932, David A. Brown, a representative of the American Jewish Joint Distribution Committee, made a special trip to Kai-feng Fu. Another meeting was called with the aid of the Christian missionaries and a considerable number responded. They pleaded for concrete aid in re-establishing their religion, especially for the organization of schools. Unfortunately, at that very time the Jews of Europe and America were being pressed by problems resulting from Hitler's rise to power in Germany. China, moreover, became a battleground as a result of Japan's aggression. Both the new and the ancient settlements of Jews in China were engulfed by the horrors of modern war.

With the cessation of hostilities in the Far East in August 1945, about 25,000 Jewish refugees from Central Europe, whom the Japanese had been keeping in a separate camp, could once more be cared for by American philanthropy. But no one can tell whether anything more than a memory remains of the ancient Chinese Jews.

7. JEWS IN THE PACIFIC ISLANDS

Jews in Japan—Jews may have arrived in Japan in the second century of the Common Era. A number of ancient inscriptions have been interpreted to stand for "David," "Ephraim," "Menasseh," and the like. It is supposed, therefore, that a group of Jewish silk merchants of that early era crossed from Korea to Japan and eventually became part of the Japanese population. Another guess, more modest in its claims, places the first contacts between Jews and Japan in the sixteenth century, when Spanish, Portuguese and Dutch Jews traded in the Far East. Both explanations are probably more interesting than truthful. All one can know for certain is that Jews were among the first merchants to deal with Japan in the middle of the last century when that country opened its doors to outsiders. Russian Jews had a synagogue and an organized community in Nagasaki in 1900, while Sephardi Jews from India and Syria enjoyed prosperity in Kobe. After World War I, more Russian Jews arrived, but the total number remained small. About 500 Jewish families lived in Japan in 1930. A considerable number of these Jews had been born and reared there.

Japan showed no hostility to the Jews, whether native or refugee, until 1936, when its government allied itself with Germany. Even then the hostility expressed itself only in words, not in action. The Japanese government placed no obstacles in the way of the European Jews who waited in Japan until relief societies in the American republics could find a permanent home for them. Several hundreds of these refugees even settled in Japan itself without objection. In 1940, a Nazi-inspired campaign of hate developed rapidly, and suddenly the Japanese discovered that the Jews were their enemies.

Jews in the Philippines—Marranos were among the first Europeans to settle in the Philippine Islands soon after their conquest by Spain in the sixteenth century. By the end of that century several of these were accused of practicing Judaism secretly. They were sent for trial and punishment to Mexico, where the nearest office of the Inquisition was located. Other cases of Marranism occurred down to the beginning of the nineteenth century. The real settlement of Jews in the Philippines began after World War I, when several hundred Russian Jews sought asylum there. Jews from other parts of the world joined them, and the community numbered about 500. But their Judaism was rather weak. A synagogue was built in Manila in 1924 and remained the only Jewish institution in the islands. The Jews, merchants for the most part, were prosperous. This enabled them to do much for the refugees from Nazi Germany who began to arrive after 1932. A plan was drawn up for the settlement of some 10,000 Jewish refugees on the island of Mindanao. But before any concrete steps could be taken, World War II engulfed the area. When the war ended, American Jewish soldiers raised funds for the rebuilding of the synagogue in Manila which had been destroyed by the Japanese.

The Dutch East Indies—The Jews of Holland played a considerable part in the development of the island empire around the equator which Holland acquired in the sixteenth century. Very few Jews, however, went to settle there and even those few were for the most part soon absorbed in the white population. Several small, scattered Jewish settlements remained. The resident white population did all it could to discourage the arrival of refugees from European lands during the 1930s.

The Jews of Australia—The earliest use to which England put Australia was as a penal colony, that is, for the punishment of men who fell afoul of the rather harsh laws which prevailed at that time. There were twelve Jews among the very first contingent of men condemned to such exile in 1788. Immigration of free settlers began in 1829. There were probably some Jews of German, Russian and Polish origin among the later as among the earlier settlers. In the middle decades of the 19th century, the Jewish immigrants were predominantly of German origin, while East European Jews began coming in larger numbers during the last two decades of the century. At whatever period they came, Jews immediately participated in the development of the subcontinent's resources. Members of the Montefiore family of England became especially prominent. Within a generation, Jews were high in the financial, industrial and political life of the country.

Their social standing, in the free atmosphere of Australia, helped them overcome what could have been a serious threat to their survival as Jews. Like every pioneering community, Australia had fewer women than men. Jews therefore intermarried in large numbers and, again as everywhere else, the next generation frequently was lost to Judaism. On the other hand, the Jewish community compensated for this situation by adhering to strict Orthodoxy. The first Jewish organization in Australia was a burial society (Hevra Kadisha), founded in 1817. Synagogues came somewhat later.

Another wave of immigrants followed World War I, so that by 1930 the Jewish population had risen to some 25,000.

Soon thereafter, when antisemitism swept over the world, Australia appeared a bit more generous in its immigration policy than most of the other nations.* In 1967, its Jewish population was estimated at about 69,000 in a total of 11,500,000.

The Jews of New Zealand—New Zealand is the youngest of the extensive land areas opened for European colonization. When the British established their first colony there in 1840, a few Jews were among the earliest settlers. By 1930 the 4,000 Jews still constituted but a small fraction of the total population (about .2 per cent). This small number, nevertheless, was invaluable for the commercial and industrial development of the dominion. Politically the Jews of New Zealand rank high; socially they have no difficulties; and in their religion they adhere to Jewish tradition.

8. New and Old Settlements in Latin America

A Twice-Tried Refuge—The relations of the Jews with the lands south of the United States began with the discovery and earliest settlement of the western hemisphere.† The Inquisition followed them, and the story of Recife illustrates their plight. When this Jewish community was plunged back into Marranism or scattered, its refugees laid the foundations not only for the Jewish community of New York, but also for those still in existence in Curaçao, Jamaica and other islands in the western Atlantic. Jewish settlements in Dutch and British Guiana were also founded at that time. As to Latin America, the Inquisition was re-established and for one hundred and fifty years made the immigration of Jews impossible.

During the nineteenth century, Latin America began for a second time to serve the Jews as a haven of refuge. By this time, the various republics had freed themselves from the reactionary domination of their European motherlands. Slowly the hard-pressed Jews of Central and Eastern Europe discovered the possibilities of making a home in these countries.‡ Once more the Jews cooperated in the commercial, industrial and even agricultural development of Latin America, and also shared in its intellectual maturing. Their numerical

* See below, pp. 663 f.
† See above, pp. 433–4.
‡ For the part played by ICA, see above, pp. 566 f.

growth has not been so rapid as that of the Jewish community of the United States. Argentina and Brazil are the only
ones with a considerable Jewish population—in 1965 they had
450,000 and 140,000 Jews, respectively. The countries south
of the Rio Grande, however, have a combined Jewish population of about a million souls. This represented seven per cent
of the total Jewish population of the world before World War
II, and an even larger percentage since the war. Several difficulties have stood in the way of their exerting as important
an influence as their numbers might justify. They were scattered; they were not well organized for Jewish religious and
educational work; and they had to contend with a powerful
reactionary spirit among the ruling class in many of the republics. These reactionary forces were strengthened by the
propaganda of the fascists and the Nazis in Latin America.
The Jews, as usual, were the first to be attacked. Immigration
laws were enacted on a racial basis so as to make it impossible for Jewish refugees from Europe to enter Latin America,
although Colombia, Venezuela and the Dominican Republic
have shown a more humane spirit.

The Rediscovered Jews—Even while the tide of reaction
was rising in various Latin American countries, the Jews of
the United States were startled to hear of the existence in
Mexico of a group of Jews who traced their descent from the
very earliest settlers in America. A similar group of Indian
Jews has long been known in Chile, but the story of the Indian Jews of Mexico is more striking and romantic. Mexico
seems to have been especially attractive to Spanish New
Christians (Marranos). An office of the Inquisition, established there about the middle of the sixteenth century, found a
great deal to do. In 1574, for example, eighty persons were
condemned to die at the stake for being "Judaizers," that is,
for practicing Judaism. Among the important personages in
the early history of Mexico was Luis de Caravajal, who came
to Mexico in 1567. He became governor of the district
around Monterrey and opened it for colonization by whites.
Some years later Caravajal received royal permission to bring
from Spain into his Mexican province one hundred persons,
among them members of his immediate family. He did not
look too closely into their religious sympathies. In 1590, Caravajal himself was brought up on charges of practicing Judaism. Although the case against him was not proved, he
was removed from office. But there was no doubt about his
nephew, also called Luis de Caravajal, and known as a poet.
He was arrested in 1595. Even in prison the younger Carava-

jal not only boasted of his Jewishness but tried to convert others to his religion, and he was executed one year after his imprisonment. The Inquisition tried its utmost to root out every vestige of the Jews, executing some and imposing severe penalties on others. All it accomplished, however, was to drive them back into the secret practice of Judaism.

For three hundred years no one knew that this small Marrano community existed in Mexico, practicing Judaism and spreading its religion among the Indians. Its existence was not revealed even after freedom of worship was established when Mexico declared its independence from Spain. It is almost miraculous that it managed to retain some knowledge of Jewish worship and ceremonies. Finally, in 1910, the Jews threw off their mask and frankly organized themselves into a Jewish congregation, and by 1925 they had a tiny synagogue in Mexico City. Even then they had not completely rid themselves of their fears, for the synagogue is hidden in a courtyard and remains without any outer symbol of its existence. About 1,000 Indian Jews live in the capital city; some 2,000 more are scattered throughout the country. Their leader, B. Laureano Ramirez, is not a rabbi but a lawyer, and most of the congregants are poor artisans. A number of Reform rabbis from the United States have taken a keen interest in their welfare, providing them with a scroll of the Torah and continuing to encourage them. The organized Jewish communities of Mexico, however, have doubted this entire story and preferred, for some reason, to have little to do with these Indian Jews whose very existence is a tribute to the power of Judaism and a living testimony to its inherent ability to survive the trials of time and the hostility of man.

CHAPTER XI

BETWEEN TWO WARS

OUR GENERATION LIVES THROUGH GOOD AND EVIL DAYS
AND TRIES BRAVELY TO MEET THE PROBLEMS THRUST
UPON IT BY THE DESTRUCTIVE FORCES IN CIVILIZATION

An Era of Light and Shadow—At its beginning, the twentieth century promised to be an age of uninterrupted peace and progress. Advances in the sciences and the arts bade fair to turn the world into the paradise long dreamed of by prophet and philosopher. The growing recognition of the individual's worth was bringing democracy even into lands governed by autocratic monarchs. The nineteenth century had bequeathed a pleasant heritage. Western civilization was reaping a plentiful harvest from its more liberal treatment of the Jews. Antisemitism was not considered anything to worry about in view of the economic and intellectual progress which mankind was making.

Before the century was many years old, the world experienced bitter disappointment in terms of more struggles, greater wars, deeper hatreds. The forces of social, political and economic reaction gained momentum and threatened to overwhelm humanity. In no case was this as evident as in the case of the Jew. On the one hand, it was a golden age, for there never had been a period in Jewish history when the small Jewish group produced so many men of light and leading, so many who contributed greatly to the political, cultural and scientific fields both within and outside of Jewish life. On the other hand, all the reactionary elements in civilization, having mobilized their powers, directed their first attacks against the Jews. Thus, even while Jewish achievements were at their highest, Jewish hearts trembled with foreboding.

1. THE JEWS AND CIVILIZATION

Jews in the Arts—In every country of the world during the past generation, Jews made contributions to the arts out of all proportion to their comparatively small numbers. As though to make up for the long centuries during which they had been denied artistic self-expression, they now entered into these fields with vigor and enthusiasm. In painting Amedeo Modigliani, Joseph Israels and Max Liebermann were three great names among many. In sculpture Moses Jacob Ezekiel, Mark Antokolski, Jo Davidson and Jacob Epstein were leaders in a field quite closed to Jews of a former day. In music, beginning with the minor contributions of Jacques Offenbach, there has been no aspect of the art without a number of important Jewish contributors, from Meyerbeer and Mahler in the nineteenth century to Ernest Bloch and a host of instrumentalists in the present. Even more important has been the fact that the Jewish population has made music, as well as other arts, part of home life and child education. Many patrons, collectors, critics and supporters of museums have been persons of Jewish origin.

Jews in Literature—The contribution of Jews to European and American literature was at least as great as that to the other arts. The mention of outstanding Jewish names in the literatures of various languages would form too long a list for inclusion here. One need but note that as authors and critics Jews sought to interpret the spirit of modern civilization in general as well as the culture of their respective lands. The best of them contributed to the sense of world unity and human brotherhood. It stands to reason that not all Jewish authors were worth while, any more than many non-Jewish authors who merely used writing to earn their livelihood. Moreover, as readers the Jews gave evidence of possessing literary interests both extensive and profound. No doubt this was the result of those many centuries during which books and study played a decisive role in Jewish life.

Jews in Science—Medicine has ever held a particular fascination for the Jews, and modern times again illustrated this fact. As soon as medical schools were opened to Jews, Jewish students flocked to them in unusually large numbers. As a result, the science of medicine is particularly indebted to Jewish researchers. There was Paul Ehrlich, and hundreds of others, in medical research. Sigmund Freud, by his writing and experiments, brought about a revolution in the study of psychology and in the treatment of nervous and mental disorders. Besides, he contributed to progress in education, to character study and training and, more indirectly, to new movements in literature. Freud's theories were no more revolutionary in the study of the mind than were those of Albert Einstein in the realm of physics. He and a number of other physicists of Jewish origin contributed materially to the release of atomic energy. Jews were prominent also in other fields of science. Unfortunately, considerable areas of industrial research had been closed to them to a large extent by prejudiced industrialists and even scientists.

Jews in Politics—The most spectacular form of Jewish participation in contemporary life has been in the field of government. Actually, this was nothing new. Jewish diplomats and financiers, personal advisers and unofficial ambassadors in many states and of many rulers did honorable and patriotic work throughout the ages. Modern times made it possible for Jews to be elected to public office and for them to render such services openly. Where antisemitism was not too rife, Jews rose to cabinet posts and on occasion even to the office of prime minister. For example, Luigi Luzzatti, one of the foremost Italian economists, was prime minister of Italy from 1909 to 1911. So, too, Léon Blum, a man of deep thought and broad human sympathies, was the leader of the mildly socialist party of France and as such twice became prime minister of that country during the 1930s and for a third time, during a critical period, in 1946. England, of course, had a good many Jews in very high office. The most notable in our time was Rufus Isaacs, Marquis of Reading, jurist, administrator and diplomat. As for the United States, one needs but mention that the Supreme Court had three Jewish members before the outbreak of World War II: Louis D. Brandeis, Benjamin N. Cardozo and Felix Frankfurter. Henry Morgenthau, Jr., was secretary of the treasury under Franklin D. Roosevelt, and Herbert H. Lehman was governor of the State of New York from 1932 to 1942. In almost every civilized land Jews figured prominently in civic and national government and their devoted labors won nothing but praise, except, of course, from the antisemites. In addition to those who were openly Jews, men of Jewish origin, but without any Jewish affiliation, have contributed to the welfare of their countries. Of Walter Rathenau mention has already been made. The name of Leon Trotsky also ranks high in a list of this sort, since he, next to Lenin, was the creator of modern Russia.

Jewish Gains and Losses—The many contributions which Jews made to human welfare within the last century thus amply repaid the Western world for the emancipation which it granted them, assuming that such emancipation needs to be justified by anything other than the rights of Jews as human beings. But, if mankind as a whole was the gainer, the Jewish group itself often proved the loser. Many of the men and women who devoted themselves to human progress all too frequently abandoned the culture of their own group. Sometimes this was due to nothing more than lack of time to cultivate the art of Jewish living; at other times it was due to the desire to be of the majority rather than of the unpopular minority. Whatever the reason, the fact remains that the loyalty of some of the greatest contributors to civilization, as well as that of many of their imitators and admirers, was completely lost to the Jewish people. Arthur Schnitzler and Jakob Wassermann, for example, both of the first rank in German literature, were so conscious of the duality of German and Jew that each wrote books which were outright pleas for the Jews to assimilate and thus destroy themselves as a group. (Yet, by the end of his life, each of them recognized that Jewish survival was inevitable and desirable.) There were even Jews who were so anxious to be accepted by the majority that they became leaders in the antisemitic movement. To a greater or lesser extent examples of such spiritual treason have appeared in every land. For, despite the valuable contributions of the Jewish group, the past generation saw anti-Jewishness rising like a tidal wave.

2. REBUILDING ZION

Pioneers and Builders—Apart from the growing contributions of Jews to the science and culture of the world, the period between the two World Wars witnessed some remarkable achievements in the rebuilding of Palestine. The Jews had so long been subjected to antisemitic propaganda that they themselves had begun to doubt their powers. Palestine, since the Balfour Declaration, proved the continued existence, not only of the spirit of self-sacrifice, but also of unsuspected pioneering ability. This was the period of the Third *Aliyah*, the third "going upward" to the Holy Land—the first having been that of the 1880s and the second that which had occurred under early Zionist inspiration from 1900 to 1914. Young men and women, brought up to be merchants or trained in some profession, left shop and school in Europe to organize colonies, drain swamps and build new cities in the ancient but neglected land. The ideal of Zion and the search for a home brought into being a type of peasant the like of whom the world had never seen—a lover of thought, art and literature who turned away from no kind of hard labor on a soil he and his ancestors had dreamed of. For the very land had to be rebuilt. Centuries of neglect had turned it into a desert; the Jewish pioneer (*halutz*) struggled with the elements to make it blossom like a rose. It became dotted with numerous colonies and settlements. Its productivity increased beyond the wildest imaginings of the former Arab owners and the present Arab neighbors. Modern machinery was introduced and the Jordan River was harnessed to electrify increasing portions of the country. Garden suburbs grew up around Old Jerusalem, and an entirely new, all-Jewish city, Tel-Aviv, came into existence on the sand-dunes near Jaffa. Herzl's vision in *Altneuland* could not have been more closely approximated.

Hebrew Language and Culture—Keeping step with the progress of the land was the progress in its Jewish culture. Hebrew once more became the language of the Palestinian Jew, a language revitalized and made supple through use. In it new poets and novelists wrote with vigor and vividness beyond the most fervent hopes of Eliezer ben Yehudah (1858–1922), compiler of the great modern Hebrew dictionary—and the one who had devoted his life to making Hebrew the vernacular of the Jews in Palestine—or of Hayyim Nahman Bialik (1873–1934) and Ahad Ha'am (Asher Ginzberg, 1856–1927), respectively the poet and the essayist of the previous generation who lived to see the modern revival. For the Jewish population of Palestine wrote much and read with unparalleled intellectual hunger. More books were published for the half million Jews of Palestine than for the five millions of America. The number of newspapers and periodicals was also exceptionally large.

The University—Characteristically, the Jewish population lost no time in establishing schools. It considered no sacrifice too great for the physical and mental development of the next generation. To crown the cultural system of the new community, the Hebrew University, opened in 1925 under the presidency of Dr. Judah L. Magnes (1877–1948), grew rapidly in the number of students and departments, until it has become the foremost cultural institution in the Near East. Its experimental work in agriculture has been of incalculable value to Jew and Arab alike. Its work in semitics, archaeology and history has contributed much to the knowledge of the past, Jewish as well as Mohammedan. The more recent addition of refugee professors from Germany made it a center of scholarship rivaling the best the West had to offer. Medical research and instruction at the university was closely integrated with the Hadassah Hospital. Hadassah, the women's Zionist organization founded by the saintly and capable Henrietta Szold (1860–1945), has evoked the enthusiastic support of the Jewish women of America. Their hospital, starting from small beginnings, soon became the finest of its kind in that part of the world. Palestine used to be a disease-ridden country. It is that no longer, either for Jew or for Arab, due to medical science introduced by the Jews.

The Jewish Agency—Before the mandate over Palestine was finally given to Britain, an agreement was reached that every Jewish group be drawn into the task of supervising the building of the Jewish homeland. A "Jewish Agency" was to be created with whom Britain would deal in matters relating to Palestine. At first, the Agency consisted of Zionists only, but it was hoped that representatives of the non-Zionists would join them. After some years of negotiation, such an Agency was finally formed at Zurich, Switzerland, in 1929. Its membership consisted of Zionists and non-Zionists equally. Dr. Chaim Weizmann, president of the World Zionist Organization, and Louis Marshall, the highly respected head of the American non-Zionists, were placed at the head of the Agency. Unfortunately, Louis Marshall died within a few weeks after this achievement of unity. He was succeeded by Felix M. Warburg.

Britain Changes Its Mind—Even while the Jews of the world were applying themselves enthusiastically to the task of upbuilding Palestine and while the Jews of the land were cheered by the remarkable results of their devoted efforts, the British government was taking back, bit by bit, what England and the League of Nations had promised the Jewish people. Every expression of violent opposition by the Arab nationalists was the occasion for a reduction by England of Jewish rights in their homeland. The results of Arab outbreaks of 1920 and 1921 have already been mentioned.* In 1922 the British Colonial Office issued a "White Paper," that is, a gov-

* See above, pp. 618–9.

ernment declaration, by which the promised homeland was deprived of any independent political foundation. It asserted "that the terms of the Declaration [of Balfour] do not contemplate that Palestine as a whole should be converted into a Jewish national home, but that such a home shall be founded in Palestine." All that this White Paper granted the Jews was a chance to build up a Jewish community on the basis of the belief that they were in Palestine "as of right and not of sufferance."

Palestine was quiet for a while thereafter, and not even an economic crisis stopped its growth. It was already clear, however, that the British government both in England and in Palestine was ready to do everything possible to win the Arabs over, if necessary at the expense of the Jews. The Arabs knew this too, and their propaganda among their peasants grew more aggressive from day to day.

In 1929, almost as though in response to the establishment of the Jewish Agency, a riot broke out in Jerusalem and spread over the rest of the country. The pretext was the use by the Jews of the Wailing Wall as a place for prayer. Although the Jews had been doing just that for centuries, the Arabs now discovered an objection. Demonstrations and counter-demonstrations excited everybody. The English administration took no precautions and the rioting cost many lives. The important thing was not so much the riot itself as the fact that it gave the English government an opportunity once more to review the entire question of the Jewish homeland.

Investigating Commissions—An investigating commission was sent to Palestine to place the blame for the disorders. The majority of the commission, employing some strange logic, decided that the Jews were to blame because their growing numbers had increased the fears of the Arabs and because their rapid acquisition of land had left some of the poor Arabs landless. The commission consequently recommended that Jewish immigration be seriously curtailed, that the acquisition of land be stopped and that everything wait until the Arabs were taken care of. The Balfour Declaration, in other words, was to be turned right around and, instead of developing a homeland for the Jews, was to become a means for the economic and political advancement of the Arabs. The fallacies in the commission's report were pointed out by one of its own members who proved that the poorer Arabs benefited from Jewish immigration and that the existence of landless Arabs was only partly due to Jewish land purchase.

Nevertheless, the colonial minister issued another White Paper accepting the conclusions of the majority. The Jewish Agency energetically protested; the English Parliament openly criticized; the Mandates Commission of the League of Nations rejected the English government's view of the situation. Thereupon, Prime Minister Ramsay MacDonald wrote a letter to the heads of the Jewish Agency practically repudiating the White Paper. The result was that nobody knew just where the English government stood, although everyone suspected its good intentions regarding the Jews in Palestine.

Enter the Axis—During the next ten years, the 1930s, while the Jews of Palestine were making progress in the development of the land and its culture, the homeland was forced to fight for its very life. A new enemy had now appeared upon the scene. The aim of fascist Italy and Nazi Germany was to break up the British empire, and in these enemies of England the politically ambitious Arabs found allies. Still the blind British colonial officials stood in the way of the efforts of the Jews to reach an understanding with the poorer Arabs. They continued to curry the favor of the mufti, that ambitious, rapacious and violent leader of the upperclass Arabs, although it was obvious that he was helping the flood of propaganda loosed upon his people from Germany and Italy. Acts of terrorism increased; murder on the highways became a frequent occurrence. Beginning with 1936 there was open insurrection. Jewish colonies were attacked and the British soldiers had to take up arms in self-defense. The mufti's henchmen, imitating Nazi tactics, used gangster methods against any Arab who refused to join them. With superhuman self-restraint the Jews adopted the policy of not retaliating for acts of terror. But this policy, too, failed to quiet the storm.

The White Paper of 1939—England sent another investigating commission. In 1937 it issued its report which advocated the partition of Palestine into Jewish, Arab and English districts, although the territorial advantages were to go to the Arabs. But the arrangement created more difficulties than it solved, and every party rejected it. As never before, Palestine was serving the Jewish cause by giving an example of Jewish heroism in the face of danger, by building in a time of general destruction, by providing a home for the homeless. On the other hand, a conference of Jews and Arabs, called in London by the British government early in 1939, showed the weakness of that government and its willingness to yield to terror in Palestine just as it was yielding to terror by Germany in Europe. It issued another White Paper in which it declared that the building of the Jewish homeland was now completed, that during the next five years only 75,000 Jews would be admitted to Palestine, and that no more would be admitted thereafter without Arab consent. It furthermore made difficult any purchase of land by Jews, and promised self-government for Palestine in ten years. The cruelest part of this White Paper was that it restricted Jewish immigration into Palestine at the very time when millions of European Jews were facing merciless destruction.

3. Confusion in Europe

The Basic Problem—The fundamental problem which had to be solved at the end of World War I was that of economic reorganization. Soldier and civilian alike, returning to normal life after four years of slaughter and emotional instability, sought in vain for the better world which had been promised them. Most of them returned to more grinding poverty and greater insecurity. Every country's statesmen were destined to be harassed by the economic question more than ever before in the history of their nation. That no happy solution was found anywhere was tragic for all humanity and infinitely more tragic for the Jews.

Reorientation in Russia—In what was left of the vast empire of the czars, the solution offered for Russia's, indeed for the whole world's, ills was communism. Private property in the means of production was abolished. The state undertook to modify each person's life so as to uproot the very idea of such individual property rights. All this affected the Jews both as Jews and as members of the middle class. A very large number of Jews, perhaps the majority, had been merchants, either on a commission basis or as small shopkeepers. Some twenty-five per cent had been artisans, doing manual labor in their own homes or employed in the factories which had been slowly developing as czarist Russia became industrialized. Only the latter, the factory workers, fitted at once into the new order of Russian society. The rest of the three million Jews had to readjust their lives almost overnight. But even if they were willing to make the readjustment, the industries were not yet there into which they might have entered.

Along with the economic, a social and religious transformation was demanded of the Russian Jews. The Russian Revolution, like the French Revolution a hundred and fifty years previously, looked upon the Church as an ally of the former regime. All religion was suspect; religious teachers were feared as counter-revolutionaries; synagogues as well as churches were closed. There could no longer be any Jewish community, nor a rabbi, nor even a teacher of Hebrew. The six-day week, which was soon introduced, made Sabbath observance almost impossible. Moreover, the new rulers of Russia objected to Zionism, Lenin and the Bolshevist party having long before taken the stand that Zionism was a movement among the Jews of the lower middle class in which the working class had no interest. They now regarded the Balfour Declaration as an expression of British imperialism. A Zionist was therefore considered a person who not only wanted to weaken Russia by urging emigration, but who also sought to transfer his allegiance to the hostile British empire. By the same token, the cultivation of Hebrew and its literature was under suspicion.

At the same time the Soviet government tried to make it unnecessary for the Jews to seek homes outside of Russia. It granted that the Jews might constitute themselves a separate nationality, like the other ethnic groups within the Soviet Union, and use their own (Yiddish) language and organize their own schools. A Jewish university was in fact established in Minsk, and several Yiddish newspapers were founded. These cultural institutions were thoroughly anti-religious. Indeed, the Jewish section of the Communist party was rabid in its opposition to Judaism. Antisemitism, however, was proscribed in the Soviet state, since it weakened Russia by creating divisions within it, and all differences in legal status between Jews and non-Jews were abolished.

To alleviate the economic hardships among the Jews, the government offered land in the Ukraine and the Crimea. In 1924, the American Jewish Joint Distribution Committee decided to supply part of the funds needed for this project. The Russian government provided the land and made many concessions to help the settlers get started. Within the new settlements, wherever the Jews were a majority of the population, they enjoyed the same rights of autonomy as other ethnic groups similarly situated. In 1929, after some 15,000 Jewish families had thus been settled in southern Russia, the government announced a much more ambitious plan, namely, the establishment of an autonomous Jewish republic in Biro-Bidjan, an almost uninhabited region of Central Siberia. Cold, distant and wild, though rich in natural resources, this territory required hardier pioneers than even colonial America had attracted. Reports on this experiment have varied widely. In 1940 the Jewish population of Biro-Bidjan was still very far from the 100,000 for which the government had hoped. A good many more must have sought refuge there during the war years, and a number of industries were established there. Nevertheless, the Jewish population of the area had, by the 1960s, sunk to 15,000.

In the meantime, more than two decades of communist rule had brought about a measure of adjustment in the rest of Russia. The old and unadjustable people died; the young were absorbed into the new system. No one twenty years previously could have predicted the extent to which the Jews would enter industry. The cultural situation, on the other hand, did not improve. Only eighteen per cent of the children in the places of old Jewish settlement attended Yiddish schools in 1940; the rest preferred to go to the general schools. The number of readers of Yiddish newspapers fell in the same year to 40,000. After 1934, to be sure, the Soviet government relaxed its anti-religious drive, and there was said to be a return to religion among the Russian Christians; but the effect of this upon the Russian Jews remained doubtful.

Reaction in Poland—No such radical solution of the ever-present economic problem was attempted in Poland and in the other states created by the treaty of Versailles. In fact, there was nothing which these states feared more than communism. Nationalist feelings ran high, but the landless peasants and the unemployed thousands of the urban population demanded something more than patriotic sentiments to live on. One obvious solution might have been the re-distribution of some land from the vast estates held by the nobility in Poland and in the other East and Southeast European states. Any such suggestion, however, was branded as communistic and, therefore, not to be considered. Starving peasants flocked to the cities and swelled the ranks of the unemployed. The best the government could think of was to make the people forget their personal difficulties by emphasizing the political and international problems above the economic. Before Poland was many years old, a military dictatorship was established, less for purposes of defense than in order to compel internal obedience in the name of unity.

Under such circumstances, the minority populations of the country were looked upon with greater suspicion than ever before. The insistence of the Jews upon minority rights was offered as proof of their lack of patriotism. First the amount of money granted the Jews for communal administration and education was cut to an insignificant sum, despite Poland's obligations under the minorities treaty upon which her independence had been conditioned. Thereafter the Jews had to tax themselves apart from the state taxes. But more important than that was the direct economic attack upon the Jewish population. In Hungary and Rumania as well as in Poland the argument ran that Christian Hungarians, Rumanians or Poles would be better off if the Jews were removed from business and industry. The history of the Middle Ages had proved that such restrictions hindered rather than improved the flow of economic life. The East European politicians, however, cared little about history. The removal of the Jews was an argument which the masses could follow. Besides, it drew the attention of the masses from a search for any real solution of their problems. The governments of these states used their taxing power to ruin many Jewish-owned businesses. They ran cooperatives which competed with Jewish stores and shops, and which refused to employ Jews. Difficulties were placed in the way of Jews entering the professions. Finally, lest any Jews manage to surmount all these obstacles, the antisemites preached a relentless boycott. There were fistfights and riots on the streets and even in the classrooms of the universities. Fortunately, the Jewish students defended themselves, or the situation might have been considerably worse.

Marshal Joseph Pilsudski, hero and dictator of Poland, who was not the ordinary militarist, acted as a restraining influence. Besides, the truly liberal elements in Poland and elsewhere recognized official antisemitism for what it was—a means for hiding the government's lack of program to solve its country's problems. The more intelligent labor union leaders did their utmost to counteract the anti-Jewish propaganda. With the death of Pilsudski (1935), the situation changed for the worse. The avowed object of the new Polish government, as well as of the governments of Rumania and Hungary, was to force the Jews to leave. The financial assistance which poured into the country, for the most part through the American Jewish Joint Distribution Committee, saved many Jews of Eastern Europe from starvation. The ORT, an international Jewish organization for the retraining of people for manual labor, helped somewhat to readjust Jewish men and women everywhere in Eastern Europe to the new situation which confronted them. But only thousands received aid where millions were in need. The most important

Jewish community in the world, that of Poland, which had supplied the reserves of Jewish spiritual strength for four centuries, was faced with ruin and dissolution.

Betrayal in Germany—The Jews of Poland were at least accustomed to poverty; antisemitism also was nothing new to them. The Jews of Germany, however, were in a different situation. The mild socialist government which succeeded that of the kaiser was incapable of solving the economic problems and powerless to heal the sense of humiliation. The Jews were blamed for the economic ruin of Germany, although it was notorious that certain Christian German capitalists had been the real economic vultures. Those who made these charges knew that they were false; but lying was their policy; and their lies, repeated frequently and energetically, sank into the minds of the people.

Two political parties grew by leaps and bounds in Germany: the communists and the national socialists (Nazis). The program of neither held out much hope for Jewish survival. The communists offered at least political and economic equality, even if they discouraged religion. The national socialists, on the other hand, boasted of the complete extermination which they would visit on the Jews, and used antisemitism with diabolical skill to advertise themselves and to gain adherents. On the defenseless Jewish group they heaped the blame for everything wrong with the world. Using the pseudo-scientific theory of racial differences, they contrasted what they called the Jewish and the Aryan "races." The latter was held up to be the supreme biological development of humanity and, therefore, deserved to rule the world, while the rest of humanity was destined for enslavement to it, especially to its purest branch—the German. The Nazis, laughed at for this mixture of false science and bloodthirsty arrogance, nevertheless kept growing in numbers. Adolf Hitler, ferocious in his hates, limitless in his promises, cunning in his lies, became the hero of the masses. The fear of communism on the part of the middle and upper classes proved a powerful ally of the Nazis. Finally, the Prussian nobility sought to protect their own interest and treacherously betrayed the German republic. In 1933 the Nazis gained control of the state and Hitler became the dictator of Germany.

Nazi Culture—Hitler made good his word regarding the Jews. Their businesses were boycotted and their possessions confiscated for the benefit of so-called Aryans; stealing, like lying, became a matter of national policy. The race doctrine was made the law of the land. The laws promulgated by the

662 THE SEARCH FOR A FRIENDLY HOME

Nazi party conference at Nuremberg in September, 1935, deprived Jews of their German citizenship and instituted racial distinctions which outdid anything the Middle Ages had imposed upon them. Nazi Germany "purified" itself of Jewish influences culturally too. One of the first acts of the Nazis after coming to power was to make a bonfire of the books which they judged hostile to their cause or, as they put it, hostile to the German spirit. Most prominent among the books burned were those of the German Jewish authors. No such books could thereafter be read; no music written by a Jew could be played.

Nazi Propaganda—Humanitarians and liberals expressed disgust with the treatment of the Jews by the Germans, but the governments of the world preferred to consider this an internal German matter with which they could not interfere. Hitler had correctly estimated the situation when he argued that generations of antisemitic propaganda had so affected the mind of the Western world that few would come to the defense of Jews and many would justify whatever action he took against them. Posing as saviors of the world from the Jews, the Nazis carried forward their plots against civilization, developed their military plans, robbed their neighbors and attacked religion and culture in Germany itself. In this way, antisemitism, from its very beginning a mask for reaction, became the means for disorganizing the mind of the world and destroying its peace. By September, 1939, the Nazis were ready to start the war for which they had been preparing.

The Search for a Refuge—The half million Jews who had been so thoroughly German, and the Christian liberals whom the Nazis persecuted with equal hate, sought to escape from the bloodthirsty masters of the German state. The Jews organized themselves into one body (Reichsvertretung der deutschen Juden) whose main object was to find places where they might emigrate and to retrain such prospective emigrants for manual labor abroad. Special attention was given to the younger people, who might still adjust themselves to life outside of Germany. In all countries the Jews established committees to aid the refugees, the National Refugee Service in the United States doing valiant work in helping the newcomers meet their new situations.

The World's Conscience—Unfortunately, the response of humanity was not adequate to the situation. In September, 1933, the League of Nations created an office to handle the problem of the German refugees, with James G. MacDonald as high commissioner. Whether because the Nazis were afraid that the would-be emigrants would gain the respect of the other nations, or simply because they wanted to bedevil the rest of the world, they tried to prevent any country from accepting the very people whom they were driving out of Germany. The weak League of Nations did not stand behind MacDonald, and he resigned in December, 1935. In various parts of the world immigration laws were made more strict. In Latin America, some countries, which could easily have absorbed all the German refugees and more, very much to their cultural and economic benefit, succumbed to the influence of Germany. Even the United States consular officers in Germany used their authority to interpret harshly the restrictive clauses of the American immigration laws. Liberal elements in various countries did, to be sure, come to the aid of the refugees. France, Holland and Belgium permitted tens of thousands of them to enter, though they usually placed obstacles in the way of their earning a livelihood. Great Britain, between 1933 and 1939, admitted about 75,000, not all of them Jews. The United States, between 1933 and 1942, admitted about 175,000 from Germany, Austria, Bohemia and other Nazi-dominated lands. But there were hundreds of thousands more who could have been saved, but were not. Moreover, Britain in 1939 shut the doors of Palestine, the one country which welcomed the refugees and where 200,000 of them (most of them from Poland), including a great many children, had found asylum since 1933—the so-called Fifth *Aliyah*.

The Evian Conference—As the situation went from bad to worse, President Roosevelt called a conference of all nations to solve the refugee problem. It met at Evian, in France, and there was hope at first that some countries would open their doors. But the Germans, carrying on their sinister propaganda, prevailed. Various Latin American countries agreed to permit small numbers to enter, provided they brought with them considerable sums of money. Thus antisemitism killed that human decency which centuries of development had produced as the finest fruits of human progress. At about that time, Austria with its 200,000 Jews fell into the hands of the Nazis; and a little later Czechoslovakia, with its 350,000 Jews, suffered the same fate. In November, 1938, the Nazis organized pogroms in every German city, burning the synagogues, looting Jewish homes and driving the Jews, almost indiscriminately, into concentration camps. There was a new

flood of refugees, the last before Germany started on its final
bid for world domination.

4. THE CHALLENGE TO AMERICAN ISRAEL

Americans All—While the Jewish situation in Europe was
moving towards tragic disintegration, and while Palestine
struggled to be reborn, American Jewry began to emerge as a
great reservoir of Jewish strength and hope. The Jewish population of the United States during that generation grew to
about 4,770,000. A third of this population lived in New
York City, and ninety per cent of the total number lived in
towns with a population of 100,000 or more. In proportion
to their numbers, the Jews were more numerous in shopkeep-
ing and in the professions and less numerous in other occupations, such as farming, in which only about 100,000 Jews
were engaged. But in a land where freedom prevails such
figures present no cause for criticism. Men live and work as
they please; all that can be expected of them is that they act
as good citizens. Their participation in the life of the nation
was so full and wholehearted that it was difficult to point to
any specifically Jewish contribution as distinct from a non-
Jewish one. Individual Jews became prominent in one or another field, especially in the cultural. Jews of the second generation in America became all but indistinguishable from
Jews or Christians whose ancestors had been native Americans for many generations. They adopted the same attitudes,
the same political views, hopes and hobbies, dress and manners. Left alone, the Jews of the United States would have
been the happiest Jewish community since the days of the
Golden Age in Spain. Unfortunately, serious economic problems at home and hostile influences from abroad disturbed
the relations between the Jewish and the Christian Americans.

Immigration and Antisemitism—Anti-Jewish feeling had
been rising slowly in the United States even before World
War I. But as long as American industry and commerce were
expanding, antisemitism was a minor social disease of which
true Americans were ashamed. It showed itself among the
newly-rich class in the form of social snobbery and among
the Christian immigrants and their descendants as part of the
mental baggage brought over from the Old World. Unfortunately, the unsettled conditions of the globe, when World
War I was over, gave unscrupulous adventurers an opportu-

nity to capitalize on these feelings. Russian communism was the great bogey, and a number of Russian czarist refugees spread among Americans the charge that the Jews, rather than the rottenness and cruelty of the old order in Russia, had brought about the victory of the Bolshevik regime. They persuaded the immensely wealthy Henry Ford to support their theory and to help them popularize in the United States the mendacious *Protocols of the Elders of Zion*. Ford publicly admitted later that he had been misled, but by that time much harm had already been done.

Even more serious was the spread of the unscientific theory of race differences. On the assumption that the United States had been built up by immigrants from Northern and Western Europe, an agitation began for restricting further immigration from Southern and Eastern Europe, whose peoples were called "undesirable." Anti-immigration propaganda was in reality directed against the Jews, since they were the greatest sufferers from the post-war conflicts in Eastern Europe and would, therefore, be the most likely applicants for admittance to the United States. A flood of prejudiced pamphlets and speeches drowned out the old concept of America as the land of refuge and its ideal of human equality. Congress passed strict anti-immigration laws over the veto of the president (1922).

Antisemitism, thus encouraged, did not stop with restricting immigration. It became more or less fashionable even among the presumably cultured classes. A restrictive policy was adopted by several of the important universities, so that openly or secretly the number of Jews admitted to colleges was limited and obstacles were placed in the way of their entering professional schools. The situation was nevertheless fairly tolerable during the days of prosperity in the 1920s. It grew worse during the depression which began in 1929 and it reached alarming proportions from 1933 on. For the Nazis and their friends in the United States, following their usual method of undermining the internal peace and unity of a country by means of antisemitic propaganda, spent many millions of dollars to stir hatred of the Jews. Only after World War II broke out in 1939 did many Americans begin to realize that antisemitism was a weapon used to destroy democracy.

The Burden of World Jewry—In addition to their growing internal problems the Jews of the United States had to assume the task of solving the problems which faced Jews in other parts of the world. The Joint Distribution Committee and the United Palestine Appeal raised about $4,000,000 every year for the building of Palestine and for the growing needs of East European Jewry. The disintegration of the German Jewish community after the rise of the Nazis added the further problem of aiding the refugees. This enormous self-taxation, unparalleled in any other group, spoke well for the sense of responsibility of American Israel.

Community Organization—Community organization made great strides forward because of these very needs. Jewish leaders at last realized that, whether it be antisemitism, Jewish education or the placement of refugees in jobs, Jewish problems in America called for the joint efforts of all American Jews. At the same time, the vastness of the effort revealed other, less happy, aspects of Jewish life in the United States. A very large number of Jews in every community failed altogether to contribute to Jewish causes and projects, thus indicating a complete loss of interest in Jewish life. Besides, of the two great problems, that of assuring the future of the Jewish heritage and that of living at peace with their neighbors, almost every official community organization all but neglected the first and interpreted the second only in terms of fighting antisemitism.

Organized Religion—Judaism as a religion in the United States became better organized during the twentieth century. Three types of religious thought emerged from the debates at the end of the previous century: Orthodoxy, Conservatism and Reform. Each type developed institutions for the furtherance of its point of view. The Hebrew Union College continued through its many highly gifted alumni to exert unusual influence upon American Jewish life. Conservative Judaism began to make good progress through the alumni of the Jewish Theological Seminary. Orthodox Judaism established many schools and synagogues. In 1915 the Rabbi Isaac Elchanan Theological Seminary, founded in 1896, was reorganized and Bernard Revel (1885–1940) became its president. Later a college of arts was added to it as well as a graduate school, the whole making up the Yeshiva University. Other theological schools of orthodox tendency were established in Chicago and Baltimore. The Hebrew Theological College, in Chicago, was founded in 1922, with Saul Silver (d. 1946) as president. Ninety of its graduates held rabbinic posts in 1947. Finally, the Jewish Institute of Religion was founded in New York in 1922 by Stephen S. Wise in an attempt at sectarian non-partisanship, so that its graduates might serve any one of the religious groupings. These rabbinical institutions give evidence of an American Israel fully independent of the religious guidance of Europe upon which it had had to rely only two generations ago.

The graduates of these schools, despite their differences in the interpretation of Judaism, had in common a desire to root this faith in American soil. In a sense they represented various experiments in the development of a Judaism adjusted to the American spirit, and they were all equally subject to the influences of the new movements within Judaism. As distinctions in the social and economic standing of their adherents disappeared, these bodies became more conscious of the actual religious differences which separated them, thus making for a religious life more healthy because less confused by externals.

The Columbus Platform—The growing awareness of religious needs as well as of the claims of Jewish tradition was illustrated by the action of the Central Conference of American Rabbis at its annual meeting held at Columbus in 1937. It was there voted to replace the Pittsburgh Platform with a new statement of Reform principles. The Columbus Platform, while retaining the basic Reform emphasis on prophetic as against rabbinic Judaism, no longer spoke in the rationalistic terminology of its predecessor and granted a place to tradition and ceremonialism. It called attention to the need for Jewish education and culture among the Jews of America. It expressed a fervent hope for the establishment of the Jewish homeland as a center of spiritual life.

Reconstructionism—A new attempt at the interpretation of Judaism appeared under the name of Reconstructionism. It cut across religious group lines. It defined Judaism as "an evolving religious civilization," and argued that, although a man's theology and observances were an important part of his life as a Jew, they were only a part. A full Jewish life demanded participation in cultural and communal activity as well as adherence to ethical conduct and moral principles. Reconstructionism therefore advocated the formation of strongly centralized Jewish communities. It was also staunchly Zionist. Religiously it was, on the whole, traditionalist, although in this respect its attitude remained rather vague.

Cultural Progress—The first generation of the twentieth century had witnessed the development in the United States of a great many cultural institutions. Jewish education emerged from the chaotic conditions of the earlier days. Many communities supported Jewish schools (*Talmud Torahs*), while most Orthodox and all Conservative congregations organized weekday schools of their own. All-day religious schools were established in a number of cities. Methods and discipline improved. Moreover, adult study groups were organized. American Jewry began to contribute its share to Jewish scholarship. A great achievement in spreading Jewish information was the publication of two comprehensive encyclopedias: the scholarly and authoritative *Jewish Encyclopedia* (1901–6) and the more popular *Universal Jewish Encyclopedia* (1939–43). Several important scientific periodicals made their appearance and a number of public bodies assumed the task of stimulating Jewish literature. Of these the Jewish Publication Society of America made the widest appeal. In 1917 it completed the translation of the Hebrew Bible into English. The committee of seven scholars who did this work thus became the latest successors to those seventy who, twenty-two centuries ago, according to Jewish tradition, produced the Septuagint.* In both cases the motive for the translation was the same, namely, to reopen the treasures of the Bible to those who, living in a land of the Diaspora, possessed an inadequate knowledge of Hebrew. Jewish culture in Hebrew and in Yiddish also made remarkable progress. The *Histadruth Ivrith* (Hebrew Culture Organization), in addition to aiding in the publication of a Hebrew weekly, *Hadoar* (The Post), published books of literary merit. Yiddish-speaking Jews of various tendencies in politics and culture established organizations and schools of their own. The YIVO (*Yiddisher Vissenshaftlicher Institut* —Yiddish Scientific Institute) functioned since 1925 in cooperation with its parent body in Vilna, and since 1939 independently, for the furtherance of scholarly research in the Yiddish language, and has a number of important volumes to its credit.

Great as has been the cultural progress of that generation, it was not enough, however, to make up for a century of cultural neglect. A large number of Jewish children still did not attend a Jewish school, and only a comparatively small number of adults fully recognized the supreme importance of cultural institutions for the survival of the Jewish group. But American Israel was undoubtedly on the way, in 1939, to high achievement in this field, when its progress was interrupted by the terrible calamity of World War II.

* See above, pp. 56.

CHAPTER XII

THE SECOND WORLD WAR AND ITS CONSEQUENCES

WORLD WAR II AND THE PERIOD FOLLOWING IT BRING
TRAGEDY AND HEROISM TO THE JEWS OF THE WORLD
AND THEIR GREATEST CHALLENGE TO THE JEWS OF
AMERICA

Humanity at the Crossroads—The tragic chapter in the history of the Jews, the one dealing with events since 1939, can be written only in superlatives. Though brief, this period saw the nations of the world gripped in the greatest and most destructive of all wars, Western civilization on the very edge of self-destruction, and the Jews overwhelmed by indescribable horrors. At the same time, the problems facing mankind had never been so apparent to so large a segment of the world's population, nor the principles of their solution so clear. Never before had so many people sensed so deeply the urgent need for human brotherhood or held so profoundly the conviction that the familiar type of nationalism was a curse to mankind. Nevertheless, after the fighting had ceased, there was still no evidence that the leaders of the nations had learned the elementary lessons of human history. The old economic rivalries, the old national lust for power and dominion, the old insistence upon class privilege still dominated the thinking of some social groups within the nations and of most molders of public opinion. As so often in the past, the fate of the Jews and the attitude of the nations towards them served as the barometer of mankind's moral health.

At the end of World War II, the Jews were faced with two herculean tasks: to recover from the terrible physical injuries inflicted upon them by a brutalized portion of mankind, and to strengthen the forces seeking justice and human brotherhood. Numerous problems rising from the inner structure and needs of the Jewish people also clamored for solution: the achievement of internal unity, a genuine equality of economic opportunity, a hospitable environment to develop the distinctive Jewish culture, and aid in finding for a distressingly large number a place which they could call their home. In the course of these few years, during and after the war, the Jews of the world displayed qualities of heroism and loyalty of which any generation in their long past could well have been proud; and Israel emerged as an independent state.

1. WHEN MURDER RULED

Brutalized Germany—After six years of militarization and self-glorifying propaganda, after personal liberty and minority opinion had been thoroughly eradicated, the Germany of poets and scientists ceased to exist and in its place goose-stepped a military state that worshipped force as the sole test of greatness and its own will as the only measure of justice. It was led by a band of fanatics and cutthroats in comparison with whom Attila the Hun was a man of honor and the Ukrainian Chmelnitzki a kindly and merciful gentleman. The Germans had bullied their neighbors into submissiveness and cowed the democratic nations into repeated compromises. But that did not satisfy the Nazis. They wanted the world to surrender to them unconditionally. The democratic peoples had not taken the warning implied in the Germans' treatment of the Jews between 1933 and 1939, and now they had to expiate their failure of mind and conscience by six years of blood, sweat and tears.

Europe Engulfed—Poland, whose governing class had admired the Nazis, adopted many of their doctrines and imitated much of their nationalistic conduct, was the first to suffer devastation. Invaded in September, 1939, and conquered within a few weeks, its cities were bombed without mercy and its population was all but enslaved. After the Polish invasion, England and France declared war on Germany; but they were not ready for the kind of warfare which the Germans waged. German propaganda had hoodwinked their governments and divided their populations into groups suspicious of and hostile to each other. In France, especially, class hatreds had been fostered and violent antisemitism was used to throw the people off their guard. When, in the spring of 1940, the Nazis, violating their repeated pledges, seized Norway, Holland and Belgium, France fell easily into German hands. The traitorous elements, who helped deliver all these countries into the hands of their enemy, were found to be identical with the preachers of antisemitism. Germany, with victory almost within its grasp, now turned eastward to annihilate Russia. Here, too, its military might at first made phenomenal progress, overrunning the rest of Poland, the Baltic states and the Ukraine, territories inhabited by millions of Jews. Several Balkan states joined the Nazis and the Italian fascists; others were conquered by them. The Jews of continental Europe, with very few exceptions, now fell into the grasp of their deadly foes.

Jews in the Allied Armies—More than a million Jews officially enrolled in the fighting forces of the nations opposed to Germany. They were divided by country as follows:

	Total Jewish Population	Number in Service
United States	4,770,000	550,000
Russia	3,000,000	500,000
Great Britain	300,000	60,000
Canada	170,000	17,000
South Africa	90,000	10,000

These figures do not include the many thousands of Jews who fought in the armies of other allies or who were active in the resistance movements in France, Italy and elsewhere, or the remarkable contribution of the Jews of Palestine.

The Fate of Europe's Jews—The Nazis had been fond of expressing in their favorite songs these two sentiments: to rule the entire world, and to see the streets run red with Jewish blood. Having all too well achieved their latter aim in Germany and Austria before 1939, they set about to accomplish it during the war years in the rest of Europe. Their arrival in any country immediately initiated the execution or deportation of German and Austrian refugees. They deprived the native Jews of the invaded country of their businesses (which were given to traitorous sympathizers with Germany as rewards); they reduced Jewish food rations to less than that of the rest of the population; and they compelled the Jews to wear a yellow Shield of David (the six-pointed star), a revival of the medieval Jewish badge. They followed this up with wholesale deportations. They set aside a number of places in Eastern Europe in which they concentrated Jews from other lands, in line with the avowed Nazi policy of "freeing" all of Europe from Jewish influence. The more vigorous deportees they picked out for labor as slaves in German factories, where they were not treated as human beings at all, but as expendable material which could be thrown away when used up.

Extermination Camps—Trains of sealed box-cars crammed with human cargo could be seen passing over every European railroad. Men, women and children were crowded within them without food, without provision for sanitation, without so much as room to sit down. The trip might take days or weeks; and many died long before they reached their destination, their corpses mixed with the miserable living. Their destination was in any case but one stop before the grave. German scientific efficiency outdid itself in experiments with poisons on living bodies, especially those of children. Human beings were killed with a sadism unparalleled in the history of crime. Yet the slaughter of individuals was not enough for the Nazis. To speed the process they invented gas chambers. Here hundreds of people could be killed at one time and at low cost, and their corpses disposed of in huge crematoriums. The process was speedy and efficient, an index of German ingenuity and racial superiority.

The Warsaw Ghetto—Those Jews who succeeded in evading the Nazis joined the underground forces of the captive countries. Their stories of individual valor are gradually becoming known as part of the heroic struggle of liberation through which so much of Europe went. One story, however, that of the Warsaw ghetto, is exclusively Jewish. The Warsaw ghetto, like similar ones in a number of Polish towns, confined the local Jewish population as well as deportees from other countries. Soon after its establishment, in October, 1940, it contained half a million people, 200,000 more than the area held ordinarily. It was surrounded by a high wall; its inmates were provided with very little food, and that the worst possible, and they were deprived of hygienic aids and medicines. The death rate was so high that the daily burials had to be made in mass graves. Nevertheless, the Jews organized a pathetic semblance of community life in which mutual assistance and the education of children were the dominant features. The Jews refused to become demoralized.

The Liquidation of the Ghetto—In July, 1942, the Germans began a systematic liquidation of the Warsaw ghetto, just as they were doing with similarly imprisoned Jewish populations elsewhere. In order to prevent resistance and rebellion, the Nazis resorted to trickery and sly subterfuge to keep their victims ignorant of their ultimate fate. No one knew for certain, but everyone suspected, what was happening to the 6,000 to 10,000 persons who were deported from Warsaw daily. By the autumn of 1942 only some 40,000 remained in the Warsaw ghetto, and for a time the deportations ceased.

On January 19, 1943, they were to be resumed, and there then occurred the first active opposition to the Germans on the part of Warsaw's Jews. The Nazis took a fearful revenge; yet this was but the prelude to a greater uprising a few months later.

Revolt in the Ghetto—From the beginning, some of the Jews had kept in touch with the underground forces outside the ghetto. At great risk they had smuggled in a quantity of small arms and ammunition which they kept hidden against the day when plans for resistance would be completed. Evidently that day had been postponed so long because of the unwillingness of the Jewish community leaders to believe the reports about the Germans. But by early 1943, the remaining Jews chose to die fighting.

On April 19, 1943, which happened to fall on the first night of Passover, a detachment of Nazis arrived in the ghetto to deport a number of Jews and their families. They were greeted with pistol shots and hand grenades. Thus began a struggle which lasted for more than a month. Practically unarmed, the population, consisting for the most part of women and children, held off all the might that the Germans could muster—their tanks, their field guns and their airplanes. Most of the ghetto was soon on fire. Any Jew who was caught was tortured to death or thrown into the flames. The Germans were acting in accordance with their Nazi training; the Jews fought with Maccabean courage and intelligence. Every house became a fortress under the flags of Zion and of Poland; every street was a battlefield. The German losses were high. On the forty-second day of fighting only one house still remained standing, and the few surviving Jews contested every floor until none was left to fight. Warsaw, the Nazis triumphantly announced, was at last "free of Jews."

The Toll—The Jews had been the first victims of the Nazi frenzy. This was, in a sense, a compliment to everything that the Jews and Judaism have stood for; but it was a very costly compliment. No people against whom the Nazis waged war, with the possible exception of the Russians, suffered so many killed. Russia, however, was a huge country with a very large population. Proportionately, therefore, the Jews made infinitely greater sacrifices, in terms of those slain for the cause of human freedom, than any other group or nation. For the Nazis had destroyed—in cold blood, and not on the field of battle—six million Jews, a third of the Jewish population of the world and more than half of the Jews of Europe. The best available figures on the number of Jews in various European countries are as follows:

	Before 1939	Alive after 1945
Russia	about 3,000,000	2,000,000
Poland	3,000,000	120,000
Rumania	850,000	300,000
Hungary	400,000	200,000
Czechoslovakia	360,000	50,000
Germany	500,000 (in 1933) reduced to 200,000 in 1939	a few hundred
Austria	200,000	3,000
France	300,000	180,000
Holland	150,000	30,000
Italy	50,000	20,000
Belgium	100,000	30,000
Greece	75,000	10,000

Cultural Losses—The Nazis were enemies not only of Jews but also of Jewish ideas. Having celebrated their conquest of the German people by a book-burning festival, in May, 1933, the Nazis continued their war against the human intellect through systematic confiscations of public and private Jewish libraries and records in every country they overran. Their object was to collect vast libraries for the purpose of reinterpreting the history of the Jews in order to justify their own actions. Books which did not serve this purpose they consigned to destruction. Had they won the war, they would no doubt have done the same to the other libraries of the world, so as to reinterpret human culture in general and deprive civilization of any possibility of refuting Nazi doctrines for generations to come. For it was a cardinal principle of the Nazis that all art, science and research must serve their cause, and most German intellectuals were not slow in cooperating with this objective. Millions of displaced Jewish books were found after the war in concentration camps of their own. Their fate, too, now that their former owners had for the most part been killed, rested in the hands of the nations victorious over Germany.

2. The Failure of the Western Spirit

Christian Aid—The largest number of Jewish lives in Europe was saved by the Russians who, upon the outbreak of war between them and the Nazis, opened their frontiers wide and permitted tens of thousands from Poland and the Baltic countries to seek refuge behind their lines. As the Russian armies retreated, they saved as many of the civilian population as they could, making no distinction between Jews and non-Jews. In Western Europe, many Christians, ofttimes at the risk of their own lives, extended protection to their Jewish fellow citizens and to refugees. Jewish children, against whom the Nazi fury raged especially, were often taken into Christian homes. In Holland, Denmark and Norway, there were occasional public demonstrations of solidarity with the Jews. When, for example, the order was given for Jews to wear a yellow Shield of David, numerous Christian Netherlanders appeared in public with similar badges. A number of clergymen, both Protestant and Catholic, were among the rescuers of Jews. In Italy, where the population had never been anti-Jewish, despite the urgings of the fascist party, the deportation and murder of Jews began only after the Allied invasion of the peninsula, when the Germans became masters of the country. There were Italian priests and monks who, like those elsewhere, went out of their way to save Jewish lives. Several thousand Jews were at one time harbored within Vatican City. The sympathies of Pope Pius XII were not outspoken, though it was known that he condemned the barbarities which were being perpetrated against the Jews. Yet all these heartening examples had no apparent effect upon the corporate conscience of Western Christendom.

When Common Decency Was Lacking—The number of Jews saved through the intervention and assistance of good people amounted to thousands, whereas the number in danger and eventually murdered amounted to millions. Could they have been saved? The extent of the slaughter was, to be sure, not quite realized by the peoples who made up the United Nations; but the governments and the newspapers must have known the truth. Several American church bodies passed general resolutions urging aid. The heads of various states among the United Nations issued pious statements promising the Jews peace and equality of treatment after the war would be won. But nothing was done until almost at the end of the war to rescue even those comparatively few who could have been transported out of German-occupied Europe by way of Switzerland and Turkey. By dint of arduous efforts on the part of Jewish relief organizations, devious subterfuges and large private funds, about 125,000 were saved during the war years. Obviously, therefore, many more of those in danger could have been rescued if the Allied governments and peoples had been more cooperative. President Franklin D. Roosevelt made two attempts to help those stricken. At his instance, a number of Allied nations sent representatives to a conference which was held at Bermuda on April 19–30, 1943, the very days when the last remnants of the Warsaw ghetto were fighting their losing battle against the Nazis. The Bermuda Conference was held behind closed doors—the nations represented were ashamed to reveal their attitude—and it bore no fruit. On January 22, 1944, President Roosevelt appointed a War Refugee Board, with John W. Pehle as chairman, and ordered consular officials in the Balkans to help save as many lives as they could.

The difficulty, apart from England's unwillingness to open the gates of Palestine to Jewish immigration, was the latent antisemitism among the democratic peoples. Hitler's propaganda had been effective in this respect, and few among the political leaders and the molders of public opinion within the democratic nations had the courage and the decency openly to counteract it. The civilized nations of the Western world obstinately refused to admit more Jewish immigrants, although, in most instances, their cultural and economic life would clearly have profited from their admittance. They preferred to permit the murder to go on, and Western civilization thus became a party to the crime. At that very time, clergymen were hailing a return to religion, and newspaper editors were interpreting the war as a battle for the sacredness of human personality—brave and no doubt truthful words.

Displaced Persons—When the war ended in Europe, on May 8, 1945, the full horror of the Jewish situation became evident to all. For a while, efforts were made to rehabilitate the broken-bodied and embittered Jews whom the Nazis had not had time to destroy. It soon became apparent, however, that the problem was not as easily solved as was at first thought possible. These people, especially the Jews who hailed from Eastern Europe, did not want to return to their former homes; they did not, as a matter of fact, have homes to return to. Their property and their means of earning a livelihood were gone; their relatives and friends had been murdered; and in most instances they would have had to live in the midst of a population which had succumbed to Hitler's doctrines of antisemitism. Until such time as a solution could be obtained for the basic problem of their finding a new home, these people were permitted to stay in temporary quarters in the American and British zones of occupation.

Difficulties arose almost at once. The occupation forces,

with the vast problem of reorganizing Germany on their hands, permitted the displaced persons to stay too long in the places and under the conditions which reminded them of the Nazis. Unintelligent military officers decided that no favor in the matter of food distribution should be shown to displaced persons over the Germans who had tortured them and had destined them for murder. When the victims voiced their complaints and insisted that their problem be solved, the occupation authorities treated them as nuisances. Only slowly and after a great deal of prodding from the Jews of the United States were conditions partly improved. In large measure the improvement was due to the activities of representatives of American Jewish organizations. Bad as conditions were in the American zone, they were worse under the British.

In August, 1945, there were 65,000 displaced persons in all zones, most of them Jews. The number increased rapidly. Thousands from the Russian zone and from Poland preferred to make their way through the military lines into the American zone of occupation, where they hoped that their migration to permanent homes would be facilitated. By 1948, there were about a million displaced persons in the British and American zones, among them over 250,000 Jews. Their choice of a new home was Palestine, the United States or Great Britain.

The Jews Who Returned Home—The desire to migrate to Palestine was not confined to the displaced persons. During the war years and soon thereafter, while optimism about a reconstructed Europe was still high, there were many who argued that the Jews ought to return to their former homes and there help their fellow citizens rebuild their respective lands. This hope proved a delusion, except in such Western countries as France, Belgium, Holland and Denmark. A large proportion of the Jews who did return home in Eastern Europe found conditions there intolerable. They came back to the cemeteries of their friends and relatives as well as of their former hopes. In many instances they knew very well that their Christian townsmen had aided the Germans in the policy of extermination. Poland, Rumania, Slovakia, Hungary and even Austria, after their liberation, remained spiritually enslaved to German doctrines, especially antisemitism. Poland was the outstanding example of this. Its reactionaries, those within Poland and those who preferred to remain in exile, had learned nothing from their experience with fascism. As on previous occasions in Polish history, they refused to remember the heroic cooperation of the Jews in the Polish underground. Murders and outright pogroms occurred frequently. There were Catholic prelates in Poland who, unlike most Catholics in other parts of the world, persisted in their pre-war policy of antisemitism. To a lesser degree the same situation obtained in Western Europe, where the return of Jewish property was long delayed. Judicial procedure for reclaiming it was slow, and those who profited directly or indirectly from Nazi confiscations organized themselves to make it still slower. Everywhere, governments showed little inclination to grant the Jews any form of reparation. Of the remaining Jews in Rumania, for example, in 1946, one third were on relief and one half were unemployed. Emigration was the only conceivable solution.

3. PALESTINE AND IMPERIAL AMBITIONS

Whither?—Among the numerous suggestions whither the Jews of Eastern Europe might migrate were Australia, Rhodesia, the Philippines, Alaska and Madagascar. The one obvious place was, of course, Palestine. There, however, callousness, imperial ambitions and unmoral politics intervened to prevent the remnant of European Jewry from saving itself.

Palestinian Jews and the War—Despite the betrayal of Jewish hopes involved in the White Paper of 1939,* the Jews of Palestine supported Great Britain wholeheartedly in its life-and-death struggle with Germany. They did so not only because Germany was the deadly enemy of the Jews everywhere, and not merely out of a desire to avenge the concentration camps and the gas chambers, but also because of the fundamental moral issues of the war—personal freedom and justice versus the military state—Jewish experience and Jewish teaching could guide the Jews in only one direction. By the beginning of 1945 the Jews of Palestine, where selective service was not practiced, had furnished more than 25,000 volunteers to the British army, whereas the Arabs, from twice the number of inhabitants, had furnished less than 10,000. These figures do not take into account the civilian assistance given by the Jewish workers and professionals. With the Mediterranean Sea all but closed as a result of the Italian entrance into the war, Jewish Palestine provided much materiél and a great deal of medical aid. By contrast, the

* See above, pp. 656–7.

Arabs, not only of Palestine but of the entire Middle East, were openly sympathetic to Nazism and fascism. This, in turn, was due not only to the years of propaganda carried on by Germany and Italy, nor merely to the Arab contempt for Britain resulting from its policy of appeasing the Moslems; it arose chiefly from the sentiments and traditions of the Arab upper classes, to whose political and social outlook fascism was much more congenial than democracy. Their neutrality was either bought, as in the case of Saudi Arabia, or won by force of arms, as in the case of Iraq and Iran.

England's Unenviable Position—Great Britain, in fact, found itself in a most uncomfortable position. It had been trying for years to bolster its weakening hold on its colonial empire. With India and Egypt clamoring for complete independence, the British colonial and foreign offices tried desperately to obtain the friendship of other Moslems. It had to have Palestine, above all, to substitute for Egypt as a military base for the protection of the Suez Canal. Russian influence, moreover, was being exerted upon the Mohammedans to a greater extent than ever, for Russia now resumed its traditional search for outlets into the Mediterranean Sea and Indian Ocean. No British government, whether Conservative or Labor, could afford "to preside over the dissolution of the Empire." It was most unfortunate that the English people, who in modern times had been so friendly and understanding towards the Jews, should have been the ones to show callousness to their suffering and considerable opposition to their aspiratons for national revival.

Continuous Sabotaging of the Homeland—The British colonial office drew an iron barrier across the road of the tens of thousands who sought to escape certain death in the German gas chambers. In November, 1940, 1,771 Jewish fugitives arrived in a Palestinian port. In despair because they were not permitted to land, the refugees caused an explosion on board the steamer *Patria* which killed about two hundred of them. The rest were thereupon sent to an internment camp on the island of Mauritius. In February, 1942, 769 men, women and children boarded the *Struma,* a boat totally unseaworthy for the trip from its Rumanian port to Palestine. They had to take that chance because civilized humanity had offered them no better means to escape from certain death. They hoped somehow, despite British opposition, to find their way into Palestine. Near a Turkish port the boat blew up and all but one of the passengers perished.

These were the spectacular results of British policy, but

they were insignificant when compared with that policy's wider implications. In every one of the conferences called to deal with the problem of saving the Jews of Europe from certain destruction, Britain stood adamant against opening the gates of Palestine. In order to fortify its own international position and to remove some of the blame from itself, the British encouraged the Arab states to organize themselves into an Arab League. The British administration during the war made every effort to minimize the share of the Jews in the fighting and the aid they extended to the Allied armies. Reports of investigators indicate that the government of Palestine had never centered its attention on the welfare of the population of Palestine—even its system of taxation was not directed towards that end—but on its police activities, with the emphasis on keeping the Moslem ruling class appeased and on preventing the Jews from competing with British industry.

The Anglo-American Committee of Inquiry—No matter how persistently the British politicians and military men tried to sidetrack the Palestine issue, they could not avoid it after the end of the war, if for no other reason than that there was no other place for the unfortunate survivors of European Jewry. Reluctantly, Britain granted a monthly immigration quota of 1,500 Jews, but it refused to take sole responsibility for a complete reopening of Palestine to Jewish immigration. When President Harry S. Truman suggested that 100,000 displaced Jews be admitted there, the British government countered with a proposal that a joint committee of Englishmen and Americans be appointed to investigate again the entire situation.

The members of the joint committee were appointed by their respective governments in December, 1945. They took testimony in the United States and England, among the displaced persons and among the survivors in various countries, as well as among Arabs and Jews in Palestine. They issued their report four months later, and the report was unanimous. Its two most important recommendations were that 100,000 Jews be admitted into Palestine at once and that further discussion as to the future political status of the country be postponed until a later date. The Jews, to be sure, were not satisfied with the denial of their hopes to establish a Jewish state, but they could at least look forward to the rescue of the 100,000. The Arab League denounced the conclusions of the committee and made dire threats if they should be carried out. The chief difficulty, however, lay in the refusal of Britain

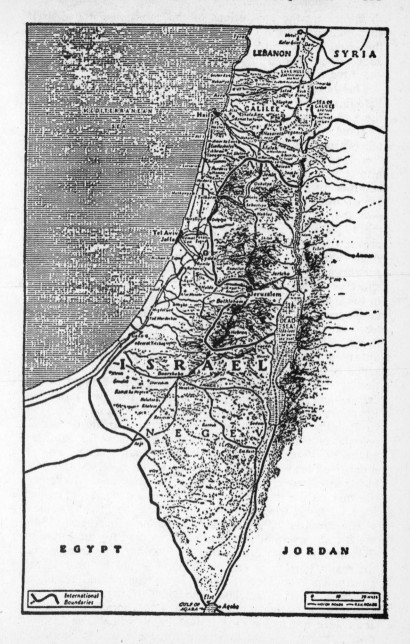

to implement the conclusions of the committee it had itself suggested, unless the United States shared in the expense and the responsibility. Ernest Bevin, the English foreign secretary, added insult to injury by giving utterance to sneering remarks about the Jews.

The Jews of Palestine Use Force—There was peace in Palestine as long as the war raged around its borders; with the end of the war the Palestinian Jews lost patience with England. For years they had watched arrogant colonial officials oppose their hopes and sabotage their efforts to arrive at an understanding with their Arab neighbors. They had also seen England yield to force on the part of the Arabs and continue to do so even now that hundreds of thousands of Jewish lives were at stake. They thereupon revived the *Haganah*, the self-defense organization which had been created in the 1920s and had continued to function, with the tacit approval of the English administration, during the years of Arab rioting in the 1930s. The primary use to which the *Haganah* was now put was to smuggle Jews into Palestine. Every effort was made to avoid bloodshed, and warning was given to the British soldiers when an attack upon their posts was to be made. A small group of extremists, however, acted on the assumption that terror alone would prove effective with the British. The latter answered both groups with martial law, arbitrary search and arrest, and military force that often resulted in death. They pointedly permitted the return to Palestine of several Arab leaders of the riots during the previous decade and let the infamous former mufti find refuge in Egypt where he could continue his plotting against the Jews of Palestine. The malevolence often characteristic of British colonial officials was displayed when they picked a Saturday (June 29, 1946) to transport to concentration camps a large number of Jewish leaders, many of whom observed the Sabbath scrupulously. The situation in Palestine began to resemble that of the days, almost two thousand years ago, when imperial Rome tried to impose its will on the Jewish people.

The Proposal of a Federated Palestine—In August, 1946, the British government made known its plan for the future of Palestine. It would divide the tiny country into three parts: the major portion of the arable land would be under Arab government; the Negev, below Beersheba, would be under the direct rule of England; the smallest part, some 1,500 square miles, would constitute the Jews' homeland. But the Jews were not to have control of immigration even in their own territory. All but local administration was to be in the hands of a super-government in which the English would play the major role. The British government called two conferences to discuss this and similar plans (September, 1946; February, 1947). They resulted only in a further postponement of any solution and in deepening misery for the displaced Jews. After the failure of the second conference, the British government put the problem in the hands of the United Nations, an act which was bound to mean more investigation and further delay.

Deporting the Refugees—In the meantime, the British government adopted a stringent policy against the admittance of Jewish refugees. The British navy was assigned the task of patrolling the coast of Palestine and preventing any Jews from landing. As ships arrived with their cargoes of human misery seeking to enter the promised homeland, they were forcibly carried away and placed in newly established concentration camps on the island of Cyprus. Each such deportation was accompanied by riots on board the refugee-laden ships as well as among the Palestinian Jews. The most spectacular event of this sort occurred in the summer of 1947. A ship, calling itself *Exodus 1947*, arrived at the coast of Palestine with 4,500 refugees. The British cabinet ordered its navy to intercept them and, not even deporting them to Cyprus, to carry them to the same concentration camps in Europe from which these unfortunates had tried to escape.

Palestine and the United Nations—On April 2, 1947, Great Britain submitted the problem of Palestine to the General Assembly of the United Nations. On April 20, a special session of the Assembly met, and, after prolonged discussion, decided to appoint a United Nations Special Committee on Palestine (UNSCOP) with broad powers of investigation. Since the great powers eliminated themselves from service on the Committee, it consisted of representatives of the following nations: Australia, Canada, Czechoslovakia, Guatemala, India, Iran, Netherlands, Peru, Sweden, Uruguay and Yugoslavia. The Committee began its work late in May. It took evidence both in and outside of Palestine, as well as in the Displaced Persons' camps of Europe. The Palestinian Arabs boycotted the Committee; but the Arab nations gave their views. The ultimate report, submitted on September 1, favored partitioning Palestine into independent Arab and Jewish states, bound together by economic ties. The Jews were given those districts in which they predominated—that is, most of the coast and part of Galilee—as well as the desert of the Negev. Jerusalem was to belong to neither side, but be administered under the supervision of the United Nations. A minority report was submitted by the representatives of India, Iran and Yugoslavia recommending an independent federal state in Palestine, with two houses, one based on population and the other on national parity.

The discussion which followed in the United Nations was tense with drama. Worldwide attention was focused on the representatives of the three great powers: Britain, the United States and Russia. The first declared that it would have nothing to do with any scheme of partition not acceptable to both Arabs and Jews—a patently impossible condition—and that it would relinquish its mandate over Palestine in May, 1948. Russia, to the surprise of most, advocated partition. The United States had the deciding voice, since its policy was followed by many of the smaller nations. It declared itself strongly in favor of the Committee's report. On November 29, the General Assembly, by a vote of thirty-three nations against thirteen, accepted the principle of establishing two states in Palestine.

With few exceptions, Jews received this decision gratefully as an indication of the world's desire to make up, at least in part, for all that it had failed to do during the tragic Hitler era. The Jews of Palestine hailed the decision with rejoicing. But much still had to be done. The chief problem was how to bring the United Nations decision into realization. After some deliberation, in which the boundaries of the proposed Jewish state were further reduced, the United Nations appointed a commission to act as its executive arms for bridging the gap between the end of the British mandate and the beginning of the two states.

The Failure of Diplomacy—The Arab states and the so-called Palestine Higher Committee, under the leadership of the iniquitous ex-mufti, now openly rebelled against the United Nations' decision. Irregular bands of Palestinian Arabs and recruits from other Moslem lands, with a considerable admixture of volunteers from among British and Polish ex-soldiers, began systematic attacks on Jewish colonies and on Jews within Palestine. Pitched battles were fought all over the country. The mandatory government seemed to the Jews of Palestine to be less than neutral in the struggle; in any event, it showed its inability to maintain order. It confessed this inability by refusing to guarantee the safety of the representatives of the United Nations and advised against their arrival in Palestine until only two weeks before it relinquished the mandate. Nor would Great Britain permit the *Haganah,* the Jewish militia, to obtain arms. Britain prevailed upon the United Nations to place an embargo on arms to the Near East, but it did not stop its own sale of arms to the Arab states, pleading that it was bound to do so by treaty. Almost unarmed and unprotected, the Jewish settlement was left alone to fight for its own survival and for the prestige of the United Nations.

These factors were not the only ones militating against the establishment of the Jewish state. The military and commercial interests of the United States also joined the opposition. The rivalry with Russia created a danger zone in the Middle East. Some American military strategists apparently believed that the feudal-minded Arab leaders would really court disaster to themselves by inviting the friendship of Russia. Profit-seeking oil companies, for their part, persuaded the United States government that the Arab states would refuse to permit the tapping of their rich oil resources unless the Arab view of Palestine was adopted. As a result, the United States, in March, 1948, announced a complete change of policy. It asked the General Assembly of the United Nations to reverse its decision of November, 1947: The UNSCOP report was to be sidetracked; Palestine was again to be ruled by the discredited system of trusteeship.

Events did not wait upon the fruitless debate which followed within the United Nations Assembly. The fighting in Palestine became intensified and the Jews showed themselves fully able to beat back the attacks of the Arabs. Britain had announced some months before that, failing an acceptable solution, it would terminate its mandate on May 16, 1948. As the British withdrew, the Jews extended their authority, so that by the date mentioned the Jewish state was actually functioning. On Friday, May 14 (5th of Iyar, 5708), before a distinguished gathering in Tel Aviv, David Ben-Gurion, head of the Provisional Government, basing himself on the historic rights of the Jewish people and the authority of the United Nations decision, called the State of Israel into being. The thrill of this electrifying declaration was heightened when, on the same day, President Truman announced United States recognition of the new nation. Guatemala and Russia followed suit, and its recognition by other powers was expected. Two days later, Chaim Weitzmann was proclaimed President of the Council of Government of Israel. The great news was marred by the invasion of Israel's territory by the Arab nations. Israel was to be reborn in battle, even while it craved and needed peace.

The Reconquest of Israel—Five regular armies had been poised for weeks on the borders of Palestine, waiting for the British mandate to expire and, in the meantime, proclaiming to a credulous world how quickly and thoroughly they would put the Jews in their place. That place, few doubted, would be the bottom of the Mediterranean. The invasion began, from every direction except the sea, during the night between the 14th and 15th of May.

Among the Jews arms were inadequate, heavy armor non-existent, experienced generalship apparently rare. But there was plenty of courage among young and old, men and women. The enemy was outgeneraled and outfought, though Jewish losses were heavy. The isolated colonies held out for weeks, despite numerous casualties. Most spectacular was the defense within and around the Old City of Jerusalem. Lack of food and water, as well as lack of defenders, eventually forced its surrender; but the New City was stoutly held, so that the Arab Legion, the best the enemy had, was stopped in its tracks.

The United Nations now belatedly attempted to end the fighting. It appointed Count Folke Bernadotte of Sweden as mediator, and he succeeded in arranging a four-weeks truce beginning June 11. At its expiration, July 9, the Arabs, still confident, resumed fighting. The Jews, however, were now better equipped, their army better coordinated. They scored victory after victory until, before long, all the territory assigned them by the United Nations was cleared of the enemy. They even penetrated a few miles into Lebanon and Arab Palestine and surrounded some important Egyptian forces. The Moslem nations more readily agreed to a second truce on July 18.

The Refusal of Peace—Count Bernadotte tried to turn the truce into an armistice on conditions which might result in permanent peace. His proposals, calling for a decrease in Israel's territory, angered the extremists among the Jews. Bernadotte was assassinated, to the shame of the new state. An armistice was nevertheless eventually effected, after months of negotiations carried on by Dr. Ralph Bunche, American successor to Bernadotte. The Arabs stubbornly refused, however, to make peace. They spoke darkly of "a second round."

The Arab Refugees—One of the most profoundly disturbing difficulties was that involving the refugees resulting from the victory. The Arab leaders of the days preceding the declaration of independence were so certain of ultimate victory that they encouraged and sometimes compelled the peasants to abandon their homes. Their object was to build up a case for the eventual dispossession of the Jews. Fear of the Jews also played its part. The victory of the Jews left these unfortunate peasants stranded and homeless. Hundreds of thousands of them clamored for a return to their former villages and towns. The Jews could not readmit them for two reasons. The Arab homes had in the meantime been occupied by Jewish refugees from Europe and Moslem lands. Besides, a large Arab population within Israel would endanger the state's security. The neighboring Arab countries, though greatly in need of population, refused to permit these refugees to settle in their midst. They preferred to use the misery of the displaced Arabs as an argument in the political bargaining about peace with Israel. Israel offered what compensation it could afford, but this was curtly rejected.

Jerusalem the Capital—The Arabs were not alone in refusing to let Israel be. There had long been sentiment within the United Nations, especially under the influence of the Catholic Church, to internationalize Jerusalem. The reason given was that none but Christians could be trusted to guard the holy places. The fact was that almost all such places were in the Old City, now under the rule of Jordan. Nonetheless, the United Nations voted to internationalize Jerusalem as a whole. Thereupon the Israel government moved its offices and the Kneset (Parliament) to the Jewish part of the City and declared it the capital of the state. Jordan for its part annexed all of non-Israel Palestine.

Democracy and Constitution—The first election for members of the Kneset was held on January 25, 1949. All persons over 18, whether Jews or Arabs, men or women, were eligible to vote. It is not surprising that the politically conscious population divided itself into some twenty different parties. MaPAI (*Mifleget Poalei Eretz Yisrael*—The Workers' Party of Israel), the socialist party, won forty-six out of the 120 seats; MaPaM (*Mifleget Poalim Me'uhedet*—The United Workers' Party), the radical socialist party, won nineteen; the Religious Bloc won sixteen; Herut, the extreme nationalists, won fourteen; the General Zionists, the middle class party, won seven; the Communists four; while six other parties won some representation. Mapai with the cooperation of the Religious Bloc, plus some of the smaller groups, organized the government with David Ben-Gurion as premier. The government set itself to solving the numerous problems which faced the state. But it did not produce the promised constitution. Many felt that the country was too young, its problems too numerous and its experience too limited for it to bind it-self by a written constitution. The basic principles, it was argued, would be developed in the course of actual application of law to life.

The Ingathering of the Exiles—Israel's problems were, in fact, overwhelming. Among the most difficult, apart from the threat to its security, was the absorption of a vast influx of immigrants. The very origin of the state was predicated on the assumption that the state's doors were open to every Jew who wanted to come in. The displaced persons of Europe came first, and the camps were soon emptied. Jews from East-European countries were also eager to come. Russia, however, was now engaged in an effort at compulsory assimilation of minorities. Under its influence communist governments prohibited the emigration of Jews. On the other hand, many tens of thousands whose life was threatened by the Moslems smarting under their defeat by Israel could go to the Jewish state provided they left practically all their possessions behind. "Operation Magic Carpet" was the name appropriately given to the transportation by air of the Yemenite and Iranian Jews to whom land and sea routes were closed. The North Africans also clamored for admittance. As a result, the Jewish population of the state practically doubled in the three years following the declaration of independence: from 665,000 in May 1948 to about 1,330,000 in June 1951, to over 1,600,000 by May 1952 including about 175,000 Arabs. Almost all the newcomers were poor, few knew a trade and a great many suffered from various ailments. The problem of providing them with work and housing was all but insuperable, while the process of their adjustment to the new environment was bound to take a long time.

Religion and the State—Another example of problems peculiar to Israel concerned religion and the state. For many centuries the term "Jew" had borne a religious connotation. But many of the foremost Zionists, especially among those who had built up the Jewish community of Palestine between the two World Wars, had been brought up under the influence of European rationalism and socialism. In many cases, if not anti-religious, they were insistent that the new state separate religion from its politics. A clash was inevitable between these people and those to whom Judaism was the breath of life. Disputes in the Kneset were frequent on such matters as *kashrut*, Sabbath observance, woman's place in law, and the like. The two viewpoints clashed, above all, on the subject of education. The argument became so bitter that it led to a split in the government and to a call for new elections.

The Second Election—The economic problems of the country played as important a role in the campaign as the religious. The government was blamed for the austerity program, the unfavorable trade balance, the slow development of industry. Yet, when the votes were counted at the end of election day, July 30, 1951, the relative standing of the parties underwent but slight change. Mapai retained first place, though still far from having a majority. The middle class General Zionists replaced Mapam as the second party in importance; while the Religious Bloc's strength emerged substantially unchanged. Ben-Gurion made an effort to form a government with the aid of the General Zionists, but in the end went back to the former coalition with the religionists. Politically the problems remained unsolved.

Israel and the Diaspora—The establishment of the state compelled Jews everywhere to re-think the relationship between these two parts of the Jewish people. Was there any further need for a Zionist organization in the Diaspora? If so, what were to be its functions? Did the Jews of the Diaspora have any right to offer advice to the Jews of Israel, since clearly problems might arise in the state which, if approached in the wrong spirit, might reflect upon Jews in other parts of the world? Shall the Jews of America send manpower to aid in the building of the land? For centuries the widely scattered Diaspora hoped for the day when spiritual instruction and example would reach them from the Holy Land, when "Torah will come forth from Zion and the word of God from Jerusalem." Just what could be done to bring that day nearer? Patience and statesmanship were needed for the ultimate development of the proper kind and degree of cooperation.

4. PROBLEMS AND PROSPECTS IN AMERICA

The Continued Search for Unity—Confronted with the European Jewish tragedy, the Jews of the United States found a greater degree of unity than at any time since the early nineteenth century. The efforts of the American Jewish Joint Distribution Committee and of the United Palestine Appeal were at last seen to be but two aspects of one and the same problem. These nation-wide organizations therefore continued their cooperation in the raising of funds and, to some extent, in their disbursement. The Jews of America recognized the vastness of the problem before them, so that when, in 1946, the appeal was made for the huge sum of $100,000,000, the response was magnificent. Equally encouraging was the cooperation shown by a number of Christian individuals and organizations in the raising of this money. Yet the immense problems of relief for the displaced persons in Europe and of security for the Jewish effort in Palestine remained. For the year 1948, therefore, the Jews of the United States undertook to tax themselves to the extent of $250,000,000, a staggering burden but obviously an inescapable one. The sums raised in later years were not so huge, though still amounting to tens of millions. On the other hand, efforts to achieve a greater degree of unity within American Jewry failed. In 1943, the B'nai B'rith, as the largest non-partisan organization of Jews in the United States, took the lead in calling an "American Jewish Conference." But by 1948 the Conference acknowledged failure and went out of existence.

The Jews and American Christendom—The broad-minded Christians of America repeatedly gave evidence of sympathy with the tragic problems which the Jews had to face. The Congress of the United States passed a resolution, on December 19, 1945, urging the President to work for the reopening of Palestine to Jewish immigration. President Truman needed no such urging; he had been doing what he could to persuade the British to adopt such humanitarian action. He made another appeal to this effect on October 4, 1946, after the consultations on the British plan of federation seemed to have reached an impasse. On the other hand, there were forces in America which made for antisemitism. Certain social, economic and pseudo-religious groups again found it advantageous to abuse the minority groups in American society, especially the Jews. Social discrimination, such as the refusal to admit Jews to clubs or to invite them to Christian homes, may bespeak a narrow mind, but a Jew has no real right to object to such practices, since everyone is free to pick his friends and associates. Economic discrimination, however, became a much more serious matter during the decade preceding the war and the period immediately following. Restrictions on the employment of Jews were widely practiced by business firms large and small. Professional schools and undergraduate institutions established quotas in the admission of Jewish students. In this way, persons in every way fit were deprived of the opportunity not only for self-development, but also for giving society the best that was in them. Moreover, an opinion-testing body in 1945 found more antisemitism among well-to-do Americans than among the poor. Jewish experience had in fact found it to be true everywhere and at all times that antisemitism grows from the top down. Left alone, the lower economic and cultural classes have no quarrel with their Jewish neighbors. It clearly would take years of prosperity among the poor and of re-education in the fundamentals of Americanism among the wealthy to undo the work of the decade of the 1930s, the decade of economic depression coupled with Nazi propaganda. The fight against communist propaganda, which rose to a very high pitch after the end of World War II, gave the reactionary antisemitic forces a new opportunity to play on the perplexities and fears of the American population. But unless America loses its Americanism, these evil influences must be overcome.

The Effect on the Jews—So terrified did many Jews become, during that generation, lest antisemitism solidify into a habitual thought process of the American Christian population, that fear became a habitual attitude among them and constituted one of the most serious problems of Jewish life. Fear attitudes practically paralyzed better community organization, healthy self-criticism and more effective Jewish education. Moreover, a considerable number rebelled against living in this constant fear and under the handicap of discrimination. They went to great lengths to sever their intellectual and social ties with all that stemmed from Jewish life. Intermarriage became more frequent, and many so far despaired of Jewish survival in the Diaspora that they made this their primary reason for supporting the Jewish state in Palestine.

Education for Survival—The years of World War II had a sobering effect upon the Jews of the United States. Not in many years had there been such widespread interest in Jewish education, both on the elementary and the adult levels. All-day Jewish schools were established in several American cities, while the summer camp movement was given a Jewish cultural turn. Serious attention was given to the problems of curriculum and teacher-training, in the quest for adjustment between Jewish and American cultural values. There were growing signs that the Jewish population would in the future show more discrimination in its choice of leaders, realizing that leaders unaware of their people's past experience and present worth, not only tended to repeat the mistakes of the past, but lacked the spiritual stamina to guide the group on its course towards the future. Granted external peace, American Jewry had every reason to believe that it would meet the challenges of our day.

CHAPTER XIII

TWO UNEASY DECADES

THE DECADES THAT FOLLOWED THE END OF WORLD WAR II
WITNESSED RADICAL TRANSFORMATIONS IN MOST DIASPORA
COMMUNITIES AND TWO MORE CONFLICTS BETWEEN THE
NATIONAL COMMUNITY AND ITS MOSLEM NEIGHBORS

A Turbulent World—Such peace as might have enabled
the Jews to move toward a solution of their internal problems
was not forthcoming. The peace that actually came after
World War II was disappointing in many respects. It did not
so much solve the old problems that afflicted the entire world
as create new ones. It initiated an era of great scientific development and of more effective communication, but also of
greater danger to the survival of mankind and of uglier manifestations of nationalism. The Jews, scattered throughout the
world and feeling themselves part of every nation, were
affected by the social and political problems that affected everybody and, in addition, by new problems that were specifically their own as Jews. They found themselves in the midst
of bitter conflicts: the icy relations between East and West,
the boiling anti-colonialism of Africa and Asia, and the stri-
dent nationalism of the Moslem states. Internally, moreover,
the problems of cultural and religious identity became more
urgent in every Jewish community, both the well-established
and the recently re-organized. At the same time, the continuous and heroic assertion of its independence by the State of
Israel served as a source of inspiration to Jews all over the
world.

1. SOVIET RUSSIA AND ITS JEWS

The Czarist Heritage—The fate of the Jews in Russia, after
as before World War II, was in many respects the result of
social habits inherited by the Russian population from the

czarist regime which preceded the Communist Revolution of 1917. The hostility toward the Jewish minority which had been fostered for centuries could not be eradicated simply by prohibiting one generation from passing its prejudices on to the next. Officially the communist state frowned on antisemitism; nevertheless, snide anti-Jewish remarks were not infrequent and sometimes led to action. Joseph Stalin, Russia's all-powerful dictator, himself made use of this wide-spread latent hostility in order to bolster his personal power. He never overcame his suspicions of other men, some of whom were of Jewish origin, who had been prominent in the leadership of early communism. Many of these had been eliminated in the purge of 1938; others were removed from positions of influence after the war. In the last year of his life, Stalin levelled against a number of physicians, most of them identifiably Jewish, the mediaeval charge that they were scheming to murder the country's leaders in order to weaken the Soviet state. The entire Jewish population of Russia would have been in danger had Stalin lived much longer. He died in 1953, and with him died the threat of an anti-Jewish frenzy.

Anti-Judaism or Antisemitism—One may accept the insistent claims of Soviet leadership that they had banished antisemitism from Russia. Equal opportunities in employment and in public office were, in fact, open to Jews; they became prominent in the arts and the sciences. Yet there was a persistent feeling that the survival of Russian Jewry was problematical. More sophisticated methods were discovered for eliminating the Jewish population. For communism's hostility to all religion was directed with special vigor against Judaism. Few synagogues were permitted to function: cities with a Jewish population of scores of thousands were allowed only one synagogue. There was no rabbinical school in the entire country to prepare religious leaders for coming generations. In a totalitarian state such institutions cannot be established without government consent, and there was a strong suspicion that applicants would be classed as counter-revolutionaries. Even cultural activities, like Yiddish theater or concerts of Jewish music, were given but grudging support by the government. None of the other ethnic-cultural groups in Russia had to bear such stringent regulation of their lives. The claim that all this was but an aspect of the struggle against religion was belied by the fact that the Russian Orthodox Church did not suffer as many restrictions and was even permitted to maintain contact with its churches in other lands, while the Jews were denied similar organizational relationships. Obviously, Russian communists did not adopt the Nazi method of physical extermination; they aimed rather at the destruction of the Jews as an identifiable group by absorbing them into the regimented mentality of the total population. The attitude of the atheist state was akin to that of the mediaeval Church.

Protests from the West—Protests by Jews and by non-Jewish liberals in various parts of the west against this suffocation of an ancient culture led to a slight improvement. Late in the 1950s, the republication of a few Yiddish books was permitted; a few theatrical performances in Yiddish and an occasional concert were allowed in a number of cities; and some selected translations were made into Russian from classical Yiddish writings. A surprisingly large number of Jews responded with enthusiasm to this meager cultural fare. On the religious level, the Russian government reluctantly agreed in 1966 to the baking of *matzah* for Passover, and consideration was given to a new edition of the Jewish prayer book, the importation of which had been forbidden, just as was the importation of prayer shawls and *tefillin*.

The Assertion of Identity—At the end of 1965, the Jewish population of European and Asian Russia was said to be slightly more than two and a half million. This represents a decrease of at least half a million from the estimated Jewish population of the same territory before World War II. Some of the loss may have been due to the war, and some may have been due to total assimilation. The 1965 figure, however, is surprising for another reason. Since the majority of the population must by that time have been born after the October Revolution of 1917 and perhaps also after the subsequent beginning of cultural repression, it is significant that so many still identified themselves as Jews. For the rate of intermarriage is high and it is possible for a child of an intermarriage to record himself with the nationality of the non-Jewish parent. A very large number picked Yiddish as their mother tongue. There were two occasions during the year when the usually empty synagogues were over-crowded: on Purim, which commemorates deliverance from the danger of physical extermination; and on Simhat Torah, which is observed in gratitude for the connection of the Jews with the Bible. A large number of young Jews would gather in front of the synagogues on these two days to dance and sing Jewish songs. No doubt these were not meant to be religious manifestations, since both holidays can be given secular interpretations, but the phenomenon did indicate that a large number of Russian Jews could be retained in the Jewish fold if the government relaxed its totalitarian anti-religious attitude, or if it permitted migration to Israel.

2. ISRAEL'S SECOND WAR

Russia's Return to an Old Policy—When the Jews of Palestine proclaimed the State of Israel, in 1948, and began their heroic defense against the invading armies of its Moslem neighbors, Russia followed swiftly upon the United States in recognizing the Jewish State. It even permitted Czechoslovakia to send arms to Israel. Within a few years, however, Russian policy underwent a change. In the weakness of the Moslem states, Russia saw an opportunity of reviving old imperialist ambitions to penetrate the lands of the south, now doubly attractive because of the riches in oil which its "Cold War" opponents were drawing from those countries. To win the so-called Arab nations over to its side against the Free World, Russia declared its sympathy for the Arab cause and pronounced Israel "a tool of the capitalist West." Egypt began to receive large quantities of arms from the communist bloc. Moreover, communist countries shut their gates more firmly against the migration of Jews to Israel, since the Arabs feared Israel's growth and expansion. In the course of the 1950s and 1960s, both Poland and Rumania appeared willing to relax their restrictions on emigration to Israel; but under Russian influence such willingness was short-lived.

Egyptian Aggression—Emboldened by the support of the communist bloc, Colonel Gamal Abdel Nasser, the Egyptian dictator, embarked on a course of empire-building. He thought he could emerge as the hero of the Moslem world by taking the lead in undermining and destroying Israel. The Jewish State had ever since its inception been subjected to occasional terrorist raids from beyond the borders of Egypt, Jordan and Syria. In 1955, the Egyptian army began the training of well-organized raiders. Almost nightly they would cross the Gaza strip, where Palestinian refugees were concentrated, steal their way across the border into Israel where they would lay mines and bomb settlements. Hundreds of Israelis were killed by them, and much property was destroyed or carried off. As a further show of his strength and independence, and secure in the diplomatic support promised him by his communist allies, Nasser challenged the western powers by taking over—he called it "nationalizing"—the Suez Canal.

The Canal had been built by and belonged to western stock-holders, primarily British and French; but the protests of these powers were disdainfully rejected.

The Sinai Campaign—Israel had something more than property at stake: the security of its citizens and its ultimate independence had been challenged. In October 1956, Israel mobilized its small but efficient army and invaded the Sinai Peninsula. Egyptian resistance crumbled. Despite the superior equipment supplied them by Russia, the Egyptians proved inferior soldiers. At this juncture, France and Britain attacked Egypt by air, demanding the return of the Suez Canal. Israel probably knew beforehand that France and Britain intended to act, but the air attack that the western powers mounted had little bearing on the success of Israel's invasion of Sinai. In fact, it turned out that the mismanaged western campaign interfered with Israel's complete victory. For, at this point, both the United States and Russia, rivalling one another for Nasser's gratitude, demanded the cessation of hostilities and the return of the situation to that preceding the beginning of hostilities. Britain and France reluctantly and angrily complied; but Israel hesitated to be deprived of the fruits of its victory.

The Inconclusive Results—Prime Minister David Ben-Gurion of Israel, despite serious protests within his own country, finally yielded. But he did so only after the United Nations and President Dwight D. Eisenhower of the United States promised to make sure that the marauding raids from Egypt would stop. They also promised to prevent Egypt from interfering with Israel's shipping by way of the Gulf of Aqaba, as well as to keep the Suez Canal open to ships going to and from Israel.

Nasser soon went back on his promise about the freedom of navigation in the Canal. But the United Nations did, before long, station soldiers recruited from several neutral nations on the Egyptian side of the border between Israel and Egypt. Thus the resumption of Egyptian raids was prevented. A further troop of soldiers was stationed on one of the tiny islands at the mouth of the Gulf of Aqaba, so that Israel's communication with the countries of Asia and Africa might suffer no interference. Israel, moreover, had destroyed or captured most of the armaments that Russia had supplied to Egypt. Nasser, however, thanks to Russia, emerged from the conflict better than anyone expected; Russia and the United States had saved him from imminent defeat, and he retained the Suez Canal. He was again free to carry on his political intrigues in the Middle East, for which Egypt had been notorious from Bible days on. He continued to dream of an empire in that part of the world. Like a pharaoh of old, he announced that the war had resulted in a great Egyptian victory.

3. The Vanishing Communities of North Africa and Asia

The Fate of the Jews in Egypt—The first victims of Nasser's vengeance, during and following the Sinai War, were the 40,000 Jews who lived in his country. Hundreds were arrested on the charge of sympathizing with Israel; their shops were looted and their property confiscated. Many of these Jews were citizens of foreign countries, and they fled to France, Italy or Greece. A small number managed to reach Israel by roundabout routes. Less than 20,000 remained in Egypt, ever under the hostile eye of the dictator and his officials, never daring to express themselves freely, their businesses in ruins, thir lives in constant jeopardy.

Disintegration of the West-Asian Communities—A similar fate had already overtaken the other Jewish communities in the Moslem states of western Asia. No sooner was the Jewish State proclaimed, in 1948, than the Moslem countries began a systematic expulsion of their Jewish populations and confiscation of their property. Jews had been living in all these countries long before the days of Islam. Now, hardly a Jew was left in Yemen and Aden. By 1953, the Jews of Iraq—ancient Mesopotamia—who had been living there uninterruptedly since the Babylonian Exile, two and a half millennia before, were reduced from 130,000 to 6,000. The much smaller communities of Syria, Lebanon and Asiatic Turkey also lost considerable numbers. All of these exiles from their homes went to Israel. For one of the first laws enacted by the Knesseth, Israel's parliament, declared that any Jew had a right to come to Israel and settle there, unless his coming endangered the life and health of the people already there. All too soon, the application of the law proved more than theoretical.

Migration from North Africa—The North African countries between Egypt and Algeria also experienced a rapid decline in their Jewish populations. Begun in the early 1950s, the process was intensified by the Sinai War. One after another, in the course of the decade, these states embarked on successful struggles to throw off the yoke of colonialism and establish themselves as independent nations. But nationalism's usual concomitants are racialism and religious uniformity. Consequently, the struggle for independence was everywhere accompanied by anti-Jewish words and acts, the excuse being that Jews were Zionists and therefore anti-Moslem. Ancient Jewish communities were broken up as a result, and obstacles were placed in the way of the exiled Jews going to Israel. Many, usually the economically less fortunate, nevertheless succeeded in making their way to the Jewish State. The majority, however, went to France or to Italy. Thus the Jewish population of Tunisia, numbering about 105,000 in 1950 (in a general population of some three and a quarter million), lost about a fourth of its number in the course of the next ten years. Morocco, with a Jewish population of about 260,000 in 1948 (in a general population of about ten million), lost about half its number by 1960. It must be noted, however, that the legal and economic positions of the Jews in these countries were not substantially impaired. Nonetheless, Jewish relief organizations in other parts of the world had to come to the aid of the North African Jews to a greater or lesser extent.

The Algerian Tragedy—No Jewish community of North Africa, outside of Egypt, was struck such a stunning blow as was that of Algeria. Its 150,000 Jews (in a general population of nearly nine million) were among the most culturally advanced of the area. Under the protection of France—in fact, French citizens since the Crémieux Decree of a century and a quarter earlier—the Algerian Jews had made tremendous progress. When the agitation against French suzerainty began, the Jews of the country were torn between two conflicting loyalties. On the one hand, they keenly felt an attachment to France and to French culture. On the other hand, as Algerians for many centuries, they sympathized with the widespread desire for national independence. They were especially drawn to the Moslem side of the argument because the large number of the Christian colonizers of the country had been, and remained, vehemently anti-Jewish. But when the Moslem side finally triumphed, the Jews discovered that their fellow Algerians had fallen under the influence of the other Moslem states and could no longer be trusted to deal with them fairly. In panic, like a great many other Algerians of European extraction, almost two-thirds of Algeria's Jewish population sadly left their homeland. They abandoned practically all their worldly goods and the institutions developed in the course of centuries and sought new homes. Most of them

went to France. Some went to Portugal and Spain from
which, in many cases, their ancestors had fled in the 14th and
15th centuries. A smaller number reached Israel.

4. Renewal and Revival in Western Europe

France—The new arrivals from North Africa to France
brought overwhelming problems to the comparatively small
French Jewish community that had survived the difficult period of World War II. In the course of those tragic years,
French Jewry had lost more than half its numbers out of a
pre-war population of some 300,000. It emerged at the end
of the war with a Jewish population of about 175,000, including new settlers from other parts of Europe. The community's physical resources were at a low ebb, and its spiritual
powers were greatly diminished. Suddenly—as historical processes evolve—within hardly a decade, the community was
faced with an avalanche of refugees from North Africa.
Early in the 1960s the Jewish population of France jumped
to a figure in excess of half a million. The newcomers settled
in Paris and in a number of other cities, especially in southern
France, whose Jewish population had been tiny or completely
non-existent. Fortunately, most of the Algerian refugees
spoke French; but the conditions of life which they encountered were entirely different from those to which they had
been accustomed. They created problems of housing, education, and economic adjustment, none of which could be
solved quickly or easily. Nor were they able to adjust easily
to the communal and religious situation which they encountered. Religious life in France consequently began to take a
new turn. Schools were established for the young, and communal life could no longer pursue its former somnolent way.

Thus two trends began to manifest themselves among the
Jews of France. One was toward a revitalization of Judaism.
The newcomers being observing Jews, to whom the traditional ways of life and thought were important, they offered
renewed promise of a religious revival, though in a Sephardi
rather than the Ashkenazi forms dominant in French Judaism
before World War II. The other trend was toward assimilation. In the free environment of pre-war France, the religious
loyalties of its Jewish population had grown weak almost to
the vanishing point, and the rate of intermarriage was very
high. The more westernized Jews of North African descent
soon joined the older residents and their descendants in ques-

tioning the traditional ways and values. French Jewry, however, quickly developed currents of rabbinic and intellectual
leadership which promised to exert a strong influence on this
emerging cultural struggle. It is interesting that the French
government began, soon after the war, to encourage scholarly
research into the Jewish past.

Italy—In pre-war years, Italy had a comparatively small
native Jewish population of about 60,000; it ended World
War II with something less than half that number, including
the refugees from other parts of Europe who stayed on to
make their home there. The immigration from North Africa,
especially from Egypt following the Sinai War of 1956, increased the number by some thousands, so that by the middle
1960s the Italian Jews numbered about 35,000. The problems
these people had to face were social and religious rather than
economic, and the re-organized community undertook to attack them with vigor and intelligence. The rabbinical school
was re-opened and elementary schools were established, the
necessary books being provided by translations from other
languages. There was a clear intention to keep alive the community's pride in its long and distinguished history, the longest and among the most distinguished in Europe. A falling
birth-rate threatened its existence; but this was primarily a
psychological rather than a communal problem.

Spain and Portugal—The two countries of the Iberian peninsula were in a different situation from either France or
Italy. A very few European Jews had settled in these countries after World War I. A small number of Jewish refugees
from Hitler-dominated parts of Europe remained in Spain
and Portugal after World War II. Some hundreds of North
African Jews settled in Portugal during the 1950s and 1960s,
while more came to Spain and increased the Spanish-Jewish
population to about 7,000. Interesting also, and perhaps destined to be significant in a more practical way, was the concern which scholarly Christians as well as members of the
government showed in Sephardi Jews, the presumed descendants of those exiled from Spain and Portugal in the last decade of the 15th century. One of the handsome former synagogues of Toledo, which in that century was turned into a
church, was rededicated in 1966 for use as a museum of Jewish interest. Every so often there were rumors that complete
equality would be granted to all religions in Spain; but no
such action was taken by either regime in the peninsula. The
Jews of Madrid, Barcelona and Lisbon organized themselves

into communities and established synagogues of modest appearance and proportions.

Germany and Austria—In 1966, there were about 30,000 Jews in West Germany and fewer than 10,000 in Austria. Many of them were older people who, having fled the Nazis, could not adjust themselves to life in the lands of their exile. Others were of non-Germanic origin who had stayed on after their liberation from the death camps or who, having tried Israel or some other country, thought they could make a better life for themselves among an energetic people certain to rise from its ruins. But no unity or organization developed among any of them. There was little Jewishness; but a sense of instability hovered over the entire group, a sense of insecurity that comes from living in the midst of a population that had, to say the least, tamely acquiesced in the extermination of other Jews. During the two decades that followed the war, the democratic government of the German republic repeatedly expressed regret over what had happened during the Hitler era. In 1951, the Parliament at Bonn voted close to a billion dollars, to be spent in the course of the following ten years, as a token of penitence for what had happened. Three-quarters of the sum were used to aid the State of Israel "which had admitted so many homeless refugees." The rest went to compensate individual survivors for some of their material losses and to rehabilitate Jewish cultural life. This action gave evidence that an official conscience existed which in time might make possible the restoration of a vigorous Jewish community on German soil. Austria, equally guilty toward the Jewish people, did considerably less. It granted only about a million dollars in restitution to that country's victims of Nazism. The Austrian government, however, promised, and perhaps did all it could, to restrain antisemitic sentiments which manifested themselves with fair frequency.

In the matter of controlling Nazi revivals, West Germany also gave rise to some misgivings. For a few years after the conclusion of the war, the new government, under Chancellor Konrad Adenauer, made earnest efforts to punish those among known former Nazis who had been guilty of atrocities. After a while, however, as Germany and the rest of the world became preoccupied with other problems, the zeal for justice cooled. Former Nazis were even accepted into the government. Trials of Nazi criminals became less frequent and their punishments less severe. A new political party appeared in West Germany, the National Democratic Party of Germany, which reflected in its pronouncements many of the old super-nationalistic attitudes. This party's popular vote kept growing in the early 1960s, especially in some of the northern provinces and in Bavaria. In one such local election in 1967 it obtained as much as 30% of the votes. The question whether Germany really has taken its experiences of the 1930s and 1940s to heart has begun to agitate the minds of liberals everywhere.

Great Britain—With a population of 450,000, Great Britain (including Northern Ireland) ranked next in size to France; but its history and problems during the two decades were vastly different. It experienced no immigration of consequence from among Jews of non-British background, and its antisemites were few and lacking in popular support. The most serious problems experienced by British Jews were internal and largely of a religious nature. Few deliberately abandoned the Jewish fold, but a growing lack of interest in Judaism was apparent and the rate of intermarriage seemed to be increasing. Orthodoxy, on the other hand, remained well organized, though rigid in its attitude. In 1961, it kept a qualified scholar from an appointment to the principalship of Jews' College, the British rabbinical institution, because he favored discussing the problems of modern Bible criticism. It was an organizational rather than a popular victory. In 1966, Rabbi Immanuel Jacobovits, who had been Chief Rabbi of Ireland and later served for some years as rabbi of an Orthodox congregation in New York, became Chief Rabbi of the United Hebrew Congregations of the British Commonwealth. Reform (Conservative in the United States) and Liberal (Reform in the United States) congregations created a union of their own. Thus there was some ferment, which may make for growing public interest and better understanding of the problems.

The Smaller States of Western Europe—There was a time, before World War II, when it was possible to speak of West and Central European Jews as having similar communal structures, as having undergone similar experiences and attained more or less the same outlook. Such was no longer the case in the two post-war decades. The Jewish populations of France, Germany, Great Britain and Italy now differed completely from one another. The differences extended to the smaller countries as well. Each was now a new and divided community. Belgium's 40,000 Jews displayed little internal unity. It had East European Jews making a new start in life, in addition to the remnants of the old Belgian community that used to model itself upon French Jewry in the pre-war

days. More than half of the Jews lived in Brussels; fewer in
Antwerp. Those of the former city leaned to assimilation;
most of the latter were traditionalist. The 30,000 Jews of the
Netherlands were equally divided in religious sentiments.
Whether Sephardim or Ashkenazim, having been reduced to
a fifth of their pre-war numbers, they showed the effects of
their wartime experiences, and their Jewish life moved at a
tired pace. The 17th-century Sephardi synagogue of Amsterdam appeared to have lost most, in spirit as in attendance.
Nor has this segment of the population been replenished by
newcomers as the Ashkenazi segment was replenished to
some extent. Surprisingly, least unity existed among the
20,000 Jews of Switzerland who, before the war, had been
under the guidance of the Jews of Germany. Physically the
Swiss Jews had not suffered from Nazism, but their Jewish
spirit seems to have been broken. The cleavage between
East European and German Jews in Switzerland was stronger
than between Sephardim and Ashkenazim in Holland. It
looked in the 1960s as if at least a generation would have to
pass before these communities became as productive, spiritually and intellectually, as their predecessors were a generation
ago. Yet there were hopeful signs, since in all these smaller
countries there was a growing urge to increase the nature and
extent of Jewish education for the young. There were occasional manifestations of antisemitism everywhere, but the authorities remained fairly vigilant and the Churches friendly.

5. THE WESTERN DIASPORA

Jewishness in the Western World—European communities
had been close to and suffered directly from the events of
World War II; the Jewish communities in the western hemisphere, though distant from the scene of conflict even when
participants in it, nevertheless entered the decade of the
1950s with their character and awareness as Jews deeply
affected. They felt the need to redefine themselves in terms of
their respective situations, their relationship to the new State
of Israel, and of the problems which affected the entire
world. But any such definition of what Judaism and the Jewish people meant in the lands outside of Israel called, in the
first place, for knowledge of the essentials of Jewish life and,
secondly, for a willingness to remain members of a minority
group. In these respects, more or less extreme attitudes were
the first to become apparent. Hasidism was attracting much

interest in the larger cities, especially in the United States, and Orthodoxy became vocal and influential. At the same time, the rate of intermarriage—always an index of the force of disintegration within a minority group—was rising rapidly. A statistical study in 1957 revealed that the rate of intermarriage in several Jewish communities had risen to as high as 18% of all marriages contracted by Jews, though of course the rate for all of the United States was lower. The same study indicated that 70% of the children of intermarriages were lost to Judaism.

Cultural Progress—The situation called for greater efforts to retain the religious and cultural loyalties of young and old; it demanded more knowledge and deeper understanding. There was, in fact, a revival of interest in Jewish education in every country of North and South America. In Mexico, Brazil and Argentina this took the form of more Jewish schools and the publication of more books of Jewish content. In Argentina a seminary was established for the training of rabbis. Communal and congregational schools in the United States intensified their curricula, and there was a steady growth in the number of all-day schools beyond the 214 reported in 1960. In that year, moreover, the Council of Jewish Federations and Welfare Funds set up a National Foundation for Jewish Culture, with headquarters in New York, with the avowed aim of encouraging scholarly research and publication. Though the inadequate financial resources made available to the new Foundation drastically limited its activity, the fact of its establishment indicated a recognition of the cultural basis for Jewish survival.

The Climate of Equality—The improved cultural climate of the western world in general, at the beginning of the second half of the 20th century, had a beneficent effect on the position of the Jewish people. The burden of restrictions on the economic opportunities open to Jews was lifted: the professions were opened to them and, with some notorious exceptions, so too were industrial and banking offices. The extent to which the cultural and intellectual hungers traditional among Jews now asserted themselves was clear from the fact that, in the 1960s, 75% of Jews of college age in the United States were continuing their studies. Jews began to rank high in the fields of literature, journalism and art. The career of Arthur Goldberg, appointed in 1965 to represent the United States in the United Nations, indicated that there were fewer obstacles to the advancement of Jews in politics.

Antisemitism in the Post-War Period—The improvement

in the general attitude was properly considered as a reaction against the spiritual blight of Nazism that had threatened America in the 1930s and 1940s. The Christian population grew somewhat ashamed of antisemitism, and the manifestations of prejudice became weak and infrequent. But they did not entirely disappear. Small but vociferous Nazi groups continued operating in the United States and in parts of Latin America. In Argentina, for example, a semi-military band of middle-class youths, calling itself Tacuara, functioned as antisemites under the guidance of Nazi refugees and Arab propagandists. The government disowned them, though somewhat half-heartedly, but their violence continued. In the United States, the most disquieting manifestations of hostility to Jews were those which developed among the American Negroes. This was the more painful because Jews had for a long time been in the forefront of those advocating the rights of the Negroes to economic opportunity and civil equality. Again, as so often in the past, the faults of a social system were blamed on an easily distinguishable minority.

6. THE CHRISTIAN CHURCHES AND THE JEWISH PEOPLE

Help in Time of Distress—As the atmosphere cleared, after the defeat of the forces of evil in 1945, it became known that many Christian men and women had been moved by sympathy and humanitarianism to come to the aid of those who were threatened with capture and death at the hands of the Nazis. Hundreds had risked their own lives by hiding individual Jews and entire families, or by smuggling them out of danger and across frontiers. Among these heroic helpers were ordinary people, Protestants and Catholics, priests, ministers and nuns; they were found in Holland, Denmark and France, occasionally within Germany itself; there were such instances even in Poland. A number of these defenders of Jews were caught and sent to extermination camps, there to perish along with those whom they tried to save. While the number thus saved by their brave and usually anonymous protectors was no more than a fraction of the total lost, their action testified to the fact that decency was not dead. Various Jewish organizations, as well as the State of Israel, made public acknowledgment of their gratitude to a number of persons whose deeds had been especially notable and self-sacrificing.

The Official Conscience—At the same time, a question in

the opposite sense thrust itself into the mind. Could more men and women and children have been saved had the Christian Churches taken official note of the situation and condemned the Nazis for their criminal assault upon the Jews of Europe? The allied governments also had done little to save the threatened. Toward the end of the war, and while the extermination camps were still at work, Britain and the United States had refused to redeem some tens of thousands of Jews out of Nazi hands; they excused themselves on the ground that the materials with which payment was to have been made would add to the resources of the German military. The organized Churches, however, were not expected to take action of this sort, but merely to arouse the conscience of their adherents in Germany and the occupied lands who stood by and were doing nothing. A strong statement by Pope Pius XII, it has been argued, in condemnation of the extermination camps, issued at any time after 1942, might have saved many lives. Whether or not the Pope expressed his disapproval privately, he made no such statement public. He was said to have feared that such a public declaration might stir up the Nazis to take reprisals against the Catholic clergy and institutions under Hitler's control. Whether the Church should have taken a public stand nevertheless, especially at the time when hundreds of Jews in Rome were being herded off to execution, is a question which for a while was earnestly debated.

The Ecumenical Council—John Joseph Cardinal Roncalli was the papal nuncio (ambassador) to Yugoslavia when the Jews of that country were being rounded up for deportation to the death camps. A saintly man, he did what little he could to help them. When Pope Pius XII died, in 1958, Cardinal Roncalli was elected Pope and took the name John XXIII. In 1960, he called an ecumenical (universal) council of the Catholic Church to meet at the Vatican, with the aim of bringing the Church into closer harmony with the modern world. He also hoped to bring greater harmony among the various Christian Churches and, if possible, to alert all the religious forces of the world to the need of resisting atheistic views of life.

Pope John's plans for the Council extended in still another, more extraordinary, direction. Perhaps he recalled what he had witnessed in Yugoslavia. He was certainly aware that many Jews as well as non-Jews were convinced that the roots of antisemitism were traceable to certain Christian teachings and interpretations of the New Testament. As early as March

1959, more than two years before the Council met, Pope John gave a hint of his attitude by ordering the removal, from the Good Friday prayer for the conversion of the Jews, of the Latin word *perfidi;* it had originally meant "unbelieving," but in the course of time had taken on an insulting connotation. In preparing for the Council, the Pope appointed the learned Augustine Cardinal Bea to prepare the draft of a statement on what the Christian attitude should be toward the Jewish people. The draft was to be submitted to the Council when it met.

But it was not till September 1963, some months after John XXIII died and was succeeded by Pope Paul VI, that the statement which Cardinal Bea prepared was submitted to the Council at its second session. Considerable opposition to the statement arose behind the scenes, on both theological and political grounds. It was understandable that conservative Churchmen would oppose a change in the traditional doctrine that accused *the* Jews of rejecting and killing Jesus. The political argument was made by those members of the Council who, under pressure by Moslem politicians, made the point that the progress, and the very institutions, of the Church in Moslem countries would be jeopardized if any statement favorable to Jews were to be adopted. It was consequently not till the fourth and final session of the Council, in the autumn of 1965, that a resolution was finally adopted—by an overwhelming vote, to be sure, but with certain verbal weaknesses. The statement represents so radical a departure from the traditional interpretation of certain Christian doctrines and teachings that a few passages from it deserve quoting.

Since then the spiritual patrimony common to Christians and Jews is so great, the Council wishes to foster and commend mutual understanding and esteem. This will be the fruit above all of biblical and theological studies and of brotherly dialogue.

True, the Jewish authorities and those who followed their lead pressed for the death of Christ; still, what happened in his passion cannot be charged against all the Jews, without distinction, then alive, nor against the Jews of today. Although the Church is the New People of God, the Jews should not be represented as rejected by God or accursed, as if this followed from the Holy Scriptures. All should see to it, then, that in catechetical works and in the preaching of the word of God they teach nothing save what conforms to the truth of the Gospel and the spirit of Christ.

Furthermore, in her rejection of every persecution against any man, the Church, mindful of the patrimony she shares with the Jews and led, not by political reasons, but by the Gospel's spiritual love, decries hatred, persecution, manifestations of anti-Semitism, directed against Jews at any time and by anyone.

Teaching and Dialogue—This revolutionary statement was generally hailed as promising very much better relations between Christians and Jews. The educational departments of the churches in various countries at once began an examination of the textbooks used in the church schools, in order to weed out those expressions and teachings that made for misunderstanding and conflict. The goal, everyone realized, would take a long time to attain. But direct conversations, or dialogues, between Christians and Jews were easy to arrange. The suggestion, however, at once evoked misgivings among some Jews. They argued that dialogues imply the possibility of a deliberate effort to arrive at a compromise on theological concepts and may therefore prove to have a conversionist tendency. On the other hand, there were Jews who welcomed the idea of dialogues as affording an opportunity to clarify the differences between Judaism and Christianity and between the Church and the Jewish people. A number of dialogues took place which did not justify the fears, nor completely realize the hopes.

The Problems of Church and State—One such difference between Christians and Jews became a topic of public discussion in the United States. Jewish experience had repeatedly proved the danger inherent in a situation where Church and State were united, so that the State placed itself at the service of some particular religious organization. Almost invariably —modern Britain being the outstanding exception—the privileged Church tried to impose its will on the religious minorities in the country. In modern Spain, for example, public worship by Protestants and Jews was restricted. It need occasion no surprise, therefore, that Jews in the United States cherished the provision, early made part of the country's basic law, by which Church and State were completely separated. Since, however, the population of the United States was overwhelmingly Christian, the Protestants being in the majority, it was only natural for the Christmas holiday to be observed in the schools and for the school day in many districts to begin with the recital of a Christian prayer and the reading of the Bible. The protests of individuals failed to stop this practice and it tended to spread more widely over the country. Jewish organizations thereupon appealed to the courts and cited the Constitutional provision. In 1961 and in 1962, the Supreme Court of the United States handed down decisions against making prayer and Bible reading a part of the school procedures. Many Christians were shocked by what they considered secularization of the schools. On the other hand, given the historical experience of the Jewish people, their attitude in the matter is not hard to understand. There was less agreement among Jews on the question of government subvention of Catholic elementary schools and Jewish all-day schools.

7. PROGRESS AND PROBLEMS IN ISRAEL

Israel's Memories—After considerable discussion, Israel signed the reparations agreement with Germany in September 1952. In the course of the ten years that followed, Israel acquired from Germany ships, machinery and many other materials the new State needed, accounting for an average of 10% of Israel's imports. It was understood from the beginning that reparations could not mitigate the horror with which the Jews thought back upon Nazism. After all, a large part of Israel's population, those who had come from Europe, could not but recall what they had gone through personally and their loss of close relatives and friends. They erected the dignified and stirring Yad Vashem memorial building, planted a forest in memory of the martyrs, and wrote numerous books on the vanished Jewish communities. But, of course, the Israelis of North African and Asian origin did not carry the same memories. Nor could the growing generation of native Israelis be expected to recall the Nazi era with the same poignancy as their elders. It was notorious, moreover, that the rest of the world was eager to forget the cruelties of and the lessons to be learned from the Nazi experience.

The Eichmann Trial—The most spectacular result of this state of mind in Israel, as well as among Jews elsewhere, was the trial of Adolf Eichmann which was held in Jerusalem in 1961. Eichmann had been among the prominent Nazi officials entrusted with the job of exterminating the Jews of Europe from 1942 to 1945; and he had performed his murderous task with a degree of ruthless efficiency which won for him the commendation of his superiors. After the defeat of the Nazis, he, like so many of the major criminals among them, went into hiding. But a group of Jews, dedicated to finding these fugitives and bringing them to justice, located Eichmann in Argentina, where he was living under an assumed name. They kidnaped him in May 1960 and brought him to Israel, where he was charged with murder and put on trial in April 1961. A prominent lawyer of his choice was brought from Germany to defend him. A justice of the Israel Supreme Court and two other of Israel's foremost judges were appointed to hear the evidence. Gideon Hausner was the prosecutor. One hundred and twelve witnesses were called in the course of the trial. It lasted for five months.

The Argentine government had vigorously protested to Israel against the violation of its sovereignty by the act of kidnaping committed on its soil. It had done nothing itself to cleanse its soil of Nazi refugees, although in this respect it was no different from many other countries. The trial repeatedly revealed how little the allied governments had done during the war to save Europe's Jews, even when the saving of life was possible. Britain, Russia and the United States, as well as Germany, were on trial along with Eichmann. During the trial—in fact, ever since his arrest—the sentiment of the civilized world was divided. Many voices were raised in condemnation of the trial, especially of holding it in Israel; but no one offered any cogent suggestion as to what other course of action was proper under the circumstances, since there was no international court for such a contingency and Germany would have been seriously embarrassed by it.

Eichmann's defense, like that of other Nazis who were ever brought before a court anywhere, was that he had been but a humble cog in the huge wheel of Hitlerite policy: his was not to question, but to obey, even when obedience meant wholesale murder. He showed himself to be clever enough personally, but a man of slight intellectual and spiritual stature, who had advanced himself by eagerly adopting the standards and ideas which prevailed in his time and which he could use to personal advantage. He received a fair trial. The judges took some months to consider the evidence. In December 1961 they issued their verdict condemning him to be hanged. His execution took place the following May.

Friends and Enemies—The dramatic Eichmann trial had as little effect on Israel's diplomatic relations as had the Sinai War several years before. The friendliness of some nations and the hostility of others were motivated, as usual, by self-interest rather than by the rights and wrongs of the situation. Even the presumably high-minded government of India still refused to recognize Israel's existence, no doubt because a large part of its population adhered to the Moslem faith. Israel's Moslem neighbors continued to seek its destruction, while Soviet Russia saw its advantage in playing Nasser's game. The western nations remained friendly. Britain supported Israel diplomatically when need arose. If the United States pursued a policy of neutrality, though with occasional ominous implications for Israel's future, this was due to the exigencies of the Cold War. By far the most disturbing element in the situation was the piling up of armaments by both sides, by Moslems as well as by Jews, which neither could afford. For the most part Israel's arms came from France; Egypt's and Syria's from Russia. The United Nations proved to be of little help. Although it was no secret that the Moslem nations were planning to shut off Israel's water supply by deflecting the waters of the Jordan; although bands of infiltrators, trained to murder, now came from the Syrian side to spread destruction within Israel, just as in former days such bands had come from Egypt; although the scandalous refugee situation was being constantly falsified and aggravated, the United Nations seemed unable to do anything about solving the problems of the Middle East.

Israel's International Helpfulness—With the opening of the Red Sea to Israeli shipping after the Sinai War, the port of Eilath could be used for contact with African and Asian nations. Israel thereupon embarked on a policy of helping under-developed countries by giving them the benefit of its experience in cooperative agriculture. It did this in two ways: by sending experts to advise and train men in their respective countries, and by opening courses of study for the training of people whom the various nations sent to Israel. In 1966, fifty-five countries in Asia, Africa and Latin America were using six hundred Israeli experts, who were training 3,600 men. At the same time, between 1958 and 1966, almost 9,000 men, representing ninety-one nations, received training within Israel.

Israel's Population—Israel's population at the end of 1965 consisted of 2,299,100 Jews, 212,400 Moslems, 57,000 Christians, and 29,000 Druses and members of other religious groups. At the end of 1966, the total population of the country was 2,656,800. Of the Jews, 45% were of Asian and North African origin. The growing imbalance in the population had long been a matter of concern to the nation's leaders, who did not like the idea of the country's losing its European character. But there was little that one could do about it, since the communist nations would not permit their Jews to emigrate to Israel, while the immigration from North and South America continued to be disappointingly small. Israel in the 1960s thus faced a problem of acculturation similar in many respects to the problem faced by a number of the diaspora communities. For Israel it meant greater efforts in the fields of culture and education.

The Problem of Water—A problem of more immediate concern was that of irrigation. The austerity that had been essential for some years after the establishment of the State could be relaxed in the mid-1950s. Foreign capital, especially American, helped found new industries. New agricultural settlements were established in the Negev, the southern desert, frequently also with an eye to defense. But the great need, in a country with as little rainfall as Israel enjoyed, was for irrigation. Pipes were laid at great expense from the Sea of Galilee in the north all the way down to the southland; but these did not yet provide sufficient water to meet the needs of the Negev, where the future of Israel's agriculture must lie. Experiments had thus far failed to make the desalting of Mediterranean water economically feasible. It therefore appeared essential for Israel to tap the waters of the Jordan river. But the Arab nations countered by announcing plans to draw enough water away from Lake Huleh, in the north, as to make the Israel plan impossible. Thus the basis was laid for further international conflict.

Cities, Old and New—When immigration into Palestine began in earnest, after World War I, a town was laid out by the side of the ancient city of Jaffa and was named Tel Aviv (Mound of Spring). It is difficult to think back to Tel Aviv as the small town of some 30,000 that it was in the late 1920s. In 1966, it was a bustling city of close to 400,000. It had two universities: the Tel Aviv University with some 7,000 students, and the religiously-oriented Bar Ilan University with about 3,000. Fifty miles to the north was the industrial city of Haifa, with a population of 200,000. On the crest of its Mount Carmel, overlooking the magnificent bay, the new buildings of the Technion rose in 1966, as Israel's engineering school. It had been crowded out from the center of the city and could now be more comfortable with its 5,000 students and greatly expanded curriculum. Farther south, below Tel Aviv, the ancient Philistine cities of Bible days, Ashdod and Ashkelon, sprang into new life. In 1966, Ashkelon began the building of a port intended to supplement, if not to rival, the port of Haifa. Inland, Beersheba, a frontier town in 1960, grew into a thriving metropolis within half a decade. Eilath, at the head of the Red Sea, consisted of a few huts before the Sinai campaign; but in 1965 it was a port of growing importance in the commerce with the south.

The New Jerusalem—Jewish Jerusalem, for all that its varied and colorful population had grown to 280,000 since the attainment of independence, was third in size of Israel's cities, though first in the respect and affection of the Jewish people. Because the Old City was in the hands of the Moslem Jordanians, the Jewish part of the city had to grow westward. The Jordanians also held the approaches to Mount Scopus. They were able to do this by the terms of the armistice agreement of 1948, so that the Jerusalem University buildings and its library, as well as the Hadassah Hospital, became inaccessible to the Jews. For more than a decade, rented and temporary quarters had to be used. In the early 1960s, a new University campus came into existence, with an administration building at one end and a magnificent library building at the other. Not far away a museum was erected and, connected with it, a House of the Book in which are displayed the newly-found Dead Sea Scrolls and other archaelogical treasures. On the other side of the University center, Hadassah erected its new hospital buildings. Overlooking the whole, was the Knesseth building to house the Israel parliament and the offices connected with the national administration; it was dedicated on August 30, 1966.

Religion and the State—The Hekhal Shelomo (the Hall of Solomon) was dedicated in Jerusalem in May 1958, to serve as the religious capital of Israel's Jewish community. There the highest religious court of Israel held its sessions. The extent of the authority exercised by this religious establishment and its influence on the government constituted one of the most serious problems confronting the country. Under the British mandate, each religious group regulated its own affairs, and the arrangement was continued after the mandate ended and the State was established. There never was any question of terminating the arrangement for the Moslems, Christians, or any other religious group; but for the Jews, who everywhere else in the world were striving for the separation of Church and State, such religious authority appeared anomalous. Yet the Orthodox part of the Jewish community insisted that no other Jewish religious viewpoint be recognized. Reform and Conservative Judaism, as practiced in western Jewish communities, found it impossible to plant their religious institutions in Israel. Their rabbis were not permitted to perform religious rites and their synagogues could not function except on an informal and personal basis. Few in Israel denied that religion was the basic test of Jewishness, and few failed to be concerned when it was discovered, in the 1950s, that Christian missionary activity was going on among Jewish children of the poor. But the extent to which the State must be guided by Orthodox religious leadership remained an open and irritating question. The nature of the political situation—the need for the votes of the Orthodox in the Knesseth government coalition—made the influence of the Orthodox secure for the time being. But dissatisfaction with the arrangement was growing. A moderating influence in the 1950s was Chief Rabbi Isaac Halevi Herzog. His death, in 1959, was the signal for an open difference of opinion about the nature of his successor, whether he was to be a moderate or a staunchly Orthodox rabbi. After several years of delay, the government was compelled to accept the conservative-minded Rabbi Israel Unterman of Tel Aviv as chief rabbi of the Ashkenazi community.

Parties and Politics—Since the major external problems facing the State did not change, the political situation was affected, down to 1967, only by internal needs and differences of opinion. Israel's third national election was held in 1955, the fourth in 1959, and the fifth in 1961. In this year the Knesseth, whose full term of office had been set for four years, dissolved itself because of a political crisis caused by an incident known as the Lavon Affair. The Mapai, a moderate workers' party, received the largest number of votes in all these elections, electing more than a third of the 120 members of the Knesseth. But since no one party received a majority, the government remained a coalition. This, in turn, implied compromise, especially in religious and economic matters. David Ben-Gurion remained prime minister throughout, except for a brief period (1954–1955) when Moshe Sharett replaced him. In 1963, however, at the age of 77, he stepped down and was followed in office by Levi Eshkol who had previously served as minister of finance. But the continued bitterness engendered by the Lavon Affair created a rift between Eshkol and his predecessor. A new parliamentary election was therefore called for in 1965. The Ben-Gurion forces entered candidates of their own under the party name of Rafi (Israel Labor List), while Mapai joined with a segment of the somewhat more radical Mapam party. The last-named united group won close to a majority in the election and formed a government in cooperation with Mapam and the religious group, with Levi Eshkol continuing as prime minister. In December 1967, the Rafi group rejoined Mapai.

In April 1963, the scholarly Itzhak Ben-Zvi, Israel's second president, died. He was succeeded by Zalman Shazar, who had been a Yeshiva student in Russia, a publicist in Palestine and Israel, and an author of considerable charm. At about the same time, Golde Meir, long Israel's foreign minister, relinquished her post to Abba Eban, former ambassador to the United States and Israel's representative at the United Nations.

Nobel Prize Winners—There could have been no better indication of the essential unity of the Jewish people—culturally at least—than the award of the Nobel Prize in Literature for the year 1966 to Samuel Joseph Agnon, formerly of Galicia and now of Israel, and to Nellie Sachs, formerly of Germany and now of Sweden. Agnon had written imaginative tales in Hebrew, drawing on Jewish piety in Eastern Europe. Nelly Sachs had written poetry in German, drawing on the tradition of West European culture and liberalism. The world in which both had grown to maturity had been destroyed during their lifetime. Each represented a part of the precious spirit which had nurtured them.

8. THE SIX-DAY WAR

Steps Leading to Conflict—During the early part of 1967, Israel was grappling with its serious internal problems, especially with such economic difficulties as a high rate of unemployment and an unfavorable balance of trade. In the background of the nation's life, frequently making the headlines of Israeli and foreign newspapers, were the frequent attacks from across the Syrian and Jordanian borders, which occasionally provoked retaliation by Israel. The firing into Israel from the fortified heights of Syria and the incursions into Israel territory had become facts of life; apart from striking back, Israel could do nothing more about them. It appeared pointless to lodge complaints with the United Nations. Russia had for years vetoed any resolution dealing with this subject in the Security Council whenever such a resolution condemned the Arabs, no matter how strong the proof of their guilt. Suddenly, in the middle of May 1967, the situation took a turn for the worse.

a. Russia had been pouring vast quantities of arms—guns and tanks and planes—into both Syria and Egypt. Yet Nasser's prestige among the other Moslems continued to sink, while Syria's presumably socialist dictatorship was again in danger of collapsing. A plan of action to counter the trends seems to have been worked out between Russia and its Moslem protégés. Early in 1967, the Syrian attacks on Israel began to take on bolder and more menacing forms, and they naturally called forth stronger retaliation on the part of Israel. A Syrian attack in early April was especially vicious. Israel's response was sure to come, but it was slow in developing. Nasser, announcing that Israel was mobilizing its forces to attack Syria, although Israel offered to prove that this was not true, mobilized the Egyptian army and, on May 14, sent most of it and many hundreds of tanks into the Gaza strip and the Sinai desert. Within a few days, Israel responded by calling up its own reserves.

b. The second step came two days later, when Nasser demanded the withdrawal of the international patrol that ever since the war of 1956 had been stationed on the borders between Egypt and Israel. Now Nasser wanted these foreign soldiers out of his way and, after some hesitation but without first consulting the Security Council, U Thant, the secretary-general of the United Nations, agreed to remove them. They could only have stayed there, he pointed out, with Egypt's consent.

c. But the most fateful step was yet to come. On May 22, Nasser announced the resumption of the blockade of the Gulf of Aqaba against Israeli shipping. That exit from the port of Eilath had been opened by the war in 1956, and a United Nations force had been stationed there as well to guarantee Israel's freedom of navigation. To close it meant to stifle Israel's developing commerce. It may be that this step went beyond Egypt's agreement with Russia; yet, once done, Russia stood by the action. By any accepted definition of international law this constituted an act of war against which Israel was bound to fight. Yet Israel held back, in the hope that the maritime powers of Europe and America would join in making it clear that the Egyptian action would not be tolerated. As it turned out, these powers would take no action. When this became clear, conflict was inevitable.

d. The pro-Israel and neutral members of the United Nations were fully aware of the dangers inherent in the situation: the act of war in blockading Eilath had to be reversed. The Security Council was called into session on May 24. If the great powers represented on the Council could have arrived at a decision to maintain a just peace, the situation might still have been saved. But the pro-Egyptian nations on the Council, still under the impression that Israel would not fight back against the overwhelming armaments in the hands of the Arabs, delayed the meetings and made action impossible. Even France, theretofore a staunch friend of Israel, appeared half-hearted in the matter. The United Nations thus showed itself powerless, and thereby convinced Israel that it could count on no help from the outside. On June 1, Prime Minister Eshkol appointed Moshe Dayan, who had on many occasions proved his generalship, to the ministry of defense.

e. Throughout the weeks of waiting, the Moslem nations carried on a furious propaganda campaign for the destruction of Israel. In posters and broadcasts and speeches, by means of parades and demonstrations they aroused their populations to a frenzy; they left no doubt of their intention to invade Israel and slaughter its Jewish inhabitants. On May 30, Hussein, King of Jordan, announced his solidarity with Egypt and Syria in the war of annihilations which they exultantly predicted. Iraq sent a part of its army into Jordan, so as to bring it closer to the scene of the coming action. Saudi Arabia, Kuwait, and the Moslem lands of North Africa gave their promise of support. Could the Moslems now be restrained? No one in Israel, or anywhere else, believed it possible.

The Fighting—Had Israel reacted at once to the blockade of Aqaba, instead of waiting for two weeks for the United Nations or some maritime powers to act, no one would have doubted that Egypt started the war. As late as June 3, Israel made the lifting of the blockade its primary condition for avoiding war. But because Israel chose not to act precipitously, the warlike nature of the blockade was pushed into the background, and Israel was charged by the pro-Moslem nations, under Russian leadership, with having been the aggressor. It is, in fact, impossible to tell from which side the first shots came. Nor is it important: by early June, the situation was beyond control.

The first major blow came from the side of Israel. Early on Monday, June 5, the Israeli Air Force accurately and thoroughly bombed the airfields of Egypt, destroying several hundred airplanes on the ground, practically the entire air fleet so painstakingly built up at Russia's expense. The airfleets of Jordan and Syria were soon to meet the same fate. Simultaneously, Israel's army moved into the Gaza strip and across the Sinai border; it soon reached the Suez Canal. Poorly trained, badly led, unable to use their superior weapons, the soldiers of Egypt were no match for those of Israel. Hussein of Jordan was urged by Israel to stay out of the fighting; but he replied by bombarding Jewish Jerusalem. On the second day of the war, the Israelis began the attack on the Old City, and Mount Scopus was the first spot to be liberated. On the third day, Israeli tanks fought their way into Jordanian Jerusalem. Forbidden the use of heavy guns, lest injury be done to the holy sites of several religions, the Jewish soldiers limited themselves to the use of small arms. Late that day, the ancient city was completely under Jewish control. By Thursday, the fourth day, the entire western sector of Jordan, including the cities of Nablus (Shechem), Jericho and Bethlehem, was in the hands of the Israeli army.

Fighting had been expected at Sharm El Sheikh, which commanded the entrance to the Gulf of Aqaba. Paratroopers who flew there on Wednesday found the place deserted, the Egyptian garrison having fled northward. Things were different on the Syrian border. For some reason, Syria waited till Thursday to commence hostilities; but by then Israeli soldiers could be detached from the other fronts and sent north. Here the fighting was heavy and costly, for the Syrians fought from the Golan Heights, which were subsequently found to have been excellently fortified by Russian engineers. It was not till Saturday that the fighting here was brought to a successful end.

The cease fire voted by the Security Council of the United Nations went into effect on Sunday, June 11.

The United Nations Debates—No sooner was the victorious advance of Israel reported than the very nations that had stood in the way of peace-making the week before began to clamor for a halt to the fighting. Oblivious of their acquiescence in the blockade of Aqaba, they now loudly proclaimed Israel the aggressor and insisted on reverting to the situation of June 4. Only when they failed in this maneuver did they agree to the cease fire resolution which went into effect on June 11. But their efforts to turn the clock of history back by compelling Israel to withdraw from all the territory it had overrun during the six days of fighting did not stop. Israel, on the other hand, through its eloquent foreign secretary, Abba Eban, insisted that it sought peace, and that such peace could be obtained only through a treaty negotiated and signed in a direct confrontation of the participants in the fighting. The old situation, in which the Moslem nations refused to recognize the existence of Israel and openly agitated for its destruction, he pointed out, could only lead to more border incidents and eventually to further warfare. Until a genuine peace could be arranged Israel would continue occupying the territory it had won.

9. CONSEQUENCES OF THE WAR

United Jerusalem—There was only one bit of land that Israel declared it expected to hold forever: the Old City of Jerusalem. It had always been the most sacred spot in Judaism; for the past two thousand years the Jews had turned toward it in prayer. But ever since the War of Israeli Independence, it had been barred to Jews. Even the so-called Wailing Wall, which Jewish tradition considers to be the last vestige of the ancient Temple, could not be visited by Jews. The Jewish cemetery on the Mount of Olives had suffered at the hands of vandals; many of its tombstones had been used for building barracks or as paving stones. On June 7, when the City fell into the hands of the Jews, an impromptu service was held at the Wailing Wall: Rabbi Shlomo Goren, Chief Chaplain of the Israel army, read the service in the presence of the prime minister and of General Dayan. The *shofar,* the ram's horn, whose strange sounds are heard in the synagogue on the most solemn days of the Jewish calendar, was sounded. Rabbi Goren then vowed that, in Jewish hands, the City would remain open to all religions and that the sites sacred to each would be protected. A few days later, the Israel government proclaimed the irrevocable union of Old and New Jerusalem. The proclamation did not sit well with some Christians who would have much preferred for the Holy City to be placed under international control. The Jews, however, were enthusiastic.

The Refugees—For almost twenty years, Israel had been under siege by a host of poverty-stricken refugees whom the surrounding Moslem nations refused to absorb. For them the existence of the refugee camps served as a remarkably effective method of anti-Israel propaganda. It made humanitarians everywhere overlook the many millions of starving people in other lands, while their resentment was continuously stirred against Israel for having presumably caused the homelessness of these unfortunate Arabs. The Six-Day War added to the problem by impelling most of the old refugees to move across the Jordan and by creating some new refugees from among those residents on the west bank of the river who refused to remain under Israeli control. The estimate of

200,000 new refugees was a vast exaggeration; but even if the number was much smaller, it served to complicate the situation. Soon after the end of hostilities, Israel agreed to permit the return of many who had family or property west of the Jordan. Peace in the Near East admittedly could not be achieved unless the refugee problem were solved.

Whenever the question of the refugees had been discussed, Israel maintained that the fate of the Jews expelled from Moslem lands, in the course of the conflicts between Israel and her neighbors, should be balanced against the fate of the Arabs who fled from Israel. For hundreds of thousands of Jewish refugees had been deprived of their homes and possessions before they fled to the new State and to other lands. The fact that the Jews were more hospitable to their kin than the Moslems were to theirs should not be held against Israel. The losses in property should be taken into account on the one side as on the other.

The Search for a Way to Peace—In the course of the six months that followed the six days of war, everyone expressed a desire for peace, but no one could suggest an acceptable way of achieving it. The Jews argued from the first that the wrong way would be for them to give up the territory they had conquered and then plead with the Arab nations to recognize their existence, their rights to free navigation and to freedom from fear of incursion by marauding bands. But the Arab nations kept insisting on a return to the old situation and refused to meet Israel's representatives face to face. Egypt refused to re-open the Suez Canal until Israel removed its soldiers from the Canal's eastern bank. The United States and Britain recognized the justice of Israel's stand, although the United States continued its embargo on arms to the Middle East and shipped to Israel only those planes which had been promised before the fighting began. Russia, however, not only took the Arab view of the situation, but began immediately to replenish the losses in armaments suffered by Egypt and Syria during the war in June. It even sent part of its fleet to Egyptian waters, perhaps to bolster Nasser's loss of self-confidence as well as his waning popularity. As to France, President Charles de Gaulle decided that his country had more to gain from becoming pro-Arab and therefore changed the traditional French pro-Israel policy; he imposed an embargo on the export of arms to Israel. Under these international circumstances, it appeared, by the end of 1967, that the war between Israel and its neighbors was far from over and that another round was inevitable. In

November 1967, the only thing the United Nations could do was to send a representative to the Middle East to search for a solution. It picked a Swedish diplomat by the name of Gunnar V. Jarring.

The Fate of Dialogue—One unexpected result of the Six-Day War was the effect it threatened to have on Jewish enthusiasm for dialogues between Jews and Christians. These friendly dialogues had been going on ever since the Ecumenical Council in Rome. But when the storm broke between Israel and the Moslem states in May 1967, with the Moslem states loudly and insistently proclaiming their intention to wipe out not only the Jewish State but also its two and a half million Jewish lives, the Christian Churches remained almost completely silent. The Christian masses were almost everywhere pro-Jewish; individual Churchmen here and there spoke up in favor of the Jewish side of the argument. But organized Christianity said not a word, though undoubtedly the various Churches would have expressed horror if the Arabs had carried out their threats of annihilation. When, however, Israel's victory was assured, some leading Churchmen saw fit to accuse Israel of aggression and expansionism. Clearly, the dialogues had in large measure failed of their purpose. The Jewish participants had failed to set forth with sufficient emphasis the part that the State of Israel had in Judaism and the hopes of the Jewish people for cultural survival. These were areas in which the Jewish and the Christian views of history clashed and where discussion was called for. Nevertheless, the usefulness of further dialogue was brought into question.

The Jewish Spirit of Battle—The conflict with the Arab states illustrated the attitude to war which prevailed among the Jewish people. There has never been a war with so much blood-lust on one side and so much self-restraint on the other. This spirit is best described in the words spoken by General Yitzhak Rabin, Chief of Staff of Israel's Defense Forces, when on June 28, 1967, he accepted an honorary degree from the Hebrew University at its old site on Mount Scopus. He said, in part:

> The entire nation was exalted and many wept when they heard of the capture of the Old City. Our *sabra* youth, and most certainly our soldiers, do not tend to be sentimental and they shrink from any public show of feeling. But the strain of battle and the anxiety which preceded it, and the sense of salvation and of direct confrontation with Jewish history itself, cracked the shell of hardness and shyness and released

wellsprings of emotion and stirrings of the spirit. The paratroopers who conquered the Wailing Wall leaned on its
stones and wept—in its symbolism an act so rare as to be
almost unparalleled in human history. . . .

And there is more to be told. The joy of triumph had seized
the entire nation. Nevertheless, a strange phenomenon can be
observed among our soldiers. Their joy is incomplete, and
their celebrations are marred by sorrow and shock. There
are even some who abstain from celebrations entirely. The
men in the front lines saw with their own eyes not only the
glory of victory, but also the price of victory—their comrades
fallen beside them soaked in blood. I know too that the
terrible price paid by our enemies also touched the hearts of
many of our men. It may be that the Jewish people has never
learned and never accustomed itself to feel the triumph of
conquest and victory, with the result that these are accepted
with mixed feelings.

10. SUMMARY OF THE EVENTFUL DECADES

The Sense of Interdependence—The threat to the Jewish
population of Israel evoked a remarkable display of solidarity
among the Jews all over the world. Even those Jews whose
interest in the existence of an independent Israel was minimal
showed deep concern over the threat that hung over the State
and the people. It was far from being a show of political loyalty; it was rather an assertion of group and cultural affinity.
In a sense it was the outcome of the millennial Jewish experience that the fate of no Jewish group leaves the rest
unaffected. "All Israelites are responsible for one another" is
the way the matter was put in talmudic days. That was a
statement of historical fact as well as an exhortation. The
echoes of Nazism everywhere in the 1930s was a recent example of the statement as historical fact; the response of Jewish
philanthropy to the expulsion from North Africa in the 1950s
was an example of the effectiveness of the statement as exhortation. The events preceding and following the six days in
June of 1967 revived this latent spirit of a unity that was
not reflected in the religious and cultural attitudes of the
contemporary Jews. It was a rare moment in recent Jewish
history. Not again within a single generation would the Jews
abandon the just cause of their people to the interests of international diplomacy and the heartlessness of other organized
groups, religious or political.

The New Face of the Diaspora—The two decades following World War II changed the spirit of the Jewish people as well as its physical make-up, in Israel as well as in Europe. This was due to the almost total disappearance of North African Jewry and to the migration westward of the remnants of the Jewish communities of Eastern Europe. The Sephardi element became dominant in France and gained numerically in Italy. The Jews of Spain and Portugal re-established congregational life after a lapse of five centuries. In Germany, the Netherlands, and to some extent in the Scandinavian countries, Jewish communities were in the process of rebuilding largely through immigration from Eastern Europe. Even Russian Jewry, should it ever obtain a measure of cultural freedom, will emerge as a new community. Having been deprived for more than a generation of the opportunity to live and think as Jews, it will have to live on vague memories of the past, and recall is never the same as continuity. Very much the same situation characterized the small remaining Jewish groups in the other communist states. The once flourishing Jewish community of Poland, for example, now a mere 30,000, was deprived of its last contact with other Jews when the officers of the Joint Distribution Committee were asked to close its doors at the end of 1967. In some respects, these changes represent a strange reversal of the historical process which took place in the sixteenth century.

The Religious Predicament—There never was a time, in the last millennium and a half, when differences of opinion on the subject of Judaism went so deep. Within every community, the State of Israel included, many of the most acculturated Jews appear to have lost touch with the Tradition. Yet there was a simultaneous awakening of interest in Jewish religious life, although such interest often extended to the cultural and spiritual values rather than to observance and ceremonial. In this respect, the diaspora looked to Israel, where re-interpretation and adaptation was possible without interference from a non-Jewish environment. Israel, however, was slow in providing such leadership, so that every diaspora community had to fall back on its own cultural resources to stem the tide of total assimilation.

The Jews and their Neighbors—With the defeat of Nazism, a tragic era for the Jews came to an end in the western countries. But tragedy overwhelmed the Jews of Moslem lands, where a revived nationalism and sympathy for fellow-Moslems defeated by Israel aroused the populations against the Jews who had for many centuries lived in their midst. Christendom, however, experienced a reaction against antisemitism. Not for almost a thousand years—since the beginning of the crusading era—had the countries of Europe and America been so free of this ugly spiritual blight as during the 1950s and 1960s. To be sure, antisemitic attitudes were known to be latent, and overt acts were met with occasionally among men of high and low degree; but they were few. The statement on this subject by the Ecumenical Council of the Catholic Church in 1965 was encouraging, as were similar statements by a number of Protestant bodies. The political and cultural equality of the Jews was taken for granted, although subjected to many restrictions in communist countries. One may cherish the hope that, in these respects, the situation will continue to improve.

LOOKING TO THE FUTURE

The Living People—The history of a living people does not come to an end. History goes on from age to age, from crisis to crisis. There were periods in the past when both friends and enemies thought they could foresee the end of the Jewish people. There have been those who thought that Jewish history ended with the destruction of the Second Commonwealth by Rome. They would therefore argue that this book has concerned itself with a fossil or has told the story of a ghost. If so, the fossil has been showing extraordinary vitality and the ghost still possesses a very lively body. We therefore conclude this book, but the not the story it has tried to tell.

Experiments that Ended in Tragedy—Jews had lived in Europe since the days of the Roman Republic. They did at least as much as any group in European society to build up the continent's civilization, cooperating in the development of its art and sciences, its literature and economics. They played a creative role in the emergence of European democracy, and they helped Europe's masses rise from semi-slavery to freedom. At the same time, they developed a Jewish way of life and a Jewish system of thought which went beyond the piety and spirituality of the Babylonian center which had gone before. They began to make a successful adjustment between Jewish and non-Jewish cultures, and this already bore cultural fruit.

All this seems to have been destroyed. Let it be remembered, however, that the Jewish communities of Europe and their rich cultures did not collapse of their own weakness. Jewish life in Europe was not a failure. Europe had failed; western civilization had failed. It threatened to collapse because it had neglected to establish peace and justice within its boundaries; and its most defenseless minority was drawn into the general catastrophe. But the Jewry of Europe did not die in vain. Its final struggle was, characteristically, against the enemy of the best in human culture. Its heroism, displayed during those crucial years as well as in the establishment of the State of Israel, lifted the hearts of Jews the world over. On the surviving communities, especially those of Israel and America, now rests the responsibility of carrying high the banner of Jewish hope and idealism through the ages to come.

The Dawn of a New Age—As had happened before in the history of the Jewish people, a reserve community was being built up in America while the European Jewish community was still flourishing. The vast migration of Jews during the nineteenth and twentieth centuries resulted in the growth of a number of Jewish centers: in South America, in South Africa, in Canada, and above all in the United States. A community of more than 5,000,000 in strength, living as part of a nation which had been taught to respect human personality and which has dedicated itself to the ideal of each man's inalienable rights to life, liberty and happiness, its roots firmly planted in religious faith—such a community, living in such surroundings, should have a promising future. But the promise will not come of itself; it must be planned and worked for. When American Jews have learned to know, appreciate and live by their own ideals, when they have acquainted themselves with their own cultural heritage and have made every effort to develop it in consonance with the ideals and culture of America, they will have opened the road to another golden age in Jewish history. In America this is possible as nowhere else. In America, therefore, the opportunity of living the Jewish life in freedom has the brightest hopes of realization.

We are moving toward an age which holds the promise of one world enjoying abundance and peace, justice and happiness. But there are also dangers, and much remains to be suffered before mankind achieves these goals. Yet, it is this eternal dream that lures mankind—the dream first dreamt on Judean hills by Hebrew prophet and sage. This beckoning future of mankind, and our cooperation in realizing it, help give meaning to Jewish life and struggle today. The Jewish group is challenged by mankind's opportunity. If the challenge is met with vision, wisdom and determination, the People Israel will continue to be a blessing among the peoples of the world.

BIBLIOGRAPHY*

GENERAL

* This bibliography is intended to suggest additional reading. The books were chosen for their availability and their popular approach, though many of them are works of profound scholarship. A small number of novels were included. In choosing these titles, the author had the advantage of consulting the late Leo L. Honor, then Professor of Education at the Dropsie College, and Doctor Azriel Eisenberg, former Executive Vice President of the Jewish Education Committee of New York City.

ABRAHAMS, ISRAEL, Chapters on Jewish Literature. Philadelphia: Jewish Publication Society, 1899.

BAECK, LEO, This People Israel (translated by Albert H. Friedlander). Philadelphia: Jewish Publication Society, 1965.

BARON, SALO W., The Jewish Community, 3 vols. Philadelphia: Jewish Publication Society, 1942.

——, A Social and Religious History of the Jews (revised edition) 12 vols. New York: Columbia University Press and Philadelphia: Jewish Publication Society, 1955–.

BEVAN, E. R. and SINGER, C. S., eds., The Legacy of Israel. Oxford, England, 1928.

DUBNOW, S M., Jewish History, An Essay in the Philosophy of History (translated by Henrietta Szold). Philadelphia: Jewish Publication Society, 1903.

ENGLEMAN, U. Z., The Rise of the Jew in the Western World. New York: Behrman's Jewish Book House, 1944.

FINKELSTEIN, LOUIS, ed., The Jews, Their History, Culture, and Religion, 2 vols. 3rd edition. New York: Harper Bros., 1960.

FRISCH, E., An Historical Survey of Jewish Philanthropy. New York: Macmillan, 1924.

GRAETZ, HEINRICH, History of the Jews, 6 vols. Philadelphia: Jewish Publication Society, 1891–8.

JACOBS, JOSEPH, Jewish Contributions to Civilization. Philadelphia: Jewish Publication Society, 1919.

KASTEIN, JOSEF, History and Destiny of the Jews. New York: Viking Press, 1935.

LOWENTHAL, MARVIN, The Jews of Germany. Philadelphia: Jewish Publication Society, 1936.

——, A World Passed By. New York: Behrman, 1938.

MARCUS, JACOB R., The Jew in the Medieval World. Cincinnati: Union of American Hebrew Congregations, 1938.

MARGOLIS, MAX L., and MARX, ALEXANDER, A History of the Jewish People. Philadelphia: Jewish Publication Society, 1927.

PINSON, KOPPEL S., editor, Essays on Anti-Semitism. New York: Conference on Jewish Relations, 1941, 1946.

RAPPOPORT, A. S., History of Palestine. New York: E. P. Dutton and Co., 1931.

ROTH, CECIL, A History of the Jews in England. Oxford, England, 1941.

——, The History of the Jews of Italy. Philadelphia: Jewish Publication Society, 1946.

——, The Jewish Contribution to Civilization. Cincinnati: Union of American Hebrew Congregations, 1940.

SCHWARTZ, LEO W., ed., Great Ages and Ideas of the Jewish People. New York: Random House, 1956.

VOGELSTEIN, HERMANN, History of the Jews in Rome. Philadelphia: Jewish Publication Society, 1940.

WAXMAN, MEYER, A History of Jewish Literature, 4 vols. New York: Bloch, 1938–41.

1. THE SECOND COMMONWEALTH: 586 B.C.E. TO 135 C.E.

AHAD HA‘AM, "Flesh and Spirit," in Selected Essays, pp. 138–158. Philadelphia: Jewish Publication Society, 1912.

BENTWICH, NORMAN, Hellenism. Philadelphia: Jewish Publication Society, 1919.

——, Josephus. Philadelphia: Jewish Publication Society, 1914.

——, Philo. Philadelphia: Jewish Publication Society, 1910.

FEUCHTWANGER, LION, Josephus. New York: Viking Press, 1932.

——, The Jew of Rome. New York: Viking Press, 1936.

——, Josephus and the Emperor. New York, Viking Press, 1942.

GINZBERG, LOUIS, "The Religion of the Pharisees," in Students, Scholars and Saints, pp. 88–108. Philadelphia: Jewish Publication Society, 1928.

GLATZER, NAHUM N., ed., Josephus: Jerusalem and Rome. New York: Meridian Press, 1960.

GOODSPEED, E. J., The Story of the Apocrypha. Chicago: University of Chicago Press, 1939.

HADAS, MOSES, Hellenistic Culture: Fusion and Diffusion. New York: Columbia University Press, 1959.

HERFORD, R. T., The Pharisees. London, 1924.

KLAUSNER, JOSEPH, From Jesus to Paul. New York: Macmillan, 1943.

——, Jesus of Nazareth. New York: Macmillan, 1925.

MARGOLIS, MAX L., The Hebrew Scriptures in the Making. Philadelphia: Jewish Publication Society, 1922.

——, The Story of Bible Translations. Philadelphia: Jewish Publication Society, 1917.

RADIN, MAX, The Jews among the Greeks and Romans. Philadelphia: Jewish Publication Society, 1915.

ROBINSON, T. H., and OESTERLEY, W. O. E., A History of Israel, 2 vols. Oxford, England, 1932.

SCHEDCHTER, SOLOMON, "A Glimpse of the Social Life of the Jews in the Age of Jesus the Son of Sirach," in Studies in Judaism, Second Series, pp. 55–101. Philadelphia: Jewish Publication Society, 1908.

ZEITLIN, SOLOMON, Who Crucified Jesus? New York, Harper, 1946.

——, Rise and Fall of the Judean State, 2 vols. Philadelphia: Jewish Publication Society, 1967.

II. THE SUPREMACY OF THE EAST

BAECK, LEO, Judaism and Christianity (translated by W. Kaufmann). Philadelphia: Jewish Publication Society, 1958.

COHEN, A., Everyman's Talmud. London, 1937.

DANBY, H., The Mishnah (English translation of the text). London, 1933.

DEUTSCH, EMANUEL, The Talmud. Philadelphia: Jewish Publication Society, 1895.

FINKELSTEIN, LOUIS, Akiba: Scholar, Saint and Martyr. New York: Covici, Friede, 1936.

——, ed., Rab Saadia Gaon: Studies in his Honor. New York: Jewish Theological Seminary, 1944.

GINZBERG, LOUIS, The Legends of the Jews, 7 vols. Philadelphia: Jewish Publication Society, 1913–1938.

GOITEIN, S. D., Jews and Arabs. New York: Schocken, 1955.

MONTEFIORE, C. J., and LOEWE, H., A Rabbinic Anthology. New York: Macmillan, 1938.

MOORE, GEORGE FOOT, Judaism in the First Centuries of the Christian Era, 3 vols. Cambridge: Harvard University Press, 1930–2.

SCHECHTER, SOLOMON, "The Talmud," in *Studies in Judaism*, III, pp. 194–237. Philadelphia: Jewish Publication Society, 1924.

SILVER, ABBA HILLEL, Where Judaism Differed. Philadelphia: Jewish Publication Society, 1957.

——, A History of Messianic Speculation in Israel. New York: Macmillan, 1927.

STEINBERG, MILTON, The Making of the Modern Jew. Indianapolis: Bobbs-Merrill, 1934; New York: Behrman, 1942.

——, As a Driven Leaf. Indianapolis: Bobbs-Merrill, 1939; New York: Behrman, 1947.

III. THE JEWS IN THE WEST

ABRAHAMS, ISRAEL, Jewish Life in the Middle Ages. Philadelphia: Jewish Publication Society, 1911.

——, The Book of Delight and Other Papers. Philadelphia: Jewish Publication Society, 1912.

ADLER, ELKAN N., Jewish Travellers. London, 1930.

BAER, YITZHAK, A History of the Jews in Christian Spain, 2 vols. Philadelphia: Jewish Publication Society, 1966.

FREEHOF, SOLOMON B., A Treasury of Responsa. Philadelphia: Jewish Publication Society, 1962.

GOODBLATT, MORRIS S., Jewish Life in Turkey in the 16th Century. New York: Jewish Theological Seminary, 1952.

GUTTMANN, JULIUS, Philosophies of Judaism. New York: Holt, Rinehart, Winston (translated by D. W. Silverman), 1964.

HALPER, B., ed., Post-Biblical Hebrew Literature, 2 vols. Philadelphia: Jewish Publication Society, 1921.

HUSIK, ISAAC, A History of Mediaeval Jewish Philosophy. Philadelphia: Jewish Publication Society, 1918.

KATZ, JACOB, Tradition and Crisis: Jewish Society at the End of the Middle Ages. Glencoe, Ill., 1961.

——, Exclusiveness and Tolerance in Medieval and Modern Times. New York: Schocken, 1959.

LIBER, MAURICE, Rashi. Philadelphia: Jewish Publication Society, 1906.

MILLGRAM, ABRAHAM E., ed., An Anthology of Medieval Hebrew Literature. Philadelphia: Associated Talmud Torahs, 1935.

NETANYAHU, B., Don Isaac Abravanel. Philadelphia: Jewish Publication Society, 1968.

NEUMAN, ABRAHAM A., The Jews in Spain, 2 vols. Philadelphia: Jewish Publication Society, 1942.

PARKES, JAMES, The Conflict of the Church and the Synagogue. London: Soncino Press, 1934.

——, The Jews in the Medieval Community. London: Soncino Press, 1938.

REZNIKOFF, CHARLES, The Lionhearted. Philadelphia: Jewish Publication Society, 1944.

ROTH, CECIL, A History of the Marranos. Philadelphia: Jewish Publication Society, 1932.

——, The Jews in the Renaissance. Philadelphia: Jewish Publication Society, 1959.

SALAMAN, NINA, and BRODY, HEINRICH, Selected Poems of Jehudah Halevi. Philadelphia: Jewish Publication Society, 1928.

SCHWARZ, LEO W., Memoirs of My People through a Thousand Years. Philadelphia: Jewish Publication Society, 1945.

SOLIS-COHEN, SOLOMON, and BRODY, HEINRICH, Selected Poems of Moses ibn Ezra. Philadelphia: Jewish Publication Society, 1934, 1946.

STERN, SELMA, The Spirit Returneth. Philadelphia: Jewish Publication Society, 1946.

Three Jewish Philosophers. Philadelphia: Jewish Publication Society, 1960.

TRACHTENBERG, JOSHUA, The Devil and the Jews. New Haven: Yale University Press, 1943.

YELLIN, DAVID, and ABRAHAMS, ISRAEL, Maimonides. Philadelphia: Jewish Publication Society, 1903.

ZANGWILL, ISRAEL, and DAVIDSON, ISRAEL, Selected Religious Poems of Solomon ibn Gabirol. Philadelphia: Jewish Publication Society, 1923.

ZEITLIN, SOLOMON, Maimonides. New York: Bloch, 1935.

IV. Retreat and Progress

Abrahams, Israel, Jewish Life in the Middle Ages. Philadelphia: Jewish Publication Society, 1911.

Buber, Martin, Tales of the Hasidim: The Early Masters. New York: Schocken Books, 1947.

Cohen, Israel, History of the Jews in Vilna. Philadelphia: Jewish Publication Society, 1943.

Dubnow, S. M., History of the Jews in Russia and Poland, vol. I. Philadelphia: Jewish Publication Society, 1916.

Feuchtwanger, Lion, Power. New York: Viking Press, 1928.

Ginzberg, Louis, "The Gaon, Rabbi Elijah Wilna," in Students, Scholars and Saints, pp. 125–44. Philadelphia: Jewish Publication Society, 1928.

Gutstein, M. A., Aaron Lopez and Judah Touro. New York: Behrman, 1939.

Horodetzky, S., Leaders of Hasidism. London, 1928.

Kastein, Josef, The Messiah of Ismir. New York: Viking Press, 1931.

Lebeson, Anita, Jewish Pioneers in America. New York. Brentano, 1931.

Lewisohn, Ludwig, The Renegade. Philadelphia: Jewish Publication Society, 1942.

Lowenthal, Marvin, tr., The Memoirs of Gluckel of Hameln. New York: Behrman, 1932.

Meyer, Michael A., Origins of the Modern Jew. Detroit, Michigan: Wayne State University Press, 1967.

Minkin, Jacob S., The Romance of Hasidism. New York: Macmillan, 1935.

Newman, Louis I., The Hasidic Anthology. New York: Scribner's, 1938.

Philipson, David, Old European Jewries. Philadelphia: Jewish Publication Society, 1895.

Roth, Cecil, History of the Jews in Venice. Philadelphia: Jewish Publication Society, 1930.

——, A Life of Menasseh ben Israel. Philadelphia: Jewish Publication Society, 1934.

Schechter, Solomon, "The Chassidim," in Studies in Judaism, First Series, pp. 1–45. Philadelphia: Jewish Publication Society, 1915.

——, "Rabbi Elijah Wilna Gaon," in Studies in Judaism,

First Series, pp. 73–98. Philadelphia: Jewish Publication Society, 1915.

——, "Safed in the Sixteenth Century," in *Studies in Judaism*, Second Series, pp. 202–85. Philadelphia: Jewish Publication Society, 1908.

STERN, SELMA, Josel of Rosheim (translated by Gertrude Herschler). Philadelphia: Jewish Publication Society, 1965.

——, The Court Jew. Philadelphia: Jewish Publication Society, 1950.

TRACHTENBERG, JOSHUA, Jewish Magic and Superstition. A study in Folk Religion. New York: Behrman, 1939.

WALTER, H., Moses Mendelssohn. New York: Bloch, 1930.

WERBLOWSKY, R. J. Z., Joseph Karo, Lawyer and Mystic. Oxford, 1962.

V. THE SEARCH FOR A FRIENDLY HOME

AHAD HA'AM, Ten Essays on Zionism and Judaism. London, 1922.

ADLER, CYRUS, I Have Considered the Days. Philadelphia: Jewish Publication Society, 1941.

BAECK, LEO, This People Israel. Philadelphia: Jewish Publication Society, 1965.

BEIN, ALEX, Theodore Herzl. Philadelphia: Jewish Publication Society, 1940.

BEN-AMI, Between Hammer and Sickle. Philadelphia: Jewish Publication Society, 1967.

BENTWICH, NORMAN, Solomon Schechter. Philadelphia: Jewish Publication Society, 1939.

——, For Zion's Sake: A Biography of Judah L. Maghus. Philadelphia: Jewish Publication Society, 1954.

BEN-ZVI, YIZHAK, The Exiled and the Redeemed. Philadelphia: Jewish Publication Society, 1957.

BIEBER, HUGO, Heinrich Heine (translated by Moses Hadas). Philadelphia: Jewish Publication Society, 1956.

CAHAN, ABRAHAM, The Rise of David Levinsky. New York: Harper, 1917.

COHEN, I., Jewish Life in Modern Times. New York: Dodd, Mead, 1914.

CRUM, BARTLEY C., Behind the Silken Curtain. New York: Simon and Schuster, 1947.

DUBNOW, S. M., History of the Jews in Russia and Poland, 3

vols. Philadelphia: Jewish Publication Society, 1916–20.

ELBOGEN, ISMAR, A Century of Jewish Life. Philadelphia: Jewish Publication Society, 1944.

FREEDMAN, MAURICE, ed., A Minority in Britain. London, 1955.

FRIEDMAN, LEE M., Jewish Pioneers and Patriots. Philadelphia: Jewish Publication Society, 1942.

FRIEDMANN, GEORGES, The End of the Jewish People? New York: Doubleday, 1967.

GOLDBERG, ISAAC, Major Noah. Philadelphia: Jewish Publication Society, 1936.

GOODMAN, PAUL, Moses Montefiore, Philadelphia: Jewish Publication Society, 1925.

HERTZBERG, ARTHUR, The Zionist Idea. Doubleday, 1959.
——, The French Enlightenment and the Jews. Philadelphia: Jewish Publication Society, 1968.

HIRSCHMANN, IRA, Life Line to a Promised Land. New York: Vanguard Press, 1946.

JANOWSKY, OSCAR I., ed., The American Jew: A Reappraisal. Philadelphia: Jewish Publication Society, 1965.
——, Foundations of Israel. New York: Anvil Original, 1959.

KAPLAN, MORDECAI M., The Future of the American Jew. New York: Macmillan, 1948.

LEHRMAN, HAL, Israel: The Beginning and Tomorrow. New York: William Sloan Associates, 1952.

LEARSI, RUFUS, Fulfillment: Epic Story of Zionism. Cleveland and New York: World Publishing Co., 1951.

LEVIN, SHMARYA, Childhood in Exile, 1929; Youth in Revolt, 1930; The Arena, 1932. New York: Harcourt.

LIPTZIN, SOLOMON, Germany's Stepchildren. Philadelphia: Jewish Publication Society, 1944.

LOWENTHAL, MARVIN, Henrietta Szold. New York: Viking, 1942.

MARCUS, JACOB R., The Rise and Destiny of the German Jew. Cincinnati: Union of American Hebrew Congregations, 1936.
——, Memoirs of American Jews, 3 vols. Philadelphia: Jewish Publication Society, 1955–56.

McDONALD, JAMES G., My Mission to Israel. New York: Simon and Schuster, 1951.

MODDER, MONTAGU F., The Jew in the Literature of England. Philadelphia: Jewish Publication Society, 1939.

PARKES, JAMES, End of an Exile. London, 1954.

PHILIPSON, DAVID, The Reform Movement in Judaism. New York: Macmillan, 1931.

POSENER, S., Adolphe Crémieux. Philadelphia: Jewish Publication Society, 1941.

RAISIN, JACOB S., The Haskalah Movement in Russia. Philadelphia: Jewish Publication Society, 1913.

REVUSKY, ABRAHAM, Jews in Palestine. New York: Vanguard Press, 1936.

ROBACK, A. A., The History of Yiddish Literature. New York: YIVO, 1940.

RUDAVSKY, DAVID, Emancipation and Adjustment. New York: Diplomatic Press, 1967.

SACHAR, H. M., The Course of Modern Jewish History. New York: World Publishing Company, 1958.

SAMUEL, MAURICE, Blood Accusation: The Strange History of the Beiliss Case. Philadelphia: Jewish Publication Society, 1966.

——, Harvest in the Desert. Philadelphia: Jewish Publication Society, 1944.

——, The World of Sholom Aleichem. New York: Knopf, 1944.

SHERMAN, BEZALEL C., The Jew Within American Society. Detroit, Mich.: Wayne University Press, 1961.

SIMMEL, ERNST, Antisemitism: A Social Disease. New York: International Universities Press, 1946.

SKLARE, MARSHALL, ed., The Jews: Social Patterns of an American Group. Glencoe, Ill., 1958.

SPIEGEL, SHALOM, Hebrew Reborn. New York: Macmillan, 1930.

STEINBERG, MILTON, The Making of the Modern Jew. Indianapolis: Bobbs-Merrill, 1934.

——, A Partisan Guide to the Jewish Problem. Indianapolis: Bobbs-Merrill, 1945.

SYRKIN, MARIE, Blessed Is the Match. Philadelphia: Jewish Publication Society, 1947.

TCHERIKOWER, ELIAS, Early Jewish Labor Movement in the United States (translated by Aaron Antonowsky). New York: YIVO, 1961.

WISCHNITZER, MARK, To Dwell in Safety. Philadelphia: Jewish Publication Society, 1948.

ZANGWILL, ISRAEL, Children of the Ghetto. Philadelphia: Jewish Publication Society, 1892.

INDEX

736